T0340083

# NETWORKS IN TELECOMMUNICATIONS

## Economics and Law

*Networks in Telecommunications* addresses fundamental issues in discussions of regulatory policy by offering an integrated framework for understanding the economics and law of networks. It extends theories on network design associated with the mathematics of graph theory, which provides insights into the complex, systemic interrelationships among network components. It also applies the principles of transaction cost economics to analyze decisions about the appropriate boundaries of proprietary network architecture. The book introduces network theory into the study of the economics and law of telecommunications. The discussion opens up the black box of the cost function in telecommunications. The analysis also goes beyond the "network externalities" approach, which focuses primarily on the size of networks. The book highlights the effects of network architecture and the tradeoffs inherent in network design.

Daniel F. Spulber is the Elinor Hobbs Distinguished Professor of International Business and Professor of Management Strategy at the Kellogg School of Management, where he has taught since 1990. He is also Professor of Law at the Northwestern University School of Law (Courtesy) and founder of Kellogg's International Business and Markets Program. Founding editor of the *Journal of Economics and Management Strategy*, Professor Spulber has received eight National Science Foundation grants, three Searle Fund grants, and two Ewing Marion Kauffman Foundation grants for economic research. His current research is in the area of international economics, industrial organization, management strategy, and law. He is the author of 11 other books, including *The Theory of the Firm: Microeconomics with Endogenous Entrepreneurs, Firms, Markets, and Organizations* (2009), *Global Competitive Strategy* (2007), *Market Microstructure: Intermediaries and the Theory of the Firm* (1999), and *Deregulatory Takings and the Regulatory Contract: The Competitive Transformation of Network Industries in the United States* (with J. Gregory Sidak, 1997), all from Cambridge University Press, and *Management Strategy* (2004), *The Market Makers* (1998), and *Regulation and Markets* (1989).

Christopher S. Yoo is Professor of Law and Founding Director of the Center for Technology, Innovation, and Competition at the University of Pennsylvania Law School. He is also Professor of Communication at the Annenberg School for Communication at the University of Pennsylvania (Courtesy). Formerly Professor of Law at Vanderbilt University, he was also Founding Director there of the Technology and Entertainment Law Program. Professor Yoo earlier clerked for Justice Anthony M. Kennedy of the Supreme Court of the United States and Judge A. Raymond Randolph of the U.S. Court of Appeals for the D.C. Circuit. He coauthored *The Unitary Executive: Presidential Power from Washington to Bush* (with Steven G. Calabresi, 2008) and has written more than three dozen book chapters and articles in the Columbia, New York University, University of Pennsylvania, Cornell, and Northwestern University law reviews, as well as the *Harvard Journal of Law and Technology* and the *Yale Journal of Regulation*, among others. Professor Yoo's research focuses primarily on how technological innovation and economic theories of imperfect competition are transforming the regulation of the Internet, representing a leading voice in the debate over network neutrality.

# Networks in Telecommunications

## Economics and Law

**Daniel F. Spulber**

Northwestern University

**Christopher S. Yoo**

University of Pennsylvania

CAMBRIDGE
UNIVERSITY PRESS

**CAMBRIDGE**
UNIVERSITY PRESS

Shaftesbury Road, Cambridge CB2 8EA, United Kingdom

One Liberty Plaza, 20th Floor, New York, NY 10006, USA

477 Williamstown Road, Port Melbourne, VIC 3207, Australia

314–321, 3rd Floor, Plot 3, Splendor Forum, Jasola District Centre, New Delhi – 110025, India

103 Penang Road, #05–06/07, Visioncrest Commercial, Singapore 238467

Cambridge University Press is part of Cambridge University Press & Assessment, a department of the University of Cambridge.

We share the University's mission to contribute to society through the pursuit of education, learning and research at the highest international levels of excellence.

www.cambridge.org
Information on this title: www.cambridge.org/9780521673860

First published 2009

*A catalogue record for this publication is available from the British Library*

*Library of Congress Cataloging-in-Publication data*
Spulber, Daniel F.
Networks in telecommunications : economics and law / Daniel F. Spulber,
Christopher S. Yoo. – 1st ed.
p.  cm.
Includes bibliographical references and index.
ISBN 978-0-521-85710-9 (hardback) – ISBN 978-0-521-67386-0 (pbk.)
1. Business networks.   2. Telecommunication.   3. Telecommunication – Law and legislation.
I. Yoo, Christopher S.   II. Title.
HD69.S8.S68   2009
384 – dc22      2008054545

ISBN   978-0-521-85710-9   Hardback
ISBN   978-0-521-67386-0   Paperback

Cover art: Aaron Spulber, *Networks*, oil oncanvas, © 1990.

*We dedicate this book to our wives, Sue and Kris, for their patience, understanding, and encouragement throughout this long project*

*D.F.S. and C.S.Y.*

# Contents

### PART III.  POLICY APPLICATIONS

# Preface

Networks in communications, transportation, and distribution are fundamental features of the modern economy. Network industries are a major source of economic growth and a key component of economic development. The expansion of telecommunications, the Internet, and mobile communications has accompanied innovations in information technology. Although electronic commerce was once viewed as a specific category of business transactions, practically all business activity has come to depend on digital communications networks.

Public policymakers are keenly aware of the critical role of telecommunications in the economy. A great shift in regulatory focus has occurred, from more traditional utility regulation to access mandates. Examining changes in public policy in telecommunications requires a more fundamental understanding of the structure and function of networks. Expansion of the economics and law literatures on networks has accompanied economic and technological developments. The purpose of this book is to evaluate the implications of this public policy shift and to achieve a better understanding of public policy toward networks.

To achieve these objectives, the book develops a comprehensive framework for the study of telecommunications networks. We draw upon important developments in the graph theory that is used to represent networks. We examine economic models of networks and apply these developments to study the legal aspects of network industries. The result is an outline of a theory of telecommunications networks that generates insights into important public policy debates, including mandatory access and network neutrality.

The book is organized as follows: The first part introduces the economics of networks. Chapter 1 considers the structure and functions of networks and introduces some basic ideas from graph theory. Chapter 2 examines the design and costs of networks and includes some basic concepts from engineering and economics. Chapter 3 studies the pricing of network services and efficient choice of capacity. It is not possible to give a complete overview of the vast fields of network mathematics, network engineering, and network economics. This book thus seeks simply to provide an introduction to networks and then to apply some of the basic concepts to the design of public policy.

The second part of the book presents a comprehensive overview of regulatory and antitrust approaches to network access. Chapter 4 examines the rationales traditionally invoked to justify regulation of communications networks, as well as the policy instruments used to implement these rationales. Chapter 5 looks at the transaction costs of providing access to networks. Chapter 6 examines market-based pricing of access to networks. Chapter 7 examines constitutional limits on the pricing of access to networks.

The third and final part of the book presents a set of four key policy applications. Chapter 8 analyzes the access to local telephone networks mandated by the Telecommunications Act of 1996. Chapter 9 examines how antitrust policy has addressed access to networks. Chapter 10 then studies access to local broadband networks, such as digital subscriber line (DSL) and cable modem systems, an issue that has been the focus of recent Supreme Court decisions and FCC proceedings. Chapters 11 and 12 address an issue known as "network neutrality," which has emerged as the most controversial issue in Internet policy, applying the insights of the economics of product differentiation and congestion.

# Acknowledgments

Daniel F. Spulber gratefully acknowledges the support of a research grant from the Searle Foundation that made his contribution to this book possible. Spulber also thanks Dean Dipak Jain and Dean Kathleen Hagerty for their support of his research work, and he thanks the Kellogg School of Management for providing a stimulating research environment.

Christopher S. Yoo gratefully acknowledges a grant from the Milton and Miriam Handler Foundation, which helped support his contribution to this book. He also thanks Deans Kent Syverud and Edward Rubin of the Vanderbilt Law School, Dean Michael Fitts of the University of Pennsylvania Law School, and his colleagues at both institutions for their support and encouragement. In addition to acknowledgment of his wife in the dedication, he also would like to express his appreciation to his children, Marshall and Brendan, who fill his life with such joy every day.

Both would like to thank Johannes Bauer, Mark Brandon, Jon Bruce, David Callies, K.C. Chiu, Andrew Daughety, Paul Edelman, James Ely, Joseph Farrell, Gerald Faulhaber, Rob Frieden, Brett Frischmann, Luke Froeb, Chris Guthrie, Todd Henderson, Jack Hirshleifer, Herbert Hovenkamp, Charles Jackson, Louis Kaplow, Vik Khanna, Jeff MacKie-Mason, Elliot Maxwell, Richard Nagareda, Randy Picker, Richard Pierce, Robert Rasmussen, Jennifer Reinganum, Jim Rossi, Greg Sidak, Robert Thompson, Michael Vandenbergh, Philip Weiser, Sang-Seung Yi, Kiho Yoon, and participants in workshops conducted at the American Law and Economics Association, Seoul National University, the Telecommunications Policy Research Conference, UCLA Law School, the University of Michigan, the University of Pennsylvania, Vanderbilt University, the Wharton School, and Northwestern University for their comments on earlier versions of this work. Elizabeth McIntyre, David Nijhawan, Robert Schmoll, and Constantin Severe provided excellent research assistance.

The book was previewed at a Research Roundtable Conference at Northwestern University Law School's Searle Center for Law, Regulation, and Economic Growth. We thank Henry Butler, Director of the Searle Center, for hosting the conference. We thank the participants for their helpful discussion and comments: Babette Boliek,

Michelle Connolly, David Gabel, Shane Greenstein, Keith Hylton, Pierre Larouche, John Lopatka, Julian Morris, William Page, Susan Perkins, William Rogerson, David Sappington, Hans-Bernd Schäfer, William Sharkey, J. Gregory Sidak, D. Daniel Sokol, James Speta, Jagannadha Pawan Tamvada, Ingo Vogelsang, and Kevin Werbach.

The book draws upon material from the following publications:

Spulber, Daniel F., and Christopher S. Yoo 2003. "Access to networks: Economic and constitutional connections," *Cornell Law Review* 88: 885–1024.
———— 2005. "On the regulation of networks as complex systems: A graph theory approach," *Northwestern University Law Review* 99: 1687–1722.
———— 2005. "Network regulation: The many faces of access," *Journal of Competition Law and Economics* 1: 635–78.
———— 2007. "Mandating access to telecom and the Internet: The hidden side of *Trinko*," *Columbia Law Review* 107: 101–82.
———— 2008. "Rethinking broadband Internet access," *Harvard Journal on Law and Technology* 22: 1–74.
———— 2008. "Toward a unified theory of access to local telephone networks," *Federal Communications Law Journal* 61: 43–117.
Yoo, Christopher S. 2005. "Beyond network neutrality," *Harvard Journal of Law and Technology* 19: 1–77.
———— 2006. "Network neutrality and the economics of congestion," *Georgetown Law Journal* 94: 1847–1908.

# Introduction

The purpose of this book is to examine the implications of network theory for public policy toward communications. Network theory provides a highly useful and powerful tool for modeling and understanding communications networks. Network theory opens the "black box" of networks to reveal the complexities of network architecture. Rather than working with the reduced form of the standard economic cost function, network theory pays attention to the nodes and links that form networks. The architecture of networks affects transmission capacity and the quality of service. The structure of networks also is important for understanding the boundaries of private networks provided by individual firms and the interconnections between networks. By applying network theory to communications, we develop a general Coasian theory of networks.

Using network theory, we develop a comprehensive framework for analyzing public policy toward communications. The discussion identifies the shift in regulatory policy from utility regulation to mandated access. Access to networks refers to the market transactions that connect a firm's network to its customers, suppliers, competitors, and partners. Our discussion presents a classification scheme for analyzing access to networks. We apply network theory based on the mathematics of graph theory tools to characterize the structure of networks. We examine how regulatory access mandates can distort access price. In competitive markets, optimization by firms and access transactions lead to efficient network boundaries and interconnections. Regulatory access mandates potentially reduce economic efficiency by changing the market-equilibrium structure and boundaries of communications networks.

## A. The Changing Network Economy

Economic growth in the modern economy has accompanied a dramatic upsurge in the importance of communications networks. Consumers and businesses have

1

become linked together with ever-faster connections transmitting a growing amount of data for electronic commerce, organizational management, and social interaction. Communications networks have joined more traditional network industries in energy and transportation in playing a pivotal role in the functioning of national economies. The information and communications technology (ICT) industries form a growing share of the global economy (U.S. Department of Commerce 2003). International trade has gone online, with worldwide electronic transmission of information, technology, services, entertainment, and money. Telecommunications companies have played a starring role in a significant number of megamergers that have transformed the business environment and also served as a driving force behind the spectacular rise and equally spectacular fall of the NASDAQ index. Perhaps most dramatically, the failure of WorldCom produced the largest bankruptcy in U.S. history.

In addition, scientific advances have rendered the technological environment increasingly dynamic, with different types of communications now available through an ever-increasing array of transmission technologies. These developments have made different communications media increasingly interchangeable and have turned different technological platforms that had previously constituted universes unto themselves into competitors. Not only has the emergence of platform competition provided consumers and firms with a wider variety of ways to access network services; it has also begun to put pressure on the traditional regulatory distinction among voice, video, and data communications, under which each type of service was governed by a separate regulatory regime (Yoo 2002). It is also forcing policy makers to abandon their traditional approach of framing regulation in largely static terms and to begin focusing on issues of dynamic efficiency, with the accompanying emphasis on providing incentives for investing in the deployment of new technologies.

These developments have heightened the importance of understanding how networks function and how regulation affects their behavior. Not only does government policy play a key role in shaping returns and investment incentives; a growing number of commentators have suggested that regulation has also played a decisive role in precipitating much of the turmoil that has wracked the industry of late, having shaped both the recent wave of mergers (Chen 1999) and the WorldCom bankruptcy (*Wall Street Journal* 2002). The direct link between regulation and industry performance makes understanding the economic implications of current regulatory policy all the more imperative.

## B. A Fundamental Shift in Regulatory Policy

The need for a more sophisticated understanding of networks has been made all the more critical by a fundamental shift in the basic approach to regulating networks. For over a century, policy makers charged with regulating networks relied almost exclusively on the set of tools associated with *rate regulation*, in which regulatory authorities used tariffs to dictate the prices that network owners could charge end customers for network services. Because rate regulation targeted final goods that represented the output of the entire system, this approach did not require much of a theory of how networks are configured or how the various network components interact with one another.

In recent years, however, regulators have begun to turn to a new approach, known as *access regulation*. Unlike rate regulation, where regulators focus on the prices that network owners charge for the services of the entire network, access regulation dictates the terms under which network owners must allow customers, partners, other network firms, and even competitors to use portions of their networks. In short, rather than following the approach dictated by rate regulation and controlling the terms under which *consumers* purchase access to *outputs*, access regulation instead controls the terms under which *competitors* may purchase access to *inputs*. This shift in regulatory approach is exemplified by the Telecommunications Act of 1996, which attempted to introduce competition into local telephone service by potentially compelling incumbent local telephone companies to provide competitors with unbundled access to every element of their networks. Access requirements are also being implemented with respect to cable television systems, networks of utility poles, and broadband technologies. Some scholars have even suggested that the shift to access regulation represents a paradigm shift in the approach to regulating network industries (Kearney and Merrill 1998). As one commentator aptly acknowledges, we do indeed live in "the Age of Access" (Rifkin 2000).

The shift to access regulation has changed the primary unit of regulatory analysis from the outputs of the entire network to the services provided by individual network elements. In so doing, it has created the need for a more comprehensive understanding of how network components interact within the context of a complex system, as well as some basis for determining the impact of access regulation on optimal network design. Absent some greater insight into these considerations, regulatory authorities will be hard pressed to shape policy in ways that are both coherent and constructive.

We demonstrate that the complexity of networks implies the need for additional regulatory forbearance. The law of unintended consequences applies with a vengeance to network access regulation. Small regulatory changes that affect network utilization and interconnection can significantly affect network performance and capacity. This raises the bar for network access regulation in comparison with traditional utility regulation.

Put differently, there must be a substantial market failure in telecommunications to justify regulatory intervention through mandatory network access. In addition, regulators must show that their intervention will address the alleged market failure. To satisfy this test, regulators must identify the potential consequences of their intervention. This requires application of the theory of networks to understand the possible effects of access regulation.

## C. The Limits of Existing Scholarship

Unfortunately, the existing economic and legal commentary on networks provides few insights into network architecture and design. The literature has been hampered by the absence of a terminology that identifies networks' essential components and captures the manner in which they interact with one another. Even more importantly, the recent upsurge in attention from economists has focused primarily on the phenomenon known as *network economic effects*, which occurs when a network's value is largely a function of the number of other users connected to it.[1] The problem with this approach is that it focuses on only one aspect of networks: their size. As a result, it is unable to provide insights into the relative benefits of different network architectures or the interrelationship among the various network components.

Legal scholarship and the substantive decisions of regulatory authorities have proven similarly unhelpful. They have reflexively adhered to the cost-based approaches associated with traditional rate regulation and have based access prices on the costs of particular network elements, with the primary policy issue centering on whether these calculations should be based on historical or replacement cost. Cost-based approaches violate one of the central precepts of economics by focusing solely on the supply side without providing a way to take demand-side considerations into account (Yoo 2003a). Even more problematically, by considering each component as if it existed in isolation, this approach fails to capture one of the central characteristics of networks, which is how the aggregation of individual network components into an integrated system causes them to interact with one another in complex ways. In the words of one noted network theorist:

> First, real networks represent populations of individual components that are actually *doing something* – generating power, sending data, or even making decisions. Although the structure of the relationships between a network's components is interesting, it is *important* principally because it affects either their individual behavior or the behavior of the system as a whole. Second, networks are dynamic objects not just because things happen in networked systems, but because the networks themselves are evolving and changing in time, driven by the activities or decisions of those very components. In the connected age, therefore, *what happens and how it happens depend on the network*. And the network in turn depends on what has happened previously.
> (Watts 2003, p. 28)

As with all complex systems, the costs and benefits associated with any one component cannot be assessed without an appreciation for the function it plays

---

1 The literature on network externalities is vast. For the seminal articles, see Rohlfs (1974); Farrell and Saloner (1985); and Katz and Shapiro (1985). For a survey appearing in the legal literature, see Lemley and McGowan (1998).

within the system as a whole. Each network is designed so that each element interacts with other elements in ways that analysis of individual elements cannot adequately take into account. Thus, the impact of compelling access to a particular network component can only be understood if one has a theoretical model of the interrelationship of the network's various constituent parts.

## D. Network Law and Economics

This book is designed to overcome these conceptual limitations and to place the issues surrounding network economics and policy on a sounder economic and legal foundation. We begin by demystifying networks as an economic phenomenon by offering a more precise definition of what constitutes a network. The terminology we establish not only provides a technical background for our study; it also provides important insights into network design.

In addition, we offer a more general theory of networks that makes it possible to analyze how networks function as integrated systems based on the critical engineering and management processes employed for the design and operation of networks. Our theory applies and extends the insights provided by the mathematics associated with *graph theory*, which has served as the foundation for a substantial scientific literature on the science of networks that has been largely overlooked by economists, legal academics, and policymakers. The rapidly developing science of networks is chronicled in a number of popular works (Watts 1999, 2003; Barabási 2002; Buchanan 2003).

Economists have begun to take into account the complexity of networks. The cost model of Gasmi, Kennett, et al. (2002) reflects the architectural structure of telecommunications networks. Cost allocation in networks is examined by Bird (1976), Sharkey (1995), and Henriet and Moulin (1996). Networks have also been studied in markets for electric power, including the application of Kirchoff's laws; see for example Bohn et al. (1984) and Hogan (1992). For an introduction to the economics of networks, see Economides (1996). We also consider some principles of network design from engineering and operations research.

Our analysis shows how demand interacts with the cost, capacity, geography, and directional flow of the various network components to create a theory of optimal network architecture. Then we present an economic analysis of pricing and efficient choice of network capacity. Applying the insights of graph theory to the economic and legal issues surrounding access regulation captures one of the essential qualities of networks, which is that the properties of the overall network cannot be understood solely in terms of the individual components, any more than the behavior of organisms can be understood solely in terms of individual cells. By providing a basis for analyzing how networks function as integrated systems, our theory makes possible an appreciation for how the entire network can be more than merely the sum of its constituent parts. The model we advance also provides insights into the complex interrelationships among network components that cause them to interact in ways that are often surprising and unpredictable.[2]

We augment the insights provided by graph theory with the economics of transaction costs, pioneered and developed by Ronald Coase (1937). This framework allows us to analyze two other elements critical to network design and management: (i) a method for understanding *market transactions* for network services and (ii) a method for understanding the *organizational governance* of networks. Transaction cost economics provides a method of integrating these two components in the analysis of network firms. Network firms own and operate networks to provide a wide variety of transmission and transportation services. The organizational structure and boundaries of network firms are determined by the relative costs of market transactions and organizational governance.

Coase explained that firms choose their activities by comparing the costs of engaging in market transactions with the costs of internal resource allocation. For Coase, firms arise as a means of economizing on market transaction costs by internalizing those transactions within the organization. The transaction-cost approach to the economic theory of the firm emphasizes the need for vertical integration as a means of avoiding contracting costs.

Network firms optimize access and network design by trading off the costs of market transactions and organizational governance. Compelled access regulations interfere with these decisions. The result will be departures from the efficient degree of vertical integration and institutional organization in network industries. Over time, there may be dynamic inefficiencies affecting investment in network capacity and research and development of network-related technology.

Economic analysis indicates that efficiency would best be promoted if access to those network services were based on market value. Reliance on market-based pricing mechanisms not only tends to allocate goods to their best use; it also provides the proper signals to parties who consider investing in network technologies. Rather than basing access prices on the market value of the network services provided, regulators continue to employ access-pricing methodologies that focus on the cost of the inputs used to establish the physical network. Such an approach might be appropriate in an ideal, frictionless world in which all welfare-enhancing transactions clear instantly. Over time, competition tends to drive the market prices of outputs and the costs of production together, so that ideally the purchase cost

---

2   One classic example of this phenomenon is the widespread failure of the power grid across much of the western United States in August 1996. The failure of a single transmission line in western Oregon interacted with a handful of other seemingly similarly minor discrepancies in the system to plunge 7.5 million people into darkness within a matter of minutes (Watts 2003, pp. 21–23). A similar problem occurred in August 2003, when the failure of three high-voltage transmission lines in Ohio cut off power to 50 million people in the northeastern and midwestern United States and parts of Ontario, Canada (see Chapter 5).

of inputs would represent a good approximation to the earning potential and thus the market value of those inputs.

In practice, however, both purchase cost and market value are moving targets. Improvements in production technology, innovations in goods and services, shifts in consumer demand, entry and exit by producers, and changes in factor prices represent exogenous shocks that temporarily prevent the market from reaching general equilibrium, during which time the market value of inputs deviates from their initial cost. The greater the rate of change of technology and other forces, the greater this disparity is likely to be. Given the unpredictability of such changes, the deviations from market value caused by basing access prices on the cost of the inputs used to create the network will tend to lead to gluts or shortages and will eventually induce entrants to over- or underinvest in certain types of network capacity. Furthermore, basing access prices on input costs ignores the fact that the whole is typically greater than the sum of its parts. So long as a firm is efficient and creative, the value of the services it provides is likely to exceed the cost of the inputs it uses.

## E. Distinguishing among Different Types of Access to Networks

Applying graph theory and transaction costs to networks provides a basis for a more specific definition of access. *Access* in our framework refers to economic transactions between network firms and their customers, partners, and other network firms. Access is the critical economic mechanism for allocating network services and organizing network industries. Our framework makes it possible to distinguish among five different types of access, each with its own distinct economic and legal implications. (1) Retail access refers to transactions between network firms and retail customers. (2) Wholesale access denotes transactions between network firms and resellers. (3) Interconnection access refers to transactions between network firms for origination, termination, and transit of transmissions. (4) Platform access is the set of transactions between network firms and suppliers of complementary services, such as programming on cable networks or Internet content providers. (5) Unbundled access includes transactions between network firms for leasing network elements such as lines and switches.

Distinguishing among different types of access in this manner provides a clearer understanding of how compelling access can have unintended effects. For example, the manner in which regulators have implemented access regimes has resulted in major distortions in market transactions for access. In addition, compelled access potentially affects the design and planning of networks, resulting in inefficient usage of existing networks and inefficient investment in network facilities over the long term. The combination of these regulatory effects further alters the tradeoff between market transactions and the internalization of particular business activities within the boundaries of the network.

## F. Toward a Market-Based Approach to Access Prices

In addition, our analysis offers a powerful critique of regulators' current tendency to implement access regimes by basing access rates on cost. The only plausible justification for basing regulated prices on costs incurred was that the absence of external markets caused by the lack of technological substitutes made it impossible to base rates on market prices. By stimulating direct facilities-based competition, the emergence of platform competition and the shift to access regulation have made market-based pricing both feasible and desirable. We refute arguments advanced by other scholars suggesting that network industries are somehow prone to unique forms of market failure that justify adhering to cost-based pricing. Economies of scale and scope, sunk costs, and network economic effects do not generally cause market prices to deviate from levels that promote efficiency and do not change the basic analysis.

Finally, we examine the constitutional implications of the emergence of access regulation by evaluating the limits that the Takings Clause places on such regulation. Because rate regulation simply restricts the terms and conditions under which parties may contract for finished goods and services, it represents the type of adjustment of economic burdens traditionally subject to the more permissive analysis applied to nonpossessory takings. Access regulation, in contrast, often requires network owners to permit third parties to place equipment on their property. When that is the case, access regulation necessarily falls within the Supreme Court's physical takings jurisprudence, which mandates that the government reimburse property owners for the market value of their property without regard to the economic impact of the regulation or whether the regulation in question furthers important public interests. Therefore, when physical collocation is involved, just compensation for compelled access exactly corresponds to economically efficient prices for compelled access.

Established principles of economics and constitutional law thus require that regulators adopt methodologies that allow voluntary access transactions, or as a second-best alternative, adopt methods that base access rates on market prices. Because access transactions are central to the organization of network industries and the organizational structure of firms in those industries, competition and efficiency require unfettered access transactions.

To summarize, we argue that the fundamental shift in regulatory approach toward compelled access demands an equally fundamental shift in the approach to setting prices. If there is to be public intervention in private access transactions, economic principles still dictate that access prices should be based on the market value of the incremental network services provided by the relevant input. In addition, to the extent that compelled access to a telecommunications network requires that competitors be permitted to place equipment on the network owner's property, access requirements constitute physical takings for which market-based compensation must be paid. Although the unavailability of market-based determinants once justified basing prices on some measure of cost, the shift in regulatory policy (especially when combined with the emergence of direct, facilities-based competition made possible by technological convergence) has caused the justifications for refusing to set rates on the basis of market prices to fall away.

Although the absence of comparable transactions in external markets historically led regulatory authorities to eschew market-based pricing in favor of cost-based pricing, platform competition and the shift to access regulation have drained this justification of its vitality. The emergence of direct facilities-based competition from alternative telecommunications networks has created market-based benchmarks that can serve as independent bases for setting rates. Contrary to the suggestion of some commentators, distinctive economic features of networks such as sunk costs, economies of scale and scope, and network economic effects do not alter this core conclusion.

Our public policy analysis focuses primarily on telecommunications networks. Although we suspect that the economic and constitutional concepts that we discuss may have implications for other network industries, such as energy and transportation, developing those ideas would require detailed consideration of the technological and regulatory conditions of those industries and would exceed the scope of this book. We therefore withhold any firm policy conclusions with respect to energy and transportation networks, although we draw on examples from the energy and transportation industries to help illustrate the analysis of networks. We believe, however, that the definitions of basic network concepts advanced here have general applicability to all network industries.

# PART I

# THE ECONOMICS OF NETWORKS

# 1

# The Structure and Functions of Networks

Economic life is critically dependent on a wide variety of privately owned networks: for communications (the Internet and broadband data, telephone, broadcast television and radio, cable television), for transportation (airlines, railroads, buses, trucks, shipping, electric power transmission and distribution, natural gas and petroleum pipelines), and for distribution of products (wholesale trade and postal services). Although different types of networks vary significantly with respect to a wide variety of technical details, they share certain technical and economic features that are critical to understanding network access.

This chapter introduces some basic aspects of network structure and design. The focus of our discussion is on physical networks, involving facilities such as telecommunications switching equipment and transmission lines. The purpose is not only to provide a technical background to our study but also to obtain some important insights into how networks are organized. Evaluating the effects of regulation on the organization or formation of networks is central to our public policy analysis.

This chapter also introduces a classification scheme that is useful for understanding the different types of access to networks. These types of access have generated a variety of public policy actions. Classifying the types of access provides insights into inconsistencies in public policies that can create economic inefficiencies. Our classification scheme provides the basis for the development of a new Coasian theory of communications networks. The boundaries of the private networks, and their pattern of interconnections, depend on a comparison of the costs of governing networks by firms and the transaction costs of interconnecting networks. Markets can be expected to generate efficiencies in the structure of private networks and the pattern of interconnections between networks.

## A. Types of Networks

There are many types of networks. The focus of our policy discussion is on communication networks. However, many of our conclusions apply to regulation of some

**Table 1.1.** *Value added by industry as a percentage of*
*Gross Domestic Product as of 2006*

| | |
|---|---|
| Utilities | 2.1% |
| Wholesale trade | 5.8% |
| Transportation and warehousing | |
|     Air transportation | 0.4% |
|     Rail transportation | 0.3% |
|     Water transportation | 0.1% |
|     Truck transportation | 0.9% |
|     Transit and ground passenger transportation | 0.1% |
|     Pipeline transportation | 0.1% |
|     Other transportation and support activities | 0.7% |
|     Warehousing and storage | 0.3% |
| Information | |
|     Broadcasting and telecommunications | 2.6% |
| Total | 13.4% |

*Source:* U.S. Department of Commerce (2008, Table 2).

types of transportation and distribution networks. For completeness, we touch briefly in this section on social and business networks, although these are beyond the scope of our later discussion.

## 1. Communications, Transportation, and Distribution Networks

The contributions of the transportation and distribution network industries to the U.S. gross domestic product (GDP) are summarized in Table 1.1. Network industries are primarily located within the Transportation and Public Utilities sector and constitute more than 13 percent of GDP. There are three parts to this sector: transportation, communications, and utilities other than communications. Network industries have historically been subject to more regulation than other sectors of the economy, including regulation by various transportation agencies, the Federal Communications Commission, the Federal Energy Regulatory Commission, and state public utility commissions.

The components of transportation are air transportation, railroad transportation, water transportation, truck transportation, transit and ground passenger transportation, pipeline transportation, other transportation and support activities, and warehousing and storage. Communications is composed of telephone and telegraph and radio and television. Finally, the sector also includes water, sanitary services, natural gas, and electric power transmission. Not all of these elements represent network contributions, because communications includes production of content such as programming, and electricity services include the production of electric power.

The Transportation sector is composed of network industries. Each mode of transportation is provided using networked facilities. Railroads are the classic example of a network industry. The nodes of a railroad include railway stations, railyards, and switching facilities, whereas the links of the system are the rails and the trains that travel on them. Railroads offer both passenger travel and freight transportation services. In 2007, railroads operated over 160,000 miles of track and had 1.77 trillion ton/miles of traffic (Association of American Railroads 2008). In the airline industry, the nodes of the network are airports and the links consist of the airline routes and the fleets of airplanes that travel those routes. In the trucking industry, the nodes are warehouses and pickup and delivery points, with links consisting of routes and the trucks that carry freight.

The energy industries depend on large networks for transportation and transmission services. As of 2006, the U.S. natural gas pipeline network had nodes consisting of hubs and terminals with links of over 1.5 million miles, of which 1.2 million are distribution mains and 300,000 are transmission pipelines (U.S. Department of Transportation 2008, Tables 1–10). The wholesale electric power grid has nodes at which large customers and utilities receive power and generators provide power and links in 2005 consisting of more than 160,000 miles of high-voltage transmission lines, defined as carrying 230 kilovolts or above (North American Electric Reliability Corp. 2007).

Communications networks such as the telecommunications network are classic examples of network design. Data networks are constantly evolving, with continual technological change in switching and transmission. The physical network that supports the Internet is composed of dozens of backbone networks connected to each other at exchange points. The backbone networks are privately built and operated by such companies as UUNet (Verizon), Sprint, AT&T, Level 3, and Qwest. In addition to the dozens of backbone providers, there are up to 10,000 regional Internet service providers (ISPs) that provide retail access and over 100,000 networks connected at the regional nodes.[1] At the nodes of the backbone are high-capacity routers and switches. The nodes of the backbone network include the exchange points between the backbone ISPs and the many connection points of the backbone network with the regional ISPs. The links of the backbone network are high-capacity circuits primarily composed of fiber optic transmission systems. Advances in computer chips that handle optical switching offer the promise of vast increases in the capacity of data transmission systems (Reed 2004).

Although the Transportation and Utilities sectors include trucking and warehousing, it might be instructive also to consider the Wholesale Trade sector as operating wholesale distribution networks, with the Wholesale sector contributing 5.8 percent of GDP. The Wholesale Trade sector includes intermediation activities and management of the distribution network, even though some trucking and warehousing is counted separately as part of transportation. Within the Retail

---

1  Information about the Internet's physical layer is drawn from Russ Haynal's ISP page at http://navigators.com/isp.html. A list of ISPs is provided at http://www.thelist.com/. Exchange point information is given at EP.net, http://www.ep.net/ep-main.html.

sector, some large retail chains also engage in their own wholesale distribution activities.

## 2. Social and Business Networks

Social and business networks, although not the subject of our analysis, are closely related to communications and transportation networks. Social networks are mechanisms that distribute wealth, transmit information, facilitate business transactions, and form personal relationships.[2] Social networks have been popularized by the idea of six degrees of separation, which refers to the high likelihood that any two members of a society are connected by fewer than six social ties.

> Fred Jones of Peoria, sitting in a sidewalk café in Tunisia, and needing a light for his cigarette, asks the man at the next table for a match. They fall into conversation; the stranger is an Englishman who, it turns out, spent several months in Detroit. "I know it's a foolish question," says Jones, "but do you by any chance know a fellow named Ben Arkadian? He's an old friend of mine, manages a chain of supermarkets in Detroit..."
>
> "Arkadian... Arkadian..." the Englishman mutters. "Why, upon my soul, I believe I do! Small chap, very energetic, raised merry hell with the factory over a shipment of defective bottle caps."
>
> "No kidding!" Jones exclaims, amazed.
>
> "Good lord, it's a small world, isn't it?"
>
> (Milgram 1967, p. 61)

Although the classic study by Milgram may well be an urban myth (Kleinfeld 2002a, 2002b), the interaction of social connections quickly widens the number of social contacts of individuals to encompass a significant share of the population.

Social networks are composed of the individuals in a society and the relationships between them. Individuals in a society coordinate their activities by forming organizations such as businesses, clubs, churches, or government units. The relationships in a society include kinship, friendship, business transactions, and political, religious, ethnic, or cultural affinity groups. Thus, individuals can be part of a network as buyers and sellers, employers and employees, friends or family members, or members of organizations or interest groups. A substantial literature in sociology studies these social networks and considers economic relationships to be *embedded* in the underlying network of social relationships. According to Polanyi (1944, p. 46), "man's economy, as a rule, is submerged in his social relationships" (see also Granovetter 1973, 1985).

---

2  See Wasserman and Faust (1994) for an introduction to social networks. They are related to networks used for communications (Monge and Contractor 2003).

The application of graph theory and network design ideas to game theory is related to the theory of social networks.[3] Myerson (1977) uses ideas from graph theory to analyze cooperative games in which only some players can cooperate with others. These cooperation structures correspond to links in a transportation or communications network. Such cooperation structures necessarily place limits on the possible outcomes of a cooperative game, in contrast to a game in which any combination of players can interact and form coalitions.

The strategic design of business networks appears in representations of markets in which players must interact through intermediaries. These intermediaries act as network organizers, bringing together buyers and sellers and reducing transaction costs (Spulber 1998, 1999). There is also a related set of studies of two-sided markets, in which buyers and sellers interact strategically through centralized communication mechanisms (Caillaud and Jullien 2003; Rochet and Tirole 2003; Spulber 2006). Analysis of the study of business and social networks contributes to an understanding of international trade in work by Rauch (1999, 2001) and others. The formal study of the structure of business networks also includes models of the organization of markets, referred to as market microstructure, as examined by Spulber (1996, 1999, 2002b) and Lucking-Reilly and Spulber (2001).

Intermediaries reduce transaction costs for buyers and sellers by establishing networks. Intermediaries provide network economies by replacing the transaction costs of direct buyer–seller contacts with indirect hub-and-spoke contacts. In contrast, when many buyers and sellers must interact directly, they encounter search costs and high costs of exchanging information. Imagine if customers shopping at a grocery store had to contact all the manufacturers and distributors that supply the store to obtain price and product information. By establishing a centralized network of suppliers and providing the products to customers, the grocery store takes on many of these transaction costs, performing the task more efficiently than individual customers could ever do. The store provides price and product information through its advertising and store displays. The store interacts with each of its suppliers on behalf of its many customers. The comparison between an intermediary network and directed exchange is represented in Figure 1.1.

A wholesale distributor lowers transaction costs for retailers and manufacturers. By serving networks of retailers, the wholesaler creates convenience for manufacturers. The wholesaler interacts with each of its retailers on behalf of the manufacturers it serves. For example, pharmaceutical wholesalers provide medicines to networks of pharmacies, doctors, and hospitals. They obtain pharmaceuticals from networks of manufacturers. These networks save greatly on communication costs, in comparison with extensive direct contacts between individual retail pharmacies and manufacturers.

---

3   See Dutta and Jackson (2003) for a collection of key articles in this literature.

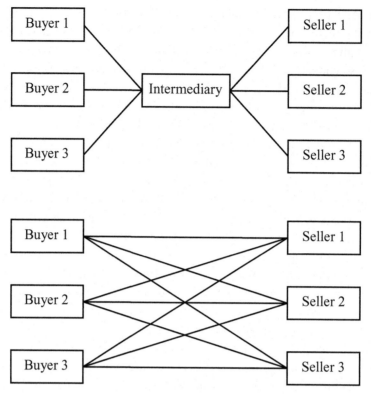

**Figure 1.1.** Intermediaries reduce the transaction costs of direct buyer–seller contacts with hub-and-spoke networks of business relationships.

Companies that are supply-chain managers perform complex network management functions. For example, Flextronics, one of the largest electronics manufacturing services companies, provides outsourcing solutions to leading original equipment manufacturers (OEMs) in such electronics industries as computers, computer peripherals, networking, telecommunications, semiconductor equipment, industrial controls, medical electronics, avionics, and consumer electronics. Flextronics maintains a vast global network of customers (OEMs) and suppliers (component manufacturers) and reduces communication costs by applying electronic data interchange, centralizing data collection and analysis, and jointly monitoring manufacturing and business transactions.[4] The centrally managed network allows outsourcing transactions to be managed at far lower costs than if the OEMs and component suppliers were to transact directly with each other.

## B. The Structure of Networks

The concept of a network is a powerful metaphor used to describe many types of systems. The network is also an even more powerful conceptual tool for analyzing

4 Flextronics, http://www.flextronics.com.

complex interactions. Scientists apply network concepts to model chemical reactions, nuclear reactions, and biological processes (Temkin et al. 1996; Shore 2002; Jeong et al. 2000). The mathematical theory of networks is used to analyze these types of interactions and to model how physical systems change over time. The mathematics of networks is itself a vast area that includes the representation of network structures using graph theory and other types of analysis (see the classic text by Berge 1976, as well Carré 1979; Anderson 1970; Beineke and Wilson 1978; Wilson and Beineke 1979; and the historical survey by Biggs et al. 1976).

Methods for describing and analyzing the structure of networks should be an essential part of network economics. Regulators need to understand the design of communications networks and the effects of regulatory policy on network architecture and performance. In this section, we examine network structures that will be useful in our discussion.

### 1. Describing Networks

A network is a general concept used to describe, among other things, systems of communication, transportation, and distribution. A network is composed of two types of objects: nodes and links. *Nodes* are the junctions of the network, and *links* are the connections between the nodes.[5] In graph theory, a *network* is defined formally as a system of nodes and links, with particular numerical values, such as costs or capacities, assigned to the links.

In what follows, we employ two different uses of the term "network" that should be readily apparent from the context. We apply the graph theory meaning of the term "network" to define a generic communications system composed of nodes and links with particular properties of the links. We also apply the economic meaning of the term "network" to indicate a privately owned communications facility provided by a firm. When speaking of network access, we mean the market transactions of a firm that provides a privately owned network.

A node in a network can be a terminal point such as the end of a subway line, or it can be a point of origin such as a subway's central station. A node can be simply a point along the line, such as a subway station. Even more simply, a node can be a point in a network where two or more lines reach a juncture. This can be a point in an electrical system where a line bifurcates. Thus, a node can be a point at which two links come together without any type of additional equipment or facilities. A node also can be something much more complex: it can be the location at which one or more pieces of specialized equipment are installed and perform various tasks. Thus, in a communications network, switching takes place at the nodes, and equipment for transmission and reception of information also is located at terminal nodes.

---

5 　The terms *nodes* and *links* are analogous to the terms *vertices* and *edges* that appear in much of the literature on graph theory.

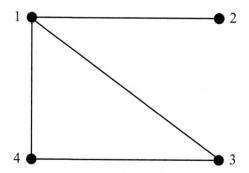

**Figure 1.2.** The set of nodes is {1, 2, 3, 4}. The set of links is {(1, 2), (1, 3), (1, 4), (3, 4)}.

In a network that is tied to a specific location, such as a railroad or an electrical system, nodes indicate geographic locations for junctures and switching equipment, such as the location of a train station in a railroad or a central office switching station in a telecommunications system. However, generally nodes need not be confined to a specific location. Mobile phones are among the nodes of a wireless network, so that nodes can move around while still being part of a network. Nodes can even jump from one network to another, as occurs when mobile phones roam across different wireless networks, or laptop computers with radio transmitters move into and out of WiFi networks.

A link in a network is any type of connection between nodes. Links can be fixed in place, such as electrical transmission lines or fiber-optic communication lines. Links can be flexible and temporary, such as the airplanes and routes that form the links of an airline system, because such links can be created or terminated by the managers of the airline. Links need not represent specific geographic corridors. For example, a transmitter within a wireless phone network may be in a specific geographic location, but the communication links with mobile phones depend on the location of the phones.

The structure of a network can be represented using a *graph* that provides a picture of the network $A$. Graph $G$ is composed of two sets. The first set in a graph is a list of the nodes of the network, which we label consecutively for convenience. For a network with $n$ nodes, the set of nodes is simply $N = \{1, 2, 3, \ldots, n\}$. The second set in a graph is a list of the links between these nodes. Thus, $L$ is a set of links $(i, j)$ where $i \neq j$ and $i$ and $j$ are elements of the set of nodes $N$.

For example, if the network has four nodes, $N = \{1, 2, 3, 4\}$, a list of the links might be $L = \{(1, 2), (1, 3), (1, 4), (3, 4)\}$. The graph with four nodes and these four links is shown in Figure 1.2. Even a simple graph with a few nodes has many possible configurations. The notation $G$ refers to the set of nodes $N$ and the set of links between those nodes $L$: $G = (N, L)$. This provides a formal description of the basic structure of the network. As we will soon see, there are many other aspects of a network that must be identified.

The description of links between nodes in a network can include specification of a direction. A picture of a network that specifies the direction of the connections

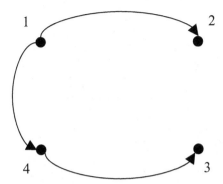

**Figure 1.3.** A one-way network in which nodes 1 and 4 are initial nodes, and nodes 2, 3, and 4 are terminal nodes.

in a network is called a *directed graph*. When the nodes have labels that describe their function, such a graph is called a *flow graph* – made popular by the widespread use of flow charts in engineering, computer science, and management. An example of a one-way network is a cable television system in which signals are transmitted to receivers. Also, a radio broadcast system constitutes a one-way network with the radio station and radio receivers as nodes, and the radio transmitter and a particular frequency on the radio spectrum as the links. A one-way network with four nodes and three links is shown in Figure 1.3. In the figure, nodes 1 and 4 are initial nodes, and nodes 2, 3, and 4 are terminal nodes. The links are shown as curved lines or arcs with arrows to indicate the direction of flow.

A two-way network can be viewed as a directed network in which there are always paths in both directions. For example, a one-way network with matching links forms an equivalent two-way network. Figure 1.4, for example, has four nodes and six matching one-way links. Because our focus is on communications networks, we restrict attention to two-way networks unless specified otherwise.

A basic example of a directed network is a direct current electric circuit, as shown in Figure 1.5. Node 1 is the *source* of the electric power, with a positive and negative terminal. Node 2 is the *load*, which is a device that is powered by electricity,

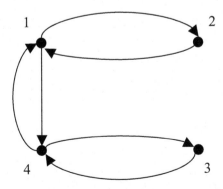

**Figure 1.4.** A one-way network with matching links forms a two-way network.

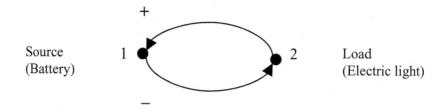

**Figure 1.5.** A direct current electric circuit.

such as a light bulb or toaster. The direction of the arcs shows the direction of the flow of the current of electrons.

Another way to think about networks is in terms of the *capacity* of the links. A natural gas pipeline can only transmit a certain amount of gas per period of time. An electric power line can only carry a certain amount of power per unit of time. For each link in a network the transmission or transportation capacity can be specified. For example, in the network in Figure 1.6, there are four links, three of which have a capacity of 12 and one of which has a capacity of 8. Thus, within any given amount of time, more can be transported from node 1 to node 4 than from node 3 to node 4. Transporting more than 8 units from node 1 to node 3 could be faster if it went through node 2 than if it went through node 4. The segment of the trip from node 3 to node 4 is a bottleneck, because the capacity is less than for other segments. However, that segment can be bypassed for transportation between node 1 and node 3 that passes through node 2.

The nodes are also subject to capacity limitations. For example, a switch in a telecommunications network can be limited in the number of calls it can direct per unit of time; see Figure 1.7. Switches and routers within data networks are subject to capacity limitations. The interaction between the capacity of switches and other devices at the nodes of a system and the capacity of the links is a complex engineering problem. Generally, bottlenecks can arise because of capacity limits at nodes or on links. There are tradeoffs between capacity at nodes and capacity of links. Network designers can take advantage of these tradeoffs by suitable choices

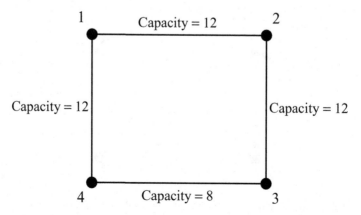

**Figure 1.6.** Three links have a capacity of 12 and one link has a capacity of 8.

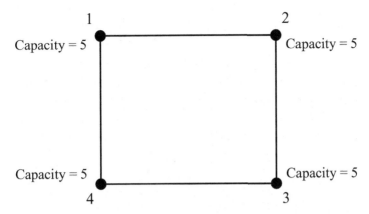

**Figure 1.7.** Capacity at the nodes of the network.

of the arrangements of nodes and links within a network. Often, upgrades in a network's transmission capacity require corresponding adjustments both of the capacity of equipment at the nodes and of the capacity of links. For example, with links in fiber optic data networks having terabit capacity, the switching and routing centers developed into bottlenecks and had to be replaced by larger-capacity optical switches and routers (McDermott 2002).

In addition to capacity, network links can also be described by geographic distance. Some networks, such as computer intranets, can be confined to a building or a campus. Telecommunications networks can be local, regional, national, or international. Undersea telecommunications cables are links that connect nodes across oceans. Satellites extend communications links into outer space. A basic telecommunications system for a regional telephone company might involve links of many different lengths that range from the basic local loop from the curb to the home to regional fiber backbones. Figure 1.8 illustrates a single network with links of varying lengths.

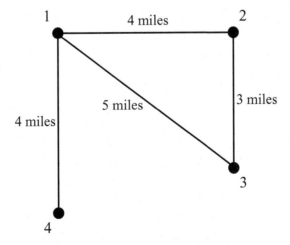

**Figure 1.8.** A network with links of varying lengths.

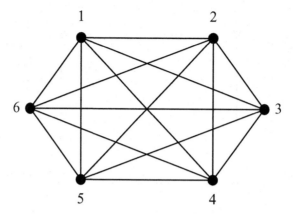

**Figure 1.9.** A complete graph representing a point-to-point network. The graph has $n = 6$ nodes and $\frac{1}{2}n(n-1) = 15$ links.

## 2. The Shapes of Networks

Networks come in many different configurations. The many shapes of networks reflect design efficiencies to take advantage of the performance of network components and the costs of various combinations of components. Network designs also reflect regulatory requirements, the costs of land, and technological alternatives. Network designs can depart from efficient configurations because networks evolve over time through additions and abandonments reflecting changing population patterns or business locations. For example, railroads and traditional phone systems tend to be the products of long-term evolution instead of rational design. In this section, we consider some basic types of networks that are useful in simplifying discussions of network design (see also Wilson and Beineke 1979, offering an introduction to different types of graphs).

One basic network directly links every pair of nodes. This type of network is represented by what is called a *complete graph*. If such a network has $n$ nodes, then it will have $\frac{1}{2}n(n-1)$ links. For example, Figure 1.9 has six nodes and fifteen links. We refer to this type of network as a point-to-point network. For example, an airline that connects all of its origins and destinations with direct flights has a route structure that is a point-to-point network. Such a network involves the greatest number of links and can potentially be replaced by an alternative network with fewer links that connect the nodes at least indirectly. If the links are costly, then it can be very inefficient to maintain such dedicated links. When switching is expensive but transportation or transmission links are relatively less costly, a point-to-point network can be desirable. Southwest Airlines operated a point-to-point network structure to connect lower congestion second-tier airports, avoiding the high time costs to passengers of changing planes at larger airports and the high costs of landing rights at those airports. They further benefited from operating efficiencies associated with longer flights in comparison to multiple short flights.

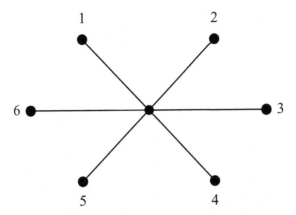

**Figure 1.10.** A star graph representing a hub-and-spoke network.

An alternative to the point-to-point network is a hub-and-spoke network. The hub-and-spoke network is represented by a *star graph*. Figure 1.10 shows a star graph that connects six terminal nodes to a hub that is a central node, with six links that resemble the spokes of a wheel. Many major airlines operate hub-and-spoke networks with regional flights connecting cities to a central hub. Passengers traveling from a city on the periphery to another city on the periphery must make connections by first traveling to the central hub. The hub-and-spoke system is a way to reduce the number of links while also keeping switching to a minimum. All switching by the network takes place at the central hub. Another advantage of hub-and-spoke systems is that they can be connected through trunk lines to form a larger network. The hub-and-spoke network performs both local and long-distance switching while collecting traffic for transport or transmission on the trunk line.

A tree network begins from an original node, with a series of branches reaching additional nodes or terminal nodes. There are no cycles in a tree. For a graph of a tree network see Figure 1.11. Tree networks are perhaps one of the most important types of networks. A tree network with a regular number of branches at each node, other than the terminal nodes, represents a process of exponential growth in the number of nodes and the number of links. For example, a tree with ten branches from each node has over a million links after only six steps! More precisely,

$$10^1 + 10^2 + 10^3 + 10^4 + 10^5 + 10^6 = 1,111,110 \text{ links.}$$

It is easy to see how a telecommunications network based on a tree structure can quickly cover a large number of households. Most telecommunications networks contain some trees within their network structure. Cable television networks traditionally have been designed as trees, with transmission originating at the root node.

The tree network is a powerful communications mechanism that lends itself in a natural way to both dissemination and gathering of information. The tree structure helps in the dissemination of information because each node need only contact a small number of nodes to pass along a message. With only a few iterations, the same

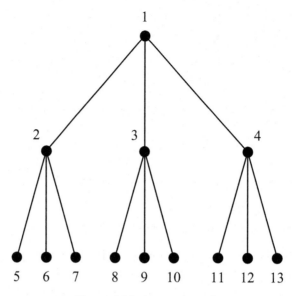

**Figure 1.11.** A tree network.

message reaches a large number of lower nodes. Furthermore, messages can easily be broken into component parts and addressed properly to lower nodes. Going in the opposite direction, information gathered at lower nodes can be aggregated, analyzed, and transmitted to higher nodes.

The tree structure is a fundamental aspect of the structure of information. All outlines of books, articles, or even plays have a hierarchical structure of sections, subsections, and other subdivisions. The tree or outline concept permeates computers through the use of directories and subdirectories that are used to organize databases or to arrange information in computer memory. The directory structure of databases and computers mirrors the structure of traditional information-filing systems. The overwhelming advantage of a tree structure is its ease of use for information storage and retrieval, because users can quickly select the appropriate label of the tree, scan the root directory, move to the appropriate subdirectory, and find the folder or file that contains the desired information. Internet search engines depend on the use of the tree structure in information storage.

A ring network connects each node to a circuit. This can be represented by a circuit graph; see Figure 1.12. In such a network, the number of connections corresponds to the number of links, usually reducing the length of each of the transmission links. More switching is needed, however, because the shortest transmission or transportation between nodes 1 and 3 necessarily must pass through node 2. More generally, Peter Huber defined the *geodesic* network structure as being one in which all nodes are connected along a geodesic – a path of minimum length. Because the nodes in a data network are computerized switches, the cost of switching is considerably lower than the cost of human or mechanical switching in a traditional telephone network. As Huber (1987, pp. 1.3, 1.14) observes, "When

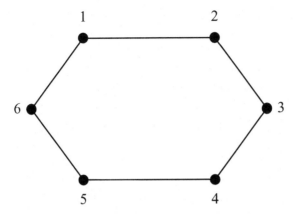

**Figure 1.12.** A circuit graph representing a ring network.

switching is cheap and transmission is expensive the efficient network is a ring." As the costs of switching fall, some networks can reduce reliance on large-scale central switching facilities. "Network functionality will therefore continue to rush out to the edges," where users are located.

## C. The Output of Networks

Industry observers and policymakers are sometimes puzzled by the question, "What does a network produce?" The answer is that networks produce transmission, transportation, or delivery services. The services produced by a network are intermediate inputs rather than final consumption goods in most cases. They are thus means to an end, rather than ends in themselves. Identifying the output of a network is critical to understanding the costs and pricing of that output. Understanding what a network produces is essential for evaluating public policies toward networks.

Perhaps the best example of a network service is the delivery of a letter by a postal service. Mailing a letter provides only indirect benefits for the sender and the recipient. The benefits to the sender and the recipient derive from the communication itself. For example, the sender may be a buyer who is ordering a product from the recipient, who is a seller. The benefits of the communication reflect the benefits from the economic transaction. Postal services do not generate benefits from the economic transaction: they only make a particular communication feasible. The substitutes for the standard postal delivery of a paper document include travel by the buyer or seller, fax transmission, telephone communication, e-mail, and Internet-based exchange of documents and data.

To illustrate the general principle, consider the most basic case of a single buyer and a single seller. The seller can provide the buyer one unit of a good at a cost $C$ to the seller. The buyer obtains a benefit $V$ from consuming the unit of the good provided by the seller. The buyer and the seller are separated by a geographic distance. They are connected by a network of length one, with the seller located at point zero and the buyer located at point 1. The cost to the network of providing the necessary transmission, transportation, or delivery service to the buyer and seller is $T$. Suppose that the buyer and the seller have no suitable alternative business partners, and that there are no alternative networks to provide a means of connecting the buyer and the seller. Then the network service makes it possible for the buyer and the seller to achieve gains from trade $V - C$ at a cost of network service $T$. The cost of the network service is thus a transaction cost and the net benefit from the transaction is thus $V - C - T$. The network service is not the transaction itself but only the mechanism of exchange.

Suppose that the buyer has an alternative transaction that yields a net benefit $V_o$, which is less than $V$. Suppose also that the seller has an alternative transaction that yields the seller a benefit of $C_o$. Then $V_o$ and $C_o$ are the respective opportunity costs of the buyer and the seller. The buyer and the seller have no alternative network service to transact with each other. Accordingly, the buyer and the seller will use the network service if and only if

$$V - C - T \geq V_o + C_o.$$

The net benefit generated by the network is then $V - C - V_o - C_o - T$. The network service must permit a transaction that is better than the alternatives for both the buyer and the seller.

Now suppose that there are two competing networks that have respective costs $T_1$ and $T_2$, with $T_1 < T_2$. Then, regardless of whether the buyer and seller have any alternatives, the second network does not offer a service of any value. The value of the service offered by the first network is simply the lower cost relative to the second network. If it used by the buyer and the seller, the net benefit generated by the first network is thus at most $T_2 - T_1$. To see why this is so, note that without the first network, the buyer and the seller would use the second network if and only if $V - C - V_o - C_o \geq T_2$. Thus, the incremental value of the first network is $T_2 - T_1$. If $V - C - V_o - C_o < T_2$, the incremental value of the first network is either $(V - C - V_o - C_o) - T_1$, which is therefore less than $T_2 - T_1$, or possibly zero, if the first network does not yield a positive benefit. Thus, with multiple substitutes for a network service, the value created by a network service is the incremental cost efficiency, if any.

There is a tendency to confuse the output of a network, that is, the network's transmission, transportation, or delivery services, with what is moved by the network. For example, the purpose of an electric power transmission network is to move electric power from a point of generation to a point of consumption, or more generally from a point of surplus to a point of deficit. The output of the electric power network is not electric power, only the transmission of that power. The output of the electric power grid is the transmission service itself.

As another example, a cable television network is used in the provision of entertainment, news, advertising, and other content to viewers. The output of the cable television network is the transmission service. The content is produced by content providers. Although important, this distinction may pose some difficulties when content providers are vertically integrated with the cable television network. However, this is similar to a manufacturer engaged in wholesale delivery. The network still represents a set of facilities and activities that are distinct from those used in the creation of content. Other than the physical difference between these types of facilities and activities, a good way to understand this distinction is by noting that some of the content carried by cable television companies is created by independent companies.

Thus, network services are distinct from what is transmitted, transported, or distributed. In addition, the network's *output* of services should not be confused with the *inputs* used to establish, operate, or maintain the network. Many types of productive inputs are used to create network services. Networks can require considerable amounts of land for rights of way and central offices. For example, railroads, electric power transmission grids, and natural gas pipelines use land for rights of way. Second, companies employ considerable amounts of labor services to construct, operate, and maintain network facilities. Third, companies employ substantial amounts of capital equipment to build the network, including heavy construction equipment. Capital equipment forms part of the network itself, including, for example, the lines and switches of a telecommunications network. Companies employ financial capital to finance the construction, operation, and maintenance of the network. However, land, labor, and capital are the inputs to the network, not its outputs.

By attaching a local loop, say a twisted copper pair, between the network and a household, a telephone company extends the transmission services of the network to the household. The local loop is an input used to provide the transmission service inbound or outbound; it is not an output of the network. This is an important issue because regulators have classified the local loop as an unbundled network element (UNE). Telecommunications companies are asked to provide other companies with the UNE as if it were an output of the network rather than a detached input of the network.

### D. Access to Networks

We define *access to networks* as the marketplace transactions between firms that provide networks and users of network services. Firms that establish networks can provide services to retail customers, wholesalers of services, suppliers of content and other complementary services, competitors, and other firms that supply network services. These transactions provide network users with access to network services.

We introduce a classification scheme that identifies the main forms of access to networks. Our analysis of access using the classification scheme allows economic modeling that distinguishes between market transactions for access to the network and governance transactions within the network. This important distinction will suggest a Coasian theory of networks, discussed in the next section.

Market transactions for network services are voluntary by their very nature. Accordingly, market participants engage in access transactions only when they anticipate obtaining gains from trade. This contrasts with regulatory mandates that place requirements on the provision of access by network firms. Such transactions are not voluntary in nature and thus may be expected to differ from what would be observed in the marketplace in the absence of regulation.

*Mandated access to networks* is a regulatory term of art. The definition of mandated access has its roots in the antitrust law of essential facilities and is spelled out at length in the 1996 Telecommunications Act and decisions by regulatory agencies. The classification system that we propose is useful for analyzing regulation and public policy toward networks.

The five types of access to networks are represented in Figure 1.13. Access requires a combination of market transactions and the necessary physical interfaces and technological standards to carry out the transactions. In the figure, networks are represented by solid nodes connected by solid lines. These indicate a network as a unified facility owned by a particular company. In the figure, the dotted lines represent the combination of market transactions and network interfaces that form access to networks.

The critical issue turns on who is seeking access – customers, competitors, or suppliers of complements. There are five main types of access: (1) retail access, (2) wholesale access, (3) interconnection access, (4) platform access, and (5) unbundled access. Retail access is provided to final customers, whereas wholesale and unbundled access are provided to competitors. Platform access means that the network facilities conform to a standard that allows other companies to provide complementary services. Platform access that is available to any and all suppliers of complements constitutes open access. Interconnection access refers to reciprocal connection agreements between networks that provide access to each other's facilities, forming a larger network in the process.

Each type of access has a corresponding set of regulations. Retail access is governed by traditional regulation of retail service, including state regulation of retail service in telecommunications, natural gas, and electricity. Such regulations include control over prices, rates of return, and service quality. Retail access is targeted through common carrier regulations that include service requirements. Wholesale and unbundled access in telecommunications regulation are addressed extensively by the Telecommunications Act of 1996 and FCC regulations. Platform access is addressed by open access regulations and antitrust enforcement, including merger conditions in the cable television industry. Reciprocal access through

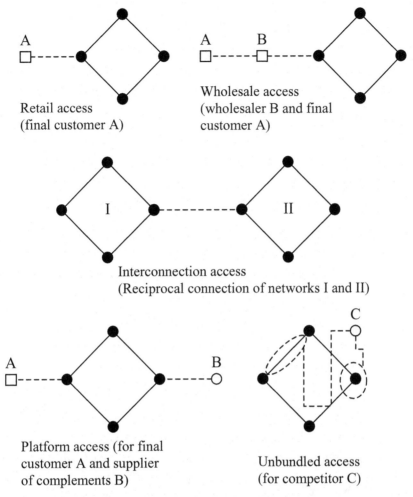

Retail access
(final customer A)

Wholesale access
(wholesaler B and final
customer A)

Interconnection access
(Reciprocal connection of networks I and II)

Platform access (for final
customer A and supplier
of complements B)

Unbundled access
(for competitor C)

**Figure 1.13.** The five forms of access to networks. Solid nodes and links indicate facilities of proprietary networks. Dashed lines indicate links combined with market transactions necessary to provide access.

interconnection is also addressed by the Telecommunications Act of 1996 and FCC rule making.

### 1. Retail Access

We interpret retail access to networks simply as the supply of a network's services to customers, just as any other type of producer would use its facilities to provide a service. Thus, retail access to postal networks is the provision of mailing services to customers, both to those customers sending mail and to those customers receiving mail. Retail access to electric power networks is the provision of electricity transmission services to companies that generate power and to companies that receive power for their own use or for retail distribution. Retail access to a telecommunications network means the ability to communicate with others who also have access to the network. Retail access to a transportation network means the ability to send or receive freight or to obtain travel services, depending on the type of transportation network. Access to a wholesale distribution network refers to the provision by wholesalers of distribution services to retailers and manufacturers.

Because retail access to a network refers to a customer's use of the network's services, which are the outputs of the network, it means more than simply a physical connection to the network. Rather, access refers to the opportunity to benefit from the services generated by network usage. Access is the subject of the economic transaction between the customer and the company that suppliers network services.

The price of retail access to a network's customers can be set by market forces just as with any other type of service. Indeed, markets exist for all types of network services, including transportation and travel, telecommunications, and distribution. Also, the prices of network services can be subject to cost-of-service regulation or other forms of government regulation. For example, state public utilities commissions regulate the prices charged by electricity companies that distribute electricity. The price regulation applies to both the resold power and the cost of retail distribution over the local power grid.

In his book *The Age of Access*, Rifkin (2000) observes that many types of services are delivered over networks. For example, entertainment and other types of content are delivered over telecommunications networks. The content provided to the final customer is owned by the company providing the content. For example, a household receives a transmission from a cable television company. The transmission is an entertainment program provided by a company that creates content, say Home Box Office (HBO). Rifkin is concerned about the fact that the final customer pays for viewing the content, but does not own anything. However, this situation is no different from any other type of rental agreement. Customers rent automobiles or apartments without any ownership. These types of rental agreements have been around for a long time and do not represent anything unfair or dangerous requiring government regulation.

Markets are as capable of pricing rentals as they are of pricing any other service. Rentals face several types of competition. First, rental companies compete with each other, so apartment rents reflect competition between apartment owners. Second, rental companies compete with the option of ownership: for example, customers renting or leasing cars compare these options with the cost of owning a car. Third, rental companies compete with companies that own or rent the necessary assets to provide the final service, so that a consumer renting a car would compare prices with the cost of taking a taxi. Finally, rental companies compete with substitute goods and services; for example, a customer considering renting a movie from a movie rental store would compare the benefits with other forms of entertainment and the opportunity costs of time.

The access to which Rifkin refers is to the content itself. That access is provided by the creators of the content. It is transmitted to the final customer through a network, but it is not the network that creates the content. Rather, the network provides transmission services; that is, the network provides access to the network itself. The fact that some types of content are transmitted over networks whereas other types of content are not – for example, movies can be transmitted over cable television or viewed in a movie theater – in itself does not provide any reason for regulation of networks.

## 2. Wholesale Access

Access to a network's services on a wholesale basis means that the network's elements are kept together, but that competitors are allowed to purchase and then resell the services provided by the entire network to final customers. Because wholesale access utilizes the entire network in largely the same manner as the network owner, the ability of the network to operate is less likely to be affected than in the case of access to only a portion of the network. The main things that are affected would appear to be the merchant activities of the network owner. The wholesale provision of network services simply removes some of the retail activities of the network operator and replaces those activities with wholesale activities. These activities are more a matter of transaction costs, including the costs of back office activities, marketing, and sales.

## 3. Interconnection Access

Interconnection access refers to any reciprocal interconnection agreements between networks. Most networks in a given industry are interconnected. For example, practically all telecommunications networks are either directly or indirectly connected, so that a telephone call originating from any wireless or wireline telecommunications system can reach anyone on any other system around the world. Interconnection is reciprocal because communication of this type is a two-way street, with each network both originating and terminating telephone calls. The Internet is a network of networks with reciprocal arrangements. Packets of data from a given communication are split up and travel separately across multiple networks. Wholesale electric power transmission grids often comprise multiple interconnected networks. Transportation networks, such as railroads, are often interconnected so that trains can travel across multiple networks.

Some connections are internal to the network, whereas others are external to it. The nodes and links that form networks generally are physical facilities, such as switches and lines in a telecommunications system. In our discussion, the switches and lines that compose a network are owned and managed by a single firm. This is the same as a manufacturing firm owning and managing its equipment and other facilities.

Access refers to connections that are external to the network and mediated by market transactions. For any given network, there are nodes and links that are outside the network. For example, in a telecommunications network, customer premises equipment and local area networks are attached to the network but lie outside its boundaries. When there are multiple networks that interconnect, each network is independently owned and managed. When independent companies have platform access, the activities of the companies that supply complementary products are outside the network even if they provide services that are transmitted by the network.

This discussion has established that the physical shapes of networks are distinct from the economic relationships that govern networks. Two sets of nodes and links may be identical in terms of physical facilities but very different in terms of the economic relationships that establish those networks. For example, one network could be owned and operated by a single firm, whereas another identical set of nodes and links may be formed by two interconnected networks, with each of the two networks owned and operated by different firms. For example, in Figure 1.13, the interconnected networks could compose one network (with a solid line showing the connection) or they could be distinct networks.

## 4. Platform Access

Platform access refers to technological standards that allow suppliers of complementary services to supply their products to customers of the network's services. Platform access can include access to the network's transmission services so that the supplier can provide services over the network and the network's customers can receive the complementary services. It can also include the ability of suppliers of complementary services to know and use the technological standards of the network in creating new types of services. A company that owns a network can in principle grant selective platform access to a select group of companies through licenses, partnerships, and other contracts. Alternatively, a network owner can open its network services and standards to any company that provides complementary goods and services. A network is said to be *modular* or to exhibit an *open architecture* if most suppliers of complementary services can gain access to the network.

The Internet is the prime example of open architecture. The transfer control protocol and Internet protocol (TCP/IP) are open standards that allow a wide variety of software applications to be transmitted over the Internet, permitting such services as search engines and Internet commerce to be provided by companies using the Internet. In addition, a wide variety of types of information including voice, data, images, and video can be transmitted over the network.

Discussions of networks often include other industries in which companies sell complementary goods, such as cameras and film. When standards are widely available and not necessarily proprietary, independent companies can produce complementary components, allowing consumers to assemble groups of products.

In information technology, the IBM standard made possible a modular set of products that are complementary so that consumers can obtain computers, software applications, and peripheral devices such as printers, monitors, and memory devices that work together. In addition, the components of the computer itself, including microprocessors, memory chips, and monitors, are sufficiently standardized to allow these products to be supplied by a variety of industries connected to information technology. Such common technological standards need not be confined to high technology, because similar modularity is observed in a variety of products such as automobiles, bicycles, audio systems, and video display systems. Multiple companies produce components for these products. Also, consumers can purchase a wide variety of add-on complementary products. The notions of a platform and an open architecture are very general ones, and include networks as well as suites of complementary products, although in the discussion that follows we restrict attention to networks.

## 5. Unbundled Access

Provision of unbundled access to networks to competitors is another matter entirely. Here regulators use the term to refer to the use of the services of inputs used to establish the network. Access to inputs, such as UNEs in the case of a telecommunications network, corresponds to the antitrust provision of access to what are termed essential facilities. This type of regulated access has significantly different economic consequences.

In the case of access to the services of network elements by a competitor, the ability of the network owner to operate the network is likely to be impaired. The network cannot provide the same level of services if network elements are operated independently or are subject to capacity constraints due to use by competitors. As we will see in a later chapter, the economically correct access price depends on what the company could have obtained by using those network services itself or by selling network services to some other party. The proper measure of the value of network access is thus the value of the network services that could otherwise have been provided, which in turn is determined by the value of the network's final output.

The types of networks on which we are focusing are physical production facilities that encompass factors of production such as land, labor services, capital equipment, and technology. Construction of these facilities requires network owners to invest in substantial fixed assets that should be viewed in the same way as other types of capital equipment such as manufacturing plants, office buildings, and commercial structures. Like other long-term assets, the network's physical production facilities do not vary directly with output in the short term. Moreover, like other capital investments, the configuration of the network's physical assets cannot be changed in the short term. Given sufficient time, however, the network's capital equipment is variable and can be adjusted to create different capacity levels.

The operation of a network's facilities often requires variable inputs as well, such as the labor used to maintain its facilities and to monitor its operations.

In combination, the productive inputs that constitute the network are used to create a stream of services, such as the transmission and distribution of communications, that are the outputs of the network. Just as natural gas transmission does not consume the physical pipeline, usage of a telecommunications network does not consume the network itself, but instead only temporarily precludes the provision of services to some other user. Of course, network use does impose some wear and tear on the network's physical production facilities. The measures of depreciation employed under generally accepted accounting principles do not accurately indicate the value of the services provided by the equipment, however. As a result, the applicable depreciation rules typically do not properly reflect the equipment's economic life.

## E. A Coasian Theory of Networks

The five types of access refer to a network's external connections. The five-part classification scheme for access to networks provides the basis for a Coasian theory of networks. The communications sector is composed of many networks. These networks often are interconnected to form a very large network of networks. This extends beyond the Internet, which itself is a network of networks, to encompass traditional telephone networks, cable television transmission networks, data networks, and mobile telecommunications.

This raises the critical question: *what determines the boundaries of a network?* The size and structure of individual networks are closely related to their boundaries. The economy's communications depend on the boundaries of individual networks and their interconnections with retail customers, wholesalers, competitors, and partners who use network elements and content providers who depend on platform access. Finally, the interconnections between networks themselves determine the form of the economy's overall communications network.

This is a special case of a much more general issue, namely, what determines the boundaries of the firm? The answer was first given by Nobel Prize winner Ronald Coase (1937, 1988, 1994) and is the foundation for the New Institutional Economics. The theory of the firm in the presence of transaction costs can be specialized to address the boundaries of networks. Network connections are internal to the firm when the organizational costs of managing the connection as part of a network are less than market transaction costs. Network connections are external to the firm and take the form of access when the organizational costs of managing the connection as part of a network are greater than market transaction costs.

Consider first retail access. Networks do not vertically integrate with buyers because retail access for final customers is a product of the network, yet even these connections have internetwork aspects. Households and business customers of telecommunications networks often have internal communications networks. The division of the network between retail customers and the network provider depends on the relative size of the costs of managing network connections internally and transaction costs of external connections.

Wholesale access is provided when the network owner finds the organizational costs of conducting retail sales greater than the market transaction costs of dealing with independent wholesalers. Unbundled access is provided when the network owner finds the organizational costs of managing particular nodes and links in the network to be greater than the transaction costs of dealing with independent operators.

Networks are connected to content providers that transmit their services over the networks. Platform access is provided when the network owner finds the organizational costs of managing the development and supply of complementary services to be greater than the transaction costs of dealing with independent suppliers. In the case of platform access, the relative inefficiencies and reduced creativity of internal provision of complementary services translate into incremental organizational costs.

Interconnection of distinct networks can be more efficient than a unified network if the additional organizational costs of managing the combined networks are greater than the transaction costs associated with interconnection. The costs of managing a network also include costs associated with providing retail access and procuring services, as well as facilities management. Thus, the cost savings from separate networks that are interconnected also reflect all the operating costs as well as other types of transaction costs. Many diverse telecommunications networks, including wireline telecommunications, mobile telephony, the Internet, and cable telephony, can coexist through interconnection.

The market for communications services involves two types of connections. Access refers to market transactions for network services that must accompany connections outside the boundaries of a network. Management transactions refer to connections within the boundaries of the network. The economy's communications systems involve a complex set of interconnections both inside and outside the boundaries of networks. The firms that provide network services by establishing privately owned networks must choose between connections that are external to their networks and connections that are internal to their networks.

The economic decisions of firms that provide network services involve choice regarding the boundaries of their networks and interconnections between networks. This suggests that the boundaries of networks and their pattern of interconnections follow a Coasian theory of networks.

---

**Network Proposition.** Network connections take the form of access when organizational governance costs exceed market transaction costs. Network connections take the form of management transactions within the network when market transaction costs exceed organizational governance costs.

---

Firms expand the boundaries of their networks to the farthest point where the incremental costs of management transactions do not exceed the incremental costs of access transactions.

The theory of networks presented in this proposition will guide the discussion throughout the rest of the book. The proposition helps to analyze the extent to which companies that own networks are vertically integrated. These issues are a special case of vertical integration, but the implications for networks need to be fully explored.

Competitive markets generate an efficient pattern of access and internal connections. In competitive markets, optimization by firms and efficient transactions should result in networks with efficient boundaries and efficient interconnections with users of the network. There should be efficient access transactions with customers, wholesalers, suppliers of complementary services, and competitors. Public policy interventions in markets for communications can be expected to affect the boundaries of networks and their interconnections. Understanding how markets generate efficient networks should prove useful in understanding the impact of public policies on the structure of networks and their pattern of interconnections.

*          *          *

The efficient boundary of firms that operate networks is an important but particular case of the boundary of the firm. Networks provide wholesale, unbundled, and platform access when the organizational costs of managing the network are greater than market transaction costs. Networks are vertically integrated when market transaction costs exceed organizational costs. Thus, the efficient boundary of a network firm is determined by tradeoff between costs of controlling the network within an organization and transaction costs of market coordination.

The goal of regulatory policy should be to realize efficiencies in the formation of networks and the organization of network firms. Our main proposition also provides guidance for merger policies toward networks. To the extent that markets realize efficient ownership structures and network design, regulatory and antitrust forbearance are called for. Public policy in the network industries, particularly compelled access, should be chosen carefully to avoid creating incentives to form inefficient networks and to allow firms to form efficient networks.

# 2

# The Design and Costs of Networks

How do network owners make decisions about network creation and configuration? This question is critical for public policy, particularly compelled access to networks. The answer is more complex than it might appear at first blush. First and foremost, private companies create networks by designing network architecture and investing in network facilities. Second, private companies create larger networks by interconnecting with other networks through contracts and physical facilities. Third, consumers help to shape networks by decisions about what types of network services to purchase. Fourth, suppliers of complementary services affect networks by the types of products they invent and sell. Thus, networks come from supply decisions by network providers, interconnection between networks, demand decisions by network customers, and supply decisions by providers of complementary services.

The regulatory actions of public policymakers can have a significant impact on supply, demand, vertical integration, and access decisions. The law of unintended consequences can make these impacts difficult to predict. Regulations that constrain access prices below market rates or compel access reduce incentives to invest in network facilities, while at the same time stimulating demand for network services. Regulatory price constraints and compelled access requirements will not be responsive to increases in market demand, in contrast to market prices, thus further lowering incentives to invest. Also, access price regulations and compelled access can distort interconnection decisions and affect access agreements between companies that build and operate networks.

Understanding the optimal design of networks is critical for public policy. There is a tendency on the part of regulators to view networks in retrospect (Sidak and Spulber 1997b). Networks are viewed as *established* facilities so that regulators can compel access with relatively little effect on network design. Of course, regulatory policies affect decisions about the design of future networks. They also affect decisions to maintain the performance of existing networks and decisions to extend the scope of a network or to upgrade its technology. This chapter examines factors that affect the design and development of networks. The complex process of network design shows how input choices are the result of a series of interconnected

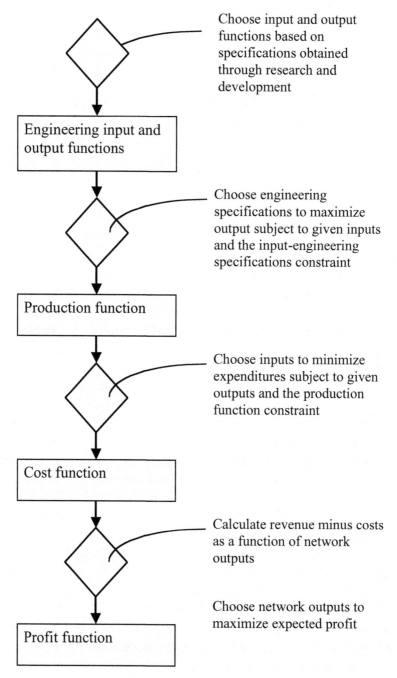

**Figure 2.1.** Building networks.

engineering and economic decisions. As a result, compelling access is likely to be inconsistent with this series of decisions by occupying a portion of a particular network component's capacity.

Building networks has four conceptual steps. These four steps are represented in Figure 2.1. First, based on research and development, network engineers obtain two sets of functions that specify the output of the network and the necessary inputs of the network, respectively. Second, network engineers choose the technical specifications that maximize the output of the network subject to available inputs and the relationship between the technical specifications and network inputs. This results in an economic production function that specifies outputs as a function of inputs. Third, the network company chooses the mix of inputs to minimize expenditures subject to given outputs and the economic production function. This specifies the economic cost function that relates total costs to output levels. Fourth, the network company calculates revenue minus costs as a function of network outputs. This yields the profit function for the network. As the conclusion of the planning process, the network firm chooses the mix of outputs to maximize expected profits. By backward induction, the profit-maximizing output mix specifies the necessary mix of inputs from the cost-minimization process, which in turn determines the engineering specifications and design of the network.

## A. The Optimal Design of Networks

To say that networks are interconnected might appear to be a tautology. However, networks are also interconnected in the sense that the whole is greater than the sum of its parts. Nodes and links can be critical; without a particular node or link the network may not provide the full set of services its designers intended. Even if a network could be assembled in a modular way, removal of a node or link could impair its overall ability to function. An automobile's tires are certainly modular, but remove one and the car does not travel far. The notion of access to unbundled network elements advanced by the Telecommunications Act of 1996 and by the Federal Communications Commission's concept of total element long-run incremental cost (TELRIC) makes the mistake of treating networks as collections of independent parts, which recalls the joke about military procurement that a B-52 was not an aircraft; it was just a lot of parts flying in close formation.

This section examines the optimal design of networks and shows that networks are more than collections of nodes and links. Because the configuration of a network is the result of optimization, the nodes and links in the final design are selected to achieve the designer's purpose. The parts of the network are necessarily interdependent.

## 1. Choosing the Network Configuration

A network designer chooses a set of nodes $N = \{1, \ldots, n\}$ and a set of links $L = \{1, \ldots, m\}$, each of which connects a pair of distinct nodes $i$ and $j$. A network designer chooses the set of nodes and the links between them to maximize profit. For a given set of services, the network designer chooses the network configuration to minimize costs. The network's projected services are chosen to maximize expected profit, which in turn determines the underlying cost-minimizing network config-uration. Both the nodes and the links of the network affect the costs of delivering the services.

The costs of nodes and links reflect the underlying costs of construction, oper-ation, and maintenance. Moreover, the costs of the nodes and links depend on a number of attributes that are critical to delivery of network services. Among these attributes are the following:

(1) *Capacity* of nodes and links;
(2) *Geographic distance* covered by the links, the related features of the terrain such as hills, valleys, and water, and economic and regulatory obstacles;
(3) *Speed of transmission* through nodes and links;
(4) *Reliability* of nodes and links;
(5) *Durability of capital equipment* needed for nodes and links;
(6) *Relative proportions* of construction, operation, and maintenance costs of nodes and links; and
(7) *Rate of technological obsolescence of nodes and links.*

All of these factors affect the cost of providing network services through a particular set of nodes and links.

A networks should be considered as an integrated whole when nodes and links potentially affect the overall cost and performance of the network. One way that links can be essential is if they provide the only connections between nodes, or even more importantly, between distinct subnetworks. This latter property corresponds to the idea of a connected graph in graph theory. A graph is said to be *connected* if it cannot be split up into two disjoint graphs. Equivalently, a graph is connected if any pair of nodes is connected by a *path*, which is a sequence that consists of connected but distinct nodes and links. If a network can be split up into distinct subnetworks, the connected subnetworks sometimes are referred to as *components* in graph theory.[1]

There are two measures of how connected a graph is. One measure is to remove nodes to see whether the remaining graph is still connected. A graph $G$ with at least $k + 1$ nodes is *k-connected* if it is still connected after $k - 1$ or fewer nodes are removed. The other measure is to remove links to see whether the remaining graph is still connected. A graph $G$ is said to be *k-link-connected* if it is still connected after $k - 1$ or fewer links are removed.

Even if a graph is *k*-connected, links need not be redundant. Rather, extra links provide reliability if some links fail to function properly. Also, extra links add capacity, so that links need not be considered duplicates. Some links are needed for additional capacity if traffic flows are not uniform or if those links provide backbone transmission that is distinct from lower-volume transmission to and from terminal nodes.

---

1  For more precise definitions, see Wilson and Beineke (1979).

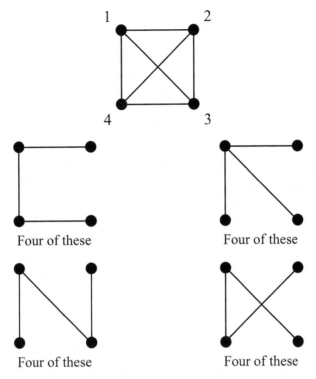

**Figure 2.2.** There are sixteen minimum spanning trees in a graph with four nodes.

## 2. Cost-Minimizing Network Design

A standard approach to network design is to begin with a set of nodes and to imagine all possible links between those nodes. With $n$ nodes, there are $\frac{1}{2}n(n-1)$ links in a complete graph. Then consider the cost of each link within the complete set. Not all of these links are necessary to achieve the desired network attributes. By only constructing the minimal set of links that are needed to achieve the desired network attributes, the network designer obtains a cost-minimizing network.

The first network attribute we consider is one in which all nodes are linked together. In graph-theory terms, a graph that connects all of the nodes with the minimum number of links is known as a *tree graph*. A tree graph that connects all of the nodes in a network is known as a *spanning tree*. In a network with $n$ nodes, such a spanning tree would consist of $n-1$ links. A tree graph has no *cycles*, which are paths along which it is possible to pass through a succession of links and eventually return to the original node without crossing any link more than once. The network designer's problem is to find the least-cost tree that includes all of the desired nodes. In graph theory terms, this tree is a *minimum spanning tree*.

The network designer begins with the complete graph, as shown in Figure 2.2. Then the network designer evaluates the cost of each link. Finally, the network designer chooses a tree that connects all of the nodes at the lowest cost, which is the minimum spanning tree. Finding the most efficient tree is complicated by the fact

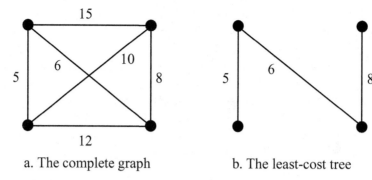

a. The complete graph              b. The least-cost tree

**Figure 2.3.** The least-cost minimum spanning tree network. Total cost is $5 + 6 + 8 = 19$.

that the number of spanning trees is very large for even a small number of nodes and quickly becomes extremely large as the number of nodes increases. Network designers resort to algorithms that run on computers to solve such problems. According to Cayley's formula (1889), the number of spanning trees in a graph with $n$ nodes is $n^{n-2}$, where $n$ is greater than 2. For four nodes there are sixteen possibilities, depicted in Figure 2.2. For ten nodes, there are 100 million possible configurations.

Consider the network designer's problem when choosing the minimum-cost spanning tree. A *network*, in graph theory, is defined as a graph with numerical values assigned to the links. Figure 2.3 shows a complete graph with the costs of links and the least-cost spanning tree.

The least-cost network can be found by Prim's algorithm (1957). Choose any node arbitrarily as the initial node and find the least-cost link connected to that node. Add that link and its end node to form the start of the tree. Find the least-cost link connected to that tree and add that link and its end node to the tree. Continue until all nodes are included.

The design of a cost-minimizing network in the tree problem shows how networks are integrated. The final network design is the best selection from the set of $n^{n-2}$ alternative configurations. The links are not chosen individually, but reflect instead the best configuration, so that the choices of what links to create are interdependent. Removing a link from the final network does more damage them simply breaking up the tree. If the network designer had known that such a link would be removed, the designer would have chosen an entirely different network configuration. Occupying the capacity of a link would have a similar effect, albeit on a lesser scale. This suggests that granting a third party access to a network element such as a link has complex consequences for the characteristics of the network.

### 3. Cost-Minimizing Design of a Cycle Network

Consider the problem of a network designer who must choose a network that links a set of nodes in a complete cycle.[2] This corresponds to the well-known traveling

---

2   A cycle that links all of the nodes in a graph is known as a *Hamiltonian cycle*.

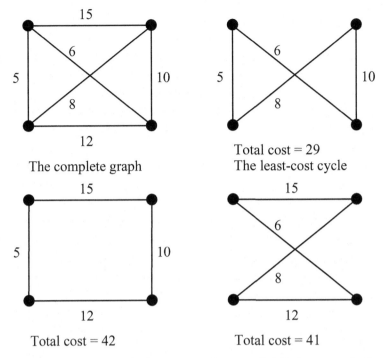

The complete graph

Total cost = 29
The least-cost cycle

Total cost = 42

Total cost = 41

**Figure 2.4.** Choosing the least-cost cycle network. Total cost equals 29.

salesman problem. A complete graph with four nodes is shown in Figure 2.3. The graph indicates the cost of establishing each of the links. The cycle network is useful for a transportation system that completes a circuit. It is also useful for a system of product distribution in which freight transportation completes a circuit between warehouses and retail outlets. The least-cost cycle network is shown in Figure 2.4.

The least-cost cycle network is an integrated network not only because each link is needed to complete the cycle, but also as a result of the optimization decision. The network designer can have multiple alternative cycles to choose from, depending on the initial graph. Accordingly, regulatory decisions that increase the cost of individual links can significantly alter the configuration of the least-cost network.

## 4. Network Configurations with Economies of Scale in Links

The characteristics of links, including the technology used for transmission, play an important role in determining the optimal network configuration. If there are sufficient economies of scale in links, the network designer may choose a network configuration that consolidates traffic. Again, the optimal network configuration is highly sensitive to the costs of links. Regulatory policy cannot treat links as separable from the network because the costs of individual links affect the choice of network design.

To illustrate this effect, consider a network with *n* nodes that are located in two clusters. The network designer must choose between two network configurations. The network designer can create a star network by establishing a central hub and

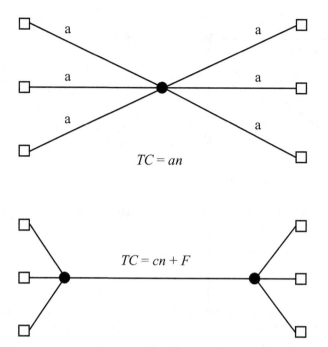

**Figure 2.5.** One hub or two? The choice between a star network and a trunk line network.

connecting all the terminal nodes with individual spokes. Alternatively, the network designer can create two hubs, one for each cluster, and connect them with a high-capacity trunk line.

Choosing between the star network and the two-hub network depends on a comparison of the cost of the spokes in the star network and the cost of the trunk line. Suppose for simplicity that there is no difference between the cost of establishing a single central hub and the total cost of establishing two peripheral hubs. Also, for ease of discussion, suppose that the cost of reaching a peripheral hub is negligible. The cost of a link in the star network is $a$. The variable cost per final customer of the trunk line is $c$ regardless of where the customers are located. The trunk line has a fixed cost of $F$. As the number of total customers gets large, the two-hub configuration becomes desirable. The critical number of customers, given that $a > c$, is

$$n^* = \frac{F}{a - c}.$$

As long as $n$ is greater than or equal to the value $n^*$, the network designer will choose a two-hub configuration. The two choices are represented in Figure 2.5.

Even though the two alternative networks appear modular, it should be clear that the optimal network design is sensitive to the costs of individual network elements and to the number of potential customers. For example, suppose that the cost of a link in the star network is $a = 20$ and the variable cost per customer of the trunk line is $c = 15$. Suppose that the fixed cost of the trunk line is 48. Then the trunk-line network only becomes attractive if there are 10 or more customers.

Suppose that a regulator were to require the addition or removal of terminal nodes through unbundled access. This would affect which network configuration was optimal because the number of terminal nodes affects the cost of each design. This conclusion applies generally to more complex types of networks and different cost structures.

## 5. The Max-Flow/Min-Cut of a Network

In addition to providing insights into how the interrelationships among particular network components affect the network's overall cost and reliability, graph theory also reveals how network configuration affects the network's maximum capacity. This section introduces a well-known principle in graph theory known as the max-flow/min-cut theorem, which provides a way to determine the maximum carrying capacity of any transportation network and the costs associated with operating it at that level.[3] Although a formal proof of the max-flow/min-cut theorem exceeds the scope of this book, the basic intuitions underlying it can be easily explained in a relatively nontechnical manner. The theorem focuses on the maximum flow capacity of a network transporting traffic from a *source* (usually denoted $s$) to a destination called a *sink* (usually denoted $t$).[4] A *cut* is a set of links that, if removed, divide the graph into two subgraphs. The two subgraphs contain distinct sets of nodes. Of greatest relevance, for our purposes, are those cuts in which the source (node $s$) and the sink (node $t$) lie in different sets. The set of nodes containing the source node $s$ is typically called $S$, and the set of nodes containing the sink node $t$ is typically called $T$. The key insight is that any traffic bound from node $s$ to node $t$ necessarily must travel from nodes contained in set $S$ to nodes contained in set $T$ and hence along the links in the cut. As a result, the total carrying capacity of the links directly connecting one of the nodes in set $S$ to nodes in set $T$ represents a constraint on the total carrying capacity of the network.

---

3  This theorem is prominently discussed in most graph theory texts. For a relatively accessible exposition, see Stein (2004).

4  The network is portrayed as a one-way network from a single source to a single sink. Certain aspects of this simplification do not affect the generality of the analysis. For example, the insights provided by the analysis of $s - t$ networks can be extended to networks with multiple sources and multiple sinks without any loss of generality (Wallis 2000). In addition, the foregoing exposition focuses solely on the capacity of links without taking into account the capacity limits on nodes. A node with a capacity constraint can be reconceptualized as two uncapacitated nodes connected by a capacity-constrained link. As a result, the entire analysis can focus solely on the capacity of links without loss of generality.

Other aspects are potentially more problematic. The most significant concern is that telecommunications networks tend to be two-way rather than one-way. It is theoretically feasible to model these flows as two different networks, although if the capacity of certain nodes is used for traffic passing in both directions, some means for trading off capacity must be devised. The problem can also be analyzed as a multicommodity flow problem. Multicommodity problems pose additional difficulties that sometimes border on the intractable (Stein 2004).

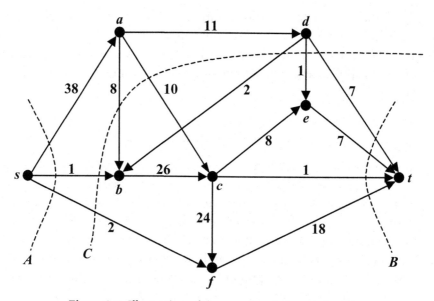

**Figure 2.6.** Illustration of the max-flow/min-cut theorem.

This insight is most easily understood by analyzing the simplest cuts in the context of the relatively simple network depicted in Figure 2.6. That network consists of eight nodes connected by a series of links; the capacity of each link is indicated on the graph.[5] Consider the cut represented by the dotted line labeled A. In this cut, which consists of the links connecting node *s* to nodes *a*, *b*, and *f*, set *S* consists of only node *s*, whereas set *T* consists of the remaining seven nodes (*a*, *b*, *c*, *d*, *e*, *f*, and *t*). Any traffic leaving node *s* must necessarily travel along one of the links connecting node *s* to node *a*, *b*, or *f*. As a result, it is clear that the total carrying capacity of the network from *s* to *t* can be no greater than the sum of the capacity of those links, which in this case is 38 + 1 + 2 = 41. A similar logic obtains with respect to cut B, which divides the network into a set *S* consisting of seven nodes (*s*, *a*, *b*, *c*, *d*, *e*, and *f*) and a set *T* consisting only of node *t*. Because only four links connect to node *t*, it is also clear that the total capacity of the network cannot exceed the total capacity of those four links (which in this case is 7 + 7 + 1 + 18 = 33). Because every traffic flow must necessarily pass through both of these cuts, the capacity of the links crossing these cuts represents a constraint on the flow capacity of the entire system. In other words, the network cannot possibly carry more than the lower of 41 or 33.

One can generalize from this insight by analyzing the entire universe of possible cuts to the network. The cut with the smallest capacity (called the *minimum cut*) represents the maximum flow that one can push through the system.[6] The

---

5   Figure 2.6 is adapted from Jungnickel (1999).

6   Although it is quite intuitive that the maximum carrying capacity of a transport network must be *less than or equal to* the capacity of the minimum cut, the max-flow/min-cut theorem actually establishes that the maximum flow of the network is *strictly equal to* the capacity of the minimum cut.

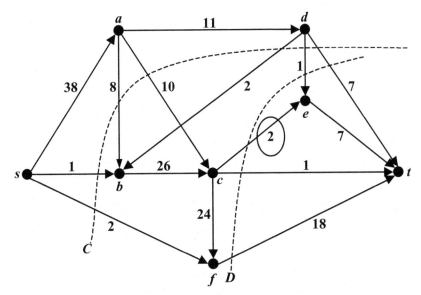

**Figure 2.7.** Impact of unbundled access on network capacity.

minimum cut in any network can be identified using an iterative algorithm. In this case, the cut with the minimum capacity is the one depicted by cut *C*, which has a capacity of 31. Because all traffic traveling between nodes *s* and *t* must necessarily travel across cut *C*, the total capacity of the links crossed by cut *C* necessarily represents the maximum carrying capacity of the network. In addition, the algorithm for identifying the minimum cut also determines the flow passing along each noncritical link when the network is operating at full capacity. This makes it possible to determine the direct cost of operating the network when it is carrying its maximum volume.[7]

Now consider the impact on the network of granting a competitor access to a network element. Access ties up some of the capacity of the leased elements, which in turn reduces the capacity available to the network owner. One of the most interesting insights of graph theory is that changing the capacity of any particular network component can have a surprising and somewhat unpredictable impact on the capacity of the network. Indeed, changes in capacity can cause the links that compose the minimum cut (which represents the constraint on the total carrying capacity of the network) to change to a completely different set of links.

Consider, for example, the situation depicted in Figure 2.7, which is the same network represented in Figure 2.6, except that now a competitor has obtained access to six units of the capacity of the link connecting nodes *c* and *e* (marked on the graph with a circle). From the perspective of the network owner, this has the effect of reducing the effective capacity of that link by that amount. In this case, the magnitude

---

7 If the network is not operating at full capacity, the optimization problem instead focuses on identifying the minimum-cost flow and requires a slightly different approach (Fleischer 2004).

of this reduction causes the links composing the minimum cut to change to the ones portrayed by the line marked *D*. As a result, granting a competitor access to a link that was not part of the minimum cut (and thus had slack in its capacity) nonetheless reduces the effective capacity of the entire network. The amount of reduction is not necessarily equal to the magnitude of the access granted. Instead, the amount of reduction depends upon the configuration of the particular network involved. In the situation portrayed in Figure 2.7, the impact of allowing a competitor to occupy six units of capacity in the link connecting node *c* with node *e* is to reduce the effective capacity of the entire network by two. The value of carrying two units from node *s* to node *t* represents the opportunity cost of granting this competitor access to the link between nodes *c* and *e*. In addition, the change in direct costs associated with granting access can be determined by recalculating the flow passing along each noncritical link when the postaccess network is operating at full capacity.

At the same time, it is quite possible that granting access to a particular link might have no effect on the total carrying capacity of the network. Whether that is the case depends on how much slack exists in the link to which access is being granted. If the link to which access is being granted is not part of the minimum cut and the additional reduction in capacity does not make it part of the minimum cut, granting access has no impact on the overall capacity or the full-capacity operating costs of the network. On the other hand, if the link is already part of the minimum cut or if granting access to that link places it on the minimum cut, granting access to that link reduces the total carrying capacity of the network.

Therefore, the retail value of the reduction in network capacity represents a good measure of the opportunity cost associated with granting access to competitors. Note, however, that the reduction in capacity is not necessarily equal to the size of access granted. The rest of the network may compensate for the reduction in the capacity of one link in ways that partially offset the impact of the reduction. In practice, access by competitors is not an isolated event but a pattern of usage that changes over time as more competitors access the network. The network's available carrying capacity will evolve over time as a consequence of the access decisions of competitors.

## B. Production Functions of Networks

Networks provide streams of services, such as transmission and transportation. The services provided by such networks are usually measurable, at least in principle. For example, the services of a telecommunications system can be measured in terms of message minutes of use per unit of time. The Internet measures traffic flows in terms of megabytes of data transmitted per unit of time or packets transmitted per unit of time. The output of a passenger transportation system, such as a railroad or an airline, might be measured in terms of passenger miles per unit of time. The output of a freight transportation system can be measured in ton-miles per unit of time. An electric power transmission grid measures capacity in terms of megawatt-miles.

Networks, however, provide outputs that are much more complex than what is represented by these total measures. The origins and destinations of network transmissions are also very important. For example, it is possible to identify origin–destination pairs for telecommunications traffic, allowing identification of inter-country traffic flows in international telecommunication. Transportation systems can identify traffic by city pairs or country pairs. Accordingly, networks should properly be viewed as providing multiple types of services. Companies that operate networks are multiproduct firms.

Network services can be classified in terms of quality of service. For example, in a freight transportation system, customers can choose various grades of service that specify the speed of delivery. Other types of network services require more subtle distinctions. A telecommunications system can offer not only distance-based services such as local and long distance calling, but also switching services such as call waiting, call forwarding, and caller identification.

In this section we examine the technological relationship between network services and the underlying structure of the network. The production function of a network specifies this relationship.

## 1. Production Functions and Engineering

Production functions in economics are schedules that associate the outputs of production processes with the inputs. Let $Q$ be the output of a production process and let $X$, $Y$, and $Z$ be the inputs. Then $Q = F(X, Y, Z)$ is a production function. For some production processes, an economic production function can be derived using an underlying set of engineering relationships.

Let $w = (w, \ldots, w_J)$ be a list of engineering variables such as weight, length, volume, speed, or strength. These engineering variables determine output through an engineering production relation

$$(1) \qquad Q = H(w_1, \ldots, w_J).$$

To achieve the desired level of the engineering variables requires the economic inputs

$$(2) \quad X = G^X(w_1, \ldots, w_J), \quad Y = G^Y(w_1, \ldots, w_J), \quad Z = G^Z(w_1, \ldots, w_J).$$

Take the level of the economic inputs $X$, $Y$, and $Z$ as fixed. Then choose the engineering variables to make the best use of the economic inputs. Thus, maximize final output $Q$ subject to the three input relationships with fixed input levels:

$$\max_w H(w)$$

$$(3) \qquad \text{subject to } X = G^X(w), \quad Y = G^Y(w), \quad \text{and} \quad Z = G^Z(w).$$

The solution is a vector of engineering variables that depends on the levels of the economic inputs, $w^* = w^*(X, Y, Z)$. Now, substitute this solution into the engineering production relationship to obtain an economic production function:

$$(4) \qquad Q = H(w^*(X, Y, Z)) \equiv F(X, Y, Z).$$

The economic production function includes the necessary information about the underlying engineering production relationships.[8]

The connection between the underlying network and the output of services depends on engineering relationships. Chenery long ago suggested that understanding the engineer's problem was a useful guide to the use of engineering data in economics. Chenery observed that in order to use engineering data it was necessary to "go back to the intermediate stage in engineering calculations at which the possibilities of using various types of inputs are considered" (Chenery 1949, p. 510).

The construction, operation, and maintenance of a transportation or transmission network involve complex engineering processes. Telecommunications, electric power, and natural gas network systems require sophisticated designs, construction methods, and operating procedures. These important and difficult aspects of creating network services are implicit in the economic production functions of networks. This does not mean policymakers can go straight to the production functions and ignore the engineering relationships. It is also not our contention that regulators should become engineers as well as economists (not to mention attorneys). Rather, we suggest that regulations that change input–output relationships have complicated effects on the underlying engineering processes.

Because a production function is constructed from engineering processes, it is difficult to extract particular inputs from a production process. Input requirements can stem from many different engineering processes. The resources, labor, and capital equipment in a production function are *aggregates*. This means they are added up from the requirements of the many individual engineering processes used to produce final outputs.

Removing some amount of one input or another, say a computer or some other piece of capital equipment, can have far-reaching effects in an optimized engineering system. The network engineer must compensate for removal of the input by necessary reductions in output, not to mention rebalancing of potentially all affected engineering processes to best produce the lower level of output. Accordingly, engineering processes that support production create connections between inputs that are not easily broken. Providing unbundled access to inputs in a production process thus is likely to have complex effects throughout the underlying engineering processes.

---

8   This approach is based on the classic analysis of Chenery (1949). See also Wibe (1984).

## **2.** Production Functions for a Single-Output Network

Networks generally require capital equipment. The nodes and links of a network can be associated with specific capital equipment, such as the switches and lines of a telecommunications network. Let $N = \{1, \ldots, n\}$ be the set of nodes of the network and let $L$ be the set of $m$ links that connect these nodes. For the purpose of this section, let $N$ and $L$ represent the services of capital equipment that are respectively associated with the nodes and links of the network.

Typically, a production function for a firm also depends on land and other resources, labor services at various skill levels, and additional parts, components, and materials. In what follows, let $X$ represent land and resources, let $Y$ represent labor, and let $Z$ represent any other purchased parts and services. The production function of a firm that operates a single-output network is defined by

(5) $$Q = F(N, L, X, Y, Z).$$

A production function represents the most efficient use of the inputs given a particular technology. Accordingly, the *network production function* shows the tradeoffs between nodes, links, and the other inputs.

The network production function describes how different links applied to a particular set of nodes affect output. Because the production function depends on the sets of nodes and links, the network's *configuration* matters, not just the number of nodes or links. The various alternative inputs in a network can refer to the types of switches at nodes or the types of lines in the links, such as copper, coaxial cable, and fiber optics. The complex engineering decisions about technologies, software, and network design thus underlie the network production function.

### *a. Natural Gas Transmission*

Interestingly, Hollis Chenery's classic illustration of an engineering production function was for a network, namely pipeline transportation of natural gas. Interstate natural gas transmission pipelines form networks through the United States. Pipelines, the links of the network, are generally made of welded steel up to 48 inches in diameter, with compressor stations located along the length of the lines (Gallick 1993). The nodes of the natural gas pipeline system are the supply points, the delivery points, and interconnections within the network. The service of the system is its natural transmission rate in terms of millions of cubic feet of gas per day. Consider the transmission rate of a single link as a proxy for a more complex web of lines. Suppose that there are a single supply node and a single demand node located one unit of distance apart. A unit of distance might equal 1,000 miles. The capacity of the pipeline depends on the specific gravity of the natural gas, its temperature in the pipeline, the number of compressor stations along the pipeline, the diameter of the pipeline, and the thickness of the steel used to make the pipeline.[9]

---

9   For further discussion of these engineering aspects, see Chenery (1949).

The rate of throughput or capacity utilization depends on the compression ratio, which is the ratio of the initial pressure to the terminal pressure. The amount of capital facilities, represented by the amount of steel to build the pipeline and the number of compressor stations, can be summarized by a variable $L$ that represents the amount of capital equipment. The set of supply and delivery nodes is $N = \{1, 2\}$, which implicitly specifies the distance. Finally, operation of the compressor stations and the nodes requires an input of energy $Z$ to drive the gas through the pipeline. The energy required depends on the ratio between the initial pressure and the terminal pressure and the amount of throughput.

Let $Q$ represent throughput as measured in millions of cubic feet of gas per day per thousand miles. The production technology is summarized by

$$(6) \qquad\qquad Q = F(\{1, 2\}, L, Z).$$

Increasing throughput can be achieved by adding to the capacity of the pipeline $L$ by increasing its diameter or the number of pumping stations. Alternatively, throughput can be raised by increasing the energy $Z$ used for compressing the gas.

Generally, a transmission pipeline system includes many nodes and many connecting links, with miles of pipelines and multiple compressor stations forming a complex network. The integrity of such a network depends on its many component elements, which are optimized to form an integrated system. The operational control structure of a pipeline illustrates the interdependence of the parts of a natural gas transmission system. Pipelines operate central command posts that monitor information about the pipeline facilities and transmit operational orders directly to automated equipment and to maintenance personnel. The gas control operator receives information transmitted by telephone, microwave, or satellite. The system employs specialized equipment for supervisory control and data acquisition (SCADA) to monitor volumes, pressures, and temperatures, as well as the operating status of pipeline facilities. SCADA equipment monitors the volume of gas being supplied to the system and the volume of gas delivered to customers. SCADA also grants the system monitor the ability to quickly identify and react to equipment malfunctions and the capability to remotely start or stop certain compressors, thereby changing flow volumes to meet changes in customer demand for natural gas (Interstate Natural Gas Association of America 2007, p. 83). SCADA systems are used in "water management systems, electric power, traffic signals, mass transit systems, environmental control systems, and manufacturing systems" (techFAQ, 2009).

The discussion of central control of pipeline operations shows how the capacities of the pipelines and the compressors combine to deliver natural gas. Clearly, the effect of an individual network element such as a compressor on pipeline services is not easily separated from the effect of the network. When a pipeline network is constructed, compressors are incorporated into the design and structure of the network. When a pipeline is operated, the pipeline's central control coordinates the functioning of the compressors to achieve desired flow volumes through the system.

## b. Telecommunications

The engineering of telecommunications networks presents problems of even greater complexity than for a natural gas transmission system. Calls must be routed between specific initial and terminal points. Calls are of random duration, origin, and destination. Telecommunications systems consist of many different types of elements of varying complexity ranging from sophisticated computer-controlled exchanges to basic parts such as regenerators (Ericsson 1997, pp. 349–50). The construction of such a complicated system requires an integrated design that allows diverse network elements to work together. The operation of a telecommunications network requires management of the interaction between operations support systems (OSS) and network elements.

The production functions for telecommunications networks are summaries of complicated engineering designs. Queuing theory is a widely used planning method for network design. Queuing analysis is employed in "switched networks, local area networks, wide area data networks, multilink networks," as well as "multiprocessor multimemory computing systems" (Saadawi et al. 1994, p. 79). Queuing theory provides models of the performance of a network subject to random arrival of demands for service and capacity constraints. By specifying the capacity of nodes and links, the models yield predictions about performance.

The performance of the network is the output of network services. The capacities of the nodes and links are the productive inputs. The structural relationship between the output of network services and the inputs of network capacity defines the network's economic production function.

To illustrate these issues, without a complete tour of queuing theory, consider a simple communications network consisting of two nodes and a connecting link. The network handles *demand* in the form of *calls*, at a rate of $\lambda$ calls per second. The calls transmitted or handled by the network could be voice calls, data packets, messages, or other types of communications. Calls are handled in the order in which they are received. Calls have a random duration.

The *capacity* of the network is represented by a service rate of $\mu$ calls per second. The service rate takes account of the capacity of the system as well as random call duration. The *load* on the system is the ratio of the rate at which calls are received to the rate at which calls are served.[10] Because calls can exceed the capacity of the system, they form a queue. To prevent infinite queues, assume that the load on the system $\lambda/\mu$ is less than one.[11] The process of call arrival and servicing just

---

10  The load on the system is also known as the utilization factor or traffic intensity factor. The dimensionless load is measured in units called "Erlangs" (Saadawi et al. 1994).

11  The uncertainty in arrival and uncertainty in servicing corresponds to a birth-death stochastic process. Queuing theory refers to this type of arrangement as an $M/M/1/\infty$ queue, where $M$

Calls (network is
serving calls)

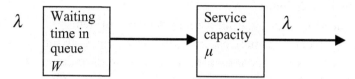

**Figure 2.8.** The output of the network is to serve the $\lambda$ calls. The input of the network is the service capacity $\mu$.

described is standard in telecommunications network planning (Robertazzi 1999). The process is represented in Figure 2.8.

If calls exceed system capacity, then a queue forms. A useful measure of service quality is the average time a call spends in the queue before being served. The average waiting time spent in the queue, $W$, is

(7)
$$W = \frac{\lambda}{\mu(\mu - \lambda)}.$$

This is calculated using Little's formula, which specifies the total of average waiting time plus service time, $1/(\mu - \lambda)$. To obtain the average waiting time subtract the service time, $W = 1/(\mu - \lambda) - 1/\mu$. The smaller the waiting time in the queue, $W$, the greater is the service quality. The formula can be rewritten in a form that lends itself to economic interpretation:

(8)
$$\lambda = \frac{W\mu^2}{1 + W\mu}.$$

The call arrival rate $\lambda$ is the *output* of the network, because it is the number of calls per second that are handled by the system. The network serves a rate of calls $\lambda$ with service quality $W$, which is the average time for a call to begin. The *input* of the network is the service capacity $\mu$, which results from capital investment in the system's nodes and links. Therefore, equation (8) is the production function of the network,

(9)
$$\lambda = F(\mu, W).$$

The network produces a service $\lambda$ of quality $W$ using capacity $\mu$. Service quality $W$ is a parameter in the production function. Increasing capacity increases output for a given service quality. Increasing service quality by reducing $W$ decreases output $\lambda$ for any given capacity $\mu$.

This approach can be generalized by allowing the network to have $m$ servers with possibly different service rates, $\mu = (\mu_1, \ldots, \mu_m)$. The production function

means the arrival process is memoryless (a Poisson arrival rate), the service of calls is memoryless (a Poisson service rate), there is one server for the calls, and there is no exogenous limit on the size of the queue.

would be a reduced form with optimal utilization of the $m$ servers.[12] In addition, the queue itself can be limited, with calls blocked and discouraged if they exceed the size of the buffer or waiting room. To represent the production function of a general network, consider a network that serves total traffic $Q$ with some quality level parameters $W$ representing such characteristics as waiting time in a queue and the number of blocked calls. The backbone network has a set of nodes $N = \{1, \ldots, n\}$ that are connected by a set of links $L = \{(1, 2), (1, 3), \ldots\}$ that is not necessarily complete. Let $K_{ij}$ be the capacity of each link $ij$ in the set of links and let $K$ represent the vector of these capacities. Let the set $N$ represent the switches and other capital equipment associated with the nodes in the backbone network. Assume that the calls are dispatched efficiently given the configuration of the backbone network. Suppose also that the network is efficiently designed and operated given its configuration and the capacity of the links. Although calculating performance measures for complex networks is difficult and can require computer algorithms, suppose that such calculations have been made by network engineers. Then it is possible to describe an economic production function that relates the output of the service provided by the backbone network to the inputs of capital facilities at the nodes and the capacity of the links. Let $X$, $Y$, $Z$ represent other economic inputs. Then the network's production function is

(10) $$Q = F(N, K, X, Y, Z; W).$$

The network production function plays an important role in determining the costs of the network.

Changes in the capacity of a link affect the network's quality of service in complex ways. These effects are mitigated by optimal dispatch of calls over the backbone network, which in turn takes account of possible congestion effects in other parts of the network. The effects of changes in the capacity of a link $K_{ij}$ cannot be presumed to have smooth effects, because of possible discrete effects on network performance. This is even more the case with the addition or removal of a critical link or node, because the configuration of the backbone network will necessarily change.

To illustrate these issues, consider a simple backbone network with four nodes and four links, as shown in Figure 2.9. Suppose that distinct sets of calls originate or terminate through node 1 or through node 3, so that calls are switched either through the path 123 or through the path 143. The performance of the network thus depends on the capacity of all four links. Suppose that any of these links is removed, say for instance the link between nodes 3 and 4. Then, given the way that calls are switched over the backbone network, the link between nodes 1 and 4 becomes useless because it is no longer possible to connect nodes 1 and 3 through node 4. Accordingly, all traffic is switched to links (1, 3) and (2, 3). The capacity of

---

12  This corresponds to an underlying $M/M/m/\infty$ queue. If the queue with $m$ servers is limited to size $k$, then it is an $M/M/m/k$ queue.

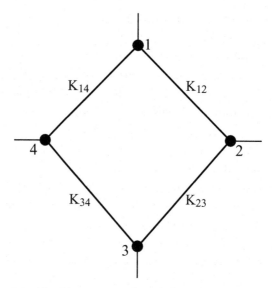

**Figure 2.9.** A backbone network with four nodes and four links.

the backbone network is then entirely dependent on the smaller of the capacities of the two links $K_{13}$ and $K_{23}$.

To give another example, suppose that all four nodes originate and terminate traffic from distinct populations. Again, remove the link between nodes 1 and 4. Then all calls must travel over the remaining three links. One interesting consequence of this is that direct connections between nodes 1 and 4 are replaced by the indirect route passing through nodes 3 and 2. Thus, the direct traffic on one link, $K_{14}$, is added to traffic on each of the other three links. If direct traffic on (1, 4) was 100 calls, then combined traffic on the other three links increases by 300 calls. Removing link (1, 4) also removes the possibility of indirect traffic that would travel on that link if there were congestion on any of the other three links. Therefore, removing one link affects service quality throughout the network. The stress on the network is far greater than the traffic that traveled on the missing segment. Again, the nodes and links of the backbone network form an integrated system. Removal of a critical node or link has effects on final network output that are not easily isolated to the specific network element.

### 3. Production Functions for a Multioutput Network

The production function of a network applies also to multiple outputs. Suppose the network produces $J$ outputs. Then

$$(11) \qquad\qquad H(Q_1, \ldots, Q_J, N, K, X, Y, Z) = 0$$

is a production function specifying the outputs $Q_1, \ldots, Q_J$ that are produced using a network with nodes $N$, links with capacities $K$, and other economic inputs *X*, *Y*, and *Z*. The list of outputs of the network can represent many things, including

- A set of point-to-point connections, such as city pairs;
- A set of outputs of varying service qualities, such as regular and priority service;
- A set of services distinguished by types of uses of the network, such as local versus long distance;
- A set of distinct services, such as data versus voice transmission or wireline versus mobile service; or
- A set of services distinguished by the classes of customers who receive that service, such as residential, commercial, and industrial customers.

The production function not only illustrates tradeoffs between inputs as alternative ways to produce particular outputs. The production function also illustrates tradeoffs between outputs for given levels of inputs. This latter tradeoff is known as the *production possibility frontier* (PPF).

It must be emphasized that networks have limited capacities. Technological innovations such as computerized switching and optical transmission have vastly expanded capacity over traditional alternatives, but greater capacity should not be understood as infinite capacity. Even if there is excess capacity relative to demand at any particular time, capacity remains bounded. Capacity is costly, so it must be considered scarce. Demand for capacity also increases with the development of higher-bandwidth applications. Accordingly, the interaction between the supply of and demand for network capacity is similar to that in most other industries.

The PPF for networks specifies alternative uses for network facilities. To pick a simple example, consider the use of a traditional telecommunications network as a means of transmitting data and voice traffic. Suppose that the technical characteristics of the data and voice services are specified, with some quality level for each and other engineering specifications; see Figure 2.10. At output ($Q_1^{**}$, 0) there is a network optimized for voice, perhaps a circuit-switched network. At output (0, $Q_2^{**}$) there is a network optimized for data, perhaps a packet-switched network. At ($Q_1^*$, $Q_2^*$) there is a hybrid network optimized for a mixture of voice and data, perhaps with voice over Internet protocol or a mixture of circuit-switched and packet-switched transmission methods. The PPF shows what is feasible given available technologies and underlying inputs.

The multiple-output production function again demonstrates the interconnected nature of network inputs. Changes in the input mix results in a shift in the production possibilities frontier; see Figure 2.11. Changes in the input mix thus fundamentally alter the tradeoffs between services that the network can provide. The set of services on the PPF is altered if network elements are detached through unbundled access.

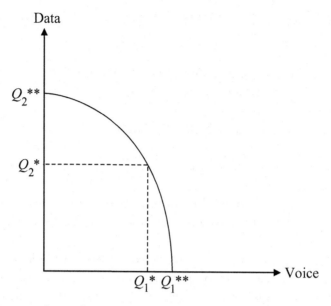

**Figure 2.10.** The production possibility frontier of a multiproduct network.

## C. Cost Functions of Networks

Costs represent a schedule of dollar amounts associated with outputs. Cost schedules do not depend directly on inputs because costs are expenditures on the most efficient combinations of inputs needed to produce final outputs. It is important to emphasize this distinction because unbundled access regulation seeks to determine final costs of the network based on inputs. The network element approach is flawed

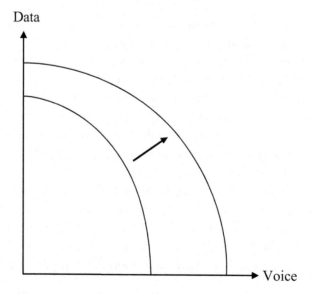

**Figure 2.11.** A change in the input mix shifts the PPF.

because costs are necessarily driven by outputs. This section considers the cost function of networks and proposes an approach to costing unbundled access.

## 1. Derivation of the Cost Function

The costs of networks refer to the total economic cost of producing the network's final services. Let $(Q_1, Q_2, \ldots, Q_J)$ represent the outputs of a network that provides $J$ types of services. Then the costs of the network are based on the level of each type of service, $C(Q_1, Q_2, \ldots, Q_J)$. The economic cost of a network, as with cost functions for any type of firm, is based on final outputs.

The cost function of a network, as with cost functions in general, is obtained by minimizing the input expenditures needed to produce a given set of outputs. Expenditures are minimized by choosing input levels that are subject to a production function constraint. In what follows, let $N$ be a vector of capital equipment associated with the set of nodes and let $K$ be a vector of capital equipment associated with the set of links, and let $p_N$ and $p_K$ be price vectors associated with these two types of capital equipment. Let the prices of other economic inputs (land and resources, labor services, and other parts and components) be $p_X$, $p_Y$, and $p_Z$. Suppress any parameters that describe network performance, because these are implicit in the network production function.

The network's total cost function is therefore derived as follows:

$$(12) \quad C(Q_1, Q_2, \ldots, Q_J) = \max_{N, K, X, Y, Z} p_N N + p_K K + p_X X + p_Y Y + p_Z Z$$
$$\text{subject to } H(Q_1, Q_2, \ldots, Q_J, N, K, X, Y, Z) = 0.$$

The cost function depends implicitly on the input prices and on the technology, as represented by the production function.[13] The characteristics of network cost functions are important for regulatory policy and legal aspects of networks.

To illustrate the network cost function and its relation to the production function, consider the basic example of a single-server network. As before, traffic arrives at the network at rate $\lambda$ and is served at rate $\mu$. Waiting time in a queue, $W$, is the quality of the network's output. The production function as specified in equation (8) is

$$\lambda = \frac{W\mu^2}{1 + W\mu}.$$

Suppose that the cost of network capacity is $c(\mu)$. Then the amount of capacity needed to provide the quantity of service $\lambda$ at quality $W$ is obtained by inverting the production function:

$$(13) \qquad\qquad \mu = \lambda/2 + (\lambda^2/4 + \lambda/W)^{1/2}.$$

---

13  Gasmi et al. (2002) construct network cost functions by examining the costs of different output combinations and using econometric models to estimate a cost function based on these simulations.

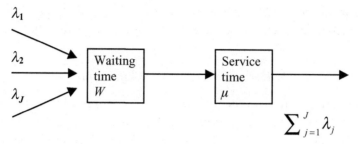

**Figure 2.12.** Combining traffic flows into a network.

Substitute for $\mu$ in the capacity and function to obtain the network cost function for output $\lambda$ and parameterized by the quality of service $W$:

$$(14) \qquad\qquad C(\lambda) = c(\lambda/2 + (\lambda^2/4 + \lambda W)^{1/2}).$$

Consider next a generalization to multiple outputs. A useful property of Poisson arrival processes is that the sum of independent Poisson processes is itself a Poisson process. Suppose that the network receives many types of traffic with independent arrival rates $\lambda_j, j = 1, \ldots, J$. Then total traffic received by the network is a Poisson process with an arrival rate that is the sum of these arrival rates:

$$\lambda^* = \sum_{j=1}^{J} \lambda_j.$$

This immediately generalizes the cost function in equation (14) to a multiproduct cost function,

$$(15) \qquad\qquad C(\lambda_1, \lambda_2, \ldots, \lambda_J) = c(\lambda^*/2 + [(\lambda^*)^2/4 + \lambda^* W]^{1/2}).$$

This type of multiproduct cost function shows the effects of congestion. To avoid increasing costs, while maintaining a given quality of service in terms of queuing time, increases in the rate of traffic flow of any type would need to be balanced by reductions in the flow rates of other types of traffic. In general, traffic flows may be correlated, either positively or negatively, rather than being independent. Also, traffic flows may differ by origins and destinations, so that system congestion varies between different parts of the network. With multiple servers of different capacities and optimal dispatch of calls through the network, the interactions between multiple traffic flows can be complex. Traffic is then unlikely to be additive, except perhaps for parts of the network. In any case, the effects of interactions between types of traffic can be represented by a general multiproduct cost function, $C(Q_1, \ldots, Q_j)$.

The cost function is useful for examining tradeoffs between types of inputs. Suppose for purposes of illustration that $N$ and $L$ represent levels of capital investment in nodes and links, respectively. Let $p_N$ and $p_L$ be the prices of these two forms of capital equipment. Suppose that the network production function has a basic Cobb–Douglas form,

$$(16) \qquad Q = AN^a L^b,$$

where $A$ is a constant and where $a$ and $b$ are productivity parameters. If $a + b = 1$, there are constant returns to scale. If $a + b > 1$, there are increasing returns to scale, and if $a + b < 1$, there are decreasing returns to scale. The marginal product of investment in nodes is $a A N^{a-1} L^b$ and that of investment in links is $b A N^a L^{b-1}$. The ratio of marginal products is called the marginal rate of technical substitution (MRTS). The MRTS reduces to

$$(17) \qquad \mathrm{MRTS} = \frac{aL}{bN}.$$

Cost minimization requires equating the marginal rate of technical substitution to the ratio of input prices:

$$(18) \qquad \frac{aL}{bN} = \frac{p_N}{p_L}.$$

This is the input mix that equates the relative productivity of inputs to their relative purchase costs. Now, combine the network production function (16) and the efficiency condition (18) to obtain necessary inputs as a function of the output level:

$$(19) \qquad N^* = \left[ \frac{Q}{A} \left( \frac{p_L}{p_N} \frac{a}{b} \right)^b \right]^{\frac{1}{a+b}}, \quad L^* = \left[ \frac{Q}{A} \left( \frac{p_N}{p_L} \frac{b}{a} \right)^a \right]^{\frac{1}{a+b}}.$$

To obtain the network cost function, substitute these results into the expenditure levels, $p_N N + p_L L$:

$$(20) \qquad C(Q, p_N, p_L) = p_N N^*(Q, p_N, p_L) + p_L L^*(Q, p_N, p_L).$$

Although expenditures depend on the efficient number of network elements, the cost function is a schedule based only on the final output level and input prices. For example, if $a = b = 1/2$, the network cost function is

$$(21) \qquad C(Q, p_N, p_L) = (Q/A) p_N^{1/2} p_L^{1/2}.$$

The configuration of the network is sensitive to the relative prices of nodes and links when these types of network elements are substitutes in production. The cost function reflects an efficient combination of network elements given their relative productivities and relative prices. Access regulations that impact either productivity or the purchase costs of network elements will alter the firm's decisions and potentially cause departures from the efficient input mix, resulting in costs higher than the efficient level.

## 2. Economies of Scale

A network is similar to other production facilities in many respects, including the potential for economies of scale. There are many sources of economies of scale in networks that are identical to those for other types of manufacturing. Some sources of scale efficiencies are specific to networks, however, so we begin with these.

Consider a network with a set of nodes $N$ and a set of links $L$ that specify connections that exist between the nodes. Suppose that the traffic flow on link $(i, j)$ is specified by $\lambda_{ij}$ and the per-unit capacity cost on that link is $c_{ij}$. Then the network designer must choose traffic flows over the network to minimize the total cost of capacity, which is the sum of capacity costs for all the links in L:

$$(22) \qquad C(Q_1, \ldots, Q_J) = \min_{\lambda_{ij}} \sum_L c_{ij} \lambda_{ij}.$$

The traffic flows to be chosen are subject to the constraint that they complete the connections for the final services $Q_1, \ldots, Q_J$, to travel over available links. For traffic on a network with many connected nodes there are many alternative paths that connect any given origin–destination pair. Given that capacity costs are linear, as in equation (22), the solution is straightforward. The cost-minimizing set of traffic flows must follow the shortest path, that is, the path between initial node $i$ and terminal node $j$ that has the smallest sum of costs $c_{lk}$. This is the well-known traveling salesman problem discussed earlier. The solution requires the shortest path because the traffic that begins at node $i$ and terminates at node $j$ travels on every link along the path. Cost minimization requires making sure that the repeated traffic has the least-cost set of links along its path.

In contrast, suppose that the costs of links are not linear in traffic but instead exhibit economies of scale. Suppose, for example, that a link $ij$ has a fixed cost $f_{ij}$ as well as a cost per unit of traffic $c_{ij}$. Then, depending on the relative levels of these costs, it might be worth avoiding the creation of some links in order not to bear the fixed cost. This means that longer routes could be more attractive. The result is a concentration of traffic on a smaller set of links, which lowers unit costs on those links and yields economies of scale for the cost function overall.[14]

To illustrate the effects of economies of scale at the level of individual links, consider a network with four nodes, $N = \{1, 2, 3, 4\}$. The nodes can be connected directly at a constant cost per unit of traffic, $c$. The traffic patterns are given by city-pair outputs, $Q_{ij}$, with every node requiring direct or indirect connections with every other node. The solution is that a complete point-to-point network is needed because direct connections are the shortest paths. Total cost is therefore

---

14   For a related discussion of economies of scale and network design, see Robertazzi (1999) and
      Yaged (1972).

represented by the constant-returns-to-scale cost function

(23)         $C(Q_{12}, Q_{13}, Q_{14}, Q_{23}, Q_{24}, Q_{34})$

$$= cQ_{12} + cQ_{13} + cQ_{14} + cQ_{23} + cQ_{24} + cQ_{34},$$

where $L$ is the set of links $\{(1, 2), (1, 3), (1, 4), (2, 3), (2, 4), (3, 4)\}$.

Now suppose that establishing a link requires a fixed cost $f$. Suppose that the traffic requirements are evenly distributed: $Q_{ij} = Q$ for all pairs $(i, j)$ in the set of links. Suppose also that fixed costs are sufficiently large relative to variable costs,

$$f > 2cQ,$$

so that it is less costly to add more traffic on three links, $3cQ$, than to add a direct link, $f + cQ$. Then we are back at the problem of choosing the least-cost tree that connects all the nodes. By the symmetry of the problem, any such tree will do, say for example $(1, 2)$, $(2, 3)$, and $(3, 4)$. Then the total cost function of the network is

(24)      $C(Q_{12}, Q_{13}, Q_{14}, Q_{23}, Q_{24}, Q_{34})$

$$= 3f + c(Q_{12} + Q_{23} + Q_{34}) + 2c(Q_{13} + Q_{24}) + 3cQ_{14}.$$

The total cost function has economies of scale due to the presence of fixed costs that come from the links.

The main point of the preceding example is that economies of scale in components of the network can imply the need to concentrate traffic. The use of central switching in hub-and-spoke configurations and the establishment of trunk lines in backbone networks take advantage of economies of scale in nodes and links, including high-capacity switches and transmission lines. Concentration of traffic to achieve economies of scale is a particularly interesting aspect of network design.

Economies of scale in networks also derive from standard sources (Spulber 1989, 1995).

(1) Networks have joint and common fixed costs that can be spread across units of output or across multiple outputs. Such joint and common fixed costs include the overhead costs of designing and managing the network, as well as fixed costs of construction and maintenance. Telecommunications companies maintain extra transmission capacity, known as dark fiber, because the cost of installing additional fiber during the initial installation is lower than the cost of later additions to capacity. With greater output of a service or of a set of services, companies can spread out the fixed costs.

(2) Economies of scale are present in telecommunications, as in other industries, because with a higher output it becomes possible to switch technologies. For example, fiber optic transmission lines, although expensive, reduce unit costs of transmission relative to copper or coaxial systems for a sufficiently high output

level. Similarly, high-capacity switches lower unit costs for a sufficiently high output level.

(3) Networks benefit from volume–surface relationships. Pipeline companies can scale up the volume of a pipeline without the same increase in surface area and thus without a proportional increase in the materials used to construct the pipeline. Telecommunications companies can use larger-volume conduits at lower unit costs.

(4) As Adam Smith pointed out with his famous pin factory example, economies of scale result from specialization and division of labor. Telecommunications companies and other network companies employ many specialized and skilled personnel in design, management, operations, and maintenance activities.

### 3. Multiproduct Cost Functions

Because a network typically provides many services, it will have a multiproduct cost function. Such cost functions generally are not separable in outputs. Thus, it is not possible to identify the total cost of any individual service or any subset of services. Any allocation of costs to specific services is necessarily arbitrary. Regulatory or accounting procedures that perform such cost allocations are easily altered to obtain wildly differing results and thus cannot serve as an effective guide to policy.

A useful benchmark for analyzing multiproduct cost functions is the standalone cost of a product,

$$(25) \qquad \mathrm{SAC}^j(Q_j) = C(0, \ldots, Q_j, \ldots, 0).$$

A firm's technology is said to be *nonjoint* if and only if it can be written as the sum of the standalone costs (Hall 1973; Van den Heuvel 1986). This is unlikely to be the case for firms in network industries because the network services are likely to be interconnected technologically, resulting in a nonseparable cost function.

Another important aspect of the multiproduct cost function is the incremental cost of each product $j$,

$$(26) \qquad \mathrm{IC}^j(Q) = C(Q) - C(Q_1, \ldots, Q_{j-1}, 0, Q_{j+1}, \ldots, Q_J),$$

where $Q = (Q_1, Q_2, \ldots, Q_J)$. The concepts of standalone cost and incremental cost can be extended to apply to sets of products. Thus, $\mathrm{SAC}^S(Q_S)$ and $\mathrm{IC}^S(Q)$ apply to the set of products $Q_S$, that is, all $Q_j$ where $j$ is in $S$.

Let $S$ and $T$ be disjoint sets of products. Then the network cost function exhibits economies of scope if the total of the standalone costs of each group of products exceeds the total cost:

$$(27) \qquad \mathrm{SAC}^S(Q_S) + \mathrm{SAC}^T(Q_T) > C(Q_S + Q_T).$$

This is called an economy of scope because the network firm realizes economies from joint production of the two sets of products. There are potential cost gains from handling multiple forms of traffic (peak and off-peak), multiple origin–destination pairs, or multiple types of transmission (voice and data).

An example of economies of scope is the sharing of a fixed cost between two or more goods:

$$(28) \qquad C(Q_1, Q_2) = F + c(Q_1) + c(Q_2).$$

Such a cost function exhibits economies of scope because producing the two goods separately would require paying the fixed cost twice.

Another source of economies of scope in networks is sharing facilities that exhibit increasing returns to scale, such as high-capacity transmission lines. Suppose that a network can carry two types of traffic, $Q_1$ and $Q_2$, and that the common transmission line has a cost function $c(Q)$ with economies of scale. The economies of scale of the transmission line mean that average cost declines with output:

$$(29) \qquad c(Q_1) > Q_1 \frac{c(Q_1 + Q_2)}{Q_1 + Q_2}, \quad c(Q_2) > Q_2 \frac{c(Q_1 + Q_2)}{Q_1 + Q_2}.$$

Adding these two conditions together implies that $c(Q_1) + c(Q_2) > c(Q_1 + Q_2)$. This implies that the network has economies of scope:

$$(30) \quad C(Q_1, Q_2) = c(Q_1 + Q_2) < c(Q_1) + c(Q_2) = C(Q_1, 0) + C(0, Q_2).$$

This sharing of a high-capacity trunk line to achieve economies of scale is illustrated in Figure 2.13.

Another source of economies of scope is the benefits from handling multiple types of random traffic. Suppose that $\lambda^* = \lambda_1 + \lambda_2$ is the combination of two types of traffic. Then the capacity requirements for a combination of two types of traffic are less than the capacity requirements for handling the two types of traffic separately:

$$(31) \qquad \begin{aligned} \mu^* &= \lambda^*/2 + [(\lambda^*)^2/4 + \lambda^* W]^{1/2} \\ &< \lambda_1/2 + [(\lambda_1)^2/4 + \lambda_1 W]^{1/2} \\ &\quad + \lambda_2/2 + [(\lambda_2)^2/4 + \lambda_2 W]^{1/2} \\ &= \mu_1 + \mu_2. \end{aligned}$$

Let the cost of the service capacity have a constant unit cost, $c(\mu) = c\mu$. Then the total cost function has economies of scope:

$$(32) \qquad C(\lambda_1, \lambda_2) = c\mu^* < c\mu_1 + c\mu_2 = C(\lambda_1, 0) + C(0, \lambda_2).$$

This result readily generalizes to multiple independent traffic flows. Simply separate one traffic flow at a time to obtain the result. Thus, networks have economies of scope that result from efficiencies in serving multiple independent traffic flows.

The concept of economies of scope is important for regulatory policy because it is another aspect of interconnection in networks. The network produces multiple services more efficiently than separate networks would. This implies that

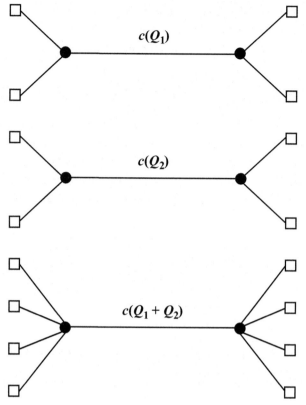

**Figure 2.13.** Sharing a high-capacity trunk line to achieve economies of scale, where $c(Q_1 + Q_2) < c(Q_1) + c(Q_2)$.

network services cannot be treated in isolation but must be considered as part of an interrelated set of services. The cost of an individual service cannot be considered independently. The cost of the service depends on the amount of other services provided by the network. The amount of the service in question that is supplied in turn affects the costs of other services.

## D. The Cost of Unbundled Access to Networks

If unbundled access is a regulatory fact of life, what are its costs? The discussion of networks in the current and previous chapters serves to establish that networks are greater than the sum of their parts. If that is the case, how can a part of a network be separated out and assigned a cost without doing something that is inconsistent with the engineering design of the network or the economic optimization of the input mix?

The proper way to think about the cost of unbundled network elements is to define the services those elements provide. Then the network firm can treat the services generated by specific elements as it does other types of network services, most of which are generated by combinations of network elements. This chapter examines problems that arise with this approach, even though it is conceptually consistent with economic cost principles. First, even if it is possible to define services corresponding to specific network elements, it is not possible to assign costs to such services, because in general multiproduct costs cannot be assigned by output in anything but a haphazard fashion. Second, defining new services that are based on network elements as final services requires redefining the firm's production and cost functions.

## 1. Allocating Multiproduct Costs

The interconnection of services provided by a network has a number of formal implications. Because there are economies of scope, the total of the standalone costs of individual outputs necessarily exceeds the total cost of producing jointly, so standalone costs are limited as a guide to dividing costs. The most that can be said is that the regulated revenue provided by a service $R_j$ should not exceed its standalone cost, because consumers would then be better off if the service were supplied by a standalone facility:

(33) $$R_j \leq \text{SAC}^j(Q_j).$$

The standalone cost condition must hold for any subset of outputs. This condition is necessary and sufficient for a regulated rate structure to avoid *cross subsidies*. A *regulated rate structure* refers to revenues for each service that sum to equal total cost:

(34) $$\sum_{j=1}^{J} R_j = C(Q).$$

The incremental cost of a service provides some guidance in dividing costs. To avoid cross subsidies, a regulated rate structure must have revenues that cover incremental costs:

(35) $$R_j \geq \text{IC}^j(Q).$$

For a regulated rate structure, the requirement in equation (35) is equivalent to the condition in equation (33) that revenues not exceed standalone costs. If the firm earns a positive economic profit, revenues should still be greater than or equal to incremental cost. Otherwise the firm loses money on that service because the firm's profit could be increased by dropping the service. The cost reduction would exceed the lost revenue. The incremental cost condition must also hold for any subset of outputs.

An important aspect of incremental costs is that if subsidy-free revenues exist, incremental costs must sum to less than total costs:

$$(36) \qquad \sum_{j=1}^{J} \mathrm{IC}^{j}(Q) \le \sum_{j=1}^{J} R_j = C(Q).$$

A sufficient condition for the existence of subsidy-free revenues is *cost complementarities*,

$$(37) \qquad C_{ij}(Q) = \frac{\partial}{\partial Q_i} \frac{\partial C(Q)}{\partial Q_j} \le 0,$$

for all $i$ and $j = 1, \ldots, J$. This is a stronger requirement on costs than economies of scope. Cost complementarities imply that the cost function exhibits economies of scope. Also, cost complementarities imply that the multiproduct cost function exhibits (weak) increasing returns to scale:

$$(38) \qquad \sum_{j=1}^{J} C_j(Q) Q_j \le C(Q).$$

Finally, cost complementarities imply that the multiproduct cost function exhibits the *natural monopoly* property,[15] also referred to as subadditivity:

$$C(Q') + C(Q'') \ge C(Q' + Q'').$$

This means that if $C(Q)$ is the cost function of a network firm, costs are lower than if the output were divided between two (or more) network firms using the same technology (Baumol et al. 1982).

Because incremental costs sum to less than total cost, when there are cost complementarities, there is a temptation for regulators to think of dividing up total costs into incremental costs plus some cost allocation of the residual cost:

$$(39) \qquad \text{Residual cost} = C(Q) - \sum_{j=1}^{J} \mathrm{IC}^{j}(Q).$$

However, any administrative allocation of residual cost is necessarily arbitrary.

Suppose that all costs can be fully attributable to each service *except* for a joint and common fixed cost $F$. Thus the cost function would be

$$(40) \qquad C(Q) = F + \sum_{j=1}^{J} c^{j}(Q_j).$$

---

15  The concept of natural monopoly is generally attributed to John Stuart Mill (1961; originally published in 1848), who emphasizes the problem of wasteful duplication of transmission facilities that can occur in utility services. The connection between natural monopoly and regulation is developed by Leon Walras (1936) with reference to the construction and operation of railroads.

Regulators have long applied *fully distributed cost* (FDC) pricing rules to divide the fixed cost among a set of services. Typically, in network industries, regulatory commissions categorize services by customer classes and distribute joint costs "on the basis of some common physical measure of utilization, such as minutes, circuit-miles, message-minute-miles, gross ton-miles, MCF, or kwh" (Kahn 1971, p. 150). Among the rules of thumb used by regulators are the relative output rule, the relative attributable cost rule, and the relative revenue rule. The arbitrariness of such rules is easily demonstrated. By choosing different measures of output, regulators can easily generate substantially different cost allocations. Moreover, actual costs do not lend themselves to such neat separations of fixed and variable costs or to such clear attributable costs. Accordingly, allocating nonattributable costs is likely to be an exercise in regulatory accounting that bears little relation to market prices.

In the FCC's TELRIC system, each component that constitutes part of a network, such as a switch or a line, can be assigned a specific cost equal to its replacement cost. Any joint costs can be arbitrarily broken up and assigned to all of the elements. If such a system were accurate, the cost of a network would be independent of its configuration. This is impossible, because varying a network's configuration affects its performance. A network's configuration thus affects the production function relationship between the network's output and its inputs. Thus, the network's cost function also reflects its configuration. It is therefore not possible to divide a network's costs among its components in a meaningful way.

## 2. Long-Run versus Short-Run Costs

Of course, the expenditures needed to establish, operate, and maintain the network can be separated into their components. These are purchase prices times the purchased amounts of individual components. In this sense, perhaps, the cost of components is easily identified based on market prices. Thus, there are market prices for switches or fiber optic equipment offered by original equipment manufacturers (OEMs). However, once they are integrated into a network, a *fundamental change* takes place in the effect of inputs on cost. Access to an unbundled component is not provided by unbolting or disconnecting the component and reselling its services. Were that the case, market prices would provide a good guide to value. The problem is that unbundled access is provided *in situ*; that is, access to the element is provided while it is a functioning part of the network. The costs of access then include (1) recovery of the costs that were incurred in including the component in the network, (2) the costs of making the component available while it is a functioning part of the network (so called make-ready costs), and (3) the impact of providing access to the component's services on total costs. The first two types of costs are more readily identified than the third type of costs, because of the complexity of network design.

The cost of network elements such as switching, transmission links, loops, and network signaling is subsumed in the total cost function. They are interconnected in the network planning functions that underlie the engineering design of networks.

Furthermore, the optimal combination and configuration of network elements are represented by the economic production function. Finally, the best mix of network components to achieve a given mix of network services is contained in the minimum expenditure that underlies the cost function. Finding the effect of inputs on the total costs of the network would require untangling these three planning stages associated with engineering specification, the production function, and the cost function.

As noted, a fundamental change takes place after network elements are incorporated into a functioning network. To represent the *forward-looking* costs of network elements accurately requires a redefinition of the firm's production function and cost function *before* the fundamental change takes place. The *long-run cost function* requires all inputs to be variable. Consider the situation in which a firm correctly anticipates that regulators will require it to make unbundled network elements available. Generally, because the elements are provided only as part of the network, it is not the element itself that is provided, only the services of that element. The network firm may be called upon only to provide a portion of these services. To make these ideas clear, suppose that $q$ represents the vector of services of network elements to be provided to competitors and let $Q$ be the vector of outputs provided to the firm's customers. Then a new augmented production function must be defined that specifies the inputs needed to produce unbundled network element services $q$ and final customer services $Q$:

$$(41) \qquad\qquad H(Q, q, N, K, X, Y, Z) = 0.$$

It should be evident that additional network services will generally require more inputs to the network if the same level of final customer services is to be maintained. This is because the network production function is the efficient combination of inputs needed to produce a given level of services subject to the underlying engineering specifications and technology. Alternatively, if the inputs to the network are fixed, particularly capital equipment and facilities, the modified production function will not sustain the same level of outputs. Also, it is likely to differ from the technologically efficient production function, which requires all inputs to be variable. Instead, with some inputs already fixed, the production function is a *short-run production function* that is suboptimal relative to the long-run production function.

The production function having been redefined, it is necessary to redefine the network firm's cost function to handle both final services and the services of unbundled network elements. The modified cost function $C^U(Q, q)$ is the minimum level of expenditures needed to produce network outputs $(Q, q)$ subject to the modified production function. With all inputs variable, $C^U(Q, q)$ is a long-run cost function. Then, notice that the standalone cost of final outputs equals the original cost function:

$$(42) \qquad\qquad C^U(Q, 0) = C(Q).$$

For the modified long-run cost function, the incremental cost of the services provided by a network element is calculated in the same manner as any type of incremental cost.

For ease of illustration, suppose that there is only one final output $Q$ and only one service from the unbundled network element $q$. Then, because $C^U(Q, q)$ is a long-run cost function, that is, with all inputs variable and chosen optimally, the long-run incremental cost of the service provided by the network element is

$$
(43) \quad \text{LRIC}^q(Q, q) = C^U(Q, q) - C^U(Q, 0)
$$
$$
= C^U(Q, q) - C(Q).
$$

This is the additional cost of building a network that anticipates providing the services of unbundled network elements.

Suppose that there are economies of scope for firms that provide both final services and the services of unbundled network elements. This assumption need not hold in practice because, as we will observe in the next chapter, various costs can arise that make such joint production less efficient. However, if there are economies of scope, then

$$
C^U(Q, q) \le C^U(Q, 0) + C^U(0, q).
$$

Accordingly, the sum of the long-run incremental costs of the final service and of the unbundled network element service is less than modified total cost:

$$
(44) \quad \text{LRIC}^Q(Q, q) + \text{LRIC}^q(Q, q) = C^U(Q, q) - C^U(0, q)
$$
$$
+ C^U(Q, q) - C^U(Q, 0) \le C^U(Q, q).
$$

The problem for regulators is how to recover the shortfall between incremental costs and total costs.

Clearly, the revenues generated by final consumers $R_Q$ and the revenues generated by competitors must cover incremental costs to avoid cross subsidization:

$$
(45) \quad \begin{aligned} R_Q &\ge \text{LRIC}^Q(Q, q), \\ R_q &\ge \text{LRIC}^q(Q, q). \end{aligned}
$$

Regulators may choose to charge only incremental costs for competitors obtaining the services of unbundled network elements: $R_q = \text{LRIC}^q(Q, q)$. The result is to shift the rest of the costs to final consumers:

$$
R_Q = C^U(Q, q) - \text{LRIC}^q(Q, q)
$$
$$
= C^U(Q, 0) = C(Q).
$$

Final consumers are no worse off than before, assuming of course that long-run cost functions are used.

Consider the situation in which the modified cost function differs from the long-run cost function because some inputs are fixed. Modifications to the network are required that raise costs above the long-run cost function because the network was designed to provide only final services $Q$, not unbundled network element services $q$. Thus, $\text{SRC}^U(Q, q)$ is a short-run cost function and $\text{SRC}^U(Q, q) \geq C^U(Q, q)$.[16] Properly defined, with zero services from unbundled elements, the standalone cost of final services should equal the initial cost, as in the long-run case: $\text{SRC}^U(Q, 0) = C(Q)$. Notice that there may be a jump in total costs from the provision of even a very small amount of unbundled network element services $q$ if there are fixed costs of modifying the network. Thus, there may be a discontinuity in $\text{SRC}^U(Q, q)$ from supplying some unbundled network element services. The incremental cost of supplying UNE services should contain all of those costs and should be thought of as the short-run incremental cost of network services, $\text{SRIC}^q(q)$, where for all $q > 0$,

$$\text{SRIC}^q(Q, q) > \text{IC}^q(Q, q)$$

for any inputs that are fixed and depart from the long-run efficient level.[17]

Now, suppose that the network's competitors are charged based on long-run incremental cost, but some inputs are nevertheless fixed. Then, if $R_q = \text{LRIC}^q(q)$, customers of final services are made worse off:

$$\begin{aligned}
R_Q &= \text{SRC}^U(Q, q) - \text{LRIC}^q(Q, q) \\
&= \text{SRC}^U(Q, q) - \text{SRIC}^q(Q, q) + \text{SRIC}^q(Q, q) - \text{LRIC}^q(Q, q) \\
&= \text{SRC}^U(Q, 0) + \text{SRIC}^q(Q, q) - \text{LRIC}^q(Q, q) \\
&= C(Q) + \text{SRIC}^q(Q, q) - \text{LRIC}^q(Q, q) \\
&> C(Q).
\end{aligned}$$

This situation can be remedied by charging for all incremental costs of UNE services, not just long-run costs as if the network were efficiently configured. Thus, with fixed inputs, short-run incremental costs reflect the actual cost increases resulting from the provision of UNE services.

Consider now the FCC's notion of total element long-run incremental cost. In our framework, there is a vector of services corresponding to each specific unbundled network element, $q = (q_1, \ldots, q_L)$, and a vector of services corresponding to initial final services generated by the network as a whole, $Q = (Q_1, \ldots, Q_J)$. Then, if there are economies of scope, total cost exceeds the sum of all incremental costs:

$$C^U(Q, q) > \sum_{j=1}^{J} \text{LRIC}^{Q_j}(Q, q) + \sum_{l=1}^{L} \text{LRIC}^{q_l}(Q, q).$$

According to TELRIC, it should be possible to divide total costs into categories that can be fully assigned to the network elements. Such costs with $L$ elements would

---

16  This follows from standard arguments based on the Le Chatelier principle. On the cost functions with investment, see Becker and Spulber (1984).

17  Because $\text{SRC}^U(Q, q) > C^U(Q, q)$ for fixed inputs that depart from long-run optimal levels, $\text{SRC}^U(Q, q) - \text{SRC}^U(Q, 0) > C^U(Q, q) - C^U(Q, 0)$ given that $\text{SRC}^U(Q, 0) = C^U(Q, 0) = C(Q)$. Therefore, for output $Q$, $\text{SRIC}^q(Q, q) > \text{LRIC}^q(Q, q)$.

correspond to revenues $R_l$, $l = 1, \ldots, L$, such that total costs were covered:

$$\sum_{l=1}^{L} R_l = C^U(Q, q).$$

There are three problems with this approach.

First, due to economies of scope in the provision of network services, each $R_l$ would necessarily equal or exceed the incremental cost of the UNE service, with at least one strictly exceeding the UNE service's incremental cost. It would certainly not be advisable or economically correct to have any attributed cost below any of the UNE service's incremental costs. Thus, the question is how to allocate the joint and common costs of the UNE services. This problem arises even if there are no final network services. This is the classic problem of allocation of joint and common costs by regulators. All administrative approaches to this problem are necessarily arbitrary, as noted earlier, no matter what are the types of services, and UNE services are no exception.

Second, there are costs that are attributable to final services, that is, the long-run incremental costs of each of those services. Assigning all shares of total costs to the services of elements presents a distorted picture of total costs or at least a distorted picture of the sources of costs, the final services and UNE services. If final services are then to be sold, the UNE incremental costs will not provide much of a guide to assigning costs to final services.

Finally, the same problem of short-run versus long-run incremental cost arises. If total costs are to be divided among elements on the basis of long-run incremental costs, but some inputs to the network are fixed, there will be a shortfall relative to short-run incremental costs:

$$\sum_{l=1}^{L} \text{SRIC}^{q_l}(Q, q) > \sum_{l=1}^{L} \text{LRIC}^{q_l}(Q, q).$$

Therefore, with fixed inputs in an existing network, short-run incremental cost may be a better guide to the attributable costs of network services. Some share of total short-run costs can be assigned to network elements to reflect the joint and common costs that are shared with final services, with the caveat that such administrative allocations are arbitrary. As later discussion shows, relative prices established by markets provide better benchmarks for UNE services.

\* \* \*

Networks are greater than the sums of their parts. Far from being collections of elements snapped together like tinkertoys, networks are interconnected in irreducible ways. Beginning with engineering specifications and technology, networks are designed to make the best use of inputs to achieve performance standards. This process generates an economic production function that reflects all of the technically efficient combinations of inputs needed to produce network services. Then the network operator chooses the least-cost mix of inputs to produce a particular set of network services. The economic cost function is the schedule of costs associated with network outputs. As we will see, the profit-maximizing mix of network outputs is chosen based on relative costs to the network operator and relative benefits to consumers of network outputs. Thus, the decision processes associated with engineering design, production functions, cost functions, and profit functions determine network architecture and the configurations of network elements.

The set of connections between network elements is reflected, for example, in the cost of UNE services. It is not possible to evaluate the separate cost of UNEs after the fundamental change takes place when these elements are incorporated in the network. Instead, the network operator must evaluate the cost of providing the services of UNEs within the three-step process of engineering design, production function specification, and cost minimization.

The science of networks principally shows that networks function as integrated systems, so that understanding individual components cannot provide a full appreciation of the properties of the network. Regulation that is based on access to individual network elements or on the costs of those elements may not reflect an understanding of the effects of regulations on the network as a whole. Communications networks function as unified systems in many ways. The network's configuration of elements matters for performance. As this chapter demonstrates, networks are unified by engineering and economic planning processes. Mandating access places additional demands on the network that are likely to affect overall performance. As the next chapter shows, the capacity of the network reflects choices based on the interaction of supply and demand.

# 3

# Pricing Network Services

Network designers choose the capacity necessary to provide the desired level of network services. The quality of service also determines the capacity required to deliver the specified quantity of network services. Because the architecture of the network is optimized by the network designers, the level of network capacity determines the underlying configuration. Different configurations are likely to accompany different capacity levels.

Choosing the aggregate level of services determines how much capacity to build into each node and link and the architecture of the network. In a telecommunications network, the capacity of switches and lines and the design of the network create constraints on the volume and type of traffic that the network can handle. Capacity usage might take the form of the number of calls and the time spent on each call in a circuit-switched network. In a packet-switched data network, capacity usage is measured by more complex definitions of bandwidth.

Pricing, that is, the selection of prices by decision makers, serves two general functions. First, prices ration consumer demand, because consumers reduce their capacity usage in response to higher prices. Second, prices stimulate capacity supply, because suppliers increase capacity offered for sale in response to higher prices. Prices implicitly communicate the scarcity of network capacity to consumers and also signal the strength of demand to suppliers. At a market equilibrium, prices tend to reflect consumer demand for network services and the supply of network capacity by firms.

The network operator chooses capacity with a view to providing retail access. Access regulation affects the demand for network capacity in two ways. First, compelled access can increase (or possibly decrease) the total demand for network services, thus affecting the efficient design of the network. Second, compelled access can alter the traffic patterns on the network, creating different usage levels in specific locations and different points of congestion. Wholesale access is likely to consume network capacity in ways that differ from retail access. Unbundled access takes up network capacity at the fundamental level of the nodes and links themselves. By tying up some of the capacity (even if not foreclosing the network owner from using the link altogether), competitors radically change the optimization decision of the network owner. Platform access can fundamentally change the demand for network services by altering the types of usage, so that different types of transmissions (voice, data, video) change demand for network capacity. Interconnection also changes the demand patterns for network capacity because originating, terminating, and transiting communication on the network changes traffic patterns.

This chapter examines the demand for network capacity and the prices that allocate network capacity. We consider the effects of uncertainty on pricing and the allocation of services. We further examine the pricing of network capacity under asymmetric information. Next, we consider network capacity pricing when usage creates congestion that reduces the quality of service. We consider pricing when there are blocked calls in a telephone network and pricing when there is information loss in a data network. Finally, we examine the demand for network capacity when consumers can buy services that are substitutes or complements for network capacity.

## A. Network Capacity and Pricing

### 1. The Basics of Pricing with Scarce Capacity

As a first approximation to the problem of pricing capacity, we assume that the demand for capacity is not subject to uncertainty. In a deterministic setting, networks can use prices to ration capacity while avoiding problems of either congestion or excess capacity. Later, we address the problem of random demand.

Suppose that there are $I$ consumers, $i = 1, \ldots, I$. Each consumer obtains a benefit from consuming network capacity, $B^i(Q^i)$, where $Q^i$ is both the network service and the amount of capacity required to deliver the network service. Assume that the consumer's income does not affect the consumer's benefit from network services and that consumption of network services does not affect the consumer's marginal utility of income. These assumptions are made to simplify the presentation by ruling out income effects on the demand for network services. Suppose that network services require a small portion of income. In practice, consumer demands for network services are affected by income. For our purposes, these differences can be modeled by allowing differences in consumer benefit functions.

Assume also that the consumer's purchases of goods other than network services need not be specified explicitly. As noted in Chapter 1, the demand for network services is a means to an end. Consumption of network services such as telecommunications depends on the demand for communication and the value of other economic transactions. Because many forces drive the consumer's needs for telecommunications services, it is sufficient to specify a benefit function for network services. It can be assumed that the purchases of other goods are adjusted optimally

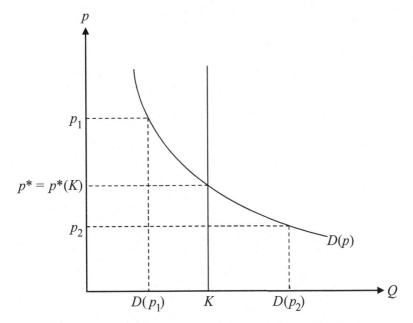

**Figure 3.1.** Allocating scarce network capacity and the market-clearing price.

by the consumer and that the benefit function for network services is a reduced form that incorporates related consumption decisions. The benefit function can be considered separable from some other types of consumption decisions.

Let $p$ be the price of the network service. The consumer's demand for the network service maximizes net benefits:

$$(1) \qquad\qquad V^i(p) = \max_Q B^i(Q) - pQ.$$

The consumer's demand for the network service equates the consumer's marginal benefit to the price,

$$(2) \qquad\qquad B^{i\prime}(Q^i) = p,$$

where demand $Q^i = D^i(p)$ solves equation (2). Total demand for network services is obtained by summing individual consumer demands:

$$(3) \qquad\qquad D(p) = \sum_{i=1}^{I} D^i(p).$$

In the *short run*, the capacity of the network is fixed, say at $K$. Then, given continual usage of network capacity, the price at which demand for and supply of capacity are equal solves

$$(4) \qquad\qquad D(p^*) = K,$$

where $p^* = p^*(K)$ solves equation (4). This solution is represented in Figure 3.1. A price above $p^*$ rations demand to the point where there is excess capacity, so at $p_1$,

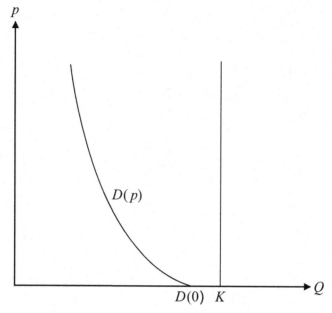

**Figure 3.2.** The efficient price is equal to zero when demand at the zero price is less than network capacity.

there is excess capacity $K - D(p_1)$. A price below $p^*$, say at $p_2$, allows excess demand $D(p_2) - K$ and results in unsatisfied customers. Regulated prices can miss the mark and lead to inefficient outcomes.

The market-clearing price is also the efficient price. The equilibrium price shown in Figure 3.1 is strictly decreasing in capacity because demand for the network service is downward sloping. Conversely, outward shifts in demand increase the equilibrium price. In this setting, without congestion effects, increases in demand result in a higher equilibrium price.

There is an important case of capacity pricing that occurs when demand at a zero price is less than capacity. This case is represented in Figure 3.2. In this case, the efficient price of capacity is the zero price. This corresponds to the situation of many fiber optic networks that have substantial amounts of transmission capacity, referred to as *dark fiber*. The price of capacity represents its per-unit economic scarcity rent. Economic rent per unit is positive with scarce capacity and zero with excess capacity.

If variable costs are present, the pricing rule must be modified accordingly. Suppose that $c$ represents constant per-unit operating costs. If prices cover per-unit operating costs, then the firm should operate at those prices. If prices do not cover per-unit operating costs, then there should be higher prices, even though the result will be excess capacity. Generally, revenues must cover avoidable costs for the firm to continue operating. This agrees with the standard neoclassical model.

The demand faced by a profit-maximizing firm corresponds to market demand if the firm is a monopolist. If the firm competes with other firms and if firms offer

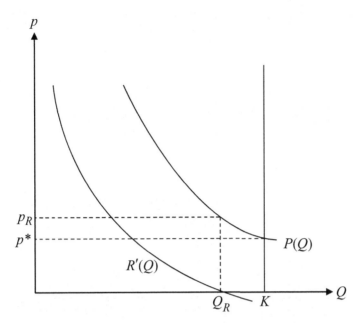

**Figure 3.3.** Let $P(Q)$ be inverse demand and let $R'(Q) = P(Q) + P'(Q)Q$ be marginal revenue as a function of output. The firm chooses the unconstrained revenue-maximizing price that is greater than $p^*$.

differentiated products, then the demand faced by the firm can be interpreted as a type of residual demand that is contingent on the pricing policies of rival firms. If competing firms offer fixed levels of capacity, then the firm's demand can be interpreted as a residual demand function, that is, as the market demand function net of the quantities offered by rival firms. Accordingly, in what follows, we allow the demand function $D(p)$ to represent a variety of such situations.

Let $R(p) = pD(p)$ be total revenue and let $R'(p) = pD'(p) + D(p)$ be marginal revenue. A profit-maximizing firm with capacity $K$ compares the revenue-maximizing output with available capacity. The revenue-maximizing price solves

(5) $$R'(p_R) = 0.$$

The revenue-maximizing output is thus $Q_R = D(p_R)$. If there is sufficient capacity $K$ to serve $Q_R$, the firm will set the price at $p_R$, which is greater than $p^*$; see Figure 3.3. Otherwise, if the firm is capacity-constrained so that $K < Q_R$, the firm will choose the price at which all capacity is used, which is exactly $p^*$; see Figure 3.4. The monopolist will not have excess demand but may have excess capacity. With increased competition, firms have incentives to lower prices and there is less incentive for firms to have excess capacity.

In the long run, capacity is variable. If the network is to be newly established, the firm can choose capacity to reflect the expected requirements of customers over some period of time. If the network already exists, the firm considers the costs of constructing additional capacity and the adjustment costs of integrating that

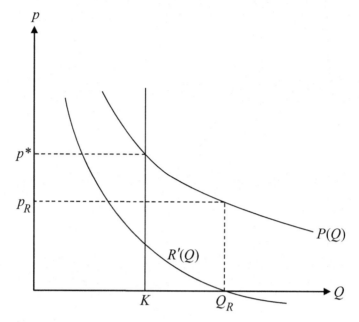

**Figure 3.4.** The constrained revenue-maximizing price equals $p^*$ if $K < QR$.

capacity within the network. To represent these situations, let $C(K)$ represent the cost of providing capacity $K$. Assume that there are no other costs of providing network services. Then the efficient price equals the marginal cost of capacity evaluated at total demand:

$$(6) \qquad\qquad p^* = C'(D(p^*)).$$

This price clears the market because total demand for network services equals the amount of capacity that is supplied: $K^* = D(p^*)$. Also, the level of capacity that is supplied is efficient because each consumer's marginal benefit equals the price, which in turn equals the marginal cost of capacity. Thus, the capacity level maximizes total benefits for consumers net of the cost of capacity.[1] The solution is represented in Figure 3.5.

The efficient price covers the costs of the firm if economies of scale do not exist at the market-clearing capacity level, that is, if marginal cost is greater than or equal to average cost:

$$C'(D(p^*)) \geq C(D(p^*))/D(p^*).$$

---

1  Define the net benefit of capacity by $G(K)$,

$$G(K) = \max_{Q^i, i=1,\dots,I} \sum_{i=1}^{I} B^i(Q^i) - C(K),$$

subject to $\sum_{i=1}^{I} Q^i \leq K$. Then $K^*$ solves $G'(K^*) = 0$ or

$$B^{i\prime}(Q^{i*}) = C'(K^*), i = 1, \dots, I,$$

where $\sum_{i=1}^{I} Q^{i*} = K^*$.

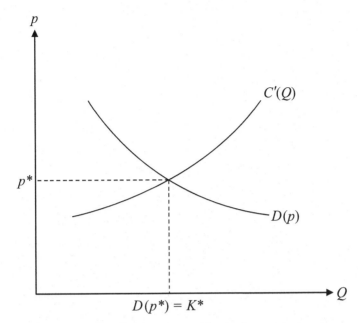

**Figure 3.5.** The efficient price and level of network capacity.

Otherwise, if there are economies of scale, and prices must be constant per unit of output, then average-cost pricing is necessary:

(7) $$p^{**} = C(D(p^{**}))/D(p^{**}).$$

At this second-best price, the firm exactly breaks even. The firm supplies capacity that serves market demand at the average-cost price.

A profit-maximizing firm adjust the price and sells the corresponding amount of network services such that marginal revenue equals marginal cost:

(8) $$R'(p_M) = C'(D(p_M)).$$

Competition between profit-maximizing firms tends to lower prices below the monopoly level and raises the total amount of network capacity that is provided. With sufficient economies of scale, smaller numbers of firms provide capacity. Price competition tends to drive prices toward average costs. These results apply to network capacity in much the same way that they apply generally to productive capacity in practically any industry. More difficult issues arise in network industries due to uncertainty in demand for capacity.

## 2. Pricing Capacity under Uncertainty

When demand is uncertain, the market-clearing price of capacity will vary. If the price of capacity is at the market-clearing level for the corresponding state of the world, then the price of capacity is the spot price. Let $\omega$ be a real-valued random variable that represents the state of the world. Let demand be dependent on the

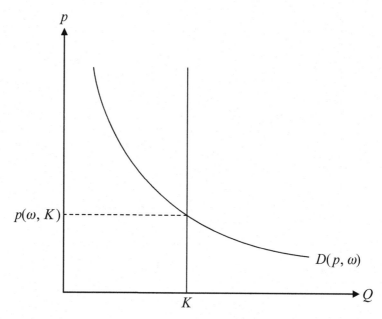

**Figure 3.6.** The spot price of network capacity or the state-contingent Arrow–Debreu security price.

realization of the random variable, $D(p, \omega)$. Then the spot price is given by the price $p(\omega, K)$ that clears the market:

$$(9) \qquad\qquad D(p(\omega, K), \omega) = K,$$

if $D(0, \omega) \geq K$. Otherwise, if $D(0, \omega) < K$, the spot price of capacity equals zero. The spot price also can respond to random variations in capacity associated with changes in the provision of capacity or reductions in network capacity that result from failures and maintenance.

   Suppose that contingent contracts are established such that individual consumers receive capacity allocations

$$(10) \qquad Q^i(\omega) = D^i(p(\omega, K), \omega), \quad i = 1, \ldots, I,$$

in state $\omega$. Note that total capacity allotments sum to total demand, which in turn equals total capacity $K$ in states of the world with a positive spot price and equals $D(0, \omega)$ in states of the world with a zero spot price. The state-contingent forward contract is priced using Arrow–Debreu state-contingent prices $p(\omega, K)$ that correspond to the spot prices. Thus, consumer $i$ purchases the state-contingent capacity allocation $Q^i(\omega)$ at the state-contingent price $p(\omega, K)$; see Figure 3.6.

### 3. Time-of-Use Pricing of Capacity

Capacity must serve customers over time. Demand for network services may vary by time of day, day of the week, or even seasonally, in the case of energy transmission.

In telecommunications, prices for network services often vary by time of day and day of the week. Capacity must be sufficient to meet demand during the time period when demand is greatest, and correspondingly, excess capacity is present in other time periods. By pricing to reduce demand at the peak, the network firm reduces the amount of capacity required to service customers. Pricing that smooths the pattern of demand over time is referred to as peak-load pricing, or more generally, time-of-use pricing.

Typically a consumer uses some network services in each period. Suppose that there are $T$ time periods, representing both times of day and days of the week. The consumer purchases network services in each time period, as represented by the vector $Q = (Q_1, \ldots, Q_T)$. The consumer takes into account the relative benefits of consuming services in the different time periods and the relative prices across the time periods. Consumers choose demand to maximize net benefits, so that $Q_t^i = D_t^i(p_1, \ldots, p_T)$ represents consumer $i$'s demand in time period $t$, $t = 1, \ldots, T$. Total demand in period $t$ is $D(p_1, \ldots, p_T)$. The set of time-of-use prices can be adjusted to increase the quantity of services demanded in some periods and to reduce the quantity of services demand in others. Time-of-use pricing makes more efficient use of capacity by matching demands to capacity.

For a given level of capacity $K$, the market-clearing time-of-use prices solve $T$ equations,

$$(11) \qquad D_t(p_1^*, p_2^*, \ldots, p_T^*) = K, \quad t = 1, \ldots, T.$$

To illustrate the solution, suppose that there is a single consumer with a quadratic benefit function and only two time periods,[2]

$$(12) \qquad B(Q_1, Q_2) = a(Q_1 + Q_2) - \left( b_1 Q_1^2 + 2\gamma Q_1 Q_2 + b_2 Q_2^2 \right) / 2.$$

Then, because marginal benefit equals the price in each period and capacity is the same, the price in period $t$ is simply

$$(13) \qquad p_t^* = a - b_t K - \gamma K, \quad t = 1, 2,$$

which is well defined if $a/(b_t + \gamma) \geq K$. Let the price equal zero otherwise. The time-of-use prices are lowered in all periods by increases in the substitution parameter $\gamma$.

Consider time-of-use pricing in the long run when the network firm chooses the level of capacity. Suppose that there is a single representative consumer. Then the optimal level of network services in each time period and the optimal level of network capacity satisfy the following condition:[3]

$$(14) \qquad \sum_{t=1}^{T} \frac{\partial B(Q_1^*, Q_2^*, \ldots, Q_T^*)}{\partial Q_t} = C'(K^*).$$

---

2  Assume that $b_1 > \gamma$ and $b_2 > \gamma$. Assume also that the two goods are substitutes, $\gamma > 0$.
3  The network service in each period is limited by capacity, $Q_t^* \leq K^*$. If $Q_t^* < K^*$, $\partial B/\partial Q_t = 0$. If $Q_t^* = K^*$, $\partial B/\partial Q_t \geq 0$.

The sum of marginal benefits of network services across time periods equals the marginal cost of capacity.

To understand this fundamental result, notice that capacity acts as a public good across the time periods. Supplying capacity in one period means that it is also available in all other time periods without additional cost. Usage in one period does not preclude usage in another time period. Of course, usage of a network is not free, because there are operating costs, but the capacity that is available in one time period is essentially available without cost in other time periods. In the public goods literature, the amount of the public good equates total marginal benefits to marginal cost.

Access to network capacity is excludable, except of course when regulators compel access. The prices of access that support the efficient outcome are time-of-use prices:

$$(15) \qquad p_t^* = \frac{\partial B(Q_1^*, Q_2^*, \ldots, Q_T^*)}{\partial Q_t}.$$

The price equals zero in periods of excess capacity $Q_t^* < K$ and is greater than or equal to zero in periods of full capacity $Q_t^* = K$. Prices are positive when the capacity constraint is binding. The efficient solution equates the marginal cost of capacity to the sum of time-of-use prices:

$$(16) \qquad \sum_{t=1}^{T} p_t^* = C'(K^*).$$

Because access is excludable, it is sufficient to post time-of-use prices in each period to gauge demand in each period. This differs from the public goods problem, in which individual users are asked how much they value the public good. As is well understood, there are incentives to free ride by understating demand, which results in underproduction of the public good because everyone free rides. Of course, simply asking users how much they value access in a particular time period would replicate the free rider problem.

To illustrate the solution, suppose that the representative consumer has quadratic utility. Then the price in period $t$ is positive if $p_t^* = a - (b_t + \gamma) K^* > 0$. The efficient capacity level satisfies

$$\sum_{t=1}^{T} [a - (b_t + \gamma) K^*] = C'(K^*)$$

if prices are positive in all time periods.[4] Otherwise, periods with excess capacity will not add to marginal benefits.

Adding usage of the network even in off-peak times adds to the marginal benefits of capacity and therefore can require an increase in capacity. Thus, granting access to network services in off-peak times should not be viewed as discovery of a free public

---

4   For a general model of peak loading pricing with a neoclassical production function, see Panzar (1976). For a discussion of the effects of cost functions on peak-load pricing, see Mitchell and Vogelsang (1991).

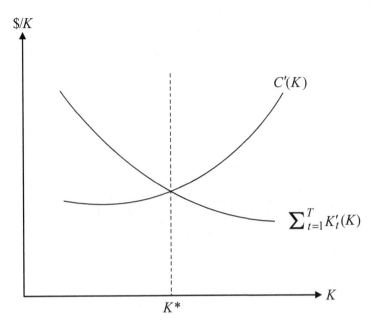

**Figure 3.7.** The optimal level of network capacity with multiple time periods of usage.

good. Of course, as with public goods generally, there is a tremendous temptation to free ride. Off-peak users would like to shift costs to peak users as much as possible. Regulators may believe that by granting retail, wholesale, or unbundled access off peak there should be no costs because capacity is only there to serve the peak users. However, as with public goods, capacity reflects the sum of benefits at least across those periods where there is full capacity utilization. With variable costs of usage that depend on the capacity of the network overall, this requires *all periods* to contribute to the cost of capacity (Panzar 1976). Accordingly, the costs of access generally should be carried by all users regardless of the period in which their usage occurs. The amount of costs can certainly vary with the intensity of usage in each period. However, variations in demand by time of use need not support free riding.

To illustrate the discussion, suppose that benefits are independent across time periods, which is a standard assumption in the literature on time-of-use pricing. Then $B_t(Q_t)$ denotes benefits in time period $t$. Suppose further that marginal benefits are positive at full capacity in each period, even though marginal benefits vary across time periods. Then, because the efficient amount of capacity equates the sum of marginal benefits to marginal cost, the solution can be illustrated as in Figure 3.7. This analysis demonstrates that greater consumption benefits in any period, including off-peak periods, raise total benefits and also increase the total of marginal benefits. The result is that the efficient level of capacity is increased by greater off-peak consumption requirements. The time-of-use price in any period equals the marginal benefit in that time period if consumption is at full capacity, as shown in Figure 3.8. Prices are greater in periods with higher benefits of consumption but are positive in all periods if there are positive marginal benefits at $Q_t = K^*$. Thus, it should not be assumed that capacity is free off peak. Off-peak usage at full

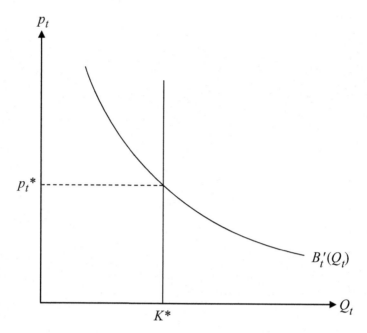

**Figure 3.8.** The time-of-use price in period $t$ equals the marginal benefit of consumption at the full-capacity level.

capacity still signifies scarce capacity, even if marginal benefits are lower. Because all periods with scarce capacity contribute to capacity payments, the efficient level of capacity is not just dependent on peak demand. Accordingly, additional usage resulting from off-peak access should require additions to the capacity of the network.

### B. Network Capacity Pricing under Asymmetric Information

#### 1. Vickrey Auctions of Capacity

Suppose that the demand functions of individual consumers are unobservable and suppose that the distribution of consumer types is unknown to the firm. Then, as a consequence, the firm does not know aggregate demand. Suppose, for ease of presentation, that each consumer has a demand for only one unit of service.[5] A consumer $i$ has a benefit function defined by

(17)
$$B^i(Q) = \begin{cases} b^i Q & Q \le 1 \\ b^i & Q > 1. \end{cases}$$

Suppose that the taste parameter $b$ is a positive, real-valued random draw from a cumulative distribution function $F(b)$, with density of $f(b)$, defined on the unit interval. Capacity is available in $K$ discrete units. Suppose that the number of

---

5   For generalization to downward sloping demand, see Spulber (1992, 1993a, 1993b).

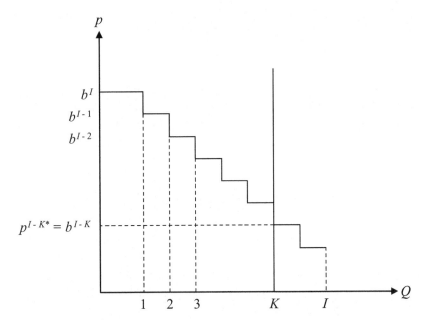

**Figure 3.9.** Demand for network capacity when the number of consumers $I$ exceeds the number of units of network capacity $K$.

consumers is greater than the capacity, so that some type of rationing is necessary, $I > K$.

Given these assumptions, the demand for capacity is a step function composed of the list of realized valuations of the good by consumers $(b^1, b^2, \ldots, b^I)$. This is represented in Figure 3.9. Clearly, only $K$ consumers can obtain a unit of the good, so some form of rationing is necessary. Because the firm does not know the realizations of consumer valuations, the aggregate demand function is not known to the firm.

Many different allocation mechanisms are available to solve the problem of selling multiple units of scarce capacity. A well-known mechanism is the Vickrey auction (1961). Each buyer submits a bid $p^i$. The winning bidders must pay the highest losing bid. Suppose that the consumer bids are in increasing order

$$p^1 < p^2 < \cdots < p^I.$$

Then the highest losing bid is $p^{I-K}$. The buyer's (weakly) dominant strategy is to bid his true valuation,

(18)                              $p^{i*} = b^i.$

To see why, note that a buyer will never bid above his valuation. If bidding above the valuation resulted in obtaining a unit of the service that the buyer would not have received when bidding at his valuation, the buyer necessarily would pay more than his valuation for the unit, resulting in a loss of consumer surplus. The buyer will never bid below his valuation, for to do so would potentially result in the loss of a unit that could have been obtained at a price below the consumer's valuation. This would mean forgoing potential consumer surplus.

Accordingly, the market clears at the highest losing bid, $p^{I-K*} = b^{I-K}$. This is the appropriate market-clearing price, so that the Vickrey auction results in an efficient allocation of the network's capacity. The $K$ highest bidders obtain units of capacity, and because these are the buyers with the highest valuations, it follows that capacity is allocated to the highest-value consumers. The equilibrium price is shown in Figure 3.9. The $K$ consumers with values $b^i > b^{I-K}$ each obtain a unit of capacity and pay $b^{I-K}$.

## 2. Reliability Pricing of Capacity

Reliability of service is represented by $Q$, which is the likelihood that a consumer receives a unit of service. The network firm offers consumers a nonlinear payment schedule based on reliability, $R = R(Q)$. Consumers choose how much reliability they want and pay in advance based on the payment schedule. Consumer $i$ chooses reliability to maximize net benefits:

$$(19) \qquad\qquad V^i(b^i) = \max_Q b^i Q - R(Q).$$

The consumer chooses a level of reliability $Q^{i*}$ that equates the marginal payment for reliability to the consumer's willingness to pay for a unit of service:

$$(20) \qquad\qquad b^i = R'(Q^{i*}).$$

It can be shown that given an optimal payment schedule, consumers with a greater willingness to pay for a unit of service choose a higher level of reliability. The reliability payment schedule must be increasing in reliability. Thus, consumers with a greater willingness to pay for a unit of service choose to pay more for reliability of service. Suppose that consumer willingness-to-pay levels are arranged in increasing order,

$$b^1 < b^2 < \cdots < b^I.$$

Then the consumers with the $K$ highest willingness-to-pay levels each receive a unit of service. Thus, the outcome of the allocation process with a reliability payment schedule corresponds exactly to the allocation in the Vickrey auction. We examine how the reliability and payment schedules compare to the Vickrey auction.

We present an intuitive approach to the design of an optimal reliability payment schedule. First, define the consumer's *virtual* marginal willingness to pay for capacity by subtracting $(1 - F(b^i))/f(b^i)$ from the consumer's willingness to pay, $b^i$:

$$(21) \qquad\qquad v(b^i) = b^i - \frac{1 - F(b^i)}{f(b^i)}.$$

This is the exact amount by which consumers understate their willingness to pay under asymmetric information.[6] Thus, define the consumer's virtual demand function by

(22)
$$D^*(\rho, b^i) = \begin{cases} 1 & \text{if } v(b^i) \geq \rho \\ 0 & \text{otherwise.} \end{cases}$$

The virtual demand function of consumer $i$ depends on the shadow price of capacity $\rho$ and the individual's value of a unit of service, which equals $b^i$.

Now, calculate the sum of virtual demands to obtain aggregate virtual demand,

(23)
$$D^*(\rho, b^1, b^2, \ldots, b^I) = \sum_{i=1}^{I} D^*(\rho, b^i).$$

Then use the aggregate virtual demand to calculate the shadow price of capacity, $\rho^*$, which clears the market,

(24)
$$D^*(\rho^*, b^1, b^2, \ldots, b^I) = K.$$

Clearly, the shadow price of capacity will depend on all of the consumer valuations of service: $\rho^* = \rho^* (b^1, b^2, \ldots, b^I, K)$. The shadow price also depends on total capacity. Now, plug the shadow price back into individual demands to obtain the output allocation rule,

(25) $$D^*(\rho^*(b^1, b^2, \ldots, b^I, K), b^i) = \begin{cases} 1 & \text{if } v(b^i) \geq \rho^*(b^1, b^2, \ldots, b^I, K) \\ 0 & \text{otherwise.} \end{cases}$$

Finally, calculate the output that a consumer of type $i$ expects to receive,

(26)
$$Q^*(b^i) = \int_0^1 \cdots \int_0^1 D^*(\rho^*(b^1, b^2, \ldots, b^I, K), b^i)$$
$$df(b^1) \ldots df(b^{i-1})df(b^{i+1}) \ldots df(b^I).$$

This is the reliability of service for a consumer of type $i$.

To find the reliability schedule, find the inverse of the reliability function, $b^* = Q^{*-1} (Q)$. The optimal price schedule for reliability is then

(27)
$$R(Q) = b^*(Q)Q - \int_0^{b^*(Q)} Q^*(b)db.$$

It is easy to see that $R'(Q) = b^*(Q)$. The consumer chooses a reliability level that equates the marginal payment to the willingness to pay for a unit of reliability. It follows that

(28)
$$b^i = R'(Q) = b^*(Q).$$

---

6  The term $(1 - F(b))/f(b)$ is the reciprocal of the hazard rate.

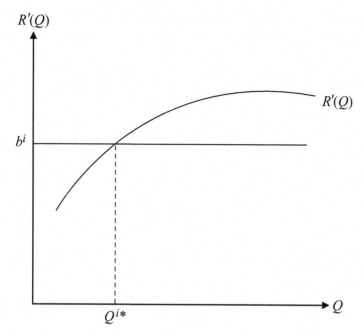

**Figure 3.10.** Consumers pay a premium for greater reliability of network service.

The consumer's choice of reliability will be the efficient level; that is, $Q^i = Q^*(b^i)$. Thus, the consumer's choice of reliability $Q^i$ reveals the consumer's type, because $b^i = b^*(Q^*(b^i))$.

Consider the properties of the reliability payment schedule. Because higher-willingness-to-pay consumers choose more reliability, the marginal payment schedule is increasing, $R''(Q) = b^{*\prime}(Q) > 0$. This means that consumers pay a quantity premium to obtain greater reliability. This is shown in Figure 3.10. Moreover, the average payment per unit of reliability is increasing in the level of reliability. From equation (27),

$$(29) \qquad \frac{\partial}{\partial Q} \frac{R(Q)}{Q} = \frac{\int_0^{b^*(Q)} Q^*(b)db}{Q^2} > 0.$$

Compare the outcome for the reliability pricing mechanism with the outcome of the Vickrey auction. In both cases, consumers with the $K$ highest willingness-to-pay levels each receive a unit of service. This suggests that the likelihood of winning the Vickrey auction for a particular consumer exactly equals that consumer's choice of reliability of service with reliability pricing. This can be demonstrated using basic order statistics. Let $s_{I-K}$ be the $I - K$ order statistic if the sample of consumer types is in increasing order, $b^1 < b^2 < \cdots < b^I$. Thus, $s_{I-K}$ is the type of the losing consumer with the highest willingness to pay. Let $F_{I-K}(b)$ be the probability distribution for the $I - K$ order statistic.[7] The probability that the $I - K$ order statistic is less than or

---

7  The cumulative probability distribution of the $(I - K)$th order statistic is $F_{I-K}(b) = \sum_{i=I-K}^{I} \binom{I}{i} f(b)^i (1 - F(b))^{I-i}$ for all $b$ in the unit interval.

equal to $b$ is equal to the probability that the number of consumers with willingness to pay $b^i$ less than or equal to $b$ is greater than or equal to $I - K$. Thus,

$$(30) \qquad F_{I-K}(b) = \Pr\{s_{I-K} \le b\} = Q^*(b).$$

So the likelihood of a type-$b$ consumer winning the Vickrey auction equals the reliability level chosen by a type-$b$ consumer with reliability pricing.

In a Vickrey auction, only winners make payments for service, and these payments are necessarily made after demand is observed by the firm. With reliability pricing, all consumers make payments, and payments are made before demand is observed. Despite this difference, the expected payment of a type-$b$ consumer in the Vickrey auction equals the payment for reliability of a type-$b$ consumer. In the Vickrey auction, all winning consumers pay the bid of the highest-type losing consumer, $p^{I-K} = b^{I-K}$. The probability distribution of the willingness to pay of the highest-type losing consumer is the order statistic for the $(I - K)$th highest type, because capacity equals $K$ and there are $I$ consumers. Thus, the expected payment in the Vickrey auction of a type-$b^i$ consumer is the expectation of the $(I - K)$-order statistic, contingent on the order statistic being less than that consumer's willingness to pay:

$$(31) \qquad \text{Expected payment} = \int_0^{b^i} b f_{I-K}(b) db.$$

It follows that the expected payment in the Vickrey auction equals the actual payment with reliability pricing,[8]

$$(32) \qquad R(Q^*(b^i)) = b^i Q^*(b^i) - \int_0^{b^i} Q^*(b) db.$$

This equivalence holds because $Q^*(b^i) = F_{I-K}(b^i)$.

## 3. Priority Pricing of Capacity

Another approach to pricing network capacity is priority pricing.[9] This widely used system assigns access priorities to consumers, with higher prices charged for higher priorities. Postal systems assign priorities for express mail deliveries as a means

---

8   Apply integration by parts to the expected payment in the Vickrey auction for a type-$b^i$ consumer to obtain

$$\int_0^{b^i} b f_{I-K}(b) db = b^i F_{I-K}(b^i) - \int_0^{b^i} F_{I-K}(b) db.$$

Therefore, since $F_{I-K}(b^i) = Q^*(b^i)$,

$$\int_0^b b f_{I-K}(b) db = b^i Q^*(b^i) - \int_0^{b^i} Q^*(b) db = R(Q^*(b^i)).$$

9   For additional discussion, see Harris and Raviv (1981). In their setting, consumer types are discrete and capacity is perfectly divisible, as opposed to our setting, with a continuum of consumer types and capacity in discrete units.

of allocating scarce capacity based on differences in how consumers value speed of delivery. In electricity and natural gas, customers paying a premium for higher priority are less likely to be curtailed given a shortage of transmission capacity.

The discussion in the previous section derived a price schedule for reliability $R(Q)$. This can be interpreted as a priority pricing scheme. Define $p$ as the price of a unit of capacity, with a continuum of priorities ranging from $p(0) = R(Q^*(0))$ to $p(1) = R(Q^*(1))$. The higher the price chosen by the consumer, the higher the priority. A consumer of type $b^i$ will select a priority price,

$$(33) \qquad\qquad p(i) = R(Q^*(b^i)), \quad i = 1, \ldots, I.$$

The firm will serve customers in order of priority prices starting from the highest price and continuing until all units of capacity have been exhausted. The $K$ highest-value consumers obtain a unit of capacity and have the same expected payment as in the case of the reliability schedule by construction. The priority pricing scheme is effectively a discriminatory auction in which every winning consumer pays his bid, with the highest $K$ bidders winning a unit of capacity.[10]

## C. Network Capacity Pricing with Congestion and Quality of Service

Allocation of network capacity is substantially more complex than dividing a cake among potential consumers. The cause of this complexity is that usage of capacity can create congestion that drives down the quality of service. This means that whereas transmission capacity can be well defined in terms of quantity, changes in the level of usage affect customer benefits from using that capacity. The effects of congestion of telecommunications networks on quality of service have been widely recognized. Increases in usage for a given capacity can lead to delays or blocked calls in a circuit-switched network or dropped packets in a packet-switched network. This chapter considers the problem of setting prices for capacity when congestion affects service quality.

It is tempting to refer to quality-of-service effects as a *congestion externality*, but there are misleading implications from this loaded term. It is certainly true that there are formal similarities to classic externalities such as pollution. The reasoning proceeds as follows. One person's consumption of network services, which lead to capacity usage, negatively affects another person's benefit from consumption of network services. A consumer takes into account the benefits received from consumption of network services, but presumably is indifferent to the costs that such consumption imposes on others. Without any rationing of capacity, congestion will increase to the point where each user's marginal benefits from consumption are exhausted. The allocation of network services would necessarily be inefficient.

---

10  Discriminatory auctions are efficient in the unit-demand case. When buyers demand multiple units, the auctions may fail to be efficient, as Vickrey (1961) recognized.

The problem with the congestion externalities approach is that network services usually are not free. Network firms charge for retail access to network services. Thus, access is rationed by price. Because the consumers of a network engage in transactions with the network, congestion effects are not external to the market. Network congestion effects are *internal* to transactions between consumers and the network. Consumers may not be aware of the congestion effects they create, but the network firm is certainly aware of these effects. The network firm chooses prices and capacity with an understanding of the effects of usage on quality of service. Thus, the network's prices internalize the effects of usage on congestion.

Congestion effects may take the form of externalities if government regulators limit the network firm's ability to ration access to capacity. Thus, if competitors have wholesale or unbundled access to network services without sufficient price rationing by the network firm, congestion effects that resemble externalities can occur. An extreme example is the granting of interconnection access to Internet service providers at a zero price. Presumably, there are ways that the network firm could negotiate access limits with its competitors if it were not prevented from doing so by regulation. Coase (1960) emphasized that without substantial transaction costs, parties can bargain to achieve efficient levels of an externality. Coase emphasized that this would be possible regardless of the initial assignment of property rights. Depending on the initial assignment of rights, the polluter would compensate the victim for pollution or the victim would bribe the polluter to reduce pollution. In principle, the network firm could attempt to pay competitors to reduce their access if congestion costs became too high, although such payments might be prohibitively costly. Also, such payments are impractical because they would encourage further entry of competitive local exchange carriers (CLECs), new entrants in the deregulated local exchange markets, and lead to further usage and congestion.

## 1. Blocked Calls

There are many aspects of the quality of service provided by a network. One important measure of quality is the waiting time to obtain service. For a telecommunications system, this could be represented by the average waiting time in a queue before initiating a communication. For data networks, this approach could be applied to study the total time of service, which is the waiting time plus the time for completion of transmission. For our purpose, it is sufficient to consider only the waiting time in a queue to show the effects of quality of service on demand. Examples of waiting in a queue are the delay in connecting by phone to an Internet service provider or to a service call center and the average time spent waiting for a dial tone.[11]

---

11  For a general approach to pricing multiple services with quality-of-service requirements, see Keon and Anandalingam (2003). For a related discussion of congestion on the Internet, see Mackie-Mason and Varian (1995a).

Suppose that each consumer obtains a benefit from the number of completed phone calls $Q$. The number of phone calls is integer-valued. The consumer's benefit is a standard increasing and concave utility function $u(Q)$. Suppose that the number of phone calls that the consumer makes is random due to exogenous factors that affect the necessity of communicating with others. Suppose further that the consumer chooses the intensity of usage $\lambda$, which determines the average rate at which calls are made within a period of time, but not the actual number of calls. Within a given period of time, the consumer's calls have an arrival rate that does not depend on prior arrivals. This is referred to as a Poisson arrival rate. The consumer's expected utility is then a function of the rate of making phone calls,

$$(34) \qquad\qquad U(\lambda) = \sum_{k=0}^{\infty} u(k) e^{-\lambda} \frac{\lambda^k}{k!}.$$

The expected utility has the standard properties of a utility function.[12]

Suppose that the network's capacity to complete calls constrains demand, which leads to the possibility of blocked calls. Let $W$ be the average waiting time for service for consumers seeking to initiate a call, as described in the previous chapter. Suppose that the consumer's benefit from the number of calls is affected by the average waiting time, $u = u(Q, W)$. An increase in average waiting time reduces the consumer's total and marginal benefit from service. The consumer's expected benefit also will depend on the waiting time, $U = U(\lambda, W)$. An increase in waiting time reduces the marginal expected benefit from service; see Figure 3.11.

The expected number of calls per period is equal to the arrival rate, $EQ = \lambda$.[13] The consumer pays a price $p$ per completed call. The consumer chooses the rate of usage to maximize the expected net benefit from network services. The consumer's resulting net benefit equals

$$(35) \qquad\qquad V^i(p, W) = \max_{\lambda} U^i(\lambda, W) - p\lambda,$$

because the consumer's expected payment is $p\lambda$. Let $\lambda^i = \lambda^i(p, W)$ be the solution to the consumer's problem. The consumer's choice of usage equates the consumer's

---

12  It can be demonstrated that $U(\lambda)$ is an increasing and concave function. Taking a derivative with respect to $\lambda$ yields

$$U'(\lambda) = \sum_{k=0}^{\infty} u(k) e^{-\lambda} \frac{\lambda^{k-1}}{k!} - \sum_{k=0}^{\infty} u(k) e^{-\lambda} \frac{\lambda^k}{k!} = \sum_{k=0}^{\infty} (u(k+1) - u(k)) \frac{e^{-\lambda} \lambda^k}{k!}$$

So $U'(\lambda) > 0$ because $u(k)$ is increasing. Taking the second derivative with respect to $\lambda$, by similar arguments we obtain

$$U''(\lambda) = \sum_{k=0}^{\infty} [(u(k+2) - u(k+1)) - (u(k+1) - u(k))] \frac{e^{-\lambda}}{k!}.$$

Thus, $U''(\lambda) < 0$ because $u(k)$ is concave.

13  The expected number of calls is $EQ = \sum_{k=0}^{\infty} k e^{-\lambda} \frac{\lambda^k}{k!} = \lambda$.

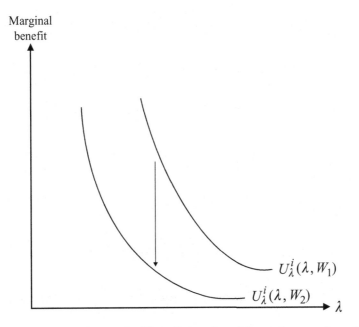

**Figure 3.11.** The consumer's marginal benefit is reduced by an increase in waiting time, which represents a reduction in network service quality, $W_1$.

marginal benefit of usage, for a given waiting time $W$, to the price of usage:

$$(36) \qquad U_\lambda^i(\lambda^i, W) = p.$$

Suppose that there are $I$ consumers. Given the demand for capacity of each consumer, the total demand for capacity can be obtained by summing consumer demands:

$$(37) \qquad \lambda = D(p, W) = \sum_{i=1}^{I} \lambda^i(p, W).$$

This is the total demand for capacity given a common waiting time $W$. Recall that with an independent memoryless arrival processes, the arrival rate of the combined traffic is also a memoryless arrival process. The arrival rate of the combined traffic is the sum of the arrival rates of the individual components. Thus, the aggregate demand in our model is the arrival rate of traffic coming to the network.

In the short run, the service capacity of the network is fixed and equal to $\mu$. Therefore, more traffic on the network creates congestion that reduces service quality. Recall the production function, as already specified in equation (8) in Chapter 2:

$$(38) \qquad \lambda = \frac{W\mu^2}{1 + W\mu}.$$

Because the capacity of the network is fixed, an increase in the amount of service $\lambda$ can be achieved only by reducing service quality $W$.

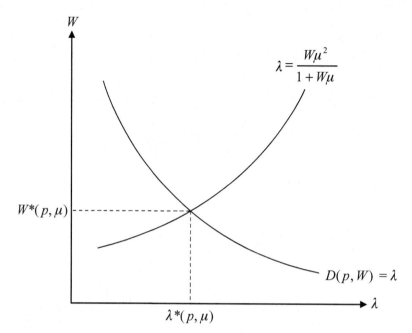

**Figure 3.12.** The equilibrium level of network congestion and capacity utilization with a fixed price $p$ and a fixed network capacity $\mu$.

For any price $p$, consumers will choose their amount of demand $\lambda^i$ based on their expectations of service quality. Thus, for any price $p$, consumer usage decisions will result in an equilibrium level of service quality, that is, an equilibrium level of congestion represented by the waiting time $W$. The equilibrium amount of congestion equates demand for service $D(p, W)$ with supply of service:

$$(39) \qquad D(p, W^*) = \frac{W^* \mu^2}{1 + W^* \mu}.$$

The equilibrium amount of congestion depends on the price of network service and the amount of network service capacity, $W^* = W^*(p, \mu)$. The equilibrium usage of the network is $\lambda^* = D(p, W^*(p, \mu))$. Therefore, congestion acts as another type of price by rationing demand. The solution is represented in Figure 3.12.

Rationing usage by congestion is necessarily inefficient because consumers may prefer a somewhat higher price with less congestion. Consider the effects of network pricing on congestion. Differentiate the equation (39) with respect to price and substitute using equation (39) to obtain

$$(40) \qquad \frac{\partial W^*(p, \mu)}{\partial p} = \frac{D_p(p, W^*)}{(D(p, W^*)/W^*\mu)^2 - D_W(p, W^*)}.$$

Demand is downward sloping in price and decreasing in waiting time. So congestion is decreasing in the price per call: $\partial W^* / \partial p < 0$.

There is no market-clearing price of capacity because of congestion effects. By specifying a desired quality of service, the price that allocates capacity can be

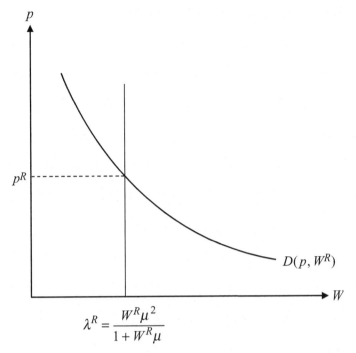

$$\lambda^R = \frac{W^R \mu^2}{1 + W^R \mu}$$

**Figure 3.13.** The price that rations network capacity is $p^R$ given an exogenously specified quality of service $W^R$.

determined. Suppose that a regulator specifies a maximum average waiting time, which sets a minimum quality of service level. The regulated quality level $W^R$ determines the available capacity by equation (38),

(41) $$\lambda^R = \frac{W^R \mu^2}{1 + W^R \mu}.$$

Therefore, the price that rations capacity with quality of service $W^R$ is the price that equates demand to available capacity,

(42) $$D(p, W^R) = \lambda^R.$$

This is represented in Figure 3.13. This is equivalent to the capacity allocation model when there are no congestion effects. Thus, with a given minimum quality of service, the model of pricing with congestion effects corresponds to the basic problem of allocating scarce capacity that was discussed previously.

The discussion of congestion thus far has assumed that network capacity is fixed. Taking a long-run perspective, suppose now that capacity $\mu$ is variable and that the cost of capacity is $C(\mu)$. The efficient level of capacity maximizes consumer benefits net of capacity costs. Capacity must be allocated efficiently across consumers and the level of service quality must maximize net benefits as well. Finally, total service, waiting time, and capacity are related by the production function in equation (38). The maximization problem is therefore

$$\max_{\{\lambda^i\}, W, \mu} \sum_{i=1}^{I} U^i(\lambda^i, W) - C(\mu)$$

$$\text{subject to} \quad \sum_{i=1}^{I} \lambda^i = \lambda \text{ and equation (38).}$$

The efficient level of capacity $\mu^*$, the efficient amount of waiting time $W^*$, and the efficient amount of service $\lambda^*$ solve the maximization problem. The solution can be represented simply by introducing a price of service, $p^*$. As before, efficient usage depends on the price of service $\lambda^{i*} = D(p^*, W^*)$. Total usage is the total of the rates of individual usage, $\lambda^* = \sum_{i=1}^{I} \lambda^{i*}$. The efficient amount of capacity equates adjusted marginal cost of capacity to the price of service:

(43) $$p^* = \left[ 1 + \frac{1}{(2 + W^*\mu^*)W^*\mu^*} \right] C'(\mu^*).$$

The upward adjustment of marginal cost represents the need to account for congestion. This means that the price of service must exceed the marginal cost of capacity due to the effects of congestion.[14]

The analysis of pricing with congestion sheds light on the pricing of access. As access to the network increases, greater congestion effects result. Optimal prices for access should reflect these congestion effects. Moreover, additional capacity usage should translate into capacity expansion. The result of additional usage is adjustments in the efficient levels of both service quality and network capacity.[15]

## 2. Information Loss

*Bandwidth* is a measure of the amount of information that can be carried by a communications network. The bandwidth of the network thus measures the *capacity* of the network. Bandwidth measures can refer to individual links or to collections of links used to provide a particular service. Just as in the previous discussion of blocked calls, there is a related problem that arises in data networks. If the amount of data being transmitted exceeds the capacity, there can be some *information loss* due to capacity constraints.

---

14   The efficient price reflects the disutility of blocked calls,

$$p^* = -\left( \frac{W^*\mu^*}{\lambda^*} \right)^2 \sum_{i=1}^{I} U_W^i(\lambda^{i*}, W^*),$$

where $\lambda^*$, $\mu^*$, and $W^*$ solve the maximization problem.

15   This analysis is closely related to the theory of externalities and to the theory of club goods (Cornes and Sandler 1986). Our analysis in this section extends the discussion of congestion to employ the queuing model that is typically used to study blocked calls in telephone networks. For a related queuing model with congestion costs, see Walrand and Varaiya (2000). See also Mackie-Mason and Varian (1995a) and Gupta et al. (1997).

A data transmission typically is divided into smaller components such as packets. The packets are independently transmitted over a link, or more generally, over the network. In a packet-switched network, a data transmission is divided into packets at or near its origin and the packets are transmitted over the network, often over different paths. The packets are addressed individually, just as are letters in a postal system. The packets are reassembled into the original data transmission at or near the destination. When the capacity of the network is exceeded, packets can be lost, resulting in lost information from data transmissions. This section presents a highly simplified discussion of information loss.

To understand the basics of information loss, suppose that a network provides a transmission service to one customer. The service can be provided with a single link or with a more general network. The capacity or bandwidth of the network is represented by $K$. The customer has uncertain data transmission needs represented by a truncated probability distribution over the amount of data transmitted per unit of time, $F(Q)/F(h)$, that is defined on the interval $[0, h]$. Let $F(0) = 0$ and let $f(Q)$ be the probability density, where the cumulative distribution $F(Q)$ is defined on $[0, \infty]$.

The quality of service that the customer receives depends on the relationship between the consumer's data transmission needs and the available bandwidth. If $h \leq K$, then bandwidth $K$ is sufficient for error-free service. Because any transmission will be less than the available bandwidth, there will be no loss of information. Conversely, if $h > K$, there is a likelihood that some transmissions may be in excess of available bandwidth, resulting in some information loss. Information loss occurs with likelihood $1 - F(K)/F(h)$, which is the probability that $Q$ is strictly greater than $K$.

How much bandwidth is needed by the consumer? A very large bandwidth may be required to guarantee error-free transmission if the range of transmission levels is substantial. However, if some information loss is tolerated, it may be possible to substantially reduce capacity requirements. By truncating the upper tail of the distribution of transmission, capacity can be reduced without much loss of information. This is illustrated in Figure 3.14. The shaded area denotes the likelihood of information loss.

The consumer obtains a benefit $u(Q)$ from a transmission of size $Q$, where the benefit function is increasing in transmission size. If the size of the transmission were to be reduced due to the network's capacity constraint, the consumer would suffer two effects. First, there would be a loss of incremental benefit since some of the transmission did not reach its destination. Second, the consumer would experience a cost of information loss. Let $g$ be the cost of information loss per unit of reduced transmission. Therefore, if $h \leq K$, the consumer's expected utility is

(44)
$$U(h, K) = \int_0^h u(Q) \frac{f(Q)}{F(h)} dQ.$$

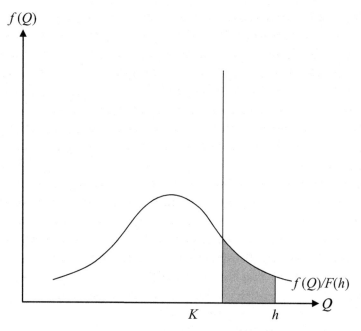

**Figure 3.14.** The probability of information loss when network capacity $K$ represents bandwidth and $f(Q)$ is the density of data transmissions defined over the range from zero to $h$.

If $h > K$, the consumer's expected utility is

$$
(45) \qquad U(h,\,K) = \int_0^K u(Q)\frac{f(Q)}{F(h)}dQ + u(K)\left(1 - \frac{F(K)}{F(h)}\right)
$$
$$
- g\int_K^h (Q-K)\frac{f(Q)}{F(h)}dQ.
$$

Even if the consumer has free access to capacity up to the available bandwidth $K$, the consumer may still choose to bear some information loss. The consumer faces a tradeoff. A greater range of transmissions, that is, a higher value of $h$, increases the average amount of data transmitted. However, increasing the range also can increase information loss if the upper limit of the range $h$ exceeds network capacity $K$. To verify that the consumer will choose some amount of information loss for any positive and finite cost $g$, differentiate the consumer's expected utility with respect to $h$ and evaluate the marginal expected utility at $h = K$. Thus, we obtain

$$
(46) \qquad U'(K,\,K) = -\int_0^K u(Q)f(Q)dQ\frac{f(K)}{(F(K))^2} + u(K)\frac{f(K)}{F(K)},
$$

which is positive because $u(Q)$ is an increasing function of the size of the transmission. Thus, the consumer will choose a transmission range $h^* > K$ that solves

$U'(h^*, K) = 0.$[16] The consumer's choice of transmission range depends on the level of available capacity, $h^* = h^*(K)$.

The consumer will tolerate less information loss the greater the cost of error $g$. However, the consumer still prefers some information loss because it is always worthwhile to increase the average transmission. Suppose that transmission capacity is obtained at cost $c(K)$. The efficient level of capacity reflects the fact that the consumer tolerates some amount of information loss. The efficient level of capacity maximizes the consumer's net expected benefit given that the range of transmission levels depends on capacity, $h^*(K)$. Thus, $K$ solves

$$\max_K U(h^*(K), K) - c(K).$$

The efficient level of capacity satisfies the condition

$$(47) \qquad (u'(K^*) + g)\left(1 - \frac{F(K^*)}{F(h^*)}\right) = c'(K^*).$$

The left-hand side of equation (47) is the marginal cost of information loss times the likelihood of information loss. The right-hand side of equation (47) is the marginal cost of capacity.

The efficiency condition (47) provides guidance on the pricing of capacity when there is the possibility of information loss. The consumer purchases capacity $K$ from the network firm at a cost per unit $p$. Suppose further that the network firm takes the price $p$ as a given and supplies capacity up to the point where the marginal cost of capacity equals the price. Then the efficiency condition (47) defines the market-clearing price of capacity $p^*$,

$$(48) \qquad (u'(K^*) + g)\left(1 - \frac{f(K^*)}{F(h^*)}\right) = p^* = c'(K^*).$$

This is represented in Figure 3.15.

At the market-clearing price of capacity $p^*$, there is still information loss because the consumer chooses a range of transmission in excess of the amount of capacity that is purchased, $h^*(K^*) > K^*$. The consumer's demand for capacity reflects the consumer's loss of benefits from truncated transmission as well as the cost of information loss. The market-clearing price gives the correct signal to both the firm and the consumer because the efficiency condition is satisfied.

The idea that individuals tolerate some level of costly information loss is behind the use of statistical multiplexing. Suppose that there are multiple individuals who

---

16  The first-order condition simplifies to

$$-\int_0^K u(Q) f(Q) dQ + u(K) F(K) - g(h^* - K) F(h^*) + g \int_k^{h^*} (Q - K) f(Q) dQ = 0.$$

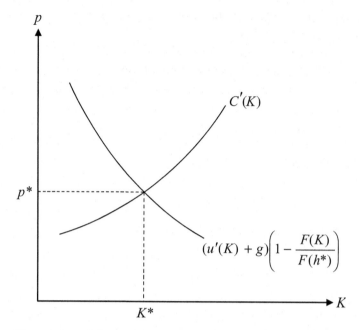

**Figure 3.15.** The supply and demand for network capacity with a price-taking network firm and a price-taking consumer.

receive network services. The capacity constraint is then

$$\sum_{i=1}^{I} Q^i \leq K.$$

An advantage of sharing capacity is that less capacity is needed to provide communications services than if each individual has a separate dedicated capacity. If different users may have peaks at different times, total capacity needs are less than would be required by adding up peak usages. This is simply an illustration of risk pooling. If capacity needs are independently distributed, or even better, negatively correlated, then the combined capacity requirements are lower than they would be with separate networks.

To illustrate the implications of shared capacity, consider the basic case of two consumers. Suppose that the range of transmission requirements for both consumers is the unit interval, $h^1 = h^2 = 1$. Also, suppose that transmission requirements are uniformly distributed for both consumers. Thus, the range of combined transmissions is between zero and two. Suppose further that the capacity of the network exceeds the maximum needs of either consumer but is less than the maximum of the combined needs:

$$1 < K < 2.$$

By standard arguments,[17] the probability that the combined transmission exceeds capacity $K$ is thus

$$\Pr\{Q^1 + Q^2 > K\} = 2 - 2K + K^2/2.$$

This is the probability of information loss when two consumers are served by a shared network with capacity $K$.

The probability of information loss with shared capacity can be compared with that for two separate networks of capacity $K/2$. The probability that a consumer does not experience an information loss is then $F(K/2) = K/2$. So the probability that at least one consumer experiences an information loss is

$$\Pr\{Q^1 > K/2 \quad \text{or} \quad Q^2 > K/2\} = 1 - K^2/4.$$

It can easily be verified that the probability of information loss is greater when consumers have separate networks.[18] By pooling information transmission, the probability of information loss is reduced.

However, congestion remains a problem. If a consumer increases the amount of information transmitted, this increases the probability of information loss for all users of the network. For example, suppose that there are many consumers using the network and each has a range of possible transmissions $[0, h^i]$, $i = 1, \ldots, I$. If a consumer increases $h^i$, expected information loss increases for all consumers. When retail access is priced based on a consumer's usage of the network, prices can be adjusted to reflect congestion effects. Sufficiently high prices for usage will fully eliminate congestion effects. If consumers choose the range of transmissions, then congestion effects are fully eliminated when

$$\sum_{i=1}^{I} h^i \leq K.$$

However, as we have seen, a consumer will tolerate some information loss in return for a higher range of transmissions. Thus, the efficient price will allow for some possibility of information loss; that is,

$$\sum_{i=1}^{I} h^i > K.$$

The price of retail access will reflect several considerations. The price will reflect the value that consumers place on transmission of information. Also on the demand side, the price of retail access will reflect the cost to consumers of information

---

17 The derivation involves application of the convolution formula for two (independent) distribution functions. If $Q = Q^1 + Q^2$ then for $Q$ in $(0, 1)$, $f_Q(Q) = Q$ and for $Q$ in $[1, 2]$, $f_Q(Q) = 2 - Q$. So $\Pr\{Q > K\} = 1 - \Pr\{Q \leq K\} = 1 - F_Q(K) = 2 - 2K + K^2/2$.

18 Thus, for $1 < K < 2$, $(1 - K^2/4) > (2 - 2K + K^2/2)$.

loss. On the supply side, the price of retail access will reflect the marginal cost of providing capacity.

The interplay between the demand and supply of capacity has important implications for access regulation. For a particular demand for capacity and supply of capacity, there is a corresponding pattern of information loss. The probability of information loss provides a measure of the quality of service. Increasing access to the network corresponds to increased demand for transmission capacity. Without any adjustments in the level of capacity, greater access results in a higher likelihood of information loss, all other things equal. Thus, increased access results in a diminished quality of service. In compelling access to data networks, regulators need to take account of network congestion and its implications for information loss.

Compelled access corresponds to congestion and reduced quality of service. If it is necessary to compel access, and regulators do not wish to cause reductions in the quality of service, access prices must increase to discourage capacity usage and to provide greater incentives for networks to provide more capacity.

The possibility of information loss occurs at times of peak demand. Clearly, there may be excess capacity in the system in times of off-peak demand. It is particularly difficult to predict peak usage on data networks because transmissions may have so-called bursts of usage. Unlike electric power usage, which can depend on weather patterns or the time of day, data networks are subject to the effects of random transmission requirements. However, periods of excess capacity should not suggest to regulators that capacity is free just because it is not in use. The level of capacity is chosen to provide a particular quality of service. Thus, excess capacity in off-peak times is simply a form of insurance against the possibility of information loss. The price of additional access should reflect the total demand for capacity, the cost of information loss, and the additional cost of capacity.

### D. Demand for Capacity: Substitutes and Complements

The demand for network services that use transmission capacity is affected by the availability of substitutes and complements. There are many substitute forms of transmission capacity that compete in the marketplace, including traditional telephone service, mobile telecommunications, broadband cable, and broadband telephony. Because different forms of transmission capacity potentially provide distinct types of services, a greater variety of services can increase total demand for telecommunications capacity. Individual network firms may experience reduced demand as a result of competition from substitutes. However, the benefits from a greater variety of services are likely to increase total demand, thus leading to greater provision of capacity by network firms.

There are also many complements to transmission capacity. After all, the demand for transmission services is a means to an end, as we have already emphasized. Consumers demand transmission services based on the demand for the communication made possible by those transmission services. The complements to transmission services are the services that are the content of communications. It is useful to view some services that are provided through transmission capacity as complementary to transmission services. Thus, the services of networks are complements to the information, entertainment, transactions, and other services that are sent over the network. The demand for network services is affected by the prices of complements. Higher prices of complementary services can reduce the demand for network services. Greater availability of complementary services increases the demand for network services. As the availability of complementary services increases – say there are more Internet services – more capacity is needed to serve the greater demand for transmission services that results.

## 1. Substitutes and Network Capacity

A greater variety of network services increases the demand for network capacity. Consumers have a higher willingness to pay for services that most closely match their desired combination of product features than for more distant substitute services. If a single network can provide a variety of services, then more services will usually increase demand. If distinct networks are needed to increase product variety, then multiple networks will have a greater total demand for capacity than would a single network with less product variety.

We now consider how the number of substitute services affects demand for capacity. Suppose that the set of products is described by a circle of unit circumference. Suppose that there are $m$ types of services and that these are located evenly around the circle. This is represented in Figure 3.16. Consumers have different preferences over product features. Suppose that the most preferred products of consumers are uniformly distributed around the circle with unit density.

A consumer's willingness to pay for $Q$ units of a product at a distance $r$ from the consumer's most preferred product is

$$(49) \qquad\qquad U = u(Q) - tr Q,$$

where $t$ is a taste parameter. The taste parameter is analogous to transport cost in the Hotelling location model. If products are all priced at the same price $p$, the consumer chooses the product closest to that consumer's most preferred type of product. The demand of a consumer at distance $r$ from the nearest available product maximizes net benefits $u(Q) - tr Q - p Q$. Thus, the consumer's demand solves

$$(50) \qquad\qquad u'(Q) - tr = p.$$

Let $Q^*(p + tr)$ be the consumer's demand for network capacity. Clearly demand is downward sloping in price $p$ and in distance $r$.

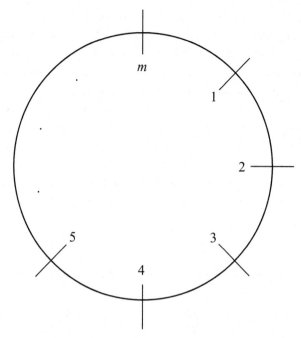

**Figure 3.16.** The product space is a circle of unit circumference with $m$ substitute services.

If there are $m$ substitute products all at the same price, total demand for capacity is

$$(51) \qquad\qquad D(p, m) = 2m \int_0^{1/(2m)} Q(p + tr)\,dr.$$

Because a consumer demands less if the nearest product is farther away, it is straightforward to demonstrate that total demand is increasing in the number of products,

$$D(p, m_2) > D(p, m_1),$$

if $m_2 > m_1$. This implies that demand for network capacity is increasing in the number of substitute products.[19] For a given level of capacity, the market-clearing price of network capacity will be greater with more substitute products. This is illustrated in Figure 3.17.

Suppose that distinct networks are needed to provide substitute services. For example, a mobile network provides the convenience of mobility whereas a fiber-optic data network provides greater transmission capacity. The benefits of multiple networks on the demand side must be traded off against the costs of operating multiple networks. Suppose that networks have economies of scale as represented by the cost function $c(K) = C + cK$, where $C$ is the fixed cost of establishing and operating network capacity and $c$ is the marginal cost of capacity. Clearly,

---

19  Differentiating $D(p, m)$ with respect to $m$, we obtain $\partial D(p, m)/\partial m = D(p, m)/m - Q(p + t/(2m))/m$. Thus, $\partial D(p, m)/\partial m > 0$ because $Q(p + tr)$ is a decreasing function of $r$.

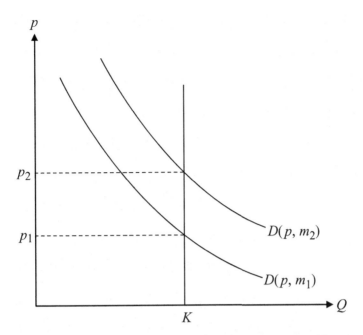

**Figure 3.17.** The market-clearing price of network capacity is greater with more substitute products, $m_2 > m_1$.

with unlimited economies of scale, the least-cost configuration is a single network without any variety of services. This situation corresponds to anecdotal characterizations of the Bell System, which provided a standardized service and benefited to some extent from economies of scale. However, multiple networks provide benefits to consumers because they prefer product variety.

The total benefits to consumers when network services are priced at $p$ and there are $m$ networks equal

$$(52) \quad B(p, m) = 2m \int_0^{1/(2m)} [u(Q(p + tr)) - tr\, Q(p + tr) - p\, Q(p + tr)]\, dr.$$

Clearly, a price increase reduces total consumer benefits.[20] Increased product variety increases total consumer benefits, because each consumer is nearer to his or her most preferred product.[21]

---

20 The effect of a price increase on consumer benefits is equal to the negative of total demand, $B_p(p, m) = -D(p, m)$.

21 Differentiating consumer benefits with respect to $m$ gives

$$B_m(p, m) = \frac{B(p, m)}{m} - \frac{1}{m}\left[u\left(Q\left(p + \frac{t}{2m}\right)\right)\right.$$
$$\left. - \frac{t}{2m}Q\left(p + \frac{t}{2m}\right) - p\,Q\left(p + \frac{t}{2m}\right)\right].$$

Thus, $B_m$ is positive because $u(Q(p + tr)) - tr\, Q(p + tr) - p\, Q(p + tr)$ is a decreasing function of $r$.

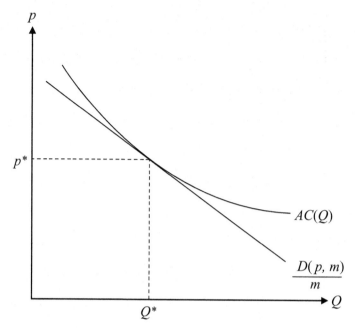

**Figure 3.18.** The free-entry condition with monopolistic competition between networks in the traditional Chamberlain model.

The socially optimal extent of product variety is examined for the case of second-best pricing. Suppose that there are $m$ networks and that each of them breaks even at the common price $p$. Because of the symmetry of the distribution of consumer preferences, each network has the same share of total demand. The break-even profit condition is therefore

$$(53) \qquad\qquad (p - c)\, D\, (p, m)\, /m - C = 0.$$

This determines a break-even price $p^*(m)$, which depends on the number of networks. It can be shown that the break-even price is increasing in the number of networks. Even though greater product variety increases consumer demand, which helps each network take advantage of economies of scale, greater product variety also means that the fixed cost of each network must be shared among fewer consumers.

The efficient number of networks is calculated by substituting the break-even price into total consumer benefits and maximizing over the number of networks. The efficient number of networks reflects the trade-off between higher prices to cover costs and the returns to variety,

$$(54) \qquad\qquad - B_p( p^*(m),\, m)\, p^{*\prime}\,(m) = B_m( p^*(m),\, m).$$

Consider a competitive equilibrium with monopolistic competition.[22] Competitive entry drives down profit until the break-even profit condition holds; see Figure 3.18. Firms compete on prices because raising one's price drives consumers

22   For a preliminary assessment, see Yoo (2005).

toward the nearest substitute good. At an equilibrium with symmetric pricing strategies, firms choose prices such that prices exceed marginal cost:[23]

$$(55) \qquad (p - c)\left[\frac{2}{t}Q(p) - \frac{1}{t}Q\left(p + \frac{t}{2m}\right)\right] = \frac{D(p, m)}{m}.$$

This condition, combined with the break-even profit condition, determines the equilibrium price $p^c$ and the number of networks $m^c$. Generally, the market equilibrium will differ from the social optimum. Thus, the market will choose different levels of total network capacity, because the optimal total capacity will differ from the capacity provided by the market with monopolistic competition. Thus, $D(p^*, m^*)$ will differ from $D(p^c, m^c)$.

The divergence of market capacity from (second-best) optimal capacity need not suggest that networks should be regulated. There is no general tendency for markets to provide either too much or too little capacity. When economies of scale are limited, product variety is higher for both the optimal benchmark and the market outcome. As the cost of establishing a network falls, price approaches unit costs in either case and product variety increases. Markets may provide insufficient product variety in this case, but this does not matter that much because the benchmark is relatively high optimal product variety. Conversely, with significant economies of scale, product variety is lower for both the optimal benchmark and the market outcome. As the cost of establishing a network rises, the price is marked up above unit cost in either case and product variety declines. Markets may provide excessive product variety in this case, but this is relative to the benchmark of relatively low optimal product variety.[24] Different market structures and competitive behaviors will yield different capacity levels. Moreover, when networks interconnect, their interaction and transfer payments will also affect the amount of capacity provided at the market equilibrium. Cooperative agreements may serve to eliminate potential inefficiencies in the market provision of capacity, as Mathewson and Winter (1997) point out.

The market provision of network capacity thus reflects the demand for product variety, economies of scale of individual networks, and cooperative interconnection agreements. Access regulations are likely to have significant effects on market equilibrium capacity and on the number of networks. Suppose that mandated access increases total demand from $D^0(p, m)$ to $D(p, m) + A$, as in Figure 3.19. The market equilibrium can be restored in several ways. First, market prices would need to rise to ration consumer demand for capacity. Second, capacity would need to expand to meet the additional access demand if prices were not adjusted. Third, demand

---

23  For a derivation of this condition, see Spulber (1989).

24  Koenker and Perry (1981) show that with a high elasticity of substitution and low scale economies, markets do not provide sufficient product diversity and vice versa. The literature provides a variety of results on the provision of differentiated products. The over- or underprovision of product variety is highly sensitive to the form of consumer preferences (Lancaster 1975; Spence 1976; Dixit and Stiglitz 1977; Salop 1979).

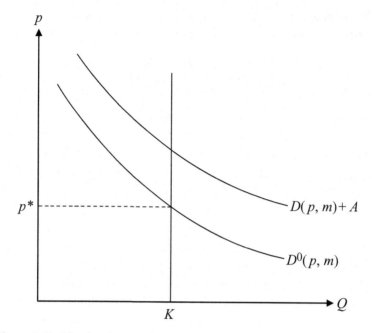

**Figure 3.19.** Mandated access increases total demand for network capacity.

could be reduced by decreasing product variety $m$. This would require consolidation of networks and would potentially generate economies of scale as usage of each network increased. Consumers would be made worse off by the reduction in product variety. Thus, accommodating the additional access to capacity requires some combination of higher prices, capacity investment, and diminished product variety. If access were not mandated but instead were met with a market response, the result could be a combination of somewhat higher prices combined with greater product variety as additional networks entered to provide capacity. Alternatively, the market might respond by maintaining the existing level of product variety, with each network expanding to provide more capacity. Thus, consumers would not experience diminished product variety, and there might be lower prices as expanded access generated benefits from economies of scale.

## 2. Complements and Network Capacity

Demand for network capacity depends on complementary services. Consumer demand for cable television depends on what types of programs are available. Consumer demand for Internet access services depends on the types of content that are available online. Generally, communications networks are not vertically integrated with providers of complementary services.

The relationship between the transmission services of a communications network and the services obtained through the network is analogous to other types of complements. The classic example is computer hardware and software. A consumer

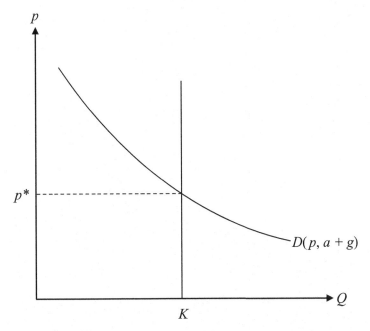

**Figure 3.20.** The demand for network services when the cost of a complementary service is $a + g$.

purchases hardware in anticipation of using various types of software. The hardware often has little value without the applications, which depend on software. This includes such functions as word processing, spreadsheets, data storage, multimedia display, and Web browsers. The greater the potential availability of software, the greater the consumer's willingness to pay for hardware.[25]

To highlight the effects of complements on demand for network services, we examine a simple model of demand. Suppose that there is a single representative consumer who purchases both network services and a set of complementary services. Let $Q$ represent the amount of network services. Suppose that the consumer purchases complementary services in the amount of one unit each, and let $M$ represent the number of complementary services. Let $p$ be the price of network services and be $g$ be the price of a complementary service, all of which have the same price. The consumer has utility $U(Q, M)$ from the consumption of network services and complementary services. The consumer can vary the relative proportions of network transmission services and complementary services that are consumed.

The availability of network services is represented by a cost parameter, $a$. The parameter represents the per-unit cost of access to the complementary service

25  This type of standard complementarity is referred to as an *indirect network effect* by Katz and Shapiro (1985). They argue that consumers are concerned about how many other consumers purchase the hardware because sales of the hardware will affect the variety of the complementary software that will be available. Liebowitz and Margolis (1994, p. 139) argue that such effects are not consumption externalities, but rather they "describe nothing more than welfare-neutral interactions that occur in properly functioning markets."

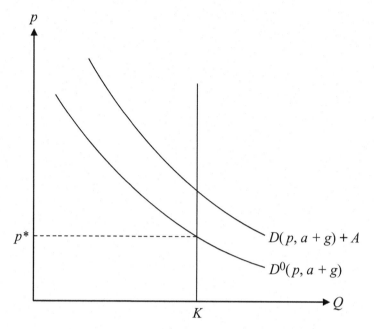

**Figure 3.21.** Additional access demand for network services when there are complementary services.

provider who is using the network. The cost may be an explicit access charge that is passed on to consumers by the service provider. Alternatively, the access cost can represent the degree of compatibility of the network with the complementary service. Consumers experience this type of access cost as a loss of service quality or as a cost of buying an adaptor. A network with more open access will have a lower value of the access cost $a$ than would a network with less open access.

The consumer's demand for network transmission services and complementary services maximizes net benefits,

$$\max_{Q,M} U(Q, M) - pQ - (a + g)M.$$

Thus, the demand for network services, $Q = D(p, a + g)$, is a decreasing function of the price of network services $p$, the cost of access to complementary services $a$, and the price of complementary services $g$. The demand for network services is represented in Figure 3.20.

Suppose now that the regulatory authority grants access to the network in the form of additional demand for network services, $A$. Without any other adjustments, there will be excess demand for network services. The effect of additional access demand for network services is shown in Figure 3.21. As already noted, one solution is to raise the price of access to existing customers and to users of access. Another solution is to raise the complementary services access costs $a$, which will reduce the availability of complementary services, thus shifting the demand function to the left. Of course, raising the price of network services $p$ or the complementary service access cost $a$ will reduce demand for complementary services and could lower the market equilibrium price $g$ of those services. This would stimulate demand for network, so $p$ and $a$ would have to be raised sufficiently to compensate for this effect. This analysis shows the potential tradeoffs between very different types of access. Greater wholesale access or unbundled access could translate into reduced platform access.

# PART II

# THE REGULATION OF NETWORKS

# 4

# Network Regulation Basics

The performance of network industries is determined not just by their underlying economics, but also by the manner in which they are regulated. The chapters in this part analyze the impact of regulation on network performance. This chapter begins the analysis by laying out the sources of market failure traditionally thought to justify widespread regulation of the telecommunications industry. It continues by reviewing the regulatory instruments employed to address those source of market failure. It then critiques the validity of those justifications, finding that they are generally based on economic theories and factual premises that are no longer regarded as viable and fail to take into account the full complexity of network behavior.

Chapter 5 offers a more complete description of the five-part system for classifying types of access mentioned briefly in the Introduction and analyzes the impact of each type of access on network capacity, configuration, and transaction costs. Chapter 6 examines the insights that graph theory can provide into the pricing of network access and uses that framework to critique existing approaches to establishing access prices. Chapter 7 considers the constitutional limitations on access imposed by the Fifth Amendment to the U.S. Constitution, which prohibits the taking of property for public use without the payment of just compensation.

## A. Economic Justifications for Regulating Networks

### 1. Natural Monopoly

Perhaps the classic justification for regulating telecommunications networks is that they have long been presumed to be natural monopolies. As noted in Chapter 2, a given production technology is said to exhibit natural monopoly characteristics if it is *subadditive*; that is, a single firm can supply the entire market demand at lower cost than could two or more firms. A sufficient condition for subadditivity is for the technology to exhibit scale economies, such as occur when a production technology requires the incurring of joint and common fixed costs that can be spread across units of output or across multiple outputs. Scale economies give the producer with the largest volume a cost advantage that allows it to underprice its competitors, which in turn allows it to capture a larger share of the market. This causes the cost advantage to widen still further until all other producers are driven from the market. Under these circumstances, a single firm will eventually dominate markets that initially consist of multiple producers.

Natural monopoly gives rise to two normative implications. First, like all monopolists, natural monopolists tend to charge prices that are inefficiently high and to produce quantities that are inefficiently low. Second, the fact that the market ultimately reaches equilibrium with only one producer implies that the fixed costs incurred by any subsequent entrant will inevitably end up being wasted, because only one set of capital assets will ultimately end up being used.

Both of these rationales have long been applied to the telecommunications industry. Indeed, throughout its early history the telephone network was widely regarded as a paradigmatic example of a natural monopoly. Concern that telephone companies would charge supracompetitive rates has long led state agencies (commonly known as public utility commissions) to regulate the rates for intrastate telephone service. The Communications Act of 1934 similarly mandated that the Federal Communications Commission (FCC) regulate the rates for interstate service as well.

In addition, the supposed danger of wasteful duplication of fixed costs investments led to the widespread belief that all telephone services needed to be provided by a single company, perhaps best exemplified by AT&T President Theodore Vail's call for "[o]ne policy, one system, and universal service" (AT&T 1911, pp. 18–19). This rationale justified limiting entry by requiring that all providers obtain a certificate of public necessity and convenience, either from the state public utility commission (for local service) or from the FCC (for interstate service), before offering telephone service.

## 2. Network Economic Effects

Another classic justification for regulating telecommunications networks is the presence of *network economic effects*. Network economic effects exist when the value of a network is determined not only by the access price charged, but also by the number of users connected to the network. The telephone system has long been regarded as a classic example of a network that exhibits such effects, because the value of a telephone network is determined in large part by the number of people with whom one can communicate through that network. The more people an individual subscriber can reach through the telephone network, the more valuable the network becomes.

The notion of network effects springs from "Metcalfe's Law," named after Robert Metcalfe, otherwise celebrated as the coinventor of the Ethernet protocol for network transmission technology. Recall from our earlier discussion in Chapter 1 that if all of the $n$ nodes of a network are directly connected to each other, the network will have $\frac{1}{2}n(n-1)$ links. This defines a complete network. Distinct from this principle of network design, consider a network with $I$ subscribers. The subscribers have access to the network's transmission services. If every subscriber can reach every other subscriber through the network, there are $\frac{1}{2}I(I-1)$ possible connections between subscribers. Those connections need not be physical connections provided by specific links; they instead refer to the completion of communications between subscribers that have access to a common network. Metcalfe's Law is the observation that because $I$ subscribers can make $\frac{1}{2}I(I-1)$ possible connections between each other, the value of the network in terms of the number of interpersonal connections rises with the square of the number of subscribers. As George Gilder originally put it, Metcalfe "is the author of what I will call Metcalfe's law of the telecosm, showing the magic of interconnections: connect any number, '$n$,' of machines – whether computers, phones or even cars – and you get '$n$' squared potential value. Think of phones without networks or cars without roads. Conversely, imagine the benefits of linking up tens of millions of computers and sense the exponential power of the telecosm" (Gilder 1993, p. S158).

Thus, Metcalfe's law refers to *potential connections*, the links that a network makes possible. This is equivalent to saying that a market with $I$ traders has a number of potential economic transactions that is proportional to the square of the number of traders. Of course, potential transactions are very different from actual transactions. The value of such a network would be weighted by the likelihood of a transaction occurring and the potential benefits of a randomly chosen successful transaction. Thus, although the value may be proportional to the squared number of traders, the proportional weight may be very small indeed. The problem is further compounded if the likelihood of a successful match decreases with the number of potential trading partners, for the usual reason that search costs are high and more traders can mean greater diversity and greater costs of finding a good match. If these costs increase rapidly, they can outweigh the benefits of having more members, so that there can be diminishing returns to larger networks. The intensity and quality of meetings may be better at a small party than at a large gathering, for example. However, with many people connected to a network, there are returns to mechanisms that reduce search costs. If such mechanisms exhibit economies of scale, this can restore the benefits of larger networks. For example, with many people connected to a telephone network, there are benefits from telephone directories. With many people on the Internet, there are benefits from establishing search engines. However, these are subtle concepts that are very different from the idea of simply squaring the number of people with access to a network.

Some economists contend that network economic effects can give rise to a kind of *externality* that can be a source of market failure (Katz and Shapiro 1985). This view draws on the fact that an individual subscriber's decision to join a network creates benefits for those who have already joined the network. These arguments assume that subscribers cannot coordinate their adoption decisions. These arguments are also based on the notion that the network firm and its subscribers cannot internalize the benefits from network effects in the terms of their transactions. New subscribers' assumed inability to capture all of the benefits generated by their adoption decisions arguably creates a wedge between private and social benefit that may cause subscribers to forego joining a network even though the social benefits of doing so would exceed the costs. The concept of network externality thus suggests that network industries may be uniquely susceptible to market failures that prevent the price mechanism from playing its usual role in generating efficient outcomes.[1]

Some theorists have also suggested that network economic effects can turn network access into a competitive weapon (Katz and Shapiro 1985).[2] By refusing to interconnect with other networks, network owners can force subscribers to choose one network to the exclusion of others. The fact that each network's value increases with the number of subscribers connected to it provides a powerful incentive for new subscribers to flock to the largest network. According to this view, network economic effects create demand-side scale economies that can be a source of monopoly power. One oft-cited example of this phenomenon is the attempt by the Bell System to use its refusal to interconnect to combat the emergence of competition in local telephone service following the expiration of the initial Bell telephone patents in 1893. The hope was that refusing to interconnect with independent local telephone systems would protect the Bell System's market share by ensuring that it would remain the largest (and thus the most valuable) local telephone provider.

## 3. Vertical Exclusion

The assumption that the telephone network was a natural monopoly gave rise to the related concern that the Bell System would use its control over the network to harm competition in vertically related markets. The specific concern was that telephone providers would discriminate against independent companies

---

1  Thomas Schelling (1978) identified the effects of *critical mass* on many types of economic and social behavior (see also Leibenstein 1950).

2  For an argument that network externalities turn telecommunications into a winner-take-all monopoly that should be regulated, see Melody (2002). Some economists apply similar arguments to suggest that the drag on the shift to new networks caused by these so-called network externalities can also cause markets to become "locked in" to existing technologies long after the arrival of new, more efficient network technologies (Farrell and Saloner 1986; Katz and Shapiro 1994).

offering complementary services that competed with the Bell System's proprietary offerings.

For example, the Justice Department's 1913 antitrust suit against AT&T was filed at a time when the lapse of the original Bell patents had permitted vigorous competition to emerge in local telephone service, while the Bell System continued to hold key patents needed to provide effective long-distance service. The claim was that the increasing importance of long-distance service put the Bell System in a position to attempt to use its dominant position in long distance to harm competition in local service by refusing to allow any independent local telephone company to interconnect with its long-distance network (discussed in greater detail in Chapter 8). As part of the consent decree settling this action, the Bell System agreed to cease pursuing such tactics and instead to open its long-distance network to all qualified independent local telephone companies.[3]

Over the next half century, concern about the Bell System's dominance of long distance would be replaced by concerns about AT&T's dominance of local telephone service. For example, concerns about vertical exclusion arose with respect to the market for *customer premises equipment* (CPE), which consisted of handsets, answering machines, fax machines, modems, and other devices located in residences and businesses that end users attached to the local telephone network in order to communicate with other parties.[4] Since 1882, the Bell System had granted its manufacturing subsidiary, known as Western Electric, the exclusive right to supply the telephone equipment used in connection with its network. Concern that this exclusivity arrangement enabled AT&T to reduce the competitiveness of the market for CPE led the federal government to bring an antitrust suit against the Bell System in 1949, although that the government eventually settled the suit in 1956 without requiring AT&T to open its network to CPE manufactured by independent providers.[5] The same concerns also underlay the landmark judicial and regulatory decisions in *Hush-a-Phone* and *Carterfone* that eventually forced AT&T to abandon its "foreign attachments" policy, which restricted end users' ability to attach non-Bell CPE to the network.[6] Concerns about vertical exclusion of CPE also played an important role in the federal antitrust suit that eventually led to the breakup of AT&T in 1984 as well as in the Telecommunications Act of 1996.[7]

Apprehensions about vertical exclusion also played a key role in shaping federal policy with respect to long distance. Under the usual arrangement, long distance

---

3 See AT&T (1914); *United States v. AT&T* (D. Or. 1914) (decree), *reprinted in* Shale (1918).

4 This is in contrast to "telecommunications equipment," which refers to the wires and switches located outside end user locations that connect those premises together.

5 *United States v. W. Elec. Co.* 1956 Trade Cas. [CCH] ¶ 62,246 (D.N.J. Jan. 24, 1956).

6 See *Hush-A-Phone Corp. v. United States*, 238 F.2d 266 (D.C. Cir. 1956); FCC (1968).

7 On the breakup of AT&T, see *United States v. AT&T* (*Modification of Final Judgment*), 552 F. Supp. 131, 190 (D.D.C. 1982), *aff'd sub nom. Maryland v. United States*, 460 U.S. 1001 (1983). On the Telecommunications Act of 1996, see 47 U.S.C. §§ 272(a)(2)(A), 273.

companies do not connect directly to subscribers. Instead, long distance companies simply interconnect to the local telephone network at a point located in the local telephone company's central office switch and rely on the local telephone company to provide the final connection needed both to initiate and to terminate long-distance calls. When AT&T had a monopoly over local telephone service, this placed local telephone companies in a key strategic position, which in turn gave rise to the concern that AT&T was using its control over local telephone networks to protect its long distance service from competition.

It was in order to preserve the nascent competition in long distance that the D.C. Circuit ordered AT&T to allow MCI to interconnect with its local telephone network and the Seventh Circuit held that AT&T's refusal to grant MCI access to its local telephone network constituted a violation of the essential facilities doctrine.[8] The desire to promote competition in long distance also underlay the 1984 antitrust decree that required AT&T to spin off its local telephone subsidiaries and required the newly independent regional Bell operating companies (RBOCs) to provide "equal access" to all long distance carriers (*Modification of Final Judgment*, 552. F. Supp. at 195–200). The same concerns also underlay a key provision of the Telecommunications Act of 1996, which prevented RBOCs from offering long-distance service until they could demonstrate that they had satisfied a fourteen-point competitive checklist designed to show that they had opened their local telephone networks to competition (47 U.S.C. § 271(2)(B)).

Concerns about vertical exclusion also arose with respect to *information services*, which are services that combine transmission with computing power to provide more sophisticated services that transcend mere voice communications.[9] For some information services, the additional computing power is located in the telephone company's central office switch, as with services such as caller ID, call waiting, call forwarding, and voice mail. Other information services rely on computing power connected to the network via modems or other devices, such as check and credit card verification systems, electronic data interchange, database access services, and Internet access services.

As was the case with CPE and long distance, policy makers have long been concerned that the Bell System would use its control over the physical network to discriminate against information services offered by independent providers. As a result, the FCC instituted a series of *Computer Inquiries* to protect independent information service providers against the threat of vertical exclusion (discussed in greater detail in Chapter 8). Similar protective measures were included in the court

---

8   For the D.C. Circuit decision overturning the FCC's refusal to order AT&T to open its local telephone network to MCI, see *MCI Telecomms. Corp. v. FCC*, 580 F.2d 590 (D.C. Cir. 1978). For the Seventh Circuit decision holding that AT&T's local telephone network constituted an essential facility, see *MCI Commc'ns Corp. v. AT&T*, 708 F.2d 1081, 1132–44 (7th Cir. 1983).

9   The FCC's earlier regulatory proceedings (most notably the *Computer Inquiries*) referred to these types of services as "enhanced services." Like the FCC, we use the phrase "information services" to include all of the services included with the term "enhanced services" (FCC 1996e).

order that led to the breakup of AT&T as well as in the Telecommunications Act of 1996.[10]

## 4. Ruinous/Managed Competition

Policymakers have not confined their regulatory activities to situations in which sustainable competition was impossible. Throughout much of the late 19th and 20th centuries, policy makers have intervened to curb the perceived problems caused by "ruinous," "excessive," or "destructive" competition.[11] The concern was that industries characterized by high fixed costs would be plagued by excess capacity, resulting in a surfeit of new entrants. The argument was that entrants would rush in to invest in a new technology without anticipating the level of investment made by other competitors. Once having sunk the fixed costs needed to enter, producing firms would not exit the industry so long as they could charge prices sufficient to cover their variable costs. The resulting competition would drive prices down to variable cost, which would prevent firms from generating sufficient revenue to recover their capital investments. Some sort of coordinated action, either through collusion or government regulation, was viewed as the only viable solution to endemic overproduction and eventual collapse into a natural monopoly (*New York v. United States*, 331 U.S. 284, 346 (1947); *ICC v. Inland Waterways Corp.*, 319 U.S. 671, 688 n. 24 (1943); *New State Ice Co. v. Liebmann*, 285 U.S. 262, 292–94 (1932) (Brandeis, J., dissenting)).

Economists and the Supreme Court have largely rejected ruinous competition as a basis for regulation.[12] (Indeed, then-Harvard law professor and now-Justice Stephen Breyer (1982) criticized this rationale as an "empty box" with no particular economic meaning or content.) Any excess capacity that might exist would only lead firms to forego making new investments as the existing capital stock was depreciated. Thus, although producing firms might suffer substantial losses in the short run, over the long run the market would tend toward the competitive equilibrium. In the meantime, the ensuing competition would yield substantial benefits to consumers, while simultaneously identifying the most efficient firm from among the contenders

---

10  On the breakup of AT&T, see *Modification of Final Judgment*, 552 F. Supp. at 180–86, 189–90. On the Telecommunications Act of 1996, see 47 U.S.C. §§ 272(a)(2)(C), 274, 275.

11  See Hovenkamp (1991) for a survey of the intellectual history of "ruinous competition."

12  For judicial rejections of ruinous competition, see *Arizona v. Maricopa County Medical Soc'y*, 457 U.S. 332, 346 (1982); *Nat'l Soc'y of Prof'l Eng'rs v. United States*, 435 U.S. 679, 689–90 (1978); *United States v. Container Corp. of Am.*, 393 U.S. 333, 338 n.4 (1969); *Fashion Originators' Guild of Am. v. FTC*, 312 U.S. 457 (1941); *United States v. Socony-Vacuum Oil Co.*, 310 U.S. 150, 220–24 (1940); *United States v. Trans-Mo. Freight Ass'n*, 166 U.S. 290 (1897). The sole modern exception is *Appalachian Coals, Inc. v. United States*, 288 U.S. 344 (1933), which allowed competing coal producers to form an agreement that limited competition so long as the intent was not to unreasonably restrain trade. That holding does not seem to have withstood the test of time. For statements by economists rejecting ruinous competition, see, e.g., Clark (1914); Knight (1921a); Taussig (1922); Clark (1923); Kaysen and Turner (1959); Noll (1989).

and providing an empirical test of whether a particular market was in fact a natural monopoly.

Even after the collapse of ruinous competition as a basis for regulation, policy makers have sometimes imposed regulation even when competition is possible. The classic situation is when a change in technology or demand opens a market previously dominated by one player to competition, although such competition may take some time to emerge and the dominant player will continue to be able to exercise market power for quite some time. When this occurs, policy makers have sometimes imposed asymmetric regulation on the dominant player to prevent it either from charging supracompetitive rates or from engaging in predatory actions to protect its market position. Although somewhat inconsistent with the growing embrace of a policy of open competition, the hope was that such asymmetric regulation would protect against anticompetitive excesses by the dominant firm while simultaneously nurturing the new entrants' ability to survive.

Another form of managed competition arises when new entrants struggle to put their entire networks in place before offering service. To allow competition to emerge before entrants had fully established their networks, policy makers have sometimes imposed interconnection access by requiring the incumbent network owners to provide new entrants with access to portions of their networks. This allowed a new entrant to pursue an incremental-entry strategy by using the existing network to provide any components that had not yet been deployed. In each case, the impact of attempts to manage competition would depend critically on the scope of the intervention, the prices that the existing network owner would be permitted to charge for the use of its facilities, and how quickly the owner of the existing network would be relieved from these regulatory obligations after effective competition had emerged.

## B. Basic Regulatory Instruments

### 1. Tariffing

As noted earlier, the tendency of monopolists to charge prices that are inefficiently high has long led state and federal agencies to regulate the rates charged for telephone service. The standard regulatory instrument employed to regulate telecommunications rates is the tariff, which in the case of intrastate service is overseen by state agencies commonly known as public utility commissions and in the case of interstate service was historically administered by the FCC. The tariffing process begins when telecommunications carriers file schedules containing all of the rates, terms, and conditions under which they will offer service. The agency then reviews the proposed rates to ensure that they are "just and reasonable." Once the tariff has been approved, the carrier must offer service under the terms specified by the tariff on a nondiscriminatory basis to any requesting party that qualifies to receive the service. Under the so-called filed rate doctrine, the tariffed terms constitute the entirety of the contractual agreement between the customer and the carrier and displace the terms of any private agreements.[13]

The Supreme Court has called determining whether a particular rate is reasonable an "embarrassing question" (*Smyth v. Ames*, 169 U.S. at 546) as well as a "laborious and baffling task" (*Mo. ex rel. Sw. Bell Tel. Co. v. Pub. Serv. Comm'n*, 262 U.S. 276, 292 (1923) (Brandeis, J., concurring in the judgment)). One of the central difficulties has been how to determine the reasonableness of any particular rate. The difficulty of this determination is best summed up by Justice Brandeis's classic concurring opinion in *Missouri ex rel. Southwestern Bell Telephone Co. v. Public Service Commission*. Brandeis recognized that the most accurate methodology for determining the reasonableness of a proposed rate would be to compare it to the prices charged for comparable products bought and sold in an open market. The problem was that "utilities, unlike merchandise or land, are not commonly bought and sold in the market"; as a result, no such market benchmarks could exist. Another commonly used, market-based approach to valuation is the capitalization of the utility's earnings. Brandeis correctly pointed out, however, that capitalizing earnings necessarily embroiled regulatory authorities in a "vicious circle," because the rate would depend on the utility's earnings, and the earnings were largely determined by the rates the utility was permitted to charge.

The principal question confronting Brandeis was whether the rate base should be calculated based on historical cost or replacement cost. Brandeis recognized that replacement cost might well represent the best evidence of present value, because replacement cost constituted a better reflection of changes in demand and technology. In the end, however, pragmatic considerations led Brandeis to advocate relying on historical costs. Determining replacement cost was an inherently speculative endeavor fraught with uncertainty. In addition, basing value on replacement cost would expose both consumers and investors to the risks associated with fluctuations in market prices. In comparison, relying on historic cost allowed less subjective and less variable determinations of value. Although shifts in demand and technological obsolescence could cause replacement cost to overstate or understate market value in some circumstances, in the absence of data based on actual transactions, replacement cost remained a useful proxy (262 U.S. at 292–308).[14] Brandeis's analysis

---

13 The seminal case on the filed rate doctrine is *Louisville & Nashville Railroad v. Maxwell*, 237 U.S. 94 (1915). For a modern reaffirmation in the context of telecommunications, see *AT&T v. Central Office Telephone, Inc.*, 524 U.S. 214 (1998).

14 To the extent that Brandeis's opinion evinces a strong desire to insulate both consumers and investors from the dislocation caused by market fluctuations, it exhibits some strikingly antieconomic tendencies. His preference for stability is perhaps explained by the desire to promote classical-style democracy that permeates his jurisprudence. A more cynical observer might suggest that his interest in protecting investors from market fluctuations followed more from the fact that he held a substantial amount of his wealth in commercial paper issued by utilities (Zacharias 1988).

quickly became one of the focal points in the debate over rate-setting methodologies. The Supreme Court has frequently invoked it to justify regulatory authorities' use of cost-based pricing when setting rates (*Verizon Commc'ns Inc. v. FCC*, 535 U.S. 467, 481–85 (2002); *Duquesne Light Co. v. Barasch*, 488 U.S. 299, 308–09 & n.5 (1989); *Fed. Power Comm'n v. Natural Gas Pipeline Co.*, 315 U.S. 575, 603 (1942) (Black, J., concurring)).

Eventually, however, the controversy between historical and replacement cost ended in a somewhat inconclusive draw. Rather than resolving this dispute on its substantive merits, the Supreme Court ultimately invoked notions of administrative deference and judicial restraint to resolve not to strike down any rate for its failure to adhere to any particular methodology. Instead, the Court opted to uphold any rate so long as it fell within a broad zone of reasonableness (*Fed. Power Comm'n v. Hope Natural Gas Co.*, 320 U.S. 591, 602 (1944); *Duquesne*, 488 U.S. at 314–16).[15] Applying these principles allowed the Court to sustain a wide variety of ratemaking methodologies based on increasingly complicated versions of historical or replacement cost (*Verizon*, 535 U.S. at 497–517, 523–8 (replacement cost); *Duquesne*, 488 U.S. at 310–12 (historical cost); *Permian Basin Area Rate Cases*, 390 U.S. 747, 761, 768–74 (1968) (historical cost for an entire area rather than a single firm); *Hope Natural Gas*, 320 U.S. at 596–98, 603–05 (historical cost)).

The unifying thread in all of these approaches was their consistent commitment to basing rates on direct cost (whether historical or replacement cost) and their consistent refusal to include a component taking opportunity cost or market-based influence into account (*Verizon*, 535 U.S. at 484, citing Kahn 1988). Fortified by this background, regulators charged with implementing access regimes have tended to follow their traditional patterns and base access rates solely on either historical or replacement cost. In failing to incorporate some dimension that reflects the earning potential of the regulated input, approaches based on direct cost, whether historical or replacement cost, fail to reflect the basic insight that has guided economics for the last century (Hovenkamp 1993; Yoo 2003a).

Rate regulation has inevitably raised additional implementation problems. State regulators have traditionally used a cost-of-service approach according to the formula

$$R = O + Br,$$

---

15  It should be noted that in basing the legal outcome on reasonable expectations, the approach taken by the Court in *Hope Natural Gas* is itself circular, because the legality of any particular rate depends on the expectations of the regulated firm. Those expectations in turn are shaped in large part by whether or not a court would uphold the rate as legal. The ratemaking methodology need not have been part of the original "regulatory contract" between the regulated firm and the regulatory authority. This contrasts with expectations damages in contract law, which reflect expectations under the contractual agreement.

where *R* is the total revenue the carrier is allowed to generate, *O* is the carrier's operating expenses, on which the carrier is not allowed to earn a rate of return (such as taxes, wages, energy costs, and depreciation), *B* is the rate base of capital investment, on which the carrier is allowed to earn a rate of return, and *r* is the appropriate rate of return. The rates are then determined by dividing the total revenue that the carrier is allowed to earn by the number of units consumers are expected to demand.

Although this formula is easy to state, regulators and courts have long recognized that it is exceedingly difficult to apply. As an initial matter, determining the appropriate rate of return has proven quite difficult, because such a determination depends on identifying other ventures bearing similar risk. This determination is complicated by the fact that small differences in rates of return can have dramatic effects on the total revenue that the carrier is allowed to generate. For the reasons described above, determining the proper rate base has also proven to be a significant regulatory challenge. Regardless of the methodology used, calculating a proper rate base was notoriously difficult, typically devolving into a battle between experts. Determining how much particular configurations of network elements would cost on the current market raised difficult problems of proof. In addition, changes in demand and technology would often render particular facilities obsolete or would imply a very difficult network configuration.

Cost-of-service ratemaking also induces a number of systematic inefficiencies. As an initial matter, cost-plus pricing regimes give firms little incentive to economize. Regulators attempt to curb this problem by only allowing recover of costs that are "prudent," but that often requires difficult determinations that are fraught with hindsight bias. Firms, moreover, are allowed to earn a rate of return on capital expenses, but not on operating expenses. Most firms usually have the choice to use production processes that are more or less capital-intensive. The ratemaking methodology discussed above thus introduces a bias in favor of capital-intensive solutions even when other solutions would be more efficient (Averch and Johnson 1962).

Eventually, traditional ratemaking gave way to the imposition of price caps, in which the maximum rates that utilities could charge in any particular year did not depend on costs, but rather on the rates set the previous year, adjusted to reflect inflation and increases in productivity. Determining initial price levels and price adjustments in subsequent years has proven to be extremely difficult (*U.S. Telecom Ass'n v. FCC*, 188 F.3d 521, 524–27 (D.C. Cir. 1999); Bernstein and Sappington 1999; Vogt 1999). The empirical literature is divided on whether price caps lead to lower or higher rates; compare, for example, Mathios and Rogers (1989) and Kaestner and Kahn (1990) with Knittel (2004).

The emergence of competition in portions of the telecommunications industry has provided some impetus toward eliminating tariffing requirements. The FCC's attempts to detariff long distance following the breakup of AT&T represent a prime example. Because MCI and Sprint did not hold a dominant position in the long distance market, the FCC tried to exempt them from having to file tariffs (FCC 1982, 1983a, 1985a). As AT&T lost its dominant position, the FCC eventually exempted it from having to file tariffs as well (FCC 1995c). The courts rejected the FCC's actions, holding that the agency lacked the discretion to forbear from enforcing the tariff requirement mandated by the statute (*MCI v. AT&T*, 512 U.S. 218 (1994); *MCI v. FCC*, 765 F.2d 1186 (D.C. Cir. 1985); *AT&T v. FCC*, 978 F.2d 727 (D.C. Cir. 1992); *Southwestern Bell Corp. v. FCC*, 43 F.3d 1515 (D.C. Cir. 1995)). Congress eventually amended the statute to give the FCC the discretion to forbear from enforcing the statutory tariff requirements when the agency found that doing so would be in the public interest (47 U.S.C. § 160). The FCC has exercised its forbearance authority so that at this point, long-distance services have been completely detariffed (FCC 1996d[16]). After initially ruling to the contrary, the FCC has also ruled that local telephone companies do not have a dominant position in offering broadband services such as digital subscriber lines (DSL) and thus do not need to file tariffs for those services (FCC 2002e).

A similar move is taking place in local phone service, as competition from wireless services is leading local phone companies to request detariffing of rates. For example, Qwest asked the Idaho Public Utility Commission to deregulate their rates in light of the emergence of effective competition. The Idaho Public Utility Commission rejected the petition on the ground that the evidence that cell phones are functionally equivalent and competitively priced with Qwest's local service was unpersuasive (Idaho Public Utility Commission 2003). Over time, state public utility commissions have largely deregulated local phone service to businesses and have begun to deregulate residential local phone service as well (Tardiff 2007).

## 2. Structural Separation

The tariff system was not sufficient by itself to eliminate the supracompetitive pricing resulting from monopoly power. A regulated firm that offered tariffed as well as untariffed services could evade the strictures of rate regulation simply by bundling its regulated service with an unregulated service and charging supracompetitive prices for the unregulated service.

In addition, to the extent that the same facilities are used to provide both regulated and unregulated services, the regulated entity can manipulate the tariffing process to gain a competitive advantage. As discussed in Chapter 2, the allocation of joint costs among multiple products is inherently somewhat arbitrary. As a result, both regulators and regulated entities possess some degree of latitude over the percentage of shared costs to allocate to the regulated instead of the unregulated service. The concern is that this latitude will allow the network owner to allocate a disproportionate share of the joint costs to the regulated service. To the extent

---

16   The Court of Appeals upheld this order on judicial review (*MCI WorldCom, Inc. v. FCC*, 209 F.3d 760 (D.C. Cir. 2000)).

that rates are based on cost, this would guarantee their ability to recover a greater proportion of the shared costs through the rates charged for their regulated services. At the same time, allocating more of the shared costs to the regulated service would also yield advantages in the unregulated market, because the provider of both the regulated and unregulated services would have to recover a smaller portion of the shared costs through the prices charged for its unregulated services, which in turn would give it a price advantage vis-à-vis competitors that did not participate in both markets.

Allowing a single company to participate in regulated and unregulated markets also greatly complicates regulatory authorities' ability to enforce nondiscrimination mandates. Determining the precise terms under which the regulated services are provided to the unregulated portion of the business is extremely difficult when the interconnection agreement is not negotiated at arm's length. The resulting opacity of the interconnection terms makes it much easier for any favoritism shown by the provider of the regulated service to go undetected.

Finally, both Congress and the FCC have become increasingly committed to the benefits of competition. As a result, both sets of policy makers have increasingly sought to limit regulation to the narrowest range possible and to permit market forces to determine outcomes in the broadest feasible range of activity.

The traditional solution to each of these problems is to require telecommunications providers to segregate their regulated services into separate subsidiaries. A subsidiary must offer unaffiliated providers of complementary services carriage on the same terms on which it offers carriage to its own complementary services. Structurally separating the regulated business from the unregulated business limits the network owner's ability to shift costs from its unregulated service to its regulated service. Forcing the regulated subsidiary to negotiate interconnection agreements through arm's-length transactions also eliminates the ability to use bundling of regulated and unregulated services to avoid rate regulation and makes nondiscrimination easier to detect and enforce.

The 1956 consent decree that settled the government's second antitrust case against AT&T represents a classic example of the use of structural separation and quarantine as regulatory tools by restricting AT&T to tariffed services and forbidding them to participate in nontariffed markets (*United States v. W. Elec. Co.*, 1956 Trade Cas. [CCH] ¶ 68,246 (D.N.J. Jan. 24, 1956)). Similarly, the *Computer Inquiries* required that the largest telephone companies only offer enhanced service through separate subsidiaries (FCC 1971;[17] 1980a[18]). The court in charge of the government's third antitrust suit against AT&T employed these same regulatory instruments when breaking up AT&T. Because long-distance services were now

---

17  The Court of Appeals upheld this order in relevant part on judicial review (*GTE Serv. Corp. v. FCC*, 474 F.2d 724, 731 (2d Cir. 1973)).

18  The Court of Appeals upheld this order on judicial review (*Computer & Commc'ns Indus. Ass'n v. FCC*, 693 F.2d 198 (D.C. Cir. 1982)).

potentially competitive, the court structurally separated them from local telephone services, which remained a regulated monopoly. The court then restricted the local telephone companies' ability to participate in markets that were unregulated and/or potentially competitive, such as long distance, information services, and equipment manufacturing (*Modification of Final Judgment*, 552 F. Supp., at 189–90). The 1996 Act contained similar restrictions, prohibiting the RBOCs to sell in-region long distance and manufacturing CPE until the RBOCs satisfied a fourteen-point competitive checklist demonstrating that they were confronting effective competition. The statute also required RBOCs that wished to offer certain information services (specifically electronic publishing and alarm monitoring) to do so through a separate affiliate for a period of several years (47 U.S.C. §§ 271–275).

The logic inherent in this approach suggests that regulation and the resulting quarantine should be limited to those services that are inherently noncompetitive. Doing so would allow competition to determine outcomes to the greatest extent possible. This rationale thus presumes that the scope of regulation should constantly contract over time, as technological change and increases in demand open larger portions of the telecommunications industry to competition.

This dynamic quality of the scope of regulation explains much of the history of telecommunications policy. As noted earlier, initially the entire telephone system was regarded as a natural monopoly. As a result, the entire network was subjected to rate regulation. Over time, it became clear that CPE manufacturing was not subject to the high fixed costs traditionally associated with natural monopoly and was instead potentially open to competition. The emergence of microwave and satellite transmission also lowered the fixed costs of providing long-distance service by allowing new long distance entrants such as MCI to compete without having to establish nationwide networks of high-volume telephone lines. As it became clear that each of these markets was now open to competition, the FCC released them from rate regulation and prohibited regulated entities from offering them on an integrated basis. Eventually, the only portion of the telecommunications industry that remained subject to rate regulation was local telephone service. Over time, even that premise has come under fire, as wireless has reduced the fixed costs needed for transmission and as computer processing has reduced the fixed costs of switching.

### 3. Unbundling

The precipitous drop in the cost of switching suggests that the only portion of the telephone network that remains a natural monopoly may be the wires connecting the central offices maintained by local telephone companies to individual residences (commonly known as *local loops*). Although the demand for local loops servicing large business enterprises is sufficiently high to permit competition, it is arguable that local loops serving residences and small businesses may remain a natural monopoly. The logic of rate regulation and structural separation would require a constant narrowing of the scope of rate regulation with every increase in the portions of the telephone network that became open to competition. In addition, it would require limiting the regulated entity to providing only those services that were inherently uncompetitive. The traditional approach would support isolating local loops into a separate company (sometimes called a "Loop Co."), requiring that it offer nondiscriminatory access to any requesting parties, and prohibiting its offering any other services. Indeed, the FCC entered into serious discussions at some point to pursue just such a solution.

Over time, however, policy makers began to exhibit greater appreciation for the insights of the theory of the firm (discussed at greater length in Chapter 5) and to acknowledge the potential benefits of combining certain functions within the boundary of a single firm. This in turn suggests that there may be a natural limit to policy makers' ability to keep narrowing the scope of activities permitted to take place within a regulated entity. In fact, forcing a telephone company to externalize certain functions can create significant costs and disrupt the firm's natural boundaries, whereas permitting telecommunications companies to offer some services on an integrated basis can give rise to efficiencies that may make integrated provision the preferred second-best alternative.

The FCC explicitly recognized that structural separation can create substantial costs with respect to information services. The issue first arose during the second *Computer Inquiry*, in which the FCC recognized that the costs of structural separation weighed particularly heavily on smaller carriers, which possessed smaller subscriber bases over which to amortize the costs of managing a separate subsidiary. Smaller carriers nonetheless retained bottleneck control over a resource upon which information service providers depended, albeit with a reduced total incentive because of the smaller size of their market. The FCC responded to the higher costs of structural separation by devising a new regulatory approach that required local telephone companies to unbundle their basic services and to offer them to all unaffiliated information service providers on the same terms that they provided to their own proprietary information service offerings (FCC 1980a).

The FCC expanded unbundling into a more general regulatory regime in its third *Computer Inquiry*. The FCC acknowledged that structural separation requirements "impose significant costs on the public in decreased efficiency and innovation." These costs include precluding information services such as voice mail and advance calling, which are integrated directly into the switch maintained by the local telephone company; foreclosing the realization of economies of scope associated with joint marketing and the joint use of technology and expertise; duplication of personnel and facilities; depriving large business subscribers of "systems solutions" provided by a single company; and preventing local telephone companies from organizing their operations in the manner best suited to the markets and customers they serve (FCC 1986a).

The FCC thus allowed large telephone companies to forego structural separation if they complied with two unbundling regimes. The first, known as *comparably efficient interconnection* (CEI), was in essence a nondiscrimination regime that required any major local telephone company that wished to provide information services without establishing a separate subsidiary to provide unaffiliated information service providers with access to the same basic services on the same terms on which it provided its own information service offerings. CEI was to be superseded by a more comprehensive unbundling regime known as *open network architecture* (ONA), which required all major local telephone companies (even those that were not offering information services) to provide unaffiliated information service providers with unbundled access to all of their network elements (FCC 1986a). During 1992 and 1993, the FCC lifted the structural separation requirements as soon as the major local telephone companies filed plans detailing how they would comply with ONA (see cases cited in FCC 1995c, n. 22). A series of judicial challenges invalidated the FCC's actions, which left the regulatory regime advanced in the third *Computer Inquiry* in limbo.[19]

Unbundling requirements also formed one of the key provisions of the Telecommunications Act of 1996. Specifically, the Act required that all carriers providing local telephone service as of the date of the statute's enactment provide any requesting carrier with access to all of their network elements on an unbundled basis at any technically feasible point. The statute restricted this so-called unbundled network element (UNE) access provision to situations in which access to proprietary network elements was "necessary" and "the failure to provide access to such network elements would impair the ability of the telecommunications carrier seeking access to provide the services that it seeks to offer" (47 U.S.C. § 251(c)(3), (d)(2)).

The FCC quickly implemented this provision, applying the unbundled access requirement to a wide range of network elements required for providing both local telephone and broadband services (FCC 1996c, 1998b, 1998f, 1999c, 1999e, 1999g, 2000c, 2001e). After a protracted series of judicial setbacks,[20] the FCC largely

---

19   The Ninth Circuit initially overturned the *Computer III* regime as arbitrary and capricious on the ground that the FCC had not adequately justified its decision to rely on nonstructural safeguards (*California I*, 905 F.2d at 1230–39). On remand, the FCC attempted to respond to the Ninth Circuit's concerns by strengthening ONA by imposing mandatory price cap regulation on the BOCs and establishing new cost accounting rules that would make anticompetitive activity easier to detect (FCC 1991b). At the same time, the FCC also simultaneously weakened ONA somewhat by shifting from a "fundamental unbundling" approach, in which ISPs could obtain access to the BOCs' networks on an element-by-element basis, to a less granular approach in which unbundling was defined in terms of network services rather than facilities (FCC 1988). The Ninth Circuit again partially vacated the FCC's ONA regime on the grounds that the FCC had failed to explain its shift away from fundamental unbundling (*California v. FCC*, 39 F.3d 919, 925–30 (9th Cir. 1994) ("*California III*")). Despite the court's invalidation of ONA, the FCC has continued to require the BOCs and GTE to comply with the ONA plans already filed with and approved by the FCC (FCC 1995a, 1995c).

20   *AT&T v. Iowa Utils. Bd.*, 525 U.S. 366, 388–92 (1999); *U.S. Telecom Ass'n v. FCC*, 359 F.3d 554, 564–77 (D.C. Cir. 2004); *United States Telecom Ass'n v. FCC*, 290 F.3d 415 (D.C. Cir. 2002); *GTE Serv. Corp. v. FCC*, 205 F.3d 416, 422–24, 425–26 (D.C. Cir. 2000); *US West Commc'ns, Inc. v. FCC*, No. 98–1410 (D.C. Cir. Aug. 25, 1999) (unpublished disposition available at 1999 WL 728555).

exempted most of the major elements needed to provide local telephone and DSL service from the UNE access requirements.[21] In the process, the FCC also resolved the issues that remained open following the Ninth Circuit's remand of the third *Computer Inquiry* by abolishing the CEI and ONA regimes (FCC 2005d).

## C. Analyzing the Rationales and Regulatory Instruments

The foregoing review demonstrates the extent to which the rationales traditionally underlying the regulation of telecommunications, as well as the regulatory instruments traditionally used to implement them, are premised on the assumption that certain features render portions of the telecommunications network inherently uncompetitive. Over time, technological advances, changes in consumer demand, and the insights provided by breakthroughs in economic theory have largely undermined these premises. The reduction in fixed costs and the emergence of new transmission and switching technologies have greatly increased the scope of the industry that is open to competition. At the same time, economic theory has raised serious doubts about the extent to which fixed costs, network economic effects, and vertical exclusion represent anticompetitive threats. Subsequent work in applied economics and experience implementing the traditional regulatory instruments has exposed the immense practical difficulties associated with the traditional regulatory regime. Last, the traditional rationales have focused almost entirely on how best to allocate the network resources that exist today. In the process, they have overlooked the equally (if not more) important question of how maximize incentives to create the optimal network of tomorrow. In other words, the approach to telecommunications regulation has placed too much emphasis on *static efficiency* and too little emphasis on *dynamic efficiency*.

### 1. Natural Monopoly

As noted earlier, one of the classic causes of natural monopoly is the presence of fixed costs sufficiently large to create scale economies that are not exhausted over the relevant range of production. This suggests that a natural monopoly can be dissipated either by a reduction in the fixed costs needed to create and operate a telecommunications network or by an increase in the total demand for the services provided by the network.

Technological and economic forces have pushed from both of these directions to undermine the natural monopoly rationale. Perhaps the most important is the

---

21  On the removal of DSL elements from the UNE requirements of the 1996 Act, see FCC (2003e), *aff'd in relevant part sub nom. U.S. Telecom Ass'n v. FCC*, 359 F.3d at 578–85. On the removal of switching and other key elements needed to provide local telephone service from the UNE requirements of the 1996 Act, see FCC (2005h).

reduction in fixed costs needed to provide local telephone service. Although the provision of local service involves a large number of components, the two that have required the greatest up-front investment in fixed costs have historically been (1) the wires needed to connect individual residences and businesses to the central office facility maintained by the local telephone company and (2) the switching equipment needed to route individual calls to their destinations.

Over time, the fixed costs needed to provide both transmission and switching have both dropped dramatically. The most dramatic development with respect to transmission has been the emergence of wireless alternatives to wireline transmission technologies. The first significant deployment of wireless transmission technologies was the use of microwave relay and satellite systems as substitutes for wireline long-distance services. This was followed by the widescale deployment of cellular telephony, personal communication services (PCS), and other wireless technologies that could serve as substitutes for conventional wireline local service. Although the fixed costs needed to deploy wireless networks are significant, they pale in comparison to the fixed costs needed to deploy wireline networks. As we discuss in greater detail in Chapter 8, improvements in computer processing technology have also effected an equally dramatic drop in the fixed costs of switching. The advent of first electronic and then digital switching has caused the fixed cost of switching technologies to plummet. Switching functions that once required equipment that occupied an entire building can now be performed by a box roughly the size of a personal computer. The net result is a dramatic reduction in the fixed costs needed to establish a telecommunications network sufficient to undercut the natural monopoly–based justifications for regulation.

In addition, the emergence of wireless transmission has brought local telephony within the ambit of the theory of contestable markets (Baumol et al. 1982), which takes issue with the prior scholarship arguing that high fixed costs necessarily represent a barrier to entry (see Bain 1956 for the classic argument and Woroch 2002a for an application to telephony). Contestability theory draws on the insight that high fixed costs need not inexorably lead to natural monopoly so long as a new entrant can resell the assets that it has to purchase should it have to exit. So long as fixed costs are not also *sunk costs*, any attempt by an existing player to charge supracompetitive prices will only invite hit-and-run entry by firms that gather the available profits and depart as soon as competition drives prices down to competitive levels.

Contestability theory underscores a critical difference between wireless and wireline transmission technologies. Because telephone wires have historically been useless for any other purpose, fixed cost investments in telephone wires can properly be regarded as sunk and thus a potential source of market failure. The same is not necessarily true for the infrastructure needed to construct a wireless transmission network. Wireless technologies require equipment located on transmission towers as well as the legal right to use particular portions of the electromagnetic spectrum. Because alternative uses exist for both of these assets (either by other wireless telephone providers or by providers of wireless broadband or other spectrum-based services), investments in wireless network technologies are less likely to be regarded as sunk costs and thus less likely to give rise to the market failures associated with natural monopoly.

The tendency toward natural monopoly created by the fixed costs is also substantially mitigated by the decommodification of telecommunications technologies and the increasing differentiation among the services provided by different network providers (Yoo 2005). It has been recognized since Edward Chamberlin's seminal work on monopolistic competition (1962) that product differentiation can allow markets to reach equilibrium with multiple producers each producing on the declining portion of the average cost curve. In other words, so long as products are differentiated, the existence of unexhausted economies of scale need not necessarily force a network to collapse into a natural monopoly.

The weakening of the natural monopoly justification associated with the reduction in fixed costs has been accompanied by an increase in the demand for the services provided by telecommunications networks. The emergence of personal computing and the analog modem made it possible for subscribers to use their connections to telecommunications networks to send data as well as voice communications. The increase in functionality made possible by the deployment of digital technologies has mitigated the tendency of telecommunications markets to collapse into natural monopolies by greatly increasing the demand for the network services. These analog technologies are in the process of being replaced with digital technologies, such as digital subscriber lines, and by fiber optics, which are enhancing the value of the network connection still further.

The increasing packetization of communications technologies is also putting pressure on the distinctions between transmission technologies, which once made sense when each medium of communications employed distinct analog encoding formats. At this point, however, voice over Internet protocol (VoIP) has already made cable modem systems a viable competitor to the voice services provided by local telephone companies, and telephone companies are working hard to offer packet-based television services. The deployment of new transmission technologies, such as third-generation wireless (3G), broadband over powerline, WiFi, and WiMax, will increase the competitiveness of last-mile telecommunications services. Once the shift toward packetization is complete, all forms of communications will simply be different applications traveling on the same data network, and the distinctions between transmission technologies that have represented the foundation of telecommunications policy since the enactment of the Communications Act of 1934 (and have sparked so many controversies over the proper regulatory classification of new communications technologies) will completely collapse.

This combination of reductions in fixed costs and increases in the demand for network services has caused much of the telecommunications network to lose its natural monopoly (Spulber 1989, 1995). Wireless networks also involve fewer transaction-specific sunk costs in comparison with wireline networks because wireless networks are not linked to specific consumers. Multiple facilities-based providers now vie to provide telecommunications to large business enterprises. In addition, intermodal competition from different wireline and wireless technologies is having the same effect on the residential and small business market as well.

## 2. Network Economic Effects

There is also reason to question theories that invoke network economic effects to justify regulation of network industries. Network effects need not create externalities. Network effects potentially create externalities only if network subscribers and the network provider somehow cannot internalize the benefits of network effects. In practice, network subscribers can address these benefits by coordinating their subscription decisions. In addition, network providers can internalize the benefits of network economic effects through pricing, service offerings, contract terms, marketing, and sales efforts (Spulber 2008a, 2008b).

A review of the theoretical literature reveals that arguments that network economic effects inexorably lead to market failure are too simplistic.[22] Network externalities arguments overlook the ability of private ordering to mitigate or eliminate any problems that may arise. These arguments based on network economic effects presume that those who adopt a new technology create benefits to those who are already members of the network that subscribers joining the network cannot internalize. The usual inference is that network economic effects create an externality that favors incumbent network owners by locking the existing network into place.

A close analysis of the seminal work on network economics reveals that the issue is significantly more complex than the conventional argument would lead one to believe. A consumer's decision to switch to a new network actually gives rise to two distinct and countervailing effects. On the one hand, the decision to join a network enhances the value of the new network for those already connected to that network and those who will join that network in the future. The inability to capture all of the benefits created by its network adoption decision gives rise to a positive externality that can cause a consumer to refuse to join a new network even when it would be socially beneficial for it to do so, a phenomenon sometimes called *lock-in* or *excess inertia*.

At the same time, the decision to join a new network also lowers the value of the old network by reducing the number of people using it. In effect, switching to a new network imposes costs on those connected to the old network that the person switching networks does not bear. Individuals who switch networks thus do not fully internalize all of the costs created by their actions. This may make that individual willing to adopt a new technology even when the costs to society exceed the benefits, a situation variously called *excess momentum* or *insufficient friction*. It is thus theoretically possible that network economic effects can cause network

---

22   The discussion that follows is based on Yoo (2002).

members to shift too quickly as well as too slowly. Which is the case depends upon which of these two countervailing effects dominates (Farrell and Saloner 1986; Katz and Shapiro 1992).

In addition, the market failures identified by the formal economic models depend on the assumption that the relevant markets are either dominated by a single firm or highly concentrated (Besen and Farrell 1994; Crémer et al. 2000; Katz and Shapiro 1986). The clear implication of these models is that policy makers should undertake a detailed examination of the structure of the relevant market before relying on network economic effects to justify regulatory intervention and that the presence of competition is likely to mitigate or eliminate any anticompetitive outcomes. For reasons introduced in the foregoing discussion on natural monopoly and discussed at greater length in Chapters 9 and 10, telecommunications networks are not likely to be sufficiently concentrated to implicate the types of market failure identified by the theoretical models.

The economic literature further indicates that private ordering may well prove quite robust in solving any economic problems created by network economic effects. One major reason is that with respect to telecommunications networks, the potential network externalities are *direct network externalities*, in that they necessarily arise through direct connections to a physical network that can be owned (Katz and Shapiro 1985; Farrell and Saloner 1985). Thus, even though individual users may not be in a position to internalize all of the benefits created by their network adoption decisions, the network owner will almost certainly be in a position to do so. The existence of a single network owner allows the problems associated with this type of externality to be solved through the same mechanism used to solve externality problems that arise in other contexts, that is, by placing property in the hands of a single owner and protecting it with well-defined property rights. Any benefits created by network participation can thus be internalized and allocated through the direct interaction between the network owner and network users (Liebowitz and Margolis 1994, 1995; Spulber 2008a).[23]

Reliance on unitary ownership of a network to internalize any network externalities that may exist does not necessarily mean that competition cannot emerge. In many cases, a network need not occupy the entire market to realize all of the

---

23  *Indirect network externalities*, in contrast, involve instances that do not involve a direct physical connection. Instead, the value of a good is determined by the number of other people who purchase the same good, with the examples commonly cited including the network of users of a particular type of format of videocassette recorder (VCR), a particular type of software, or a particular computer operating system. To date, scholars have focused on the fact that indirect network externalities typically arise in markets that involve complementary goods and that proprietary control of a network can provide network users with some assurance that a ready supply of complementary goods will remain available (Katz and Shapiro 1994; Speta 2000). Stan Liebowitz and Stephen Margolis argue that such effects are not consumption externalities, but rather are pecuniary externalities that simply transfer wealth between market actors. As such, they "describe nothing more than welfare-neutral interactions that occur in properly functioning markets" (Liebowitz and Margolis 1994, pp. 133, 139).

available demand-side economies of scale. When this occurs, no unexploited gains from trade regarding network size remain, and the equilibrium solution is competition among multiple proprietary networks. The point can be illustrated through the now classic problem presented by overfishing a lake. Because individual anglers do not internalize all of the costs of their actions, they lack sufficient incentives to undertake efficient levels of conservation and investment. The solution is to vest property rights to the entire lake in a single owner. Doing so will not necessarily eliminate competition in the market for fish, because giving owners unitary property rights over a particular lake is not the same as giving them control over all lakes. Instead, one would expect the various owners of different lakes to compete with one another in the market to supply fish. Placed in the context of networks, the proper policy question becomes one of defining property rights in a way that ensures that networks achieve sufficient size to realize all of available network economies. This does not mean that only one network will necessarily emerge and that government intervention is required to ensure that that network is the "right" one (Liebowitz and Margolis 1994).

Even assuming for the sake of argument that circumstances permit network economic effects to give rise to the problems of monopolistic dominance and technological lock-in, it is far from clear that other features of the market and the structure of consumer preferences might not mitigate, if not eliminate, these adverse effects. For example, the market may also dislodge an existing network technology so long as the new network provides additional value that exceeds the value derived from the size of old network.[24] This is particularly true given that, after networks have captured a sufficient number of subscribers, the marginal benefit from adding another subscriber is likely to be low, which would greatly reduce the magnitude of any potential externality (de Fontenay and Lee 1983; Breslaw 1985; Mitchell and Vogelsang 1991; Yarrow 1996; Albon et al. 1997).

In addition, network externalities may be substantially mitigated if user preferences are nonuniform. As Michael Katz and Carl Shapiro have noted, "Customer heterogeneity and product differentiation tend to limit tipping and sustain multiple networks. If the rival systems have distinct features sought by certain customers, two or more systems may be able to survive by catering to consumers who care more about product attributes than network size. Here, market equilibrium with multiple incompatible products reflects the social value of variety" (Katz and Shapiro 1994, p. 106; see also Liebowitz and Margolis 1996).

The existence of large users may further mitigate any problems caused by network economic effects. If a single user controls a significant portion of the network, that user will be able to internalize more of the benefits of its adoption decision,

---

24 Katz and Shapiro (1994, p. 106) observe that new, incompatible standards may emerge despite the presence of network externalities if "consumers . . . care more about product attributes than network size." Liebowitz and Margolis (2001, pp. 21–22) similarly note that the "greater the gap in performance between the two standards, . . . the more likely that a move to the efficient standard will take place."

which will help minimize any slippage caused by the existence of the network externality. Furthermore, because large users are in a position to capture a disproportionate share of the benefit resulting from the adoption of a new technology, they have a significant incentive to make the investments needed to begin the shift toward the new technology (Katz and Shapiro 1986, 1994; Liebowitz and Margolis 1995).[25] Indeed, formal models of such market structures indicate that "the sponsor of a new technology earns greater profits than its entry contributes to social welfare. In other words, markets with network externalities in which new technologies are proprietary exhibit a bias towards new technologies" (Katz and Shapiro 1992, p. 73).[26] Far from being a bane, the existence of large players may be a blessing in disguise.

In addition, significant growth in market size can render network externalities irrelevant. If an industry is undergoing explosive growth, market outcomes are determined by the adoption decisions of future users, and not the decisions of the users who have already committed to a particular network. In such cases, the fact that a particular network may currently dominate a market is of little consequence. People concerned about lock-in will focus on the network that will exist in the future, not the one that exists today.[27]

Determining the optimal number of networks and the optimal timing of technological change requires a careful balance of the relevant costs and benefits. In striking this balance, policy makers should bear in mind that standardizing on a single network and slowing the pace with which one network is superseded by another can reduce transaction costs by facilitating compatibility between complementary products. Allowing multiple networks and allowing network technologies to shift too rapidly can also give rise to significant transaction costs, because production of new technological platforms and adaptation of existing network infrastructure to incorporate innovations can be quite costly (Bresnahan 1999). Accordingly, some delay in the introduction of new products may reflect efficiency, not market failure. Absent a compelling reason to believe that network externalities are causing efficiency losses that the market cannot properly redress, regulations designed to counteract network economic effects cannot be justified.

The fact that markets seem fully capable of resolving most of the supposed market failures identified by the theoretical literature on network economics suggests that any attempt to remedy these supposed problems should be approached with considerable caution. Indeed, it would seem appropriate to insist on empirical

---

25  The fear of being held up after committing to a network might make consumers reluctant to join proprietary networks. Katz and Shapiro (1994) describe a number of ways that a network owner can allay such fears.

26  Price discrimination helps internalize potential benefits, although price discrimination is not a necessary condition for such internalization. Price discrimination is consistent with competition and thus does not require monopoly providers of network services.

27  See Katz and Shapiro (1992); Shapiro (1995); Liebowitz and Margolis (1996); and Spulber (2008b).

proof that such problems actually exist before authorizing governmental action to redress them. Proponents of network externality theories have yet to offer any systematic evidence to support their theories. Instead, most of these theorists have opted to invoke a handful of well-known anecdotes concerning supposed technology lock-in, such as the persistence of the traditional typewriter keyboard layout (commonly known as the QWERTY keyboard) and the triumph of VHS over Beta as the leading format for video cassettes.

The lack of systematic evaluation has allowed the proponents of network externality theories to be somewhat imprecise about what constitutes lock-in. The absence of a clear definition of terms ignores the fact that no technological standard is permanent and that over a long enough time horizon all technological standards are subject to change. Whether a technology has become locked in is thus in no small part a function of the period of time deemed relevant for evaluating such a change. The failure to explain terms essentially renders the concept of lock-in currently employed in the literature arbitrary and obscures any attempt to prove or falsify its existence empirically.

Furthermore, close analysis of the historical record reveals that none the key examples that form the empirical basis for network externality theory can properly be regarded as market failures. Specifically, the evidence suggests that the QWERTY keyboard does not represent an obsolete technology locked into place by network externalities. On the contrary, it appears that the QWERTY keyboard first emerged as the winner of a vibrant competition on the merits, in which various keyboard designs were tested against one another in a series of typing contests. In addition, the evidence supposedly demonstrating the Dvorak keyboard's superiority is riddled with conflicts of interest, because all of the key studies, including the Navy tests that represent perhaps the primary support for these claims, were conducted by the person who invented and patented the Dvorak keyboard. Modern ergonomic studies suggest that any technical difference between the QWERTY and the Dvorak keyboards remains nominal at best (Liebowitz and Margolis 2001).

The historical record also contradicts the suggestion that VHS's emergence as the prevailing standard for videocassettes represents the perseverance of an obsolete technology. Any suggestion that VHS's victory was the result of inefficient lock-in effects is belied by the fact that Beta was deployed first and was the early leader in VCR technology. The evidence instead suggests that the final resolution of the competition between Beta and VHS turned on a design tradeoff, with Beta incorporating a smaller cassette in order to enhance portability and VHS opting for a larger cassette in order to provide longer playing and recording time. VHS's victory over Beta thus seems to have resulted from consumers' preference for videotapes capable of recording a two-hour movie on a single cassette rather than from any market failure that frustrated the efficient outcome. If anything, then, the final outcome of the battle between Beta and VHS is more properly regarded as an example of how differences in product value and the availability of an expanding customer base can displace an existing technology, rather than as an example of inefficient lock-in. The other anecdotal examples upon which network externality theorists rely have been similarly critiqued (Liebowitz and Margolis 2001).

Against the absence of empirical evidence indicating that network externalities have caused markets to fail are arrayed a large number of instances in which new technologies have displaced incumbent technologies that were firmly entrenched. For example, vinyl and cassette recordings have been displaced by compact disks, and the VHS video format has been displaced by the digital video disc (DVD) format, which in turn has given way to the Blu-Ray high-definition DVD format. In short, the empirical record provides little reason to believe that networks are in any way sufficiently prone to market failure to justify more intrusive regulation than any other type of industry. If anything, the history of technological change suggests the contrary. Particularly given that even the theoretical models on which this literature is based suggest that network economic effects can cause market failure only under certain limited circumstances, claims of market failures caused by network economic effects that are not backed by firm empirical support should be approached with considerable skepticism.

Last, even proof of the existence of the necessary empirical preconditions for network-induced market failure would not necessarily support regulatory intervention. Consider, for example, the particular regulatory decisions associated with any state-sponsored attempt to solve the problems of technological lock-in. Such intervention would necessarily require the government to replace clear winners in the technology marketplace with what it believed represented the superior technology. Moreover, in order to be effective, the government must do so at an early stage in the technology's development, when making such determinations is the most difficult. Regulators would also typically have to make such determinations on extremely thin information that in most cases would be provided by parties with a direct interest in the outcome of the regulatory process. In addition, decisionmakers would have to insulate themselves from the types of systematic biases traditionally associated with political decisionmaking processes. It is for these reasons that even supporters of network externality theories caution that governmental intervention might well make the problem worse, not better (Katz and Shapiro 1994; Bresnahan 1999).

## 3. Vertical Exclusion

Technological and theoretical developments have also substantially undercut the plausibility of basing regulation on the dangers posed by vertical exclusion. The same forces that are increasing the competitiveness of every portion of the telecommunications industry are eliminating the plausibility that any network provider will have a dominant market position to use as leverage over an adjacent market. At the same time, the conventional wisdom with respect to vertical integration has undergone a sea change over the past half century. Although economic theorists during the 1950s and 1960s were quite hostile toward vertical integration and vertical contractual restraints (such as exclusive dealing and long-term contracts) that were tantamount to the same thing, vertical integration is now generally recognized to be less problematic than previously believed.[28] On the contrary, it can often be quite economically beneficial.

The driving force behind this transformation is the emergence of the so-called "one-monopoly-rent theorem," which holds that monopolists have little, if any, incentive to engage in vertical exclusion. Because there is only one monopoly profit available in any vertical chain of production, a monopolist can capture all of that profit without having to resort to vertical integration simply by charging the monopoly price (for the seminal statements, see Director and Levi 1956; Bowman 1957).

A simple numerical example, based on a classic opinion written by then-Chief Judge Stephen Breyer,[29] illustrates the intuitions underlying the one-monopoly-rent theorem. Suppose that a firm with a monopoly over refining ore into copper ingots sells its output into a competitive market in which firms fabricate the ingot into copper pipe. Suppose further that the cost of refining ore into ingots is $40, that the cost of fabricating the ingot into pipe is $35, and that the monopoly price for the final good is $100. If the monopolist were to vertically integrate into fabrication, it could charge $100 for the final good and thereby earn a profit of $25 per unit (i.e., $100 − $40 − $35). The monopolist need not vertically integrate to capture this profit, however. All it needs to do is price the ingot at $65, which would allow it to earn the same profit of $25 per unit (i.e., $65 − $40). Because the firms fabricating the ingot into pipe face competition, they will simply set their markup equal to their costs. This results in the price of the final good also being set at its profit-maximizing price of $100 (i.e., $65 + $35). Thus, under these circumstances, the monopolist gains nothing by vertically integrating into fabrication. All it needs to do to capture all of the available profit is to price the input so that the final good is priced at the monopoly level.

Furthermore, it is impossible to state a coherent theory of vertical exclusion unless two structural preconditions are met. First, the firm possesses monopoly power in one market (typically called the *primary market*), because without such power the network owner would not have anything to use as leverage over the upstream market for complementary services (Director and Levi 1956; Posner and Easterbrook 1982). Second, the market into which the firm seeks to exercise vertical exclusion (called the *secondary market*) must be protected by entry barriers. If no such barriers to entry exist, any attempt to raise price in the secondary market will simply attract new competitors until the price drops back down to competitive levels (Posner 1976).

Unless these structural preconditions are met, the most that vertical integration would do is rearrange distribution patterns. To use an example based on one of the

---

28  For overviews of this literature, see Yoo (2002, 2006).

29  *Town of Concord v. Boston Edison Co.*, 915 F.2d 17, 32 (1st Cir. 1990) (Breyer, C.J.).

leading Supreme Court cases on vertical integration,[30] suppose that a shoe manufacturer whose output composed ten percent of the overall shoe market decided to stop distributing its products through the 100 available independent shoe retailers. Instead, this manufacturer purchases ten of the available shoe retailers and sells its shoes only through those outlets. Would this decision reduce competition in either shoe manufacturing or shoe retailing? Although competing manufacturers will not be able to sell their products through the ten shoe retailers that now only sell shoes produced by the vertically integrated manufacturer, the ninety remaining independent shoe retailers should now have extra capacity from the withdrawal of sales from the vertically integrated manufacturer sufficient to provide distribution for all of the other manufacturers' output. The competitive manufacturers who produce ninety percent of the market are not excluded from the market at all, because they will still have ninety percent of the retail distribution capacity available to them. In this case, vertical integration only serves to realign the patterns of distribution without affecting the market shares of either the manufacturers or the retailers. Nor is it likely that the vertically integrated manufacturer could foreclose the retail market by purchasing more than ten percent of the available retailing capacity. In the absence of entry barriers, any attempt to lock out other manufacturers by tying up retailers or to extract supracompetitive returns in the retailing market would only stimulate entry by new retail outlets that would be ready and willing to distribute the products of the other manufacturers (Director and Levi 1956; Stigler 1968; Peltzman 1969; Posner 1976; Bork 1978).

The theoretical literature acknowledges the existence of exceptions to the one-monopoly-rent theorem under which vertical integration can be profitable. As noted earlier, a monopolist subject to rate regulation may well find it profitable to integrate vertically. Gaining control of a second, unregulated level of production would allow the firm to earn the profits foreclosed by regulators (Bowman 1957; Bork 1978; see also Brennan 1987 for an application to telephony). In such cases, it is arguably appropriate to prohibit vertical integration in order to isolate and quarantine the monopolist. Such regulation is justified, however, only when any attempt to break up the monopoly would ultimately prove futile. As the market at issue becomes increasingly open to competition, both rate regulation and the concomitant prohibition of vertical integration become equally unwarranted.

Scholarship associated with the post-Chicago school of antitrust law and economics has used game theory to identify other circumstances under which vertical integration can harm competition. Interestingly, these models presuppose the existence of dominant-firm and oligopoly market structures in the primary market, which necessarily presupposes that both the primary and secondary markets are highly concentrated and protected by entry barriers. In the absence of such structural features, these formal models recognize that vertical integration may be just as likely to lower price and increase welfare and that the ability of existing players

---

30  *Brown Shoe Co. v. United States*, 370 U.S. 294 (1962).

or new entrants to expand their outputs will be sufficient to defeat any attempt to increase price above competitive levels (Salop and Scheffman 1983; Salinger 1988, 1991; Hart and Tirole 1990; Ordover et al. 1990; Whinston 1990; Riordan and Salop 1995; Riordan 1998).

The post-Chicago literature has thus done little to disturb the basic conclusions that vertical integration is unlikely to harm competition unless the relevant markets are concentrated and protected by entry barriers and that vertical integration may yield efficiencies.

At the same time, economic theorists increasingly recognized that vertical integration could yield substantial efficiencies. For example, if two layers of a vertical chain of distribution are monopolistic or oligopolistic, firms in each layer will have the incentive to try to extract the entirety of the available supracompetitive returns, which would lead to an aggregate price that would be even higher than the monopoly price. Vertical integration can eliminate this so-called double marginalization problem, because a company that spans both layers would rationalize the decisionmaking between the two levels of production and would avoid the uncoordinated action that would make the supracompetitive pricing even worse (Spengler 1950; see also Machlup and Taber 1960, reviewing the early scholarship on successive monopoly theory).

In addition, to the extent that the inputs can be used in variable proportions, any attempt to charge supracompetitive prices for one input creates incentives for firms to substitute alternative inputs whenever possible. The resulting substitution creates an alternative potential source of inefficiency, as production processes deviate from the most efficient input mix. Allowing the provider of the monopolized input to vertically integrate into manufacturing can allow it to prevent inefficient input substitution (McKenzie 1951; Bowman 1957; Burstein 1960; Vernon and Graham 1971). The welfare implications of input substitution are ultimately ambiguous, because prohibiting input substitution enhances the monopolist's ability to exercise market power, which can create welfare losses sufficient to offset the welfare gains from preventing customers from deviating from the most efficient input mix. Determining which of the two countervailing effects will dominate can be quite difficult.[31] The consensus is that any reduction in welfare from preventing input substitution is likely to be small enough not to pose a problem significant enough to be worth redressing (Perry 1989; Salinger 1991; Reiffen and Vita 1995).

Finally, scholars building on Coase's seminal work on the theory of the firm (1937) have demonstrated how vertical integration can reduce transaction costs.

31  Scherer and Ross (1990, pp. 523–24) note that "The mathematical conditions underlying this result are complex." Specifically, the welfare tradeoff described above turned largely on the elasticity of substitution and the elasticity of demand for the final good. Economists who have assumed that the final product market is perfectly competitive have disagreed over the range of elasticities that lead to a price increase. Compare Hay (1973), Schmalensee (1973) and Warren-Boulton (1974) with Mallela and Nahata (1980) and Westfield (1981). Scholars that have modeled the final product market as oligopolistic have reached a similar disagreement. Compare Waterson (1982) with Abiru (1988).

One example is the elimination of free riding. For example, suppose that a firm manufactures a technically complicated product that requires significant presale services, such as the demonstration of the product. Telser (1960) shows that retailers may have the incentive to shirk in providing such services in the hope that other retailers will bear the costs of providing them. If all retailers respond to these incentives in the same way, the total amount of presale services will fall below efficient levels. A manufacturer facing the possibility of such free riding can either rely on a vertical contractual restraint that specifies the level of presale services that each retailer is required to offer or eliminate the incentive to free ride by granting territorial exclusivity (Mathewson and Winter 1984). Alternatively, the manufacturer can vertically integrate into distribution. All of these solutions effectively align the retailers' incentives with the manufacturers'.

Another oft-cited transaction cost efficiency associated with vertical integration stems from the existence of relationship-specific investments, which exist whenever the cost of a capital asset exceeds the value of its next best use. Relationship-specific investments can create *appropriable quasi-rents*, because they allow others to hold up the investing party in an attempt to extract a greater proportion of the joint benefits. Firms confronting such risks can eliminate them either by entering into a vertical contractual restraint (such as an exclusive dealing requirement or long-term contract) or by vertically integrating. Either solution eliminates the incentives for engaging in opportunistic behavior designed to affect the division of profits between the two firms (Klein et al. 1978). Although a lively debate has emerged over the frequency with which vertical integration will represent the preferred solution over a vertical contractual restraint,[32] both sides agree about the potential benefits associated with some greater exercise of vertical control.

Despite their differences about the likelihood that vertical exclusion will be profitable, post-Chicago scholars agree that vertical integration may lead to efficiencies

---

32  The classic example discussed in the literature is GM's 1926 acquisition of one of its component manufacturers, Fisher Body. Klein et al. (1978) argue that the shift from wooden to metal automobile bodies required Fisher Body to make a relationship-specific investment in new metal stamping technology unique to GM's cars that created the possibility that GM would act opportunistically against Fisher Body after the investment costs had already been sunk. To mitigate this risk, GM and Fisher Body entered into a long-term exclusive dealing agreement that was well designed to protect Fisher Body against opportunistic behavior by GM, but not well designed to protect GM against opportunistic behavior by Fisher Body. A dramatic increase in the demand for metal-bodied automobiles put GM in the position of being held up by Fisher Body. Unable to manage its relationship with its input supplier through contractual devices, GM was left with no choice but to vertically integrate backward into body fabrication by acquiring Fisher Body. Other scholars, including Coase himself, have disputed this account. These critics argue that vertical contractual restraints were more than sufficient to protect GM's interests and point out that at the time that Fisher Body supposedly acted opportunistically, GM already owned sixty percent of Fisher Body's common stock (Coase 1988, 2000; Casadesus-Masanell and Spulber 2000; Freeland 2000). Klein, in turn, responded by arguing that the relevant quasi-rents resulted from firm-specific human (rather than physical) capital and by placing greater emphasis on Fisher Body's supposed refusal to locate its plants near GM's (Klein 1988, 2000).

sufficient to offset any concomitant anticompetitive effects. Whether a particular instance of vertical integration impedes or promotes competition depends on which of these two effects dominates.[33]

Determining whether a particular form of vertical integration will enhance or reduce economic welfare is thus an empirical question that turns on the particular market structure and the nature of the available efficiencies. Although some have questioned whether the empirical literature is sufficiently developed to support any clear policy inferences,[34] recent surveys of the empirical literature on vertical integration and vertical restraints found that the existing studies overwhelmingly support for the proposition that vertical integration and vertical restraints tend to promote, rather than harm, competition.[35]

All of the rationales discussed up to this point focus on how best to allocate the network that already exists, by organizing production so that it consumes the fewest resources and by allocating outputs to those consumers who can put them to the best use. In focusing on allocating the network that already exists today, these rationales overlook the equally (if not more) important question of how to create incentives to invest in new network technologies that will compose the optimal network of tomorrow. In other words, the current policy debate has placed too much focus on *static efficiency* and given too little emphasis to the maximization of *dynamic efficiency.*

When competitive entry is possible, the traditional regulatory tools can have a detrimental impact on incentives to invest in alternative network technologies. So long as competitive entry remains feasible, supracompetitive returns should not prove sustainable over the long run, and prices should tend toward competitive levels. In the short run, however, shifts in demand, changes in technology, and other exogenous changes can cause markets to deviate from their long-run equilibrium position. When this is the case, prices that permit short-run supracompetitive returns allocate the scarce network resources, signal industry participants that the market is in short-run disequilibrium, and provide incentives to invest in additional network capacity.

The emphasis on short-run economic profits is sometimes mistakenly compared to the type of competition proposed by Joseph Schumpeter (1942), in which the market is dominated by a series of monopolists and firms compete by vying to discover the next breakthrough innovation that will give them a cost or quality advantage decisive enough to allow them to displace the current monopolist and dominate the market in its place. This argument ignores the key role that short-run supracompetitive returns play in horizontal competition within a market, in which multiple players offer substitute products to consumers and in which any

---

33   See Krattenmaker and Salop (1986); Ayres (1988); Salinger (1988); Hart and Tirole (1990); Klass and Salinger (1995); Riordan and Salop (1995).

34   See Page (1989); Jacobs (1995); Muris (2001).

35   See Cooper et al. (2005); LaFontaine and Slade (2008).

supracompetitive returns will prove transient and quickly dissipated. In fact, using regulation to prevent the earning of supracompetitive returns would eliminate the primary impetus for competitive entry, in which case the supply curve would never shift outward to bring the market back into long-run equilibrium (Yoo 2005). This tendency to forestall competitive entry implicitly presumes that rate regulation will persist indefinitely. Such a surrender to the monopoly only makes sense if competitive entry is infeasible.

Mandating access to the existing network creates similar disincentives to investments in alternative transmission technologies. Because any benefits gained from investments in capital or research must be shared with competitors, forcing a monopolist to share its resources discourages incentives to improve their facilities and pursue technological innovation. As Garrett Hardin (1968) pointed out in his path-breaking work on "the tragedy of the commons," resources that are in effect jointly owned tend to be overused and receive suboptimal levels of investment. Hardin's insights apply with equal force to compelled sharing of telecommunications networks.

In addition, denying providers of complementary services guaranteed access to the existing network gives them powerful incentives to enter into strategic partnerships with firms interested in constructing alternative network capacity in competition with the existing network. Using regulation to provide those same providers with guaranteed access to the existing networks would destroy any incentives to enter into such arrangements. In effect, forcing a monopolist to share an input rescues other firms from having to supply the relevant input for themselves. As a result, compelled access can have the perverse effect of entrenching any supposed bottleneck facility by forestalling the emergence of the substitute network technologies. This is particularly problematic in technologically dynamic industries, in which the prospects of developing new ways either to circumvent or to compete directly with the alleged bottleneck are greatest.

This analysis underscores the extent to which debates over access to networks have all too often focused on the wrong policy problem. One of the key insights of vertical integration theory is that markets yield efficient outcomes only if every link of the chain of production is sufficiently competitive. As a result, competition policy should focus on identifying the link that is the most concentrated and the most protected by entry barriers and design regulations to increase its competitiveness. This implies that regulatory decisions should be guided by their impact on competition in the last mile, which remains the portion of the industry that is the most concentrated and the most protected by barriers to entry. Most access proposals are intended to preserve and foster competition in markets for complementary services that depend on the last mile, such as long distance, CPE, or information services, which are the portions of the industry that are already quite competitive and sufficiently unprotected by entry barriers to be likely to remain that way. Although the promotion of competition in complementary services was arguably an appropriate second-order policy goal when the first-order policy goal of promoting competition in the last mile was likely to prove futile, the growing feasibility of last-mile competition strongly supports refocusing telecommunications policy back on the first-order concerns.

Indeed, the ensuing reductions in incentives to invest in alternative transmission technologies could have the unfortunate effect of cementing the existing last-mile oligopoly into place, which would somewhat perversely turn access regulation into the source of, rather than the solution to, market failure. It is conceivable that investment disincentives could be minimized if policy makers engaged in asymmetric regulation that freed new entrants from rate and access regulation while continuing to subject the dominant player to such restrictions. If entry is truly feasible, it is not entirely clear whether such regulation would be economically necessary. In addition, administering such a regime would require policy makers to make difficult determinations about when the market became sufficiently competitive to deregulate the activities of the formerly dominant player. Such a determination is likely to be particularly difficult when technology and consumer demand are changing rapidly.

The foregoing analysis underscores the extent to which regulators seeking to impose rate or access regulation must thread a very narrow needle even under the best of circumstances. Any such an intervention will only yield economic benefits if it forces prices closer to competitive levels. If the regulated price is set too high, the regulatory intervention will have no beneficial effect. If set too low, the intervention will deter investment while effectively forcing the incumbent network owner to cross subsidize providers of complementary services and new entrants. And any such intervention will be completely unnecessary to the extent that competitive entry into last-mile transmission is feasible. The alternative would be to allow the short-run supracompetitive returns to stimulate entry by alternative last-mile providers. By the standards imposed under modern competition policy, the availability of three (or perhaps four) last-mile options should be sufficient to dissipate any concerns about anticompetitive pricing in the last mile or vertical exclusion in complementary services. It is for this reason that courts and policy makers have been reluctant to compel access to a resource that is available from another source, even if it is only available at significant cost and in the relatively long run.[36]

Some scholars have asserted that because the dynamic efficiency gains will be compounded over time, they will necessarily exceed the short-run static efficiency losses.[37] This approach seems too simplistic. Whether the dynamic efficiency gains will dominate the static efficiency losses depends on the relative magnitude of the gains and losses, the speed of entry, and the appropriate discount rate. That said, a

---

36  See *Iowa Utils. Bd.*, 525 U.S. at 388–9; *Nat'l Cable & Telecomms. Ass'n v. Brand X Internet Servs.*, 545 U.S. 967 (2005); *U.S. Telecom Ass'n v. FCC*, 290 F.3d 415, 428–9 (D.C. Cir. 2002); Areeda and Hovenkamp (2008c).

37  See Bolter et al. (1984); Ordover and Baumol (1988).

number of institutional considerations militate in favor of the dynamic efficiency side of the balance. For example, calibrating the prices needed to implement rate regulation and access regulation will necessarily require the government to engage in an exquisite exercise in line drawing that requires a careful and fact-intensive balance of opposing considerations. This is made all the more complicated by the rapid pace with which the underlying technology and the demands that consumers are placing on the network are changing. The fact that regulatory processes invariably take several months to complete makes it inevitable that, even under the best of circumstances, rate and access regulation will be subject to a degree of regulatory lag. In the worst case, as many noted commentators have observed, it can cause regulation to endure long after technological change has eroded its justifications (Posner 1969; Kahn 1971; Breyer 1982). On the other hand, promoting dynamic efficiency allows regulatory authorities to focus on stimulating entry by new network platforms, which should represent a policy goal that is considerably easier to implement. Perhaps even more importantly, promoting entry has embedded within it a built-in exit strategy. Once a sufficient number of broadband network platforms exist, regulatory intervention will no longer be necessary. This stands in stark contrast to rate regulation and access-oriented solutions, which implicitly presume that regulation will continue indefinitely.

The impact of this critique has been quite influential. The conventional wisdom has now largely abandoned its hostility toward vertical integration.[38] The manner in which technology is in the process of increasing the competitiveness of all segments of the telecommunications industry and the real efficiencies from vertically integrated provision already identified by the FCC have effectively undercut the threat of vertical exclusion as a justification for regulating telecommunications networks.

---

38  See Markovits (1970); Areeda and Turner (1978); Williamson (1987); Areeda and Hovenkamp (2008c); Hovenkamp (2005).

# 5

# Economic Effects of Regulating Access
# to Networks

On the afternoon of August 14, 2003, a major power blackout struck the northeastern and midwestern United States and parts of Ontario, Canada. The power outage cascaded across cities and states, forcing businesses to close, cutting power to households, and shutting down communications networks, affecting over 50 million people. The outage stranded commuters with traffic jams, closed bridges and tunnels, and stalled public transportation systems. The problem began in Ohio when three high-voltage transmission lines of First Energy Corporation made contact with trees. Because of malfunctioning control-room equipment at First Energy, the utility failed to detect the problem and to warn other utilities. The downed lines caused power to overload the grid, which in turn led to further breakdowns in the transmission network. The Midwest Independent System Operator and the reliability control area for Pennsylvania, New Jersey, and Maryland (the PJM Interconnection) lacked the information and procedures to address the transmission problems.[1]

The dramatic story of the Northeast power outage illustrates the complexities of networks – both in balancing the supply and demand for network capacity and in coordinating the interconnection of networks. Monitoring the performance of a single network is hard enough, and the transaction costs of coordinating network interactions are even higher.

Although communications networks face different types of problems than electric power networks, they also involve highly complex problems of network management and interconnection. Regulatory efforts to mandate access to communications networks can substantially increase this complexity. Mandated access puts stress on network capacity that requires networks to rethink their design. If the system has substantial excess capacity, then mandated access may not require the regulated firm to reconfigure its network. However, if mandated access adds sufficient demand relative to the capacity of the system or substantially changes

---

1  See U.S. Canada Power System Outage Task Force (2004).

traffic patterns, the regulated firm may need to invest in additional capacity and to reconfigure the network.

Mandated access also creates substantial transaction costs for networks, for which cost-based regulation often does not account. Compliance with regulations mandating retail, wholesale, unbundled, platform, and interconnection access entails different transaction costs for each. Regulators should take such transaction costs into account in evaluating the total costs of access and include them in the costs of establishing and operating networks.

Network firms are able to address problems of determining network capacity and configuration through market mechanisms. The size and configuration of networks will reflect the supply and demand for network capacity and related services. Moreover, the extent to which networks are vertically integrated will reflect the transaction costs of networks. The complexity of network design suggests that regulators should exercise forbearance and leave these problems to market mechanisms. Mandated access will bias market mechanisms in the selection of inefficient network capacity and design.

## A. Classifying Types of Access to Networks

*Access to networks* refers to physical connections that are external to the network and mediated by market transactions. We classify different types of access in terms of the type of entity to whom access is provided (e.g., customers, competitors, or suppliers of complementary products and services), as well as the specific network facilities to which access is provided; see Chapter 1.

Each of the types of access in our classification scheme has a corresponding set of regulations. Retail access is implemented through common carrier regulations. Wholesale, interconnection, and unbundled access in telecommunications regulation are addressed extensively by the Telecommunications Act of 1996 and FCC regulations. Platform access is addressed by open access regulations and antitrust enforcement, including merger conditions in the cable industry. In addition, the basis for determining the rates paid for access varies considerably. In some cases, access prices are determined through private negotiations. In other cases, regulatory authorities set them pursuant to varying methodologies.

### 1. Retail Access

*Mandated retail access* gives end users rights to obtain the network's services, whereas wholesale, interconnection, and unbundled access are provided to competitors. Customer access to a telecommunications network means the ability to communicate with others who also have access to the network. Because retail access to a network refers to a customer's use of the network's services, which are the outputs of the network, access means more than simply a physical connection to the network. The physical connection is necessary but not sufficient for access. Rather, access refers to the opportunity to benefit from the services generated by network usage.

Retail access has its origins in the common law duty to serve that applies to all common carriers (Sidak and Spulber 1997a). With respect to intrastate communications, states typically implement retail access through public tariffs, which specify terms of service that the carrier must make available to any requesting customer. With respect to interstate communications, the Communications Act of 1934 requires carriers to provide service to any customer making a reasonable request for service (47 U.S.C. § 201(a)). Although interstate rates were once governed by tariffs as well, following a long battle that eventually involved the Supreme Court and Congress, retail access to interstate services is now provided on a nontariffed basis (Schoenwald 1997; Huber et al. 1999).

In telecommunications, retail access is sometimes accompanied by regulation of retail rates charged. For example, retail rates for local wireline telephone service are regulated. As noted in the previous chapter, the traditional approach assesses the reasonableness of a particular rate in light of the carrier's historical costs. Because the retail rates tend to be uniform throughout the service area, customers in low-cost areas implicitly cross-subsidize customers in high-cost areas. Retail rates for emerging services, such as wireless telephony and digital subscriber lines, tend not to be regulated.

## 2. Wholesale Access

*Mandated wholesale access* gives purchase rights to a network owner's competitors, who can then resell network services to end users. Wholesale access involves the same services as retail access, but the party obtaining access is different. In retail access, access is provided to the customer. In wholesale access, access is provided to a competitor. It also differs from unbundled access in that the network's elements are kept together and purchased as a whole.

Incumbent telecommunications firms voluntarily provide wholesale access services to a wide range of local, national, and international companies, including competitive local exchange carriers (CLECs) with or without their own facilities, long-distance carriers (known as interexchange carriers or IXCs), international long-distance carriers, wireless carriers, enhanced service providers (ESPs), Internet service providers (ISPs), and national resellers. For example, Qwest offers what it terms wholesale products in the following categories: combined access and transport, billing, customer premises equipment, interconnection facility-based, interexchange access, Internet and data, resale, non-facility-based, voice solutions, and wireless. In the most basic wholesale category of switched access, Qwest offers complex bundles of switched transport, local switching, and carrier common lines. As part of its national and international service, Qwest offers direct local access to its network that enables "wholesale customers to maximize advanced communications services, including dedicated Internet access (DIA), asynchronous transfer mode (ATM), frame relay, and dedicated private lines" (Qwest Web site).

In other situations, wholesale access is mandated by regulation. For example, the 1996 Act requires all local exchange carriers (LECs) to permit resale of their telecommunications services without imposing any "unreasonable and discriminatory conditions or limitations." Incumbent LECs (ILECs), which are LECs providing service at the time of the 1996 Act's enactment, are further required to allow resale at wholesale rates. The statute requires that wholesale rates be based on retail rates "excluding the portion thereof attributable to any marketing, billing, collection, and other costs that will be avoided by the local exchange carrier."[2] The FCC defined *avoided costs* as "those that an incumbent LEC would no longer incur if it were to cease retail operations and instead provide all of its services through resellers" (FCC 1996a, p. 15956).

## 3. Interconnection Access

*Mandated interconnection access* refers to reciprocal connections between networks that provide access to each other's facilities, forming a larger network in the process. Interconnection is a dominant characteristic of most network industries. For example, practically all telecommunications networks allow a telephone call originating from any wireless or wireline telecommunications system to reach anyone on any other system around the world. A classic instance is the interconnection between independent telephone systems and the Bell System, such as previously occurred when both GTE and Pacific Bell (now Verizon and SBC) served customers within the same calling area in California. Some type of interconnection was essential if GTE customers were to be able to make calls to and receive calls from Pacific Bell customers. The Internet is a network of interconnected networks with reciprocal arrangements. Interconnection is reciprocal because communication of this type is a two-way street, with each network both originating and terminating telephone calls. Although the common law and early federal statutes did not require the Bell System to interconnect with competitors or providers of complementary services, the 1996 Act imposed the requirement that all telecommunications carriers interconnect directly or indirectly with other carriers.[3]

The compensation regime for mandatory interconnection access varies. The rates for many types of interconnection remain unregulated. For example, rates for interconnection between wireless telephone networks are currently unregulated. Similarly, interconnection among backbone providers is not compulsory.

In other situations, the law dictates interconnection rates. For example, the 1996 Act requires all LECs to establish reciprocal compensation arrangements with one another and mandates that they "provide for the mutual and reciprocal recovery

---

2   47 U.S.C. §§ 251(b)(1) & (c)(4), 252(d)(3).
3   Huber et al. (1999); 47 U.S.C. § 251(a)(1).

by each carrier of costs associated with the transport and termination... of calls that originate on the network facilities of the other carrier." The FCC authorized state public utility commissions (PUCs) to impose default proxy prices or to base interconnection access prices on TELRIC, which is a forward-looking, replacement-cost methodology. The Act also requires ILECs to interconnect with all other telecommunications carriers on just, reasonable, and nondiscriminatory terms.[4]

The logic underlying reciprocal compensation stems from the fact that telecommunications systems have typically operated on the principle that the calling party pays. When this is the case, the network originating a call is the only one that receives any revenue even though the network that terminates the call also incurs costs. Some mechanism for compensating the terminating carrier for the costs it incurs would thus seem reasonable. In recent years, there has been growing interest in "bill and keep" arrangements, in which each network recovers the costs of terminating traffic received from other networks. Bill and keep arrangements have long been a common way to handle interconnection between independent telephone companies and the Bell System, and the 1996 Act specifically provides that its reciprocal compensation requirement should not be construed to preclude bill and keep arrangements.[5] Indeed, the FCC has opened proceedings to consider whether it should adopt bill and keep as the sole basis for reciprocal compensation (FCC 2001d).

### 4. Platform Access

*Mandated platform access* requires that a firm's network facilities conform to a standard that allows other companies to provide complementary services. We define a *platform* as a collection of related technological standards. In telecommunications networks, platforms permit compatible transmission of communications and interconnection of equipment. In computers, a platform is a "reconfigurable base of compatible components on which users build applications" and is identified with "engineering specifications for compatible hardware and software" (Bresnahan and Greenstein 1996, p. 7; see also Greenstein 1998; Bresnahan and Greenstein 1999). For example, IBM devised standards for the personal computer that were adapted by manufacturers of components and software designers. In turn, software designers use Microsoft's standards for personal computer operating systems to create applications that are compatible with its operating systems.

When standards are widely available and not necessarily proprietary, independent companies can produce complementary components, which in turn allows consumers to assemble groups of products. In information technology, the IBM standard allowed a modular set of products that are complementary so that consumers can combine computers, software applications, and peripheral devices such

---

4   47 U.S.C. §§ 251(a)(1),(b)(5), & (c)(2), 252(d)(2)(i); 47 C.F.R. § 51.705(a)(1).
5   47 U.S.C. § 252(d)(2)(B)(i).

as printers, monitors, and memory devices that work together. In addition, the components of the computer itself, including microprocessors, memory chips, and monitors, are sufficiently standardized to allow these products to be supplied by a variety of industries connected to information technology. In markets for electronic equipment and software, a platform often refers to standardization through a collection of technical specifications that permit interchangeable products. Such common technological standards need not be confined to high-tech industries; similar modularity is observed in a variety of products such as automobiles, bicycles, audio systems, and video display systems. Multiple companies produce components for these products. Also, consumers can purchase a wide variety of add-on complementary products. The notion of an open platform is a very general one and includes networks as well as suites of complementary products, although in the discussion that follows we restrict attention to networks.

*Platform access* requires network owners to conform to a set of standards that allows other companies to provide complementary services to the network's customers. It usually also includes the ability of suppliers of complementary services to know and use the technological standards of the network when creating complementary products and services. Platform access also typically includes access to the network's transmission services so that the supplier can provide services over the network and the network's customers can receive the complementary services. In principle, a company that owns a network can grant selective platform access to a limited group of companies through licenses, partnerships, and other contracts. Alternatively, a network owner can open its network services and standards to any company that provides complementary goods and services. A network is said to be *modular* or to exhibit an *open architecture* if most suppliers of complementary services can gain access to the network.

Platform access has long been a part of telecommunications law. For example, the FCC standardized the interface for telephone handsets and other customer premises equipment (CPE) and required network owners to permit the interconnection of any CPE that met those standards (FCC 1975).[6] Platform access was also mandated during the breakup of AT&T. As part of the effort to introduce competition into long distance services, the court required the newly divested Regional Bell Operating Companies (RBOCs) to reconfigure their switches to provide a standardized interface accessible to any long-distance carrier.[7] During its *Computer Inquiries*, the FCC also required the RBOCs to "'make available standardized hardware and software interfaces that are able to support transmission, switching,

---

6  The Court of Appeals upheld this order on judicial review (*N.C. Utils. Comm'n v. FCC*, 552 F.2d 1036 (4th Cir. 1977). These standards were later repealed (FCC 2000a).

7  *United States v. AT&T*, 552 F. Supp. 131, 196, 223–34 (D.D.C. 1982), *aff'd mem. sub nom. Maryland v. United States*, 460 U.S. 1001 (1983). As Robinson (1988) has pointed out, this aspect of the court order mandating the breakup of AT&T completed a process that was begun by the FCC.

and signaling functions identical to those utilized in the enhanced service provided by the carrier'" (FCC 1986b, p. 1039).[8] The 1996 Act similarly authorizes
the FCC to work with industry standard-setting organizations to develop interconnectivity standards to govern public telecommunications networks (47 U.S.C.
§ 256(b)(2)).

The critical debate on platform access focuses on the Internet. The predominant communication standard on the Internet is known as the transfer control
protocol/Internet protocol (TCP/IP). The ubiquity and openness of TCP/IP allow
a wide variety of applications to be transmitted over the Internet, permitting such
services as search engines and Internet commerce to be provided by companies
using the Internet. In addition, TCP/IP makes possible the transmission of a wide
variety of types of information including voice, data, images, and video. Increases
in the volume and heterogeneity of traffic have created some pressure on network
owners to deviate from TCP/IP in favor of alternative protocols that can guarantee greater reliability in throughput rates. As discussed in more detail in the last
three chapters of this book, critics have responded by calling upon policymakers to
mandate adherence to TCP/IP.

## 5. Unbundled Access

*Mandated unbundled access* requires network owners to lease portions of their
networks to their competitors. Like wholesale access, unbundled access is provided
to competitors. Rather than providing the services of the entire network, as is the
case under wholesale access, unbundled access involves the use of the services of
selected inputs.

Unbundled access represents the culmination of a long-standing movement in
network regulation. Regulatory authorities initially regarded the entire telephone
network as a natural monopoly. As competition began to emerge in portions of
the network, regulatory authorities adopted a policy of restricting rate regulation
to the narrowest possible scope and deregulating the competitive portions of the
network. This approach had the benefit of allowing the broadest possible scope of
the industry to be governed by competition. Separating the regulated and unregulated lines of business also made it easier to enforce nondiscrimination mandates
and to prevent regulated entities from including costs properly attributable to the
competitive line of business in their regulated rates.

This rationale is what led Judge Harold Greene to order AT&T to segregate its
now-competitive long distance business from its local telephone operations. It also
underlay the structural separation requirements embodied in the first and second
*Computer Inquiries*. Both proceedings implicitly treated local telephone service as
if it remained a natural monopoly. Since that time, however, the dramatic drop
in the cost of switching has opened even portions of local telephone service to

---

8   As discussed in Chapter 4, this order was the subject of ongoing litigation.

competition. At this point, the only portion of the telecommunications network that even plausibly exhibits natural monopoly characteristics is the local loop.[9] Carried to its logical conclusion, this approach would lead to creation of "Loop Cos," in which physical wires connecting central offices to individual residences and businesses would be segregated from switching and other functions associated with local telephone service.

Over time, however, policymakers began to recognize that structural separation often exacted some fairly significant costs. As noted in Chapter 4, vertical integration often yields real efficiencies that cannot be realized if regulated businesses are required to be segregated into separate companies. As a result, the FCC initiated a third *Computer Inquiry*, which amended the rules to allow major local telephone companies to avoid being subject to the structural separation requirement so long as they made every element of their networks available to any enhanced service provider on an unbundled basis. Unbundled access rates under the third *Computer Inquiry* were based on historical cost.

A similar approach was embodied in the UNE access provision of the 1996 Act, which requires ILECs to provide access to all of their network elements on an unbundled basis at any technically feasible point. In determining which network elements would be subject to the UNE access requirement, the statute required the FCC to consider whether "access to such network elements as are proprietary in nature is *necessary*" and whether "the failure to provide access to such network elements would *impair* the ability of the telecommunications carrier seeking access to provide the services that it seeks to offer."[10] As was the case with interconnection access, the FCC implemented the unbundled access requirements of the 1996 Act through TELRIC.[11]

## B. Capacity and Configuration Effects of Access Regulation

This section explores the consequences of the incremental demand associated with the various forms of access regulation. Mandated access may cause the total demand for capacity to rise or fall, depending on the regulated price of access and whether access involves some types of demand that were not present before. If mandated access increases total demand for capacity, compelling access may necessitate changes in network capacity and configuration. If the network firm has sufficient excess capacity to meet any additional demands placed on the network, either across

9 As noted in Chapter 4, the emergence of intermodal competition from wireless has rendered this premise questionable. In addition to providing direct competition to wireline local loops, the fact that spectrum can be resold converts the upfront investments needed to establish network service from sunk costs into fixed costs, thereby arguably bringing local telephone service within the ambit of the theory of contestable markets.

10 47 U.S.C. § 251(c)(3) & (d)(2)(A)–(B).

11 47 C.F.R. § 51.505(a).

the network or at specific locations on the network, then mandated access may not affect the capacity and configuration of the network. If so, the effects of mandating access are restricted to the transaction costs of compliance and the opportunity costs of lost earnings from displaced demand.

If the network firm lacks sufficient excess capacity to meet any increases in demand due to access, then the network firm must adjust its capacity accordingly. Adjusting network capacity to meet additional demand generally entails more than capacity expansion; it also requires reconfiguring the network. The costs of expanding an existing network reflect the medium-term costs of expanding its capacity and the adjustment costs of incorporating new facilities into its system. If the network firm were to establish at least parts of its network after compelled access, then its costs of capacity would reflect more long-term costs more closely. Furthermore, even if access caused network demand to fall, it might still require the network to be reconfigured if traffic patterns changed or demand for capacity increased only at particular locations in the network.

## 1. Retail Access

Mandating access to a network alters the market equilibrium for network capacity. Unless there is substantial excess capacity to cover the mandated access, the result could be an imbalance of demand and supply and economic inefficiency. Even if total demand for capacity decreases or stays constant, there may be changes in the distribution of capacity requirements across the incumbent firm's network that require reconfiguration of the network. Accordingly, we propose a principle of network capacity.[12] *Restoring market equilibrium requires that mandated access to a network be accompanied by compensating adjustments – higher prices, greater capacity, or reduced services – that correct imbalances in the demand for and supply of network capacity.* There may, however, be practical or regulatory constraints that foreclose some of these compensating mechanisms.

In sizing its network, the network owner must forecast what the likely demand for network resources will be and design a network to accommodate it. These decisions are complicated by the fact that capacity typically cannot be expanded in a continuous manner. Instead, the indivisibility of fixed cost investments often forces network owners to add capacity before it is actually needed. More importantly, capacity generally cannot be expanded instantaneously. The network owner must precommit to a particular level of capacity based on the anticipated network demand.

---

12   This type of problem arises when some exogenous force disturbs an equilibrium. In chemistry, the Le Chatelier principle (Le Chatelier 1888) states that "Every change of one of the factors of an equilibrium occasions a rearrangement of the system in such a direction that the factor in question experiences a change in a sense opposite to the original change." Newton's third law of motion, which states that "for every action there is an equal and opposite reaction," provides an analogous principle to physics. The Le Chatelier principle is used in physics as well. Paul Samuelson (1947) recognized this principle in his development of comparative static analysis in economics.

Consider the basic capacity and configuration decision faced by the typical network firm. Let the expected retail demand for network services be given by $Q = D_e(p)$, and let the actual retail demand for network services be given by $Q = D_a(p)$. The network firm will configure its network with capacity $K$, where $K$ equals the profit-maximizing quantity given the expected demand. The variability of demand makes capacity decisions particularly complicated. Peaks in network traffic can saturate portions of the network, which in turn causes queues to form and the quality of network service (in terms of throughput rates) to degrade. As a result, network owners must calibrate their networks to handle the peaks plus an additional margin to serve as insurance against unanticipated variability in demand. The amount of excess capacity will depend on the tradeoff between network cost and reliability. Clearly, information about the expectations for the magnitude and variability of traffic flows play a critical role in setting network capacity.

The price that rations retail demand before access regulation is $p^*$, which solves

(1) $$D_e(p^*) = K.$$

Suppose that regulatory authorities cap retail prices below $p^*$. In that event, demand will increase along the demand curve to the point where it exceeds the available capacity. The natural response is for the network firm to exercise the right that businesses typically enjoy to refuse to deal with other firms as they see fit and simply decline to meet the excess demand. To the extent that the network firm is subject to retail access, this response is foreclosed.

A related problem exists if the actual network demand diverges from expectations. If demand falls short of expectations, $D_a(p)$ will be to the left of $D_e(p)$. Such an occurrence is not likely to require significant reconfiguration of the network. Over the long run, the natural response is to reduce capacity to meet the lower demand. In the short run, the network owner can compensate by dropping price in order to bring the market back into equilibrium.

A different situation arises if actual network demand exceeds expectations, as represented in Figure 5.1. In this case, the network owner lacks sufficient capacity to satisfy the increase in demand and faces three possible solutions to the excess demand for capacity. The first solution is the expansion of network capacity through investment in facilities, or through the entry of additional firms to provide network services. Although this response may be feasible over the long run, the fact that capacity expansions take some time may render it infeasible in the short run.

The second solution is to increase the prices of retail access to give incentives for consumers to reduce demand along the demand curve.[13] The price of retail

---

13   Indeed, the economics of congestion supports the notion that a price increase would be a particularly appropriate response. As we discuss in Chapter 12, the standard result is that prices should be set equal to the customer's marginal contribution to congestion. The unexpected increase in demand naturally means that, for a given capacity, congestion would be higher than expected, and thus that the congestion cost associated with adding an additional user would also be higher (Sidak and Spulber 1998).

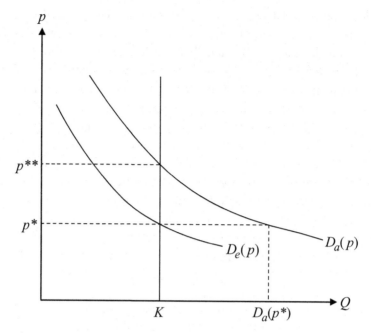

**Figure 5.1.** Excess demand for capacity as a result of retail access.

access must be such that the demand for capacity is rationed. This means that the new price of retail access $p^{**}$ must allocate capacity. This requires that total demand for capacity, including retail demand and access demand, must equal network capacity:

(2) $$D_a(p^{**}) = K.$$

This solution is likely to be the most efficient solution, at least in the short run, when network capacity is fixed. It may, however, be foreclosed by regulation. To the extent that retail prices are subject to rate regulation, such price increases may not be permitted.

The third solution is to find a way to reduce demand for network capacity by shifting the retail demand curve to the left to compensate for the excess demand. There are many different ways to achieve such reductions in demand. Demand can be reduced by shifting peak demand to off-peak periods, thus reducing the need for peak capacity. Demand can be reduced by tolerating a lower quality of service, allowing more blocked calls in a circuit-switched telecommunications network or more information loss in a packet-switched communications network. Demand can be reduced by reducing the variety of services offered by the network firm. If platform access is not mandated by law, demand also can be reduced by decreasing platform access, thus lowering the number of types of complementary services delivered on the network, which will reduce consumer demand for network capacity.

Imposition of retail access thus places the network owner on the horns of a dilemma. The duty to serve prevents it from protecting the quality of its services by refusing to deal with additional customers. The inevitable lag in adding capacity renders it unable to meet the unexpected increase in demand by expanding capacity. The price controls associated with rate regulation prevent it from adjusting price so that it rations capacity. In effect, retail access leaves network owners with no choice but to respond to unanticipated increases in demand with a degradation of service. This is the only means available to bring demand and capacity back into balance. Networks can try to anticipate and guard against this problem, but that would require undertaking additional costs and altering network configuration in uneconomical ways.

Retail access places another burden on network design. Because retail access gives any customer who leaves a carrier the right to return, carriers must maintain excess capacity against the possibility that their competitors may fail and the customers of their competitors may seek access to their networks. In effect, retail access forces carriers to act as insurers of their competitors. The problem is that during the time when the customers subscribe to other networks, they make no contribution toward the costs incurred by the carrier in maintaining the standby capacity. In essence, retail access leaves network owners vulnerable to a form of free riding, in which the remaining customers pay the premium on the insurance consumed by customers residing on other networks (Sidak and Spulber 1997a).

## 2. Wholesale Access

At first glance, the capacity effects of wholesale access would appear to be minimal. All of the traffic will continue to reside on the same network. The only difference is that the marketing functions will be transferred to another firm. Viewed in this manner, the amount of traffic on the network would appear to remain the same.

On closer inspection, the situation becomes somewhat more complicated. Because total network demand depends upon the interaction of two prices, the impact of wholesale access becomes more ambiguous. To the extent that new entrants underprice the network owner, they may be able to increase demand along the demand curve. If the new entrants are able to bundle the resold services with attractive complementary services or otherwise enhance the resold services, total demand may increase. This means that the new entrants take business from the incumbent firm, but also increase the size of the market. Total retail and wholesale demand for the network firm's services can increase, depending on the characteristics of the firms that purchase wholesale access and the types of services that they offer.

Let the expected retail demand for network services without wholesale access be given by $Q = D^0(p)$. Again, the network firm will configure its network so that its capacity $K$ equals the profit-maximizing quantity. The price that rations retail demand before access regulation is $p^*$, which solves

$$(3) \qquad D^0(p^*) = K.$$

The imposition of wholesale access puts the network owner in competition with firms that purchase wholesale access. Wholesale access may displace the retail access as the incumbent firm's customers purchase their retail services from the competitor. Let $\rho$ be the regulated wholesale price of access, and let $A = A(p, \rho)$ be the demand for wholesale access by the network firm's competitors. The demand for wholesale access depends on the network firm's retail price $p$ to reflect retail competition with the firms that purchase wholesale access. Let $Q = D(p, \rho)$ represent the retail demand for the network firm's services after access is granted. The demand for the network firm's retail services depends on the price of wholesale access because the price of wholesale access affects the prices that competitors can charge for their retail services.

Total retail and wholesale demand for the network firm's services can increase or decrease. This means that $D(p, \rho) + A(p, \rho)$ may be greater than, equal to, or less than $D^0(p)$. The regulated price of wholesale access will affect the retail demand for the incumbent firm's services and the demand for wholesale access.

Wholesale access need not be a problem if total demand falls or if there is sufficient excess capacity to satisfy the increased demand. If $p^*$ is the initial price, and $\rho$ is the regulated wholesale rate, then the incumbent firm may accommodate the shift in demand to wholesale users in the short run if $D(p^*, \rho) + A(p^*, \rho) \leq K$.

The price of retail access and the price of mandated access must be such that the demand for capacity is rationed. This means that the new price of retail access $p^{**}$ and the price of mandated access $\rho^*$ must allocate capacity. This requires that total demand for capacity, including retail demand and access demand, must equal network capacity:

$$(4) \qquad D(p^{**}, \rho^*) + A(p^{**}, \rho^*) = K.$$

Because there are two prices, the condition does not specify what the two prices should be. Rather, it determines combinations of the two prices that ration retail and wholesale access to the network firm's capacity. The model is illustrated in Figure 5.2 for the situation in which total demand is increased by wholesale access.

The possible solutions are similar to those discussed with respect to retail access. The first solution is the expansion of network capacity. The fact that the addition of capacity takes time to add may render capacity adjustments infeasible as a short-run solution. The second solution is to adjust the price of retail access to give incentives for consumers to reduce demand along the demand curve. This also requires adjustment of the regulated price of wholesale access to ration the demand for capacity. This is likely the most efficient solution, at least in the short run, when network capacity is fixed. However, to the extent that retail and wholesale access

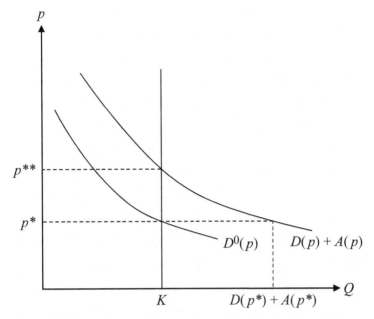

**Figure 5.2.** Excess demand for capacity as a result of wholesale access.

rates are both regulated, as is often the case with telecommunications networks, this solution will be foreclosed.

The only solution that may be feasible in the short run is to reduce demand for network capacity by degrading quality of service, either in terms of reliability or by reducing the variety of services available to the network. In other words, mandating access must necessarily be accompanied by one of the compensating adjustments identified above: higher prices, greater capacity, or reduced services.

Our focus in this section is on the costs of providing capacity to serve this incremental demand. To simplify matters, up to this point we have assumed that all inputs are variable, so that the firm is able to adjust capacity flexibly without incurring adjustment costs. To give regulation the benefit of the doubt, the network firm is able to move along its long-run marginal cost function. Let $C(Q)$ and $\mathrm{MC}(Q)$ be the network firm's long-run cost and marginal cost, respectively.

Finally, suppose that incumbent network firms act as competitive firms that take retail prices as given. The network firm chooses output to maximize profit, $\max_Q pQ - C(Q + A)$, so that network firms equate marginal cost of retail and wholesale access to the retail price:

(5) $$p = \mathrm{MC}(Q + A).$$

Thus, the representative supply curve of a network firm reflects the provision of both retail and wholesale services,

(6) $$Q = S(p) - A,$$

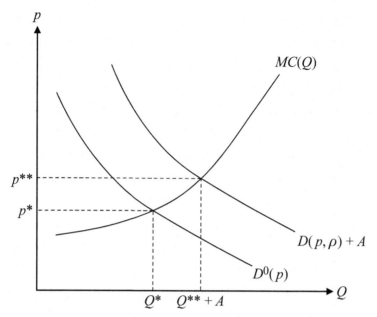

**Figure 5.3.** The market demand for retail access given incremental demand for wholesale access $A$.

where $S(p)$ is the inverse of the marginal cost curve. Taking the regulated wholesale demand for capacity as given, the market-clearing retail price $p^{**}$ solves

$$(7) \qquad\qquad D(p^{**}, \rho) + A = S(p^{**}).$$

Consider the case in which wholesale access shifts out total demand relative to initial demand, as shown in Figure 5.3. Total capacity requirements increase, $Q^{**} + A > Q^*$. If the incumbent firm's demand is less than or equal to its initial demand, it follows from $p^{**} > p^*$ that $Q^{**} = D(p^{**}, \rho)$ is strictly less than $Q^* = D^0(p^*)$.

What are the consequences of such an increase in capacity? All other things equal, particularly if the network firm maintains its quality of service, additional capacity requirements must be met by adding nodes and links to the network or by expanding the capacity of individual nodes and lines. As capacity increases, it may become necessary to change transmission technology, increasing the carrying capacity of switches and lines. The network firm might upgrade parts of the network to incorporate different technologies, such as enhancements in fiber optic facilities. In addition, the efficient configuration of the network is likely to change with substantial increases in capacity. For example, traffic can be consolidated in trunk lines to take advantage of scale economies. This requires the creating of additional hubs and trunk lines.

Changing the level of service provided by the network changes not only the total costs, $C(Q)$, but also the underlying mix of cost-minimizing inputs, because a different mix of inputs is associated with different output levels. In turn, the underlying output and input mix changes the engineering specifications of

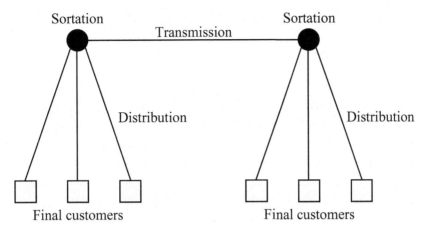

**Figure 5.4** The three stages of production of a network firm: transmission, sortation, and distribution.

the network, which can result in changes in the architecture of the network, as discussed in Chapter 3.

Conversely, if wholesale access shifts total demand down relative to initial demand, the system can operate with less capacity. If the wholesale services are identical, this will reduce capacity utilization and reduce congestion. If wholesale services are distinctly different, there may still be a need to reconfigure the network. Capacity shortages can develop at specific locations in the network that may require configuration.

It is useful to consider the vertical structure of telecommunications. The *operations* of network firms in telecommunications have a three-part vertical structure consisting of three stages of production: (1) transmission, (2) sortation, and (3) distribution. This vertical structure corresponds to what network engineers refer to as *service layers*. The three stages of production in a telecommunications network are evident in postal systems (Sidak and Spulber 1996). The transmission stage in a postal system is the long-distance transportation of large mail shipments that links postal regions. The sortation stage in a postal system refers to the aggregation of mail collected within a region or the disaggregation of mail collected elsewhere for delivery within a region. This sortation or wholesale level includes regional transportation warehouses and both inward and outward sortation. Finally, the distribution stage in postal service refers to delivery to individual customer premises by truck and on foot and to collection from customer premises. The distribution stage also includes local post offices that provide local sortation and serve the delivery and collection functions. The three stages of production or service layers are represented in Figure 5.4.

Consider now the three service layers or stages of production in telecommunications networks. First, the *transmission* stage uses the facilities of the backbone network, including all the nodes and links that connect the large-scale portion of the network. The transmission stage provides *transport services* for aggregate traffic. The aggregate traffic carries telephone calls or data packets in a combined form, much as large containers are used in long-distance freight transportation. The backbone network uses high-capacity trunk lines and switches. The technology of large-scale data pipes generally is fiber optics with various methods of data aggregation and transmission.

Second, *sortation* employs facilities, including switches and routers, that aggregate traffic that is received from the distribution stage or disaggregate traffic that is received from the transmission stage. Traffic originating from the distribution stage must be directed to the proper long-distance transmission facilities, and traffic received from transmission must be directed to the proper local distribution facilities. The sortation stage provides *routing services* that intermediate between access services and transmission services. In a circuit-switched network, we use the term sortation to refer to connections between local distribution and long-distance transmission. In a packet-switched network, individual data packets are aggregated for transmission and disaggregated for distribution, with addresses on individual packets allowing assembly of messages and distribution to final customer premises.

Finally, *distribution* employs links to customers such as the local loop. This production stage is sometimes referred to as part of the "last mile," or the neighborhood, or household-to-the-curb connections. The plant and equipment that connect the customer's facilities to the network provide retail access service to customers. The access service layer originates or terminates the communications of individual customers. Generally, customers are located on the periphery of the network.

Provision of wholesale access places demands on the transmission, sortation, and distribution facilities of the network. The configuration of the network will be altered as the network expands the carrying capacity of these facilities or adds new transmission lines, switches, and distribution facilities to serve competing carriers. These changes are likely to require alteration of the configuration of the network. If the parties obtaining wholesale access serve different customers, there will be changes in distribution facilities. If the pattern of traffic changes due to changes in distribution services, this will create the need for changes at both the sortation and transmission levels.

## 3. Interconnection Access

Like wholesale access, interconnection access has an ambiguous impact on the total demand for network capacity. The addition of customers residing on other networks can induce the customers on the primary network to increase network usage. The increase in traffic can require additional capacity. At the same time, interconnection access can cause demand for network capacity to decrease. Under wholesale access, all of the customers still reside on the primary network. In other words, all of the functions associated with the three service layers described above are still performed by a single network. Although there may be some substitution in terms of which carrier fulfills the merchant activities, the transmission, sortation, and distribution functions are still performed by the primary network.

Interconnection access, in contrast, clearly envisions that some customers will reside on other networks. This means that some of the transmission, sortation, and distribution functions will be satisfied by capacity provided by other networks rather than the primary network. In the most common case, one network will perform the distribution and sortation services associated with origination and a portion of the transmission services before handing the communication off to another network to provide the balance of the transmission services and the sortation and distribution services associated with termination. The fact that many customers will reside on other networks necessarily implies that the other networks may serve as substitutes for, rather than complements to, the primary network. Thus, there is a greater possibility of a reduction in demand for network capacity under interconnection access than under the other forms of access we have discussed.

Interconnection access also has implications for network configuration. Regardless of whether total traffic is increased by interconnection, satisfying regulatory requirements for connection to other networks can require multiple points of entry with elimination of bottlenecks for related traffic. Furthermore, decisions about which technologies to employ in constructing a network depend on the magnitude of the projected demand as well as the feasibility of aggregating traffic to take advantage of the available economies of scale. As noted in Chapter 2, when traffic is large enough, it makes sense for networks to deploy higher fixed-cost technology that reduces the per-unit variable costs of transmission. By diverting traffic onto other networks, imposing interconnection access can render network configurations uneconomical that would otherwise be efficient.

### 4. Platform Access

The impact of platform access on the demand for network capacity is also ambiguous, although for reasons that are different from those for wholesale and interconnection access. Whether it increases or decreases demand depends on the relative benefits of standardization and product variety.

On the one hand, standardization ensures that customers have access to the full range of complementary services that are available. Greater accessibility to complements has the effect of increasing demand for network services. In addition, the fact that providers of complementary services are guaranteed access to all network customers reduces the level of business risk that they confront, which increases the economic viability of complementary service providers. The broader range of complementary service providers should enhance the demand for network capacity still further.

On the other hand, platform access has the inevitable effect of favoring some applications and disfavoring others. Take TCP/IP, for example. One of the most distinctive features about TCP/IP is that it routes packets on a first come, first served basis without regard to the origin of the packets or the application with which they are associated. Although this approach is well suited to traditional Internet applications, such as e-mail and Web browsing, in which delays of a quarter second are unproblematic, it is less well suited to applications that are less tolerant of variations in throughput rates, such as streaming media and Internet telephony (also known as "voice over Internet protocol" or "VoIP"). Moreover, the packet anonymity inherent in TCP/IP restricts the ability to add security features designed to foster e-commerce or to protect against viruses and the other hostile elements that are proliferating on the Internet. To the extent that platform access forecloses the emergence of new, beneficial applications, it causes the demand for network capacity to decrease.

The net impact on network demand thus ultimately depends upon whether the value of standardization dominates the value of product variety, or vice versa. Indeed, if the value of network diversity is sufficiently large, deviating from platform access can change the fundamental structure of the industry. This is because differentiation represents a classic solution to the pressures toward concentration created by the presence of large fixed costs. Varying protocols in ways that target subsegments of the potential customer base can allow networks to generate sufficient revenue to cover costs, notwithstanding their lower sales volumes and higher per-unit costs. It is conceivable that three different networks could coexist: one optimized for traditional Internet applications such as e-mail and Web site access, another for security-sensitive applications such as e-commerce, and a third for time-sensitive applications such as VoIP. By mandating adherence to standardized protocols, platform access can forestall the process by which multiple competitors might emerge.

Platform access also affects the way that networks are configured. The precise location of the points of interface within the network must be determined before the standardized interfaces can be designed. Platform access in effect requires network owners to design their networks to provide service at those interface points according to the relevant standards. The problem is that technological change often causes the optimal interface design as well as the optimal location of the interface points to change over time. Indeed, the inevitable attempts by network providers to shift the points of interconnection in ways that enlarge the scope of services that they provide can represent a valuable source of competition (Bresnahan 1999). By dictating the protocols and locations, platform access can short-circuit the process of network reconfiguration by effectively locking the existing interfaces into place. At best, the natural evolution of network configuration will be delayed. At worst, platform access will preempt the process altogether and prevent innovation.

This danger of an adverse impact on network configuration becomes particularly apparent once it is acknowledged that standard setting is an inherently political process. Whether implemented by the government, consortia of industry participants, or independent standard-setting organizations (ISOs), standard-setting processes have long been subject to accusations of substantive biases, anticompetitive

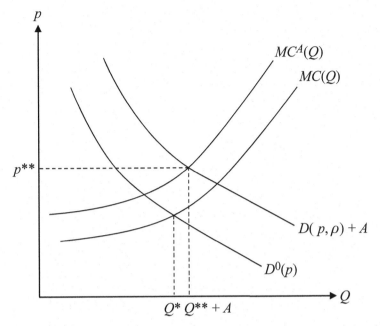

**Figure 5.5.** The effects of unbundled access on costs and demand.

activity, and capture. Platform access has the unfortunate effect of institutionaliz-ing centralized decision making at the expense of allowing decisions about network configuration to take place through a myriad of private choices.

## 5. Unbundled Access

Unbundled access also represents incremental demand for network services that consume network capacity. Thus, unbundled access has effects that are similar to wholesale access. However, unbundled access has significant additional effects. Usage of a portion of the network's elements to provide services affects the perfor-mance of the network overall because the capacity of individual network elements such as lines and switches is limited. Usage of network elements potentially creates bottlenecks that generate congestion for the network overall. Congestion effects translate into increased costs if the network firm maintains quality of service. Because the network does not function as it was designed, the network firm must find a way to restore its functions by rerouting traffic and changing the network's configuration.

To represent these effects, suppose that marginal cost $MC(Q)$ increases to $MC^A(Q)$. This situation is represented in Figure 5.5. Thus, unbundled access shifts out the demand for network capacity while increasing the marginal cost of providing capacity. The result is that the equilibrium retail price increases to reflect both increased capacity usage from the outward shift in demand and increased cost from the upward shift in the marginal cost curve. There is greater crowding out of retail demand. In Figure 5.5, total capacity usage increases, because the demand effect outweighs the cost effect.

However, total capacity usage may fall if the cost effect outweighs the demand effect. In that case, crowding out of retail demand due to increased marginal cost would exceed the mandated demand for capacity due to network access. Thus, unbundled network access would cause total network usage to fall. Regulators should not conclude from this outcome that incremental usage did not affect the network because the reduction in usage is the result of increased costs due to unbundled access.

Consider the impact of unbundled access on the three service layers of the network. At the transmission layer, the network must provide access to transport, including dedicated transport connecting the network switches or wire centers. At the sortation layer, the network must provide various types of services using its switching facilities. Also, the network must provide unbundled access to signaling networks that are used to operate the network. Finally, at the distribution layer, the network must provide the services of local loops to the customers' premises.

Unbundled access is likely to have significant effects on the configuration of the network. Recall that the formal representation of a network involves nodes, links, and values assigned to the links that can represent such information as capacity and costs. By granting competitors access to particular network elements or combinations of network elements, unbundled access affects the characteristics of those network elements from the point of view of the network firm. If another firm has access to a particular link, for example, the capacity available to the network firm is reduced. The network firm would encounter additional costs if it were to expand the capacity of the link. The capacity and cost values assigned to the link must therefore be modified to reflect access to that network element.

A change in the cost of one or more links can significantly alter the design of a network to connect a set of nodes. A change in the cost of one or more links can change the configuration of the least-cost minimum spanning tree network or the least-cost cycle network. Because the design of a network reflects the best combination of elements, unbundled access affects the network design problem in complex ways that extend far beyond the particular network elements affected by access. The reconfiguration of the system thus can involve many network elements that are not directly involved in access.

Because competitors are given the choice of elements in unbundled access regulation, there can be incentives to choose access strategically. Competitors not only will choose those elements they need to create their own system, but they also may choose elements that increase costs to the incumbent network. The firm obtaining unbundled access need only pay for the incremental costs of the elements it obtains under the TELRIC pricing system. However, the firm providing unbundled access pays for the system-wide reconfiguration costs and bears the costs of additional elements called for indirectly by unbundled access because they are not provided to competitors.

## C. Transaction Cost Effects of Access Regulation

If there is displacement of the network firm's demand on a one-for-one basis without any changes in traffic patterns on the network, then the effects of access include the *opportunity costs* of lost returns. The effects of access also include the *transaction costs* to the incumbent network firm that result from dealing with independent distributors. Such transaction costs are incurred whether or not there is displacement of the incumbent network's retail sales.

### 1. Retail Access

The transaction costs of providing retail service are substantial. Telephone companies engage in marketing and sales to individual customers, both households and businesses. They perform the full range of marketing activities including advertising, pricing, promotion, and product design. In contrast to product manufacturers, network firms are service providers who must meter network usage of individual customers including the time, duration, and distance of individual calls and usage of switched services. Corresponding to these metering activities are costly back-office processes for billing customers and receiving payments. In addition, the network firm must make sure that the network's capacity is sufficient to provide services to individual customers. The indivisibility and inherent lag associated with expanding capacity and the sensitivity to variability render decisions about network configuration particularly complex.

This is compounded by the transaction costs associated with making retail services available to all customers. The traditional method for implementing retail access is by having the carrier file a public tariff containing the terms under which the carrier will provide service to any customer. Tariffs are usually subject to regulatory approval before going into force. The process of filing tariffs is notoriously cumbersome, expensive, and time-consuming. The emergence of simplified, notice-oriented regimes has eased these burdens somewhat, but even these regimes impose significant transaction costs on network providers. Having to preannounce and preclear all terms of services also necessarily slows down the pace of change, can deter innovation in pricing and services, and can even facilitate collusion.

Retail access would mean little if the carrier could render it a nullity by charging an exorbitant price. As a result, retail access regimes typically include the requirement that rates be reasonable. The traditional cost-of-service approach to determining the reasonableness of rates is notoriously onerous and difficult to implement, requiring allocations of shared costs and determinations of proper rates of return and the prudence of investment that border on the arbitrary. It also distorts economic efficiency by biasing regulated entities away from production functions that emphasize operating expenses and toward more capital-intensive solutions. Although the institution of price caps was supposed to ameliorate many of these problems, they ultimately did not prove to be the panacea that many thought they would be.

Tariffing also affects the transaction costs faced by customers. The filed-rate doctrine dictates that the tariff defines the entirety of the network–customer relationship. Any deviations from the tariff are preempted, even when both parties agree to alternative terms. This means that customers cannot rely on the representations of the carrier regarding the terms of service and instead must verify the terms of services published in the tariffs. In recent years, regulatory authorities have relaxed this restriction and allowed carriers to petition for waivers that allow them offer more customized services. Whether on balance the transaction costs of negotiating terms of service will exceed or fall short of the cost of verifying the tariff terms is an empirical question. Indeed, the uniformity of application mandated by tariffs effectively prevents networks from customizing solutions to the needs of particular customers. Furthermore, although networks are permitted to impose supply-side price discrimination by imposing price differentials that are cost-justified, tariffs prevent networks from mitigating the effects of nonmarginal cost pricing necessitated by the presence of large fixed costs by engaging in demand-side price discrimination through regimes such as Ramsey pricing.

Imposing retail access thus creates significant transaction costs that would not otherwise exist. These costs must be included in any assessment of the efficiency of imposing retail access.

## 2. Wholesale Access

Wholesale access compels network firms to permit their competitors to act as distributors that perform the merchant activities needed to procure the network services and resell them to final customers. A critical way to determine whether wholesale access is economically efficient is to examine the types of transaction costs that are associated with it. Under the classic Coasian theory of the firm, a function will be brought within the boundary of the firm whenever the transaction costs associated with external provision exceed the costs of monitoring and coordinating the function internally.

Transaction costs thus affect whether vertical integration of merchant activities increases efficiency or whether delegating retail activities to the network's competitors is preferable. Wholesale access compelled by regulators corresponds to vertical divestiture of some of the network firm's retail merchant activities. To examine whether such an arrangement is cost-efficient requires consideration of the transaction costs that the network firm encounters when it deals with an independent retailer or distributor. These transaction costs must be compared with the organizational costs the firm would incur if it were vertically integrated and carried out its own retail activities. These transaction costs and organizational costs are notoriously difficult to measure, but it is worthwhile examining what drives such costs. Most firms, whether manufacturers or service providers, must choose between these two alternatives: contracting with independent distributors versus providing one's own distribution.

Historically, firms that operate telecommunications networks, whether for local or long-distance services or some combination of the two, share an important economic feature. These firms have tended to be vertically integrated. They provide retail services directly to customers, they operate internal processes that correspond to wholesale services, and they are manufacturers of network services by operation of the network. Before the breakup of the Bell System in 1984, AT&T went even further into vertical integration upstream, not only providing both local and long-distance services, but manufacturing customer premises equipment and its own networking equipment through its Western Electric unit. Even further upstream, AT&T conducted extensive R&D through its renowned Bell Laboratories.

One explanation for the full vertical integration of AT&T was that it was a protected and regulated monopoly. As a regulated monopoly, the company may have favored vertical control of any and all activities related to telecommunications. Another explanation is that many firms in the early 1900s favored extensive vertical integration. For example, General Motors, which was founded in 1908, pursued extensive vertical integration under Alfred P. Sloan, and Henry Ford wanted the Ford Motor company to be "From Mine to Finished Car; One Organization" (Thompson 1954, p. 12). AT&T's leader Theodore Vail expressed a similar philosophy in 1908: "One Policy, One System, Universal Service" (AT&T 1911, pp. 18–19). Modern telecommunications firms such as SBC and Verizon are also vertically integrated, combining retail, wholesale, and manufacturing. This might be an accident of history, because the RBOCs are the offspring of AT&T. It might also be that telecommunications firms such as the RBOCs share a legacy of regulation with other network industries that are also vertically integrated, particularly electric power and natural gas.

Because telecommunications companies such as the RBOCs are still subject to state regulation by PUCs and to federal regulation by the FCC, it is difficult to determine what effect regulation has had on their extent of vertical integration. However, some inferences may be drawn by observing the many diverse types of carriers in telecommunications. These companies are subject to different degrees of regulation in the United States and in other countries. The fact that these firms frequently combine retail services with network operation in different market settings and under different regulatory regimes suggests that there are some transaction cost advantages from vertical integration downstream. It is possible that vertical integration at the retail distribution level in telecommunications also may be the result of economic efficiency rather than regulation.

The three stages of production of network services described in the previous section are only a partial description of the network firm. Companies that own and operate networks do much more than manage operations. They perform a host of marketing activities and related management tasks. Network firms, such as telephone companies, perform retail merchant activities. They engage in marketing and sales to provide services to final customers. They operate internal processes that correspond to wholesale merchant activities, aggregating information necessary to

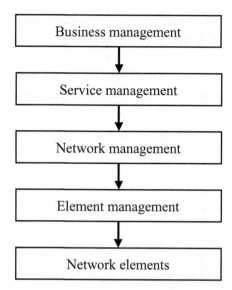

**Figure 5.6.** The five layers of the telecommunications management network (TMN).

providing retail services and interacting with internal manufacturing of network services.

The marketing and coordination functions performed by a network firm are summarized by the telecommunications management network (TMN) concept developed by the International Telecommunications Union, articulated in ITU-T Recommendation M.3000 (1994), and depicted in Figure 5.6. At the highest level is the business management of the company that operates the network; this includes management strategy and budgeting and is referred to as the business-management layer. Next, the service-management layer interacts with customers, for sales and service, and with service providers, for procurement. Then, the network-management layer coordinates the interaction of all network elements to create a functioning network through configuration of the network structure and operations management. The element-management layer is responsible for handling individual network elements, including maintenance and gathering of data on activities and performance for use by network managers. Finally, the network-element layer includes the full range of physical equipment and managed information that form the network facilities.

The TMN concept of hierarchical layers is a good illustration of the complex connections between organizational tasks in a network. At the service management level, the organization interacts in the marketplace with customers and suppliers. These market interactions must be translated into organizational responses through network management. The critical interface between market transactions and network management is where the configuration of the network occurs. The key question is why the three activities – service management, network management, and element management – should be contained within the same organization. The fact that telecommunications firms tend to engage in retail merchant functions suggests that the retail transaction costs are lower for a vertically integrated firm than for a standalone reseller of retail services.

The core activities of the telecommunications management network – service management, network management, and element management – require extensive coordination within the organization. This type of coordination might be difficult to replicate with arm's-length contracts. In principle, under the right market conditions, these activities need not be contained within the same organization. Service management includes retail and wholesale activities that the network firm could outsource to external service providers. Network management could be outsourced to others, just as many companies outsource the management of their internal communications systems. Finally, element management could be outsourced to one or many service providers, just as companies have external service providers that operate or service pieces of equipment such as computers, copy machines, or specialized capital machinery.

The outsourcing question is especially critical for regulatory policy. The outsourcing of service management, particularly the retail service stage, is important because it corresponds to wholesale access. Recall that wholesale access means that the network firm makes its services available on a wholesale basis to a competitor who in turn acts as a retailer. The competitor resells the service to retail customers. Were a company to outsource retailing to dedicated agents, it would retain a considerable measure of control, just as, for example, insurance companies contract with dedicated agents. Alternatively, a company can outsource retailing through contracts with independent distributors who provide additional services. For example, automobile manufacturers form agreements with dealers who also provide repair services in addition to marketing and sales. The provision of wholesale services to competitors involves additional problems such as possible displacement of the firm's own retail sales. However, it is still useful to view wholesale access as analogous to outsourcing of distribution.

Generally, the retail function is outsourced in a competitive market if the transaction costs of dealing with independent retail distributors are less than the organizational costs of dedicated retail within the organization. The firm compares the transaction costs of relying on others with the costs of doing it itself. There is little inherent in telecommunications technology that should prevent outsourcing of the retail function. Indeed, cell phone networks sign up customers through all kinds of independent resellers, including electronics retailers such as Best Buy, Circuit City, or Radio Shack.

The Coasian make-or-buy decision is applied to the choice of whether or not to vertically integrate downstream into retailing. Companies solve this problem in different ways. Most manufacturers rely on independent wholesalers and retailers. Franchise operators, particularly in the restaurant business, often contract with independent owner-operators for retail activities. Most apparel is sold through independent retailers, although a few clothing chains that operate retail and wholesale distribution choose also to manage contracts for manufacturing or even to make their own clothing. In services, such as the insurance industry, the use of an internal sales force versus external independent agents varies across companies. Transportation companies, particularly the airlines, sell both through internal resources and through external retailers, including travel agents and Web-based merchants such as Orbitz, Travelocity, and Expedia.

Thus, retail and wholesale functions tend to be separate from manufacturing. These examples suggest that the transaction costs of using the market tend to be less than the organizational costs of vertical integration into retailing. Some of the advantages of independent retailing stem from the fundamental differences between the activities required for interaction with customers and manufacturing activities. Retailers specialize in marketing, sales, and service, achieving expertise that comes with specialization and division of labor. Retailers obtain economies of scale and scope from large-scale distribution operations, including the operation of large retail stores.

Manufacturers benefit from sales through multiple retailers, each of whom addresses different market segments by offering different locations, shopping experiences, price levels, selections of other products, degrees of convenience, and complementary services. Manufacturers can benefit from competition between retailers, which lowers retail margins to avoid double marginalization. Competition between retailers can increase customer service in some cases, although there is also the risk of a free-rider problem. If discount stores can free ride on customer information provided by specialty stores, then specialty stores will not be able to sustain the markups needed to support provision of information.

Some of the benefits from independent retailing may not be readily available to network firms in telecommunications. The key reason is that the network firm continues to do many of the retailer's jobs. Thus, the network firm continues to perform all activities associated with delivering and distributing the service to the final customer. For example, a telecommunications company provides the retail access plant, such as the local loop that services the household or the commercial establishment. The network firm still keeps track of each individual customer's usage of network services, such as the types of services chosen by the customer (e.g., call waiting, caller ID, call forwarding), as well as metering usage (such as time of day and duration of calls). When manufacturers hand off goods to retailers and wholesalers, they avoid all of the costs of distribution, such as transportation, storage, and operating retail stores, as well as the transaction costs of retail, such as marketing, sales, billing, and record keeping.

This is not the case for network firms that provide wholesale access. Their internal systems still provide almost all of the information used for retail billing and record keeping. In addition, wholesale access is provided to competitors, which places additional demands on the record keeping of the network firm. The network firm must keep track of which customers have been retained and which customers purchase from the competitor, while still generating the same amount of retail service information that would be required without the wholesale access. Because the information is used by the competitor to bill the final customer, the network firm must prepare the billing information for use by the competitor through electronic data interchange (EDI). This again creates transaction costs for the network firm. Thus, owing to the nature of network services, the advantages of outsourcing retail appear to be of limited value. The transaction costs of external retail, other than perhaps the initial signing up of customers, are likely to be higher relative to internal provision. Compelled wholesale access is inefficient if transaction costs of wholesale access exceed the cost of internal retail activities.

To understand the complexity and difficulty of these activities, it is useful to consider operations support systems (OSS) in telecommunications. These systems are used for ordering and providing service for voice, data, and Internet services. A customer places an order for service that leads to various internal systems for the network firm: "workflow, ordering, inventory, circuit design/engineering, provisioning, and activation." Each of these systems has associated software, information, and management processes. Additional systems connect these processes to make sure that the right network facilities are made available and the necessary network elements are activated (International Engineering Consortium [IEC] n.d.).

According to the IEC, "the largest problem [ILECs] face is facilitating access to information residing within their OSSs." The IEC points out that OSSs are "standalone, proprietary mainframe systems that were never designed to share information with external systems or trading partners" (IEC). However, under the 1996 Act, ILECs must allow CLECs access to OSS functions used for obtaining customer data, ordering service, and providing service. To comply with the Act and FCC enforcement requirements, ILECs must invest in substantially modifying or replacing automated internal information systems. There is a substantial cost to making available the network firm's internal systems that can provide service requested by the customers of another firm.

In addition, ILECs must provide external interfaces to allow information exchange with the information systems of CLECs. To achieve systems integration between their systems and those of CLECs, ILECs must invest in complex software and hardware systems for electronic data interchange. CLECs must invest in corresponding systems to gather preorder customer information from ILECs and to transmit order information to ILECs (IEC n.d.). Not only must ILECs and CLECs exchange ordering and confirmations upon customer signup, but also they must share ongoing service usage data for billing purposes. It should be evident that OSS interfaces between ILECs and CLECs require substantial investment and operating costs.

The preceding discussion demonstrates that wholesale access represents a substantial increase in transaction costs in comparison with the internal costs of a vertically integrated telecommunications company. The incumbent telecommunications company experiences little or no reduction in costs from the partial outsourcing of the retail function but substantial incremental costs of modifying systems to give wholesale access to internal management and service systems and incremental costs of systems for interfacing with competitors. CLECs also incur substantial transaction costs to gain access to ILECs' OSSs. Thus, total costs rise because of higher incremental transaction costs.

The problem is that the approach to pricing wholesale access created by the 1996 Act ignores the impact of transaction costs. As noted earlier, the Act requires state PUCs to base wholesale rates on retail rates less *avoided costs*, defined to be the costs "that an incumbent LEC would no longer incur if it were to cease retail operations and instead provide all of its services through resellers" (FCC 1996a, p. 15956). This approach mistakenly ignores the transaction costs associated with wholesale access to resellers (Larson 1997; Larson and Mudd 1999). Thus, the proper discount should be based on net avoided costs:

$$\text{Discount} = \text{Avoided Retail Transactions Costs}$$
$$- \text{Incremental Wholesale Transaction Costs.}$$

The 1996 Act and the FCC consider only the positive component of avoided costs.

The discussion in this section has two main implications. First, the discount based on avoided retailing costs is likely to be *low* because ILECs continue to perform many retail functions and thus avoid very few costs. Second, the incremental transaction costs of selling wholesale services are likely to be *high* because ILECs must reconfigure their OSSs and develop new systems for EDI with CLECs and for provisioning services within its network. Therefore, properly calculated avoided costs may be small or even negative if wholesale transaction costs exceed avoided retail transaction costs.

The fact that such costs may be negative should suggest that compelled wholesale access can be inefficient in a network industry. This is particularly likely when the ILEC continues to provide service to final customers. Such inefficiencies might not deter the FCC because the agency is charged with enforcement of the Act regardless of economic efficiency. Also, wholesale access is directed at other policy goals, such as increasing competition in local exchange services, allowing other carriers to develop brand recognition and to bundle local exchange services with other services such as long distance. However, achieving its other policy objectives does not relieve the government from the obligation to compensate the ILEC for additional transaction costs of wholesale by netting those costs with avoided retail costs in calculating wholesale access rates. If the avoided costs turn out to be negligible or negative, there is little room for other carriers to enter as resellers due to the costs they will incur in marketing and sales and in transacting with the ILEC to procure the wholesale services. The FCC should resist the temptation either to tax the ILEC due to improper calculations of avoided costs or to subsidize the CLEC from some other source of funds such as new taxes on telecommunications services. Instead, regulators should draw the appropriate conclusion that some forms of vertical integration can be cost-efficient relative to market transactions. Delegation of retailing to other firms should be voluntary so that network firms can choose between distribution contracts and vertical integration based on their relative efficiency.

### 3. Interconnection Access

Interconnection access involves somewhat different transaction costs than other forms of access. For example, under wholesale and retail access, access is provided solely at the edges of networks, where customers receive their service. These forms of access do not necessarily require creating new systems to measure network traffic, because the network must necessarily have some basis for metering customer usage already in place. Under interconnection access, in contrast, traffic is handed off at nonterminal points in the core of the network. It thus requires the network to create new systems for metering usage at points that it would not otherwise measure. As the debate about bill and keep demonstrates, the transaction costs of creating such intermediate metering systems can be quite substantial.

Furthermore, as discussed in Chapter 2, decisions about network capacity and configuration depend on detailed information about the magnitude, patterns, and variability of network demand. Accurate information about these parameters is essential if network owners are to calibrate total capacity and configure their networks in a way that preserves reliability and cost-effectiveness. Under both retail and wholesale access, all of the traffic flows remain under the control of the network owner. The same is not true under interconnection access. The fact that traffic will originate and terminate outside the network means that the network owner will not have available all of the information needed to make these decisions. The inability to observe all of the necessary information greatly increases the transaction costs of network management under interconnection access. The problem becomes even more difficult after one recognizes that networks must depend upon their competitors for that information. Imposition of interconnection access thus guarantees that networks will have to incur substantial transaction costs when obtaining and verifying information about network flows.

### 4. Platform Access

Platform access also requires the incurring of substantial transaction costs. Before one can compel a network owner to adhere to certain standards, those standards must be established either by the government, an industry consortium, or an ISO. The process of establishing a standard is time-consuming and costly. In addition, as noted earlier, standards established through a centralized, institutionalized process run the risk of being subject to substantive biases. Furthermore, once the standards have been established, they must be disseminated. The need to provide advance notice of any changes that may affect the interface with providers of complementary services exacerbates the transaction costs still further.

In addition, imposing standards on a network that has already been established can be quite costly. A classic example occurred during the breakup of AT&T, when the court ordered the BOCs to provide "equal access" to all long-distance providers. The problem was that the BOCs had not originally configured their switches to accommodate multiple long-distance providers and had instead employed interfaces that were tightly integrated and rich in information requirement and varied considerably from market to market. The process of reconfiguring and reprogramming the switches was protracted and expensive (Faulhaber 2003).

Regulatory authorities that have imposed platform access have found that simple promulgation of the standards has not been enough. As the Supreme Court has recognized, if the interface is complex, an unwilling network owner will have a virtually unlimited number of means available to frustrate platform access in subtle and essentially undetectable ways (*Trinko*, 540 U.S. at 414). Platform access has historically required that regulators supervise almost every aspect of the business relationship between network owners and complementary service providers. The insertion of the regulators into what would otherwise be a private interaction represents another source of transaction costs.

Nor do these transaction costs end once the standards have been deployed. In a world in which technology changes rapidly, standard setting is necessarily a dynamic process. Optimal interface design and location change over time. This requires ongoing involvement in the standard-setting process. At a minimum, the lag inherent in any standard-setting process and the effort needed to change standards are potential sources of transaction costs. Even worse, to have any beneficial effect, the standard-setting authority must intervene at an early stage in the technology's development, when such judgments are hardest to make (Bresnahan 1999). As such, it may demand a level of technical expertise and ability to anticipate subsequent developments that exceeds the standard-setting body's institutional capability.

At the same time, nonstandardization creates transaction costs of its own. In the absence of a standardized interface, customers and providers of complementary services would have to expend considerable resources determining the compatibility of various services. It cannot be determined *a priori* which set of transaction costs would be larger.

## 5. Unbundled Access

Under the 1996 Act, ILECs must provide CLECs with unbundled access to their network elements and allow the collocation of CLEC equipment. Contrary to popular parlance, CLECs do not buy UNEs from ILECs; they lease facilities, such as lines, switching, or transport. Put differently, CLECs purchase the services of UNEs, so some capacity of an individual UNE owned by an ILEC is devoted to providing services to a CLEC. Thus, UNEs are unbundled contractually, not physically, because they remain bolted in place as part of the existing network.

Providing unbundled access entails transaction costs for the incumbent network firm. The network firm faces two broad categories of transaction costs. First, it incurs organizational costs associated with providing unbundled access to its network to fulfill its side of the transaction. Second, it incurs costs of transacting with the competitors who are purchasing the newly created unbundled services.

The 1996 Act requires ILECs to provide unbundled access to network elements "at any technically feasible point" (47 U.S.C. § 251(c)(3)). In addition to the physical elements employed to provide service, such as transport, switching, signaling, and local loops, unbundled access also involves equipment used in the management of network elements. Also, unbundled access involves equipment used in the management of the network itself. However, unbundled access under the 1996 Act extends far beyond the network element layer. The ILEC must also supply access to call-related databases, such as those used for line information, number portability, toll-free calling, operator services/directory assistance, and the advanced intelligent network database. These databases are at higher logical layers such as element management, network management, or even service management (FCC 2003e).[14]

In addition, ILECs also must provide services that are based on bundles of elements, such as the local loop, switching, and transport. Combinations of elements extend the requirements of unbundled access to higher logical layers of the network firm, particularly to network management and service management. These activities entail organizational costs that are part of the transaction costs of providing unbundled access.

Moreover, the ILEC must also provide CLECs with access to its OSS. This moves UNE access to the highest logical layer – business management systems. This form of UNE access extends regulatory control far beyond network elements into the back office and business management of the network firm. The transaction costs involved in such access are potentially significant because they reach into the very management of the network firm.

Under traditional cost-of-service regulation of telecommunications, electric power, and natural gas utilities, regulators deferred to company management in their control of the firm and confined their attention to rate making and related activities. UNE regulation that extends to regulation of the network firm's management controls has the potential to be significantly more intrusive. Further granting discretion to the network firm's competitors as to what types of management systems are to be accessed only worsens the situation. It is difficult to evaluate the transaction costs of such unbundled access, because management control systems are at the heart of the incumbent firm's decisions about revenues and costs. Suffice it to say that the costs of such interference are potentially equal to the value of the network firm itself. This suggests that regulatory forbearance is preferable to cost recovery for management control systems.

In the absence of unbundled access, the network elements remain at the most basic logical layer of the network. They are the capital equipment that provides services within the context of overall network organization. Network elements provide service inputs to the element management layer, which in turn provides services to the network management layer. Network management integrates the

---

14    This order was vacated on other grounds on judicial review (*U.S. Telecom Ass'n v. FCC*, 359 F.3d 554 (D.C. Cir. 2004)).

many individual elements into a coordinated whole. Service management receives as its inputs the network's output of services that are integrated to form final services. These services are then given to the business management layer, which in turn presents these final services as products to the customers of the network firm.

Unbundled access short-circuits this process, bypassing the internal governance of the network firm. The business management of the network firm must procure the services of individual network elements and bundles of elements. To maintain the system's logical layers requires a fundamental change in organizational structure. The network firm must develop systems that monitor usage of network elements for the purposes of leasing transactions with competitors who have unbundled access to those elements. The network firm must create systems that internally provision the services of network elements for competitors.

The network firm must also develop systems that communicate with competitors to receive orders for the services of network elements. These systems are analogous to the internal systems of the network firm that formerly communicated information about the need for network elements to provide final services to retail customers. Under unbundled access, the incumbent firm's network effectively creates a host of new services that are needed for serving customers who wish to lease network elements.

Just as with wholesale access, unbundled access requires ILECs to provide external interfaces to allow for information exchange with the information systems of CLECs for the leasing of UNEs. The extension of unbundled access also requires systems integration between ILECs and CLECs. The provisioning of a multitude of UNEs requires substantially more detailed software and hardware systems for EDI for gathering CLEC orders and billing for usage of UNEs. These transaction costs are not part of the TELRIC calculation, which is based on the cost of elements to the incumbent network firm. Yet transaction costs can be substantial when so many specific elements are involved. Transaction costs may outweigh equipment costs when facilities leasing involves relatively limited capacity usage.

The notion in the 1996 Act that UNEs should be accessed at any technically feasible point manifestly ignores the economic cost of transactions, because some points of access will be more cost-efficient than others. This issue concerns transaction costs as well. Because of the potentially significant information costs of providing and billing specific network elements, unbundled access should reflect the most efficient means of access in terms of transaction costs for incumbents and their competitors.

### D. The Possibility of Regulatory Arbitrage

Organizing the different types of access into distinct categories inevitably poses significant definitional challenges, particularly in an industry undergoing dynamic technological change. The differences in compensation regimes allow providers to engage in regulatory arbitrage by altering access rates simply by changing the way that service is characterized or by making relatively small technological changes.

Consider, for example, the proper categorization of the first generation of Internet service providers, such as the original services offered by CompuServe, Prodigy, and America Online, which established local offices housing modem banks through which consumers could connect to the Internet through their dial-up modems. It is possible to conceptualize the access provided to these companies in any one of four ways. First, these companies could be regarded simply as end users purchasing business lines from the local telephone company, in which case they would be provided service through retail access (FCC 1983c, 1997). Second, these companies could also be characterized as providing complementary services, in which case they would receive service via platform access. Third, these companies could declare themselves to be specialized local telephone companies serving a single customer and seek service through interconnection access. Fourth, these companies could use unbundled access to purchase all of the elements they needed to provide service to their end customers.

These difficulties would be of little concern if a single, consistent pricing regime applied to all of these different types of access. Unfortunately, different types of access are governed by different ratemaking approaches and are often imposed by different regulatory entities. The result is that different methodologies apply to rates established for each different type of access. The inconsistency raises the possibility that firms will attempt to manipulate the categories of access in order to engage in regulatory arbitrage. The most prominent example of this is the controversy over UNE-P. During the early years following the enactment of the 1996 Act, a carrier that wished to compete without providing any facilities of its own had two choices. The most straightforward way was to invoke the resale provisions of the 1996 Act and purchase wholesale access to the entire network at wholesale prices. Regulators set wholesale access rates at 15–25 percent below full retail (Hazlett 2006). At the same time, resale access could be duplicated simply by using unbundled access to purchase all of the elements necessary to provide local service. In contrast to the top-down approach to wholesale access prices, in which wholesale access prices are based on deductions from full retail prices, UNE access prices are calculated from the bottom up based on the long-run incremental cost of particular network elements. Until the deregulation of mass market switching effectively abolished UNE-P in 2005, new entrants were able to leverage the differences in the pricing to obtain wholesale access at rates substantially below those regulators deemed appropriate.

The opportunity for regulatory arbitrage will remain so long as access mandates remain in place and differences in the methodologies for calculating access rates persist. Eventually, the advent of competition will obviate the need to harmonize these pricing regimes by eliminating the need for imposing access requirements in the first place.

## E. Markets and the Design of Networks

In its 2003 Triennial Review, the FCC stated that in interpreting the access standards it would consider the standards of whether access was "necessary" for entrants and whether entrants' supply plans would be "impaired" otherwise. The FCC also considered the following desired outcomes in its unbundled access regulations: (1) "the rapid introduction of competition in all markets – whether the availability of an unbundled network element is likely to encourage requesting carriers to enter the local market in order to serve the greatest number of consumers as rapidly as possible," (2) "promotion of facilities-based competition, investment and innovation the extent to which the unbundling obligations we adopt will encourage the development of facilities-based competition by competitive LECs, and innovation and investment by both incumbent LECs and competitive LECs, especially for the provision of advanced services," (3) "reduced regulation the extent to which we can encourage investment and innovation by reducing regulatory obligations to provide access to network elements, as alternatives to the incumbent LECs' network elements become available in the future," (4) "certainty in the market how the unbundling obligations . . . can provide the uniformity and predictability that new entrants and fledgling competitors need to develop national and regional business plans[, as well as] . . . whether the rules . . . provide financial markets with reasonable certainty so that carriers can attract the capital they need to execute their business plans to serve the greatest number of consumers," and (5) "administrative practicality whether the unbundling obligations . . . are administratively practical to apply" (FCC 2003e, pp. 16,999–17,000).

The FCC identified a number of factors justifying its continued access regulation including alleged entry barriers, economies of scale, sunk costs, first-mover advantages, and absolute cost advantages. Network effects have sometimes been alleged to confer first-mover advantages (FCC 2003e). But even if the necessary empirical preconditions for network-induced market failure were present, regulatory intervention would not necessarily improve matters. As noted earlier, government-imposed solutions often fall short of efficient outcomes, even when they are implemented to correct a market failure. Not only can a regulatory access regime harm allocative efficiency if access prices are set at inefficient levels, but also regulation can harm dynamic efficiency by causing investment incentives to fall below efficient levels and by creating de facto entry barriers.[15] Thus, regulators confronting a market failure must ask themselves the logically subsidiary question of whether government intervention is likely to improve matters or make them worse.

---

15   Under rate regulation, the traditional governmental response to market failure, regulators explicitly prohibit competitors from entering the market. Although access regulation does not involve any *de jure* prohibition of market entry, it can forestall the emergence of facility-based competition to existing networks by rescuing users from having to invest alternative capacity.

Consider, for example, the particular regulatory decisions associated with any state-sponsored attempt to solve the problems of technological lock-in. Concerns about externalities are inappropriate in the context of a physical network that can be owned. As discussed in Chapter 4, even if customers cannot internalize all of the benefits of their technology adoption decisions, the network owner is in a position to do so through introductory pricing discounts and other inducements. Such intervention would also necessarily require the government to replace clear winners in the technology marketplace with what it believed to be the superior technology. Moreover, in order to be effective, the government must intervene at an early stage in the technology's development, when making such determinations is most difficult. Regulators typically would have to assess technological superiority on the basis of extremely thin information that in most cases would be provided by parties with a direct interest in the outcome of the regulatory process. In addition, decision makers would have to insulate themselves from the types of systematic biases traditionally associated with political decision making (Yoo 2002). Thus, even supporters of network externality theories caution that government intervention might well make the problem worse instead of better (Katz and Shapiro 1994; Bresnahan 1999).

In short, there is ample reason to be skeptical of claims that network economic effects will cause widespread market failure in network industries. Not only are such claims problematic as a theoretical matter; as noted in Chapter 4, they also appear to be essentially devoid of any empirical support. Thus, there appears to be little justification for the belief that basing access rates on actual market transactions would lead to inefficient outcomes. On the contrary, basic economic principles indicate that market-based pricing represents the most appropriate way for ratemaking authorities to ensure that access rates are set at levels that promote both allocative and dynamic efficiency. Two fundamental transformations – the emergence of platform competition and the shift to access regulation – have made direct, facilities-based competition feasible. As a result, the only plausible explanation for failing to implement market-based access rates, that the absence of technological substitutes made market-based pricing impossible, has been drained of its vitality.

\*　　\*　　\*

Our discussion raises the critical question: *what determines the boundaries of a network?* This is closely related to the question of the boundaries of the firm. The answer was first given by Nobel laureate Ronald Coase and is the foundation for the New Institutional Economics. The Coasian theory of the firm in the presence of transaction costs can be specialized to address the boundaries of networks.

Access and the shape of networks depend on organizational costs and market transaction costs. Network connections are external to the firm and take the form of access when the organizational cost of managing the connection as part of a network are greater than market transaction costs. Network connections are internal to the firm when the organizational costs of managing the connection as part of a network are less than market transaction costs.

In the absence of regulatory distortions, transaction costs affect the extent to which companies that own networks are vertically integrated. Of course, retail access for final customers is a product of the network, so networks do not vertically integrate with buyers. Wholesale access is provided when the network owner finds the organizational costs of conducting retail sales greater than the market transaction costs of dealing with independent wholesalers. Unbundled access is provided when the network owner finds the organizational costs of managing particular nodes and links in the network to be greater than the transaction costs of dealing with independent operators. Platform access is provided when the network owner finds the organizational costs of managing the development and supply of complementary services to be greater than the transaction costs of dealing with independent suppliers. In the case of platform access, the relative inefficiencies and reduced creativity of internal provision of complementary services translate into incremental organizational costs. These issues are a special case of vertical integration, but the implications for networks need to be fully addressed.

Interconnection of distinct networks can be more efficient than a unified network if the additional organizational costs of managing the combined networks are greater than the transaction costs associated with interconnection. The costs of managing a network also include costs associated with providing retail access and procuring services as well as facilities management. Thus, the cost savings from separate networks that are interconnected also reflect all the operating costs as well as other types of transaction costs. The costs of interconnecting diverse networks are relatively low compared to the costs of managing networks. Accordingly, the many diverse telecommunications networks, including wireline telecommunications, mobile telephony, the Internet, and cable telephony, can coexist through interconnection.

The efficient boundaries of firms that operate networks are an important but particular case of the boundary of the firm. Networks provide wholesale, unbundled, and platform access when the organizational costs of managing the network are greater than market transaction costs. Networks are vertically integrated when market transaction costs exceed organizational costs. Thus, the efficient boundary of a network firm is determined by tradeoff between costs of controlling the network within an organization and transaction costs of market coordination.

The goal of regulatory policy should be to realize efficiencies in the formation of networks and the organization of network firms. The preceding discussion provides guidance for regulatory and competition policies toward networks. To the extent that markets realize efficient ownership structures and network design, regulatory and antitrust forbearance is appropriate. Public policy in the network industries, particularly compelled access, should be carefully chosen to avoid creating incentives to form inefficient networks.

Access regulations affect the boundaries of networks in a number of important ways. Mandatory access rules and access price regulations affect both the demand and supply of network services. Access regulations are also likely to increase the transaction costs of providing the various forms of access. Network firms compare the costs of market transactions with the governance costs of the network. Access regulations will affect the decisions of networks in terms of network boundaries, network architecture, and interconnection.

If there are distortions in access pricing and in the associated costs of access transactions, firms will make incorrect decisions in designing networks. If access prices and transaction costs are too high due to regulation, some network firms will rely more on internal governance, which could lead to inefficient expansion of network boundaries. If access prices are too low due to regulatory controls, some network firms will have an incentive to reduce the provision of network services, which could lead to inefficient contraction of network boundaries.

Distortions in access prices and transaction costs due to regulation may also affect the demand for network services. Mandatory wholesale and unbundled access will give competitors incentives to rely on other networks rather than expanding or establishing their own networks. Compulsory interconnection at any feasible point may lead competitors to seek inefficient interconnections and to use regulation of interconnection strategically against market rivals. Lowering the costs of interconnection below market rates could provide some networks with an incentive to rely on interconnection when expansion of their own network through investment would be more efficient. Mandatory platform access potentially increases demand for services at inefficient interface points and will increase the costs of network owners who must design their networks to meet regulatory standards at those interface points.

Markets rather than regulators should determine access to networks. Market pricing of access requires the avoidance of mandatory access regulations. Access prices should be determined by voluntary interaction among networks and between networks and their customers, suppliers, and partners. The Coasian analysis of networks shows how distortions in the market for access affect the boundaries and structure of networks.

# 6

# Pricing of Access to Networks

The consensus economic position is that so long as competition is sufficiently robust, market prices represent the best reflection of value. The market price is the outcome of the forces of supply and demand. The supply side of the market reflects the costs to sellers of providing a good; the demand side reflects the benefits to buyers from consuming the good. At market equilibrium, prices are thus determined by the *marginal* cost to sellers of providing a good and the *marginal* benefit to buyers of consuming it. Prices are adjusted through the process of exchange to balance supply and demand and to clear the market, so that prices are further reflections of scarcity, the meeting of consumer wants, and supplier capacities.[1]

Because the services of a network are comparable to the output of other types of production facilities, market processes can allocate them. Markets refer to the interaction of buyers and sellers,[2] with market prices mediating between what buyers are willing to pay and what sellers are willing to accept. Market prices are determined through the activities of suppliers, customers, and intermediaries such as retailers and wholesalers. In the short run, firms raise prices when demand exceeds supply and lower prices when supply exceeds demand. In the long run, suppliers make production decisions by comparing the prices of goods to their costs and to the prices of alternative goods the supplier might provide. Firms will supply a good at some price if the cost of each unit provided and the cost at the margin (the last unit provided) are less than or equal to the market price.

---

1 Classical economists, such as Adam Smith and David Ricardo, well understood that the determination of market equilibrium prices and value results from the interaction of supply and demand, at least in the short run. The classical economists had various cost-based explanations for the determination of the long-run prices of land, labor, and capital. Beginning in the nineteenth century, the marginalist revolution that led to today's neoclassical economy extended the supply-and-demand analysis consistently to output and input markets, in both the short and long run (Jevons 1879; Marshall 1898; Menger 1950; Walras 1954; Blaug 1968).
2 On the role of intermediaries in market allocation mechanisms, see Spulber (1999).

Conversely, consumers make purchasing decisions based on the benefits that they derive from each good and the availability of substitute goods. Consumers will purchase a good at some price if the benefits of each unit consumed at the margin (the last unit consumed) equal or exceed the market price. The price will eventually adjust until the market clears, at which point supply and demand will be in balance and the benefits to consumers will equal or exceed the costs to suppliers. The market price equals the marginal benefit of the good and thus indicates its economic value.

Markets are the best mechanism for allocating network services, so that from the point of view of efficiency, access transactions are preferable to mandatory access. It bears emphasis that markets are effective mechanisms for pricing not only physical products such as automobiles and food, but also services such as transportation or restaurant services. Many types of services are routinely purchased and sold. For example, video rental stores supply their customers with entertainment services corresponding to viewing a movie at home. Movie theaters provide similar entertainment services that require viewing the movie at the theater. Automobile renting and leasing companies supply customers with transportation services. Economic theory does not distinguish between the market allocation of physical products and the market allocation of services. Accordingly, markets can allocate network-generated services just as they do any other type of physical products or services.

The theory of networks is highly useful for modeling network architecture and the boundaries of networks. The theory of networks also is useful for examining the various types of network services and the various types of access transactions. The structure of networks and their associated costs affect the costs of providing different types of network services. Network theory is useful for determining the costs of network facilities as well as the opportunity costs of providing different types of network services. Network theory is an analytical tool and as such it is neutral in terms of its implications for what type of pricing methodology should be used by regulators. Network theory can be applied to study total element long run incremental costs (TELRIC), the efficient component pricing rule (ECPR), or other pricing methodologies.[3]

Network theory does shed light on these methodologies, however. The structure of a network affects its total costs and performance. Because network architecture is important, it may not be feasible to relate total costs to the collection of network elements, because the way that the elements are combined also affects total costs. The interaction between network elements may affect the costs of giving competitors access to network elements. Network theory can be used to understand how access mandates impact the capacity and performance of the network, which can be helpful in determining the opportunity cost component of ECPR.

---

3  The debate over pricing methodologies involves many additional issues, such as historical costs versus replacement costs, the anticipation of obsolescence, and the recovery of opportunity costs of foregone sales.

## A. The Economic Case for Market-Based Pricing of Network Access

### 1. Market Prices, Regulated Prices, and Efficiency

Market prices promote *allocative* and *dynamic* efficiency. As noted in Chapter 4, efficient allocation of goods occurs when the purchasers of a particular good are those who obtain the greatest benefit from consumption and the suppliers of the good are those who incur the lowest cost of production. By allocating the good or service to the person or firm willing to pay the most, the price mechanism ensures that goods and services are placed in the hands of those able to put them to their best use. The price mechanism further ensures that goods and services are provided by the most efficient suppliers.

Dynamic efficiency is attained when economic actors make efficient investment decisions. Investment decisions are efficient when the present discounted value of the marginal returns to invest equals the marginal cost of investment. Market prices provide incentives for efficient investment decisions because the market prices of services created by capital facilities are the best measure of the marginal benefit derived by users of those services. A firm deciding whether to invest in production facilities makes efficient decisions by considering the market value of the products and services to be created with those facilities in comparison to the cost of investment. Similarly, a firm choosing whether to purchase a good or service or to construct its own production facilities makes efficient decisions by comparing the market price of purchasing the good or service with the costs of constructing and operating its own facilities. Because market prices allocate productive capacity efficiently, signaling marginal benefits and marginal cost, they provide an accurate guide for investment decisions.

Regulated prices based on costs tend not to reflect accurately either the value of a good or service or the economic costs of producing the good or service. This results from the failure of regulatory authorities to process information about costs and benefits as effectively as the many buyers and sellers that make up a market (Hayek 1989). Even worse, the government typically must rely on information provided by the regulated entities, which of course have a vested interest in the outcome.

As a result, it is not uncommon for regulated prices to cause allocative inefficiency. To the extent that the regulated prices deviate from market prices, they send incorrect signals to both users and suppliers of access. For example, regulation that sets the price of network access below market rates in effect requires network owners to subsidize competitors. This in turn leads those competitors to adjust the mix of inputs so that they employ reduced quantities of other inputs and greater quantities of network access. In addition, because access is an input used in the production of other goods and services, pricing it below market rates can cause competitors to make inefficient decisions about which markets to enter. Below-market pricing may mislead competitors into believing that the benefits of serving a particular market exceed the costs by understating the true economic costs associated with entering that market. The result not only creates allocative inefficiency in the primary market by stimulating excess demand for network access; it also creates secondary distortions in the markets for other inputs by increasing or reducing demand for those inputs. To the extent that the suppliers of access are regulated utilities, customers as well as the utilities will bear the burden.

In addition to impeding allocative efficiency, regulated pricing can also impede dynamic efficiency.[4] Pricing access at below-market levels discourages existing network owners from investing in additional network capacity. At the same time, it also discourages competing companies from investing in alternative capacity, including substitute network technologies. This effect underscores the extent to which access requirements represent a policy anomaly. The central focus of competition policy is to prevent monopolies from emerging and to break them up whenever they occur. Access requirements, in contrast, leave the bottlenecks in place and instead simply require the monopolist to share its facilities. In addition, by rescuing competing firms from having to supply the relevant input for themselves, compelled access destroys the incentive to invest in alternative network technologies and thus deprives providers of emerging substitute technologies of their natural strategic partners. As a result, compelled access can entrench any supposed bottleneck facility by forestalling the emergence of alternative network technologies. This perverse effect is particularly problematic in technologically dynamic industries, in which the prospects of developing new ways either to circumvent or to compete directly with the alleged bottleneck are the brightest. And even if a regulatory regime were defensible when imposed, it all too often endures long after technological change has eroded its justifications (Posner 1969; Kahn 1971; Breyer 1982).

Finally, there is good reason to question the extent to which rate-making authorities will make the pursuit of economic efficiency their primary goal. As demonstrated by the burgeoning literature on public choice, governmental institutions are subject to a wide variety of pressures that can cause them to redirect competition policy towards noneconomic ends.[5] The system of cross subsidies in telephone pricing aptly illustrates how governmentally established pricing can be directed toward political and social goals, and how such pricing is an imperfect guide to allocating goods and services or making investment decisions (Kaserman and Mayo 1994). A review of a previous attempt by the FCC to promote competition through access requirements provides little basis for optimism in this regard (Yoo 2005).

The end result is similar to any system of rent controls, with demand for the service exceeding supply at the regulated price. Regulated prices do not fully serve their function of rationing user capacity and stimulating the provision of supplier capacity. In contrast, market prices send correct signals to companies that seek

---

4 For an earlier discussion of the dynamic efficiency problems posed by access regulation, see Yoo (2002).

5 See Posner (1969); Stigler (1971); Peltzman (1976); Baumol and Ordover (1985); McChesney (1995).

access as well as to utilities that provide access. Competing companies will have incentives to make economically correct decisions about the amount of services to obtain from the network access supplier and the extent to which they should invest in their own network services.

## 2. The Difference between Market Prices and Unit Costs

As the foregoing discussion demonstrates, the market price of a good is the best indication of its value. The market price of a good can differ from the costs incurred in obtaining the inputs to produce the good because many forces affect market prices through changes in demand and supply. New methods of production that increase efficiency can increase supply at any given price. Changes in the relative prices of inputs, including finance capital, wages, land rents, and the prices of parts and components, have complex effects on supply. The entry and exit of producers and decisions to expand or contract production capacity also impact supply. The introduction of innovative products can create shifts in both demand and supply toward these new products. Changes in consumer tastes and income, as well as changes in the prices of substitute and alternative goods, can also change demand at any given price. Accordingly, the market prices of output are unlikely to correspond to the past costs incurred to produce that output. Even if individual producers try to anticipate output prices in their decisions, market uncertainty will defeat their efforts, leading to randomness in profit margins.

Even if market prices were to reflect accurately the costs of the marginal producer, they would depart from the costs of the inframarginal producer. Costs tend to vary across firms because of differences in business methods, management techniques, production processes, and technological knowledge. Moreover, output value can depart from input costs because firms combine inputs in different ways, creating different products and addressing customer needs differently. Firm heterogeneity strongly implies that the unit costs of any individual firm are likely to differ from the market price. Under the textbook paradigm of perfect competition with identical firms and static demands, efficient entry guarantees that the market price eventually equals the unit cost of firms. This need not be the case when unit costs vary across firms.

Because of uncertainty regarding changes in output markets, there are likely to be deviations between output prices and unit costs. Some firms will earn economic profits and others will suffer economic losses. Moreover, firms often change prices in anticipation of developments because they respond to buyers' and sellers' expectations of future market conditions.[6]

---

6  "The question of fact is thus whether entrepreneurs as a class receive on the average more or less than the normal competitive rate of return on the productive services of person or property which they furnish to the business. The question does not admit to any definitive answer on inductive grounds" (Knight 1921b, p. 364).

Even though competitive forces tend to move market prices toward cost through the exit or improvement of inefficient producers, the past costs of producing a good are likely to differ substantially from current and future costs. Costs fluctuate due to changes in input prices and technology. Market prices correspond more to current and forward-looking demand and supply conditions than to past costs. Traditional cost-of-service regulation *at best* adjusts prices to reflect past costs, thereby permitting regulated rates to depart substantially from market prices. The fundamental reason for this departure is that the economic cost of inputs used to produce some output is not the same as the market price or economic value of an output produced with those inputs. Thus, market prices are necessarily better than regulated rates based on the costs of production.

## B. Determining Market Price

### 1. Pricing Based on External Market Transactions

Arguing that regulatory authorities should base network access rates on market prices leaves open the question of how to determine the prevailing market price. Market transactions constitute the most (if not the only) reliable indicator of individual preferences (Samuelson 1948). Thus, regulators should develop market benchmarks if they choose not to defer to market mechanisms for allocation.

Under standard valuation techniques, the most reliable indicator of market price tends to be the *comparable sales approach*, in which the price charged for the hypothetical transaction in question is determined by prices charged in actual market transactions involving similar goods. Two types of market transactions can serve as external benchmarks for comparable sales. The easiest case occurs when a network owner sells into an external market the same type of access mandated by the government. In that situation, market value determination is simple because comparable sales can serve as a reliable proxy for the services provided.

In addition, market value may be inferred from the price charged for access to a substitute transmission technology providing similar services. Although the historical balkanization of communications has long made such determinations impossible, platform competition has made resort to this type of external benchmark increasingly feasible. Admittedly, transactions involving substitute technologies can be more difficult to apply as benchmarks than transactions using the same type of network. Differences in network configuration can complicate direct comparisons between alternative technologies. For example, although cable television and digital broadcast satellite (DBS) systems have emerged as direct competitors, the wire-based distribution of cable operators is necessarily restricted to a limited geographic area, whereas the footprint of DBS providers is inherently national in scope (Yoo 2003b). In addition, different network technologies provide different performance and reliability levels. As a result, prices must be adjusted to reflect differences in the type of network before any comparisons can be drawn. However complicated such adjustments can be, they are by no means so intractable as to render transactions occurring on alternative networks useless as external benchmarks for inferring market prices.

The other principal market-based valuation method is the *income capitalization approach.* When commercial property is involved, regulators can use a discounted cash-flow analysis to determine the present value of the income that the input is projected to earn. Because the earnings are based on the prices charged in the output markets, it is possible to apply this method even if the input being priced is not sold in any external markets. In addition, because the income capitalization approach is based on data derived from actual market transactions, it is still generally regarded as a reasonably reliable means for determining market value.

## 2. The Second-Best Solution in the Absence of External Markets

If a market benchmark is not available, then an estimate based on the economic costs of providing the service may be necessary. Such an estimate should approximate the market value of all the inputs used to create and operate the network, with the understanding that the market price of network access may be greater or less than that estimate. Over time, the market price of access should reflect the economic cost of all of the inputs used to provide network services. In the short run, however, market prices may deviate from economic cost. If network access is scarce, the market price of access would likely be greater than the replacement cost of the network. Conversely, with a glut of network capacity or obsolescence of network technology, the market price of access would likely be less than the replacement cost of the network. For example, a glut in fiber optic capacity would likely reduce the price of access to below the cost of the network. Accordingly, it is important to distinguish the market value of a good from the economic cost of providing it. However, the economic cost of providing that good, properly estimated, provides a second-best alternative.

The *economic cost* of producing a product or service equals the total opportunity costs of all the inputs used to produce that product or service. An input's *opportunity cost* refers to the value of the best opportunity necessarily foregone, that is, the return from the best alternative employment of that input. The economic cost of producing network services in telecommunications includes the opportunity costs of such inputs as capital, land and land rights, wires, utility poles, towers and fixtures, switches, control systems, construction costs, operation and maintenance expenses, and management costs. The *user costs of capital* associated with owning plants and equipment is equal to the foregone return from the best alternative investment of expenditures made for the plant and equipment.

For most productive inputs, the most accurate measure of opportunity cost is their market value, which is simply the current market price of the input less the avoidable direct costs associated with providing it. The best estimate is based on the opportunity cost of the input. For example, if a company owns a plot of land that it could rent to another company for $500, the opportunity cost of using the land is $500.

*Replacement cost,* which refers to the cost of purchasing an input at current market prices, in turn provides a reasonable approximation of market value. Replacement costs are forward-looking costs of constructing the network and include all costs that the utility would incur to rebuild its system, including capital, land, labor services, and management. Accordingly, the market value of the inputs used to create a network includes the replacement costs of facilities and equipment, as well as the user cost of capital evaluated using the market cost of capital, land and land rights evaluated using current market rents, and current operation and maintenance expenses. A good proxy for replacement cost is the recent purchase cost of the input. Of course recent purchase cost is not a perfect measure, because the market price may have changed since the most recent purchase. Nonetheless, in the absence of indicia that more directly measure market value, replacement cost estimates based on comparable transactions provide a workable measure of market value.

It is now generally accepted that replacement cost is superior to historical cost as a measure of market value, because, as noted by then-Professor Stephen Breyer, "[a] competitive marketplace values assets, not at their historical price, but at their *replacement* value the present cost of obtaining the identical service that the old asset provides" (Breyer 1982, p. 38). Historical costs suffer from several well-recognized infirmities. For example, the market value of an input may have increased or decreased since its purchase. In addition, historical costs will typically be based on the book values of plant and equipment (also known as "embedded costs"). The depreciation schedules allowed under the applicable accounting rules and tax laws often fail to constitute proper economic measures of depreciation. Replacement cost, in contrast, more accurately reflects changes in value. It is true that replacement cost is not without its own complications and that short-term changes can temporarily cause it to rise above or fall below equilibrium levels. Nonetheless, replacement cost provides a reasonably reliable measure of the direct costs of providing network services.

The costs of supplying network access also include transaction costs, discussed at greater length in Chapter 5. The network operator must devote management and employee resources to handling the provision of network services, including arranging network connections, monitoring usage, and billing for network use. In the face of mandated access, the owner of the network must determine the existing demands for capacity and provide additional capacity to meet regulatory requirements. For example, in the case of pole attachments, the FCC initially required that a utility take "all reasonable steps" to expand the capacity of its poles, ducts, conduits, and even rights of way upon request by telecommunications carriers and cable operators. Moreover, the FCC still requires that electric utilities verify the amount of space that they would like to reserve for themselves. This provision of pole attachment services may also require that utility owners accommodate those telecommunications or cable TV companies seeking access that is more convenient or less expensive than producing their own system of poles (FCC 1996c).[7] Transaction costs significantly affect prices and decisions in competitive markets. They may appear intangible to regulators and thus may be difficult for those subject to access requirements to recover.

### 3. The Efficient Component Pricing Rule

As emphasized thus far, pricing access to a network refers to the prices attached to the services generated by the entire network. An alternative regulatory approach to network access grants users the services of particular *inputs* to the network rather than the output of services from the network as a whole. This regulatory scheme originated with railroad trackage rights, whereby the Interstate Commerce Commission gave third-party operators access rights to other railroads' track (49 U.S.C. § 11102(a)). The scheme continues in the Telecommunications Act of 1996, which mandates a very different type of network access based on the use of the services of individual *components* of the network rather than the services of the network itself. Thus, this approach focuses on the services of network inputs rather than the outputs. For example, with regard to network components such as the local loop, switches, or other facilities (called "network elements"), the 1996 Act requires that incumbent local exchange carriers (LECs) provide "nondiscriminatory access . . . on an unbundled basis at any technically feasible point." Such an access requirement is analogous to requiring that a manufacturer provide another company with the use of a piece of capital equipment, such as a machine tool. Incumbent LECs also have the duty to provide "physical collocation of equipment necessary for interconnection or access to unbundled network elements at the premises of the local exchange carrier" (47 U.S.C. § 251(c)(3) & (6)). Collocation corresponds to a manufacturer allowing another company to locate its equipment in the manufacturer's factory.

Regulating access to inputs raises some of the same issues as regulating access to the services provided by the network as a whole. The best way to price access to inputs is to consider the market price of similar access. If a market benchmark for access is not available, it is necessary to resort to cost-based estimates of providing access to the input.

It is misleading to assume, as does the FCC, that the cost to the network of providing the use of an input is confined to the direct cost of that input.[8] The input is

---

7  This order was affirmed in part and reversed in part on judicial review (*Southern Co. v. FCC*, 293 F.3d 1338, 1346–47 (11th Cir. 2002)).

8  As will be discussed in greater detail in Chapter 8, the FCC issued regulations requiring that prices for the unbundled access to network elements be based on each element's total element long run incremental cost (TELRIC). This cost notion corresponds with the direct cost that a manufacturer would incur in providing another company with the usage of a piece of capital equipment in the manufacturer's factory. It does not include any factors designed to capture opportunity costs.

part of a network, and accordingly, another company's use of a network component necessarily has an impact on the output of services using the network. The network element's capacity to provide network services is correspondingly diminished, thus reducing the output of services by the network itself. To take a simple example, a set of tires for an automobile may cost only $400, but allowing another motorist to use the tires precludes the owner using the automobile. The foregone value of the entire automobile might then be $20,000. In the same way, the cost of allowing competing telecommunications companies access to unbundled network elements depends not only on the direct cost of providing that element, but also on the indirect cost of removing the services of that element from the incumbent telephone company's network. Accordingly, the cost of providing access to unbundled network elements should be measured in terms of the reduction in overall network services that results from another company's use of a network element for another purpose.

The proper cost valuation of making an input available is the direct cost of the input plus the reduction in the value of the output. Thus, prices set at the economic cost of an input must represent the sum of the direct incremental cost of providing the input and the opportunity costs associated with providing the input to a competitor. The analytical methodology for setting input access prices at these levels is known as the efficient component pricing rule (ECPR),[9] which would set access prices according to the following formula:

access price = incumbent's per-unit incremental cost of providing access
+ the incumbent's opportunity cost of providing the unbundled
input.

Because another company's use of network elements potentially reduces the services that the network can provide, the correct price of those network elements depends on what the company could have obtained by selling network services in a competitive market. Thus, the market price of network services, the *outputs* of the network, should be used as the basis for determining the value of access to the services of network components, the *inputs* of the network. In the absence of market prices for network output, the opportunity cost calculation can be based on the regulated rates for the incumbent firm's output.

We acknowledge that allocating the retail markup among multiple products using ECPR (or any other access pricing method) poses conceptual and administrative problems. For example, if a competitor were to lease two or more network elements from an incumbent LEC, it would be improper to include the entire retail

---

9 The ECPR concept originally appeared in Willig (1979); see also Baumol (1983) and Baumol and Sidak (1994), suggesting that local exchange carriers be allowed to sell necessary inputs to their competitors at a price that reflects all costs, including opportunity costs. For further discussion, see Sidak and Spulber (1997a). For a model of competition with ECPR pricing, see Sidak and Spulber (1997c).

markup in the opportunity cost component for both elements, as this would in effect allow the incumbent LEC to recover twice for the same markup. The retail markup could be divided among the various elements, but doing so would require some method (probably based on cost accounting) for apportioning the markup to particular elements. While this problem is seen most clearly when the same competitor leases both elements, the identical problem would arise if two different competitors were to lease the same elements or even two different elements in the same chain of production. Although the allocation of foregone retail margin to particular components is inevitably arbitrary, such problems are endemic to any system of establishing prices for inputs. Apportioning the foregone retail margin should not prove any more intractable than the apportionment of common costs that must occur under any regulatory scheme that relies on compelled access (FCC 1996c). In any event, the pricing of the element should at least cover its direct incremental cost, to avoid cross subsidization.

The market-determined efficient component pricing rule (M-ECPR) adjusts the calculation of opportunity costs by using a benchmark market price (if one exists), rather than regulated rates, for the incumbent firm's output. It is again likely that regulated rates for network services will not correspond to the market price of competing alternatives. Thus, the M-ECPR provides a method of adjusting access prices to reflect market prices of network services, thus promoting efficient allocation of network services as well as dynamic efficiency of investment decisions (Sidak and Spulber 1997a).

Any regulatory method that bases access prices solely on production costs without taking market demand into account will likely lead to allocative and dynamic inefficiency. The cost of providing access is not simply production cost, but also includes the value to the owner of the best opportunity foregone. Thus, access prices must include an opportunity cost component, preferably based on market prices, to reflect market demand for access. Including opportunity costs in access reflects the most fundamental economic principles.

## C. The Consistency between Network Costs and Market Pricing

Fundamental economic principles thus indicate that efficiency would best be promoted if network access prices were based on the market value of the relevant inputs. If direct market-based indicia are not available, regulatory authorities should use a methodology such as ECPR that includes the direct costs as well as the opportunity costs of providing the input. That said, some markets contain features that can cause them to fail to produce outcomes that promote efficiency. In particular, barriers to entry by new competitors may constitute a cause of market failure, particularly if the incumbent is a monopolist. The existence of barriers to entry can provide a monopoly incumbent with the market power to distort prices away from efficient levels. As noted in Chapter 4, some commentators have suggested that network industries possess features, such as sunk costs, economies of scale and scope, and network economic effects, that may deter entry in ways that can cause market outcomes to deviate from efficient levels.

The analysis that follows refutes those arguments. As a preliminary matter, the standard discussions of entry barriers assume that they are an exogenous feature of technology (Stigler 1968). In fact, companies choose their technology, by carrying out research and development and by choosing production methods and product features. Because many aspects of technology are endogenous, it is thus likely that competitors will find their way around technological impediments to entry (Spulber 2002a). Moreover, most of these features, which are not unique to network industries, are easily taken into account by traditional price mechanisms. Because these network features do not serve to deter entry, potential competition by new entrants will discipline established firms and is likely to lead to competitive pricing and innovation. Even if entry barriers exist, multiple incumbents may compete with each other, leading to competitive prices.

## 1. Economies of Scale and Scope

As we explained in Chapters 2 and 4, economies of scale and scope exist in networks. Economies of scale exist for a single-product firm if unit costs decline as a function of output.[10] For a multiple-product firm, economies of scale mean that total production costs exceed the total of each output multiplied by its marginal cost. Networks certainly exhibit economies of scale. Large-scale networks can employ advanced high-capacity switches. Moreover, a firm building and operating a large network benefits from economies of scale because it can spread the overhead costs associated with construction and maintenance over a larger set of activities. Economies of scale may also be present because of volume–surface relationships, so that the volume of a conduit can be expanded with a less-than-proportional increase in the surface. Moreover, the unit costs of capacity in a transmission line decline because the necessary cost of constructing the conduit remains fixed regardless of the number of transmission wires placed inside the conduit. Therefore, telecom companies find that the incremental cost of installing additional fiber capacity during initial installation is less than the actual unit cost of installing fiber capacity.

Economies of scope exist if a company achieves cost economies by producing goods in combination rather than separately. Because networks can use common facilities to provide multiple services, networks also contain economies of scope. For example, the same switch can provide multiple services such as call waiting and call forwarding. A network's economies of scope can also derive from its structure. For example, if a network's products are viewed as connections between pairs of network users, then rather than operating a point-to-point network, traffic can be aggregated in trunk lines with points reached by distribution or feeder lines. By

10   Much of the discussion in this section draws upon Spulber (1995, 2002a).

realizing economies of scale in the trunk lines, the firm achieves economies of scope in the production of multiple connections.

Economies of scale and scope exist in practically any industry. For example, in the automobile industry, the unit cost of producing an automobile is lower the more automobiles a manufacturer produces. Producing only a few cars requires making them practically by hand. Producing many cars allows a manufacturer to develop a large plant that benefits from automation as well as specialization and division of labor, as recognized by Adam Smith (1776). Economies of scope also explain why an automobile manufacturer can save costs by producing many types of cars: the company shares the common costs of manufacturing, engineering, and management across multiple product lines.

Contrary to the suggestions of some scholars,[11] the presence of cost economies in manufacturing does not prevent markets from allocating goods and services that are produced with economies of scale. Multiple producers can have economies of scale and scope and compete with each other in supplying goods and services. For example, automobile manufacturers compete with each other to sell cars unhindered by the presence of cost economies in manufacturing. There is no *a priori* reason that markets for telecommunications services should differ in any way. Multiple networks can operate with economies of scale and scope and still compete to supply services to customers. Market prices thus continue to be an accurate measure of value.

Sufficient scale relative to the size of the market results in a natural monopoly. A given industry is said to exhibit natural monopoly characteristics if the cost function derived from the underlying technology is subadditive, that is, if a single firm can supply the entire market at lower cost than could two or more firms. If the technology of local telephone service were to exhibit natural monopoly characteristics, then a single firm could construct and operate that network at a lower cost than could two or more firms. Multiproduct cost functions are said to exhibit natural monopoly characteristics if and only if the cost function derived from the underlying technology is subadditive across products. That is, cost functions exhibit natural monopoly characteristics when the costs incurred by a single firm producing the entire set of products are less than the costs that would result if the same production were divided between two firms.

The existence of a natural monopoly does not necessarily preclude competitive entry, however. For example, even if a particular telecommunications technology were to exhibit natural monopoly characteristics, providers could still achieve efficient retail prices if they were required to compete through periodic auctions for the right to serve the market.[12] Moreover, proponents of contestability theory (introduced in Chapter 4) have demonstrated that so long as entry and exit are easy, the potential for new entry can drive prices toward competitive levels even if

---

11  For our initial discussion of entry barriers, see Chapter 4.

12  Demsetz (1968); Posner (1972); Zupan (1989). But see Williamson (1976) challenging Posner's proposal.

the technology makes it most efficient for a single firm to serve the entire market (Baumol et al. 1982). Thus, even if the incumbent firm prices at cost, there will still be situations in which it cannot set a price that sustains its position against entry.

Moreover, natural monopoly technology need not impede competition, because the technology of entrants can differ from that of incumbents. The standard textbook definition of natural monopoly, which underlies most public policy discussions, presumes that incumbents and entrants have the same cost function and the same underlying technology. Under this theory, there is not enough room in the market for more than one firm, and an entrant could add little to productive capacity (Baumol et al. 1982). It is unrealistic, however, to assume that the incumbent and the entrant will employ the same technology. Given the rapid pace of technological change in telecommunications, an entrant can operate a network with a different configuration than the incumbent's. For example, an incumbent might operate a traditional telecommunications network with twisted copper wire, a century-old technology, whereas an entrant might offer wireless service. Other transmission technologies including coaxial cable television systems, fiber-optic cable, various land-based wireless systems, and satellite-based systems have different cost and performance properties. Transmission networks' various functions, including telephony, mobile communications, data transmission, and video, suggest that different transmission technologies are suited to different uses. As a result, entrants that offer specialized networks targeted to particular applications are likely to utilize technologies different from those used by the incumbent. Moreover, the entrant can target specialized market segments without duplicating the incumbent's system (Spulber 1995, 2002a). Competition from Internet telephony, cable telephony, and wireless provides alternatives to the traditional telephone system. Thus, competitive markets for network services can form, and market prices continue to be an accurate measure of value.

## 2. Sunk Costs

The substantial sunk costs in establishing telecommunications networks, particularly the traditional wireline network, do not prevent markets from allocating network services or prevent market prices from representing an accurate measure of value. Sunk costs are present in most industries, to an extent, and are generally accepted as reasonable business risks with few implications for the performance of market transactions. For example, expenditures for research, development, and marketing are generally regarded as sunk investments. Moreover, most forms of manufacturing entail sunk costs in the form of capital equipment, whether used for manufacturing automobiles or extracting crude oil. These costs in no way prevent market allocation of the end products. In other words, the method of manufacture does not alter the ability of market transactions to allocate a good or service. The telecommunications industry works similarly, although it requires nonrecoverable expenditures in plant and equipment, namely wires and switches.

Commentators and judges often argue that sunk costs prevent competition in telecommunications services and hence cause market failure.[13] In particular, sunk costs are an entry barrier if entrants need to make irreversible investments in capacity whereas incumbents have already incurred these costs.[14] These commentators and judges argue that the incumbent need only price goods or services to recover operating expenses and incremental capital expenditures, because it has already overcome the irreversible investment costs of entry. An entrant, in contrast, must anticipate earnings exceeding operating costs, incremental investment, and the irreversible costs of establishing its facilities before deciding to enter.[15] Richard Posner points out, however, that nonrecurring costs of entry are "irrelevant if there are small firms in the market that can grow to be large firms." Moreover, "there is grave doubt whether there are important nonrecurring costs of entry barriers to entry in the true sense." Posner further notes that the capital required for entry is not a barrier because this cost should be comparable to that of firms already in the market (Posner 1976, p. 92).

Potential entrants into an industry have many ways to reduce the risks associated with nonrecoverable expenditures, including contracting with customers before making irreversible investments and entering into joint ventures or mergers with incumbents.[16] Furthermore, in competitive markets, duplication of investment often occurs. The entry of excess or insufficient capacity can take place as a consequence of uncertainty regarding costs, technology, or market demand. Temporary overcapacity is part of the competitive process and certainly does not indicate the presence of market failure. Indeed, periods of excess capacity, often observed in a variety of industries, demonstrate that sunk costs are unlikely to deter vigorous competition. The same reasoning applies to the telecommunications industry in the absence of regulatory intervention that favors or penalizes incumbents.

Technological change further mutes the impact of sunk costs on entrants. Entrants commit capital resources in those markets or market segments in which they expect to earn competitive returns on their investments. The sunk costs involved in establishing a telecommunications system, given currently available technologies, are no different from irreversible investments in any other competitive market. Concern over sunk costs in telecommunications may be due to the substantial level of investment needed to establish a traditional telecommunications network, and in particular to the ubiquity of the regulated Bell System monopoly.

---

13　On the view that sunk costs constitute a barrier to entry, see Baumol and Willig (1981); Baumol et al. (1982); see also Goldberg (1976) arguing that sunk costs justify regulatory intervention. For the argument that sunk costs create a barrier to entry in the telecommunications industry, see *United States v. W. Elec. Co.*, 673 F. Supp. 525, 538 (D.D.C. 1987), *aff'd in part, rev'd in part*, 900 F.2d 283 (D.C. Cir. 1990); Hausman (1995). But see Kaserman and Mayo (2002) criticizing Hausman's conclusions.

14　*Verizon Commc'ns Inc. v. FCC*, 535 U.S. 467, 546–47 (2002).

15　Baumol and Willig (1981). According to George Stigler (1968), barriers to entry are long-run costs that are imposed on entrants but not on incumbents.

16　The following discussion is based on Spulber (1989, 1995).

This is a quantitative difference but hardly a qualitative one; entrants can invest smaller amounts to create networks targeted at particular customers and specific services.

As in natural monopoly analysis, the argument that sunk costs are a barrier to entry also depends in part on the similarity of the incumbent's and entrant's technology. Yet an entrant need not duplicate the incumbent's network. An entrant with lower operating costs could be assured of recovering at least the difference between the incumbent's operating costs and the entrant's own operating costs, which could well be sufficient to recover the costs of entry. This scenario is likely because technological change in telecommunications, such as the application of microprocessors in switching, potentially lowers the costs of operating networks. By differentiating its offerings through branding, customer service, and location, an entrant gains incremental revenues to cover the costs of entry. New technologies offer enhanced performance, such as the mobility of wireless services and the increased bandwidth of coaxial and fiber-optic systems, thus allowing competition with established networks.

Technological change has even altered the need to sink costs into a telecommunications network. For example, wireless technologies avoid customer-specific, irreversible investment for the "last mile" to the customer's location, because wireless transmission towers can be relocated. Thus, even if substantial sunk costs are required to reproduce the incumbent's wireline network, a wireless alternative may be an effective competitor without the same sunk costs. Accordingly, sunk costs in telecommunications need not impede the market allocation of telecommunications services.

## D. Regulatory Approaches to Setting Rates in Regulated Industries

Conventional economic theory suggests that access rates in network industries promote economic efficiency only if they are based on market prices. If market-based pricing is unavailable, then the appropriate second-best solution is to base rates on the economic costs of providing access, a concept that embraces both direct incremental costs and opportunity costs. The classic rate-making approach taken by regulatory authorities, however, focuses solely on direct incremental costs and excludes opportunity costs. Even regulatory authorities that are willing in principle to regard opportunity costs in their rate-making calculus in practice eliminate opportunity costs by positing that they are zero. The following discussion analyzes the flaws in both of these approaches.

### 1. Direct Cost

The overwhelming majority of regulatory authorities have established rates solely on the basis of direct costs. The dominant initial position was the "fair value" principle associated with the landmark decision in *Smyth v. Ames*, which required that rates be based on the replacement cost of the assets used to provide the service. The Court based its preference for replacement costs on the recognition that if the regulated entity constituted a natural monopoly, by definition no external transactions would exist that could serve as the basis for market-based pricing.[17] At the same time, parties who obtained service under a regulated rate always had the option of constructing a substitute facility. This meant that in the long run, replacement cost would tend to reflect market demand. Although in some circumstances technological and functional obsolescence could cause replacement cost to be a misleading reflection of market value, in the absence of data based on actual transactions it remained a useful proxy. As discussed in Chapter 4, pragmatic considerations of implementability led Justice Brandeis to favor basing rates on historical cost.

Over the decades, regulatory authorities have employed both replacement cost and historical cost methodologies in implementing both rate regulation and access regulation. The unifying thread to these approaches was their commitment to basing rates on direct cost and their refusal to take opportunity cost or market-based influence into account. As discussed in Chapter 4, regulatory approaches that base rates solely on direct costs fail to reflect that value is determined by demand-side considerations as well as supply-side considerations and that basic economic theory requires the inclusion of some factor to reflect the earning potential of the regulated input.

The only conceivable justification for failing to base rates on market prices is that the absence of comparable transactions rendered such an attempt inherently circular. Indeed, as the foregoing discussion reveals, Justice Brandeis and the regulatory authorities and courts that followed his lead relied on this reasoning to justify their advocacy of cost-based approaches. What modern regulatory authorities have failed to recognize is that the emergence of platform competition and the shift from rate regulation to access regulation have now made it possible to base rates on market benchmarks. The possibility of input substitution allows external markets for inputs to exist even in the absence of external markets for final goods. In addition, the *raison d'être* of access regulation is to foster competition in final goods markets. Any success in doing so will only serve to further undercut the justification for refusing to base rates on market transactions. The shift from output to input regulation has also undermined the previously proffered reasons for rejecting the income capitalization approach. When regulation focuses on the rate charged for an input rather than for a final good, the regulated price becomes only one of many factors that determines the good's overall earning potential. As

---

17   169 U.S. 466, 544–47 (1898). Although using replacement cost as the rate base is associated with *Smyth v. Ames*, the opinion offered a laundry list of considerations to guide the rate-making determination. Replacement cost did not become clearly established until the next year in *San Diego Land & Town Co. v. City of National City*, 174 U.S. 739, 757 (1899). See generally Siegel (1984).

long as the input remains only one component of the overall good, the income capitalization approach is not tautological. The degree of circularity will be limited to the percentage of the total cost of the final good represented by the regulated input.

Equally important is the manner in which technological change has allowed competition among different network platforms to develop. The availability of substitute networks employing alternative means of transmission has in turn created external markets that now make it possible for regulatory authorities to base rates on prices charged in actual market transactions. In addition, the advent of facilities-based competition in turn can lead to deregulation of the rates charged for the final good, which will eliminate the circularity inherent in the income capitalization approach.

In short, two fundamental changes are transforming the basic approach to regulating network industries: the development of platform competition and the shift to access regulation. These changes undercut the rationale underlying rate-making authorities' decisions both to base rates on some measure of direct costs and to exclude from their calculus components designed to reflect earning potential. Together, the development of platform competition and the shift to access regulation have rendered continued adherence to that approach untenable and mandate, as a matter of economic policy, that regulatory authorities begin to base access rates on market prices.

## 2. Excess Capacity and Zero Opportunity Costs

Courts that have recognized the importance of ensuring that access rates contain some measure of opportunity cost have begun to employ a different gambit to justify basing access rates solely on direct incremental costs by positing that opportunity costs are zero. In *Loretto v. Teleprompter Manhattan CATV Corp.*, for example, the State of New York replaced a privately negotiated system, in which cable companies that wished to lay cable television wires across a given apartment building would pay the building owner a standard rate of five percent of the revenue realized from that building, with a regulatory regime that accorded building owners a grand total of one dollar in compensation.[18] In a decision that was ultimately overturned by the U.S. Supreme Court, the New York Court of Appeals ruled that this nominal compensation represented a fair return to the building owner, given that the equipment in question occupied "an area of the building for which she does not claim to have any other use."[19] According to the court, then, the opportunity cost of occupying property not currently employed for other purposes was, in effect, zero. The concurring opinion sounded a similar note when it offered that "if the

---

18  458 U.S. 419, 423–25 (1982). The U.S. Supreme Court's *Loretto* opinion is analyzed in greater detail in Chapter 7.

19  423 N.E.2d 320, 333 (N.Y. 1981), *rev'd*, 458 U.S. 419, 421 (1982).

installation of a cable substantially interfere[d] with the owner's present or future use of the building, we must presume that the [State] would award reasonable compensation for the taking pursuant to its regulations."[20]

The point is made even more dramatically in the Eleventh Circuit's decision in *Alabama Power Co. v. FCC*, sustaining the compensation regime established under the Pole Attachments Act. In that case, the court acknowledged the importance of according the owners of networks of utility poles the fair market value of access to their poles, which included the pole owner's opportunity costs. The court nonetheless sustained a regime that based rates solely on direct incremental costs on the ground that one person's use of the network does not necessarily preclude another person's use. Thus, so long as excess network capacity exists, the grant of a right of access does not foreclose any opportunities to sell space to other interested firms. The court concluded, then, that the opportunity cost of allowing another party to access the network was zero. Therefore, the court held that access rates need not include compensation for opportunity costs unless (1) the network was at full capacity and (2) other parties sought access, or the network owner had a higher-valued use for that capacity.[21]

These opinions ignore certain aspects of networks' infrastructure investments that make excess capacity inevitable. Capacity in network industries is notoriously "lumpy" in that it can only be efficiently added in large, discrete quantities. In addition, if the needs of network users are to be met, such capacity must necessarily be added before it is actually needed, a problem that is particularly acute for carriers of last resort who are obligated to provide service to anyone who requests it.[22] The tendency toward excess capacity is exacerbated further by the manner in which excess capacity can enhance network reliability and provide insurance against unforeseeable variability in demand. These qualities make excess capacity a feature that is endemic to all networks. In addition, these courts have fallen into the same trap as computer system managers that have allowed additional users free use of what, at the time, appeared to be excess capacity. That is, this approach overlooks the fact that use of what appears to be excess capacity imposes real costs by hastening the need for additional capacity. The fact that the use of the facility does not consume the facility is of no consequence. As we have pointed out earlier, this is a quality that is inherent in all physical networks and, to some extent, in capital assets generally.

Finally, even assuming for the sake of argument that the costs associated with allowing access to a building were zero, it does not necessarily follow that nominal compensation is sufficient to make the building owner whole. Economic analysis indicates that the price charged by the building owner would be determined in part by the amount that other potential users of the same resources might be willing to

---

20   423 N.E.2d at 336 (Gabrielli, J., concurring).

21   311 F.3d 1357, 1367–71 (11th Cir. 2002).

22   See Sidak and Spulber (1997a) and Baumol and Sidak (2002).

pay. The price would also be determined by the value of that access to the person purchasing it.[23] In other words, the assumption that networks with excess capacity face zero opportunity costs ignores the fact that market value is determined in part by demand-side considerations that are independent of any supply-side, cost-oriented considerations. The mere fact that access to the facility has value to the party seeking access gives the facility's owner both the incentive and the ability to insist on receiving more than nominal compensation.

The facts of *Loretto* provide an apt illustration of these basic concepts. The value of the right to attach a cable wire to an apartment building is not determined by the costs of constructing a half-inch strip across the roof and down the face of an apartment building, as a rate-making approach based on historical or replacement cost might suggest. In addition, the fact that attaching a cable television wire to a building does not consume the building does not mean that the right to attach has no real value absent proof that the building owner had some other use for the same space. Our analysis indicates instead that the value of the right to attach the cable wire to an apartment building is determined by the value of the services that are provided through those wires. Indeed, it is no surprise that the pricing arrangement negotiated among the parties before the state began regulating such access was based on a percentage of the value of the services provided by the cable company.

23   To use a concrete example, the fact that a summer home may be unoccupied during the winter would arguably justify regarding the home as having excess capacity. It does not follow, however, that the government would be justified in forcing the owner to rent the home to another person who wished to occupy it during the winter for only a nominal fee. The rent that normally would be charged would depend upon the number of other possible renters as well as the amount that the owner could obtain by refusing to contract at a particular price.

# 7

# Constitutional Limits on the Pricing
## of Access to Networks

The emergence of platform competition and the shift from rate regulation to access regulation compel a different constitutional analysis of regulation. Because rate regulation simply adjusts the terms under which parties can contract, it represents the type of nonpossessory regulation traditionally subjected to a rather permissive standard of review under the Takings Clause. This standard requires only that the rate fall within a zone of reasonableness. Compelling access to a physical network, in contrast, invariably requires the network owner to permit third parties to locate equipment on its property. As such, access regulations are subject to the more restrictive standards associated with the Court's physical takings jurisprudence. Unlike nonpossessory regulations, in which reductions in the value of property are not necessarily compensable, physical takings necessarily command market-value compensation. Principles of constitutional law thus reinforce the basic economic conclusion that network access should be priced at market levels.

### A. The Distinction between Physical and Nonpossessory Takings

#### 1. The Emergence of the Nonpossessory Takings Doctrine

Initially, the Takings Clause was believed to protect only against direct government appropriations of private property or invasions that effectively divested the owner of possession as though the government formally condemned the property. Government actions that merely reduced property value did not qualify as takings.[1] The Court subsequently recognized two types of takings that can arise without a physical occupation. First, the Court acknowledged that a rate regulation may

---

1 *Legal Tender Cases*, 79 U.S. (12 Wall.) 457, 551 (1871); *Transp. Co. v. Chicago*, 99 U.S. 635, 642–43 (1878); *Meyer v. City of Richmond*, 172 U.S. 82, 99 (1898). For reviews of early Takings Clause jurisprudence, see *Tahoe–Sierra Pres. Council, Inc. v. Tahoe Reg'l Planning Agency*, 535 U.S. 302, 325 n. 21 (2002); and *Lucas v. S.C. Coastal Council*, 505 U.S. 1003, 1014 (1992).

effect a taking if the rate is set so low as to be confiscatory. Second, the Court recognized that the government may effect a taking without physical occupation or appropriation if it "goes too far" in limiting the owner's use of his or her property.

### a. Confiscatory Rate-Making

Confiscatory rate-making doctrine is rooted in the notion that although regulators may limit the prices that certain industries charge for their services, "it is not to be inferred that this power of limitation or regulation is itself without limit. This power to regulate is not a power to destroy, and limitation is not the equivalent of confiscation."[2] As a result, the Court acknowledged that the Constitution forbids rates that are set so low as to be confiscatory.[3] Although earlier Court opinions were unclear as to whether confiscatory rate-making doctrine was based on takings or due process principles, subsequent decisions clarified that the doctrine stems from the Takings Clause (Ely 1995).

The methodology on which a particular rate is based does not determine whether it is confiscatory. Instead, determining whether a particular rate falls within the zone of reasonableness involves a "balancing of the investor and the consumer interests." Rates are constitutional so long as they provide a return on equity that is sufficient to cover operating expenses, allow returns that are "commensurate with returns on investments in other enterprises having corresponding risks," and are "sufficient to assure confidence in the financial integrity of the enterprise, so as to maintain its credit and to attract capital." In so holding, the Court made clear that the mere fact that a particular rate reduced the value of the utility's property is not by itself sufficient to render a rate confiscatory. As the Court acknowledged, "Rate-making is indeed but one species of price-fixing. The fixing of prices, like other applications of the police power, may reduce the value of the property which is being regulated. But the fact that the value is reduced does not mean that the regulation is invalid" (*Hope Natural Gas,* 320 U.S. at 601, 603; accord *Duquesne Light,* 488 U.S. at 312).

Some Justices have emphasized that the Court's confiscatory rate-making jurisprudence occupied a sphere that was distinct and separate from its physical takings jurisprudence. For example, Justice Brandeis's landmark concurring opinion in *Missouri ex rel. Southwestern Bell Telephone Co. v. Public Service Commission* recognized that the Court's decisions regarding the determination of value in condemnation cases played no part in determining value for rate-making purposes (262 U.S. 276, 310–11 (1923)). Justice Black offered a similar observation in *Federal Power Commission v. Natural Gas Pipeline Co.,* stating that "[i]n condemnation cases, the value of property, generally speaking, is determined by its productiveness, the profits which its use brings to the owner." In addition, "when property is taken under the power of eminent domain the owner is entitled to

2   *R.R. Comm'n Cases,* 116 U.S. 307, 331 (1886).
3   See *Covington & Lexington Tpk. Rd. Co. v. Sandford,* 164 U.S. 578, 597 (1896).

the full money equivalent of the property taken, and thereby to be put in as good position pecuniarily as it would have occupied if its property had not been taken." Those principles, Black pointed out, "have no place in rate regulation." All rate regulation necessarily reduces the value of the regulated property, but this fact does not "stay the hand of the legislature or its administrative agency in making rate reductions" (315 U.S. 575, 603 (1942) (Black, J., concurring) (internal quotation marks omitted)).

### b. Regulatory Takings

Regulatory takings are the second type of nonpossessory taking recognized by the Supreme Court. As Justice Holmes acknowledged in his seminal opinion in *Pennsylvania Coal Co. v. Mahon*, regulatory takings necessarily involve a difficult balance of interests. On the one hand, the government must have wide latitude in regulating the use of property, even if such regulation reduces the property's value. Indeed, "[g]overnment hardly could go on if to some extent values incident to property could not be diminished without paying for every such change in the general law." On the other hand, the government's ability to impose limits on the use of property "must have its limits" if the constitutional protection of property is to be meaningful. Without some restriction on the government's ability to qualify the manner in which owners can use their property, "the natural tendency of human nature [would be] to extend the qualification more and more until at last private property disappears." Thus, "[t]he general rule at least is, that while property may be regulated to a certain extent, if regulation goes too far it will be recognized as a taking" (260 U.S. at 413, 415, 416).[4] Although the Supreme Court's regulatory takings jurisprudence originally emerged in the context of land-use restrictions, the Court has since applied the analysis to any government-imposed nonpossessory restriction on property.[5]

In the landmark decision in *Lucas v. South Carolina Coastal Council*, the Court squarely held what it had frequently noted in dicta in other cases[6]: a nonpossessory regulation may constitute a per se taking if it deprives the owner of "all economically beneficial or productive use of land." When a restriction reaches this level, it can no

---

4   Although *Pennsylvania Coal* is generally regarded as the seminal opinion on regulatory takings, it was not without its historical antecedents. See, e.g., *Commonwealth v. Perry*, 28 N.E. 1126, 1127 (Mass. 1891) (Holmes, J., dissenting); *Hadacheck v. Sebastian*, 239 U.S. 394, 410–11 (1915). For more recent restatements of this rationale, see *Tahoe–Sierra*, 535 U.S. at 325 n. 21, and *Lucas*, 505 U.S. at 1014.

5   *Andrus v. Allard*, 444 U.S. 51, 64–8 (1979) (eagle feathers; *United States v. Sec. Indus. Bank*, 459 U.S. 70, 78 (1982) (liens on real property); *Ruckelshaus v. Monsanto Co.*, 467 U.S. 986, 1004–19 (1984) (pesticide formulas); *Bowen v. Gilliard*, 483 U.S. 587, 603–09 (1987) (welfare payments); *Concrete Pipe & Prods. of Cal., Inc. v. Constr. Laborers Pension Trust*, 508 U.S. 602, 641–45 (1993) (pension plans); *Phillips v. Wash. Legal Found.*, 524 U.S. 156, 172 (1998) (interest on attorney trust accounts); *E. Enters. v. Apfel*, 524 U.S. 498, 522–37 (1998) (plurality opinion) (retiree benefits).

6   *Agins v. City of Tiburon*, 447 U.S. 255, 260 (1980); *Hodel v. Va. Surface Mining & Reclamation Ass'n*, 452 U.S. 264, 295–96 (1981); *Nollan v. Cal. Coastal Comm'n*, 483 U.S. 825, 834 (1987).

longer be considered a regulation that "simply adjust[s] the benefits and burdens of economic life," but instead is more properly regarded as "the equivalent of a physical appropriation" (*Lucas*, 505 U.S. at 1015, 1017 (internal quotation marks omitted)).

A more difficult issue arises when a restriction that falls short of eliminating all economically beneficial use nonetheless constitutes a regulatory taking. Holmes did not elaborate on the proper way to balance the interests of property owners and the government, although he did note that "this is a question of degree" (*Pa. Coal*, 260 U.S. at 416). The Court did not offer much additional guidance until 1978, when it issued its opinion in *Penn Central Transportation Co. v. City of New York*. In *Penn Central*, the Court recognized that, although determining whether a particular governmental action constitutes a taking is an "essentially ad hoc, factual inquir[y]," it is possible to identify three factors with particular significance. Specifically, the Court focused on (1) "the economic impact of the regulation" on the property owner, (2) "the extent to which the regulation has interfered with distinct investment-backed expectations," and (3) "the character of the governmental action." The Court immediately thereafter emphasized that "[a] 'taking' may more readily be found when the interference with property can be characterized as a physical invasion by government than when interference arises from some public program adjusting the benefits and burdens of economic life to promote the common good" (438 U.S. 104, 124 (1978)).

What is perhaps most striking about *Penn Central* is the suggestion that physical and regulatory takings might be governed by the same analysis. The Court's observation that a taking may "more readily" be found when the regulation effects a physical invasion arguably implies that a physical invasion of property is not by itself a taking. Instead, it is simply one consideration that can be overcome by countervailing considerations. The Court seemed to confirm this conclusion in *PruneYard Shopping Center v. Robins*, in which the Court upheld a California decision requiring that the owner of a shopping center permit a group of high school students to engage in political speech on his premises. In holding that this requirement did not violate the Takings Clause, the Court stated that the students' physical invasion of the shopping center "cannot be viewed as determinative" (447 U.S. 74, 84 (1980)). Many noted scholars have downplayed the importance of this language and argued that *PruneYard* can be explained largely on First Amendment grounds (see, e.g., Tribe 1988). Nevertheless, a number of lower courts following *PruneYard* held that the *Penn Central* factors govern takings that effect physical invasions as well as nonpossessory restrictions on the use of property.[7]

The Supreme Court soon removed any remaining doubts about the issue. In the first of two leading cases on the proper takings analysis applied to compelled access to communications networks, the Court in *Loretto v. Teleprompter*

---

7  See, e.g., *Loretto v. Teleprompter Manhattan CATV Corp.*, 423 N.E.2d 320, 331–34 (N.Y. 1981), *rev'd*, 458 U.S. 419 (1982).

*Manhattan CATV Corp.* firmly distinguished between its physical and regulatory takings jurisprudence.


### 2. *Loretto* and the Distinction between Physical and Regulatory Takings

The issue in *Loretto* concerned cable operators' ability to string coaxial cables on New York apartment buildings for the provision of cable television services. Such cables served two distinct purposes. First, they allowed cable operators to provide service to each building's tenants. Second, even if no tenant in a particular building subscribed to cable, the cable operator often needed to string a "crossover" line in order to service customers in adjacent buildings. In 1970, the previous owner of the plaintiff's building allowed the local cable operator to install a thirty-five-foot crossover line that was less than one-half inch in diameter and that ran eighteen inches above the building's roof. The operator also attached directional taps, measuring four inches per side, on the front and rear of the roof and two silver boxes, measuring 18 by 12 by 6 inches, along the roof cables. When the building's tenants subscribed to the service, the cable operator installed another cable running down the front of the building to the first floor.

The cable operator originally compensated building owners for such access by paying them a standard rate of five percent of the gross revenues realized from the property. In 1973, however, the State of New York enacted a statute requiring that landlords permit cable operators to install equipment on their property and providing that a state agency would set the rate of compensation. The agency eventually set the compensation at a one-time rate of one dollar. The plaintiff, the owner of a Manhattan apartment building, challenged the statute on the ground that it violated the Takings Clause. The New York Court of Appeals, consistent with the suggestion of the language in *Penn Central* and *PruneYard* quoted above, held that a government-authorized physical occupation is not necessarily a taking (423 N.E.2d at 330–32).

The Supreme Court responded with a ringing reaffirmation of the distinction between physical and regulatory takings. In particular, the Court rejected the conclusion that the takings determination should in all cases be governed by the ad hoc standards announced in *Penn Central*. Instead, the Court held that any regulation that authorizes a permanent physical occupation of property constitutes a per se taking. This proposition held regardless of whether the government itself occupied the property or simply empowered a third party to do so (458 U.S. at 432 & n. 9).

The Court based its decision on three considerations. First, the Court looked to precedent, finding that that "when the 'character of the governmental action' is a permanent physical occupation of property, our cases uniformly have found a taking to the extent of the occupation, without regard to whether the action achieves an important public benefit or has only minimal economic impact on the owner." Indeed, the Court indicated that it was the "historical" and "traditional" rule to treat a permanent physical occupation as a per se taking. In so holding, the

Court explicitly limited or rejected language in *Penn Central* and *PruneYard* that suggested otherwise (458 U.S. at 427–35).[8]

Second, the Court drew support for its conclusion from the general policies underlying the existence of property rights. Permanent appropriation of property is "perhaps the most serious form of invasion of an owner's property interests." In so reasoning, the Court invoked the familiar metaphor of property as a bundle of rights encompassing three separate strands: the rights to possess, use, and dispose of the property. Unlike regulatory takings, which affect only the property-use strand, physical invasions "chop [ ... ] through the bundle, taking a slice of every strand." Specifically, physical occupations necessarily foreclose owners from either possessing or using the occupied portion of property. Although the owner retains the theoretical right to dispose of the occupied space, the presence of equipment attached to that space essentially "empt[ies] the right of any value." In addition, the Court concluded that these deprivations are particularly severe when the government authorizes a stranger to invade and occupy the owner's property. As a result, the Court concluded that a permanent physical occupation "is qualitatively more severe than a regulation of the *use* of property, even a regulation that imposes affirmative duties on the owner, since the owner may have no control over the timing, extent, or nature of the invasion" (*Loretto*, 458 U.S. at 435, 436, 441).

Finally, the Court invoked practical considerations. Treating permanent physical occupations as per se takings "avoids otherwise difficult line-drawing problems." Unlike the ad hoc quality of the *Penn Central* balancing test, determining the presence of a permanent physical occupation under *Loretto* poses fewer problems of proof. For example, "[t]he placement of a fixed structure on land or real property is an obvious fact that will rarely be subject to dispute." As a result, when the government action is in the form of a permanent physical occupation, that factor by itself becomes "determinative." Although the size and economic impact of the occupation are relevant in ascertaining the amount of compensation, those considerations play no role in determining whether a taking has occurred (*Loretto*, 458 U.S. at 434–35, 436–38).[9]

---

8   The Court reasoned that nothing in *Penn Central* "repudiate[s] the rule that a permanent physical occupation is a government action of such a unique character that it is a taking without regard to other factors that a court might ordinarily examine." The Court emphasized that the "permanence and absolute exclusivity" of the physical occupation at issue in *Loretto* "distinguish[ed] it from [the] temporary limitations on the right to exclude" at issue in *PruneYard*. The Court also distinguished *PruneYard* on the grounds that the invasion in that case was "temporary and limited in nature" and that "the owner had not exhibited an interest in excluding all persons from his property." *Loretto*, 458 U.S. at 432, 434, 435 n. 12. Moreover, in *PruneYard*, "the owner had already opened his property to the general public, and . . . permanent access was not required." *Nollan*, 483 U.S. at 832 n. 1. For a recent analysis of *PruneYard*, see Epstein (1997).

9   Addressing the cable company's argument regarding the small size of the equipment it installed, Justice Marshall quipped, "whether the installation is a taking does not depend on whether the volume of space it occupies is bigger than a breadbox." *Loretto*, 458 U.S. at 438 n. 16.

The Court was careful to emphasize that its holding was not at odds with the "substantial authority" upholding the state power to restrict an owner's use of his property. Citing *Penn Central*, the Court observed that "[s]o long as these regulations do not require the [property owner] to suffer the physical occupation of a portion of his building by a third party, they will be analyzed under the multifactor inquiry generally applicable to nonpossessory governmental activity" (458 U.S. at 440, 441). The reference to *Penn Central* indicates that the Court was referring to traditional regulatory takings doctrine.

*Loretto* thus established two principles that play a central role in our analysis. First, the opinion articulated a strong rationale for subjecting physical takings to the highest degree of protection under the Takings Clause. If a regulation requires a property owner to allow third parties to install permanent equipment on his property, it constitutes a per se taking, regardless of the size of the physical invasion or the public purposes that the regulation advances.[10] Second, *Loretto* reasserted the sharp distinction between the Court's physical and regulatory takings jurisprudence. When a physical taking is involved, regulatory takings precedent does not apply.

### 3. *Florida Power* and the Distinction between Physical Takings and Confiscatory Ratemaking

The Supreme Court advanced similar themes in *FCC v. Florida Power Corp.*, the other leading case involving a takings challenge to regulation compelling access to a communications network. As noted in *Loretto*, the distribution of cable television depended on the operator's ability to establish a web of coaxial cables connecting individual households. Although in urban areas this could be accomplished by compelling building owners to allow cable operators to string cable across their properties, in suburban and rural areas, the network of utility poles owned by telephone and electric companies was the only feasible means of establishing the necessary infrastructure. Congress was concerned, however, that utility companies were exploiting their monopoly position by overcharging cable operators for the right to attach coaxial cables to existing utility poles. As a result, in 1978 Congress enacted the Pole Attachments Act authorizing the FCC to regulate the terms and conditions of pole attachment agreements in any state that did not already impose such regulation (*Statutes at Large* 1978, pp. 35–36 (codified as amended at 47 U.S.C. § 224)).

---

10  It bears emphasizing that this argument is far narrower than the one advanced in Sidak and Spulber (1997a), which claimed that *Loretto* required compensation for any deviation from investment-backed expectations resulting from a change in regulatory systems and that a third party's introduction of a data stream constituted a physical occupation. Instead, we limit ourselves to what is indisputably *Loretto*'s core holding that regulations authorizing the permanent placement of equipment on another person's property constitute a physical taking. Thus, even those who question the former interpretation of *Loretto* are unlikely to find this interpretation controversial.

Nothing in the original version of the Pole Attachments Act gave "cable companies any right to occupy space on utility poles, or prohibit[ed] utility companies from refusing to enter into attachment agreements with cable operators." Instead, the Act simply regulated the rents charged by those parties who voluntarily chose to enter into such agreements. As a result, the Court held that the Act did not constitute the type of permanent physical occupation that *Loretto* held to be a per se taking because it lacked the necessary "element of required acquiescence." The Court found *Loretto* dispositive, concluding that, "'[s]o long as these regulations do not *require* the landlord to suffer the physical occupation of a portion of his building by a third party, they will be analyzed under the multifactor inquiry generally applicable to nonpossessory governmental activity'" (480 U.S. 245, 251, 252 (1987), quoting *Loretto*, 458 U.S. at 440).

Having held that the Pole Attachments Act fell outside *Loretto's* per se rule governing physical takings, the Court evaluated whether the Act nonetheless represented a nonpossessory taking. Rather than applying the *Penn Central* factors, as its quotation of *Loretto* suggested, *Florida Power* held that the Takings Clause simply required that the set rates not be confiscatory. The Court concluded that the pole attachment rates established by the statute allowed sufficient return on investment to satisfy the requirements of its confiscatory rate-making jurisprudence (480 U.S. at 253–54).

*Florida Power* thus reinforced the same key principles underlying the Court's decision in *Loretto*. First, although it did not address the issue explicitly, the Court implied that had the Pole Attachments Act compelled utilities to give cable television systems access to their poles, the Act would have constituted a per se taking under *Loretto*. Second, *Florida Power* underscored the sharp distinction between the Court's physical takings and confiscatory ratemaking precedents. Echoing the admonitions of Justices Brandeis and Black that physical takings and confiscatory ratemaking occupy distinct jurisprudential spheres, the Court established that its confiscatory rate-making precedents did not apply to cases involving physical takings (480 U.S. at 251–52 & n. 6).

## 4. Toward a Possible Synthesis of Regulatory Takings and Confiscatory Ratemaking Doctrine

Although courts and scholars typically treat regulatory takings and confiscatory rate-making as conceptually distinct (Sidak & Spulber 1997a), the Court's opinions in *Loretto* and *Florida Power* suggest that both lines of precedent may represent a single concept. It is easy to conceptualize a restriction on the amount that one can charge for access to a piece of property as either a restriction on the property's use or a "public program adjusting the benefits and burdens of economic life to promote the common good" (*Penn Cent.*, 438 U.S. at 124). Moreover, similar concerns appear to animate both lines of precedent. Each recognizes that almost every government action necessarily affects the value of private property and that imposing too stringent a leash on regulatory action conflicts with the exigencies of modern governance.[11] At the same time, both recognize that excess power to regulate can constitute the power to destroy.[12] In addition, both employ almost identical methodologies that emphasize the fact-specific nature of the claims[13] and that focus primarily on the restriction's economic impact on the regulated entity[14] and investor expectations.[15]

Finally, some case law suggests that these two approaches may be fungible. For example, in *Florida Power* the Court invoked its regulatory takings jurisprudence when it suggested that unless a regulation required that utilities permit cable companies to occupy existing poles permanently, it would be "'analyzed under the multifactor inquiry generally applicable to nonpossessory governmental activity.'" Immediately following that observation, however, the Court held that in the absence of such compulsion, the Pole Attachments Act was properly analyzed under the Court's confiscatory rate-making precedent. The juxtaposition of these two observations indicates that the Court may have viewed these two lines of precedent as simply variations on the same theme (*Fla. Power*, 480 U.S. at 252–54, quoting *Loretto*, 458 U.S. at 440).

The Court's reasoning in rent control cases gives rise to a similar inference. For example, the Court analyzed the rent control ordinance at issue in *Pennell v. City of San Jose* in terms of the Court's confiscatory rate-making precedent (485 U.S. 1, 11–13 (1988)). In contrast, the Court analyzed the rent control ordinance in *Yee v. City of Escondido* in terms of its regulatory takings jurisprudence, stating that

11  Compare, e.g., *Pa. Coal Co. v. Mahon*, 260 U.S. 393, 413 (1922) ("Government hardly could go on if to some extent values incident to property could not be diminished without paying for every such change in the general law"), with *Fed. Power Comm'n v. Hope Natural Gas Co.*, 320 U.S. 591, 601 (1944) ("The fixing of prices . . . may reduce the value of the property which is being regulated. But the fact that the value is reduced does not mean that the regulation is invalid").

12  Compare *Pa. Coal*, 260 U.S. at 415 (noting that, without some limit on the government's ability to restrict owners' use of their property, "the natural tendency of human nature [would be] to extend the qualification more and more until at last private property disappears"), with *R.R. Comm'n Cases*, 116 U.S. 307, 331 (1886) ("[I]t is not to be inferred that this power of limitation or regulation [of rates] is itself without limit. This power to regulate is not a power to destroy, and limitation is not the equivalent of confiscation").

13  Compare *Penn Cent.*, 438 U.S. at 124 (calling the regulatory takings standard an "essentially ad hoc, factual inquir[y]"), with *Hope Natural Gas*, 320 U.S. at 602 (observing that determining whether a rate is confiscatory depends upon a series of fact-intensive inquiries focusing on the rate's net effect).

14  Compare *Penn Cent.*, 438 U.S. at 124 (identifying "[t]he economic impact of the regulation on the claimant" as a factor in the regulatory takings analysis), with *Hope Natural Gas*, 320 U.S. at 603 (recognizing the importance of ensuring that the regulated entity receives "enough revenue not only for operating expenses but also for the capital costs of the business").

15  Compare *Penn Cent.*, 438 U.S. at 124 (identifying "the extent to which the regulation has interfered with distinct investment-backed expectations" as a factor in the regulatory takings analysis), with *Hope Natural Gas*, 320 U.S. at 603 (noting that investors have "a legitimate concern with the financial integrity of the company whose rates are being regulated").

the rent control ordinance at issue "merely regulate[s] petitioners' *use* of their land by regulating the relationship between landlord and tenant." Indeed, the Court specifically equated rent ceilings imposed on landlords with other use restrictions and declared that both types of restrictions were properly analyzed under classic regulatory takings precedents such as *Pennsylvania Coal* and *Penn Central's* progeny (503 U.S. 519, 522–23, 528, 529 (1992)).[16] The parallel between the two doctrines is further underscored by the Court's opinion in *Lucas v. South Carolina Coastal Council*, which described the strand of regulatory takings doctrine used to invalidate regulations prohibiting all economically beneficial land use as being directed against "confiscatory" regulations (*Lucas*, 505 U.S. at 1029, 1032 n. 18).

It is thus arguable that the Court's regulatory takings and confiscatory rate-making jurisprudence amount to slightly different aspects of a single doctrine. Unfortunately, the Court has never clearly addressed the relationship between these two lines of precedent, and scholarly analysis has shed little light on the issue.[17] In addition, it would be anachronistic to suggest that the Court had a unified takings jurisprudence in mind from the outset. The Court's confiscatory takings jurisprudence long antedates its recognition of regulatory takings in *Pennsylvania Coal*, let alone its announcement of ad hoc factors in *Penn Central*. In fact, because states primarily regulated rates and the Takings Clause was not applied to the states until *Chicago, Burlington & Quincy Railroad Co. v. Chicago*, 166 U.S. 226, 241 (1897),[18] the earliest confiscatory rate-making cases arose under the Due Process Clause, rather than the Takings Clause. The historical dichotomy is further reinforced by the views of Justice David Brewer (1891), perhaps the primary architect of the Court's early takings jurisprudence. His famous speech at Yale Law School on the subject clearly evinced his belief that rate regulation and use restrictions represent distinct lines of authority.

## 5. The Importance of the Shift to Access Regulation

Fortunately, we need not resolve the precise relationship between regulatory takings and confiscatory rate-making in order to press our argument. Although the cases do not shed much light on whether regulatory takings and confiscatory rate-making represent distinct concepts or slightly different aspects of the same doctrine, for our purposes it is sufficient that the Court has emphasized the importance of distinguishing both categories from its physical takings jurisprudence. If a regulation authorizes a third party to establish a permanent physical invasion, *Loretto* and

---

16  For an earlier analysis along the same lines, see *Block v. Hirsh*, 256 U.S. 135, 155–56 (1921) (Holmes, J.).

17  Drobak (1985) asserts, without analysis, that the Court's regulatory takings and confiscatory rate-making precedents are equivalent. Goldsmith (1989) identifies similarities in the Court's regulatory takings and confiscatory rate-making precedents, but concludes that confiscatory rate-making is based on due process considerations.

18  *Chi., Burlington & Quincy R.R. Co. v. Chicago*, 166 U.S. 226, 241 (1897).

*Florida Power* dictate that it constitutes a per se taking regardless of any other factors typically invoked in regulatory takings and confiscatory rate-making cases.

Equally important, the Court has frequently reiterated that its physical and nonpossessory takings cases occupy separate doctrinal spheres, and that its decisions involving nonpossessory takings have no application to physical takings. For example, the Court held in *Yee* that a regulatory takings challenge was not fairly included in a physical takings challenge, because "[c]onsideration of whether a regulatory taking occurred would not assist in resolving whether a physical taking occurred as well." In so holding, the Court emphasized that the two questions "exist side by side, neither encompassing the other" (*Yee*, 503 U.S. at 537). The Court struck a similar note in *Palazzolo v. Rhode Island* when it recognized that physical takings "present[ . . . ] different considerations than cases alleging a taking based on a burdensome regulation" (533 U.S. 606, 628 (2001)).

The Court reaffirmed these principles in *Tahoe–Sierra Preservation Council, Inc. v. Tahoe Regional Planning Agency*. The Court held that whenever a physical taking occurs, the government has a categorical duty to compensate the owner, regardless of the size of the occupation or whether the government only takes part of a larger parcel. Echoing its more extended discussion in *Loretto*, the Court found it appropriate to treat physical takings categorically because "physical appropriations are relatively rare, easily identified, and usually represent a greater affront to individual property rights." As a result, when determining whether a physical taking has occurred, the Court does not evaluate the magnitude of the economic impact on the property owner or inquire into the substantiality of the governmental interest underlying the regulation; any physical invasion, no matter how small, is sufficient to trigger the duty to compensate. Most importantly for our purposes, the *Tahoe–Sierra* Court emphasized that these differences "make[ . . . ] it inappropriate to treat cases involving physical takings as controlling precedents for the evaluation of a claim that there has been a regulatory taking, and vice versa." *Tahoe–Sierra* thus reaffirmed the core substantive holding of *Loretto* by reiterating that permanent physical occupations constitute per se takings without regard to the economic impact or the public purpose served by the invasion. *Tahoe–Sierra* also offered the Court's plainest statement to date that its regulatory takings decisions do not constitute precedent in cases involving physical takings (535 U.S. at 320–24 (internal quotation marks omitted)).

## B. Physical Takings Jurisprudence Applied to Network Access

Determining whether a takings violation has occurred thus requires resolution of two separate questions. First, has the government action in question effected a taking? As the foregoing discussion underscores, the resolution of this question varies depending on whether the regulation at issue is alleged to be a physical taking. Second, has the government provided just compensation for its actions?

## 1. Determining Whether a Taking Has Occurred

In contrast to the analysis applied to both regulatory takings and confiscatory rate-making, which attempts to balance the interests of the public with those of the utility and which carefully examines the regulation's economic impact, physical takings are governed by a simple bright-line rule. As the Court held in *Loretto* and reaffirmed several times since, government action is a per se taking if it authorizes a permanent physical occupation, such as giving third parties the right to place telecommunications equipment on another person's property. This fact under-scores the constitutional significance of the shift from rate regulation to access regulation. If a permanent physical occupation occurs, it does not matter whether the action furthers an important public interest or achieves an important public benefit. Nor does the size or economic impact of the invasion matter.[19] Indeed, a permanent physical invasion constitutes a per se taking even if it increases the value of the property. The Court reasoned: "[This] conclusion . . . [is] premised on our longstanding recognition that property is more than economic value; it also consists of 'the group of rights which the so-called owner exercises in his dominion of the physical thing,' such 'as the right to possess, use and dispose of it.' While the [property] at issue here may have no economically realizable value to its owner, possession, control, and disposition are nonetheless valuable rights that inhere in the property" (*Phillips v. Wash. Legal Found.*, 524 U.S. 156, 170 (1998), quoting *United States v. Gen. Motors Corp.*, 323 U.S. 373, 378 (1945)).[20]

As will be discussed below in greater detail in Chapter 8, regulations that compel access to wireline telecommunications networks often require the placement of third-party equipment on the network owner's property. As a result, the shift from rate regulation to access regulation generates an equally fundamental shift in the constitutional analysis. Finding that a taking has occurred, however, is only the first step in the constitutional inquiry.

## 2. Determining Just Compensation

Once a court determines that a taking has occurred, the constitutionality of the regulation in question depends on whether the government provides just compensation for the property taken. The *Loretto* Court did not address the question of compensation, remanding it for consideration by the state courts (458 U.S. at 441). In addition, most courts confronted with this issue held that it was not ripe for judicial consideration.[21]

---

19  *Loretto*, 458 U.S. at 426, 436–37, 438 n. 16; *Nollan*, 483 U.S. at 831–32; *Yee*, 503 U.S. at 530; *Lucas*, 505 U.S. at 1015, 1028; *Tahoe–Sierra*, 535 U.S. at 322.

20  See also *Loretto*, 458 U.S. at 437–38 n. 15.

21  *Verizon Commc'ns Inc. v. FCC*, 535 U.S. 467, 524–25 (2002); *Ill. Bell Tel. Co. v. FCC*, 911 F.2d 776, 780 (D.C. Cir. 1990); *Iowa Utils. Bd. v. FCC*, 120 F.3d 753, 818 (8th Cir. 1997), *rev'd & remanded in part on other grounds sub nom. AT&T v. Iowa Utils. Bd.*, 525 U.S. 366, 396 (1999); *Gulf Power*

### a. Market Value as the Preferred Measure of Just Compensation

The Court often has averred that the guiding principle for determining just compensation is that the owner should be put "'in as good a position pecuniarily as if his property had not been taken.'"[22] As a result, the Court established that the predominant measure of just compensation should be "market value." As Justice Frankfurter reasoned in *Kimball Laundry Co. v. United States*: "Most things . . . have a general demand which gives them a value transferable from one owner to another. As opposed to such personal and variant standards as value to the particular owner whose property has been taken, this transferable value has an external validity which makes it a fair measure of [just compensation]" (338 U.S. 1, 5 (1949)).[23]

The external validity identified by Justice Frankfurter has both a theoretical and a practical basis. As a theoretical matter, market value reflects the seminal economic insights that effectively transformed *value* from the intrinsic concept of a good to the result of market transactions between buyers and sellers. A good's market value provides observable evidence a market price of the benefits to buyers and the costs to sellers. Market value thus sheds light on property rights by considering the returns in transferring those rights. In evaluating the value of assets used in production, market value provides tangible evidence of the property's earning potential. This shift was evident in *Monongahela Navigation Co. v. United States*, the first case in which the Court addressed just compensation principles. The Court determined that the Takings Clause required compensation not only for the tangible property taken, a lock and a dam, but also for the tolls the facility would have earned by using that property. The Takings Clause required payment of "a full and perfect equivalent for the property taken," which, "generally speaking, is determined by its productiveness, the profits which its use brings to the owner." "The value, therefore, is not determined by the mere cost of construction, but more by what the completed structure brings in the way of earnings to its owner." As a result, the income that the lock and the dam would have earned was considered part of the property's value

---

Co. v. United States, 187 F.3d 1324, 1338 (11th Cir. 1999); *Gulf Power Co. v. FCC*, 208 F.3d 1263, 1272–73 (11th Cir. 2000), *rev'd on other grounds sub nom. Nat'l Cable & Telecomms. Ass'n v. Gulf Power Co.*, 524 U.S. 327, 342 (2002).

22  *United States v. 564.54 Acres of Land*, 441 U.S. 506, 510 (1979) ("*Lutheran Synod*"), quoting *Olson v. United States*, 292 U.S. 246, 255 (1934). As Richard Epstein (1985, p. 182) has noted, "In principle, the ideal solution is to leave the individual owner in a position of indifference between the taking by the government and the retention of the property." For other early statements of this principle, see *Monongahela*, 148 U.S. at 326, and *Seaboard Air Line Railway Co. v. United States*, 261 U.S. 299, 304 (1923).

23  See also *New River Collieries*, 262 U.S. at 344; *Olson*, 292 U.S. at 255; *United States v. Miller*, 317 U.S. 369, 374 (1943); *Gen. Motors*, 323 U.S. at 379; *United States v. Commodities Trading Corp.*, 339 U.S. 121, 123 (1950); *Almota Farmers Elevator & Warehouse Co. v. United States*, 409 U.S. 470, 474 (1973); *Lutheran Synod*, 441 U.S. at 511; *Kirby Forest Indus. v. United States*, 467 U.S. 1, 10 (1984); *United States v. 50 Acres of Land*, 469 U.S. 24, 29 (1984) ("*Duncanville Landfill*"). Although the cases at times refer to this standard as "fair market value," as the Court noted in *Miller*, the two formulations essentially amount to the same thing (317 U.S. at 374).

(*Monongahela*, 148 U.S. at 326, 328, 329). The Court reaffirmed this principle on numerous occasions (see, e.g., *Lucas*, 505 U.S. at 1017; *Kimball Laundry*, 338 U.S. at 9).

Practical considerations provide additional reasons for preferring exchange-oriented approaches over cost-oriented approaches when determining just compensation. As the Court observed, the shift to the market-value standard was driven in part by the "need for a clear, easily administrable rule governing the measure of 'just compensation.'"[24] The use of external measures of value eliminated many of the "serious practical difficulties in assessing the worth an individual places on particular property at a given time."[25] Permitting such subjective considerations to determine what constitutes just compensation "would enhance the risk of error and prejudice."[26]

The Court has held that the market-value standard is not constitutionally mandated and thus might not require strict adherence.[27] Indeed, the Court has long recognized that market value fails to give "full and literal force" to the principle of putting property owners in as good a position as if their property had not been taken. In particular, the Court has frequently observed that just compensation does not necessarily require compensation for the special value that a piece of property may have for a particular user.[28] Furthermore, the Court does not allow recovery of any transaction costs imposed by the taking.[29] As a result, the market-value standard has been criticized for failing to make whole those whose property is taken.[30]

The Court has nonetheless concluded that the market-value standard offers an appropriate accommodation for the exigencies of modern governance. In most cases market value "achieves a fair 'balance between the public's need and the claimant's loss,'"[31] thereby mediating "the conflict between the people's interest in public projects and the principle of indemnity to the landowner."[32] Although a failure to consider subjective valuation can impose real costs on those whose property is taken, this loss is "properly treated as part of the burden of common citizenship."[33] As a result, any exceptions to the market-value rule remain very narrow.[34]

24 *Kirby Forest*, 467 U.S. at 10 n. 15.

25 *Lutheran Synod*, 441 U.S. at 511. See also *United States ex rel. Tenn. Valley Auth. v. Powelson*, 319 U.S. 266, 280 (1943).

26 *Duncanville Landfill*, 469 U.S. at 36.

27 *Toronto, Hamilton & Buffalo*, 338 U.S. at 402; *United States v. Fuller*, 409 U.S. 488, 490 (1973); *Lutheran Synod*, 441 U.S. at 512; *Kirby Forest*, 467 U.S. at 10 n. 14; *Duncanville Landfill*, 469 U.S. at 30–31; see also *United States v. Cors*, 337 U.S. 325, 332 (1949) (cautioning against making a "fetish" of market value).

28 *Lutheran Synod*, 441 U.S. at 511.

29 *United States v. Petty Motor Co.*, 327 U.S. 372, 377–78 (1946).

30 See commentary collected in Risinger (1985) and DeBow (1995).

31 *Duncanville Landfill*, 469 U.S. at 33, quoting *Toronto, Hamilton & Buffalo*, 338 U.S. at 402.

32 *Powelson*, 319 U.S. at 280.

33 *Kimball Laundry*, 338 U.S. at 5.

34 See Gergen (1993); Lunney (1993); DeBow (1995).

### b. Determining Market Value under the Takings Clause

Market value is the amount that would be paid for the property in a transaction between a willing buyer and a willing seller.[35] Consequently, market value takes into account any aspect of the property that affects the price that a reasonable buyer would be willing to pay.[36] For example, in *Boom Co. v. Patterson*, the Court held that in determining the value of condemned land, "the same considerations are to be regarded as in a sale of property between private parties. The inquiry in such cases must be what is the property worth in the market, viewed not merely with reference to the uses to which it is at the time applied, but with reference to the uses to which it is plainly adapted" (98 U.S. 403, 407–08 (1878)). The Court reiterated these principles in *Olson v. United States*. In *Olson*, the Court noted that in determining the price upon which a willing buyer and a willing seller would settle, "there should be taken into account all considerations that fairly might be brought forward and reasonably be given substantial weight in such bargaining." The Court acknowledged the importance of opportunity cost by stating that "[t]he highest and most profitable use for which the property is adaptable and needed or likely to be needed in the reasonably near future is to be considered, not necessarily as the measure of value, but to the full extent that the prospect of demand for such use affects the market value while the property is privately held." In addition, "to the extent that probable demand by prospective purchasers or condemnors affects market value, it is to be taken into account" (292 U.S. at 255–57).

Consistent with the economic principles identified above, the Court has held that an evaluation of comparable sales represents the most reliable way to determine the amount a willing buyer would have agreed to pay a willing seller had the property been transferred on the open market. As the Court observed in *Kimball Laundry*, "If exchanges of similar property have been frequent, the inference is strong that the equivalent arrived at by the haggling of the market would probably have been offered and accepted, and it is thus that the 'market price' becomes so important a standard of reference" (338 U.S. at 6).

Other evaluation methodology may be required when the property being valued is traded so infrequently that, in effect, no market for it exists.[37] In the absence of comparable sales, when valuing commercial property the Court has sanctioned the income capitalization approach, in which market value is equal to the net present value of the property's projected income.[38] Although this approach has the advantage of being based on data derived from actual market transactions, the Court

---

35   See *Miller*, 317 U.S. at 374; *Lutheran Synod*, 441 U.S. at 511; *Kirby Forest*, 467 U.S. at 10.

36   See *Almota*, 409 U.S. at 474, 477–78.

37   See, e.g., *Miller*, 317 U.S. at 374; *Toronto, Hamilton & Buffalo*, 338 U.S. at 402; *Kimball Laundry*, 338 U.S. at 5; *Commodities Trading Corp.*, 339 U.S. at 123; *Lutheran Synod*, 441 U.S. at 512; *Kirby Forest*, 467 U.S. at 10 n. 14; *Duncanville Landfill*, 469 U.S. at 29.

38   *Kimball Laundry*, 338 U.S. at 16 ("One index of going-concern value offered by petitioner is the record of its past earnings."); *Lutheran Synod*, 441 U.S. at 515 ("[T]he uses to which commercial property is put can often be valued in terms of the capitalized earnings produced"). For an

has recognized that it does carry some risks. Estimates of value based on income capitalization are only as reliable as the data upon which they are based. For example, projections of future income are typically based upon a particular property's past earnings. Although such data are often reliable indicators of future earnings, at times they may fail to reflect the full range of technological and economic developments.[39]

In addition, the Court has suggested that in the absence of better measures of value, courts can appropriately consider replacement cost when determining whether the government has provided just compensation (*Kimball Laundry*, 338 U.S. at 5–7). As noted earlier, replacement cost is better than historic cost at reflecting changes in value over time. Replacement cost also provides a useful price ceiling, because all those who purchase access can create the input themselves. At the same time, the Court's takings decisions recognize that replacement-cost approaches to valuation suffer from several conceptual limitations. First and foremost, such approaches do not necessarily reflect exchange value.[40] In addition, by failing to incorporate any element that reflects demand, the replacement-cost approach may fail to account for technological obsolescence and thus may require compensation even "when no one would think of reproducing the property."[41] Moreover, in order to compensate for functional obsolescence, courts must analyze the replacement cost of an equally efficient plant by allowing for physical depreciation. Failing to do so would bestow a windfall on the property owner due to the difference in quality between the replacement facility and the older facility. Factoring in depreciation does, however, add considerable uncertainty to the valuation process.[42]

The Court reserved its heaviest criticism for historical cost, the valuation approach upon which authorities have relied most often when regulating network industries.[43] As the Court explained in *United States v. Toronto, Hamilton & Buffalo Navigation Co.*, historical cost all too often represents a "false standard of the past" that bears no necessary relationship with present value. As a result, historical cost is often a backward-looking measure that is unreliable in determining a current fair market value (338 U.S. at 403). Moreover, the Court in *Olson* pointed out that market value "may be more or less than the owner's investment. He may have acquired the property for less than its worth or he may have paid a speculative and exorbitant price. Its value may have changed substantially while held by him. . . . The public

---

application of these principles in the telecommunications context, see *Illinois Bell*, 988 F.2d at 1262–63.

39  See, e.g., *Toronto, Hamilton & Buffalo*, 338 U.S. at 398–403 (finding that development of new ferry routes rendered earnings records of prior years' routes unreliable indicators of future income).

40  See Sackman (1995).

41  See, e.g., *Toronto, Hamilton & Buffalo*, 338 U.S. at 403.

42  See *Duncanville Landfill*, 469 U.S. 24 at 34–35.

43  The Court's criticism of historical-cost methodologies dates back to its earliest takings decisions. See, e.g., *Monongahela*, 148 U.S. at 328 ("The value, therefore, is not determined by the mere cost of construction. . . . ").

may not by any means confiscate the benefits, or be required to bear the burden, of the owner's bargain. . . . He must be made whole but is not entitled to more" (292 U.S. at 255; accord Sackman 1995).

Because of the problems associated with these other methodologies, the Court has consistently indicated that the comparable-sales approach represents the best evidence of market value.[44] Indeed, the Court has gone so far as to characterize other valuation methods, including replacement cost, as exceptions to the comparable-sales approach and to hold them inapplicable whenever there are market-based transactions in similar properties.[45] The Court offered its most dramatic statement to this effect in *United States v. New River Collieries Co.*, in which it held that "[w]here private property is taken for public use, and there is a market price prevailing at the time and place of the taking, that price *is* just compensation." As a result, because comparable sales data were available, the Court properly held inadmissible income and replacement cost evidence (262 U.S. at 344 (emphasis added)). Only if such data are unavailable should courts resort to other methods. Furthermore, if it is necessary to resort to other methods of determining market value, courts should turn first to the income capitalization approach and then to the replacement-cost approach before resorting to historical cost valuation.

Justice Brandeis used historical cost in evaluating takings challenges to conventional rate regulation. At no point, however, did either Justice Brandeis or the Court suggest that cost-based methodologies are superior to the comparable-sales approach under the principles of economics and fairness embodied in the Takings Clause. Instead, the Court made clear that it was sanctioning the cost-based methodologies only because market-based methodologies were unavailable. Implicit in this argument is the recognition that the emergence of market-based benchmarks would require a return to market-based compensation principles.

The foregoing analysis underscores the constitutional significance of both transformations that we have identified. The fundamental shift from rate regulation to access regulation makes it far easier for regulatory authorities to incorporate external reference points that reflect the demand side of the valuation equation. Because

---

44  Sackman (1995, § 12B.04[3], at 12B–23) calls the comparable-sales approach "the preferred way to compute market value." DeBow (1995, p. 582) states that "it is widely understood that in practice the Supreme Court shows a strong preference for the comparable sales approach." Lunney (1993, p. 728) notes that the Court "has preferred that a party establish market value through the comparable sales approach."

45  *Toronto, Hamilton & Buffalo*, 338 U.S. at 402; *Lutheran Synod*, 441 U.S. at 512–13; *Duncanville Landfill*, 469 U.S. at 29. The Court has also suggested in dicta that the market value standard may be set aside when its application "'would result in manifest injustice to owner or public'" (*Duncanville Landfill*, 469 U.S. at 29, quoting United States v. *Commodities Trading Corp.*, 339 U.S. at 123). The Court has never provided much guidance as to when this exception might arise, and has rejected every attempt to invoke it. See, e.g., *Commodities Trading Corp.*, 339 U.S. at 30–36; *Lutheran Synod*, 441 U.S. at 514–17. The language of these opinions and the Court's failure to apply this exception strongly suggest that it is extremely narrow, at best, and possibly even empty.

conventional rate regulation sets prices that utilities can charge for final outputs, any attempt to base regulated rates on final prices is hopelessly circular. Access regulation, in contrast, alleviates this problem by allowing market-based competition to determine the prices utilities charge for final goods. It is true that the access regulation approach is somewhat circular as well. For example, regulatory authorities still must establish rates to govern the terms under which incumbent firms must provide access to competitors, and the rates they set will have some influence on the prices charged for final goods. Network access nonetheless remains only one of several inputs required to produce the final good. Circularity is not a problem with respect to nonbottleneck inputs.

The emergence of direct, facilities-based network competition also is of considerable constitutional importance. Indeed, the emergence of direct competition undercuts the justifications for imposing access regulation as a matter of principle. But even setting aside the question whether access represents good policy, the emergence of substitute network technologies has profound implications for the implementation of any access regime. By facilitating the emergence of alternative networks capable of providing market-based indicia of competitive pricing, converging telecommunications technology is vitiating the justification for setting rates according to cost-based methodologies. Once competition leads to market benchmarks, continued reliance on cost-based methodologies will be improper, under precedent.

### 3. Partial Takings of Utility Property

The Supreme Court's takings jurisprudence recognizes that government compensation should generally reflect the earning potential of the property taken. The government need not compensate for a property's going concern value when it takes the entire fee and divests the current owner of title. As the Court explained in *Kimball Laundry*, "the denial of compensation in such circumstances rests on a very concrete justification: the going-concern value has not been taken." In such circumstances, "only the physical property has been condemned, leaving the owner free to move his business to a new location." The Court further reasoned that "there is no more reason for a taker to pay for the business' going-concern value than there would be for a purchaser to pay for it who had not secured from his vendor a covenant to refrain from entering into competition with him" (338 U.S. at 11; see also *Gen. Motors*, 323 U.S. at 379).

Nonetheless, the Court identified two circumstances in which compensation for the going-concern value is appropriate. The first occurs when the government takes a public utility that possesses natural monopoly characteristics. "Since a utility cannot ordinarily be operated profitably except as a monopoly, investment by the former owner of the utility in duplicating the condemned faculties could have no prospect of a profitable return." In such cases, "[t]he owner retains nothing of the going-concern value that it formerly possessed." Therefore, because taking over a public utility "has the inevitable effect of depriving the owner of the going-concern value of his business," it is properly regarded as a taking for which compensation must be paid (338 U.S. at 12–13).

The second situation arises when the government physically takes less than the fee interest in the owner's property. For example, the Court in *United States v. General Motors Corp.*, noted that although the government need not compensate for a property's going-concern value when it takes the full fee interest, "[i]t is altogether another matter when the Government does not take [the owner's] entire interest, but by the form of its proceeding chops it into bits, of which it takes only what it wants, however few or minute, and leaves [the owner] holding the remainder." Because only part of the property was taken, it was effectively impossible for the property owner simply to reestablish its business elsewhere. In such a case, the proper measure of compensation is not just the cost of the property taken, but also the going-concern value of the property as reflected by rental fees that could be obtained on the open market (323 U.S. at 379, 382; see also *Kimball Laundry*, 338 U.S. at 7, 14–16).

These situations underscore the constitutional problems that would result if network access rates were based solely on direct cost and support rates that reflect the probable demand for network services. To the extent that compelled access to any particular portion of a network is justified, it must be because that portion bears natural monopoly characteristics. Because it is infeasible for the network owner to establish similar facilities elsewhere, the physical occupation of its facilities requires that the owner be compensated for the going-concern value of the property taken. In this case, the value of the property is reflected by the value of the network services provided. In addition, the partial nature of the physical taking effected by access requirements provides yet another reason for requiring the government to compensate network owners for lost profits. Access necessarily involves a physical taking that is considerably less than the full fee, thus interrupting the owner's use of the property and leaving it inextricably intertwined with others' use. Because these encumbrances effectively prevent the owner from using the property for other purposes, compensation for such a taking must reflect the property's going-concern value.

* * *

It is no doubt tempting for regulatory authorities and courts to resolve takings challenges to network regulations according to the same principles applied in conventional rate regulation cases. Those principles are based on balancing tests that regard as constitutionally unproblematic those regulations backed by strong public policy justifications and having minimal economic impact. In addition, adherence to preexisting approaches allows regulators to continue employing the cost-based methodologies with which they are familiar. Rate-making authorities can thus maximize the leverage they have gained from regulatory tools developed in previous rate-making efforts.

Blind application of existing principles, however, ignores the constitutional import of the shift from rate regulation to access regulation. As noted earlier, access regulation typically requires network owners to permit permanent physical occupations of their property. Unlike rate regulation, access regulation effects a physical taking for which the government *must* pay compensation without regard to the magnitude of the invasion, its impact on investment-backed expectations, or the importance of the policy interests furthered by the regulation. The Court has made clear that the regulatory takings and confiscatory rate-making precedents upon which regulatory authorities have previously relied in rejecting takings challenges do not apply to cases involving physical takings.

The Court's takings jurisprudence also makes clear that the best measure of just compensation is market value, which is best determined through actual market transactions. Although at one point the absence of external, market-determined benchmarks may have justified reliance on cost-based valuation methodologies, the emergence of platform competition and the shift from regulating outputs to regulating inputs have made it increasingly possible for regulatory authorities to determine value on the basis of actual market transactions. This shift implies that the theoretical and technological transformation of regulated-industries law commands, in turn, a similar transformation of the principles used to evaluate takings challenges to access regulation of network industries. Front-line policymakers, those in charge of implementing access regulations, have largely ignored these implications. Therefore, the obligation to enforce these principles will fall to the courts as they begin to address the merits of takings challenges to this type of regulation.

The emergence of platform competition and the shift to access regulation have made basing rates on market prices more feasible than ever before. Although we expect the level of competition in the relevant markets, which include local telephony, multichannel video programming distribution, and broadband services, to vary, the competition likely to emerge in each industry should be sufficiently robust to justify basing rates on market prices. We demonstrate in regulatory case studies in the following chapters how some types of access to networks necessarily require a permanent physical invasion, which adds a constitutional dimension that reinforces the economic analysis.

# PART III

# POLICY APPLICATIONS

# 8

# The Regulation of Local Telephone Networks

In this part, we apply the framework developed in the earlier chapters to a series of current issues in telecommunications policy. The first issue, discussed in this chapter, is the regulation of local telephone networks. Chapter 9 examines how antitrust law has been applied to the telecommunications industry. Chapter 10 uses the framework we have developed to analyze the regulation of broadband networks. Chapters 11 and 12 examine one of the most high-profile recent issues in telecommunications policy: "network neutrality."

## A. The History of the Regulation of Local Telephony

### 1. Early State and Federal Regulation and the Communications Act of 1934

Under the system of federalism enshrined in the U.S. Constitution, the authority of the federal government is limited to *inter*state commercial activities. The regulation of *intra*state telephone rates fell under the jurisdiction of the states.[1] Although early legislation in five states had authorized some degree of regulation over local telephone companies, state regulation of local telephone service did not begin in

---

1  *Smith v. Ill. Bell Tel. Co.*, 282 U.S. 133, 148–49 (1930). Such a vision of dual federalism can be hard to maintain with respect to network industries such as telephony, in which the same capital assets are used for both intrastate and interstate service. With respect to other network industries, such as the railroads, the Supreme Court has acknowledged that intrastate and interstate rates "are so related that the government of the one involves the control over the other" and has recognized that the federal government cannot create a coherent regulatory system without authority over both (*Houston & Tex. Ry. v. United States* (*The Shreveport Rate Case*), 234 U.S. 342, 351 (1914); accord *Wickard v. Filburn*, 317 U.S. 111, 125 (1942) (recognizing that purely intrastate activities can have a tangential impact on interstate commerce sufficient to bring those activities within federal jurisdiction)). This reasoning was not extended to telephony prior to 1996 (*La. Pub. Serv. Comm'n v. FCC*, 476 U.S. 355 (1986); *Smith*, 282 U.S. at 148–49).

earnest until 1907, when states began authorizing their public utility commissions to oversee the reasonableness of local telephone rates. By 1921, all but three states had instituted some form of regulation of local telephone rates (U.S. House 1921).

Federal regulation of interstate telephone service began in 1910 with the enactment of the Mann–Elkins Act, which gave the Interstate Commerce Commission (ICC) the power to review the reasonableness of interstate and international telephone rates (*Statutes at Large* 1910, pp. 544–46). Although the Act obligated interstate telephone providers "to provide service on request at just and reasonable rates, without unjust discrimination or undue preference," it did not give the ICC the authority to require the filing of tariffs or mandate interconnection ex ante, which had the effect of limiting it to ex post review of rates.[2] In addition, with its attention fixed primarily on the railroads, the ICC did little to exercise the regulatory jurisdiction it did possess, undertaking only four telephone rate cases during the twenty-four years during which it had jurisdiction over the telephone industry.[3]

Congress addressed many of the deficiencies of the Mann–Elkins Act when enacting the Communications Act of 1934. In addition to giving the newly created Federal Communications Commission the authority to ensure that interstate telephone rates were just, reasonable, and nondiscriminatory, the Act also addressed the ICC's lack of authority to require tariffs by requiring all interstate carriers to file schedules of charges. At the same time, the Act preserved the preexisting division between federal and state authority by including language providing that "nothing in this Act shall be construed to apply or to give the Commission jurisdiction with respect to . . . charges, classifications, practices, services, facilities, or regulations for or in connection with intrastate communication service of any carrier." The Act also gave the FCC the authority to oversee what became known as the "separations" process, through which the agency would determine what proportion of the costs of capital equipment used for both local and long distance would be allocated to each service (47 U.S.C. §§ 152(b), 201(b), 202(a), 203, 221(c)).

## 2. The Emergence of Competition in Complementary Services

From the time of the enactment of the 1934 Act until the mid-1960s, regulators and the Bell System entered into a symbiotic relationship. The regulatory authorities

---

2  *W. Union Tel. Co. v. Esteve Bros.*, 256 U.S. 566, 573 (1921); *Clay County Produce Co. v. W. Union Tel. Co.* (*Unrepeated Message Case*), 44 I.C.C. 670, 673–74 (1917).

3  *White v. W. Union Tel. Co.*, 33 I.C.C. 500 (1915); *Malone v. N.Y. Tel. Co.*, 40 I.C.C. 185 (1916); *Commercial Cable Co. v. Sw. Union Tel. Co.*, 45 I.C.C. 33 (1917); *Whittaker v. W. Union Tel. Co.*, 59 I.C.C. 286 (1920). *See generally* U.S. House (1934, p. 69) observing that "it is known to everyone that the Interstate Commerce Commission has never found it practical to do anything toward the regulation of telephone rates." Sharfman (1931, p. 110) observes that "[i]n practice, . . . there has been no extensive exercise of these broad powers" over interstate communications by the ICC. Robinson (1989, p. 7) notes "a general consensus that the ICC did not aggressively implement its new mandate."

condoned Bell System's monopolization of all aspects of the telephone network. Monopoly control in turn allowed regulators to authorize charging above cost for certain services and use the excess returns to cross-subsidize below-cost service for other services. For example, the FCC used its control over the separations process to allocate to long-distance rates an ever-increasing proportion of the costs of the capital equipment used to provide both local and long-distance service, such as telephone handsets, the wires connecting individual customers' premises to central offices (commonly known as "local loops"), and the switching equipment located in central offices. The higher long-distance charges were thus used to keep monthly charges for local telephone service low. State regulatory authorities similarly used higher charges on business users to cross-subsidize the rates paid by residential users. Finally, regulatory authorities used a system known as "rate averaging" to mandate that all telephone subscribers in the state pay the same rates for service. The effect was to require lower-cost urban users to cross-subsidize the service for higher-cost rural users. The Bell System, which by this time had established a pattern of cooperating with regulatory authorities, acceded. So long as the resulting rates protected its aggregate rate of return, it had little concern over the allocation of that revenue across different customers and services (Temin 1987).

Over time, outside forces began to undercut this cozy arrangement. First, after a long period of rate decreases during the 1940s and 1950s, the Bell System began to seek increases in long-distance rates. Complaints from members of Congress and the General Services Administration prompted the FCC to initiate its first systematic analysis of the Bell System's costs, which revealed wide disparities in rates of return across seven different classes of interstate service. As a result, the FCC abandoned its system of "continuing surveillance," in which long-distance rates were established through informal negotiations between AT&T and the agency, in favor of a more formal regulatory regime based on cost-of-service ratemaking (FCC 1965c).

In addition, competition began to emerge from providers of complementary services. For example, producers of the telephone equipment located in people's houses and individual offices, known as CPE, began to seek access to the Bell System's local telephone networks. "Foreign attachments" provisions contained in the Bell System's tariffs prohibited the interconnection of any CPE not manufactured by the Bell System's manufacturing subsidiary, Western Electric. As noted in Chapter 4, prompted by the D.C. Circuit's *Hush-a-Phone* decision, the FCC issued its landmark *Carterfone* decision, which eventually led to the adoption of the Part 68 rules requiring the Bell System to open its network to any CPE that met specified requirements (FCC 1968, 1975, codified at 47 C.F.R. pt. 68).

The emergence of microwave transmission as a means of transmission allowed competition to emerge in long distance as well. A new company called Microwave Communications, Inc. (later known by its acronym, MCI) realized that it could expand its private line services, which were designed to serve companies with multiple offices in distant locations both by connecting those offices together and by providing connections to the local telephone networks surrounding each location, to provide long-distance service as well. Again after some prodding by the courts,[4] the FCC (1980b) acceded and allowed long-distance competition to emerge.

In addition, a new set of services, originally called "enhanced services" and later called "information services," began to emerge that combined computing power with transmission to provide innovative new services that went far beyond traditional voice communications. Some of these services were dial-up services that were the predecessors to the modern Internet, which used analog modems to make it possible for the first time to connect computers to the network. Other services harnessed computing power in the network itself, typically in the newly digitized switches, to provide new services, such as voice mail, call waiting, and caller ID. Because these functions were most efficiently provided through the switch itself, they became known as "vertical switching services."

Policymakers soon became concerned that the incumbent local telephone companies would be able to use their monopoly control over the local telephone networks to favor their own proprietary enhanced and information service offerings. As a result, the FCC initiated its first and second *Computer Inquiries*, which required that any leading local telephone companies wishing to provide data processing or enhanced services do so through separate corporate subsidiaries and required that those companies serve all enhanced service providers on a nondiscriminatory basis (FCC 1971, 1980a).[5]

The FCC later concluded in its third *Computer Inquiry* that the costs of the separate subsidiary requirement outweighed the benefits and that nonstructural safeguards could protect against anticompetitive activity just as effectively. Consequently, it allowed local telephone companies to avoid the separate subsidiary requirement so long as they adhered to a two-phase system of alternative regulatory requirements. The first phase was in essence a nondiscriminatory access mandate known as CEI, which required local telephone providers to provide unaffiliated enhanced service providers with access to the same facilities on the same terms and conditions provided to their own proprietary enhanced and information service offerings. The second phase, known as ONA, in essence required unbundled access to all of the incumbent's network elements (FCC 1986a). A series of judicial challenges prevented the alternative regime created by the *Third Computer Inquiry* from ever being fully implemented.[6]

As we discuss at greater length in Chapter 9, the consent decree ordering the breakup of AT&T also required the local telephone companies to provide equal access to all long distance and information service providers. This regime was later

---

4   See *MCI Telecomms. Corp. v. FCC*, 561 F.2d 365 (D.C. Cir. 1977); *MCI Telecomms. Corp. v. FCC*, 580 F.2d 590 (D.C. Cir. 1978).

5   Both orders were affirmed on judicial review (*GTE Serv. Corp. v. FCC*, 474 F.2d 724 (2d Cir. 1973); *Computer & Commc'ns Indus. Ass'n v. FCC*, 693 F.2d 198 (D.C. Cir. 1982)).

6   For the difficulties that the third *Computer Inquiry* faced in surviving judicial review, see Chapter 4.

extended to mandate equal access to CPE as well. These measures made no attempt to introduce competition into local telephony. Instead, they conceded that local telephone service remained a natural monopoly and instead attempted to foster competition in complementary services (FCC 1996b).

### 3. The Emergence of Competition in Local Telephony

Eventually, competition began to emerge not just in services that were complementary to local telephony, but also with respect to local telephone service itself. The arrival of fiber optics fostered the emergence of a new type of companies known as competitive access providers (CAPs). CAPs initially focused on offering long-distance bypass services, which allowed corporate customers to place long-distance telephone calls without having to access the Bell System's local telephone facilities. The eventual expansion of CAP networks to cover the entire core business districts of major metropolitan areas made it possible for CAPs to begin to offer local telephone service in direct competition with the incumbents.

CAP-provided services possessed many advantages over those provided by the incumbent local telephone companies. First, CAP networks tended to employ more modern technology, which allowed them to offer a greater range of features and a more attractive price structure than could the incumbent local telephone companies.[7] Unlike the incumbents, moreover, CAPs were not required to provide uniform services according to published tariffs approved by the FCC. As a result, they were able to respond more quickly to market demands and to tailor pricing and terms of service to each customer's needs. Last, the untariffed nature of CAP services also allowed them to avoid the cross subsidies embedded in the system of access charges created by the FCC.

The FCC recognized that the emergence of CAPs meant that some local telephone calls would originate on one carrier's network and terminate on another's. The incumbent local telephone company could use its dominant position to forestall the CAPs' ability to compete effectively, either by interconnecting with the CAPs on unattractive terms or by refusing to interconnect with them altogether. Thus, if CAPs were to compete with the incumbent local telephone companies, they needed to interconnect with the incumbent networks on the same terms and conditions that the incumbent provided for their own circuits.

As a result, the FCC's *Expanded Interconnection* proceeding gave CAPs the right to interconnect with the incumbent's network on nondiscriminatory terms. As part of this regime, the FCC gave CAPs the right to place in the incumbent's central offices any equipment needed to terminate calls. The FCC believed that

---

7   Specifically, the use of fiber optics provided dramatic improvements in the amount of bandwidth available. It also decreased service costs in general and made them much less distance-sensitive. Fiber optics also allowed CAPs to take advantage of the efficiencies made possible by computer processing, such as improved switching and digital compression.

this right, which the FCC dubbed "physical collocation," was necessary to ensure that the interconnection provided to the CAPs was comparable to that used by the incumbent for itself. If the incumbent's central office lacked the physical space to accommodate physical collocation, the incumbent could instead provide "virtual collocation," which required the incumbent to install and maintain on its property equipment that allowed the requesting carrier to interconnect with the incumbent's network through a location outside of the incumbent's central office. Interconnection prices for both physical and virtual collocation would be governed by price caps. As in other price cap regimes, initial rates would be based on historical cost. The FCC also rejected arguments that the physical collocation requirement violated the Takings Clause on the grounds that physical takings doctrine was not applicable to public utility property, which was governed exclusively by the framework applied to regulatory takings. Even assuming that physical collocation did constitute a taking, the FCC argued in the alternative that the compensation provided was sufficient to render it constitutional. State regulatory authorities issued similar orders in order to facilitate CAP entry into local telephone service (FCC 1992b, 1993a).

The D.C. Circuit struck down the FCC's collocation rules on the grounds that they exceeded the FCC's statutory authority. The court reasoned that giving CAPs the right to place equipment in the incumbent's central offices represented precisely the type of permanent physical occupation that constituted a per se taking under *Loretto*. As a result, the physical collocation requirement ran afoul of the principle that statutes should not be construed to create "an identifiable class of cases in which application of a statute will necessarily constitute a taking" (*Bell Atl. Tel. Cos. v. FCC*, 24 F.3d 1441, 1445–47 (D.C. Cir. 1994), quoting *United States v. Riverside Bayview Homes, Inc.*, 474 U.S. 121, 128 n. 5 (1985)).

The FCC responded to this decision by ceasing to make physical collocation mandatory and by giving the incumbent local telephone companies the option of providing virtual collocation instead. The FCC continued to maintain that mandatory physical collocation did not constitute a per se taking, but argued that, regardless of whether that were true, offering virtual collocation as an option eliminated any such constitutional infirmity (FCC 1994). Before the courts could address the validity of these revised regulations, the entire scheme was rendered moot by the enactment of the Telecommunications Act of 1996.

## 4. The Telecommunications Act of 1996

The Telecommunications Act of 1996 was designed to "open [ . . . ] all communications services to competition," including local telephone service (U.S. House 1995, p. 48). Policymakers envisioned that competition in local telephone markets might emerge through one of three paths. First, a new entrant might obtain *all* of the necessary elements from the incumbent local telephone company and resell them. Resale rates would be based on retail rates less "any marketing, billing, collection, and other costs that will be avoided" when local telephone services are provided by another carrier (47 U.S.C. §§ 251(c)(4), 252(d)(3)).

Second, a new entrant might construct an entirely new network. Because any new entrant would need to be able to place calls to and receive calls from the incumbent local telephone companies' customers, the 1996 Act requires that incumbents allow any requesting telecommunications carrier to interconnect with their networks at any technically feasible point on terms that are equal in quality to those that the incumbent provides for its own circuits and that are "just, reasonable, and nondiscriminatory" (47 U.S.C. § 251(c)(2)(B)–(D)).

The Act recognized, however, that not every facilities-based entrant would be able to have its entire network in place at the time it began to offer local service. In order to allow competition to emerge before entrants had fully established their networks, Congress established a third path for entering local telephone markets by requiring every incumbent local telephone company to interconnect with any requesting carrier and to provide other carriers with access to all of its network elements on an unbundled basis. Such access must be provided at any technically feasible point under rates, terms, and conditions that are just, reasonable, and nondiscriminatory. In determining which network elements would be subject to the unbundled access requirement, the statute required the FCC to consider whether "access to such network elements as are proprietary in nature is *necessary*" and whether "the failure to provide access to such network elements would *impair* the ability of the telecommunications carrier seeking access to provide the services that it seeks to offer" (47 U.S.C. § 251(c)(3), (d)(2)(A) & (B) (emphasis added)). As we discuss in greater detail below, because the initial list of UNEs developed by the FCC contained all of the elements needed to provide local telephone service, non-facilities-based competitors were initially able to bypass resale access altogether by using UNE access to create the so-called UNE-Platform (UNE-P) to offer the same services provided under resale at lower cost.

Prices for interconnection and access to unbundled network elements are to be determined through voluntary negotiations between the incumbents and the requesting carriers, at times aided by mediation by a state public utility commission. If the parties are unable to reach a voluntary agreement, the statute gives state public utility commissions the authority to set rates through binding arbitration, which would be governed by one of two statutory mandates. First, rates for interconnection and access to unbundled network elements set by arbitration shall be "based on the cost . . . of providing the interconnection or network element," provided that cost is "determined without reference to a rate-of-return or other rate-based proceeding." Second, the statute required that compensation for traffic originating on one network and terminating on another be governed by the principle of "reciprocal compensation," which "provide[s] for the mutual and reciprocal recovery by each carrier of costs associated with the transport and termination on each carrier's network facilities of calls that originate on the network facilities of the other carrier." Such costs must be determined "on the basis of a reasonable approximation of the additional costs of terminating such calls," although carriers may waive mutual recovery in favor of other arrangements, such as bill-and-keep systems (47 U.S.C. § 252(d)(2)(A)(i)). The result was a widescale federalization of local telephony, including many areas of regulation that had previously fallen within the jurisdiction of the states.[8]

By their nature, both interconnection and access to UNEs typically require the requesting carrier to place some of its equipment on the incumbent local telephone company's property. In addition, UNE access presupposes some ability to combine the incumbent's network elements with facilities supplied by the new entrant. In either case, requesting carriers must be allowed to establish physical connections between their equipment and the incumbent's network. The element most likely to be accessed in this manner is the local loop, which possesses the characteristics of a natural monopoly more than perhaps any other network element. A carrier who requests unbundled access to the local loop needs to be able to terminate that loop by connecting it to the requesting carrier's switching equipment.

As result, the 1996 Act included collocation requirements that were quite similar to those adopted by the FCC in its *Expanded Interconnection* proceedings. Specifically, the statute requires incumbents to permit "physical collocation of equipment necessary for interconnection or access to unbundled network elements." When technical considerations or space limitations render physical collocation impractical, incumbents need only provide virtual collocation (47 U.S.C. § 251(c)(6)).

The FCC implemented the local competition provisions of the 1996 Act in a massive order issued just three months after the statute's enactment. The FCC implemented the provisions governing interconnection and UNE access rates through a methodology known as TELRIC, which bases rates on the element's "economic costs," defined as the sum of the incremental costs directly attributable to the specified element and a reasonable allocation of common costs. TELRIC's most distinctive feature was the fact that it assessed both the incremental and common costs on a forward-looking basis by focusing on what it would cost to replace a particular network element rather than its historical cost. TELRIC avoids the problems caused by the distinction between fixed and variable costs by measuring incremental costs from a "long run" perspective, which is defined to be a period long enough so that all of a firm's costs become variable or avoidable. The FCC believed that basing rates on forward-looking incremental cost represented the best way to replicate, to the extent possible, the conditions of a competitive market. In addition, TELRIC further accommodates technological change by requiring that costs be determined on the basis of the most efficient technology available and the lowest cost network configuration given the existing location of the incumbent's current wire centers. It declined to incorporate an element to reflect the opportunity cost borne by the network owner providing unbundled access to network elements to competitors (FCC 1996c).

---

8   See *AT&T v. Iowa Utils. Bd.*, 525 U.S. 366, 378 n. 6 (1999).

Although the statutory mandate underlying TELRIC on its face applied only to compensation for interconnection and access to unbundled network elements, the FCC determined that TELRIC should also govern compensation for physical collocation. In addition, the FCC determined that TELRIC represented the appropriate interpretation of "the additional costs of terminating such calls" that govern reciprocal compensation, although the statue explicitly reserves the possibility of bill and keep (FCC 1996c).

In so ruling, the FCC rejected arguments that imposition of TELRIC violated the Takings Clause. In contrast to the reasoning advanced in its *Expanded Interconnection* proceedings, which argued that takings of public utility property are governed by the Court's regulatory takings jurisprudence, the FCC argued that the guiding principle for determining whether regulation of public utilities violates the Constitution depends on whether the rates are confiscatory. Alternatively, assuming for the sake of argument that physical collocation constitutes a physical taking, the FCC found that its ratemaking methodology satisfies the just compensation standard, because the constitutional requirement that the government pay the fair market value of the property taken as compensation did not permit recovery of monopoly rents (FCC 1996c, 2000c).

## B. The Rationales for Regulating Local Telephone Networks

The regulation of local telephone service provides an opportunity to examine the application of the regulatory rationales introduced in Chapter 4. The impact of these regulatory efforts and the challenges that state and federal regulators confronted illustrate the difficulty of attempting to impose regulation on such a technologically complex and dynamic industry, as well as how the emergence of competition is undermining these regulatory rationales.

## 1. Natural Monopoly

One of the bedrock assumptions of telecommunications policy is that local telephone networks are natural monopolies, primarily because of the large fixed cost investments associated with establishing telephone switches and the network of wires needed to transmit telephone calls. Natural monopoly represented one of the central justifications for early regulatory efforts in the 1920s as well as the regulatory scheme created by the Communications Act of 1934 (U.S. Senate 1921b, 1934a, 1934b). Indeed, the entire telephone network was generally regarded as a natural monopoly until the 1960s.[9] Even after the FCC began to use regulation and the breakup of AT&T to promote competition in services complementary to local telephony, such as CPE, long distance, and information services, policymakers

---

9  See Faulhaber (1987); Huber et al. (1999).

continued to believe that local telephone networks remained natural monopolies, largely by virtue of the high fixed costs associated with laying the wires needed to make local distribution possible.[10] As noted in Chapter 4, unless products are differentiated, the presence of economies of scale that are not exhausted over the entire range of industry output is a sufficient condition for natural monopoly. It was not until the enactment of the Telecommunications Act of 1996 that policymakers began attempting to promote local competition in earnest.

A close analysis of the cost structure belies any suggestion that local telephone service constituted a natural monopoly during the early years of the telephone industry. The primary source of diseconomies of scale was switching.[11] Initially, an operator at a switchboard made telephone connections manually. Switching was relatively simple so long as the number of subscribers connected to any particular exchange was relatively small. Increases in the number of subscribers eventually required the installation of additional switchboards interconnected through trunk lines, which in turn caused switching to become more complex. For example, in an exchange with two switchboards, one-half of all calls would require the participation of two operators to set up and take down each call, whereas calls to exchanges with three and four switchboards would require multiple operators for two-thirds and three-quarters of all calls, respectively. In addition, the presence of multiple switchboards increased the organizational problem considerably. Operators had to keep track of the board on which each customer resided and which trunk lines were open at any particular time. The problem becomes all the more difficult after one considers, as we point out in Chapter 2, that the number of connections increases quadratically with the number of users. Thus, increases in the subscriber base drastically increased both the cost of service and the complexity of the organizational problem.

The diseconomies of scale in switching became a major problem for the Bell System, which had to seek rate increases as its subscriber base grew. It also became a trap for the independents, who often entered based on the promise of lower rates, only to find that their very success in attracting business away from the Bell System rendered those rates unsustainable.[12] The result was that duplication of networks did not necessarily cause costs to increase. Although the deployment of mechanical switches eventually caused switching to become less important as a source of

---

10   *Verizon*, 535 U.S. at 475–76 (noting that at the time of the breakup of AT&T, local telephone service was "thought to be the root of natural monopoly in the telecommunications industry"); *United States v. W. Elec. Co.*, 673 F. Supp. 525, 537–38 (D.D.C. 1987), *aff'd*, 894 F.2d 1387 (D.C. Cir. 1990) (concluding that local telephone service "is characterized by very substantial economies of scale and scope" and that "[t]he exchange monopoly of the Regional Companies has continued because it is a natural monopoly"); Kahn (1971, p. 127) ("That the provision of local telephone service is a natural monopoly is generally conceded"); Breyer (1982, p. 291) ("Local telephone service seems to be generally accepted as a natural monopoly").

11   For an excellent discussion of the diseconomies of scale in switching, see Mueller (1989).

12   Weiman and Levin (1994); Mueller (1997).

diseconomies of scale, the Bell System did not begin widescale deployment of mechanical switches until 1919 (U.S. House 1939). The explanation for the reassertion of the Bell System's dominance after 1907 lies elsewhere.

Disputes over the extent to which the local telephone network constituted a natural monopoly persisted well into more recent times. Leading treatises on regulated industries acknowledge the persistence of disputes over whether the telephone industry was characterized by increasing or decreasing average costs (Bonbright 1961). A vibrant empirical literature emerged debating whether local telephone networks were natural monopolies. Some studies concluded that local telephone service was subadditive (Charnes et al. 1988; Röller 1990a, 1990b; Wilson and Zhou 2001; see also Gabel and Kennet 1994; Gasmi, Laffont, et al. 2002). Other studies drew the opposite conclusion (Evans and Heckman 1983, 1984; Shin and Ying 1992; Berg and Tschirhart 1995).

Subsequent technological developments have largely rendered these disputes moot. The advent of digital technologies has caused a precipitous drop in the cost of switching. In 2003, the FCC removed switches serving large business customers from the list of elements to which new entrants could obtain UNE access. At the same time, it continued to allow UNE access to switches serving residences and small businesses, not because of high fixed costs, but rather because of operational problems associated with "hot cuts," during which the line serving a particular customer is disconnected from the incumbent's switch and reattached to the new entrant's. Both findings could be rebutted on a case-by-case basis (FCC 2003d).

The D.C. Circuit upheld the FCC's decision with respect to large business customers, observing that "[t]here appears to be no suggestion that mass market switches exhibit declining average costs in the relevant markets, or even that switches entail large sunk costs" and that deployment of duplicate switches did not appear to be either "uneconomic" or "wasteful." At the same time, the court overturned the FCC's refusal to deregulate switching for residential and small business customers (*U.S. Telecom Ass'n*, 359 F.3d 554, 568–73, 586–87 (D.C. Cir. 2004)).

On remand, the FCC harmonized the two findings by ruling that mass market switching was no longer subject to UNE access requirements, largely because of the widescale deployment of competitive circuit switches and the investment disincentives created by sharing requirements (FCC 2005a). This time the court sustained the FCC's action (*Covad Commc'ns Co. v. FCC*, 450 F.3d 528, 546–49 (D.C. Cir. 2006)).

Competition has even begun to emerge with respect to the local loop, the portion of the local telephone network thought most likely to retain natural monopoly characteristics. State public utility commissions have begun to deregulate local service to large business customers (Tardiff 2007), although the FCC continues to subject high-capacity loops (except for dark fiber) to UNE access obligations (FCC 2005a). Wireless has also emerged as a vibrant competitor in local telephone service in the residential and small business markets, with the number of wireless subscribers surpassing the number of wireline subscribers since 2004 and with

30 million American adults (roughly 14 percent) relying solely on their wireless phones for service.[13] Competition from VoIP provided via coaxial cable is starting to emerge for residential and small business customers as well. Although state and federal regulators have exhibited some reluctance to deregulate local telephone service on the basis of intermodal competition, as noted in Chapter 4, they have begun the process of deregulating local telephone service as well.

## 2. Network Economic Effects

Policymakers have also invoked network economic effects as a justification for widescale regulation of local telephone service. The leaders of the Bell System clearly understood the importance of network economic effects. As it noted in its 1908 Annual report, "A telephone without a connection at the other end of the line is ... one of the most useless things in the world. Its value depends on the connections with other telephones – and increases with the number of connections" (AT&T 1908, p. 21; see also Bonbright 1961). Indeed, the Bell System attempted to use network economic effects to leverage its initial dominance by refusing to interconnect with independent telephone systems during the early years of competition. Some scholars have suggested that network economic effects played a key role in the Bell System's return to dominance after 1907.[14] Some argue that the Bell System reasserted its dominant position by refusing to interconnect with the independents' *local* telephone networks. According to this argument, the network economic effects from connecting with other local customers created demand-side scale economies that gave Bell a decisive advantage.[15] Others focus on the network economics effects provided by Bell System's refusal to allow the independents to interconnect with its *long-distance* network. Under this argument, key potential long-distance technologies, such as the Pupin coil, enabled the Bell System to provide superior long-distance service, which in turn increased the value of the network by increasing the number of customers any subscriber could reach through the network. These network economic effects, according to this variant of the argument, gave the Bell System a decisive competitive advantage that it could use to drive out the independents simply by refusing to allow them to interconnect with its long distance network.[16]

As we discussed in Chapter 4, competition already provides powerful incentives for networks to interconnect, and in the absence of a dominant player, any one firm's refusal to interconnect is unlikely to harm competition. As the FCC reasoned when declining to require wireless telephone networks to interconnect with one another, "In view of the growth of competition in the [wireless] market, ... we continue to

---

13   FCC (2005i); *New York Times* (2007).
14   Lipartito (1989, p. 250 n. 4) calls "[t]he notion that Bell's refusal to interconnect was a potent competitive weapon" an "article of faith in the telephone literature."
15   Lemley (1996); Shelanski and Sidak (2001).
16   Brooks (1975); Langdale (1978); Brock (1981); Faulhaber (1987); Noll and Owen (1989).

believe that the best way of achieving interconnection is through voluntary private agreements" (FCC 2000b, p. 13534).

A close analysis of the history of the era reveals that the refusal to interconnect likely played little role in allowing the Bell System to reassert its dominance.[17] The Bell System's long-distance network was unlikely to serve as a source of demand-side economies of scale. During this period, long distance represented only a tiny fraction of the overall demand for telephone service.[18] Indeed, contemporary observers acknowledged that its ability to provide superior long-haul long-distance service was "of little commercial or social importance." Short-haul long-distance service could be provided simply by interconnecting adjacent exchanges. Again, the Bell System held no competitive advantage for this type of traffic, because AT&T and the independents were employing the same technology (Mueller 1997).

Neither were the Bell System's local telephone networks likely to have served as the source of significant network economic effects. As we explained in Chapter 4, network economic effects are unlikely to be a source of anticompetitive problems in markets undergoing rapid growth, as was the case in the early telephone industry. The Bell System had patterned its initial business strategy on Western Union's, which primarily provided long-distance communications to business customers located in large commercial centers. As a result, the Bell System largely ignored small cities, rural areas, and residential areas, not even making much of an effort to connect larger cities to their suburbs. The skeletal nature of the Bell System's network left substantial areas of the country in which new, independent telephone companies could enter without facing any opposition. The independents were thus free to pursue the large number of unserved customers who had no allegiance to the Bell System. Indeed, once the independents had established themselves in these unserved areas, it was they and not the Bell System who benefited from network economic effects.

The traditional account is also belied by the business strategy pursued by the independents. If AT&T had been in a dominant position, one would expect the independents to have been clamoring to interconnect with it. In fact, the independents did not want to interconnect with AT&T any more than AT&T wanted to interconnect with the independents. It was only after the Bell System changed policy and liberalized its interconnection policies that it began to reassert its dominance.

The early telephone industry thus most closely resembles the type of competition, identified in the theoretical literature and described in Chapter 4, in which two equal-sized players refuse to interconnect and instead engage in a race for the market in which "[t]he successful competitor strives to become the surviving monopolist" (Gabel 1969, p. 354). Interestingly, though, this type of competition does not lead

---

17 The discussion that follows draws on the excellent, but often overlooked revisionist literature on the early telephone industry. See Gabel (1969); Bornholz and Evans (1983); Weiman and Levin (1994); Mueller (1997).

18 *Smith v. Ill. Bell Tel. Co.*, 282 U.S. 133, 147 (1930). See also Mueller (1997).

to the delays in technology adoption and supracompetitive returns associated with refusals to interconnect by dominant firms. It also has the virtue of promoting the rapid buildout of new network technologies (Besen and Farrell 1994).

Spurred into a race for the market, both the Bell System and the independents began investing heavily in expanding their networks. Annual growth rates, which had been languishing at around 6 percent during the monopoly period, skyrocketed to over 20 percent during the competitive era. By 1907, the independent telephone industry had captured more subscribers than the Bell System and competed with Bell in 59 percent of cities with populations over 5,000. At this point, the independents could defeat whatever advantage AT&T might have gained by its refusal to interconnect simply by banding together to form a network of equal size (Noll and Owen 1989).

It is thus unlikely that network economic effects played a significant role in allowing the Bell System to reassert its dominance. As we shall discuss below, the true causes of the return of the Bell monopoly lay elsewhere.

### 3. Vertical Exclusion

Although initially the entire telephone system was regarded as a monopoly, the emergence of potential competition in portions of the network raised the possibility that the Bell System would use its control over the portions of the network that remained a natural monopoly, such as local telephone service, to harm competition in those portions of the network where competition was now possible. Vertical exclusion was thus the central concern underlying the Part 68 rules mandating that the Bell System open its local telephone networks to CPE manufactured by other companies. The same concern motivated requiring the Bell System to open its local telephone networks to competing long distance companies. It also underlay the *Computer Inquiries* requirement of structural separation and equal access to unaffiliated information service providers. As we discuss in greater detail in the next chapter, each of these decisions was reinforced by the consent decree settling the government's case against AT&T, which similarly mandated structural separation and equal access for long distance and information service providers.

All of these restrictions were eventually incorporated into the Telecommunications Act of 1996, which prohibited the local telephone companies formerly affiliated with the Bell System, known as Bell operating companies (BOCs), from providing long-distance services, manufacturing equipment, or engaging in two designated information services (specifically electronic publishing and alarm monitoring) in their home regions. The 1996 Act permitted the BOCs to offer other information services immediately and to offer electronic publishing so long as they did so through separate affiliates (47 U.S.C. §§ 271(b)(1), 273(a), 274(a), 275(a)(1)).

As we explained in Chapter 4, concerns about vertical exclusion depend on the assumption that local telephone service remains monopolized. The sunset provisions of the 1996 Act reveal the expectation that concerns about vertical exclusion would ultimately be dissipated by the emergence of competition in local telephone service. By the terms of the statute, the restrictions on information services expired in 2000 and 2001. The statute eliminated the prohibition against providing long-distance service and manufacturing equipment for BOCs either facing facilities-based competition or satisfying a fourteen-point competitive checklist establishing that they were providing nondiscriminatory access to their local telephone networks, although the BOCs seeking to offer those services had to do so through separate affiliates for an additional three years (47 U.S.C. §§ 271(c)(2), (d)(1), 272(f)(2), 273(a), 274(g)(2), 275(a)(1)). The FCC has ruled that sufficient progress has been made in every state except Alaska and Hawaii to justify permitting BOCs to begin offering long-distance service (FCC 2007b). With the increasing competitive pressure being brought by wireless carriers and broadband providers offering VoIP, it appears to be just a matter of time before vertical exclusion by local telephone companies ceases to be a regulatory concern.

In addition, certain services depend on a degree of vertical integration that structural separation and equal access requirements render impossible. Two persistent problems raised by the *Computer Inquiries* illustrate the problem. The advent of digital switching placed computing power in the switch that was capable of supporting a vast new array of vertical switching services, such as voice mail, call waiting, call forwarding, and advance calling. Although independent providers could offer such services, the services appeared to function most efficiently when their capabilities were designed directly into the telephone switch. Allowing local telephone companies to offer these services on an integrated basis, however, was inconsistent with the regime of nondiscriminatory access, interoperability, and transparency implicit in equal access and structural separation and needed an express regulatory waiver before they could be provided in this manner (FCC 1986b). Estimates of the cost of the delay in the introduction of such services caused by regulations to protect against vertical exclusion exceed $1 billion per year (Hausman 1997).

Another classic example of the problems associated with attempts to regulate vertical exclusion is the emergence of digital transmission, during which local telephone companies began moving away from routing traffic on a synchronous circuit-switched basis and began to employ asynchronous packet-switched protocols in portions of their networks. The shift to digital transmission technologies required the network to engage in protocol conversion at different points, which again was inconsistent with the regime of interoperability and transparency implicit in equal access and structural separation. After considerable regulatory wrangling, the FCC concluded that the costs of the regulations exceeded their benefits and permitted protocol conversion notwithstanding its inconsistency with the commitment to vertical disintegration embodied in the second *Computer Inquiry* (FCC 1983b, 1985b, 1985c, 1986a, 1996e).[19]

These examples illustrate some of the efficiency losses associated with attempting to regulate vertical exclusion in telecommunications. Technological

---

19  The Court of Appeals sustained the 1996 order on judicial review (*Bell Atl. Tel. Cos. v. FCC*, 131 F.3d 1044 (D.C. Cir. 1997)).

developments can cause interfaces that were once natural points of separation between companies to shift or collapse. These costs render all the more attractive the regulatory alternative of eliminating the problems of vertical exclusion by promoting facilities-based competition rather than by attempting to mandate structural separation and equal access.

### 4. Managed Competition

The Bell System raised the classic argument that entry by the independents had caused the industry to engage in ruinous competition. For example, in several Annual Reports, AT&T President Frederick Fish repeatedly complained that competition had driven rates too low to allow AT&T to recover its fixed costs (AT&T 1901, 1905, 1907). Theodore Vail picked up this refrain after he assumed the presidency of AT&T in 1907, complaining that "[d]uplication of plant is a waste to the investor" and that "[d]uplication of charges is a waste to the users." Competition simply forced "the public [to] pay double charges, on double capital, double operating expenses and double maintenance" (AT&T 1908, p. 18). Concerns about the costs to consumers from wasteful duplication also appeared in the report of the Study that laid the foundation for the Communications Act of 1934 (U.S. Senate 1934a). The avoidance of wasteful duplication was reflected in the fact that the order breaking up AT&T made no attempt to promote competition in local telephone service,[20] as well as the intention of UNE access requirements of the 1996 Act to permit competitors to share those portions of the network that remained a natural monopoly.[21]

As we noted in Chapter 4, ruinous competition has long been discredited as a justification for regulation. The duplication of costs about which Vail complained is an inevitable part of the market-based economy. As Richard Gabel (1969, p. 342) noted in his landmark study of the early telephone industry, "All competition involves *some* redundancy of plant facilities and work effort. The question is whether the pressure of competing market forces produces a better or cheaper product than a single supply service." As the independent telephone industry pointed out at the time, "What forces the business man to take two telephones? The same thing that forces him to advertise his goods in two newspapers in a town instead of one – to reach the people" (*Telephony* 1906, p. 11, quoted in Mueller 1997, p. 95). A newspaper monopoly would obviate the need for placing advertisements in multiple newspapers, but at the cost of lower circulation and higher prices.

The evidence suggests that, on balance, competition between local telephone providers provided significant benefits to consumers.[22] Subscribers who purchased

---

20  *United States v. W. Elec. Co.*, 673 F. Supp. 525, 537–38 (D.D.C. 1987).

21  *Iowa Utils. Bd.*, 525 U.S. at 416–17 (Breyer, J., concurring in part and dissenting in part); *Verizon*, 535 U.S. at 545 (Breyer, J., concurring in part and dissenting in part).

22  In the discussion that follows, we again draw on the excellent revisionist histories of the early telephone industry cited in note 17 as well as several other leading histories. See Brock (1981); Robinson (1989).

service from both the Bell System and the independent were able to obtain access to five to ten times the number of subscribers for a total price that was roughly the same as or less than that paid during the monopoly period.[23] At the same time, the benefits from eliminating competition in favor of unified service provided through a single telephone network were attenuated by the fact that most telephone subscribers only sought to communicate with a relatively small group of other people. As we noted in Chapter 4, heterogeneity of consumer preferences can render an equilibrium with multiple incompatible systems optimal. Indeed, most customers needed only to purchase one service, as groups tended to segregate themselves into discrete user communities clustered on one phone system or the other. As a result, the benefits of unifying these systems were minimal, and even those benefits could be easily realized by using public pay phones or the free phone service provided by bars and other local merchants. Thus, the elimination of competition provided few benefits to consumers.

Instead, the Bell System's arguments are better understood as part of what Gabel (1969, p. 358) has described as a deliberate "flight from competition." By 1907, the corporate leadership of the Bell System acknowledged that its initial strategy of trying to expand its network, cut rates, and refuse to interconnect with the independents was a colossal failure. The price cuts had a devastating effect on the Bell System's profitability, with revenue dropping from $88 per subscriber in 1905 to $43 per subscriber in 1907. Establishing local telephone service in the areas it did not yet serve required enormous amounts of capital, which the Bell System struggled to raise. Committed as the Bell System was to a business strategy centered on long distance, service provided by it required higher-quality equipment, which in turn made its local telephone networks more costly than the independents'. In contrast, the independent companies were able to construct systems at lower cost financed largely by local sources of capital raised by local residents who were able to leverage preexisting business relationships. Interconnecting with adjacent local systems allowed the independent telephone companies to establish regional long-distance networks that were just as effective for short-haul toll calling as the Bell System.

Spurred into a race for the market, both the Bell System and the independents began investing heavily in expanding their networks. As noted earlier, annual growth rates more than tripled and by 1907 the independent telephone industry had achieved parity with the Bell System in terms of total subscribers and competed with Bell in 59 percent of cities. At this point, if the independents had coordinated their activity, they could have defeated whatever advantage AT&T might have gained by its refusal to interconnect simply by banding together to form a network of equal size.

The failure of its initial response led the Bell System to switch strategies in 1907, when the New York-based Baker–Morgan banking interests took control from the Boston-based Forbes family and replaced company president Frederick Fish with

---

23 Bornholz and Evans (1983); Weiman and Levin (1994); Mueller (1997). Johnston (1908) also describes the dramatic drop in the Bell System's rates.

Theodore Vail. The Bell System stopped trying to outbuild the independents and instead attempted to coopt them through a pair of classic anticompetitive tactics. The first was merger to monopoly, in which the Bell System offered to buy out key competing systems. If the independent refused, the fallback strategy was division of markets, in which the Bell System agreed to withdraw from the independent telephone company's service area in return for the independent's promise to restrict its activities to a "small and compact" territory and the agreement to interconnect exclusively with the Bell System's long-distance network. The Bell System combined these classic anticompetitive strategies with an aggressive public relations campaign emphasizing the inconvenience and wasteful duplication associated with maintaining two different telephone systems and the benefits of being able to contact all telephone subscribers through a single network. The primary downside to the disappearance of competition would be the simultaneous disappearance of downward pressure on rates. Vail's response to this concern was to drop Bell's longstanding opposition to government intervention and instead to endorse direct regulation of telephone rates (AT&T 1908, 1911; Vail 1913; U.S. House 1939).

The primary beneficiary of unified service and the concomitant elimination of price competition would not be consumers, but rather the shareholders of the Bell System. Unification of local telephone service also benefited those classes of business that depended on the ability to contact regional and national business centers, such as banks, railroads, hotels, and wholesale suppliers, and thus were the only customers that felt compelled to purchase service from both the Bell System and the independents. Unified service provided few benefits to small businesses and residences, who placed a substantially lower value on the ability to contact a broader range of people. For example, in the case of Norfolk, Virginia, the Bell System's acquisition of the independent allowed the 700 business customers who purchased both services to reduce their monthly charges by 25 percent. The 2,100 business customers who previously only purchased one service would pay higher rates, an increase of 20 percent for customers served by Bell prior to the merger and an increase of 100 percent for customers previously served by the independent (Weiman and Levin 1994).

It was the business users who subscribed to both systems who provided the key political support for the government's eventual acquiescence in the return of monopoly. After some initial resistance, the independents decided to cooperate with the Bell System's efforts. Having already built out much of the unserved areas of the country, the independents had faced a transition to the far more demanding strategy of pursuing more intensive development of established markets. Bell mergers with selected independents also fragmented their ability to provide short-haul long-distance service by directly interconnecting adjacent exchanges, despite Bell's assurances to the contrary, until the Bell System's so-called Vail Commitment of 1912 promised to leave the independent toll-line connections established by any acquired company unchanged. The independents' efforts to establish their own long-distance network were hampered by the fact that they were not a unified enterprise, which made coordination difficult and left them vulnerable to divide-and-conquer strategies, as well as by the Morgan banking interests' ability to persuade the Widener family to withdraw its financial support. Faced with dim prospects, the independents realized that merger was their best option.

This change in strategy reversed the downward trend in the Bell System's market share. The number of noncompeting independent telephone systems that had accepted the Bell System's offer of accommodation jumped from 25 percent to 79 percent between 1907 and 1909 and rose to 89 percent by 1913. The number of cities with population of over 5,000 in which competition existed plummeted from 59 percent in 1907 to 37 percent in 1913. By 1934, the Bell System's market share had once again reached 80 percent. With a few exceptions, the independent companies that remained served discrete areas in which the Bell System did not operate.

Thus, monopoly was not the justification for regulation. Regulation was instead the justification for monopoly. Regulation, moreover, proved ineffective at curbing rates. Consider first state regulation of intrastate rates. Debates over the proper method for determining the rate base prevented state regulatory authorities from developing a coherent basis for setting rates. The complexity of the corporate structure, in which the parent company owned the operating companies and rented telephone equipment to them through Western Electric, made it difficult for individual state authorities to discern each operating company's actual financial results, let alone regulate their profits. The regulatory challenge was made all the more difficult by the facts that state commissions were almost completely dependent on the Bell System for the information they needed and that the parent company was regulated at the federal level, whereas the operating companies were regulated at the state level and Western Electric was not regulated at all (U.S. House 1934). Thus, even histories of the early telephone industry that are largely sympathetic to the Bell System agree that "regulation, coming late and still almost non-existent in several of the States, has had relatively little effect in influencing the growth and financial success of the Bell telephone system" (Stehman 1925, p. 262).

Federal regulation of interstate rates was similarly unsuccessful. In the words of Gerald Brock (2002, p. 53), "The early FCC was an ideal regulatory agency from AT&T's perspective. It provided very little control or restriction on AT&T's interstate rates and activities but it did help prevent competition from arising." For the first three decades following the enactment of the 1934 Act, the FCC failed to undertake any formal investigations or to create any systematic basis for evaluating the reasonableness of AT&T's rates. Instead, the FCC engaged in a system of "continuing surveillance," in which long-distance rates were established through informal negotiations between AT&T and the agency.

The experience of the early telephone industry eloquently demonstrates why the conventional economic wisdom now uniformly rejects ruinous competition as the basis for regulation, as we noted in Chapter 4. Eventually, regulated monopoly was justified by the ability to use cross subsidies to support providing service in areas that would not otherwise have service. Although the conventional wisdom holds that promoting universal service in this manner was an objective since the enactment of the Communications Act of 1934,[24] such cross subsidies were not mentioned during the legislative deliberations over the Act and did not emerge until the 1970s, when AT&T began to face competition from new long-distance providers. The timing suggests that relying on cross subsidies is better understood as a flight from competition than as a principled justification for regulated monopoly.

Although policymakers have rejected ruinous competition as a justification for using regulation to eliminate competition altogether, they have attempted to manage competition for the purpose of facilitating entry. For example, the FCC has long imposed asymmetric regulation that subjected incumbents to rate regulation even after competition had emerged, although refusing to subject new entrants to the same strictures. The FCC was concerned that as long as the incumbent remained dominant, it continued to possess sufficient market power to charge supracompetitive prices. The FCC was also concerned that dominant carriers might engage in predatory pricing. Regulators were thus simultaneously concerned that dominant firms might charge prices that were either too high or too low (FCC 1980d).

The most prominent example of asymmetric rate regulation was with respect to long distance during the 1980s, during which time competition was just beginning to become established.[25] For example, until 1987, the FCC required AT&T to pay access charges to local telephone companies that were 55 percent higher than those paid by other long-distance carriers (FCC 1983c).[26] In addition, the FCC exempted new long distance companies, such as MCI and Sprint, from most tariffing requirements, while continuing to subject AT&T to rate regulation until its dominance over the long distance market dissipated in 1995 (FCC 1995e). As noted in Chapter 4, the courts invalidated the FCC's detariffing decisions, ruling that the agency lacked the power to exempt any long-distance carriers from rate regulation. The 1996 Act gave the FCC the discretion to forbear from enforcing regulations it found to be unnecessary to protect consumers or to promote the public interest (47 U.S.C. § 160). The FCC exercised this new authority to forbear from enforcing the tariffing requirements against long-distance carriers (FCC 1996d). This time, the decision was upheld by the courts (*MCI WorldCom, Inc. v. FCC*, 209 F.3d 760 (D.C. Cir. 2000)).

In addition, the FCC also attempted to facilitate entry by new long distance companies by requiring AT&T to lease portions of its long-distance network to its competitors. Although the FCC initially invoked a number of different rationales,

---

24   See, e.g., Bonbright (1961); Temin (1987).

25   Indeed, some commentators have suggested that the FCC's regulatory efforts did more to promote long distance competition than did technological change. These scholars argue that by the time of the breakup of AT&T, fiber optics had replaced microwave as the primary technology for long-distance transmission. Because fiber optics is essentially a wireline technology, long distance once again bore the natural monopoly characteristics (MacAvoy and Robinson 1983; Huber 1993; MacAvoy 1996).

26   The Court of Appeals affirmed this order in relevant part (*Nat'l Ass'n of Regulatory Util. Comm'rs v. FCC*, 737 F.2d 1095 (D.C. Cir. 1984)).

the concern that emerged as the most important was that the capital needed to establish long-distance service might impede new entrants from offering nationwide service from the outset, which in turn made it more difficult for new entrants to compete with AT&T. The FCC therefore imposed regulations providing new entrants with access to portions of AT&T's network to fill in the transitional coverage gaps that existed as they built out their networks, in the hope that new entrants would use access as a stepping stone to true facilities-based competition (FCC 1980c).[27] Congress, the FCC, and the Supreme Court also invoked this rationale to justify the provisions of the 1996 Act mandating access to local telephone networks (U.S. House 1996; FCC 1996a; *Verizon*, 535 U.S. at 491–92).

As we discussed in earlier chapters, access requirements can be quite problematic from the standpoint of both dynamic efficiency and administrability. As Justice Breyer noted in his partial concurrence and dissent in *Iowa Utilities Board*:

> [A] sharing requirement may diminish the original owner's incentive to keep up or to improve the property by depriving the owner of the fruits of value-creating investment, research, or labor. . . . [One cannot] guarantee that firms will undertake the investment necessary to produce complex technological innovations knowing that any competitive advantage deriving from those innovations will be dissipated by the sharing requirement.
>
> (*Iowa Utils. Bd.*, 525 U.S. at 428–29)

Justice Breyer similarly noted his partial concurrence and dissent in *Verizon* that compelling incumbents to share the cost-reducing benefits of a successful innovation destroys the incumbent's incentives to innovate in the first place (535 U.S. at 550–51). As we shall discuss in greater detail in Chapter 9, in *Trinko* a majority of the Supreme Court later embraced Justice Breyer's concerns about access requirements' impact on the incumbents' incentives to invest in their networks.

The concerns identified by the Supreme Court underscore the extent to which access requirements require regulators to strike a very delicate balance. If access prices are set too high, no one will avail themselves of the opportunity, and mandating access will simply impose costs without providing any corresponding benefits. If access prices are set too low, new entrants will forego facilities-based investment and will instead simply take advantage of the pricing offered through regulation. Investment distortions can be avoided only if access prices are set at the precise level that would mimic competitive outcomes. Establishing those prices is extremely difficult in the absence of external, unregulated markets that can serve as benchmarks and when regulators are dependent on the regulated entity for most of their information, as is often the case in local telephony. The pricing challenges are likely to be particularly problematic in industries that are technologically dynamic.

A growing empirical literature confirms that rate regulation has deterred entry by new competitors (Abel 2002). In addition, access regulation has largely failed to

---

27 This order was affirmed on judicial review (*S. Pac. Commc'ns Co. v. FCC*, 682 F.2d 232 (D.C. Cir. 1982)).

serve as a stepping stone toward full facilities-based competition (Ros and McDermott 2000; Eisner and Lehman 2001; Zolnierek et al. 2001; Crandall et al. 2004; Pindyck 2004; Hausman and Sidak 2005; Hazlett 2006; Quast 2008). The consequence is that a growing number of advocates who previously supported mandating access to telecommunications networks have become increasingly skeptical that doing so will provide any substantial economic benefits (see, e.g., Joskow and Noll 1999).

The FCC has also encountered considerable difficulty in determining the number of network elements that fall within the incumbent local telephone companies' UNE access obligations. Indeed, on three separate occasions, courts vacated the FCC's proffered unbundling rules for failure to comply with the 1996 Act's mandate that UNE access be limited to proprietary elements that are "necessary" and without which new entrants would "impair" the new entrants' ability to compete.[28] It was not until the fourth try that the FCC was able to issue rules that could withstand judicial scrutiny, more than a decade after the Act's enactment.[29] And by this time, the unbundling rules had largely become moot with respect to local telephone service, as the FCC had deregulated unbundling of network elements providing service to large businesses, small businesses, and residential customers.

The Supreme Court eventually upheld TELRIC as a matter of statutory construction in *Verizon Communications, Inc. v. FCC.* As several lower courts had done previously, the Court declined to reach the merits of the underlying takings claim. Instead, it explicitly adopted the clear implication of its previous decisions and held that takings challenges to ratemaking methodologies were generally inappropriate until the methodology in question had been embodied in an actual rate order. Although the Court entertained the possibility that a ratemaking methodology might have such sweeping implications that would justify addressing the constitutionality of a methodology on its face, the facts of the case before the Court did not justify doing so (*Verizon,* 535 U.S. at 524–56).

## C. The Different Types of Access to Local Telephone Networks

In addition to providing an opportunity to examine the different theoretical justifications for regulation, local telephone service also offers case studies in each of the five types of access we have identified. A close examination reveals how each type of access can have different impact on network demand, the optimal network configuration, transaction costs, implementation difficulties, and dynamic efficiency.

---

28  *Iowa Utils. Bd.,* 525 U.S. at 734–76; *U.S. Telecom Ass'n v. FCC,* 290 F.3d 415 (D.C. Cir. 2002); *U.S. Telecom Ass'n v. FCC,* 359 F.3d 554 (D.C. Cir. 2004).

29  *Covad Commc'ns Co. v. FCC,* 450 F.3d 528 (D.C. Cir. 2006).

## 1. Retail Access

Although the Federal Communications Commission has largely deregulated retail access for *interstate* services, state public utility commissions have continued to mandate retail access to *local* telephone networks. Although new carriers are often allowed to pick and choose among their customers, the incumbent local telephone company is typically designated the "carrier of last resort" and is unable to deny service to anyone who requests it. Because carriers could render retail access a nullity simply by charging exorbitant prices, retail access is generally accompanied by direct regulation of retail rates.

Retail access interferes with a network owner's ability to manage its network. As we noted in Chapter 5, networks owners configure their network based on the predicted level of network demand to provide service that satisfies consumers' expectations about reliability at the least cost. Unanticipated increases in demand leave the network owner with the options of increasing network capacity, refusing to accept new customers, rationing demand by increasing prices, or bringing demand back into line with supply by allowing service to degrade. Although expanding network capacity remains the best long-term solution, the simple reality that network capacity cannot be expanded instantaneously means that that may not be a short-run option. Retail access has the effect of foreclosing the second and third solutions by preventing the network owner from refusing customers and by limiting the prices it can charge. Although excess investment in network capacity has alleviated this problem in many areas over the past decade, such missteps do not always occur, and such problems are likely to emerge in the future.

In addition, designating the incumbent as the carrier of last resort gives rise to a moral hazard problem that has been termed "the return of the prodigal son" (Sidak and Spulber 1997a). In effect, retail access creates the possibility that a customer that leaves the incumbent for a competitor might return, in which case the incumbent would have no choice but to provide service. An incumbent whose customers demand certain levels of quality will thus have to maintain excess capacity as insurance against this possibility. The resulting distortion in the optimal network configuration requires the incumbent to cross-subsidize its competitors. More importantly, by forcing the network owner to deviate from the optimal network configuration, retail access inevitably results in an increase in cost.

As noted in Chapter 4, the rate regulation inevitably associated with retail access has raised additional implementation problems. State regulators have struggled to determine the appropriate rate base as well as the appropriate rate of return. As noted in Chapter 4, cost-of-service ratemaking also induces a number of systematic inefficiencies by failing to give owners incentive to economize and by biasing them toward capital-intensive solutions. The shift to price cap regulation has not completely eliminated these problems.

Retail access can also dull competitive forces in other ways. Filing tariffs requires local telephone companies to give their competitors advance notice of any changes in strategy. In addition, collusion is easier to maintain when products are undifferentiated and when the prices charged are visible. The tariffing process serves both of these functions and even places the state public utility commission in a position to punish any deviations from the cartel price. Even absent overt collusion, standardizing products and increasing price transparency facilitates noncooperative oligopoly behavior as well.

Retail access can also foreclose welfare-enhancing forms of price discrimination. When fixed costs are so large relative to variable cost, as is traditionally the case in local telephone service, the average cost curve lies above the marginal cost curve over the entire industry output. Thus any price that allows the network owner to cover its costs necessarily creates some degree of deadweight loss. Discriminatory pricing regimes, such as Ramsey pricing (1927), can ameliorate this deadweight loss by allocating a larger proportion of the fixed costs to those customers whose demand is most inelastic and allocating a smaller proportion to those customers who are most price-sensitive. In fact, price discrimination can theoretically lead to efficient outcomes if fixed costs are allocated in perfect inverse proportion to elasticity of demand.

Retail access can also increase transaction costs. Historically, many of the transaction costs have been the direct costs of participating in the tariffing process. Retail access also increases transaction costs indirectly. As an initial matter, tariffing provides incentives for competitors to challenge rates even when those challenges are unlikely to succeed on the merits. To the extent that retail access requires that all customers pay uniform rates for uniform services, it also limits network owners' ability to customize their offerings to the needs of particular customers.

As noted earlier, retail access can also adversely affect the incentives for both incumbents and competitors to invest in network capacity. If retail access prices are set too high, they will have no effect. If retail access prices are set too low, competitors will find entry and expansion of their networks unremunerative, because the regulated price will dampen customers' incentive to change networks. At the same time, low access prices reduce the incumbents' incentive to reinvest in their networks as well. The alternative is to follow the more orthodox mechanism of allowing the presence of short-run supracompetitive returns to signal competitors that the market is in long-run disequilibrium and to provide incentives for them to expand production. This mechanism can only function if retail access prices are set at market levels.

The best way to promote economic efficiency would thus be to base retail access rates on the price of local telephone service on the open market. Although local telephone service has long been regarded as a natural monopoly in which direct competition is impossible, the emergence of platform competition has begun to provide a wide range of possible external markets that can serve as bases for determining market value. New entrants have followed the lead of the CAPs and have constructed fiber optic networks that offer increasing competition with the incumbent LECs' networks.

Even more importantly, providers of wireless telephone services have success-fully emerged as direct competitors to the incumbent LECs. The FCC chose to deploy the first generation of wireless devices, composed of analog cellular telephones, by only issuing two licenses per city, with one of those licenses automatically going to the incumbent LEC servicing that city (FCC 1981). Thus, wireless initially offered only modest improvements to the competitive environment. The arrival of sec-ond generation wireless devices, known as "Personal Communication Services" (PCS), significantly increased the number of competitive options (FCC 1993b). The result is that the wireless telephone industry has become highly competitive, with ninety-three percent of the U.S. population able to choose from among four different wireless providers (FCC 2006b). As a result, Congress preempted state regulation of wireless rates in 1993 (*Statutes at Large* 1993, pp. 394–95 (codified at 47 U.S.C. § 332(c)(3)(A)). Once third generation wireless devices ("3G") are fully deployed, competition in the wireless industry is likely to provide sufficient competition to drive market prices toward efficient levels. As noted in Chapter 4, after some reluctance to regard wireless as competitive with conventional local telephony, competition from wireless carriers has led the FCC to begin the process of deregulating local telephone service. Once that is completed, the distortions associated with retail access will disappear.

## 2. Wholesale Access

Policymakers have also experimented with various forms of wholesale access over the years. The issue first arose when the New York Public Service Commission (NYPSC) and the FCC approved Rochester Telephone's voluntary decision to spinoff its local telephone network into a separate company that would offer basic network services to all comers on a wholesale basis (NYPSC 1994; FCC 1995b). Wholesale access was mandated without structural separation by the resale pro-visions of the Telecommunications Act of 1996, which required all companies providing local telephone service on the day the statute was enacted "to offer for resale at wholesale rates any telecommunications service that the carrier provides at retail to subscribers" (47 U.S.C. § 251(c)(4)(A)). The Pennsylvania Public Util-ity Commission (2001), although rejecting requests to divide Verizon's wholesale and retail units into separate companies, nonetheless required Verizon to provide wholesale access to Verizon's competitors.

For the reasons we discuss at greater length in Chapter 5, wholesale access can adversely affect network performance. As noted in the discussion on retail access, unexpected deviations in demand can alter the optimal network configuration. The fact that demand under wholesale access depends on two prices – the prices of retail and wholesale access – renders the impact of wholesale access on network demand ambiguous. Depending on these two prices, network demand may either increase or decrease, which in turn adversely affects network cost, capacity, and the reliability of the network. Either result will have an adverse impact on the efficiency with which the network owner can provide service.

By externalizing the marketing functions, wholesale access can also increase transaction costs. At a minimum, wholesale access requires local telephone companies that were not already offering wholesale access services to the public to establish new systems through which competitors can order wholesale access and to track the quantity of services being provided. Furthermore, according to the Coasian theory of the firm, discussed in greater depth in Chapters 4 and 5, network owners minimize transaction costs by internalizing functions if and only if the internal monitoring and organizational costs associated with producing a particular input internally are lower than the transaction costs to contract for a particular service externally. Indeed, we see a wide variety of arrangements with respect to local telephone service. Consider the wireless telephone industry, for example. In some cases, wireless companies sell part of their output to consumers through proprietary outlets, while simultaneously selling part of their output through independent retailers, such as Circuit City, Radio Shack, and Best Buy. In addition, some wireless providers voluntarily provide wholesale access to mobile virtual network operators (MVNOs), which buy network services wholesale and combine them with other services, such as customized handsets and priority placement of certain content, to provide a unique product for the customer. Wholesale access disrupts this balance by forcing local network owners to make their entire networks available at wholesale prices even when it is not transaction-cost-minimizing for them to do so.

Congress thought that this non-facilities-based competition made possible by wholesale access might be the only form of competition possible in many markets in which a facilities-based competitor was unlikely to emerge in the near term (U.S. House 1995). As the D.C. Circuit has noted, wholesale access provides a "completely synthetic" form of competition (*U.S. Telecom Ass'n*, 290 F.3d at 424; *Covad*, 450 F.3d at 548). Because all firms are providing service on the same network, there is no opportunity for firms to compete either by lowering cost or by providing innovations in service. Herbert Hovenkamp describes the type of competition in the following terms:

> Imagine that a town has only one seller of bananas, which is the local Kroger grocery store. Seeking to promote banana competition, the town passes a banana competition ordinance requiring Kroger to sell bananas at a steeply discounted wholesale price to individual entrepreneurs who push banana carts around the store, perhaps underselling Kroger itself by a few cents. In this case Kroger supplies the store facility, storage, heat, light, and even the bananas themselves, with the small sellers supplying little more than their labor.
>
> The banana competition ordinance simply confuses competition with large numbers of retailers. True banana competition would require individual stores with their own facilities, purchasing bananas on the market and retailing them to consumers. Nevertheless, this is what the 1996 Telecommunications

Act does. Small CLECs can lease most of their inputs from the Bells and even locate some of their equipment on Bell property. They are entitled to purchase the equipment and services they need at regulated wholesale prices, and then resell the services in competition with the Bells.

(Hovenkamp 2004, pp. 369–70)

It is for this reason that most commentators have found little value in the type of competition induced by wholesale access (Joskow and Noll 1999; Beard et al. 2001; Rosston and Noll 2002; Ness 2006). Under wholesale access, the only way that providers can compete with one another is by squeezing their profit margins until prices converge to cost. Regulatory authorities could dissipate any rents just as effectively simply by setting retail prices at appropriate levels. Indeed, because wholesale access prices are typically based on retail prices less any avoided costs, wholesale access mandates raise all of the problems associated with regulating retail rates, with the added complication that regulators must also determine the magnitude of the marketing and operational costs are actually avoided.

Wholesale access also has the potential to impair dynamic efficiency. To have any benefit, wholesale access prices must be set very precisely. If they are set too high, the entire wholesale access regime does not constrain the incumbent and instead simply imposes regulatory costs without providing any compensating benefits. If they are set too low, wholesale access destroys incentives for competitors to invest in their own networks and dampens the incentives for the incumbent to invest in its own facilities, because any benefit that it develops will have to be shared at wholesale cost. Indeed, the incumbent faces a moral hazard problem, in that its competitors can avoid the risks of opening new markets simply by waiting until the incumbent undertakes the necessary investments and then entering only those markets that prove profitable.

These difficulties are aptly demonstrated by the two major instances in which wholesale access has been mandated. Consider first Rochester Telephone's Open Market Plan, which proposed placing its local telephone network into a separate company that would serve all comers on a wholesale basis (Crandall and Sidak 2002). The NYPSC soon became concerned that the system of structural separation embodied in the Open Market Plan was unworkable. At the same time, the NYPSC received repeated requests for decreases in wholesale access prices, increasing the discount from full retail price from 5% to as much as 19.6%, as well as complaints about delays and difficulties in the process of ordering service. The wholesale access provisions of the Open Market Plan were eventually superseded by the Telecommunications Act of 1996 and by Global Crossing's acquisition of Rochester. During the period during which the Open Market Plan was in effect, the NYPSC (1998) acknowledged that "competition ha[d] yet to develop to any noticeable extent."

Studies analyzing the wholesale access provisions of the 1996 Act have similarly concluded that wholesale access has failed to serve either as a basis for competition among resellers or as a stepping stone toward facilities-based competition. In fact, the growth of wholesale access appears to be correlated with a drop in investment in facilities by both new entrants and incumbents, a connection largely corroborated in financial analysts' reports. Likewise, abandonment of wholesale access was accompanied by a move toward facilities-based competition through VoIP and emerging wireless technologies (Hausman and Sidak 2005; Hazlett 2006). Indeed, competitors and financial analysts agreed that wholesale access was uneconomical as a competitive strategy.[30]

### 3. Interconnection Access

Interconnection access arises any time two local telephone companies serve the same calling area. Because of the Bell System's strategy of either acquiring competing local systems or ceding the field to those competitors that refused to merge, Bell-owned local telephone companies rarely operated in the same calling areas as independent local telephone companies. It did happen on occasion, such as in the Los Angeles area, where GTE and Pacific Bell both provided local service to different parts of the Los Angeles area. As noted earlier, after the emergence of CAPs providing local telephone service in central business districts, the FCC mandated interconnection access. The 1996 Act formalized this requirement by mandating that all incumbents provide interconnection access.

Interconnection access disrupts network management to a much greater degree than retail and wholesale access. As noted in Chapter 5, the impact of interconnection access on network demand is ambiguous. On the one hand, by increasing the number of customers that subscribers can reach, interconnection access causes the value of the network to increase, which in turn should cause network demand to increase. On the other hand, the presence of alternative local telephone networks means that some customers may choose to become customers of other local telephone providers, which places downward pressure on network demand. Whether on balance network demand will increase or decrease depends on which of these two effects dominates.

The possibility that network demand may fall means that network owners may no longer have sufficient volume to take advantage of cost-reducing technologies. In addition, in contrast to retail and wholesale access, which only mandate access at the edges of the network where the network owner already offers service, interconnection access requires the creation of new points of entry at major nodes in the middle of the network. Networks that do not voluntarily offer service at these points will have to create new interfaces to permit interconnection and to meter service at these locations. Permitting access at these points also introduces a new source of flows in the middle of the network, which can have a major impact on

---

30  *Communications Daily* (1997); *Communications Today* (1998); *Telecommunications Reports* (1998a); *Telecommunications Reports* (1998b); *Wall Street Journal* (2004).

optimal network configuration and may cause congestion in portions of the network located quite far from the access point. The fact that traffic now originates and terminates outside of a single network also increases the cost of obtaining the information necessary for network planning and creates the possibility of strategic behavior to take advantage of the information asymmetries.

Some commentators have also warned that incumbent local telephone companies can use the refusal to provide interconnection access to harm competition. They argue that in the absence of interconnection, network economic effects will lead customers to flock to the largest network. Once the market reaches its tipping point, the value of the network of the dominant player will so far outstrip that of its competitors that the market collapses into a natural monopoly. Once tipped, the difficulties that new entrants face in generating sufficient volume to untip the market can cause the resulting monopoly to become locked in (Economides et al. 1996; Noam 1997; Shelanski 2007).

The analysis is not quite so simple, however. Because so much of the literature focuses on the potentially anticompetitive consequences of network economic effects, it is often overlooked that network economic effects also provide powerful incentives in favor of interconnection. For example, in a market with five equally sized players, any player that refused to interconnect would put itself at a tremendous competitive disadvantage (Katz and Shapiro 1985; Faulhaber 2005). As noted above, this conclusion is reflected in the FCC's current policy toward interconnection access in the wireless industry, in which it concluded that the presence of multiple similarly sized providers created sufficient incentive to ensure interconnection access even in the absence of regulation.

As noted in Chapter 4, refusal to interconnect is less likely to harm competition in markets undergoing rapid growth, because the primary focus in such markets is the acquisition of new users. The only scenario in which equally sized players have an incentive not to interconnect is when two equally sized firms engage in a race for the market. Interestingly, though, this type of competition does not lead to the delays in technology adoption and supracompetitive returns associated with refusals to interconnect by dominant firms (Besen and Farrell 1994). It also has the virtue of promoting the rapid buildout of new network technologies. Indeed, this appears to be precisely the type of competition that ensued during the early competitive era of local telephone service between 1896 and 1907, described above, during which time mandating interconnection would only have served to slow the buildout of the network. Once the telephone industry used mergers and division of markets to eliminate competition in local telephony, individual companies no longer had any incentive not to interconnect, because telephone companies with nonoverlapping local service monopolies have every incentive to interconnect with one another.

Mandating interconnection access necessarily requires regulatory authorities to establish access prices. The 1996 Act requires local carriers to interconnect and to settle the charges through a system of mutual and reciprocal compensation, which the statute provided would be based on "a reasonable approximation of the additional costs of terminating such calls" (47 U.S.C. §§ 251(b)(5), 272(d)(2)(A)). The FCC determined that reciprocal compensation rates would be based on TELRIC (FCC 1996a).[31]

As we have discussed in earlier chapters, any approach that bases prices on the cost of particular network components in essence treats each component as if it existed in isolation. In doing so, these approaches fail to capture networks' defining characteristic: that they are complex systems in which the value of any one component depends on its relationship with and the flows carried by the rest of the network. One of TELRIC's central failings is its inability to take the network's configuration and systemic interactions into account.

The problem of determining rates is made all the worse by the mandating of interconnection "at any technically feasible point" (47 U.S.C. § 251(c)(2)(B)). This requirement prevents the network owner from minimizing the adverse impact to its system by choosing which facilities to employ when fulfilling any particular request for service. In the worst case scenario, the right to designate the point of interconnection gives competitors the opportunity to act strategically by basing their access requests not on their needs, but rather on what would inflict the greatest harm on the network owner. A network owner may wish to hedge against this possibility by maintaining excess capacity in case one of its competitors decides to request access to a key portion of its network. This has the drawback of forcing the network owner to make capital investments that may never be used. Indeed, competitors that are acting strategically may well take into account whether the network owner maintains such excess capacity when deciding whether and where to request access. If so, the mere fact that the network owner has added excess capacity to hedge against the possibility of a strategic access request effectively guarantees that access will be sought elsewhere.

The emergence of local telephone competition has begun to provide market benchmarks that can obviate the need to establish interconnection access rates through regulation. As noted earlier, wireless telephone services have successfully emerged as direct competitors to wireline telephony. The emergence of the wireless industry is important because wireless-to-wireless interconnection is currently unregulated. As a result, the terms of interconnection between wireless carriers are determined through arms-length negotiations that can provide precisely the type of external benchmark needed to determine the market value of transport and call termination services. Admittedly, interconnection between wireless carriers does involve somewhat different considerations than interconnection with incumbent

---

31   The FCC allowed for two alternatives. First, state public utility commissions could adopt a proxy range set by the FCC (at 0.2 and 0.4 cents per minute for termination) (FCC 1996c). The Eighth Circuit struck down the use of proxy prices in *Iowa Utilities Board v. FCC*, 219 F.3d 744, 756–57 (8th Cir. 2000), *rev'd on other grounds sub nom. Verizon Commc'ns, Inc. v. FCC*, 535 U.S. 467 (2002). This portion of the Eighth Circuit's decision does not appear to have been challenged before the Supreme Court.

LECs. Direct comparisons are complicated by the significant differences in utilization rates as well as the emergence of wireless pricing schemes that do not differentiate between local and long distance service. The comparison is rendered more complicated by the fact that wireline telephony is based on a calling-party-pays regime, whereas in wireless both calling and receiving parties pay for their own connectivity. In addition, the ratio of usage costs to access costs is much higher for wireless networks than for wireline networks. The analysis is further obscured by the fact that such interconnection between wireless carriers is often accomplished indirectly through the LECs (FCC 2000b).[32] Still, as wireless and other facilities-based competitors grow, rates charged for interconnection between wireless competitors will continue to emerge as a market-based reference point that can be used to resolve pricing problems. The number of external benchmarks will only continue to grow as local cable operators and other types of broadband providers begin to offer local telephone service.

In the absence of external benchmarks based on actual market transactions, resort to some cost-based second-best measure of market value becomes necessary. As noted earlier, economic theory suggests that cost-based measures should follow ECPR, which sets rates as the sum of the direct incremental costs of providing an input and the opportunity costs that the incumbent incurs when the new entrant provides the services instead of the incumbent.[33] The opportunity cost should include not only the lost profit opportunities associated with access, but also the value of the network facilities rendered useless by the diversion of network elements to competitors. TELRIC includes elements designed to reflect the direct costs, but not the opportunity costs. The key problem with the FCC's analysis is its refusal to include any factor to reflect opportunity cost. In setting prices without considering the value of foregone alternatives, TELRIC in essence ignores the insights of neoclassical economics by basing value solely on cost without taking any demand-side effects into consideration. As such, TELRIC is fundamentally inconsistent with the analysis of markets that serves as the foundation for all modern economic theory.

32  Historically, such comparisons were complicated still further by the FCC's decision to award one of the two available first-generation cellular licenses to the incumbent LEC, which in turn produced reasons to question whether interconnection agreements between wireless carriers in fact represented arms-length transactions. The deployment of competitive wireless networks on a national scale, the subsequent emergence of PCS, and the impending arrival of third-generation wireless devices should eliminate this problem in the near future, if they have not done so already.

33  One of us has elsewhere advanced the argument that, in addition to ECPR, the rates charged for access to unbundled network elements should also include a nonbypassable end-user charge to compensate incumbent LECs for costs stranded by deregulatory innovations that caused investment-backed expectations to fail (Sidak and Spulber 1997a). Extended discussion of these issues falls outside the scope of this book. For the time being, it suffices to point out that the argument advanced in this article, while consistent with the imposition of such user charges, does not require it.

Although the FCC considered and rejected arguments that it should base access rates on ECPR, its reasons for doing so do not withstand analysis. The first reason was that it believed that the statutory requirement that prices be based on "cost" precluded it from considering opportunity cost (FCC 1996c). The *Verizon* Court specifically rejected this reasoning when it found the term "cost" to be "too protean" to support any such plain language argument (535 U.S. at 500–01). If anything, the FCC's argument is directly undercut by the fact that it is now an economic truism that opportunity costs represent a true economic cost borne by the incumbent LEC (Sidak and Spulber 1997a). Indeed, the Supreme Court in effect recognized as much when it cited "opportunity cost" as an example of a forward-looking "cost" that fell within the purview of the statute (*Verizon*, 535 U.S. at 499 n. 17).

The FCC's second reason for rejecting ECPR is equally misplaced. The FCC asserted that because ECPR calculates opportunity cost on the basis of current retail prices, it simply locks in monopoly rents without providing a mechanism for moving prices toward competitive levels (FCC 1992b, 1996c). This argument suffers from two fundamental flaws. First, it ignores the fact that as competition emerges in the retail markets, ECPR will dynamically readjust the opportunity-cost factor downward to reflect the increased competition in the downstream market. Indeed, once the downstream market becomes fully competitive, regulation of the input market will no longer be necessary. Second, the existence of any monopoly rents in retail prices is more properly regarded as the result of the failure of rate regulation at the state level rather than any theoretical flaw in ECPR. Such a failure would justify improving the manner in which state regulatory authorities establish retail prices. It does not provide a justification for incurring the myriad problems that would result from distorting access prices (Sidak and Spulber 1997a).

Although the Supreme Court upheld the FCC's ratemaking methodology in *Verizon*, it would be a mistake to construe the Court's action as a specific endorsement of TELRIC and a rejection of ECPR as a matter of economic policy. On the contrary, the Court carefully eschewed expressing any opinion about the relative merits of any particular economic approach to ratemaking. Instead, the Court based its decision on the deferential standard of review that gives agencies a wide range of discretion in resolving any interpretive ambiguities that exist in the statutes that they administer so long as the construction advanced falls within a wide zone of reasonableness. As a result, the Court's decision does not necessarily foreclose the possibility that the FCC might justifiably apply a ratemaking approach based on market prices or ECPR in the future.[34]

Regulators are also experimenting with alternative institutional arrangements that obviate the need to set access rates altogether. The statute made clear that it did not preclude arrangements that waive mutual recovery, such as bill-and-keep (47 U.S.C. § 272(d)(2)(B)(1)). Indeed, local telephone companies serving the same area, such as Pacific Bell and GTE, have long exchanged traffic on a bill-and-keep

---

34  See *Verizon*, 535 U.S. at 497–522, 541; *Iowa Utils. Bd.*, 525 U.S. at 426 (Breyer, J., concurring in part and dissenting in part).

basis (FCC 2001c). The rationale is that the payments one network would receive for terminating traffic from the other network would be largely offset by the payments that network would have to pay for traffic passing in the opposite direction. Whatever slight differences exist in traffic would not justify incurring the transaction costs needed to account for and bill the interchange of traffic.

The FCC's initial order implementing the Telecommunications Act of 1996 recognized that transaction costs can render flat-fee pricing of congestible resources efficient. One of the primary purposes of the 1996 Act was to foster the development of competition in local telephone services. As competition for local services emerged, some calls would inevitably originate on one company's local telephone network and terminate on the local telephone facilities of another company. In the process, both the originating and terminating carrier would incur costs. Because local telephone service in the United States has traditionally operated on a calling party pays basis, only the originating carrier would generate revenue from the call. As a result, the 1996 Act mandates that the FCC establish a system of "reciprocal compensation" through which originating carriers could compensate other carriers for the costs they incurred terminating their calls (47 U.S.C. § 251(b)(5)). The statute provides for reciprocal compensation based on a reasonable approximation of the costs incurred by each carrier. The statute specifically provides that it should not be construed to preclude bill-and-keep arrangements, in which each carrier recovers its costs from its own customers without receiving any additional payment from the other carrier (47 U.S.C. § 252(d)(2)(A)–(B)).

In implementing these provisions, the FCC expressed skepticism about bill-and-keep, based largely on the concern that failing to compensate terminating carriers for their costs might give originating carriers both the ability and the incentive to impose costs upon terminating carriers. As with club goods, the concern is that the resulting externalization of costs can lead to overutilization of the terminating carrier's resources. As a general matter, the FCC thus regarded bill-and-keep regimes as "not economically efficient" (FCC 1996c, p. 16055).

At the same time, the FCC acknowledged that circumstances may exist under which bill-and-keep may make economic sense. If the traffic exchanged between carriers is roughly symmetrical, the compensation that each carrier would pay the other for terminating its calls would simply offset that from the other. When that is the case, eliminating usage-sensitive pricing would not have any significant adverse impact on the carriers. At the same time, it might yield economic benefits by allowing both carriers to avoid the administrative burdens and transaction costs needed to create and implement metering regimes (FCC 1996c). In other words, the presence of transaction costs may well make flat-rate pricing the preferred institutional arrangement.

Indeed, historical patterns suggest that bill-and-keep may make economic sense even when the traffic exchanged between carriers is not symmetrical. When each carrier's originations and terminations are balanced and the pattern of calls is evenly distributed across the customer base, bill-and-keep is efficient even if the total traffic generated by one carrier is much larger than the total traffic generated by the other. The point is most easily understood through the following example. Suppose that two local networks operate in the same area, with the incumbent carrier serving ninety customers and the new entrant serving ten customers. Each customer makes ten calls randomly distributed throughout the entire customer base. One would expect the customers of the dominant carrier to initiate 900 calls. Ninety percent (or 810) of those calls would terminate on the incumbent's network, whereas ten percent (90) would terminate on the new entrant's network. At the same time, one would expect the new entrant's customers to place 100 calls, ten percent (10) of which would terminate on the new entrant's network and ninety percent (90) of which would terminate on the dominant carrier's network. Thus, if originations and terminations are symmetric and randomly distributed, 90 calls would pass from the incumbent's network to the new entrant's network, and the same number of calls would pass in the other direction. Under these circumstances, metering actual usage would provide no economic benefits even though the total traffic handed by each network would be far from balanced. As noted above, GTE and Pacific Bell interconnected on a bill-and-keep basis when serving adjacent neighborhoods in Los Angeles despite the fact that the size of their customer bases was far from symmetrical. The implication is that the transaction cost economies associated with avoiding metering costs outweighed what little benefit would have resulted from a more accurate accounting for the actual traffic flows.

Note that a far different situation holds if the distribution of calls is not random. In addition, the symmetry of terminations and originations does not hold if one carrier only terminates calls, such as would occur carriers providing service to paging service providers, call centers, or Internet service providers. In that case, the resulting asymmetry on a calling party pays system would lead to substantial distortions (FCC 1996c).

Economic theory has identified one way in which even last-mile providers without market power in the national market can nonetheless use their terminating access monopoly to harm competition. This market failure results from what is in essence a common pool problem stemming from the fact that the United States follows the practice that the calling party pays the long-distance carrier for the entirety of the long-distance call. Long distance carriers are, of course, not the only carriers that incur costs when a customer places a long-distance call. The LEC for the party originating the call must incur costs to provide a connection between the customer's premises and the long-distance carrier's point of presence in the originating LEC's central office. Furthermore, the terminating LEC must also incur the cost of connecting the call from its central office to the customer premises of the party to whom the call is placed. Long-distance carriers compensate originating and terminating LECs through a series of federally mandated access charges, which under current law must be uniform across all carriers and all customers. In other words, the cost of terminating access is covered by requiring customers to make uniform contributions to a common pool (Crandall and Waverman 1995; Laffont and Tirole 2000; FCC 1999d).

The key question is what impact the deregulation of access charges would have on originating and terminating LECs' pricing behavior. The FCC has concluded that the possibility that the originating carrier might charge excessive access charges is effectively limited by the fact that the calling party chooses its local service provider, decides whether to place the call, and ultimately bears the cost of the call. The calling party, either directly or indirectly through its long-distance carrier, is thus well situated to exert price discipline over originating access charges. The same is not true, however, for terminating access charges. Because neither the calling party nor its long-distance carrier has any influence over the called party's choice of LEC, neither can exert any price discipline over terminating access charges. Furthermore, the common pool aspect of the access charge regime means that a LEC's customers will not bear the full brunt of any increase in terminating access charges. Instead, the impact of the higher prices will be spread over the entire universe of local telephone subscribers. This, in turn, gives terminating LECs both the ability and the incentive to raise terminating access charges above competitive levels in order to draw a disproportionate amount of compensation out of the common pool. The impetus to increase terminating access charges exists regardless of whether competition exists in local access or the terminating LEC is small. Indeed, small carriers may well have the greatest incentive to increase terminating access charges, because the percentage of the increase that their own customers pay will be disproportionately small. At the same time, such pricing behavior might give long distance carriers greater incentive to enter the local access market in order to avoid paying these charges (FCC 1999d).

A number of mechanisms exist to solve this problem without mandating interconnection. For example, the incentive to increase terminating access charges would disappear if the FCC were to mandate bill and keep. Indeed, any uniform access pricing regime would eliminate the ability of terminating LECs to take advantage of the common pool problem, although economic efficiency would ultimately depend on ensuring that access prices were set at competitive levels. In addition, LECs' incentive to increase terminating access charges could also be eliminated by mandating that terminating access charges be reciprocal, although reciprocity may have implications for entry (Laffont et al. 1997, 1998). Reciprocity is not as effective when LECs do not originate and terminate traffic in a roughly symmetrical manner, as illustrated by disputes over carriers that only serve customers that receive calls, such as Internet service providers, conference call companies, and chat rooms, as evidenced by the recent dispute over "traffic pumping."[35] Finally, the terminating

---

35  This dispute arose when a small group of rural Iowa LECs left the uniform tariffs established by the National Exchange Carrier Association and negotiated relatively high compensation rates designed to cover their costs at their historically low volumes. After establishing these rates, these LECs began to solicit customers offering services that only terminated calls, such as conference calling or free adult chat-line services. These customers then advertised their conference calling and chat-line services on the Internet as free services. The result in one case was for terminating traffic for 175 customers to jump from 15,000 minutes to 6.4 million minutes in a five-month span and a transfer payment of $10–15 million to these small LECs (*Omaha World Herald* 2007).

access charges used by the incumbent LEC with which the new entrant competes can be used as a benchmark for determining the reasonableness of the new entrant's terminating access charges (FCC 2001d, Uri 2001). A complete resolution of this issue exceeds the scope of this chapter. For our purposes, determining which of these different mechanisms would best promote consumer welfare is less important than the fact that institutional mechanisms may exist for solving the terminating access problem that do not require imposing an access mandate.

## 4. Platform Access

Platform represents the type of access most often granted through regulation. For example, the FCC's Part 68 Rules, which can be traced to the FCC's landmark decision in *Carterfone,* have long required the Bell System to open its local telephone networks to all providers of CPE. As a result of MCI's long battle with AT&T, the FCC has also required the Bell System to open its local telephone network to all providers of long-distance services. Furthermore, the FCC's *Computer Inquiries* required local telephone companies to open their networks to all providers of information services. As we shall discuss in greater detail in the next chapter, similar mandates were included in the consent decree breaking up AT&T and the related consent decree regarding GTE. In each case, this regulation is properly regarded as platform access, because it involves opening up the network to providers of complementary services.

The Telecommunications Act of 1996 essentially left this system undisturbed. With respect to long distance, 47 U.S.C. § 251(c)(2) requires all carriers providing local telephone service on the day the statute was enacted to provide interconnection to any carrier for the transmission and routing of long distance access that is equal in quality to the interconnection the local telephone company provides to itself on rates, terms, and conditions that are just, reasonable, and nondiscriminatory. The FCC construed this provision to apply only to the physical linking of the two networks and not to the charges for transporting and terminating long-distance traffic (FCC 1996c). Indeed, as the Eighth Circuit reasoned in upholding the FCC's decision, section 251(g) specifies that the preexisting equal access and interconnection requirements would remain in place until specifically superseded by the FCC (*Competitive Telecomms. Ass'n v. FCC,* 117 F.3d 1068, 1071–73 (8th Cir. 1997)). Because the advent of competition would put pressure on any cross subsidies embedded in access charges, the FCC initiated an access charge proceeding designed to make transport pricing entirely cost based (FCC 1997b).

The 1996 Act similarly left undisturbed the mandate that local telephone companies must provide equal access to information service providers (FCC 1998a). It augmented those requirements with a number of other provisions, including requiring incumbents to allow information service providers to resell local telephone services at wholesale rates and to provide unbundled access to key elements of their networks. Concerns about preserving platform access also underlay the statutory provisions in the 1996 Act prohibiting the former Bell operating companies from offering long distance, information services, or alarm monitoring. The idea was that until competition emerged in local telephone service, these firms would have the incentive to discriminate against nonproprietary complementary service offerings (47 U.S.C. §§ 251(c)(4), 271, 274, 275).

As noted in Chapter 5, providing greater accessibility to complementary services, reducing the business risk faced by providers of those services, should cause network demand to increase. At the same time, platform access inevitably involves a number of collateral requirements that can become sources of inefficiency and place downward pressure on network demand. For example, local telephone networks give rise to certain technological efficiencies that can only be realized if the same carrier provides both the complementary and the local telephone service. Classic examples include voice messaging services, such as voice mail and advance calling, and vertical switching services, such as caller ID, call forwarding, and call waiting, which are most efficiently provided when integrated directly into the circuit switch (FCC 1986a). The FCC eventually exempted such innovations from its platform access requirements for the simple reason that failure to do so would have prevented these innovations from emerging (FCC 1984, 1985b, 1986a, 1996e).

Platform access also necessarily requires regulators to designate the location within the network where the interface with the complementary service provider will occur, as well as the format in which the complementary service is configured. As noted in Chapter 5, the optimal level of standardization depends largely on the magnitude of the demand-side scale economies and the heterogeneity of consumer preferences. If preferences are sufficiently heterogeneous, the value that consumers derive from consuming a service that is a better match with their preferences will dominate the benefits from belonging to a larger network, in which case an equilibrium with multiple standards may well be optimal.

Standardization also inevitably favors applications based on certain architectures. For example, the introduction of digital transmission technologies required the deployment of protocols that were not interoperable with the existing analog network. This necessitated the introduction of computer processing into the core of the network to engage in "protocol conversion" (FCC 1983b, 1985b, 1985c, 1986a). Absent a waiver of the platform access mandate, the interoperability mandated by the *Computer Inquiries* would have obstructed this innovation from being deployed (FCC 1984, 1985b, 1986a, 1996e). It is impossible to conclude a priori that standardizing on a single network architecture represents the optimal solution. The process is rendered even more challenging if the technology is undergoing rapid change. Under the best of circumstances, regulation will lock the existing interface into place, at least until the regulatory process can update it. At worst, such technological decisions will be affected by the biases inherent in regulatory processes, in which the concerns of the incumbents tend to be overrepresented.

The standardization implicit in platform also commoditizes network services and narrows the dimensions along which local telephone networks can complete.

Product standardization and price transparency make both collusive and noncooperative oligopoly behavior easier to maintain. Commoditization also limits networks to competing solely based on price and network size, considerations that reinforce the advantages enjoyed by the largest players. Differentiation can play a particularly important role in industries such as telecommunications, in which the presence of fixed costs that are large relative to marginal costs forces network providers to produce on the declining portion of the average cost curve. As noted in Chapter 4, product differentiation can create stable equilibria with multiple producers, each producing on the declining portion of the average cost curve. Thus, smaller players can survive despite cost and size disadvantages by targeting subsegments of the market.

Platform access also gives rise to significant transaction costs, both in terms of establishing the governing standards and in terms of establishing the interfaces and putting into place at those interfaces processes for monitoring and billing the service provided to existing customers and for provisioning service to new customers. As Justice Breyer noted in *Iowa Utilities Board*, such an interface is likely to be particularly hard to police when the interface is complex and embedded in the middle of the network and the information requirements needed to regulate the interface are high (525 U.S. at 428–29). The breakup of AT&T provides a useful example. Implementing the divestiture decree's equal access mandate required the local telephone companies to redesign their switches so that they could accommodate multiple long distance providers, a process that entailed considerable cost and delay, as well as close regulation of both the price and nonprice terms and conditions of interconnection. Such oversight is particularly onerous when the interface and the information needed to implement it are complex (Faulhaber 2003).

Furthermore, like any form of access, platform access requires direct regulation of prices in order to be effective, both in terms of nondiscrimination and in terms of price levels. For the reasons discussed in Chapter 4 and with respect to retail access, there is little reason to be optimistic that such regulation will prove beneficial.

Most problematic is platform access's long-run impact on dynamic efficiency. As noted earlier, the primary policy goal should be to promote entry in those segments of the industry that are the least competitive. Only if competition in a particular segment proves unsustainable should policymakers pursue the second-best policy goal of promoting competition in complementary services. Once local telephone competition became possible, platform access became counterproductive. Providers of complementary services were the natural strategic partners for new entrants in local telephone service. Platform access short-circuited this natural alliance by obviating the need for any complementary service providers to enter into such partnerships.

At the time when most of the platform access mandates discussed above were put into place, competition in local telephone service was believed to be impossible. The FCC recognized when eliminating the regulatory requirements imposed by the *Computer Inquiries* that those rules "were developed before separate and different broadband technologies began to emerge and compete for customers" and could no longer be justified under contemporary circumstances (FCC 2005d, pp. 14,876–7). In short, it is now clear that wireline competition is feasible with respect to large business customers and that wireless telephony has emerged as a vibrant competitor as well.

As we discuss in Chapter 4, because platform access necessarily involves complementary products, network owners have powerful incentives to provide it voluntarily. The economic consensus is that competition among local telephone providers is sufficient to prevent those providers from engaging in anticompetitive behavior against providers of complementary services. Even if the local telephone market is not competitive, moreover, network owners are still likely to provide platform access voluntarily, because opening networks to the broadest possible array of complementary services typically represents the best way for a carrier to maximize the value of its local telephone network. Although economic theorists have identified a set of circumstances under which that would not be true, those exceptions are fairly narrow and require the satisfaction of fairly restrictive conditions.

Unfortunately, policymakers have been loath to take wireless competition into account when deciding whether to release local telephone companies from platform access mandates. For example, the legislative history of the 1996 Act indicated that competition from cellular telephone companies should not be considered in determining whether an incumbent local telephone company faced sufficient competition to justify releasing it from the prohibition from offering long distance services (U.S. House 1996). The FCC would later retreat from this position and acknowledge wireless as a direct competitor to wireline local telephone service after the deployment of the second-generation wireless technology known as personal communications services (PCS) (FCC 1998d, 2003a, 2003b).

Over time, policymakers have narrowed the scope of local telephone networks' platform access obligations. With respect to long distance, the FCC has ruled that the local telephone companies created by the breakup of AT&T now face sufficient competition to justify permitting them to offer in-region long-distance service in every state except Alaska and Hawaii (FCC 2008c). As discussed in greater detail in Chapter 9, the dissipation of the need for platform access to preserve long distance competition is demonstrated most eloquently by the regulatory authorities' approval of SBC's acquisition of AT&T and Verizon's acquisition of MCI, which reconsolidated local and long distance services.

In addition, the FCC has eliminated the platform access for information services. As the FCC recognized when eliminating the regulatory requirements imposed by the *Computer Inquiries*, those rules "were developed before separate and different broadband technologies began to emerge and compete for customers" and could no longer be justified under contemporary circumstances (FCC 2005d, pp. 14876–77).

Last, the FCC has acknowledged that the increase in competition has weakened the ability of last-mile providers to discriminate in favor of proprietary CPE.

For example, in 1992 the FCC abolished the prohibition on bundling CPE with wireless telephone services. The FCC issued this order at a fairly early stage in the wireless industry's development, when the evidence of the competitiveness of the wireless industry was "inconclusive." As noted earlier, the FCC initially established the wireless industry in 1981 through a duopoly market structure and had not yet begun to auction PCS licenses. The FCC nonetheless found the possibility that some cellular providers might possess a degree of local market power insufficient to justify prohibiting the bundling of CPE with wireless telephone service, because any one cellular provider represented a tiny fraction of the national equipment market. Any CPE manufacturer foreclosed from distributing its products in one geographic area remained free to sell its products in other areas. As the Federal Trade Commission's comments during this proceeding note, "If individual cellular service companies do not possess market power in the sale of cellular service on a *national* level, it is unlikely that foreclosure of the CPE market can be successful." The FCC agreed, concluding that "it does not seem likely that individual cellular companies which operate in local markets possess market power that could impact the numerous CPE manufacturers operating on a national and international basis." The proper question is thus not the number of subscribers that a network controls in any one metropolitan area, but rather the network's market share in the national market. In short, it is national reach, not local reach, that matters. The FCC found that not only is bundling an efficient way to distribute CPE, but also "the high price of CPE represented the greatest barrier to inducing subscription to cellular service. Bundling wireless service with CPE allows wireless carriers to reduce the upfront cost of subscribing to cellular, which in turn will support greater competition and promote more efficient use of the spectrum" (FCC 1992a, pp. 4029–31).

The FCC similarly concluded in 2001 that the growth in competition among local exchange carriers justified abolishing its prohibition of bundling CPE with wireline telecommunications services. Even though local exchange markets were not yet perfectly competitive, the FCC concluded that the growth of local competition and the consumer benefits of bundling, such as reduction of transaction costs and increase in innovation in services, sufficiently mitigated the risk of anticompetitive harm (FCC 2001b). The FCC has also abandoned its previous role in establishing the technical criteria for interconnecting CPE, although the FCC stopped short of repealing the interconnection requirements altogether (FCC 2000f).

## 5. Unbundled Access

Local telephone networks have long represented one of the central laboratories in which regulatory authorities have experimented with unbundled access as a way to guard against vertical exclusion without foreclosing the benefits of vertical integration. As discussed above, the ONA regime created by the third *Computer Inquiry* represents perhaps the seminal example of FCC-mandated unbundling, and the UNE access provision enacted by Congress constitutes perhaps the most important provision of the Telecommunications Act of 1996, with UNE access prices being based on TELRIC. Other important antecedents include state unbundling initiatives between 1984 and 1996 as well as the unbundling model developed by the U.S. Department of Justice in negotiations to allow Ameritech to begin selling in-region long distance services (Huber et al. 1999).

Unbundled access is the form of access that has the greatest potential to cause economic inefficiency. Like wholesale and interconnection access, the fact that unbundled access simultaneously supports the creation of new services and diverts traffic off of the network renders the impact of unbundled access on network demand ambiguous. Both increases and decreases in network demand change the optimal network configuration, by making either the creation of links in particular locations or cost-reducing, traffic-aggregating technologies economically feasible or infeasible.

At the same time, unbundled access disrupts network management to a far greater degree than other forms of access. Unlike the other forms of access, which generally introduce traffic at the major nodes where customers or providers of complementary services would naturally interconnect with the network, unbundled access can introduce traffic deep within the heart of the network. Unbundled access has the potential to occupy isolated resources at multiple, disconnected points in the network, in contrast to other forms of access, which involve using large, integrated portions of the network to route traffic in patterns that are roughly similar to the patterns of traffic served by the network owner.

As we described in Chapter 2, graph theory reveals how occupying isolated resources in one part of a network can adversely affect the performance of portions of the network located far from the element being accessed. Graph theory demonstrates the potential flaw in the idea that the costs of unbundled access are confined to the network elements that are directly involved. Instead, interconnection by competitors is likely to introduce new sources and sinks into the network. Thus, substantial amounts of traffic may originate and terminate at points in the network that differ from the host network's initial points of origin and termination. This will alter traffic patterns. A network that is designed with a maximum flow/minimum cut pattern designed around particular sources and sinks will no longer be appropriate for traffic coming from new sources and sinks. The nodes at which interconnection occurs will not be the only nodes affected. Rather, the effects will be distributed across all nodes and links within the network. This invalidates the notion that only the incremental costs of providing the interconnection should be recovered. The interconnection affects the network's performance and creates costs throughout the network.

Moreover, graph theory shows that one should not expect the effects of UNE access to be confined to those elements. When individual elements are viewed in isolation, the TELRIC methodology seems quite reasonable. Typically, UNE access occupies only a few of the elements of an incumbent LEC's network. Those elements, however, can be critical to overall traffic patterns that connect the network's sources and sinks. The reduction of available capacity at critical links in the network will affect the network's maximum flow. Thus, UNE access can impose costs on the host network that extend well beyond the elements that are affected. In some cases, the costs of UNE access may even exceed interconnection costs. If usage patterns associated with interconnection are similar to those of the incumbent LEC's own traffic, absent any capacity constraints, there will be less of an impact on the network owner's decisions about network configuration. There will be no change in the network elements that compose the minimum cut and, thus, in the components that constitute bottlenecks. The situation is quite different when usage patterns associated with interconnection differ from the patterns of the incumbent's own traffic. When that is the case, granting access to critical UNEs can create bottlenecks where none previously existed and can have a dramatic impact on the network's maximum flow. Under these circumstances, UNE access can have a dramatic impact on the cost, capacity, and configuration of networks.

These problems are exacerbated by the fact that the 1996 Act obligates the network owner to permit unbundled access "at any technically feasible point" (47 U.S.C. § 251(c)(2)). The introduction of traffic flows at disaggregated points chosen by competitors deep in the heart of the network where such traffic would not otherwise occur also has a much greater potential to cause discontinuous and unpredictable disruptions to the network than other forms of access.

In addition, unbundled access increases transaction costs to a greater degree than other forms of access. For example, a network owner attempting to manage its network will need a great deal of information about the magnitude, timing, and variability of traffic associated with each element to which unbundled access is sought. The fact that much of the traffic will originate and be transmitted in part under other networks' control places much of this information outside the network owner's control. In addition, it forces network owners to develop systems for provisioning and monitoring network usage at points that would not otherwise be available to customers or other carriers. As Justice Breyer noted in criticizing the 1996 Act's UNE access requirements in *Iowa Utilities Board*:

> The more complex the facilities, the more central their relation to the firm's managerial responsibilities, the more extensive the sharing demanded, the more likely these costs will become serious. And the more serious they become, the more likely they will offset any economic or competitive gain that a sharing requirement might otherwise provide.

He further observed that unbundled access "can have significant administrative and social costs inconsistent with the Act's purposes." If taken to an extreme, "[r]ules that force firms to share *every* resource or element of a business would create, not competition, but pervasive regulation, for the regulators, not the marketplace, would set the relevant terms."

Most problematically, unbundled access delays the emergence of facilities-based competition by deterring investment in alternative last-mile facilities. Justice Breyer described how unbundled access reduces incumbents' incentives to invest in their own networks when he pointed out that unbundled access

> may diminish the original owner's incentive to keep up or to improve the property by depriving the owner of the fruits of value-creating investment, research, or labor.... [One cannot] guarantee that firms will undertake the investment necessary to produce complex technological innovations knowing that any competitive advantage deriving from those innovations will be dissipated by the sharing requirement.
>
> (525 U.S. at 428–29)

In *Verizon v. FCC*, Justice Breyer reiterated the negative impact of unbundled access on incumbents' incentive "either to innovate or to invest in a new 'element.'" Unbundled access envisions "that the incumbent will share with competitors the cost-reducing benefits of a successful innovation, while leaving the incumbent to bear the costs of most unsuccessful investments on its own. Why would investment not then stagnate?" Unbundled access also reduces the investment incentives of new entrants as well as incumbents. TELRIC bases UNE access prices on the costs of a hypothetical, most efficient network. Justice Breyer observed that this pricing approach essentially guarantees that new entrants will find it more cost-effective to obtain unbundled access to elements of the existing network than to build or buy those network elements elsewhere. Furthermore, new entrants must take into account the fact that any future technological improvements will cause UNE access rates to fall still further. Thus, any firm considering building its own facilities faces the real possibility that regulation will place it at a cost disadvantage, as TELRIC ensures that other competitors will be able to take advantage of any cost reductions that take place in the future without having to undertake the risk of making any investments. This not only will harm any new entrants who invest in facilities; it also induces firms to compete by sharing the existing network even though lower-cost alternatives exist. Although the FCC claims that unbundled access "will sometimes 'serve as a transitional arrangement until fledgling competitors could develop a customer base and complete the construction of their own networks,'" Justice Breyer asks, "Why, given the pricing rules, would those 'fledgling competitors' ever try to fly on their own?" (*Verizon*, 535 U.S. at 550–51, quoting FCC 1999i, p. 3700).

Last, Justice Breyer acknowledged that unbundled access leads to an extremely thin form of competition:

> That is because firms that share existing facilities do not compete in respect to the facilities that they share, any more than several grain producers who auction their grain at a single jointly owned market compete in respect to *auction services*. Yet rules that combine a strong monetary incentive to share with a broad definition of "network element" will tend to produce widespread sharing of entire incumbent systems under regulatory supervision – a result very different from the competitive market that the statute seeks to create.
>
> (535 U.S. at 550–51)

A majority of the Supreme Court would ultimately endorse all aspects of Justice Breyer's reasoning in the *Trinko* decision, which we discuss at greater length in Chapter 9. As we noted earlier, empirical studies have demonstrated the negative impact that unbundled access has on investments in local telephone facilities.

It is for this reason that the unbundled access provisions of the 1996 Act contain some limiting principles. Specifically, it limits UNE access to proprietary elements to which access is "necessary" and without which a new competitor would be "impaired" in its ability to offer competing services (47 U.S.C. § 251(d)(2)(A) & (B) (emphasis added)). These limitations recognize that little is to be gained and much is to be lost by compelling access to elements available on the open market for other sources.

The FCC has faced nearly insuperable difficulties in construing these limitations in a way that makes economic sense. As noted earlier, the FCC needed four tries to develop rules that could withstand judicial scrutiny. And by this time, the unbundling rules had largely become moot, as the FCC had deregulated unbundling of network elements providing service to large business customers and had deregulated key network elements needed to provide local telephone service to small business and residential customers.

## 6. Regulatory Arbitrage

As first noted in Chapter 5, the absence of a unified approach that is consistent across all of the different types of access leaves the regulatory regime vulnerable to regulatory arbitrage. A brief review of the way that access to local telephone networks is priced underscores the nature of the problem.

Retail access is regulated by state public utility commissions employing either cost-of-service ratemaking or price caps. Retail rates often include a wide variety of specialized waivers and reflect a wide range of internal cross subsidies, through statewide rate averaging and through differential pricing of business and residential services. The fact that prices are not always set in a way that reflects cost within a single jurisdiction raises the possibility of arbitrage even within retail access.

Wholesale access is typically based on retail rates less any avoided costs, such as marketing, billing, and collection. The fact that these rates are based on rates incorporating implicit cross subsidies again leaves wholesale access vulnerable to regulatory arbitrage. Further inefficiency may result from difficulties in determining precisely which retailing costs are avoided when another provider invokes wholesale access.

Platform access rates vary depending on the nature of the complementary service being provided. Long-distance providers pay access charges that have historically exceeded actual cost in order to allow long distance service to cross-subsidize local service. Although the FCC is in the process of reforming the access charge regime to provide access charges closer to cost, long-distance providers are required to pay into the universal service fund, whereas information service providers are not.

Unbundled access rates are calculated in a different manner. The statute requires that UNE access rates be "based on the cost (determined without reference to a rate-of-return or other rate-based proceeding) of providing the interconnection or network element" (47 U.S.C. § 252(d)(1)(A)(i)). The FCC implemented this requirement through TELRIC, which is based on the forward-looking incremental costs of a hypothetical network providing service through the most efficient technology at the locations of the existing wire centers.

Finally, interconnection access is governed by the reciprocal compensation provisions of the 1996 Act, which mandates that rates provide for "the mutual and reciprocal recovery by each carrier of costs associated with the transport and termination on each carrier's network facilities of calls that originate on the network facilities of the other carrier." The statute specifically does not "preclude arrangements that afford the mutual recovery of costs through the offsetting of reciprocal obligations, including arrangements that waive mutual recovery (such as bill-and-keep arrangements)" (47 U.S.C. § 252(d)(2)(A)(i), (B)(i)). As noted above, the FCC has implemented interconnection access through TELRIC, although it is considering replacing TELRIC with bill and keep.

The result is that different methodologies apply to rates established for each different type of access. The inconsistency raises the possibility that firms will attempt to manipulate the categories of access in order to engage in regulatory arbitrage. As noted in Chapter 5, the most prominent example of this is the controversy over UNE-P, in which resale competitors avoided the higher rates charged for wholesale access simply by requesting unbundled access to all of the elements needed to provide local telephone service. Such manipulation of the regulatory regime will continue to occur until all forms of access are priced on a consistent and unified basis.

## D. Constitutional Arguments in Favor of Market-Based Pricing

In addition to the problems of economic theory discussed above, the manner in which access has been imposed on local telephone networks also raises serious constitutional problems. We will focus our analysis primarily on the access provisions of the 1996 Act, because the takings implications of those provisions have received the greatest attention from both regulators and commentators.

### 1. Physical Collocation

The FCC tended to downplay the takings implications of its implementation of the 1996 Act. According to the FCC, TELRIC simply limits the prices that can be charged for the use of the incumbent LECs' network elements. Although courts and the FCC have expressed reluctance to address takings issues until a particular methodology has been embodied into an actual rate order, they have suggested that the principles of confiscatory ratemaking or regulatory takings are likely to govern such challenges.[36]

The problem with this analysis is that it focuses on TELRIC as a general matter without focusing on the constitutional implications of the 1996 Act's physical collocation provisions. As the FCC has itself recognized, both interconnection and access to unbundled network elements typically require the network owner to permit requesting carriers to place equipment in its central office on an indefinite basis. As a matter of first principles laid out in Chapter 7, the physical collocation associated with interconnection and unbundled access provisions represents the type of permanent physical invasion deemed to constitute a per se taking under the Supreme Court's decision in *Loretto*.[37]

This conclusion has been reinforced by a number of lower court decisions reviewing different aspects of the 1996 Act. For example, the D.C. Circuit's decision in *Bell Atlantic* held that the physical collocation regime upon which the FCC modeled its implementation of the 1996 Act constituted a physical taking (24 F.3d at 1445–47). This conclusion draws further support from the D.C. Circuit's decision in *GTE Service Corp. v. FCC*, in which the court repeatedly emphasized its concern that the FCC's interpretation of the physical collocation provisions may result in "unnecessary takings" of LEC property (205 F.3d 416, 421, 423, 426 (D.C. Cir. 2000)).

Most instructive of all is the decision of the Court of Federal Claims in *Qwest Corp. v. United States*, which is one of the few decisions to address the merits of a takings challenge to the 1996 Act. In that case, a requesting carrier obtained access to fourteen loops that served one particular customer and connected those loops to its own switching equipment contained in a collocation cage located in the incumbent LEC's central office. The incumbent LEC brought a takings challenge arguing that the compensation that it received was constitutionally insufficient. The incumbent did circumscribe its argument in one, somewhat unusual way. It conceded that it was already receiving adequate compensation for the space occupied by the collocation cage. As a result, it restricted its takings claim to the loops leased by the new entrant.

The court resolved the case by relying on the distinction between physical and nonpossessory takings. In particular, the court accepted the notion that "government-mandated co-location of one party's equipment on another party's premises constitutes a physical taking of the occupied space." As a result, it acknowledged that requesting carrier's collocation cage "is analogous to the rooftop

---

36  For cases applying confiscatory ratemaking doctrine to such claims, see *Verizon*, 535 U.S. at 524; *US West Communications, Inc. v. MFS Intelenet, Inc.*, 35 F. Supp. 2d 1221, 1236 (D. Or. 1998); FCC (1996c). For cases applying regulatory takings doctrine to such cases, see *Tex. Off. of Pub. Util. Counsel v. FCC*, 183 F.3d 393, 429 n. 59 (5th Cir. 1999), *cert. granted sub nom. GTE Serv. Corp. v. FCC*, 530 U.S. 1213, *cert. dismissed*, 531 U.S. 975 (2000); FCC (1992b).

37  Even scholars who are skeptical of broader readings of *Loretto* accept that regulations that require physical collocation effect per se takings (Baynes 1995; Chen 1999; Rose-Ackerman and Rossi 2000).

equipment in *Loretto*" and emphasized that it would have had little trouble holding that the restriction represented a per se taking had the incumbent LEC focused on the collocation cage itself. In contrast to the equipment contained in the collocation cage, however, the leasing of loops by the new entrant by itself simply involved restrictions on the use of the incumbent LEC's property and did not require the incumbent LEC to submit to the permanent physical occupation of its property by any equipment. As a result, the court concluded that the claim based on the loops did not constitute a physical taking. The court once again emphasized that in holding that access to the loops did not constitute a physical taking did not negate its prior conclusion that "the implementation of mandatory access provisions requiring a telecommunications provider or utility to make space available on its premises for a competitor to affix its own equipment ... constitut[ed] a physical taking under *Loretto*" (48 Fed. Cl. 672, 689–90, 691, 693–94 (2001)).

The FCC has attempted to avoid this conclusion by asserting that takings claims involving public utility property are governed by the more permissive principles embodied in the Supreme Court's confiscatory ratemaking and regulatory takings precedents (FCC 1992b, 1996c). The fundamental problem with this analysis is that ignores the distinction between physical and nonpossessory takings drawn by the Supreme Court in *Loretto* and *Florida Power* and reaffirmed in *Tahoe–Sierra*, detailed in Chapter 7. Because the 1996 Act's physical collocation mandate unambiguously requires incumbent LECs to permit competing carriers to place equipment on their property, it constitutes a classic physical taking under *Loretto*. Thus, in sharp contrast to what would be true under the Court's confiscatory ratemaking or regulatory takings jurisprudence, the magnitude of the regulation's economic impact and the public purposes served by the regulation are of no consequence.

It thus follows that the owners of local telephone networks are entitled to just compensation for the physical invasion mandated by the 1996 Act. As discussed in Chapter 7, to the extent that external markets for a particular input exist, the principles of just compensation entitle the incumbent LECs to the market value of the inputs that are physically taken. Although the absence of direct competition in local telephony previously deprived regulators of any such market-based benchmarks, the emergence of cellular telephony and other forms of wireless communications as direct competitors to local telephone companies has now created an external basis for determining the value of the services provided by the local loop. Under such circumstances, basing access pricing on replacement cost contradicts the Court's established takings jurisprudence. Perhaps sensing the weakness of its position, the FCC offered the alternative argument that, assuming that a taking had occurred, fair market value would not properly include monopoly rents (FCC 1996c). The legal support for this claim, however, is suspect.[38] And even if the FCC's legal conclusion

---

38 The FCC cites but a single lower court decision as its authority for the proposition that just compensation does not permit recovery of monopoly rents (FCC 1996c). A perusal of that decision reveals that it does not in fact stand for the proposition for which the FCC cites it. In

were somehow proven to be sound, there is also reason to doubt the factual premises underlying the argument. The emergence of direct facilities-based competition and the fact that retail prices for local telephone service are subject to rate regulation indicate that it is unlikely that there were any monopoly rents included in the prices set by the open market.

## 2. Virtual Collocation

Although we find the conclusion that the physical collocation requirements of the 1996 Act effect a physical taking inescapable, we recognize that virtual collocation poses a much closer question. The Supreme Court specifically reserved this in *Loretto*, observing that regulations requiring property owners to install certain types of network-related equipment might present a different question. In such a case, the property owner would own the equipment, which would give it full authority over the placement, manner, use, and possibly disposition of the equipment outside of the mandate of the specific regulation in question. In addition, the property owner would have the latitude to decide how to comply with the applicable regulations and therefore "could minimize, the physical, esthetic, and other effects of the installation" (458 U.S. 419, 440 n. 19 (1982)). The FCC followed this reasoning in its *Expanded Interconnection* proceeding. Without conceding that that mandatory physical collocation would constitute a per se taking, the FCC argued that offering the LECs virtual collocation as an option eliminated any remaining constitutional infirmities (FCC 1994).

Unfortunately, the courts have never had the opportunity to address whether virtual collocation effects a physical taking, because before the courts could address

that case, a manufacturer of patented rubber and metal mountings critical to allowing aircraft to fly in adverse weather conditions had developed a dominant market position that allowed it to earn profits ranging from fifty-nine to one hundred forty-seven percent. During World War II, the federal government ordered the manufacturer to sell its products to the government at prices determined by the government to be "fair and reasonable," which allowed the manufacturer a profit of only ten and one-half percent. The manufacturer challenged the action under the Takings Clause. The court conceded that "[i]f these were ordinary times," the manufacturer would have been allowed to earn supracompetitive profits. "[T]hese were not ordinary times," however, because the war had in effect caused the free and untrammeled market necessary for a fair market value determination to disappear (*Lord Mfg. Co. v. United States*, 84 F. Supp. 748, 751–55 (Ct. Cl. 1949)). The true holding of *Lord Manufacturing* is thus that circumstances may exist during which current market price is no longer a good indicator of fair market value, which is defined as the price to which a willing seller and a willing buyer would agree after ample time to find a purchaser (see also *BFP v. Resolution Trust Corp.*, 511 U.S. 531, 537–38 (1994), discussing how transient exigencies can force prices below or above fair market value). *Lord Manufacturing* assuredly does not stand for the proposition that monopoly profits are not properly considered part of fair market value. On the contrary, in the language quoted above, the Court of Claims explicitly recognized that the opposite was true (see also *City of Tucson v. El Rio Water Co.*, 415 P.2d 872, 875 (Ariz. 1966), recognizing that monopoly profits are properly regarded as part of fair market value).

the issue, the virtual collocation provisions of the *Expanded Interconnection* proceeding were rendered moot by the physical collocation provisions contained in the
1996 Act. On the one hand, the D.C. Circuit's opinion in *GTE Service Corp.* noted
that "[v]irtual collocation... minimizes the takings problem, because competitors
do not have physical access to a LEC's property" (205 F.3d at 419). At the same time,
language in the D.C. Circuit's *Bell Atlantic* opinion suggests that virtual collocation may pose the same takings concerns as physical collocation. Both virtual and
physical collocation allow CAPs to physically connect their networks to the LECs'
networks. Requiring a physical interconnection is enough to constitute a physical
taking, regardless of who owns the property on which the interconnection occurs
(24 F.3d at 1446). Indeed, a subsequent court drew largely the same conclusion
when it held that an administrative order requiring an incumbent LEC to reconfigure the wires it was using to provide telephone service to a multibuilding complex
in order to accommodate an competitive service provider constituted a physical
taking (*GTE Sw. Inc. v. Pub. Util. Comm'n*, 10 S.W.3d 7, 9, 11 (Tex. Ct. App. 2000)).
The fact that the reconfiguration occurred in an apartment complex rather than on
land owned by the LEC played no role in the decision, which in turn suggests that
virtual and physical collocation may be constitutionally indistinguishable.

### 3. Wireless Interconnection

An even more difficult problem is posed when regulation compelling access to
a wireless network is involved. In contrast to wireline communications, which
depend on having a physical connection to the network, regulations mandating
access to wireless networks do not necessarily require the installation of third-
party equipment on the network owner's property. For example, the D.C. Circuit
recently rejected a takings challenge to an FCC order intended to ensure access to
different forms of television service by, in essence, requiring property owners to
allow residents to install antennas needed to receive DBS service, broadcast signals,
and other forms of television programming. The court concluded that, because the
regulation in question did not compel a physical invasion of property by a third
party, it did not constitute a per se taking under *Loretto* and was properly analyzed
as a regulatory taking (*Bldg. Owners & Managers Ass'n Int'l v. FCC*, 254 F.3d 89, 99
(D.C. Cir. 2001)).

It appears, then, that the constitutional arguments for basing access rates on
market prices are weaker with respect to wireless networks than with respect to
wireline networks. The economic arguments for basing access rates on market
prices are the same in each case, as the harm effected by the third party's occupation
of productive capacity is the same. As a result, we would still urge the FCC and
state public utility commissions to base access rates on market prices as a matter of
policy.

# 9

# Antitrust as Applied to Network Industries

Antitrust courts have played a pivotal role in shaping the telecommunications industry, most significantly through the private antitrust suits brought against AT&T by MCI and the predecessor to Sprint in the 1970s and the case brought by the federal government against AT&T that culminated with the breakup of AT&T in 1984. All three of these cases relied upon the essential facilities doctrine, which requires owners of bottleneck elements unavailable elsewhere in the marketplace to make those elements available to competitors on reasonable terms.[1]

The essential facilities doctrine has proven quite controversial, inspiring a welter of largely critical commentary challenging its conceptual validity, its administrability, and the extent to which it actually benefits consumers.[2] After years of signaling ambivalence about the doctrine,[3] the Supreme Court once again returned to the subject in *Verizon Communications Inc. v. Law Offices of Curtis V. Trinko, LLP.* Although the Court found "no need either to recognize . . . or to repudiate" the doctrine, it endorsed many of the criticisms advanced in the commentary (540 U.S. 398, 411 (2004)).

---

1  *United States v. AT&T (Modification of Final Judgment)*, 552 F. Supp. 131, 1352–53, 1360–61 (D.D.C. 1982), *aff'd mem. sub nom. Maryland v. United States*, 460 U.S. 1001 (1983); *MCI Commc'ns Corp. v. AT&T*, 708 F.2d 1081, 1132–33, 1147–48, 1174 (7th Cir. 1983); *S. Pac. Commc'ns Co. v. AT&T*, 740 F.2d 980, 999, 1007–09 (D.C. Cir. 1984). This suit was the third case brought by the federal government against AT&T (*United States v. W. Elec. Co.*, 1956 Trade Cas. (CCH) ¶ 68,246 (D.N.J. Jan. 24, 1956); *United States v. AT&T*, No. 6,082 (D. Or. Mar. 26, 1914) (decree), *reprinted in* Shale 1918). The 1956 suit is also regarded as based on the essential facilities doctrine (Sullivan and Grimes 2006).

2  Werden (1987); Gerber (1988); Areeda (1990); Reiffen and Kleit (1990); Hylton (1991); McGowan (1996); Lipsky and Sidak (1999); Hovenkamp (2005); Areeda and Hovenkamp (2008c). More sympathetic assessments of the essential facilities doctrine also exist. See, e.g., Ratner (1988); Soma et al. (1998); Pitofsky et al. (2002).

3  *Aspen Skiing Co. v. Aspen Highlands Skiing Corp.*, 472 U.S. 585, 611 n. 44 (1985); *AT&T v. Iowa Utils. Bd.*, 525 U.S. 366, 428 (1999) (Breyer, J., concurring in part and dissenting in part).

Most striking is the language in *Trinko* questioning the antitrust courts' institutional competence to implement access remedies. Since the opinion was issued, courts and commentators have struggled to determine how broadly to read this language. Some have suggested that the presence of a regulatory regime leaves no role for antitrust courts. Others have read *Trinko* more narrowly, arguing that the scope of judicial authority depends on a more nuanced assessment of the nature of the regulatory regime. Until the Court resolves this uncertainty, it remains possible that courts will use the antitrust laws to compel access to telecommunications networks.

The lingering possibility of antitrust enforcement in this area makes understanding the scope of compelled access permissible after *Trinko* absolutely critical. The commentary on the essential facilities doctrine has generally treated access as a unitary concept without analyzing in sufficient detail how differences in the type of access can affect its costs and benefits. The *Trinko* opinion contains tantalizing hints suggesting how the nature of the party seeking access, the number of network elements to which access is sought, the technological complexity of the interface, and whether the access sought is already being provided to other customers can each affect the analysis. Unfortunately, the opinion merely offered these observations in passing without developing them in a systematic way.

The five-part classification system introduced in Chapter 5 offers a basis for differentiating among different types of access that have fallen under the larger umbrella of the essential facilities doctrine based on the nature of the party seeking access, the portion of the network to which access is sought, and the nature of the services that the party seeking access intends to provide. This framework allows us to evaluate the effect that each form of access has on the demand for network services, the network's maximum carrying capacity, its optimal configuration, and its cost structure. At the same time, this framework underscores the impact that the differences between the forms of access can have on transaction costs, both by increasing the cost of obtaining the information needed to manage the network and by forcing the network to deviate from its natural institutional boundaries. In the process, this framework offers the first systematic basis for understanding how the precise nature of each type of access should guide the actions of antitrust courts.

## A. The Origins of the Essential Facilities Doctrine

The principal provision of the antitrust laws governing unilateral action taken by firms is Section 2 of the Sherman Act, which provides that "[e]very person who shall monopolize, or attempt to monopolize, or combine or conspire with any other person or persons, to monopolize any part of the trade or commerce among the several States, or with foreign nations, shall be deemed guilty of a felony" (15 U.S.C. § 2). The use of the active verb, "monopolize," is generally interpreted as criminalizing not the mere possession of monopoly power, but rather the anticompetitive conduct used to create and sustain monopolies.[4] Thus, courts have generally concluded that Section 2 was not meant to reach monopolies obtained through natural features of the market or through competition on the merits. In the words of Learned Hand's landmark decision in *United States v. Aluminum Co. of America* (*Alcoa*):

> A market may, for example, be so limited that it is impossible to produce at all and meet the cost of production except by a plant large enough to supply the whole demand. Or there may be changes in taste or in cost which drive out all but one purveyor. A single producer may be the survivor out of a group of active competitors, merely by virtue of his superior skill, foresight and industry.
>
> (148 F.2d at 430).[5]

Proposals to criminalize "no fault" monopolization have appeared from time to time, based on the grounds that the mere existence of a monopoly increases price and reduces quantity regardless of whether it arises innocently or through anti-competitive acts.[6] Courts, however, have declined to condemn the mere possession of monopoly power out of concern that doing so would deter firms from engaging in the competition on the merits (through product innovation and cost reduction) that the antitrust laws are designed to foster.[7] As Hand so eloquently put it, "[t]he successful competitor, having been urged to compete, must not be turned upon when he wins" (*Alcoa*, 148 F.2d at 430).

As a result, courts have long held that a Section 2 violation requires more than just proof of monopoly power; it also requires proof of exclusionary conduct, defined in one case as "the willful acquisition or maintenance of that power as

---

4  See, e.g., *Standard Oil Co. v. United States*, 221 U.S. 1, 61–62 (1911); *United States v. Aluminum Co. of Am.* (*Alcoa*), 148 F.2d 416, 429 (2d Cir. 1945).

5  See also *United States v. United Shoe Mach. Corp.*, 110 F. Supp. 295, 342 (D. Mass. 1953) (noting that Section 2 does not criminalize monopolies obtained through "superior skill, superior products, natural advantages, . . . economic or technological efficiency, . . . low margins of profit maintained permanently and without discrimination, or licenses conferred by, and used within, the limits of law, (including patents on one's own inventions, or franchises granted directly to the enterprise by a public authority)"), *aff'd mem.*, 347 U.S. 521 (1954). This reading of Section 2 also draws support from the scant legislative history that exists. In the words of Senator George Frisbie Hoar:

> I suppose, therefore, . . . a man who merely by superior skill and intelligence . . . got the whole business because nobody could do it as well as he could was not a monopolist, but that it involved something like the use of means which made it impossible for other persons to engage in fair competition, like the engrossing, the buying up of all other persons engaged in the same business.
>
> (*Cong. Rec.* 1890, 21, 4:3,152)

6  U.S. President's Task Force on Antitrust Policy (1968); Williamson (1972); Areeda and Turner (1978); National Commission for the Review of Antitrust Laws and Procedures (1979); Ratner (1988). These proposals draw support for their position from language in *United States v. Griffith*, 334 U.S. 100, 107 (1948) and *Alcoa*, 148 F.2d at 428.

7  Areeda and Hovenkamp (2008a); Hovenkamp (2005); Sullivan and Grimes (2006).

distinguished from growth or development as a consequence of a superior product, business acumen, or historic accident" (*United States v. Grinnell Corp.*, 384 U.S. 563, 570–71 (1966)). As a general matter, then, monopolists do not violate Section 2 simply by charging monopoly prices[8] or by refusing to deal with a particular party.[9] At the same time, the Court has indicated that "[t]he high value that we have placed on the right to refuse to deal with other firms does not mean that the right is unqualified" (*Aspen Skiing*, 472 U.S. at 601).

The essential facilities doctrine is the result of treatise writers' efforts to make sense of early decisions requiring monopolists to deal with their rivals.[10] The doctrine, which made its first explicit appearance in a judicial decision in 1977, imposes a duty on firms controlling effectively irreproducible bottleneck resources to share those resources with their competitors on reasonable terms.[11] Since 1977, lower courts have invoked it with respect to a wide range of different facilities (Lipsky and Sidak 1999).

This doctrine is typically traced to the Supreme Court's decision in *United States v. Terminal Railroad Ass'n* (224 U.S. 383 (1912)), which is usually described as arising from a monopolist railroad's refusal to allow other railroads to run their rolling stock over the only bridge crossing the Mississippi River near St. Louis. A close examination of *Terminal Railroad*'s facts, however, reveals its inaptness as a foundation for limiting a monopolist's unilateral refusal to deal. As an initial matter, the bottleneck in question was controlled not by a monopolist, but rather by a consortium of fourteen of the twenty-four railroads terminating traffic in St. Louis. As such, the conduct in question is more properly analyzed under Section 1 of the Sherman Act, which governs "combination[s] . . . in restraint of trade," (15 U.S.C. § 1), than under Section 2, which applies to single-firm action. Furthermore, the initial bridge owned by the supposed monopolist actually faced competition from a second bridge as well as three ferry companies, each of which the consortium acquired as part of a concerted effort to foreclose competition.[12] Thus, as the Supreme Court would ultimately recognize in *Trinko*, the conduct at issue in *Terminal Railroad*

---

8   *Trinko*, 540 U.S. at 407; *Berkey Photo, Inc. v. Eastman Kodak Co.*, 603 F.2d 263, 276, 294 (2d Cir. 1979).

9   *United States v. Colgate & Co.*, 250 U.S. 300, 307 (1919).

10   Neale (1960); Sullivan (1977).

11   *Hecht v. Pro-Football, Inc.*, 570 F.2d 982, 992 (D.C. Cir. 1977) (citing Neale 1970, p. 67).

12   For example, when Congress authorized the construction of the second bridge, it attempted to protect against merger to monopoly by prohibiting anyone from owning stock in both bridges. This was repealed in what the United States described as a "mysterious manner" before the Association obtained control of the second bridge (Statement and Brief of the Attorney General of the United States at 53, *Terminal R.R.* (No. 386); see also Reiffen and Kleit 1990 describing acquisition of second bridge by Association). The Association acquired the ferry companies only after a rival railroad attempted to purchase one of the ferries as part of a plan to begin providing service in St. Louis. The bidding war between the Association and the rival railroad ended when the Association acquired the ferry while simultaneously agreeing to admit the Rock Island and seven other railroads to the consortium (Reiffen and Kleit 1990).

cannot be characterized as the unilateral actions of a solitary monopolist, but rather as the efforts of a cartel pursuing a conscious plan of merger to monopoly (540 U.S. at 410 n. 3).[13]

Two other Supreme Court decisions offer more appropriate modern foundations for the essential facilities doctrine. The first case, *Otter Tail Power Co. v. United States*, involved a power company that provided three types of services to a number of cities in Minnesota and the Dakotas. First, it generated electric power. Second, it provided wholesale distribution of electric power via its long-haul lines, either by transporting electric power from its generation facilities to individual cities or by "wheeling" power generated by third parties located outside Otter Tail's service area. Third, it provided retail distribution under municipal franchises obtained from cities that did not operate their own municipal distribution grids. Four towns that had previously granted Otter Tail retail distribution franchises terminated those franchises and announced plans to establish their own municipal distribution systems. Otter Tail responded by refusing to sell any power to those systems or to wheel power obtained from other sources. The Supreme Court held that Otter Tail was using its monopoly position in wholesale distribution to foreclose potential entrants in retail distribution. Accordingly, the Court upheld a decree enjoining Otter Tail from refusing to sell wholesale power to these cities, leaving it to the Federal Power Commission to resolve disputes over the particular terms and conditions of interconnection, even though Congress had explicitly refused to give the Federal Power Commission the authority to require companies like Otter Tail to wheel power (410 U.S. 366, 368–72, 374–78 (1973)). Although the district court had based its decision on reasoning similar to the essential facilities doctrine,[14] the Supreme Court did not mention it at all.

*Otter Tail* has been heavily criticized for both the thinness of its reasoning and its conceptual incoherence.[15] As Professors Philip Areeda and Herbert Hovenkamp note in their leading antitrust treatise (2008c, p. 362), claims seeking wholesale access so that the purchased products can be resold at retail "would ordinarily be rejected in the unregulated setting.... Antitrust would not ordinarily countenance the intending car dealer's claim, for example, that it has a right to purchase the monopoly manufacturer's cars at wholesale and resell them at retail, when the manufacturer prefers to retail them directly." As a result, Areeda and Hovenkamp

---

13  Areeda and Hovenkamp (2008c, pp. 234–36) similarly describe *Terminal Railroad* Court's emphasis on combination of companies operating bridge and attempting to exclude rivals. Hovenkamp (2005, p. 309) points out that because *Terminal Railroad* "involve[ed] an agreement among multiple firms who controlled the facility," it "makes a poor ancestor for the essential facilities doctrine." Ratner (1988, pp. 336–37) argues that *Terminal Railroad* is more appropriately classified as "a classic group boycott" or "horizontal agreements in restraint of trade in violation of Section 1."

14  *United States v. Otter Tail Power Co.*, 331 F. Supp. 54, 61 (D. Minn. 1971) (invoking the "bottleneck" theory), *modified*, 410 U.S. 366 (1973).

15  Areeda and Hovenkamp (2008c, p. 362) note that *Otter Tail* court did not "adequately elaborate[]" upon underlying grounds for decision. Kauper (2005, p. 1627) notes, "Virtually no discernible principle can be found in *Otter Tail*...."

suggest that *Otter Tail* is best understood in light of its "peculiarities." The mandate to wheel power ought to be read in light of the historical common law duty to deal imposed on public utilities. The case is also "unique in its remedial aspects," in that the Federal Power Commission was available to oversee the terms and conditions of the interconnection mandate (see also Kauper 2005).

The second decision, *Aspen Skiing Co. v. Aspen Highlands Skiing Corp.*, arose from a dispute between operators of ski areas near Aspen, Colorado. Starting in 1962, the three independently owned ski facilities in the area – Ajax, Buttermilk, and Highlands – jointly offered a multiday, all-Aspen ticket that could be redeemed at any of the facilities. The owner of Ajax eventually acquired Buttermilk and opened a new ski area called Snowmass. The combined entity, now known as Ski Co., continued to cooperate with Highlands to offer a multiarea pass, now covering all four ski areas. Revenues were divided based on the number of tickets redeemed at each mountain, with the share of the revenue allocated to Highlands ranging from a high of 18.5 percent during the 1974–5 season to a low of 13.2 percent in 1976–7. For the 1977–8 season, Ski Co. asked Highlands to fix its compensation at 13.2 percent of the multiarea pass's revenues. Subsequent negotiations increased Highlands's compensation to 15 percent. The following year, Highlands rejected a proposal that would have reduced its share of the total revenue to 12.5 percent. In response, Ski Co. terminated the all-Aspen ticket and instead offered a three-area ticket covering only the ski areas that it owned. In addition, it frustrated Highlands's attempts to reconstruct the four-area ticket by refusing to sell its three-area tickets to Highlands at the full retail price. The Supreme Court held that Ski Co.'s termination of the joint venture constituted monopolization under Section 2 of the Sherman Act. In the process, it upheld the district court's injunction, which required that the parties jointly offer an all-Aspen ticket modeled on a multiarea ticket that Ski Co. offered at another nearby resort area. In so concluding, though, the Supreme Court declined to follow the doctrinal lead of the court of appeals, which explicitly based its decision on the essential facilities doctrine (472 U.S. at 587–94, 598 n. 23, 599, 605–11, and n. 44).

The decision in *Aspen Skiing*, like the decision in *Otter Tail*, has been subject to extensive scholarly criticism. Perhaps the most trenchant criticism involves the definition of the appropriate geographic market. The jury found that the relevant product market was "destination ski resort[s]," whose primary clientele is out-of-town vacationers, as opposed to "day ski area[s]," which cater to local residents (472 U.S. at 587, 594, 596 n. 20). By definition, patrons of destination ski resorts are free to choose from among the many ski areas in the western United States and Canada. Commentators generally agree that implicitly assuming that these customers were locked into Aspen caused the Supreme Court to define the geographic market too narrowly (Campbell 1985; Easterbrook 1986; Wiley 1986b; Lipsky and Sidak 1999; Areeda and Hovenkamp 2006b; Hovenkamp 2005).

Furthermore, there is some evidence that Highlands was free riding on Ski Co.'s facilities and marketing efforts. For example, Highlands's inability to attract more than 18.5 percent of the overall business suggests that its ski area was below average in attractiveness. From this perspective, Highlands was simply diverting revenue from skiers attracted by the higher-quality mountains provided by Ski Co (Easterbrook 1986). Furthermore, Ski Co. purchased national advertising to bring vacationers to Aspen; Highlands did not. If Ski Co. were to advertise optimally, it should increase its advertising until the marginal return no longer exceeded the marginal cost of increasing advertising any further. To the extent that Highlands siphoned off some of the business generated by this advertising, Ski Co.'s returns to advertising would look artificially low and would cause Ski Co. to stop further advertising even when it would be efficient to continue to do so. Highlands's free riding would thus ultimately impede Ski Co.'s ability to compete with other ski areas (Wiley 1986b).

Another possible problem is that the pro rata division did not reflect the marginal benefits provided by each ski area. Although Highlands accounted for between 13.2 percent and 18.5 percent of the usage while the four-area pass was in use, its share eventually dropped to 11 percent after discontinuation of the pass (472 U.S. at 595). This suggests that its marginal contribution might be somewhat smaller than its pro rata usage might suggest. In other words, the value that skiers place on a four-area pass might be only 11 percent more than the value they would place on a three-area pass. Thus, the proportion in which skiers actually distribute their custom may overstate Highlands's incremental contribution. From this perspective, the dispute between Highlands and Ski Co. may have been nothing more than a disagreement over what the proper baseline was for dividing the benefits created by their joint venture. This is precisely the type of dispute in which antitrust courts should avoid becoming entangled (Areeda and Hovenkamp 2008c).

Last, Ski Co.'s history of selling multiarea tickets both in Aspen and at its other resorts greatly facilitated the remedy in *Aspen Skiing*. The Court could use these parallel transactions as a basis for fashioning a remedy without having to establish the terms and conditions for such a multiarea ticket out of whole cloth. In cases in which such external benchmarks do not exist, courts will doubtlessly find fashioning appropriate remedies in duty-to-deal cases to be much more difficult.

These criticisms, and the decisions' failure to rely upon the essential facilities doctrine, have not stopped lower courts from invoking *Otter Tail* and *Aspen Skiing* when requiring monopolists to provide competitors with access to their facilities. What remains controversial is the precise scope of the duty to deal mandated by these cases.

### B. A Critique of the Essential Facilities Doctrine

Even supporters of the essential facilities doctrine recognize that it "has long been a controversial subject under U.S. antitrust law" (Pitofsky et al. 2002, p. 443).[16] Essential facilities claims assert that a firm is using its control of a monopoly input

---

16　*Byars v. Bluff City News Co.*, 609 F.2d 843, 846 (6th Cir. 1980), similarly calls the essential facilities doctrine "one of the most unsettled and vexatious in the antitrust field."

to restrain competition in a vertically related market, either by charging companies requesting access to that resource excessive prices or by denying those companies access to the resource altogether. Rather than selling the input into the open market and allowing other purchasers to combine it with other inputs and sell their finished products on a competitive basis, the input monopolist excludes certain purchasers either by internalizing production, and thereby becoming the sole source of finished goods, or by entering into strategic partnerships with certain purchasers and giving them preferential terms.

The central concern of the essential facilities doctrine is thus vertical exclusion.[17] As such, the essential facilities doctrine is susceptible to – and, therefore, should reflect – the economic critique of vertical exclusion that has emerged over the past half-century (see Yoo 2002 for a review). In addition, the doctrine must take into account the emerging debate over the proper division of authority between antitrust courts and regulatory agencies in supervising access mandates.

## 1. The Economics of Vertical Exclusion

As noted in Chapter 4, the conventional wisdom about vertical integration has undergone something of a sea change over the past half century. Antitrust scholars once generally accepted the notion that firms could use monopoly power in one level of production to reduce the competitiveness of vertically related levels of production (see, e.g., Kaysen and Turner 1959). Accordingly, the Supreme Court was quite receptive to vertical exclusion claims until the mid-1970s. In case after case, the Court struck down vertical mergers by firms controlling as little as 5 percent of the market, largely out of concern that vertical integration would reduce competition in the downstream market.[18] This hostility toward vertical exclusion became enshrined in the initial Merger Guidelines issued by the Justice Department in 1968, which disfavored vertical mergers involving firms controlling as little as 6 percent to 10 percent of their markets (U.S. Department of Justice 1968, § 12). The Supreme Court followed a similar pattern with respect to vertical contractual restraints, either holding them illegal per se[19] or striking them down at such low

---

17 Werden (1987); Areeda and Hovenkamp (2008c).

18 *Brown Shoe*, 370 U.S. 294, 303, 327, 331–34 (1962) (striking down vertical merger between shoe manufacturer with 4% of U.S. market and shoe retailer with less than 2 percent of U.S. market); *Ford Motor Co. v. United States*, 405 U.S. 562, 568, 578 (1972) (striking down vertical merger resulting in 10% foreclosure).

19 On resale price maintenance, see *Dr. Miles Med. Co. v. John D. Park & Sons Co.*, 220 U.S. 373, 398–409 (1911), *overruled by Leegin Creative Leather Prods., Inc. v. PSKS, Inc.*, 127 S. Ct 2705 (2007); *Albrecht v. Herald Co.*, 390 U.S. 145, 149–54 (1968), *overruled by State Oil Co. v. Khan*, 522 U.S. 3 (1997). On tying, see *IBM Corp. v. United States*, 298 U.S. 131, 134–40 (1936); *Int'l Salt Co. v. United States*, 332 U.S. 392, 396–98 (1947); *N. Pac. Ry. Co. v. United States*, 356 U.S. 1, 5–7 (1958); *United States v. Loew's, Inc.*, 371 U.S. 38, 45 (1962); *Fortner Enters., Inc. v. U.S. Steel Corp.*, 394 U.S. 495, 498–99 (1969). On territorial exclusivity, see *United States v. Arnold, Schwinn & Co.*, 388 U.S. 365, 379–80 (1967), *overruled by Cont'l T.V., Inc. v. GTE Sylvania Inc.*, 433 U.S. 36 (1977).

levels of concentration as to be tantamount to the same thing.[20] In *Griffith*, the Court went so far as to indicate that liability could lie even in the absence of any intent or ability to acquire a second monopoly in another market (334 U.S. at 106–08). The Second Circuit took a similar position in *Berkey Photo*, indicating that "the use of monopoly power attained in one market to gain a competitive advantage in another is a violation of § 2, even if there has not been an attempt to monopolize the second market" (603 F.2d at 276). These decisions spawned a circuit split over whether Section 2 requires at least proof that the vertically related market was structured in a way that made the threat of monopolization credible.[21]

Since that time, antitrust law has largely internalized the scholarly critiques reviewed in Chapter 4, which have emphasized that certain structural preconditions must generally be met before the producer of an input can plausibly have any *ability* to harm competition in a vertically related market. First, the firm must possess monopoly power over the input market. If not, any attempt to charge supracompetitive prices in any market will simply lead the firm's customers to turn to other sources. In addition and more importantly for our purposes, the vertically related market must be concentrated and protected by entry barriers for a threat to the competitiveness of that market to be credible. If not, any attempt to raise price in the vertically related market will cause existing competitors to increase their production or will attract new competitors until the price is forced back down to competitive levels.[22] The post-Chicago models identifying circumstances under which input producers have the incentive to engage in vertical exclusion are based on dominant-firm and oligopoly market structures that presuppose that the relevant markets are highly concentrated and protected by entry barriers. In the absence of such structural features, these formal models recognize that vertical integration may be just as likely to lower price and increase welfare and that the ability of existing players or new entrants to expand their outputs will be sufficient to defeat any attempt to increase price above competitive levels.[23] In other words, the post-Chicago literature incorporates the same structural preconditions discussed above for vertical integration to harm competition.

The primary exception to this conclusion is a scenario contained in Michael Whinston's seminal analysis of tying (1990),[24] in which an input producer assumed

---

20  See, e.g., *Standard Oil Co. v. United States* (*Standard Stations*), 337 U.S. 293, 295, 314 (1949) (holding that exclusive dealing contracts may be held illegal even absent proof of any tendency to create monopoly and that foreclosure of 16% of market was sufficient to render exclusive dealing contract illegal); *Brown Shoe Co.*, 62 F.T.C. 679, 687 ¶ 10, 691 ¶ 33 (1963) (invalidating exclusive dealing arrangement even though it only foreclosed less than 1% of retail outlets), *aff'd*, 384 U.S. 316, 321–22 (1966).

21  *Eleven Line, Inc. v. N. Tex. State Soccer Ass'n*, 213 F.3d 198, 206 n. 16 (5th Cir. 2000) (recognizing circuit split). *Lantec, Inc. v. Novell, Inc.*, 306 F.3d 1003, 1024 n. 11 (10th Cir. 2002) (same); cases collected in Areeda and Hovenkamp (2008a, pp. 135–40).

22  Peltzman (1969); Blair and Kaserman (1985); Areeda and Hovenkamp (2008c).

23  Salinger (1991); Riordan and Salop (1995).

24  The analysis of Whinston that follows draws on Yoo (2007a, 2008).

to face competition from an inferior product uses a credible precommitment to tying in order to harm competition in an adjacent market, a situation that Whinston recognized was equivalent to vertical integration.[25] Interestingly, Whinston's model assumes a wide variety of restrictive conditions that not only largely incorporate the structural preconditions discussed above, but also require that certain assumptions fall within a very narrow range.[26] Furthermore, Whinston found that even when vertical exclusion was possible, the welfare implications were ambiguous. Whinston accordingly concluded that the normative implications of his model were unclear and that even when tying led to vertical exclusion, permitting it might actually benefit consumers.[27] Consequently, any court considering an antitrust claim based on the exception identified by Whinston must ensure that its restrictive assumptions are met and should undertake a complete analysis of the welfare implications before imposing liability.

Over time, antitrust law began to reflect the characterization of vertical exclusion found in the scholarly commentary. Of particular relevance for our discussion are the Court's most recent tying decisions, which like the essential facilities decisions are based on unilateral conduct and thus fall within Section 2. In those decisions, the Supreme Court has begun to require proof that the structural preconditions discussed above are met before finding liability. For example, the Supreme Court has required that a tying defendant possess monopoly power in a properly defined market.[28] Lower courts have followed the Supreme Court's lead and have

25 The primary scenario Whinston analyzes assumes that the market for good *A* is a monopoly, the market for good *B* is characterized by economies of scale, and consumers of good *A* represent a significant percentage of consumers of good *B*. For example, assume that 75% of the consumers of good *B* also purchase good *A* and that the minimum efficient scale for the market for *B* is 25%. Tying *B* to *A* forces all other producers of good *B* below minimum efficient scale and can therefore give the firm producing *A* a monopoly over *B* as well. In the process, the *A* monopolist is able to exert monopoly power over the 25% of the consumers of *B* who do not purchase *A*. Whinston (1990); see also Carlton and Waldman (2002), extending Whinston's work.

26 For example, the model assumes that *A* consumers constitute a sufficiently large proportion of the market for *B* relative to minimum efficient scale to crowd out other producers of *B*. At the same time, if *A* consumers represent too large a proportion of the market for *B*, tying would yield few benefits aside from those that the monopolist could extract simply by charging the monopoly price for *A*. In addition, the minimum efficient scale must be sufficiently large to facilitate crowding out without being so large as to render the market for *B* monopolistic or to create efficiency benefits from the elimination of double marginalization. Furthermore, the slope of the average cost must be sufficiently steep to render entry at output levels below minimum efficient scale infeasible. If the slope is relatively shallow, the scale economies will not provide sufficient cost advantage to prevent entry (Yoo 2008).

27 Whinston (1999); see also Carlton and Waldman (2002), similarly concluding that the possibility that exclusion could benefit consumers justifies cautioning against "trying to turn the theoretical possibility for harm shown here into a prescriptive theory of antitrust enforcement."

28 *U.S. Steel Corp. v. Fortner Enters., Inc.*, 429 U.S. 610, 620 (1977); *Jefferson Parish Hosp. Dist. No. 2 v. Hyde*, 466 U.S. 2, 12–15 (1984); *Eastman Kodak Co. v. Image Technical Servs., Inc.*, 504 U.S. 451, 462, 464, 481 (1992); *Ill. Tool Works Inc. v. Indep. Ink, Inc.*, 547 U.S. 28, 34–5 (2006); accord *Nw.*

begun to incorporate these structural preconditions into the essential facilities doctrine. These decisions have always required the practical unavailability of the input from other sources,[29] now formalized into the requirement of proof of a monopoly position in a properly defined market.[30] The need for proof of concentration in the primary market draws further support from *AT&T v. Iowa Utilities Board*, in which the Court addressed a statutory provision requiring incumbent local telephone companies to provide competitors with access to any element of their networks that was "necessary" and without which competitors would be "impair[ed]" in their ability to provide service (47 U.S.C. § 251(d)(2)). The majority declined to decide whether this provision incorporated the standard embodied in the essential facilities doctrine, but Justice Breyer found the two principles to be "analogous." Tellingly, both the majority and Justice Breyer declined to compel access to any input that was available from other sources (525 U.S. at 388–92, 428). Courts implementing other statutory access mandates have been similarly reluctant to compel access to inputs that are available from other sources.[31] Acceptance of this structural precondition is also reflected in the nonhorizontal merger guidelines issued by the Justice Department, which now require that the primary market must surpass a certain threshold level of concentration before antitrust authorities will seriously consider challenging a vertical merger.[32]

These decisions also incorporated another of the structural preconditions suggested by the economic theory by requiring proof of substantial foreclosure in the secondary market before subjecting a restraint to antitrust scrutiny.[33] The Supreme Court was even more explicit in *Spectrum Sports, Inc. v. McQuillan*, holding that even concededly bad conduct cannot support a monopolization claim in the absence of evidence of actual monopolization or a dangerous threat of monopolization, of the secondary market.[34] Lower courts have similarly made a threat to a vertically

*Wholesale Stationers, Inc. v. Pac. Stationery & Printing Co.*, 472 U.S. 284, 296–97 (1985) (applying equivalent requirement to group boycotts).

29  See, e.g., *MCI*, 708 F.2d at 1132; *Hecht*, 570 F.2d at 992; cases collected in Areeda and Hovenkamp (2008c, pp. 242–45).

30  *Consul, Ltd. v. Transco Energy Co.*, 805 F.2d 490, 494–95 (4th Cir. 1986); *City of Malden v. Union Elec. Co.*, 887 F.2d 157, 160 n. 4 (8th Cir. 1989); *Ill. Bell Tel. Co. v. Haines & Co.*, 905 F.2d 1081, 1087 (7th Cir. 1990), *vacated*, 499 U.S. 944 (1991).

31  *Nat'l Cable & Telecomm. Ass'n v. Brand X Internet Servs.*, 545 U.S. 967, 1001–02 (2005); *U.S. Telecom Ass'n v. FCC*, 290 F.3d 415, 428–29 (D.C. Cir. 2002).

32  U.S. Department of Justice (1984, § 4.213). The 1992 statement that accompanied the issuance of the new Horizontal Merger Guidelines indicated that Section 4 of the 1984 Guidelines continued to provide the relevant guidance for nonhorizontal mergers (U.S. Department of Justice 1992). The Clinton Administration considered revising the Non-horizontal Merger Guidelines but chose not to do so (Yoo 2002).

33  *Jefferson Parish*, 466 U.S. at 12–16; *Kodak*, 504 U.S. at 462, 464, 481.

34  506 U.S. 447, 459 (1993); see also *Brooke Group Ltd. v. Brown & Williamson Tobacco Corp.*, 509 U.S. 209, 224–25 (1993) ("Earlier this Term, we held in the Sherman Act § 2 context . . . that the plaintiff [must] prove 'a dangerous probability that [the defendant] would monopolize a particular market,'" quoting *Spectrum Sports*, 506 U.S. at 459).

related market a structural precondition of the essential facilities doctrine (*Alaska Airlines*, 948 F.2d at 546–47), whereas the U.S. Department of Justice's 1984 Merger Guidelines (§§ 4.211–4.212) require that the secondary market be concentrated and protected by entry barriers. Furthermore, in at least one case, four justices of the Court explicitly recognized the one-monopoly-rent theorem, as have some lower courts implementing the essential facilities doctrine.[35]

The presence of regulation can also affect incentives to integrate vertically. Regulators may explicitly encourage or discourage vertical integration into particular lines of business. The effect of regulation on incentives is illustrated by the classic example sometimes called the "Bell Doctrine" or "Baxter's Law" because of the role it played in the breakup of AT&T during Stanford law professor William Baxter's tenure as head of the Antitrust Division (Baxter 1983). It relies upon the fact that an input producer cannot extract all of the available profit simply by charging the monopoly price when the government limits the price it can charge for that input. Vertical integration into an unregulated market allows the monopolist to earn the profits denied to it in the regulated market by charging higher prices in the unregulated market (U.S. Department of Justice 1984, § 4.23). Such rate regulation, therefore, potentially gives monopoly producers the incentive to vertically integrate into an unregulated market and require all of their customers to purchase both products at prices that include the full monopoly markup.[36] These incentives can be offset by competitive incentives to attract business in the unregulated market.

A more subtle version of this argument applies when a firm subject to cost-of-service rate regulation provides an unregulated service that shares joint costs with the regulated service.[37] In that case, it is alleged that the monopolist can attempt to allocate a disproportionate amount of the joint costs to the regulated service and recover those costs through its regulated rates, which is a real possibility given the inherent arbitrariness and uncertainty surrounding methodologies for allocating joint costs. Shifting a disproportionate amount of the joint costs onto the regulated market allows firms to reduce the size of the markup to cover joint costs included in the prices charged in the unregulated market. The firm's nonvertically integrated competitors, however, will have to charge prices that reflect the genuine allocation of the joint costs to the unregulated market. As a result, some commentators have argued that the essential facilities doctrine has greater potential relevance in the context of regulated industries.[38]

Although the Bell Doctrine was once an important consideration with respect to telecommunications, economic and technological progress have undercut its

---

35  *Jefferson Parish*, 466 U.S. at 36 (O'Connor, J., joined by Burger, C.J., and Powell and Rehnquist, JJ., concurring in judgment); *Byars*, 609 F.2d at 861.

36  *Jefferson Parish*, 466 U.S. at 36 n. 4 (O'Connor, J., concurring in judgment); *Byars*, 609 F.2d at 861; *Olympia Equip. Leasing Co. v. W. Union Tel. Co.*, 797 F.2d 370, 374 (7th Cir. 1986); Bowman (1957); Brennan (1987); Ratner (1988); Joskow and Noll (1999); Farrell and Weiser (2003).

37  Brenner (1996); Farrell (1996); Sullivan (1996); Huber et al. (1999); Joskow and Noll (1999).

38  Werden (1987); Gerber (1988); Ratner (1988); Areeda and Hovenkamp (2008c).

significance. As an initial matter, it has no applicability to wireless and broadband communications, which are not subject to rate regulation.[39] The emergence of competitive wireline alternatives has caused federal and state regulators to deregulate almost all aspects of conventional wireline telephone service provided to businesses. Competition from wireless providers and Voice over Internet Protocol (VoIP) has led state regulatory authorities to begin the process of deregulating wireline residential telephone services as well (Tardiff 2007). Once this transformation is complete, the Bell Doctrine will cease to have any continuing application to the telecommunications industry.

In the absence of some anticompetitive explanation for vertical exclusion, what explains why firms engage in the practice? Even post-Chicago economic theorists recognize that vertical exclusion can yield substantial efficiencies.[40] Some efficiencies are attributed to technological effects. Building on the copper ingot example introduced above, if the input monopolist sold ingot into the open market, purchasers would have to incur the costs of reheating the ingot before fabricating it into pipe. A vertically integrated operation could reduce costs by beginning the pipe fabrication process while the ingot was still hot, although presumably these arrangements could be made between independent firms absent transaction costs. To use another example more closely related to the telecommunications industry, the Federal Communications Commission (FCC) attempted to promote competition in so-called "enhanced" telecommunications services (i.e., services that went beyond mere voice communication) by requiring that they be provided on a vertically disintegrated basis. As noted in Chapter 5, the digitization of telephone switches means that certain enhanced services, such as caller ID, call forwarding, and call waiting, are most efficiently provided through the data processing capacity already built into the switch itself. Forcing these services to be provided on a vertically disintegrated basis delayed introduction of these services by several years. Other efficiencies are more price-theoretic, such as the elimination of double marginalization or the rationalization of input substitution discussed in Chapter 4. To the extent that concerns about vertical exclusion are justified, this makes it quite likely that allowing some degree of vertical coordination will yield welfare benefits. Still other efficiencies relate to transaction costs, particularly in protecting against opportunistic behavior.

The Supreme Court eventually embraced this emerging vision in its landmark decision in *Continental T.V., Inc. v. GTE Sylvania*, in which it accepted the reduction of the transaction costs needed to guard against opportunism as a pro-competitive business justification sufficient to support holding exclusivity agreements. In the

---

39  FCC (2005c); Woroch (2002a).

40  Ayres (1988); Salinger (1988); Hart and Tirole (1990); Klass and Salinger (1995); Riordan and Salop (1995); see also Krattenmaker and Salop (1986), conducting a similar analysis with respect to vertical restraints. For discussions of the potential efficiencies associated with vertical exclusion in the context of the essential facilities doctrine, see Werden (1987); Gerber (1988); Areeda and Hovenkamp (2008c).

process, the Court rejected buyer and trader freedom as independent values that justify regulatory intervention even in the absence of any showing of harm to competition (433 U.S. at 53 n. 21, 54–55). If competition is sufficiently robust, the reduction in the freedom of some consumers or manufacturers does not rise to the level of antitrust concern, as consumers who wish to avoid the strictures of the exclusivity arrangement can do so simply by shifting their purchases to another provider.[41]

*Sylvania* marked a sea change in competition policy with respect to vertical integration. In subsequent cases, the Supreme Court has shown greater willingness to entertain efficiency justifications for vertical restraints.[42] The Court's willingness in *Aspen Skiing* to consider possible business justifications for apparently anti-competitive conduct established that efficiencies can justify monopolization (472 U.S. at 609–11). As a result, lower courts applying the essential facilities doctrine have considered whether possible efficiencies might justify a monopolist's unilateral refusal to deal.[43] Section 4.24 of the Department of Justice's nonhorizontal merger guidelines (1984) also explicitly recognizes that vertical mergers that violate the structural preconditions may nonetheless be permitted if they create sufficient efficiencies. Thereafter, antitrust law has become increasingly hospitable to vertical integration and vertical contractual restraints.[44]

These theoretical insights are corroborated by the growing empirical literature on vertical restraints. For example, a recent survey of twenty-three empirical studies of vertical integration and vertical restraints conducted by four members of the FTC staff found "a paucity of support for the proposition that vertical restraints/vertical integration are likely to harm consumers." Indeed, only one of the studies under review found that vertical integration was harmful to consumers, and even in that study the welfare losses were found to be "miniscule." In contrast, "a far greater number of studies found that the use of vertical restraints in the particular context studied improved welfare unambiguously" (Cooper et al. 2005, pp. 660–61).

Another recent survey divided empirical studies of vertical restraints into two categories: studies of those that were voluntarily adopted and of those that were mandated or prohibited by the government. This survey found that of the twelve published studies of vertical restraints that were voluntarily adopted, nine found that the vertical restraint under study enhanced consumer welfare, whereas only

---

41   *N. Pac. Ry.*, 356 U.S. at 6–7; *Jefferson Parish*, 466 U.S. at 11–12.

42   *Monsanto Co. v. Spray–Rite Serv. Corp.*, 465 U.S. 752, 762–63 (1984); *State Oil*, 522 U.S. at 18.

43   See, e.g., *City of Vernon v. S. Cal. Edison Co.*, 955 F.2d 1361, 1365–67 (9th Cir. 1992); *Ill. ex rel. Burris v. Panhandle E. Pipe Line Co.*, 935 F.2d 1469, 1481–82 (7th Cir. 1991); *Byars*, 609 F.2d at 862–63; cases collected in Areeda and Hovenkamp (2008c, pp. 253–58).

44   See, e.g., *Bus. Elecs. Corp. v Sharp Elecs. Corp.*, 485 U.S. 717 (1988); *Spectrum Sports*, 506 U.S. at 459; *State Oil Co. v. Khan*, 522 U.S. 3 (1997); *Leegin Creative Leather Prods., Inc. v. PSKS, Inc.*, 127 S. Ct. 2705 (2007); *Barry Wright Corp. v. ITT Grinnell Corp.*, 724 F.2d 227, 236–37 (1st Cir. 1983) (Breyer, J.).

three found that the practices reduced consumer welfare. In contrast, among the eleven studies of vertical restraints that were either mandated or prohibited by the government, nine found a reduction in consumer welfare, with the welfare impact of the remaining two studies being ambiguous. Although these authors recognize that the small number of studies made it difficult to make definitive claims, they describe the evidentiary record as "quite striking," "surprisingly consistent," and "compelling" in its support for the proposition that privately imposed vertical restraints benefit consumers or at least do not harm them. At the same time, "[w]hen the government intervenes and forces firms to adopt (or discontinue the use of) vertical restraints, in contrast, it tends to make consumers worse off." The survey concluded that the empirical record thus provides "consistent and convincing" evidence against government intervention to protect against vertical exclusion (LaFontaine and Slade 2008).

The discussion up to this point has focused exclusively on courts' consideration of how best to allocate the network that exists today. These rationales overlook the impact that the essential facilities doctrine can have on incentives to invest in the network of tomorrow. In other words, the current policy debate has placed too much focus on *static efficiency* and given too little emphasis to the maximization of *dynamic efficiency*.

When competitive entry is possible, the essential facilities doctrine can have a detrimental impact on incentives to invest in alternative network capacity. Exogenous factors – such as shifts in demand, cost-saving changes in technology, and the developments of new substitutes and complements – frequently cause markets to deviate from their long-run equilibrium. Antitrust law solves this problem through what one leading treatise calls "a uniquely American, market-affirming response to [market] power." It "assumes that strong incentives promote efficiency" and that in the absence of entry barriers, market power "will erode under the pressure of market developments." Tolerating a degree of short-run disequilibrium plays an essential role in this process of reequilibration. Indeed, "where supracompetitive pricing accompanies power, erosion of the power is thought to be more likely because high prices signal the need, and promise a reward, for entry" (Sullivan and Grimes 2006, pp. 84–85).

This emphasis on allowing monopolists to charge supracompetitive prices in the short run is sometimes mistaken for the type of competition envisioned by Joseph Schumpeter (1942), in which the market is dominated by a succession of monopolists and firms compete by vying to discover the next breakthrough innovation that will give them a cost or quality advantage decisive enough to allow them to displace the current monopolist and dominate the market in its place.[45] This characterization, however, ignores the key role that short-run supracompetitive returns play in the horizontal competition within a market characterized by perfect competition in which multiple players offer substitute products to consumers and

---

45  For an example of commentary describing *Trinko* as Schumpeterian, see Weiser (2005).

in which any supracompetitive returns will prove transient and quickly dissipate (Yoo 2005). Thus, short-run supracompetitive returns not only allocate the scarce network resources, but also signal industry participants that the market is in short-run disequilibrium and provide incentives to invest in additional network capacity.

The essential facilities doctrine threatens to derail this process of reequilibration. Those forced to pay supracompetitive prices for a monopoly input or denied access to that input altogether have powerful incentives to invest in alternative sources of supply. As a result, essential facilities plaintiffs are natural candidates either to develop independent capacity themselves or to enter into strategic partnerships with firms interested in becoming alternative suppliers of the input. Rather than simply requiring that the monopoly be shared, entry by independent providers of the input would break up the monopoly, which in turn would lead to long-run, sustainable consumer benefits without any continuing oversight by antitrust authorities. Conversely, anything that discourages investments in alternative sources of supply threatens to impede rather than promote technological and economic development.

The problem is that the essential facilities doctrine threatens to dampen investment incentives in two ways. First, investing in alternative capacity is quite risky and can require substantial capital investment. Forcing the monopolist to share its input rescues other firms from having to undertake the risks associated with supplying the relevant input for themselves.[46] Second, if the essential facilities doctrine is to yield any consumer benefits, it necessarily requires subjecting the owner of the bottleneck facility to some form of price regulation. This reduction in price reduces the incentives for others to invest in the development of alternative sources of supply of the input. Instead of entering under a price umbrella created by the input monopolist's efforts to maximize its own profits, any new entrant will confront a market with lower price–cost margins, which in turn makes sustainable entry even more difficult.[47] As a result, compelled access can entrench the supposed bottleneck facility by forestalling the emergence of the substitute sources of supply of the input, which in turn has the perverse effect of cementing the input owner's monopoly position into place.

Compelled access also dampens the incentives of the essential facilities defendant to invest in improvements in its facilities, because price regulation will limit the returns it can earn on such investments and force it to share successful investments with its competitors.[48] Furthermore, because the monopoly is never displaced, the essential facilities doctrine implicitly presumes that supervision by antitrust courts will be indefinite. This is particularly problematic in technologically dynamic

---

46  Hylton (1991); Areeda and Hovenkamp (2008c).

47  Areeda and Hovenkamp (2008c) argue that, in the absence of price regulation, compelled access does not preclude supracompetitive pricing. Ratner (1988) notes that monopoly pricing is a stimulus to develop independent capacity.

48  Areeda and Hovenkamp (2008b) discuss the decrease in incentive to develop facilities arising from price regulation.

industries. Even if the court strikes the proper balance at the time it renders its decision, subsequent developments may alter the appropriate input price or may render
competition in the input market possible. At best, economic welfare will suffer from
some degree of delay, as the legal processes adjust to catch up with these changes.
At worst, the disincentives created by the essential facilities doctrine will prevent
competition from ever emerging.

Of course, concerns about dampening incentives for investing in alternative
sources of supply only make sense if competitive entry is feasible. If not, competition policy's traditional response is to abandon the first-order policy goal of
using antitrust law to break up the input monopoly and instead subject the input
monopoly to rate regulation and pursue the second-order policy goal of promoting competition in complementary markets through access requirements. This
explains the rationale underlying the breakup of AT&T. The court's assumption
that competition in local telephone service was not viable caused it to focus on promoting competition in complementary services, such as long distance, information
services, and customer premises equipment (CPE). Once technological progress
renders competition in the input market feasible, antitrust courts should abandon
the second-order policy goal of promoting competition in complementary services
and return to the first-order policy goal of promoting competition in the last mile.
The problem is that mandating access will make it difficult for antitrust courts to
determine when it is possible to do so. In the worst case, the investment disincentives
created by mandated access can cause it to be a source of, rather than the solution
to, market failure by forestalling last-mile competition from emerging long after it
has become viable.

For this reason, commentators have consistently insisted that the allegedly
essential facility not be duplicable or available from other sources (Areeda 1990).
It is not sufficient that duplication of the facility might require significant capital
investment and take a long time.[49] Simply put, late is better than never.

Finally, courts have exhibited greater sensitivity to dynamic efficiency. In the
words of the Ninth Circuit in *Alaska Airlines, Inc. v. United Airlines, Inc.*, "[e]very
time the monopolist asserts its market dominance" by denying rivals access to a
bottleneck input, it gives the rival "more incentive to find an alternative supplier,
which in turn gives alternate suppliers more reason to think that they can compete
with the monopolist. Every act exploiting monopoly power to the disadvantage
of the monopoly's customers hastens the monopoly's end by making the potential
competition more attractive" (948 F.2d at 549).

Thus, by the time the Supreme Court decided *Trinko*, the law had begun to
reflect the theoretical critique of the essential facilities doctrine set forth in the
scholarly literature. As we shall see, *Trinko* gave this critique an additional, albeit
modest, endorsement.

---

49   Areeda and Hovenkamp (2008c, p. 266) show that essential facilities doctrine can be anticom-
     petitive when "the facility can be duplicated or some substitute developed, even in the relatively
     long run."

## 2. The Allocation of Authority between Antitrust Courts and Regulatory Agencies

Courts and commentators have also expressed concern about the proper division of responsibility between antitrust courts and regulatory agencies. Responding to these concerns, courts have developed a number of doctrines to prevent conflicts between antitrust law and regulatory regimes from arising. Two doctrines determine whether federal or state law provides outright immunity from antitrust scrutiny. Two additional doctrines address the timing of judicial consideration by postponing it until after a state or federal regulatory agency has had a chance to consider the issues in the first instance. As a general matter, these doctrines have not been particularly restrictive and have tended to give antitrust courts wide latitude to entertain antitrust claims requesting access to telecommunications networks. Scholarship on the essential facilities doctrine, however, has begun to question whether current law strikes the correct balance.

### a. Immunity from Antitrust Scrutiny

*Displacement of the Antitrust Laws by a Federal Regulatory Scheme.* Courts have long recognized that the enactment of a federal regulatory scheme can immunize particular conduct from antitrust scrutiny. In rare cases, a federal regulatory statute explicitly repeals the antitrust laws with respect to certain conduct. For example, from 1921 until 1996, federal law gave the FCC the authority to exempt telephone company mergers from antitrust scrutiny by the Justice Department and the FTC.[50] Such explicit repeals are relatively rare, though, and courts have construed them narrowly.[51]

In the absence of statutory language explicitly exempting conduct from the antitrust laws, defendants can still argue that the regulatory scheme is so pervasive as to give rise to implied immunity from the antitrust laws.[52] The Supreme Court has made clear, however, that "[r]epeal of the antitrust laws by implication is not favored and not casually to be allowed." As a result, courts have generally insisted that there be "a plain repugnancy between the antitrust and regulatory provision" before holding conduct impliedly immune from the antitrust laws, and upheld implied immunity "even then only to the minimum extent necessary" to make the regulatory scheme work (*Gordon v. N.Y. Stock Exch.*, 422 U.S. 659, 682, 683 (1975) (internal quotation marks omitted)).[53]

---

50  This provision was originally enacted as part of the Willis–Graham Act (*Statutes at Large* 1921, pp. 27–28). It was subsequently incorporated into the Communications Act of 1934 (*Statutes at Large* 1934, p. 1080 (previously codified at 47 U.S.C. § 221(a)). It was eventually repealed by the Telecommunications Act of 1996 (*Statutes at Large* 1996, p. 143).

51  See, e.g., *Indus. Commc'ns Sys., Inc. v. Pac. Tel. & Tel. Co.*, 505 F.2d 152, 156 (9th Cir. 1974).

52  See, e.g., *Credit Suisse Sec. (USA) LLC v. Billing*, 127 S. Ct. 2383, 2392 (2007).

53  See also *Nat'l Gerimedical Hosp. & Gerontology Ctr. v. Blue Cross of Kan. City*, 452 U.S. 378, 388–89 (1981), calling these general principles "well established."

Satisfying the "plain repugnancy" standard requires that the agency have imposed affirmative obligations on the regulated entity. Mere agency jurisdiction over particular conduct is not enough. Thus in *United States v. Radio Corp. of America (RCA)*, the Supreme Court held that the fact that conduct was subject to FCC regulation under the public interest standard was not enough to exempt it from the antitrust laws (358 U.S. 334, 345–46 (1959)). Similarly, in *Otter Tail*, the Court held that a federal agency's residual authority to compel access as "necessary or appropriate in the public interest" in the electric power industry did not satisfy the requisites for implied exemption from the antitrust laws. On the contrary, in forgoing direct agency regulation of interconnection, Congress had "rejected a pervasive regulatory scheme . . . in favor of voluntary commercial relationships. When these relationships are governed in the first instance by business judgment and not regulatory coercion, courts must be hesitant to conclude that Congress intended to override the fundamental national policies embodied in the antitrust laws" (410 U.S. at 372–75; see also *Gordon*, 422 U.S. at 692–93 (Stewart, J., concurring)).

As a result, a wide range of lower courts have rejected claims that the federal regulatory scheme overseen by the FCC immunizes telephone companies' refusals to allow other companies to interconnect with their networks from antitrust scrutiny.[54] Although 47 U.S.C. § 201(a) authorizes the FCC to mandate interconnection if it finds that doing so is "necessary or desirable in the public interest," *Otter Tail* established that such residual authority to order interconnection is insufficient to confer implied immunity. Even though the FCC has the right to review tariff filings presenting the terms and conditions under which telephone companies will permit others to interconnect with their networks, in practice it can only investigate a small percentage of them.[55] The fact that the vast majority of tariff filings go into effect without FCC review and approval renders antitrust immunity improper, because

---

54  For cases holding that regulations governing the interconnection of local and long-distance services did not impliedly immunize conduct from the antitrust laws, see *Mid-Tex. Commc'ns Sys., Inc. v. AT&T*, 615 F.2d 1372, 1377–81 (5th Cir. 1980); *MCI*, 708 F.2d at 1101–05; *S. Pac. Commc'ns*, 740 F.2d at 999–1000; *United States v. AT&T*, 461 F. Supp. 1314, 1320–30 (D.D.C. 1978). For a similar decision regarding the interconnection of paging systems, see *Indus. Commc'ns*, 505 F.2d at 156. For similar decisions regarding the interconnection of CPE, see *Essential Commc'ns Sys., Inc. v. AT&T*, 610 F.2d 1114, 1116–25 (3d Cir. 1979); *Sound, Inc. v. AT&T*, 631 F.2d 1324, 1327–31 (8th Cir. 1980); *Ne. Tel. Co. v. AT&T*, 651 F.2d 76, 82–84 (2d Cir. 1981); *Phonetele, Inc. v. AT&T*, 664 F.2d 716, 726–35 (9th Cir. 1981), *modified*, Nos. 77–3877 and 77–2936, 1982 WL 11277 (9th Cir. Mar. 15, 1982); *Macom Prods. Corp. v. AT&T*, 359 F. Supp. 973, 976 (C.D. Cal. 1973); *Int'l Tel. & Tel. Corp. v. Gen. Tel. & Elecs. Corp.*, 449 F. Supp. 1158, 1163–69 (D. Haw. 1978); *Jarvis, Inc. v. AT&T*, 481 F. Supp. 120, 123–24 (D.D.C. 1978). The only exceptions are two district court decisions that were later overturned on appeal – see *Phonetele, Inc. v. AT&T*, 435 F. Supp. 207 (C.D. Cal. 1977), *rev'd*, 664 F.2d 716 (9th Cir. 1981); *Dasa Corp. v. Gen. Tel. Co.*, 1977–2 Trade Cas. (CCH) ¶ 61,610 (C.D. Cal. May 10, 1977), *rev'd sub nom. Phonetele, Inc. v. AT&T*, 664 F.2d 716 (9th Cir. 1981) – and a third, thinly reasoned decision that relied entirely on the authority of the two previous decisions – see *Monitor Bus. Machs. v. AT&T*, 1978–1 Trade Cas. (CCH) ¶ 62,030 (C.D. Cal. May 5, 1978) (relying on *Phonetele* and *Dasa*).

55  *United States v. AT&T*, 461 F. Supp. at 1326.

the tariffs are the result of the telephone companies' business judgment rather than regulatory coercion.[56]

*State Action Immunity.* Since its landmark decision in *Parker v. Brown* (317 U.S. 341 (1943)), the Supreme Court has also recognized that state regulatory schemes can confer antitrust immunity in much the same manner as federal regulatory schemes. The Supreme Court has identified two standards that must be satisfied before state action immunity can attach. "First, the challenged restraint must be one clearly articulated and affirmatively expressed as state policy; second, the policy must be actively supervised by the State itself" (*Cal. Retail Liquor Dealers Ass'n v. Midcal Aluminum, Inc.*, 445 U.S. 97, 105 (1980) (internal quotation marks omitted)). The Court noted in a later case:

> The [active supervision] requirement is designed to ensure that the state-action doctrine will shelter only the particular anticompetitive acts of private parties that, in the judgment of the State, actually further state regulatory policies. To accomplish this purpose, the active supervision requirement mandates that the State exercise ultimate control over the challenged anticompetitive conduct. The mere presence of some state involvement or monitoring does not suffice.
> (*Patrick v. Burget*, 486 U.S. 94, 100–01 (1988))

Thus, the Supreme Court has held that for state action immunity to apply, the state must actively review the rate increases in question; mere authority to review those rates is not sufficient.[57] Although some courts have concluded that the state tariffing process is enough to immunize retail access,[58] others have refused to confer state action immunity on the refusals of local telephone companies to open their networks to independent providers of long-distance services and CPE.[59] In addition, the enactment of the Telecommunications Act of 1996 gave the federal government jurisdiction over areas of local telephone service that had previously been the exclusive province of the states, further narrowing the potential scope of state action immunity.[60] Moreover, as noted earlier, the emergence of competition in last-mile distribution has led state public utility commissions to begin deregulating

---

56 *Essential Commc'ns*, 610 F.2d at 1124; *Sound*, 631 F.2d at 1330–31; *Phonetele*, 664 F.2d at 733–34; *MCI*, 708 F.2d at 1103–05; *United States v. AT&T*, 461 F. Supp. at 1326–28; *Jarvis*, 481 F. Supp. at 123–24.

57 *FTC v. Ticor Title Ins. Co.*, 504 U.S. 621, 638 (1992).

58 *DFW Metro Line Servs. v. Sw. Bell Tel. Co.*, 901 F.2d 1267, 1269 n. 6 (5th Cir. 1990); *Sonitrol of Fresno, Inc. v. AT&T*, 629 F. Supp. 1089, 1094–1101 (D.D.C. 1986); *Metro Mobile CTS, Inc. v. NewVector Commc'ns, Inc.*, 661 F. Supp. 1504, 1508–21 (D. Ariz. 1987), *aff'd on other grounds*, 892 F.2d 62 (9th Cir. 1989); *Davis v. S. Bell Tel. & Tel. Co.*, 755 F. Supp. 1532, 1539–42 (S.D. Fla. 1991).

59 For long distance services, see *Mid-Tex. Commc'ns*, 615 F.2d at 1381–82; *Modification of Final Judgment*, 552 F. Supp. at 156–59. For CPE, see *Essential Commc'ns*, 610 F.2d at 1125; *Sound*, 631 F.2d at 1331–35; *Phonetele*, 664 F.2d at 735–7; *Jarvis*, 481 F. Supp. at 124.

60 *Iowa Utils. Bd.*, 525 U.S. at 37 n. 6.

retail services. As this process proceeds to its logical conclusion, the basis for state action immunity will eventually disappear.

### b. Doctrines Affecting the Timing of Antitrust Scrutiny

The foregoing discussion reveals that the existing state and federal regulatory schemes are unlikely to insulate telecommunications companies from claims seeking access to their networks under the antitrust laws. Although the presence of regulatory schemes may not provide antitrust immunity, it may nonetheless forestall judicial consideration of the merits of claims until after the relevant agency has had the opportunity to address the issues in the first instance.

*Abstention.* When the regulatory regime at issue arises under state law, the timing of judicial consideration is determined by one of two abstention doctrines. The first, known as administrative or *Burford* abstention,[61] applies when "the exercise of jurisdiction by the federal court would disrupt a state administrative process" (*County of Allegheny v. Frank Mashuda Co.*, 360 U.S. 185, 189 (1959)).[62] The Supreme Court recently described *Burford* abstention as follows:

> Where timely and adequate state-court review is available, a federal court sitting in equity must decline to interfere with the proceedings or orders of state administrative agencies: (1) when there are difficult questions of state law bearing on policy problems of substantial public import whose importance transcends the result in the case then at bar; or (2) where the exercise of federal review of the question in a case and in similar cases would be disruptive of state efforts to establish a coherent policy with respect to a matter of substantial public concern.
>
> (*New Orleans Pub. Serv., Inc. v. Council of New Orleans* (*NOPSI*), 491 U.S.
> 350, 361 (1989) (internal quotation marks omitted))

Lower courts have generally declined to apply *Burford* abstention to challenges to denial of access to telecommunications networks either because the state law at issue was relatively clear[63] or because the issue was purely a question of federal law.[64] As a result, there was little risk of disrupting the policies reflected in the state administrative processes.

The second, known as *Younger* abstention, is based on the premise that the federal government should not interfere with those governmental functions that are more properly regarded as falling within the province of the states under the system

---

61  *Burford v. Sun Oil Co.*, 319 U.S. 315, 317–18 (1943) (establishing doctrine); Bator et al. (1988, p. 1364), calling the form of abstention initiated by *Burford* "administrative abstention" (internal quotation marks omitted).

62  See also *Lumbermen's Mut. Cas. Co. v. Elbert*, 348 U.S. 48, 53 (1954); *Zwickler v. Koota*, 389 U.S. 241, 249 n. 11 (1967).

63  *GTE N., Inc. v. Strand*, 209 F.3d 909, 920–21 (6th Cir. 2000).

64  *Bell Atl.-Pa., Inc. v. Pa. Pub. Util. Comm'n*, 107 F. Supp. 2d 653, 665–66 (E.D. Pa. 2000).

of federalism established by the Constitution. The paradigmatic state function into which the federal government should not intrude, illustrated by the *Younger* case itself, is the prosecution of state crimes.[65] Subsequent decisions have extended *Younger* to state administrative proceedings implicating important state interests, including attorney malpractice,[66] claims of sex discrimination,[67] and misconduct by state police and prosecutors.[68] The Supreme Court has noted that *Younger* has only been applied to administrative proceedings that were essentially backward-looking. Forward-looking proceedings, such as ratemaking, are more closely allied with the legislative than the judicial process and thus are poor candidates for *Younger* abstention.[69] As a result, lower courts have generally declined to subject challenges to denial of access to telecommunications networks to *Younger* abstention.[70]

*Primary Jurisdiction.* When the regulatory regime at issue is a federal one, the timing of judicial consideration is determined by a doctrine known as "primary jurisdiction," which requires courts to permit agencies responsible for administering federal regulatory schemes the opportunity to be the first to address issues within their competence. As a result, the doctrine of primary jurisdiction requires the federal courts to stay its proceedings or dismiss a claim without prejudice until the relevant agency has had a chance to address the issue.[71]

The Supreme Court examined the foundations of primary jurisdiction in *RCA*, which addressed whether the existence of FCC regulation prevented federal courts from considering an antitrust claim:

> [W]hen rates and practices relating thereto were challenged under the antitrust laws, the agencies had primary jurisdiction to consider the reasonableness of such rates and practices in the light of the many relevant factors including alleged antitrust violations, for otherwise sporadic action by federal courts would disrupt an agency's delicate regulatory scheme, and would throw existing rate structures out of balance.
>
> (358 U.S. at 348)

Primary jurisdiction is the only doctrine ever to serve as a meaningful limit on antitrust courts' jurisdiction over claims seeking access to telecommunications networks. A number of early courts relied on primary jurisdiction to require that antitrust courts defer their consideration of requests for access until after they

---

65  *Younger v. Harris*, 401 U.S. 37, 44, 46 (1971).

66  *Middlesex County Ethics Comm. v. Garden State Bar Ass'n*, 457 U.S. 423, 431–37 (1982).

67  *Ohio Civil Rights Comm'n v. Dayton Christian Sch., Inc.*, 477 U.S. 619, 627–28 (1986).

68  *Rizzo v. Goode*, 423 U.S. 362, 378–80 (1976).

69  *NOPSI*, 491 U.S. at 370–71.

70  *GTE N., Inc. v. Strand*, 209 F.3d at 921; *Bell Atl.–Pa.*, 107 F. Supp. 2d at 666.

71  See, e.g., *United States v. W. Pac. R.R.*, 352 U.S. 59, 65–69 (1956); *Pan Am. World Airways, Inc. v. United States*, 371 U.S. 296, 309–12 (1963); *Ricci v. Chi. Mercantile Exch.*, 409 U.S. 289, 302–06 (1973).

had been addressed by the FCC.[72] Later decisions have accorded antitrust courts a greater scope of authority. For example, the district court hearing the case that would lead to the breakup of AT&T took a narrower view of primary jurisdiction, permitting the antitrust case to go forward while reserving the right to refer issues to the FCC at a later point in the litigation.[73] This position had the effect of bringing the doctrine of primary jurisdiction more into line with the other doctrines discussed above.

### c. The Rationales Underlying the Balance between Antitrust and Regulation

Over the years, the Supreme Court has offered several justifications for its doctrines allocating decisionmaking authority between antitrust courts and administrative agencies. First and foremost is the need to avoid conflict between the mandates of the antitrust courts and those of the relevant regulatory regime. With respect to immunity implied from other federal statutes, the Court has held that the law must ensure that "the federal agency entrusted with regulation in the public interest could carry out that responsibility free from the disruption of conflicting judgments that might be voiced by courts exercising jurisdiction under the antitrust laws" (*United States v. Nat'l Ass'n of Sec. Dealers (NASD)*, 422 U.S. 694, 734 (1975)). It has invoked similar rationales in the context of state action immunity,[74] *Burford* abstention,[75] and primary jurisdiction.[76]

In the context of state action immunity, the Supreme Court also has invoked federalism as an additional consideration. As the Court noted in *Parker*, "In a dual system of government in which, under the Constitution, the states are sovereign, save only as Congress may constitutionally subtract from their authority, an unexpressed purpose to nullify a state's control over its officers and agents is not lightly to be attributed to Congress" (317 U.S. at 351). The Court based *Younger* abstention on notions of "comity" and "Our Federalism," which it described as "a proper respect for state functions, a recognition . . . that the entire country is made up of a Union of separate [States], and a continuance of the belief that the National Government will fare best if the States . . . are left free to perform their separate functions in their separate ways" (401 U.S. at 44). The inclusion of federalism as a justification with respect to these two doctrines, though, did not make them any broader than when

---

72  For an invocation of primary jurisdiction in an antitrust suit challenging AT&T's refusal to allow independent long distance companies to connect with its network, see *MCI Commc'ns Corp. v. AT&T*, 496 F.2d 214, 219–24 (3d Cir. 1974). For invocations of primary jurisdiction in the context of CPE, see *Carter v. AT&T*, 250 F. Supp. 188, 190–92 (N.D. Tex. 1966), aff'd, 365 F.2d 486 (5th Cir. 1966); cases collected in Huber et al. (1999, pp. 664–65); see also *Carter*, 365 F.2d at 498 n. 23 (citing four unreported district court cases in which courts invoked doctrine of primary jurisdiction when confronted with antitrust challenges to foreign attachments tariffs).

73  *United States v. AT&T*, 427 F. Supp. 57, 61–62 (D.D.C. 1976); *United States v. AT&T*, 461 F. Supp. at 1329, 1336, 1349–50.

74  *Cantor v. Detroit Edison Co.*, 428 U.S. 579, 592 (1976).

75  *Burford*, 319 U.S. at 327.

76  *RCA*, 358 U.S. at 346, 347–48.

federalism was not implicated. As the Court noted in *Cantor*, "Congress could hardly have intended state regulatory agencies to have broader power than federal agencies to exempt private conduct from the antitrust laws. Therefore, . . . the standards for ascertaining the existence and scope of [this] exemption surely must be at least as severe as those applied to federal regulatory legislation" (428 U.S. at 596–97).

Interestingly, the Supreme Court's decisions on primary jurisdiction and *Burford* abstention added a third consideration: the differences in institutional competence between antitrust courts and regulatory agencies. For example, the Court's opinion in *RCA* underscored that, in addition to the need to avoid conflicting mandates, primary jurisdiction was also based in part on "the need for administrative skill commonly to be found only in a body of experts in handling the intricate facts" needed to regulate an industry (358 U.S. at 346 (internal quotation marks omitted)).[77] *Burford* similarly relied on the need to allow state agencies and the state courts reviewing those agencies' decisions "to acquire a specialized knowledge which is useful in shaping the policy of regulation of the ever-changing demands in this field" (319 U.S. at 327). Concerns about institutional capabilities also appeared in lower court decisions applying primary jurisdiction to the telecommunications industry, which based the doctrine in part on "the court's lack of expertise with the subject matter of the agency's regulation" (*MCI*, 496 F.2d at 220).

### d. Implications for the Essential Facilities Doctrine

Considerations of institutional competence have particular resonance for the essential facilities doctrine. Commentators have recognized that the doctrine necessarily presupposes some form of price regulation. In the absence of price regulation, the owner of the bottleneck facility would simply provide access at the monopoly price. While such access would be beneficial to the monopolist's competitors, simply requiring that the monopoly be shared would provide no benefits to consumers, because the monopoly would be left intact without any improvements in price or output.[78]

Setting prices is not a function to which antitrust courts are institutionally well suited. If courts were to adopt a role in setting prices, they would be forced to address the problems of valuing assets, distinguishing between prudent and imprudent investments, separating capital from operating expenses, allocating shared costs across multiple products, and determining the appropriate rate of return that have long plagued the administrative ratemaking process. This difficulty explains why the Supreme Court noted in *United States v. Trenton Potteries Co.* that "[t]he reasonable price fixed today may through economic and business changes become the unreasonable price of tomorrow" and warned against "placing on the government

---

77  *United States Nav. Co. v. Cunard S.S. Co.*, 284 U.S. 474 (1932); *Far E. Conference v. United States*, 342 U.S. 570 (1952); *Fed. Mar. Bd. v. Isbrandtsen Co.*, 356 U.S. 481, 497–99 (1958).

78  Posner (1976); Areeda and Hovenkamp (2008c); Hovenkamp (2005); Sullivan and Grimes (2006).

in enforcing the Sherman Law the burden of ascertaining from day to day whether it has become unreasonable through the mere variation of economic conditions." The Court continued:

> [I]n the absence of express legislation requiring it, we should hesitate to adopt a construction making the difference between legal and illegal conduct in the field of business relations depend upon so uncertain a test as whether prices are reasonable – a determination which can be satisfactorily made only after a complete survey of our economic organization and a choice between rival philosophies.
>
> (273 U.S. 392, 397–98 (1927))

Subsequent decisions by both the Supreme Court and lower courts have reiterated the difficulties that antitrust courts face in determining what constitutes a reasonable price.[79]

Commentators have invoked the difficulties that antitrust courts face in implementing access mandates when criticizing the essential facilities doctrine. As Philip Areeda notes in his now-classic critique of the essential facilities doctrine (1990, p. 853), "No court should impose a duty to deal that it cannot explain or adequately and reasonably supervise. The problem should be deemed irremediable by antitrust law when compulsory access requires the court to assume the day-to-day controls characteristic of a regulatory agency."[80]

Areeda elaborated on this critique in his treatise. As the current version (now coauthored with Herbert Hovenkamp) notes, if access is compelled without any restrictions being placed on the price charged, the essential facilities doctrine will provide no benefits to consumers through decreases in price and increases in output, as the monopolist will simply charge the full monopoly price. Antitrust courts will likely find, however, that their attempts at regulating prices are extremely difficult to administer. Because the monopolist has already evinced a lack of willingness to deal with its competitor, it is likely that disputes over the terms and conditions of the compelled access will surround the relationship:

> The plaintiff is likely to claim that the defendant's price for access to an essential facility is (1) so high as to be the equivalent of a continued refusal to deal, or (2) is unreasonable, or (3) creates a "price squeeze" in that the defendant charges

---

79  *Cline v. Frink Dairy Co.*, 274 U.S. 445, 462–63 (1927); *United States v. Socony–Vacuum Oil Co.*, 310 U.S. 150, 212–14 (1940); *United States v. Masonite Corp.*, 316 U.S. 265, 281–82 (1942); *Catalano, Inc. v. Target Sales, Inc.*, 446 U.S. 643, 647 (1980); *Town of Concord v. Boston Edison Co.*, 915 F.2d 17, 25 (1st Cir. 1990); *Chi. Prof'l Sports Ltd. P'ship v. NBA*, 95 F.3d 593, 597 (7th Cir. 1996); *cf. Trans-Mo. Freight Ass'n*, 166 U.S. at 331–42 (pre-*Trenton Potteries* decision citing difficulties in determining reasonableness of rates as justification for "leav[ing] the question of reasonableness to the companies themselves"); cases cited and reviewed in Areeda and Hovenkamp (2008b, pp. 4–7).

80  Areeda acknowledges that compelling access is more justifiable where the monopolist is a consortium that can admit additional members or where a regulatory agency already exists to control the terms of dealing.

so much for access and so little for the product it sells in competition with the plaintiff that the latter cannot earn a reasonable profit.

The disputes, moreover, will not be limited just to price. The parties are likely to disagree on nonprice terms and conditions as well. Should the demand outstrip the existing capacity, compelled access would force network owners not merely to sell out of excess capacity, but to reduce their own output or expand their plants in order to service rivals. As a result, mandating access requires "price regulation of the kind undertaken by regulatory agencies – something for which both the federal courts and the antitrust litigation process are extremely ill-suited and which is, in any event, inconsistent with antitrust's fundamental 'market' orientation to problems of lack of competition" (Areeda and Hovenkamp 2008c, pp. 195, 275–80, 338). Other commentators have drawn similar conclusions.[81]

These criticisms of antitrust courts' institutional competence to oversee access mandates are part of a broader debate about the relative merits of structural and conduct remedies.[82] Richard Posner's statistical study of antitrust enforcement (1970) distinguished between "once-for-all" decrees that render a market structurally competitive and thereafter do not require continuing judicial oversight, and "regulatory" decrees, which require antitrust courts to maintain continuing supervisory relationships. Posner questioned the institutional competence of courts to superintend regulatory decrees. In addition to requiring scrutiny over price, regulatory decrees require antitrust courts to allocate market share and restrict the lines of business that the entities subject to the decree may enter, actions that require an extraordinary level of intervention into the market and can limit competition. Most importantly, Posner questioned the expedience of creating ad hoc regulatory regimes administered by scattered district courts. Indeed, he found that "the entry of such a decree is tantamount to a confession that the antitrust action has not succeeded in restoring competitive conditions." Posner later elaborated in the casebook he coauthored with Frank Easterbrook:

> There is a sense in which the entry of a regulatory decree signifies that the case should never have been brought. The decree is an acknowledgement that competition will not work in the particular circumstances of the case.... The question is thus posed whether antitrust enforcement, the cardinal purpose of which is to prevent and destroy monopolies, is also a suitable tool for domesticating those monopolies that are ineradicable at acceptable cost.
>
> (Posner and Easterbrook 1981, pp. 762–63)

81 Werden (1987); Hylton (1991). But see Ratner (1988), recognizing that antitrust courts are not well suited to regulate price, but arguing that intervention is the only meaningful remedy available to increase output toward competitive levels.

82 Compare O'Connor (1976), advocating structural over conduct remedies, with Crandall (2001), arguing that structural remedies provide insufficient benefit to consumers, and Piraino (2000), criticizing judicial use of structural remedies as failing to consider underlying market conditions and requiring expertise lacking in courts. This debate has gained new salience with the proposal of structural relief in the Microsoft case.

The remedial difficulties associated with the essential facilities doctrine have led courts granting relief under the doctrine to be rather vague regarding the terms and conditions of access.[83] The degree of ongoing supervision required by a regulatory decree is aptly demonstrated by *Terminal Railroad,* in which the Supreme Court was constantly called upon to adjudicate the application of the decree.[84] Although such problems might be minimized if the monopolist already sold the product to other customers, because an antitrust court could simply order that it provide access on a nondiscriminatory basis,[85] evaluating claims of discrimination is notoriously difficult. In any event, this solution is completely unavailing if the bottleneck owner does not sell its input externally and instead devotes all available capacity to its own output.

It is easy to make the case that complex subjects such as telecommunications should be the province of administrative agencies and not courts. Agencies enjoy advantages that go beyond technical expertise. Unlike courts, agencies can set their own agendas, and they are less dependent on the parties for the development of the factual record and legal arguments than are courts. Administrative processes also provide greater opportunities for public participation than do judicial processes, in which interested third parties are generally limited to filing amicus briefs. Agencies are also in a better position to take all aspects of a regulatory scheme into account than are courts, which by their nature will limit their consideration to the dispute at hand. Permitting courts to entertain antitrust suits might simply invite disappointed parties who failed to obtain relief from the agency to try to take a second bite of the apple.

These considerations suggest that regulatory agencies are in a better position to supervise access mandates than are antitrust courts. As we shall see, these concerns would find voice in the Supreme Court's decision in *Trinko.*

## C. The Impact of *Trinko*

The Supreme Court's *Trinko* decision arose out of a dispute over the speed with which Verizon and its predecessors[86] were meeting the obligation that the Telecommunications Act of 1996 imposed on existing local telephone companies, called incumbent LECs, to provide access to all of their network elements on an unbundled

---

83  Werden (1987); Areeda and Hovenkamp (2008c).

84  *Ex parte United States,* 226 U.S. 420, 421 (1913); *Terminal R.R. Ass'n v. United States,* 236 U.S. 194, 195–96 (1915); *Terminal R.R. Ass'n v. United States,* 266 U.S. 17, 27 (1924); see also Lipsky and Sidak (1999), discussing continuing judicial involvement and repeated interpretation of the original decree.

85  Areeda and Hovenkamp (2008c).

86  Over the course of the litigation, the company originally named NYNEX first merged with Bell Atlantic and then merged with GTE to form a new corporation called Verizon. We will follow the Supreme Court's convention by referring to all of these entities as Verizon (540 U.S. at 402 n. 1).

basis. The specific source of concern was the computer system that Verizon used to process requests for service, known as its OSS. Verizon's competitors complained that Verizon was not fulfilling the orders that they placed through the OSS in a timely manner. Parallel investigations by both federal and state regulatory authorities led both agencies to adopt orders providing some relief. A customer of one of Verizon's competitors filed an antitrust suit arguing that the same conduct violated Section 2.

The Supreme Court rejected the customer's claims in an opinion that accepted many of the criticisms of the essential facilities doctrine discussed above. In so doing, the opinion touched off a lively debate about the proper scope of Section 2 liability and in particular about the future of the essential facilities doctrine.

### 1. The Economics of Vertical Exclusion

The Supreme Court's discussion of the substantive antitrust claim began by noting that the antitrust laws do not penalize the mere possession of monopoly power absent proof of exclusionary conduct. Indeed:

> The mere possession of monopoly power, and the concomitant charging of monopoly prices, is not only not unlawful; it is an important element of the free-market system. The opportunity to charge monopoly prices – at least for a short period – is what attracts "business acumen" in the first place; it induces risk taking that produces innovation and economic growth.

Because investments in telecommunications networks represent a legitimate form of competition on the merits, antitrust principles must be structured so that they do not deter such procompetitive conduct. As the Court noted later in the opinion, expansions of Section 2 liability that penalize procompetitive conduct can be particularly harmful "because they chill the very conduct the antitrust laws are designed to protect" (540 U.S. at 407–08, 414 (internal quotation marks omitted)).

The Court's concern was that requiring a monopolist to share its bottleneck facility could impede dynamic efficiency. The Court noted, "Compelling such firms to share the source of their advantage . . . may lessen the incentive for the monopolist, the rival, or both to invest in those economically beneficial facilities." Later portions of the opinion emphasized "the uncertain virtue of forced sharing" and how mandating access under Section 2 "seem[ed] destined to distort investment." It is for this reason that "as a general matter, the Sherman Act 'does not restrict the long recognized right of [a] trader or manufacturer engaged in an entirely private business, freely to exercise his own independent discretion as to parties with whom he will deal'" (540 U.S. at 407–08, 414, quoting *Colgate*, 250 U.S. at 307).

At the same time, the Court recognized that "[t]he high value that we have placed on the right to refuse to deal with other firms does not mean that the right is unqualified," although the Court "ha[s] been very cautious in recognizing such exceptions." The Court noted that the leading case supporting antitrust liability for a refusal to cooperate with a rival is the *Aspen Skiing* decision summarized above, which the Court described as "at or near the outer boundary of § 2 liability." According to the Court, the fact that Ski Co. was willing to terminate unilaterally "a voluntary (*and thus presumably profitable*) course of dealing suggested a willingness to forsake short-term profits to achieve an anticompetitive end," as did the fact that Ski Co. was unwilling to renew the all-Aspen ticket even if compensated at full retail price. Verizon, in contrast, had never dealt with its rivals voluntarily, but instead did so only under regulatory compulsion at regulated, wholesale prices. In the absence of a preexisting relationship, Verizon's actions did not reveal any "anticompetitive bent." The Court also distinguished *Otter Tail* as a case in which the network owner "was already in the business of providing a service to certain customers . . . and refused to provide the same service to certain other customers." This fact rendered *Otter Tail* inapposite, as Verizon had never publicly marketed wholesale access to the OSS at issue in *Trinko* in the absence of regulation (540 U.S. at 408, 409–10 (internal quotation marks omitted)).

These distinctions represent sharp limitations on the scope of liability for a network's unilateral refusal to deal. They clearly suggest that liability will not lie in the absence of a preexisting joint venture or a demonstrated willingness to offer the service to others at a full retail price, because *Trinko* regarded the willingness to sacrifice profits as a key indicator that the conduct in *Aspen Skiing* was anticompetitive. Some commentators have argued that the presence of a preexisting course of dealing reveals little, if anything, about a practice's likely competitive impact[87] and that attaching significance to the abandonment of an initial willingness to deal ignores the fact that circumstances change[88] and risks discouraging firms from dealing in the first place.[89] Others have suggested that a preexisting willingness to deal provides at least some evidence that the joint venture was efficient.[90]

There is also language in the opinion that appears to recognize the structural preconditions that are necessary for vertical exclusion to be plausible. For example, as noted earlier, the Court recognized that "the indispensable requirement for invoking the doctrine is the unavailability of access to the 'essential facilities'" and the doctrine "serves no purpose" when the input in question is available through other means. In so holding, it implicitly recognized that proof of a monopoly over an input is a necessary condition for stating a vertical exclusion claim. The emphasis on monopoly power is further reinforced by the Court's concern that forced cooperation with rivals also risks becoming a focal point for collusion. In addition, the opinion accepted the reading of *Spectrum Sports* discussed above when it underscored that any claim that a monopolist is attempting to use the leverage provided by its monopoly to attack a second market must show "a 'dangerous probability of success' in monopolizing [the] second market" (540 U.S. at 408, 411,

---

87   Campbell and Sandman (2004); Lopatka and Page (2005).
88   *MetroNet Servs. Corp. v. Qwest Corp.*, 383 F.3d 1124, 1132 (9th Cir. 2004).
89   Fox (2005).
90   Areeda and Hovenkamp (2008c).

415 n. 4, quoting *Spectrum Sports*, 506 U.S. at 459). This language has been widely interpreted as requiring proof of market concentration and entry barriers in the secondary market before a monopolization claim will lie.[91]

Read together, this language represents a sweeping acknowledgement of how compelling access to bottleneck facilities may impair economic efficiency. When alternative sources of supply exist, simply allocating the resource that exists is not the best solution. The better course is to allow any supracompetitive returns to serve as the signal and the incentive for others to develop independent sources, which in turn will provide sustainable benefits to consumers without the continuing oversight of the terms and conditions of sharing by antitrust courts.

## 2. The Allocation of Authority between Antitrust Courts and Regulatory Agencies

*Trinko* directed its strongest language toward the proper division of authority between antitrust courts and regulatory agencies. As an initial matter, the Court concluded that the Telecommunications Act of 1996 did not constitute an implied repeal of the antitrust laws. The Court noted that the extensive access requirements imposed by the Telecommunications Act of 1996 were sufficiently detailed to be "a good candidate for implication of antitrust immunity, to avoid the real possibility of judgments conflicting with the agency's regulatory scheme that might be voiced by courts exercising jurisdiction under the antitrust laws" (540 U.S. at 406 (internal quotation marks omitted)). However, any such conclusion was vitiated by the fact the Act contained an antitrust savings clause specifically providing that "nothing in this Act . . . or the amendments made by this Act shall be construed to modify, impair, or supersede the applicability of any of the antitrust laws" (47 U.S.C. § 152 note). Although some lower courts had initially held that the 1996 Act represented more specific legislation that took precedence over the antitrust laws,[92] the Supreme Court held that the antitrust savings clause definitively foreclosed any suggestion that the 1996 Act could serve as the basis for implied antitrust immunity (540 U.S. at 406).

The balance of the opinion, however, adopted a quite narrow view of antitrust courts' institutional competence. The Court noted, "Enforced sharing . . . requires antitrust courts to act as central planners, identifying the proper price, quantity, and other terms of dealing – a role for which they are ill suited." Moreover, the existence of a regulatory framework capable of remedying the relevant harm dictated that subjecting the conduct in question to antitrust scrutiny would yield only slight benefits. In particular, disputes over access to telecommunications networks "are difficult for antitrust courts to evaluate, not only because they are highly technical, but also because they are likely to be extremely numerous, given the incessant,

---

91    Kauper (2005); Areeda and Hovenkamp (2006, ¶ 652 pp. 286, ¶773(g) p. 372).
92    *Goldwasser v. Ameritech Corp.*, 222 F.3d 390, 401 (7th Cir. 2000).

complex, and constantly changing interaction of competitive and incumbent LECs implementing the sharing and interconnection obligations." Policing this "death by a thousand cuts . . . would surely be a daunting task for a generalist antitrust court." Also, "[j]udicial oversight under the Sherman Act would seem destined to distort investment and lead to a new layer of interminable litigation, atop the variety of litigation routes already available to and actively pursued by competitive LECs." Furthermore, "[m]istaken inferences and the resulting false condemnations are especially costly, because they chill the very conduct the antitrust laws are designed to protect" (540 U.S. at 408, 412–13, 414 (internal quotation marks omitted)).

Because "[e]ffective remediation of violations of regulatory sharing requirements will ordinarily require continuing supervision of a highly detailed decree," supervising access requirements "may be . . . beyond the practical ability of a judicial tribunal to control." Indeed, the Court cited with approval Areeda's conclusion (1990) that "[n]o court should impose a duty to deal that it cannot explain or adequately and reasonably supervise" and that "[t]he problem should be deemed irremedia[ble] by antitrust law when compulsory access requires the court to assume the day-to-day controls characteristic of a regulatory agency." In short, "[a]n antitrust court is unlikely to be an effective day-to-day enforcer of these detailed sharing obligations" (540 U.S. at 414–15 (internal quotation marks omitted)).

### 3. *Trinko*'s Implications

Although *Trinko* did not explicitly repudiate the essential facilities doctrine, commentators generally acknowledge that its reasoning certainly cast serious doubts on the doctrine's continuing vitality.[93] *Trinko* also substantially narrowed the potential for antitrust law to serve as a source of access mandates. What is less clear is just how much narrower the scope of antitrust law will be.

On the one hand, the Court's acceptance of Areeda's admonitions that "'[n]o court should impose a duty to deal that it cannot explain or adequately and reasonably supervise'" and that "'[t]he problem should be deemed irremedia[ble] by antitrust law when compulsory access requires the court to assume the day-to-day controls characteristic of a regulatory agency'" (540 U.S. at 415, quoting Areeda 1990, at 853) represents a rejection of courts' capacity to oversee access mandates. Indeed, *Trinko*'s challenge to the courts' institutional competence goes

---

93  See, e.g., Bauer (2006, p. 1228) notes that *Trinko* called essential facilities doctrine "into serious question." Fox (2005, p. 154) claims that *Trinko* "nearly obliterated" essential facilities doctrine. Geradin and O'Donoghue (2005, p. 396 n. 104) argue that *Trinko* "cast[s] serious doubt on future reliance on the 'essential facilities' doctrine." Jacobs (2006, p. 1183) notes that *Trinko* "cast[s] very serious doubt on the vitality of [the essential facilities] doctrine." Keyte (2005, p. 44) notes that *Trinko* "clearly signaled that the demise of the essential facilities doctrine . . . may be on the horizon." Noll (2005, p. 613 n. 47) notes that *Trinko* "all but abandoned the essential facilities doctrine." Shelanski (2007, p. 101) notes "the absence . . . of a meaningful essential-facilities doctrine in U.S. antitrust law" after *Trinko*.

far beyond the critiques appearing in the earlier doctrines designed to allocate authority between courts and agencies. More than suggesting that courts should take advantage of agencies' superior expertise and factfinding capability by postponing judicial consideration until after the agency had considered the matter, the language of the *Trinko* opinion, read for all it is worth, arguably takes mandating access to essential facilities outside the scope of Section 2 altogether (Hay 2005).

Alternatively, other scholars have advanced narrower readings of *Trinko*. Building on the requirement that state regulatory authorities must be actively supervising the conduct in question before courts will defer to their jurisdiction, these scholars suggest that determining the proper allocation of authority between antitrust courts and regulatory agencies requires a closer assessment of the details of the regulatory regime. The stronger form of this argument, advanced by Philip Weiser (2005, p. 562), would require courts to evaluate whether the regulatory regime is "reasonably effective at addressing the relevant anticompetitive conduct" before yielding the field to an agency. Weiser's proposal is reminiscent of earlier proposals that would assess whether particular regulatory regimes furthered particular economic goals[94] or were the result of failures in the political process before conferring antitrust immunity.[95] Even taken on their own terms, these proposals will require courts to determine whether a particular regulatory scheme is socially beneficial, an assessment that will vary depending on the assumptions employed. Even if measured in purely economic terms, determining the effectiveness of a regulatory program is likely to be extremely controversial, and courts are understandably chary of making antitrust liability turn on their assessment of another government entity's performance. Assessing the effectiveness of political process is further complicated by the lack of any consensus normative conception of a properly functioning regulatory system that can serve as a benchmark for evaluation, as well as the fact that regulation is often motivated by multiple concerns that are often openly redistributive and noneconomic in character (Hovenkamp 2005).

A more modest version of this proposal can be constructed from language in the Supreme Court's opinion in *FTC v. Ticor Title Insurance Co.*, which took the position that the active supervision requirement did not require courts "to determine whether the State has met some normative standard, such as efficiency, in its regulatory practices." Instead, in determining whether an agency was actively supervising particular conduct, courts should simply ask whether the regulation in question represents the "independent judgment and control" of the state, and "not simply . . . agreement among private parties." Framed in this manner, "[t]he question is not how well state regulation works but whether the anticompetitive scheme is the State's own" (504 U.S. at 634–35). Under this standard, as developed by Herbert Hovenkamp, it is not necessary that the conduct in question "have been reviewed and approved by the agency"; it is sufficient if the conduct is "under

94  Cirace (1982); Spitzer (1988).
95  Wiley (1986a); Elhauge (1991); Inman and Rubinfeld (1997); Squire (2006).

ongoing study" or if the agency has "manifested its ability and will to evaluate the conduct if asked" (Hovenkamp 2004, p. 352).

Finally, although many observers have assumed that *Trinko* effectively eliminated Section 2 liability in regulated industries such as telecommunications,[96] some lower courts have read *Trinko* narrowly, concluding that it barred essential facilities claims, but did not invalidate other types of monopolization claims.[97] Although these courts did not analyze the issue in these terms, a close examination of the regulatory regime erected by the Telecommunications Act of 1996 reveals the complexity of these issues. The Act envisions that interconnection will occur primarily through voluntary agreements negotiated by the parties. Only if those negotiations fail is the interconnection dispute submitted to binding arbitration before the state public utility commission (47 U.S.C. §§ 252(a)(1), 252(b)(1)). The fact that the terms of interconnection are more a reflection of business judgment than of regulatory coercion counsels against allowing immunizing this conduct from antitrust scrutiny.

### 4. The Impact of *Trinko*'s Varying Interpretations

*Trinko*'s ultimate impact will be determined by how broadly later courts read the decision. The broadest reading of *Trinko* would hold that antitrust courts' institutional unsuitability to supervising access requirements would bar such claims. A narrower reading that makes judicial authority to entertain antitrust claims turn on the effectiveness of the agency's efforts to address the anticompetitive conduct would require courts to evaluate the success and failure of the regulatory efforts, finding it sufficient that an agency is monitoring the conduct in question and has exhibited some willingness to step to curb any anticompetitive conduct that may occur. An intermediate reading would undertake a more specific assessment of the impact of the steps the agency has taken.

It is too soon to say with any certainty which of these positions will eventually emerge as the enduring reading of *Trinko*, with the early lower court decisions evincing some desire to strike a middle ground. The importance of how broadly to read *Trinko* is underscored when one considers how it would apply to one of the most hotly debated issues of the last Congress: network neutrality. As discussed in Chapter 10 in some detail, the FCC possesses general authority to regulate broadband networks, is currently monitoring market developments, and has stated that it stands ready to intervene should anticompetitive conduct emerge. It is not yet clear whether that level of agency activity will prove sufficient to forestall antitrust

---

96   Salop (2006); *Covad Commc'ns Co. v. Bell Atl. Corp.*, 398 F.3d 666, 671–75 (D.C. Cir. 2005).

97   *Covad Commc'ns Co. v. BellSouth Corp.*, 374 F.3d 1044, 1049–50 (11th Cir. 2004); *Linkline Commc'ns, Inc. v. SBC Cal., Inc.*, 503 F.3d 876, 881–5 (9th Cir. 2007), *cert. granted*, 128 S. Ct. 1137 (2008); *Z-Tel Commc'ns, Inc. v. SBC Commc'ns, Inc.*, 331 F. Supp. 2d 513, 535–43 (E.D. Tex. 2004).

claims seeking access to last-mile broadband networks. Until that issue is resolved, courts may well be willing to entertain claims that a telecommunications company's refusal to provide other firms with access to its networks violates the antitrust laws.

### D. The Different Types of Access under Antitrust Law

The real possibility that antitrust law will continue to serve as a basis for compelling access to telecommunications networks counsels in favor of plumbing the *Trinko* opinion for additional indications about precisely how antitrust law might apply. The existing commentary has largely overlooked the fact that the *Trinko* opinion contains some tantalizing hints about certain considerations that may play a key role in the analysis. For example, the language in the opinion contrasting access provided to consumers with access provided to rivals suggests that the application of the antitrust law might depend on the nature of the party to whom access is granted. The opinion also drew a distinction between access to services that are already sold into the open market and access to network elements that are only available to the public because of regulation. In addition, *Trinko* indicated that unbundled access can only be provided "at considerable expense and effort," because network elements "exist only deep within the bowels of Verizon" and because "[n]ew systems must be designed and implemented" to make access to those network elements possible. Later in the opinion, the Court mentioned that unbundled access requirements "are difficult for antitrust courts to evaluate, not only because they are highly technical, but also because they are likely to be extremely numerous, given the incessant, complex, and constantly changing interaction of competitive and incumbent LECs implementing the sharing and interconnection obligations" (540 U.S. at 414). This language suggests that the application of the antitrust laws may depend on certain key aspects of the type of access sought, such as whether access is to only a portion of the network or to its entirety and whether the network owner already offers the services sought to other customers.

The problem is that the *Trinko* opinion did not analyze these considerations in a systematic manner. Equally importantly, it failed to take into account that networks are complex systems whose elements interact in ways that can be sharply discontinuous and hard to predict. The absence of an analytical framework that captures the interaction among network elements makes it impossible to assess how altering the costs of particular elements and introducing additional flows into a network can affect network design, capacity, and reliability. It also prevents any realistic assessment of the impact that different types of access can have on transaction costs. The conceptual framework that developed in Chapter 5 offers a basis for analyzing the impact of various types of access in a way that reflects networks' key attributes, that is, the manner in which the whole exceeds the sum of the parts.

## 1. Retail Access

*Retail access* is a right given to customers to use the services provided by the entire network. It has its roots in the common law duty to serve all customers applied to common carriers. Typically, retail access takes the form of a regulatory mandate implemented through public tariffs, which announce the terms under which the carrier will provide service to all comers. In its modern form, retail access normally is justified by the theory of natural monopoly. An industry is a natural monopoly if one firm can serve the entire market demand at lower cost than could two. When that is the case, even markets that begin as competitive will eventually come to be dominated by single players. Retail access protects consumers against denial of service under circumstances where alternative sources of supply are unlikely to exist. To ensure that consumers benefit from the mandated sharing of the monopoly, retail access is often accompanied by rate regulation, typically based on the cost of providing service.

Retail access can interfere with a network owner's ability to manage its network. As noted earlier, a network owner will configure its network in a manner that minimizes costs, brings capacity into line with demand, and guarantees the appropriate level of reliability based on its prediction of the likely network demand. Should the network demand exceed forecast levels, a network owner has four alternatives for restoring equilibrium. First, the network owner can increase network capacity. Because capacity cannot be expanded instantaneously, this solution is typically infeasible in the short run. Second, the network owner can simply refuse to meet the excess demand by limiting the service provided to existing customers and by turning away new customers. A retail access mandate prevents a network owner from employing this solution. Third, the network owner can increase retail price, which will reduce quantity demanded along the demand curve until it no longer exceeds network capacity. To the extent that the network is subject to price controls that typically accompany a retail access mandate, this solution is also foreclosed. Fourth, the network owner can restore equilibrium by degrading the quality of service. This will cause the demand curve to shift backward until demand is brought back into balance with network capacity. Although relatively unpalatable, the presence of a retail access mandate may make degradation of quality the only viable short-run option.

A rational network owner faced with the infeasibility and unattractiveness of the four alternatives described above will be forced to carry excess capacity to guard against the possibility that it will gain new customers unexpectedly if its competitors fail. In effect, retail access forces the network to carry capacity as insurance against failure by its competitors, with the premium for that insurance being paid by the network's customers (Sidak and Spulber 1997a). The resulting deviation from the optimal network configuration inevitably results in an increase in cost. Subjecting the network to the price controls associated with retail access also has the effect of reducing incentives for upgrading the existing network and for others to build out alternative network capacity.

Retail access can also increase transaction costs by forcing network owners to gather and format the information necessary to preannounce and preclear all of their service offerings. The tariff process also imposes delays in service innovation and requires carriers to bear the costs of defending their tariff filings against challenges filed by competitors. Tariffing also facilitates oligopolistic behavior by making prices and service offerings both transparent and homogeneous. To the extent that retail access requires that all customers pay uniform rates for uniform services, it also limits network owners' ability to customize their offerings to the needs of particular customers and bars potentially welfare-enhancing forms of price discrimination. A complete analysis of the issues raised by price discrimination exceeds the scope of this chapter.[98] For our purposes, it suffices to point out that price discrimination can be particularly beneficial in industries like telecommunications, which involve large, up-front fixed costs. When fixed costs are so large relative to the variable cost that the average cost curve lies above the marginal cost curve over the entire industry output, the prices charged to individual customers must cover a portion of the fixed cost as well as marginal cost. The fact that prices necessarily exceed marginal cost makes some degree of deadweight loss inevitable. Discriminatory pricing regimes, such as Ramsey pricing (1927), can take advantage of variations in different customers' price sensitivity to minimize those deadweight losses. Customers who are extremely price-sensitive (i.e., have highly elastic demands) are likely to curtail their consumption in response to a price increase to a greater degree than customers who are relatively price-insensitive (i.e., have fairly inelastic demands). Firms can thus minimize deadweight loss by allocating a smaller proportion of the fixed costs to price-sensitive customers and allocating a greater proportion of the fixed costs to price-insensitive customers. If fixed costs are allocated in inverse proportion to each consumer's elasticity of demand, price discrimination can lead to the efficient outcome.

That said, retail access is not as disruptive as other forms of access. Because access is provided only to the network in its entirety at locations that the network already serves, the traffic patterns are likely to be quite similar to those already in the network, and thus retail access may have only a minimal impact on the network's optimal configuration. Retail access also obviates the need for carriers to negotiate service contracts with each customer. In addition, because all of the traffic travels through a single network, the network owner should be able to obtain all of the information it needs to determine the optimal configuration fairly easily.

To our knowledge, no court has ever mandated retail access under the essential facilities doctrine. As noted earlier, the essential facilities doctrine requires that network owners provide *competitors* with access to the services of bottleneck *inputs*. Retail access, in contrast, provides *customers* with access to the services provided by the *entire network*. Indeed, retail access does not fit naturally with any aspect of antitrust law. As noted earlier, antitrust law does not impose liability on firms

---

98  For an overview of price discrimination, see generally Varian (1989).

that obtain monopolies through natural features of the market.[99] In the words of a leading court of appeals decision on the subject, "a natural monopoly market does not of itself impose restrictions on one who actively, but fairly, competes for it, any more than it does on one who passively acquires it" (*Union Leader Corp. v. Newspapers of New England, Inc.*, 284 F.2d 582, 584 (1st Cir. 1960)). To hold otherwise, in the words of another leading court of appeals decision, would be to "require the impossible – a competitive market under conditions of natural monopoly" (*Omega Satellite Prods. Co. v. City of Indianapolis*, 694 F.2d 119, 126 (7th Cir. 1982)).[100] In the absence of other anticompetitive behavior, such firms are generally free to charge the full monopoly price and to refuse to deal with whomever they wish. Indeed, if the market is a natural monopoly, retail access would simply dictate how the output of the monopoly is distributed. Not only would this require antitrust courts to make the type of regulatory assessments that *Trinko* recognized they are ill suited to perform but, in addition, simply managing output falls outside antitrust's purpose, which is to make markets more competitive by breaking down monopolies rather than merely requiring that they be shared (Areeda and Hovenkamp 2008c; Speta 2006).

Judicial imposition of retail access has been based not on the antitrust laws, but rather on the common law duty to serve imposed on businesses "affected with the public interest." This concept received its fullest exposition when the Court established in *Munn v. Illinois* that businesses affected with a public interest represented an exception to the constitutional limits on regulation imposed by the *Lochner* era conception of economic rights protected by substantive due process (94 U.S. 113, 126 (1876)). The Court abandoned this line of jurisprudence in its landmark opinion in *Nebbia v. New York*, in which the Court concluded that "there is no closed class or category of businesses affected with a public interest." The Court further elaborated:

> In several of the decisions of this court wherein the expressions "affected with a public interest," and "clothed with a public use," have been brought forward as the criteria of the validity of price control, it has been admitted that they are not susceptible of definition and form an unsatisfactory test of the constitutionality of legislation directed at business practices or prices.
>
> (291 U.S. 502, 536 (1934))[101]

---

99  This is true regardless of whether the natural monopoly arises because of declining average costs or network economic effects (Lemley and McGowan 1998).

100  See also *Am. Football League v. Nat'l Football League*, 323 F.2d 124, 131 (4th Cir. 1963); *Lamb Enters., Inc. v. Toledo Blade Co.*, 461 F.2d 506, 515 (6th Cir. 1972); *Greenville Publ'g Co. v. Daily Reflector, Inc.*, 496 F.2d 391, 397 (4th Cir. 1974); *Hecht*, 570 F.2d at 990–91; *Alaska Airlines*, 948 F.2d at 548.

101  See also *Jackson v. Metro. Edison Co.*, 419 U.S. 345, 353 (1974), applying the same reasoning in the context of a public utility's refusal to serve a customer.

The collapse of the conceptual foundation for the common law duty to serve essentially eviscerated it as a basis for judicial imposition of retail access to telecommunications networks.

## 2. Wholesale Access

*Wholesale access* is a right given to a network owner's competitors to resell the network's services to end users. As is the case with retail access, under wholesale access the network's elements are kept together and purchased as a whole except for certain retail merchant activities. The key distinction is that in retail access, access is provided to the customer, whereas in wholesale access, access is provided to a competitor.

Wholesale access has two primary effects. First, it changes the overall demand of the network, which in turn changes its cost, capacity, reliability, and optimal configuration. Wholesale access thus confronts network owners with the same quandary as retail access, complicated still further by the fact that market demand now depends on two prices – the price of wholesale access and the price of retail service – rather than just one. The existence of two prices makes the net impact on demand ambiguous. To the extent that wholesale access carries with it a nondiscrimination mandate, it can also prevent network owners from using price discrimination to minimize welfare losses.

Second, wholesale access takes the marketing functions outside the boundaries of the firm. Forcing the externalization of functions is problematic from the standpoint of the theory of the firm because it forces the network to deviate from the configuration that minimizes its transaction costs. Forcing firms to externalize their marketing functions requires the creation of mechanisms to allow those invoking wholesale access to obtain the services of the network. Although the fact that the network owner already offers this service to its own customers means that systems already exist for placing orders and requesting service, wholesale access would still require that these systems be redesigned to make them accessible to outside personnel.

The complexity of this analysis is demonstrated by the variety of distribution channels employed by the wireless industry, described in Chapter 8. This system of "dual distribution," in which output is sold simultaneously through company-owned and independent retailers, can reduce distribution costs, encourage the provision of presale services, and provide manufacturers with better information about customers' responses to their products. Although dual distribution systems have sometimes raised anticompetitive concerns, commentators generally agree that such concerns are misplaced. In the words of one leading antitrust scholar:

> A manufacturer who has no market power cannot use dual distribution to create it. Furthermore, even a monopoly manufacturer generally cannot increase

its market power by insulating its wholly-owned retail outlets, even if the effect is to injure competing, independent retailers. If the manufacturer has market power, any monopoly profits earned at the retailer level could also be earned at the manufacturer level.

(Hovenkamp 2005, p. 490)

At the same time, dual distribution systems are less vulnerable to collusion, since concerns about double marginalization will give the manufacturer-owned outlets no incentive to participate in a cartel seeking to create market power at the retail level. That said, dual distribution systems are more vulnerable to free riding, because independent dealers will recognize that retail outlets owned by the manufacturer are essentially guaranteed to provide the full range of presale services. It is reasonable to expect manufacturers employing dual distribution systems to impose territorial restrictions on independent retailers and mandate a degree of exclusivity in order to protect against free riding (Hovenkamp 2005, p. 490).

The extent to which wholesale access would benefit consumers is thus far from clear. As noted in the passage from the Areeda and Hovenkamp antitrust treatise quoted in Part I, antitrust law typically allows manufacturers to sell their products directly if they so choose and does not require them to sell their products to other retailers at wholesale prices. As Areeda and Hovenkamp rightly conclude, "Why price regulation of the output should make any difference is not clear, since customers are no better off by the forced insertion of an intermediary and – if costs increase as a result – they could be worse off." The only exception is if wholesale prices were regulated, in which case vertical integration into retailing might be an attempt to evade rate regulation at the wholesale level (Areeda and Hovenkamp 2008c, pp. 363–65).

Courts have been quite reluctant to use the antitrust laws to mandate wholesale access. The closest that the Supreme Court has come to doing so is *Otter Tail*, in which the Court required an electric power company to provide wholesale distribution of power to cities seeking to replace the retail distribution franchises they had previously granted to Otter Tail with municipally owned retail distribution power grids. The analogy to wholesale access is not perfect. By seeking to create the infrastructure needed to provide retail distribution, the cities were seeking to do more than just replace the marketing functions provided by Otter Tail. Even so, leading commentators have described the situation presented in *Otter Tail* as being analogous to wholesale access (Areeda and Hovenkamp 2008c).

As noted earlier, scholarly commentators have raised serious doubts about *Otter Tail*'s vitality as a precedent. The language in *Trinko* distinguishing *Otter Tail* on the grounds that "the defendant was already in the business of providing a service to certain customers . . . and refused to provide the same service to certain other customers" arguably suggests a more limited version of wholesale access (540 U.S. at 410). Although this reasoning does not place network owners that are not currently offering wholesale access under any obligation to provide such access, it can be read as requiring firms that already offer wholesale access to do so on a nondiscriminatory basis (*Z-Tel Commc'ns, Inc.*, 331 F. Supp. 2d at 536–39).

That said, attempts to turn *Otter Tail* into a basis for imposing wholesale access must come to grips with the language in *Trinko* discussing *Aspen Skiing*. According to *Trinko*, the problem in *Aspen Skiing* was not that Ski Co. refused to sell lift tickets to Highlands at *wholesale prices*, a practice Ski Co. followed without drawing any criticism from the *Trinko* Court. Instead, the problem was that Ski Co. was unwilling to sell lift tickets to Highlands at the *full retail price*, which the Court believed "revealed a distinctly anticompetitive bent" (540 U.S. at 409). This latter observation appears to be at least somewhat probative of anticompetitive behavior, since the literature on transfer pricing indicates that a firm that offers a product that is used both as a final good and as an input in making other goods maximizes both its profits and welfare when it charges a uniform price for the good (Milgrom and Roberts 1992). This language thus provides no support for a duty by monopolists to permit competitors to access their networks at wholesale prices. At most, this language suggests that monopolists may have some duty to serve those who are willing to pay the full retail price (*MetroNet Servs.*, 383 F.3d at 1132–34). Moreover, to the extent that courts have been willing to mandate access at full retail prices, the duty has been limited to customers and has not been extended to competitors.[102]

Any arguments that firms providing wholesale access must do so on a nondiscriminatory basis must address the long line of Supreme Court precedent recognizing the benefit of allowing manufacturers to enter into exclusivity arrangements with certain retailers. Although the Supreme Court was once quite hostile to agreements giving preferential treatment to certain retailers over others,[103] it has recognized over time that restrictions on *intra*brand competition can promote *inter*brand competition. As the Supreme Court reasoned in its landmark decision in *Continental T.V., Inc. v. Sylvania*:

> Economists have identified a number of ways in which manufacturers can use . . . restrictions [on the distribution of their products] to compete more effectively against other manufacturers. For example, new manufacturers and manufacturers entering new markets can use the restrictions in order to induce competent and aggressive retailers to make the kind of investment of capital and labor that is often required in the distribution of products unknown to the consumer. Established manufacturers can use them to induce retailers to engage

---

102 *St. Louis, Iron Mountain & S. Ry. Co. v. S. Express Co.* (*Express Cases*), 117 U.S. 1, 26–29 (1886); *Pac. Tel. & Tel. Co. v. Anderson*, 196 F. 699, 703 (E.D. Wash. 1912); Areeda and Hovenkamp (2008c); Huber et al. (1999).

103 *Eastman Kodak Co. v. S. Photo Materials Co.*, 273 U.S. 359, 375 (1927) (invalidating exclusive dealing contract despite the absence of direct evidence of purpose to monopolize); *Standard Stations*, 337 U.S. at 314 (striking down exclusive dealing contract that foreclosed 16% of the market); *FTC v. Brown Shoe Co.*, 384 U.S. 316, 320–21 (1966) (rejecting exclusive dealing arrangement involving small fraction of retailers).

in promotional activities or to provide service and repair facilities necessary to the efficient marketing of their products.... The availability and quality of such services affect a manufacturer's goodwill and the competitiveness of his product. Because of market imperfections such as the so-called "free rider" effect, these services might not be provided by retailers in a purely competitive situation, despite the fact that each retailer's benefit would be greater if all provided the services than if none did.

(433 U.S. at 54–55)

The Supreme Court has reiterated these concerns in subsequent cases and has developed an elaborate jurisprudence to ensure that manufacturers remain free to enter into exclusivity agreements with some retailers and to refuse to deal with others.[104]

Given the amount of information that customers interested in purchasing telecommunications services need about service plans and necessary equipment, telecommunications markets would seem susceptible to this type of market failure. Conversely, limiting network owners' ability to shift to proprietary sales forces or exclusive retail outlets would serve only to give manufacturers the incentive to vertically integrate into retailing or to enter into exclusivity arrangements from the outset, an outcome that would have the perverse effect of harming retailers.[105]

A wide range of justifications thus exist for providing wholesale access in a discriminatory manner and permitting producers to internalize or externalize marketing functions as they see fit. The compelling nature of these economic arguments and the weight of Supreme Court authority make the imposition of wholesale access by an antitrust court very unlikely.

### 3. Interconnection Access

*Interconnection access* refers to reciprocal connections between networks that provide similar services to similarly situated customers. One example would be requiring all wireless telephone networks operating in the same area to terminate calls originating on other wireless telephone networks. Another example would be requiring top-level backbone providers to interconnect with all other top-level backbone providers.

Interconnection access complicates network management to a much greater degree than retail and wholesale access. Increasing the number of users causes the number of possible connections to increase geometrically. The net effect on the demand on any particular firm's network is unclear, however. Making it possible to

---

104  *Monsanto,* 465 U.S. at 762–3; *Bus. Elecs. Corp. v. Sharp Elecs. Corp.,* 485 U.S. 717, 723–25 (1988). For a discussion of other cases approving a manufacturers' shift to an exclusivity arrangement, see *Spectrum Sports,* 506 U.S. at 454–55.

105  *Dr. Miles,* 220 U.S. at 411 (Holmes, J., dissenting); *Standard Stations,* 337 U.S. at 309–12; *Sylvania,* 433 U.S. at 57 n. 26; *Bus. Elecs.,* 485 U.S. at 725; *State Oil,* 522 U.S. at 16.

reach other firms' customers may cause demand for network capacity to increase. On the other hand, the presence of other networks can place downward pressure on network demand, as customers substitute away and the other networks fulfill some of the functions previously provided by the primary network.

In addition, unlike retail and wholesale access, under which service is provided at points at the edge of the network where service is already available, interconnection access requires network owners to permit interconnection at new points of entry in the middle of the network, although they are likely to be at major nodes. Not only does this require designing new interfaces to permit interconnection at locations other than customers' premises; it also alters the traffic on the network by introducing flows into the network at points where flows would otherwise not occur. The resulting diversion of traffic to other networks can disaggregate traffic to the point where it is no longer economical to take advantage of the scale economies provided by higher-volume networking technologies. The fact that traffic now originates and terminates outside of a single network also increases the cost of obtaining the information necessary for network planning and creates the possibility of strategic behavior to take advantage of the information asymmetries.

The impact of interconnection access on total network demand is complicated by the presence of "network economic effects," which arise when the value of a network increases with the number of end users connected to it. The increase in value caused by providing customers with access to the customers of other networks can cause network traffic to increase relative to a noninterconnected network. At the same time, the fact that some traffic now originates and terminates outside the incumbent's network raises the possibility of diversion of traffic below the levels that would exist under retail and wholesale access, in which all traffic originates and terminates on a single network. The impact of interconnection access on the demand for network services is thus ambiguous.

As noted in Chapter 4, some commentators have also warned that networks can harm competition by refusing to engage in interconnection access. Network economic effects are often described as giving rise to demand-side economies of scale. In the absence of interconnection, customers will naturally flock to the largest network. Once the market reaches its tipping point, the value of the network of the dominant player will so far outstrip those of its competitors that the market collapses into a natural monopoly. Once tipped, the difficulties that new entrants face in generating sufficient volume to untip the market can cause the resulting monopoly to become locked in.

Network owners presented with a request for interconnection access are thus subject to conflicting impulses. Interconnection would enable customers to reach a larger number of other end users, which would increase the value of their network. Refusing to interconnect, on the other hand, would lead to a race to become the dominant player. Firms will choose among these conflicting strategies based on the skewness of the potential returns from winning and losing the resulting competition and the likelihood that they will emerge as the dominant player (Besen and Farrell 1994; Woroch 2002b).

As noted earlier, it is often overlooked that the primary effect of network economic effects is to provide powerful incentives in favor of interconnection. For example, in a market in which five equally sized players are already interconnected, any player that refused to interconnect would put itself at a tremendous competitive disadvantage. In addition, commentators from a wide range of perspectives acknowledge that lock-in is less likely in markets undergoing rapid growth, in which new entrants will be able to compete for new users. Conversely, the formal models demonstrating how refusal to interconnect can harm competition have generally been based on duopoly and dominant-firm market structures. In the absence of such market concentration, a firm cannot plausibly use its interconnection policies to harm competition. Even if risks of anticompetitive conduct exist, private ordering offers a variety of potential solutions aside from regulation. Furthermore, mandating access in an attempt to redress such anticompetitive problems risks delaying entry by additional providers and inducing the adoption of inefficient network technology. Thus, when markets are sufficiently competitive, imposing interconnection access is superfluous at best and may even be harmful.

This conclusion is reflected in the FCC's current policy toward wireless-to-wireless interconnection, discussed in Chapter 8, in which the FCC has concluded that, in the absence of a dominant player, competition already provides wireless providers with sufficient incentives to interconnect. As discussed in Chapter 10, the FCC has taken a similar position with respect to backbone interconnection.

The theoretical literature does identify one scenario in which participants in a market without a dominant player may nonetheless refuse to interconnect. If the market consists of two players of equal size, they may reject compatibility and instead engage in a race for the market. Interestingly, though, this type of competition does not necessarily lead to the delays in technology adoption and supracompetitive returns that are associated with refusals to interconnect by dominant firms (Besen and Farrell 1994). It also has the virtue of promoting the rapid buildout of new network technologies.

As discussed in Chapter 8, competition during the early years of the telephone network may have followed this precise pattern, and AT&T turned to a strategy of merger to monopoly to escape from it. This change in tactics prompted the federal government to bring its first major antitrust suit against the Bell System, which was ultimately settled by the so-called Kingsbury Commitment, named after the AT&T vice president who negotiated the terms of the consent decree with Attorney General J.C. McReynolds. Under the Kingsbury Commitment, the Bell System agreed to stop acquiring independent local telephone companies with which it competed, although the agreement permitted the Bell System to acquire independent local telephone companies operating in areas that it did not serve. AT&T also agreed to allow the independent telephone companies to interconnect with its long distance network (AT&T 1914). Although the Kingsbury Commitment ostensibly forbade the Bell System to acquire competing independent telephone systems, the government immediately backtracked on this position, announcing that the settlement was not meant to prevent communities from eliminating dual service if they so chose (*United States v. AT&T*, No. 6082 (D. Or. Sept. 7, 1914), reprinted in Shale 1918). In practice, the government permitted Bell acquisitions of competing independents so long as the Bell System and the independents swapped lines so that neither obtained a net increase in total subscribers. As a result, during the time the Kingsbury Commitment was in effect, the federal government nonetheless approved the Bell System's acquiring a total of 241,000 additional stations while transferring 58,000 stations to the independents (Gabel 1969; Mueller 1997). The result was a division of markets in which both the Bell System and the independents ended up with monopolies within their service areas.

In the end, the regulatory regime created by the Kingsbury Commitment was abolished (with the full support of the independents) by the enactment of the Willis–Graham Act, which immunized telephone mergers from antitrust scrutiny (*Statutes at Large* 1921, pp. 27–28). Instead, antitrust mergers would be reviewed by the Interstate Commerce Commission (ICC), which effectively became a rubber stamp that approved essentially all telecommunications mergers (ICC 1937). As we noted in Chapter 8, during this period, both the Bell System and the independents also endorsed rate regulation of local telephone services by state public utility commissions.

This history underscores the extent to which refusal to interconnect need not be anticompetitive. It may also yield some insights into current broadband policy. It suggests that refusing to require interconnection could foster a race for the market between cable modem and DSL that could help meet the FCC's and state public utility commissions' statutory obligations to "encourage the deployment on a reasonable and timely basis of advanced telecommunications capability to all Americans" (47 U.S.C. § 157 note). The primary worry is that the race logically ends with one of the two competitors emerging as the dominant player. An end result with a single dominant player, as noted earlier, no longer becomes a stable outcome if a third (and possibly a fourth) competitor emerges. According to *Trinko*, therefore, solutions that alter market structure to make them competitive are preferred to solutions like interconnection access, which require continuing price regulation (540 U.S. at 414–15). Furthermore, as the ongoing deployment of broadband fiber optic service demonstrates, the pace of technological change may dictate that the winner of an initial race may find its dominance destabilized by a new race to deploy a new technology.

Skepticism about mandating interconnection access does not require embracing this Schumpeterian vision of competition. As one of us has argued at length elsewhere, networks may deviate from perfect interoperability in order to distinguish their service offerings from those of their competitors. Not only does this differentiation allow the network to provide new services that depend on a different network architecture, but also it allows multiple players to survive notwithstanding the presence of supply-side and demand-side economies of scale through a niche strategy that targets subsegments of the market that place a particularly high value on different types of network services. The result is not the promotion of *vertical* competition in which a succession of monopolists compete *for* the market, but rather the enhancement of more conventional *horizontal* competition in which multiple providers compete *in* the market (Yoo 2005).

Interconnection access claims have not fared well under antitrust law, even when asserted against a dominant firm. For example, the literature often ignores the fact that MCI's private antitrust suit against AT&T involved two distinct essential facilities doctrine claims. The more celebrated claim, which we discuss in greater detail in the next section, involved what we call platform access, in which MCI sought access to a monopoly input controlled by AT&T (local telephone service) in order to sell a complementary service (long-distance telephone service). The often-overlooked claim is that MCI also sought to interconnect its long distance network with portions of AT&T's long distance network that reached areas that it did not yet serve. In this claim, MCI did not seek access to AT&T's network to sell complementary services. Instead, it sought connection with the larger network in order to sell the same services to similarly situated customers. Its concern was that its smaller network size put it at a competitive disadvantage. As a result, it sought interconnection to put itself on an equal footing with AT&T. The court of appeals overturned a jury verdict in favor of MCI on the interconnection access claim for the simple reason that "[t]here was no sufficient explanation as to why MCI, on the one hand, was building its own network, and, on the other, was entitled to access in the interim to AT&T's facilities" (*MCI*, 708 F.2d at 1132–33, 1147, 1148).

At first glance, this answer seems somewhat anomalous. AT&T was clearly a dominant firm and thus arguably posed a serious anticompetitive threat. The court's focus on the supply-side feasibility of constructing alternative network capacity ignored the demand-side scale economies associated with network economic effects. If refusing to allow MCI to interconnect with AT&T's long-distance network prevented MCI's customers from calling AT&T's customers, the demand-side scale economies would reinforce AT&T's market dominance regardless of the feasibility of constructing a second long-distance network.

One possible solution to this puzzle lies in the fact that AT&T did not have complete control over long distance calls placed by its subscribers. Long-distance calls also require the services of local telephone companies. Those local telephone companies were required by a D.C. Circuit interpretation of the specialized common carrier tariff that AT&T filed with the FCC to terminate calls from MCI as well as AT&T,[106] a conclusion that would later be reinforced by the "equal access" provisions of the decree ordering the breakup of AT&T.[107] The fact that the local

---

106 *MCI Telecomms. Corp. v. FCC*, 561 F.2d 365, 378–79 (D.C. Cir. 1977); *MCI Telecomms. Corp. v. FCC*, 580 F.2d 590, 594–99 (D.C. Cir. 1978).

107 *Modification of Final Judgment*, 552 F. Supp. at 195–200.

telephone company, rather than AT&T, controlled access to the customer meant that AT&T could not prevent MCI's customers from calling AT&T's customers simply by refusing to allow MCI to interconnect with its long-distance network. The regulatory and antitrust obligations that prevented local telephone companies from discriminating against MCI made mandating interconnection access unnecessary.

The closest analogue to interconnection access in Supreme Court precedent is *Aspen Skiing*. Recall that in *Aspen Skiing*, the owner of one ski area sought to compel the owner of three other ski areas located near Aspen, Colorado, to continue marketing a multiarea pass good for all four facilities. Although skiing facilities are not usually regarded as networks, it is possible to conceive of this arrangement as a form of interconnection access. The fact that the courts found Ski Co. liable thus provides some doctrinal support for mandating interconnection access under at least some circumstances.

As noted earlier, *Aspen Skiing* has been heavily criticized. Indeed, the *Trinko* Court distanced itself from *Aspen Skiing*, calling it "at or near the outer boundary" of antitrust liability. After *Trinko*, *Aspen Skiing* can at most be read as imposing some obligation to assert a valid business justification before discontinuing a preexisting business relationship and refusing to allow a competitor to resell a monopolist's services at the full retail price (540 U.S. at 409). The Supreme Court thus flatly rejected the idea that *Aspen Skiing* could serve as the basis for granting access to a competitor with whom the network owner has not previously done business. There is thus little reason to believe that a court will issue a general mandate of interconnection access.

## 4. Platform Access

*Platform access* requires network owners to open their networks to providers of complementary services sold through the network. It requires a network owner to provide carriage to any provider of a complementary service that presents its traffic at a designated interface in a standardized format. The early cases involved requests to force local telephone systems to open their networks to providers of long distance, information services, and CPE, described in Chapter 8. The current debate over network neutrality, described in Chapters 11 and 12, focuses on compelling broadband systems to provide platform access to all Internet content and applications providers.

It is widely recognized that network owners already possess powerful incentives to provide platform access. That is because enabling customers to reach the broadest possible range of complementary services generally represents the best way to maximize the network's value (and thus the amount that the network owner can charge for service) (Besen and Farrell 1994; Yoo 2002; Farrell and Weiser 2003).

At the same time, the standardization implicit in platform access imposes a number of costs. As discussed at greater length in Chapter 11, standardization decreases welfare by reducing product variety. Indeed, standardization on any protocol has the inevitable effect of favoring some applications and disfavoring others. Standardization also has the inevitable effect of commoditizing network services. By preventing service differentiation, platform access forces network owners to compete solely based on price and network size, which are considerations that reinforce the advantages enjoyed by the largest players. Conversely, incompatible networks may simply represent the natural outgrowth of heterogeneous consumer preferences (Katz and Shapiro 1994; Liebowitz and Margolis 1996).

Differentiation can play a particularly important role in industries such as telecommunications, in which the presence of fixed costs that are large relative to marginal costs forces network providers to produce on the declining portion of the average cost curve. As noted in Chapter 4, product differentiation can create stable equilibria with multiple producers each producing on the declining portion of the average cost curve. Thus, smaller players can survive despite cost and size disadvantages by targeting subsegments of the market.

Platform access also involves significant transaction costs, both in terms of establishing the governing standards and in terms of reconfiguring the network to open it to providers of complementary services. In addition, the governing standard must be updated to reflect changes in technology. In the meantime, standardization locks the location of the interface into place, an effect that is particularly problematic in industries in which technological change is forcing the natural interfaces between firms to shift constantly. As discussed in Chapter 8, the FCC and the court overseeing the breakup of AT&T and the FCC had to create an elaborate set of rules forcing the local telephone companies to undertake certain modifications, limiting their ability to change their interfaces, and requiring them to provide advance notice of any changes that would be approved. The platform access mandated by the *Computer Inquiries* had a similar effect. Forcing such questions to be decided as a matter of regulation represented a significant hindrance in such a technologically dynamic industry.

Furthermore, like any form of compelled access, platform access requires direct regulation of prices in order to be effective. As *Trinko* recognized, price regulation is not a task to which antitrust courts are particularly well suited. For example, as noted earlier, the Kingsbury Commitment required that AT&T make its long distance network available to independent local telephone companies. The problem was that the decree allowed AT&T to charge prices that were so unattractive as to render this form of platform access useless (Mueller 1997).

Most problematic is platform access's long-run impact on dynamic efficiency. As noted earlier, the primary policy goal should be to promote entry in those segments of the industry that are the least competitive. Only if competition in a particular segment proves unsustainable should policymakers pursue the second-best policy goal of promoting competition in complementary services.

At the time of the consent decree settling the government's 1974 antitrust suit against AT&T, entry by competitive local telephone providers was thought to be infeasible, making the promotion of competition in long distance and information services a legitimate policy goal. After competition between local telephone providers became feasible, platform access became counterproductive. Long distance providers were natural strategic partners for companies wishing to enter into local telephone service, yet they had no incentive to undertake such investments so long as the antitrust decree breaking up AT&T provided them with access to the existing network. The recent patterns of investment following the Supreme Court's *Brand X* decision bear out this dynamic. Once the Supreme Court made it clear that regulation would no longer guarantee providers of complementary services access to existing broadband networks, content and application providers and device manufacturers began pouring capital into alternative network technologies such as wireless broadband and broadband over powerlines. Proper administration would thus require the court to monitor technological developments in the telecommunications industry and to release the local telephone companies from their equal access obligations the minute that competition from other local telephone companies became sustainable. It is doubtful that any antitrust court, no matter how well intentioned, would be up to such a task.

Despite these problems, platform access represents the most common form of access imposed under the antitrust laws. For example, MCI's and the government's antitrust suits against the Bell System both attempted to promote competition in the complementary service of long distance by mandating platform access to the Bell System's local telephone networks. The order breaking up AT&T also extended this equal access requirement to the predecessors to the providers of Internet content (then called information service providers).[108] Although the Modification of Final Judgment did not initially address platform access for CPE, later modifications brought CPE within the equal access mandate as well.[109] The court also imposed similar equal access requirements on GTE, the largest non-Bell provider of local telephone service, when approving its merger with Sprint.[110] The proposed consent decree that would have approved AT&T's 1994 acquisition of the largest cellular provider contained a similar equal access requirement before the case was mooted by the Telecommunications Act of 1996.[111]

To facilitate enforcement of equal access, the Modification of Final Judgment included line-of-business restrictions prohibiting the newly divested local telephone companies from offering long distance or information services or manufacturing CPE. To ensure that the local telephone companies did not evade rate regulation by entering into an unregulated complementary market, the Modification of Final Judgment included a catch-all line of business restriction prohibiting them from

---

108  *MCI*, 708 F.2d at 1132–3; *Modification of Final Judgment*, 552 F. Supp. at 195–97.

109  Kellogg et al. (1992).

110  *United States v. GTE Corp.*, 603 F. Supp. 730, 743–44 (D.D.C. 1984).

111  Huber et al. (1999).

"provid[ing] any other product or service, except [local telephone service], that is not a natural monopoly service actually regulated by tariff" (*Modification of Final Judgment*, 552 F. Supp. at 228).

There is considerable irony that platform access is where antitrust plaintiffs have fared the best. The economic logic suggests that the anticompetitive risks surrounding platform access are much lower than those of other forms of access and are in the process of being rendered nonexistent in the telecommunications industry by the emergence of wireless and other alternatives to conventional local telephone service. As noted earlier, an exception exists when the underlying markets are subject to rate regulation. This exception, however, is largely inapposite in the telecommunications context, because many telecommunications markets, such as broadband and wireless, have never been subject to rate regulation, and the others have already been rate deregulated or are now on their way to becoming so.

Indeed, the extent to which the emergence of last-mile competition has undercut the justification for imposing platform access is well illustrated by the D.C. Circuit's decision holding that the emergence of last-mile alternatives justified waiving the Modification of Final Judgment's line of business restriction on information services[112] as well as the catch-all restriction on untariffed services.[113] Controversies over the remaining line of business restrictions continued until the Modification of Final Judgment was superseded by the Telecommunications Act of 1996.[114]

The Justice Department's and the FCC's recent approvals of the Verizon–MCI and SBC–AT&T acquisitions further attests to the extent to which control of the local loop has ceased to be a justification for imposing platform access. Indeed, as recently as 1997, a merger between a long distance company and one of the local telephone companies that used to make up the Bell System was regarded as "unthinkable" (Hundt 1997). But the FCC approved these two mergers, disposing of requests for platform access in a few brief paragraphs finding that the level of competition and the existence of excess capacity were sufficient to guard against anticompetitive harms (FCC 2005g, 2005h). Indeed, the judicial decision evaluating the acquisitions under the antitrust laws did not even mention platform access.[115]

The experience implementing the platform access provisions of the Modification of Final Judgment provides an eloquent demonstration of how difficult administering platform access can be. The court overseeing the decree was bombarded with complaints charging the local telephone companies with failing to live up to their equal access obligations. The technological dynamism of the telecommunications industry forced the court to confront hundreds of requests to waive the line-of-business restrictions.[116] These requests often took from three to four

---

112  *United States v. W. Elec. Co.*, 993 F.2d 1572, 1578–80 (D.C. Cir. 1993).

113  *W. Elec. Co.*, 673 F. Supp. at 599.

114  Huber et al. (1999).

115  See *United States v. SBC Commc'ns, Inc.*, 489 F. Supp. 2d 1 (D.D.C. 2007).

116  Kellogg et al. (1992); Kellogg et al. (1995).

years to process, with estimates of the total welfare loss associated with these delays exceeding $1 billion (Rubin and Dezhbakhsh 1995).

These developments provide a useful perspective on the ongoing debate over platform access to the Internet, which goes by the name of "network neutrality." One key question is whether antitrust law permits last-mile broadband providers to give preferential access to particular content and application providers.[117] Indeed, the FTC recently held a public workshop exploring whether the antitrust laws should impose platform access to the Internet (FTC 2007). Just as the existence of alternative sources of network capacity undercuts the justification for platform access on behalf of information services, so too does competition between cable modem and DSL systems and the imminent emergence of other broadband alternatives undercut the justification for imposing network neutrality.

## 5. Unbundled Access

*Unbundled access* requires network owners to lease portions of their networks to their competitors. Like wholesale access, unbundled access is provided to competitors. Rather than provide the services of the entire network, as is the case under wholesale access, unbundled access involves the use of the services of selected inputs.

Unbundled access has an impact on the demand for network services that is similar in some ways to that of wholesale access. Because unbundled access can create new services, it can cause demand to increase. At the same time, diverting traffic off the network can cause the demand for network services to decrease. These changes in network demand can alter the optimal network design by changing the cost of certain components, by changing the variability of network flows, and by diverting traffic onto other networks to the point where traffic-aggregating technologies will no longer be cost-effective.

That said, unbundled access disrupts the network in ways that are far more intrusive than wholesale access. Unlike wholesale access, which involves access to the entire network, unbundled access ties up only isolated portions of the network. Because networks are complex systems, tying up network elements in one part of the network can have an adverse impact on portions of the network located far from the element being accessed. Like interconnection access, unbundled access also introduces new sources of network flows at places other than customers' premises. The problem is that the interconnection points for unbundled access are far more varied than those for interconnection access. Therefore, unbundled access's impact on the network's cost, capacity, and reliability is likely to be quite unpredictable.

Unbundled access also requires the network owner to establish systems for provisioning and metering components deep within its system at points that do not normally serve as external interfaces with other firms. As the protracted

117 See Yoo (2007a) exploring implications of antitrust for network neutrality.

litigation surrounding the provisions of the 1996 Act demonstrates, implementation of unbundled access is unusually complex.

Antitrust courts have entertained requests for mandating unbundled access from time to time. For example, the court overseeing the Modification of Final Judgment was asked to approve a proposed modification that would have provided unbundled access to Ameritech's local telephone network in return for allowing Ameritech to offer long-distance service (Huber et al. 1999). As noted earlier, the failure to provide unbundled access also formed the foundation for *Trinko*.

The Supreme Court's *Trinko* decision was quite critical of the effect that using the antitrust laws to compel unbundled access to a telecommunications network can have on dynamic efficiency. These critiques are discussed at length above and need be revisited only briefly here. Specifically, the Court rejected calls for imposing unbundled access under the antitrust laws because "[c]ompelling [infrastructure] firms to share the source of their advantage is in some tension with the underlying purpose of antitrust law, since it may lessen the incentive for the monopolist, the rival, or both to invest in those economically beneficial facilities."

In addition, mandating unbundled access poses significant problems of administrability. In the words of the Court, "[e]nforced sharing also requires antitrust courts to act as central planners, identifying the proper price, quantity, and other terms of dealing." Furthermore, because unbundled access affects network elements "deep within the bowels" of a local telephone network, they can only be made available if "[n]ew systems [are] designed and implemented simply to make that access possible." Additionally, requests for unbundled access "are difficult for antitrust courts to evaluate, not only because they are highly technical, but also because they are likely to be extremely numerous, given the incessant, complex, and constantly changing interaction of competitive and incumbent LECs implementing the sharing and interconnection obligations." The "uncertain virtue of forced sharing and the difficulty of identifying and remedying anticompetitive conduct by a single firm" made the Court loath to mandate unbundled access under the antitrust law (540 U.S. at 407–08, 410, 414).

In sum, all five forms of access share a number of common characteristics. For example, access invariably has a dramatic impact on the cost, capacity, and reliability of the network. In addition, by requiring networks to externalize certain functions that would otherwise be internalized, access forces networks to diverge from the natural boundaries dictated by the Coasian theory of the firm. Every form of access also has the inevitable effect of reducing incentives for both incumbents and competitors to invest in alternative network capacity. Judicially imposed access also inevitably requires antitrust courts to undertake price-setting and output-allocation functions to which they are institutionally poorly suited.

That said, these overarching similarities do not justify disregarding the differences among the various types of access. By capturing how various network components interact with one another within the context of a complex system, our framework shows how the nature and the magnitude of each of these problems varies with the precise type of access being sought. The saving grace is that the emergence of competition in the last mile is in the process of undermining the conceptual justification for imposing all forms of access, although the degree of competition and the precise nature of the potential competitive problems vary across the different types. Until the expansion of wireless and other alternative network technologies renders access superfluous, courts and policymakers will continue to need tools to analyze the unique problems that each type of access poses.

\*    \*    \*

The antitrust laws continue to represent an uncertain basis for mandating access to telecommunications networks. Not only have the theories upon which the essential facilities doctrine rests long been under conceptual attack, but also scholars have increasingly questioned courts' institutional competence to supervise access decrees. Both of these concerns came together in the Supreme Court's decision in *Trinko*. After that decision, the presence of a regulatory regime with authority to impose access affects more than just the timing of judicial review; it may serve as a substantive bar to judicial imposition of access requirements.

The *Trinko* opinion also contains clues underscoring the mistake of treating all types of access alike. This book offers a framework for organizing and analyzing different types of access. To the extent that antitrust survived *Trinko* as a source of access requirements, we hope this framework provides some guidance. Interestingly, the courts have been most sympathetic to platform access, particularly in opening up AT&T's local telephone networks to long distance competitors, and the issue has taken center stage in the debates about network neutrality. Based on our analysis, this is the type of access to networks in which antitrust and regulatory intervention is the least justified.

# 10

# The Regulation of Last-Mile
# Broadband Networks

Telecommunications has moved from traditional analog voice service to high-speed digital transmission, referred to as broadband. The explosion of new forms of transmission and new types of content (data, audio, video), has changed the debate over access to networks. Under the general umbrella of "network neutrality," advocates of mandatory access argue for extensive regulation of prices and products.

The Supreme Court's recent decision in *National Cable & Telecommunications Association v. Brand X Internet Services* cleared the way for the FCC to resolve how to fit the leading broadband technologies, such as cable modems and digital subscriber line (DSL) services, into the existing regulatory regime (545 U.S. 967 (2005)). The fact that Congress largely failed to take the Internet into consideration when enacting the Telecommunications Act of 1996 has left policymakers with little definitive guidance.[1] Regulatory decisionmaking is further complicated by the dynamism of the technological environment. The demands that end users are placing on the Internet are changing rapidly, as evidenced by the increasing popularity of bandwidth-intensive applications, such as streaming media, peer-to-peer downloads, and virtual worlds. In the meantime, a host of new communications platforms are waiting in the wings, such as third-generation mobile communications devices (3G) and wireless hotspots employing WiFi technology.

## A. The History of Last-Mile Broadband Regulation

Cable modems and DSL represent the two leading platforms for last-mile broadband service (FCC 2008b).[2] Cable modem service generally provides more bandwidth than DSL, but requires end users to share bandwidth in ways that make the network

---

1   For example, Werbach notes (2002, p. 42) that "[t]he 1996 Act simply did not contemplate the radical changes the Internet would bring to the communications world."

2   The FCC's definition of high-speed lines was initially developed in 1999 and has become somewhat out of date. The FCC is in the process of updating its definitions (FCC 2008a).

provided to any one end user dependent on the number of other users. DSL service, although providing more limited bandwidth than cable modem service, employs dedicated connections that allow greater reliability. Despite these differences, end users typically regard the two services as relatively good substitutes for one another (Crandall et al. 2002; FCC 2005d[3]). Mobile wireless has emerged as an important competitor, skyrocketing from no subscribers at the beginning of 2005 to over 35 million subscribers by the end of 2006. In addition, Verizon is investing $24 billion in its new fiber-based FiOS network, which delivers unprecedented speeds. FiOS had already captured over one million subscribers by mid 2007 and hopes to reach seven million customers by 2010 (Verizon Communications, Inc. 2007).

Despite the functional similarities between cable modem and DSL service, governmental authorities have taken strikingly different approaches when regulating them. Whereas cable modem services have been largely deregulated, DSL services have often been subject to extensive access requirements.

## 1. Regulation of Cable Modem Systems

Cable modem systems provide service through the network of coaxial cables originally designed for cable television, although some modifications to the network configuration are required. For example, the cable network must be transformed from the typical tree-and-branch configuration associated with one-way television transmission into the ring or star-type configuration needed for data transmission. This is usually accomplished through a hybrid fiber–coaxial (HFC) architecture in which fiber optic cables are used to connect the central cable facility (known as the "headend") to satellite facilities arranged in a ring, known as neighborhood or fiber nodes. The final connection between the fiber node and individual subscribers is made through copper-based coaxial cables. Cable modem service also requires special equipment at the headend, known as a cable modem termination system (CMTS), to manage the flow of data between cable subscribers and various types of broadband services, such as e-mail, IP telephony, content cached locally, and content residing on the World Wide Web (see Figure 10.1).

The regulation of cable modem systems has been influenced by the framework of overlapping municipal and federal regulation that governs cable television. Municipalities have asserted regulatory jurisdiction over cable television since the first cable system was established in 1949, largely as a result over their control over the public rights of way upon which cable depends to provide service. From the outset, municipalities imposed access requirements and regulated retail rates in an effort to limit any exercise of cable operators' monopoly power throughout the entire history of the cable industry.

---

3 This order was affirmed on judicial review (*Time Warner Telecom, Inc. v. FCC*, 507 F.3d 205 (3d Cir. 2007)).

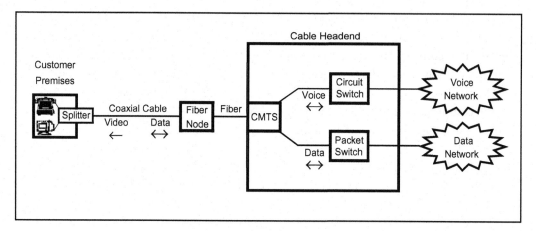

**Figure 10.1.** Typical configuration of cable modem system.

Federal regulation of cable television, in contrast, has hardly been a model of consistency. The FCC initially ruled that it lacked jurisdiction over the cable industry and called on Congress to give it explicit statutory authority (FCC 1958, 1959). Despite Congress's failure to enact such legislation, the FCC soon reversed course, tentatively concluding in 1965 that it had jurisdiction over cable, although the FCC disavowed any intention to preempt the "local components" of cable television, including ratemaking, franchise fees, and the nature of the services provided (FCC 1965b; see also FCC 1962, 1965a). The FCC made this tentative conclusion official the following year, asserting jurisdiction over cable, requiring that cable systems provide free carriage to all television stations operating in their service areas (known as "must carry"), and prohibiting cable systems in the 100 largest media markets from expanding their service or importing any additional distant television signals until a more comprehensive regulatory scheme could be developed (FCC 1966).[4] The Supreme Court would subsequently uphold the FCC's assertion of jurisdiction and its so-called "freeze" on further expansion of cable service and distant signal importation.[5] Throughout this period, the FCC continued to espouse a vision of dual federal–local regulation (FCC 1970b), although the precise division of authority between municipal and regulators remained unclear.

The FCC interest in regulating the cable industry continued to grow during the early 1970s. Most notably, in 1972 the FCC issued sweeping new rules based on a "consensus agreement" designed to replace the freeze on cable growth with a more permissive (albeit still highly restrictive) regulatory regime. At the same time, the FCC began to intrude into areas traditionally reserved to municipal authorities, requiring that all cable operators obtain certificates from the FCC and establishing minimum criteria that a franchising authority must meet before such a certificate

---

4   This order was affirmed on judicial review (*Black Hills Video Corp. v. FCC*, 399 F.2d 65 (8th Cir. 1968)).

5   *United States v. Sw. Cable Co.*, 392 U.S. 157, 167–78 (1968).

would be issued, including most notably for our purposes a minimum degree of rate regulation and a minimum level of access requirements (FCC 1972).[6]

This heightened level of interest would soon prove to be short-lived. Beginning in 1974, the FCC soon began issuing a series of orders leading to federal deregulation of cable television. Most importantly for our purposes, in 1976 the FCC eliminated the federal standards governing rate regulation and instead left those decisions to local authorities (FCC 1976b). The FCC initially retained the access requirements, with some modifications, only to abandon these requirements as well the following year (FCC 1976a, 1977). Ambiguity about the federal–municipal division of jurisdiction led to a patchwork of often inconsistent regulation[7] as well as additional Supreme Court decisions about the proper scope of federal authority.[8] Widespread criticism emerged about the ineffectiveness and abuses of the local regulatory process.[9]

At this point, the central locus of federal regulation shifted from the FCC to Congress when it enacted the Communications Policy Act of 1984. The 1984 Act endorsed the existing regime of dual regulation by giving the FCC explicit statutory authority to regulate the cable industry while simultaneously recognizing municipalities' discretion over whether to include certain types of access mandates as franchise conditions. At the same time, the 1984 Act preempted local regulation of cable rates and services (*Statutes at Large* 1984, pp. 2782–84, 2788, 2801). The D.C. Circuit invalidated must carry the following year,[10] and the FCC's subsequent attempt to revive it failed in 1988.[11] The invalidation of must carry and sharp increases in cable prices caused Congress to backtrack somewhat in 1992, when it reinstated cable rate regulation and mandated must carry as a statutory matter. At the same time, it strengthened leased access and limited municipal authority by prohibiting the issuance of exclusive franchises (*Statutes at Large* 1992, pp. 1465–66, 1471–82, 1484–85). Congress reversed course again when it included provisions in the Telecommunications Act of 1996 once again deregulating cable rates (*Statutes at Large* 1996, p. 116).

---

6 This order was affirmed on judicial review (*ACLU v. FCC*, 523 F.2d 1344 (9th Cir. 1975)).

7 FCC (1972); U.S. Senate (1983); U.S. House (1984).

8 See, e.g., *City of New York v. FCC*, 486 U.S. 57 (1988) (upholding federal preemption of state regulation of cable signal quality standards); *Capital Cities Cable, Inc. v. Crisp*, 467 U.S. 691, 704, 698–711 (1984) (upholding federal preemption of state regulation of carriage of cable signals and invalidating state regulation of cable advertising as inconsistent with federal regulation); *Cmty. Commc'ns Co., Inc. v. City of Boulder*, 455 U.S. 40, 48–49 (1982) (holding that the city's three-year moratorium on cable system expansion was not immune to federal antitrust scrutiny); *FCC v. Midwest Video Corp.*, 440 U.S. 689 (1979) (invalidating federal leased access requirement for exceeding the FCC's authority).

9 See, e.g., Sloan Commission on Cable Communications (1971); Barnett (1972).

10 *Quincy Cable TV, Inc. v. FCC*, 768 F.2d 1434, 1440–43 (D.C. Cir. 1985).

11 FCC 1986b, *pet. for review granted sub nom. Century Commc'ns Corp. v. FCC*, 835 F.2d 292, 296–97 (D.C. Cir. 1987), *clarified*, 837 F.2d 517 (D.C. Cir. 1988).

The regulation of cable modem service followed a similar pattern. The FCC repeatedly declined to resolve the regulatory classification that it thought should apply to cable, let alone decide the scope of any access obligations that might apply, with its reluctance to do so drawing a rebuke from two members of the Supreme Court.[12] In the absence of a clear assertion of federal authority, several municipal regulatory authorities attempted to exert jurisdiction over cable modem systems, either by mandating access to those systems by municipal ordinance[13] or as a condition for the transfer of licenses needed to complete the wave of major mergers that swept through the cable industry between 1999 and 2002.[14] This municipal-based strategy was soon cut short by a series of judicial decisions holding that federal law prevented municipal franchising authorities from exercising jurisdiction over cable modem systems.[15]

The FCC finally addressed the proper regulatory classification of cable modem service in its 2002 *Cable Modem Declaratory Ruling*, in which it determined that cable modem service was an interstate "information service" that fell outside both the common carriage regulations established under Title II of the Communications Act of 1934 to govern telecommunications services and the regulatory regime established by Title VI to govern cable television services. Instead, cable modem systems fell within the FCC's general rulemaking authority under the agency's Title I ancillary jurisdiction. In exercising this ancillary jurisdiction, the FCC declined to impose the tariffing and unbundling requirements created by the *Computer Inquiries* to cable modem systems, noting that the agency previously "has applied these obligations only to traditional wireline services and facilities, and has never applied them to information services provided over cable facilities" (FCC 2002c, pp. 4820–39). These aspects of the FCC's decision were sustained by the Supreme Court's 2005 decision in *Brand X* (545 U.S. at 1001).

Declaring that cable modem systems constituted information services did not resolve exactly how cable modem systems would be regulated. On the contrary, the FCC specifically sought comment on what, if any, access requirements it should impose on cable modem service. Also, concerned that a patchwork of inconsistent state and local regulation could discourage investment and innovation, the FCC sought comment on whether it should preempt state regulation, including access requirements (FCC 2002c). Until the agency addresses the issue directly, the possibility remains that state and local authorities will exercise concurrent jurisdiction over cable modem service that leaves them free to mandate access. That said, because services classified as information services in the past had been subject to

12  *Gulf Power*, 534 U.S. at 348–49, 353–56, & nn. 5–6 (Thomas, J., joined by Souter, J., concurring in part and dissenting in part).
13  See, e.g., *Comcast Cablevision of Broward County, Inc. v. Broward County*, 124 F. Supp. 2d 685, 686–87 (S.D. Fla. 2000).
14  See, e.g., *MediaOne Group, Inc. v. County of Henrico*, 257 F.3d 356, 360 (4th Cir. 2001); *City of Portland*, 216 F.3d at 875.
15  See *MediaOne*, 257 F.3d at 363–64; *City of Portland*, 216 F.3d at 878–79.

minimal regulatory requirements, classifying cable modem service as an information service was thus generally regarded as a signal that the FCC was unlikely to impose any access requirements. In addition, the fact that the FCC had preempted state regulation in the *Computer Inquiries* also suggested that to many the FCC was likely to do the same with respect to cable modem services.[16]

## 2. Regulation of Digital Subscriber Lines

The other principal technology for providing last-mile broadband Internet service is known as DSL. DSL takes advantage of the fact that conventional voice communications only occupy the lower transmission frequencies (typically those ranging from 300 to 3,400 hertz). It is thus possible to use the higher frequencies (i.e., those above 20,000 hertz) to convey data communications through the same telephone line without interfering with voice communications.

Several technical changes must be made to a local telephone network before it can be used for DSL. First, it is not uncommon for incumbent LECs to have added devices to their loops, such as bridge taps, low-pass filters, and range extenders, that are designed to improve the quality of voice calls. Unfortunately, these devices also interfere with the provision of DSL service. Thus, before loops can be used for DSL, they must be "conditioned" by removing all of these devices. In addition, for a single telephone line to be used to carry both voice and data traffic, the network owner must install equipment in its central office to separate voice traffic from data traffic. This typically involves the installation of a device known as a digital subscriber line access multiplexer (DSLAM). The relevant loops are connected to the DSLAM, which routes voice communications into a conventional circuit-switched network and routes data communications into a packet-switched network. The fact that resistance increases with the length of the copper wire places a natural limit on the range of DSL. For asymmetric DSL, which is the most commonly deployed DSL technology, customers must be located no farther than twelve to eighteen thousand feet from the DSLAM. For faster DSL technologies, such as very high-data-rate digital subscriber line (VDSL), customers must be located no more than four thousand feet from the DSLAM (see Figure 10.2).

This scenario changes somewhat in situations in which a local telephone company has deployed a technology known as digital loop carriers (DLCs). Instead of using an all-copper loop to transmit analog signals between the central office and the customer's premises, DLC systems use fiber optics to establish a digital connection between the central office and a satellite facility known as a remote terminal, where the transmission is converted into an analog format and distributed to the customer's premises through a copper subloop.[17] The improved efficiency and

---

16 See, e.g., Kiser and Collins (2003); Nakahata (2002).

17 For simplicity, Figure 10.3 omits the fact that remote terminals are actually deployed in a ring configuration.

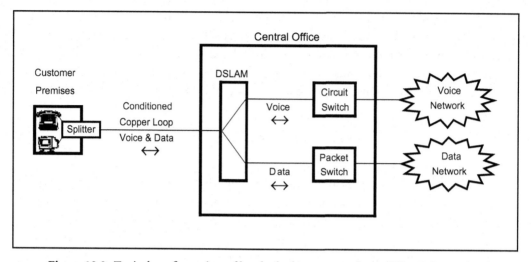

**Figure 10.2.** Typical configuration of local telephone network providing DSL service.

range provided by the fiber optic connection greatly enhance the performance and quality of voice transmissions. DLCs, however, can impede the deployment of DSL. This is because DSL depends on the ability to send and receive signals in an analog format through an all-copper connection. Because the portion of the DLC system between the central office and the remote terminal employs digital transmissions through a fiber optic connection, local telephone companies that wish to provide DSL service on a network containing DLCs must either deploy DSLAMs in remote terminals, which also increases the number of end users potentially served by DSL by reducing the distance between the DSLAM and individual customers, or find an alternative copper loop running between the customer and the central office (see Figure 10.3).

In stark contrast to the tentativeness of the FCC's regulatory approach to cable modems, the agency did not hesitate to assert jurisdiction over DSL. From the

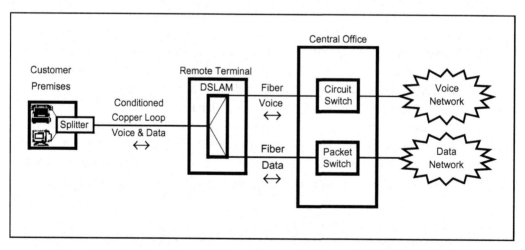

**Figure 10.3.** Configuration of DSL service provided through digital loop carriers.

beginning, the FCC concluded that DSL was analogous to private-line services offering dedicated connections providing direct access to long distance providers. So long as interstate traffic represented more than ten percent of the total traffic, DSL was properly tariffed at the federal level and not at the state level (FCC 1998e). The net result was that DSL was typically offered as a tariffed service (FCC 1999h).

The FCC has also wrestled with how to apply the Telecommunications Act of 1996 to the Internet, which Congress all but ignored when enacting the legislation. The major access provisions of the 1996 Act applied only to incumbent local telephone companies that provided "telephone exchange service," which is the use of the local telephone network to reach other local customers, or "exchange access," which is the use of the local telephone network to connect to long distance providers to reach long distance customers. The FCC's *Advanced Services Order* concluded that DSL service constituted either telephone exchange service or exchange access (without resolving into which category DSL service fell) and thus was subject to the 1996 Act's resale, interconnection, UNE access, and collocation mandates. The order also initiated a rulemaking seeking comment on precisely how to apply these resale, unbundling, and collocation requirements and proposing that DSL be allowed to avoid the restrictions imposed incumbent local telephone companies so long as they provided service through a separate subsidiary (FCC 1998f). After US West sought judicial review of the *Advanced Service Order*, the FCC moved to remand the matter voluntarily so that it could consider the arguments raised in US West's brief.[18] On remand, the FCC reaffirmed its conclusion that DSL represented either telephone exchange service or exchange access (FCC 1999f). On judicial review, the D.C. Circuit vacated and remanded the order. Agency and judicial precedent dictated that telephone exchange service and exchange access represent exclusive categories that occupy the entire field and thus that traffic had to be classified as either local or long distance. The FCC's failure to resolve into which category DSL properly fell represented a want of reasoned decisionmaking sufficient to justify invalidating the agency's action (*WorldCom, Inc. v. FCC*, 246 F.3d 690, 695–96 (D.C. Cir. 2001)).

The FCC has also struggled to determine precisely which DSL-related network elements are subject to the 1996 Act's UNE access requirements. Initially, the agency adopted a permissive, if somewhat grudging, stance. Because the statute limits UNE access to elements used in telephone exchange service and exchange access, the initial order implementing the 1996 Act declined to subject packet switches to UNE access requirements and ruled that collocation did not extend to equipment used to provide enhanced services, although it included multifunction equipment supporting both conventional telephone and enhanced services so long as it was necessary to providing conventional telephone service. Furthermore, any company obtaining interconnection or UNE access to provide telecommunications services may offer information services through the same arrangement. The order did

18 US West Communications, Inc. v. FCC, No. 98–1410 (D.C. Cir. Aug. 25, 1999).

mandate UNE access to all loops connecting central offices to end users, including the loops used to provide DSL. The order obligated incumbent local telephone companies to fulfill any requests to condition existing loops to make them DSL-compatible (FCC 1996c). A subsequent order confirmed that collocation included multifunction equipment that could be used to provide both voice and data services (FCC 1999c). Perhaps most importantly, the FCC's *Line Sharing Order* mandated UNE access to the high-frequency portion of the loop used to carry DSL so that two competitors could provide services over the same loop, with one offering conventional telephone service and the other offering DSL (FCC 2000c).

The courts soon began to question the breadth of the FCC's rulings, beginning with the Supreme Court's decision in *AT&T v. Iowa Utilities Board*, which remanded the initial UNE access rules for construing the "necessary" and "impair" standards too broadly (525 U.S. 366, 387–92 (1999)). On remand, the FCC reiterated that incumbent local telephone companies must condition DSL loops upon request. Although UNE access to loops generally included all attached electronics, the FCC specifically excepted packet switches and DSLAMs, on the grounds that the incumbents did not maintain a monopoly position with respect to these functions and that granting UNE access to them would deter investment in a nascent market. The FCC did permit UNE access to DSLAMs located in remote terminals that were too small to permit physical collocation (FCC 1999g).

In 2000, the D.C. Circuit struck down the FCC's decision permitting the collocation of multifunction equipment as a violation of the statutory provision authorizing collocation only if "necessary for interconnection or access to unbundled network elements" (*GTE Serv. Corp. v. FCC*, 205 F.3d 416, 422–24 (D.C. Cir. 2000), quoting 47 U.S.C. § 251(c)(6)). In response, the FCC revised its rules in 2001 to limit collocation of multifunction equipment to equipment whose primary purpose is to provide the requesting carrier either with interconnection that is "equal in quality" to that provided by the incumbent LEC for its own services or with "nondiscriminatory access" to an unbundled network element, a revision that survived judicial review (FCC 2001e). These revisions to the collocation rules were sufficient to survive judicial scrutiny (*Verizon Tel. Cos. v. FCC*, 292 F.3d 903 (D.C. Cir. 2002)).

These judicial decisions led the FCC to retreat from extending the regulatory regime applicable to conventional telephone service to DSL and other wireline broadband technologies. In 2002, shortly before adopting its *Cable Modem Declaratory Ruling*, the FCC issued its *Wireline Broadband NPRM*, which tentatively concluded that DSL and other broadband services provided by local telephone companies constituted "information services" that were not subject to the tariffing and common carriage requirements of Title II. At the same time, the FCC sought comment on whether changes in technology and the competitive environment justified modifying or eliminating the regulatory regime it had created under its general Title I authority in its *Computer Inquiries* (FCC 2002b). Later in 2002, the FCC detariffed DSL services that SBC offered through its separate subsidiary (FCC 2002e).

In 2002, the D.C. Circuit also struck down the FCC's decision requiring line sharing, reasoning that the FCC's findings that DSL faced robust competition from cable modem providers meant that line sharing violated the "necessary" and "impair" requirements of the 1996 Act (*United States Telecom Ass'n v. FCC*, 290 F.3d 415, 428–29 (D.C. Cir. 2002)). This led to further deregulation of DSL in the FCC's landmark *Triennial Review Order* in 2003, which eliminated line sharing and lifted UNE access obligations to most high-capacity loops. The FCC also eliminated the limited exceptions it had recognized for UNE access to DSLAMs and other packet switching equipment (FCC 2003d). This decision was affirmed in relevant part by the D.C. Circuit (*U.S. Telecom Ass'n v. FCC*, 359 F.3d 554, 578–85 (D.C. Cir. 2004)).

Finally, in 2005, the FCC issued its *Wireline Broadband Internet Access Services Order* (2005d), which as of now represents the most complete statement of the FCC's last-mile broadband policy. This order in effect extended to DSL the same reasoning followed with respect to cable modem service by the FCC's *Cable Modem Declaratory Ruling* and endorsed by the Supreme Court in *Brand X*. The FCC ruled that DSL and other broadband services provided by local telephone companies constitute information services that are not subject to Title II's common carriage and tariffing requirements. In addition, the order eliminated all *Computer Inquiry* requirements with respect to all broadband technologies used to provide Internet service, although this ruling did not extend them to broadband technologies used to provide traditional telephone service, such as frame relay services, standalone asynchronous transfer mode (ATM) services, and gigabit Ethernet services.[19]

Since the *Wireline Broadband Internet Access Services Order*, the FCC has taken additional steps to deregulate broadband services provided by local telephone companies. For example, the FCC has granted waivers giving Verizon, AT&T, and Qwest pricing flexibility for certain business-oriented broadband technologies subject to price cap regulation (FCC 2005f, 2007b, 2007c). Most importantly, the FCC has granted waivers to both Verizon and AT&T deregulating the broadband services still subject to the *Computer Inquiry* rules following the *Wireline Broadband Internet Access Services Order* on the grounds that wireline broadband services face enough competition from other providers to justify no longer subjecting them to retail access requirements (FCC 2006d, 2007e). The net result is the removal of most of the remaining retail access requirements on broadband services provided by local telephone companies.

### 3. The Debate over Network Neutrality

During the Internet's initial, narrowband phase of development, Internet service providers (ISPs) pursued a variety of architectural approaches. Some ISPs, such as CompuServe, Prodigy, and America Online, initially adopted relatively restrictive

---

19 The *Wireline Broadband Internet Access Services Order* was sustained on judicial review (*Time Warner Telecom, Inc. v. FCC*, 507 F.3d 205 (3d Cir. 2007)).

policies, which only provided end users with access to proprietary applications and content and charged them for network usage on a per-minute basis. Others followed a more permissive approach, opening up their networks to all content and applications providers on a nondiscriminatory basis and allowing end users to download any content, run any application, and attach any device for a flat monthly fee. The latter approach ultimately proved more attractive to consumers, and end users became accustomed to a world in which they faced few restrictions either on the ways they could use their network connections or on the amount of bandwidth they consumed.

This same debate has resurfaced as the Internet has begun to migrate from a narrowband to a broadband architecture. Once again, network owners have begun to experiment with more restrictive approaches. Some cable modem systems began entering into exclusive arrangements with one particular ISP. The merger between America Online and Time Warner raised the specter that the merged company would turn the second largest provider of cable modem service into a "walled garden" through which customers could not reach nonproprietary content.

Parties began to request that the FCC require cable modem providers to open their networks to more than one ISP (an issue initially called "open access" and eventually known as "multiple ISP access") as a condition for obtaining regulatory clearance for several major cable industry mergers, including most notably AT&T's 1999 acquisition of TCI, AT&T's 2000 acquisition of MediaOne, America Online's 2001 acquisition of Time Warner, and AT&T's 2002 sale of its cable assets to Comcast. The FCC also sought comment on multiple ISP access in its 2000 *Cable Modem Notice of Inquiry* (FCC 2000d).

The FCC took somewhat inconsistent positions with respect to these requests to impose multiple ISP access. In 1999 and 2000, the FCC declined to require multiple ISP access as a condition of AT&T's acquisitions of TCI and MediaOne (FCC 1999b, 2000a). In 2001, however, the FTC and the FCC imposed just such a requirement when approving America Online's acquisition of Time Warner (FTC 2000, FCC 2001a). The FCC returned to its initial position in 2002 when it again declined to require multiple ISP access when approving Comcast's acquisition of AT&T's cable assets (FCC 2002d). When issuing its *Cable Modem Declaratory Ruling and NPRM* in 2002 ruling that cable modem was an information service, the FCC declined to resolve the issue, instead asking parties to refresh the record and to clarify their positions (FCC 2002c). At roughly the same time, the FCC sought comment on whether it should impose multiple ISP access on DSL systems (FCC 2002b).

During these regulatory proceedings, numerous parties submitted comments addressing the issue of multiple ISP access (FCC 2002c, Yoo 2004b). At the same time, two coalitions of content providers, software companies, and device manufacturers proposed a series of "connectivity principles" that would prohibit network operators from restricting end users' ability to access content, run applications, or attach devices, provided that the end users' activities did not harm the network, enable theft of services, or exceed the bandwidth limitations of the particular service plan (High Tech Broadband Coalition 2002; Coalition of Broadband Users and Innovators 2003). Professors Tim Wu and Lawrence Lessig (2003) submitted a similar proposal.

In 2004, then-FCC Chairman Michael Powell called upon the industry to voluntarily embrace a series of "Internet freedoms" that would ensure end users' ability to access content, use applications, and attach personal devices, subject only to restrictions needed to manage networks, ensure quality experiences, prevent disruption of the network, and prevent theft of service,[20] although subsequent comments have made clear that Powell would not support turning his Internet freedoms into a regulatory mandate (*B2Day* 2006). Concerns about network neutrality were heightened still further when a small local telephone company known as Madison River Communications blocked its DSL customers from using the ports needed to access Internet telephony (also known as voice over Internet protocol or VoIP) (FCC 2005b). Aside from this isolated incident, little evidence emerged that last-mile broadband providers were blocking or degrading end user access to any content.[21] Indeed, even network neutrality proponents concede that such reports remain "isolated."[22]

The FCC finally addressed these concerns shortly after *Brand X* sustained its conclusion that broadband technologies constitute information services that are governed by the agency's Title I ancillary jurisdiction. In its 2005 *Wireline Broadband Internet Access Services Order*, the FCC declined to mandate nondiscriminatory access to content and applications providers, finding insufficient evidence to justify imposing such a restriction. The FCC pledged to continue monitoring market developments and reserved the right to change its mind should circumstances warrant doing so (FCC 2005d). At the same time, the FCC issued a policy statement recognizing its intention to preserve consumers' rights to access content, run applications, and attach devices as they see fit (FCC 2005e).

These steps were not sufficient to placate network neutrality proponents' concerns. The policy statement recognized an exception for "reasonable network

20  Powell (2004). Chairman Powell also called for the industry to provide consumers with clear and meaningful information regarding the terms of their broadband service plans.

21  The *Boston Globe* (2003) quotes FCC Commissioner Jonathan Adelstein acknowledging the lack of evidence that last-mile providers were limiting end users' ability to access content and calling network neutrality "a solution awaiting a problem." *CNET News.com* (2003) quotes FCC Chairman Michael Powell as stating, "I don't know yet that I see anything that says we need a rulemaking on [network neutrality]." The *Wall Street Journal* (2005b) quotes FCC Chairman Kevin Martin as saying, "'We haven't seen any evidence of this being a problem.'" *InformationWeek* (2006) quotes former FCC Chairman Michael Powell as saying that there were "no perceptible transgressions" against network neutrality.

22  U.S. Senate (2006a). The *Wall Street Journal* (2005b) notes that "Congressional proponents of net-neutrality legislation acknowledge that it isn't a problem now."

management" and explicitly acknowledged that it has no legal effect until incorporated into formal rules (FCC 2005e, p. 14988 n. 15). In addition, the statement released by FCC Chairman Kevin Martin in conjunction with the policy statement expressed his confidence that competition would remain sufficiently robust so that such regulation would prove unnecessary (Martin 2005). In subsequent statements, Chairman Martin indicated that although he would oppose any attempt to completely block access to particular content and applications, he would not oppose allowing networks to charge content and applications providers for different tiers of service (*National Journal's Insider Update* 2006). The continuing controversy ultimately became front-page news in *The Wall Street Journal* (2005b), which predicted that the issue would be of major concern when Congress began its consideration of proposals to overhaul the communications laws. A number of national media outlets published editorials and opinion pieces on both sides of the issue.[23]

Network neutrality emerged as one of the hottest issues in communications policy and became the most controversial issue in Congress's consideration of major telecommunications reform legislation in 2006. On the House side, proposed legislation with strong bipartisan support that included a network neutrality provision unraveled, and House Republicans, with the support of a small group of House Democrats, began to push forward a bill that did not contain a network neutrality provision. The House Subcommittee on Telecommunications and the Internet voted 8–23 and the House Energy and Commerce Committee voted 22–34 to reject amendments that would have added a broad network neutrality mandate to the bill. After House Speaker Dennis Hastert denied the House Judiciary Committee's request for concurrent jurisdiction over the legislation, the House Judiciary Committee favorably reported on a different measure that would have incorporated network neutrality into the federal antitrust laws, only to attempt to offer that bill as an amendment blocked by the House Rules Committee. When the full House debated the version of the legislation reported by the House Commerce Committee on June 8, it rejected a network neutrality amendment offered by Rep. Edward Markey by a vote of 152–269 before approving the entire bill by a vote of 321–101.

Network neutrality proved even more controversial on the Senate side. The Senate Commerce Committee conducted hearings on network neutrality in February 2006 (U.S. Senate 2006a) and eventually rejected a network neutrality amendment by a vote of 11–11. The Senate Judiciary Committee also conducted hearings in June and engaged in active discussions with the leadership of the Senate Commerce

---

23  For editorials favoring network neutrality, see *Business Week* (2005); *Christian Science Monitor* (2006); *New York Times* (2006); *Newsweek* (2006); *San Francisco Chronicle* (2006); *San Jose Mercury News* (2006). For editorials opposing network neutrality, see *CED Magazine* (2006); *Reason Online* (2006); *Wall Street Journal* (2006); *Washington Post* (2006).

Committee as to whether network neutrality could be addressed through antitrust (U.S. Senate 2006b; *Congress Daily PM* 2006). The legislation died at the end of the 109th Congress after the full Senate failed to act on any of these proposals. Senators Byron Dorgan and Olympia Snowe reintroduced standalone network neutrality legislation in 2007, which languished in Committee (U.S. Senate 2007).

Other policymakers began to focus attention on the issue as well. In a major policy speech, FTC Chairman Deborah Platt Majoras "urge[d] caution" and warned of the dangers of mandating network neutrality "absent clear evidence of market failure or consumer harm" (Majoras 2006, p. 15). At the same time, the Federal Trade Commission formed an Internet Access Task Force to study issue, which conducted two days of hearings in February 2007 and issued a report recommending that policymakers should hesitate before mandating network neutrality in the absence of a clear demonstration of market failure or consumer harm (FTC 2007). The U.S. Justice Department (2007) has adopted a similar position, noting the absence of evidence of harmful practices and pointing out how imposing restrictions prophylactically can foreclose practices that would benefit consumers.

The FCC continued to address the issue as well, most notably when clearing Verizon's acquisition of MCI and SBC's acquisition of AT&T in 2005, the disposition of Adelphia's cable properties in 2006, and AT&T's acquisition of BellSouth in 2007. In each case, the FCC reaffirmed its 2005 decision not to mandate that last-mile broadband providers offer nondiscriminatory access to content and applications providers, pointing to the lack of evidence in the record that any network provider had engaged in such practices and concluding that competition was sufficiently robust to prevent network providers from discriminating against any particular content or applications (FCC 2005g, 2005h, 2006a, 2007a). In March 2007, the FCC issued a notice of inquiry seeking specific examples of network providers disfavoring particular content and seeking comment on the impact of any such behavior on consumers (FCC 2007d).

In late 2007, news outlets began to report that Comcast was taking steps to limit the bandwidth consumed by certain peer-to-peer applications such as BitTorrent (see, e.g., *Seattle Times* 2007). Two advocacy organizations and an online video distributor that relied on BitTorrent filed separate complaints with the FCC challenging these practices. On March 27, 2008, while the FCC was considering these complaints, Comcast and BitTorrent announced that they had reached an agreement to work together to resolve the problems of network congestion associated with the BitTorrent traffic. After conducting hearings at Harvard, Stanford, and Carnegie Mellon Universities, the FCC ruled in August 2008 that Comcast's actions contravened its 2005 policy statement in ways that did not fall within the exception for reasonable network management. Accordingly, it gave Comcast 30 days to submit a compliance plan describing how it would modify its practices (FCC 2008c).

## B. The Rationales for Regulating Last-Mile Broadband Networks

The emergence of last-mile broadband technologies has a dramatic impact on the applicability of the regulatory rationales introduced in Chapter 4. The competition in last-mile services made possible by digital convergence opens up the policy space in important ways and undercuts many of the classic bases for regulation. In addition, the increased importance on investment incentives, the complexity of the relevant interfaces, and the rapid pace of technological change also effect fundamental changes to the policy analysis.

### 1. Natural Monopoly

The FCC has noted, "At the time the *Computer Inquiry* rules were adopted, there was an implicit, if not explicit, assumption that the incumbent wireline platform would remain the only network platform available to enhanced service providers" (FCC 2005d, p. 14877).[24] In short, previous regulation mandating access to last-mile broadband services was based largely on the presumption that last-mile broadband services constituted a natural monopoly.

Scholars have long debated whether local telephone companies or local cable operators have represented *intra*modal natural monopolies. The debate over whether local telephone service represented a natural monopoly is discussed in Chapter 8 and will not be reviewed here. A similar disagreement exists with respect to cable television. Because local distribution of cable programming required the deployment of a network of wires as extensive as that required to establish local telephone service, it too was generally regarded as a natural monopoly.[25] This led municipal and federal regulators to impose rate regulation, entry restrictions, access obligations, and a wide variety of other regulations (Brenner 1990). The Justice Department justified its decision not to oppose mergers between competing cable systems by its conclusion that cable was a natural monopoly (U.S. Department of Justice 1985, quoted in Manishin 1987, p. 87). Courts have also invoked the natural monopoly rationale when sustaining cable regulations against a variety of legal challenges.[26]

Other scholars have questioned whether the cost functions of the cable industry exhibited sufficient natural monopoly characteristics to justify entry restrictions and

---

24  See also *Brand X*, 545 U.S. at 1001; FCC (2002b, 2003c).

25  See, e.g., Cabinet Committee on Cable Communications (1974); Webb (1983); Noam (1985).

26  *Lamb Enters. v. Toledo Blade Co.*, 461 F.2d 506, 511 (6th Cir. 1972); *Cmty. Commc'ns Corp. v. City of Boulder*, 660 F.2d 1370, 1378–79 (10th Cir. 1981); *Omega Satellite Prods. v. City of Indianapolis*, 694 F.2d 119, 126 (7th Cir. 1982); *Hopkinsville Cable TV, Inc. v. Pennyroyal Cablevision, Inc.*, 562 F. Supp. 543, 547 (W.D. Ky. 1982); *Berkshire Cablevision of R.I., Inc. v. Burke*, 571 F. Supp. 976, 985–86 (D.R.I. 1983); *Erie Telecomms., Inc. v. City of Erie*, 659 F. Supp. 580, 586 (W.D. Pa. 1987), *aff'd*, 853 F.2d 1084 (3d Cir. 1988); see also *Affiliated Capital Corp. v. City of Houston*, 735 F.2d 1555, 1563 (5th Cir. 1984) (accepting as true the allegation that cable was a natural monopoly).

rate regulation[27] and have debated whether some alternative institutional regime, such as franchise bidding, might redress any problems that might arise.[28] Some courts have followed suit, questioning whether cable was a natural monopoly.[29] The three cases in which full trials were conducted on whether cable represents a natural monopoly split on the issue, with the first jury concluding that it was not a natural monopoly[30] and the second and third juries drawing the opposite conclusion.[31]

Most importantly for our purposes, commentators began to suggest that inter-modal competition from broadcasters and local telephone companies might provide sufficient competition to vitiate cable's natural monopoly status.[32] Consistent with this insight, a provision of the Cable Communications Policy Act of 1984 authorized the FCC to determine when cable operators face effective competition sufficient to justify eliminating rate regulation (*Statutes at Large* 1984, p. 2788). The FCC initially ruled that broadcasting could represent effective competition to cable sufficient to justify lifting rate regulation, while also ruling that cable operators faced effective competition if another cable provider could provide service to 50% of the homes in any service area and actually provided service to 10% of those homes.[33] Congress

27 Hazlett (1986) concludes that cable television is probably not a natural monopoly and that even if it is, the benefits from temporary competition probably outweigh the costs of permitting entry. Lee (1983) notes the lack of empirical proof that cable television is a natural monopoly and warns of the dangers of improper market definition. Owen and Greenhalgh (1986) conclude that the scale economies in cable are not sufficiently substantial to preclude the possibility of competition.

28 Posner (1973) argues that periodic auctioning of cable franchises can replace rate regulation. Williamson (1976) identifies contracting problems with Posner's proposal and providing an empirical example in which franchise bidding was not superior to regulation. Zupan (1989) discusses possible solutions to contracting problems and provides more systematic empirical evidence supporting Posner's claim.

29 *Quincy Cable Television, Inc. v. FCC*, 768 F.2d 1434, 1449–50 (D.C. Cir. 1985) (questioning the natural monopoly rationale for regulating cable); *Cmty. Commc'ns Co. v. City of Boulder*, 485 F. Supp. 1035, 1039–40 (D. Colo.), *rev'd*, 603 F.2d 704 (10th Cir. 1980), *rev'd*, 455 U.S. 40 (1982) (disagreeing that the evidence showed that cable television was a natural monopoly); *Cmty. Commc'ns Co.*, 603 F.2d at 712 (Markey, C.J., dissenting) (expressing his agreement with the district court's conclusion); see also *Preferred Commc'ns, Inc. v. City of Los Angeles*, 754 F.2d 1396, 1404 (9th Cir. 1985) (accepting as true allegation that sufficient economic demand existed to support more than one cable operator), *aff'd*, 476 U.S. 488, 493–94 (1986) (same); *Tele-Commc'ns of Key West, Inc. v. United States*, 757 F.2d 1330, 1335–36 (D.C. Cir. 1985) (same).

30 *Pac. W. Cable Co. v. City of Sacramento*, 672 F. Supp. 1322, 1328, 1339, 1349 (E.D. Cal. 1987).

31 *Nor-W. Cable Commc'ns P'ship v. City of St. Paul*, No. 3–83 Civ. 1228, 1998 WL 241122 (D. Minn. June 10, 1988); *Central Telecomms., Inc. v. TCI Cablevision, Inc.*, 610 F. Supp. 891, 901 & n.33, 908 (W.D. Mo. 1985), *aff'd*, 800 F.2d 711, 713–18 (8th Cir. 1986).

32 Noam (1983); Shapiro et al. (1983).

33 The FCC initially ruled that cable operators face effective competition whenever they face competition from at least three over-the-air broadcast stations, which effectively eliminated rate regulation for 96.5 percent of all cable systems (FCC 1985b, *aff'd sub nom. ACLU v. FCC*, 823 F.2d 1554, 1564–65 (D.C. Cir. 1987)). The FCC later raised the threshold of effective competition

overruled the FCC with respect to whether broadcasting could serve as effective competition, but ratified the decision that cable operators might face competition from other multichannel video providers (while raising the threshold of homes actually served to 15%) (*Statutes at Large* 1992, p. 1470). The fact that DBS has now captured more than 30% of the market has led to widescale deregulation of cable rates. As of January 1, 2005, competition had already been sufficient to eliminate rate regulation in more than 1,000 cable communities (FCC 2006c).

The insight that intermodal competition can eliminate natural monopoly has even stronger implications for broadband data networks. The shift to digital transmission has allowed networks that once were dedicated exclusively to voice or to video to compete with one another. Cable companies have begun to offer voice services and promote them aggressively. Telephone companies have begun to roll out fiber-based transmission networks, such as Verizon's FiOS service, and have begun to offer multichannel television. Most importantly for our purposes, digitization has allowed both telephone and cable companies to compete directly with respect to last-mile broadband services. Thus, regardless of whether cable or conventional telephone was once a natural monopoly with respect to the services they used to provide, they now clearly compete with one another.

The FCC specifically rejected the conclusion that last-mile broadband services constituted a natural monopoly in its 1999 report on broadband deployment, in which it found that "no competitor has a large embedded base of paying residential consumers" and "[t]he record does not indicate that the consumer market [for broadband services] is inherently a natural monopoly" (FCC 1999a, p. 2423). The D.C. Circuit emphasized the same point when invalidating the FCC's *Line Sharing Order* on the ground that fierce competition from cable modem service rendered the agency's conclusion that competitors would be impaired without access to the high-frequency portion of the loop unreasonable (*U.S. Telecom Ass'n*, 290 F.3d at 428–29). More recently, the FCC's *Wireline Broadband Internet Access Services Order* also noted that "broadband Internet access services have never been restricted to a single network platform," which stood "in stark contrast to the information services market at the time the *Computer Inquiry* obligations were adopted, when only a single platform capable of delivering such services was contemplated and only a single facilities-based provider of that platform was available to deliver them to any particular end users." Any tendencies toward natural monopoly are further alleviated by the increase in demand created by innovative broadband service offerings. The presence of such intermodal competition, combined with the growth of demand, eliminated the need for the access requirements imposed by the *Computer Inquiries* (FCC 2005d).

In short, the emergence of intermodal competition eviscerates claims that any particular last-mile broadband service is a natural monopoly. The natural monopoly

to six over-the-air stations, which effectively limited rate deregulation to 30 percent of all cable subscribers (FCC 1991a).

justification would thus appear to have little purchase with respect to last-mile broadband services. Instead, the ultimate market structure is likely to have a degree of competition, although the data suggest that such competition might be limited to three players. Such oligopolistic competition would nonetheless alter the policy balance in significant ways. When the alternatives are regulated and unregulated monopoly, the large welfare losses associated with monopoly pricing can arguably justify regulation despite the well-recognized defects and distortions that plague direct regulation of prices. When the decision shifts to a choice between regulated and unregulated oligopoly, the policy balance is quite different. Theoretical and economic research has shown that oligopolies, although still falling short of the competitive ideal, perform far better than monopolies, to the point where the policy balance shifts away from ex ante regulation (Nakahata 2002; Shelanski 2007).

## 2. Network Economic Effects

Some commentators have invoked network economic effects as a justification for regulating access to last-mile broadband networks. The classic argument is that network economic effects give the early leaders in the broadband marketplace (i.e., cable modem providers) a decisive advantage. Because the value of the network increases with the number of others users connected to the network, new customers will flock to the technology that gets off to the fastest start, with the subsequent increase in network size causing the advantages created by network economic effects to increase still further. These demand-side scale economies allow cable modem providers to exercise market power against end users. At the same time, so the argument goes, the deployment of proprietary protocols can exercise market power against providers of complementary services, such as applications and content, by increasing the costs of serving more than one market. Once that early technology becomes established, network economic effects may cause customers and content/applications providers to become locked in despite the emergence of subsequent competition from DSL (Hausman et al. 2001).

Mark Lemley and Lawrence Lessig (2001) invoke similar concerns when they emphasize how much content and applications providers benefit from interoperable architectures that allow them to reach the widest customer base possible. The early lead established by cable modem providers can give them the power to harm competition. Specifically, the deployment of proprietary protocols can allow cable modem providers to act strategically to chill innovation in content and applications by reducing the number of end users who can be reached through a single network. In so arguing, they emphasize the early lead taken by cable modem systems, as well as cable modem's advantages in delivering high-bandwidth applications such as video (see also Lessig 2002).

As we noted in Chapter 4, concerns about existing market share are largely misplaced in markets undergoing rapid growth. As the theoretical literature emphasizes, equilibria in markets subject to network economic effects depend not on current market shares, but rather on the market structure after the market has reached maturity. Put a different way, lock-in is unlikely to occur when competitors can compete for new customers.

More fundamentally, the extensiveness of the literature analyzing how refusals to interconnect can harm competition often overshadows the fact that the primary impact of network economic effects is to provide powerful incentives for network owners to interconnect with one another. Furthermore, as we note in Chapter 4, the models in which network economic effects enable network owners to harm competition presume that the market is an oligopoly or dominated by a single firm. Competition among a sufficient number of equally sized players should be sufficient to eliminate any anticompetitive incentives to refuse to interconnect.

Indeed, the FCC's *Wireline Broadband Internet Access Services Order* took these considerations into account when it rejected arguments based on current market data as "limited and static" and incomplete for "fail[ing] to recognize the dynamic nature of marketplace forces." Emerging markets such as broadband are "more appropriately analyzed in view of larger trends in the marketplace, rather than exclusively through the snapshot data that may quickly and predictably be rendered obsolete as this market continues to evolve." In particular, at the time of the order, broadband penetration rates had only reached 20%, whereas industry analysts forecast that penetration would eventually reach 90%. Thus, it mattered little that the cable modem industry had taken the early lead. DSL continued to emerge as an effective competitor. In addition, "emerging broadband platforms exert competitive pressure even though they currently have few subscribers compared with cable modem service and DSL-based Internet access service." Competition among current and emerging broadband platforms provided sufficient incentives to provide access in the absence of government intervention to justify deregulation of last-mile wireline broadband networks (FCC 2005d, pp. 14880–85, 14895).

### 3. Vertical Exclusion

Calls for regulation of last-mile broadband networks often invoke the threat of vertical exclusion. Concern that local telephone companies would use their monopoly control over the local loop to discriminate against unaffiliated enhanced and information service providers represented the central concern underlying the *Computer Inquiries* as well as the initial application of the UNE access requirements of the 1996 Act to DSL. Vertical exclusion also represents the central justification for proposals for multiple ISP access to cable modem systems. It also undergirds the ongoing debate over "network neutrality" (discussed at greater length in Chapter 11 and 12), which would give content and application providers nondiscriminatory access to all last-mile broadband networks.

As we discuss in Chapter 4, certain structural preconditions must be met in order to state a claim of vertical exclusion. Specifically, the primary and secondary markets must be concentrated and protected by entry barriers before vertical exclusion can plausibly harm competition. Our foregoing discussions of the natural monopoly and network economic effects justifications for regulating last-mile broadband networks demonstrate that these structural preconditions are not satisfied. Indeed, the D.C. Circuit emphasized the emergence of intermodal competition between cable modem and DSL providers when striking down the FCC's *Line Sharing Order*. The availability of broadband access from other providers meant that the dangers of vertical exclusion were not substantial enough to justify incurring the costs of mandating UNE access to the high-frequency portion of the loop (*U.S. Telecom Ass'n*, 290 F.3d at 428–29). The FCC drew the same conclusion when eliminating line sharing on remand and refusing to mandate UNE access to the hybrid copper/fiber loops used in DLC systems (FCC 2003d).

The FCC drew similar conclusions in the *Wireline Broadband Internet Access Services Order*, which eliminated the *Computer Inquiry* rules with respect to last-mile broadband technologies used to provide Internet service. As the FCC noted, the broadband market is characterized by vibrant intermodal competition between cable modem and DSL providers. In addition, those providers faced the real prospect of entry and increased penetration by satellite, fixed wireless, and other alternative transmission technologies. In the face of such competition, last-mile broadband providers have little to gain from engaging in vertical exclusion. On the contrary, the FCC concluded that the desire to spread fixed costs over the largest revenue-base possible gives them powerful incentives to maximize the traffic on their networks by accommodating as many unaffiliated content and applications providers as possible (FCC 2005d).

In addition, an economic consensus exists that vertical integration and vertical restraints can yield substantial efficiencies that must be taken into account in any vertical analysis. As the FCC noted, regulations designed to prevent vertical exclusion by drawing a distinction between transmission and enhanced services were preventing the realization of certain technological efficiencies resulting from integrated provision of broadband services. Indeed, the *Computer Inquiry* rules were based on the now outmoded belief that "because computer processing occurred at the network's edge or outside the network, the major innovation would occur there too." The rules thus "reflect[ed] a fairly static picture of network development, and an assumption that a line could be drawn between the network functions and computer processing without impeding technological innovation." Technology had invalidated this distinction. Indeed, in the current environment, "[i]nnovation can occur at all network points and at all network layers as well as in non-network applications and equipment. Continued application of the *Computer Inquiry* rules ... would prevent much of this innovation from occurring" (FCC 2005d, p. 14890).

The industry is thus structured in such a way as to mitigate last-mile broadband providers' ability to engage in vertical exclusion. Continued measures designed to prevent vertical exclusion thus only imposed regulatory costs, deterred innovation, and threatened to prevent the network from evolving toward new architectures that depend on a tighter integration of the network's functionality and its transmission capabilities.

## 4. Managed Competition

Scholars commenting on the cable television industry have sometimes expressed concern about the ruinous competition that would result from "overbuilding," in which a second cable company would enter into an area already served by an incumbent cable company and begin to compete with it (see, e.g., Johnson and Blau 1974; Smiley 1989). The concern was that the duplication would lead to higher rates. Judge Posner echoed these concerns in a 1982 opinion upholding a city's decision to issue an exclusive cable franchise. As Posner reasoned, "This duplication may lead not only to higher prices to cable television subscribers, at least in the short run, but also to higher costs to other users of the public ways, who must compete with the cable television companies for access to them. An alternative procedure is to pick the most efficient competitor at the outset, give him a monopoly, and extract from him in exchange a commitment to provide reasonable service at reasonable rates" (*Omega Satellite Prods. Co. v. City of Indianapolis*, 694 F.2d 119, 126 (7th Cir. 1982)). Other commentators have challenged these claims, arguing that overbuilding leads to lower, not higher, prices (see, e.g., Hazlett 1990; Levin and Meisel 1991). However questionable this conclusion might have been at the time, any claims of ruinous competition have been undercut by the emergence of apparently sustainable intermodal competition from DBS.

Claims of ruinous competition appear to be even less sustainable with respect to broadband. Academic studies suggest that competition among multiple last-mile broadband providers is viable in most of the country (Faulhaber and Hogendorn 2000). The FCC has concluded, moreover, that DSL and cable modem providers are already engaged in vigorous competition and that the continuing growth of the market is likely to support entry by additional broadband technologies (FCC 2005d). The large investments currently being made in 3G, WiMax, WiFi, broadband over powerline, and other alternative broadband technologies underscore the widespread nature of the belief in the viability of alternative broadband platforms.

Other scholars offer a more limited argument in favor of managed competition through asymmetric regulation, in which some portions of the industry are subject to regulation, whereas others are not. For example, former FCC Chief Economist Joseph Farrell has argued that asymmetric regulation would permit experimentation with different policy approaches. Farrell acknowledges that asymmetric regulation "may distort market shares, investment, and other decisions," "may increase incentives for lobbying and strategic behavior of various inefficient kinds," may reduce consumer welfare, and would place regulators in the position of picking technological winners and losers, but nonetheless argues for experimentation in different regulatory forms for its own sake until policymakers have a clearer picture of what works (Farrell 2006, pp. 207–09; see also Wilkie 2004).

Another former FCC Chief Economist, William Rogerson (2000b), offers a more conventional argument in favor of asymmetric regulation in which he proposes subjecting the legacy technology (DSL) to access regulation without imposing such regulation on the new technology (cable modem service). Rogerson argues that DSL can be deployed simply by adding additional equipment to the end of the loop without making substantial investments in the loops themselves. As a result, the adverse impact of DSL regulation on investment incentives would be minimal. The deployment of cable modem service, in contrast, requires huge investments and upgrades to physical plant. Mandating access to cable modem systems would thus cause unacceptable deterrence to investment.

Asymmetric regulation has been heavily criticized by scholars favoring both regulatory and deregulatory approaches (Lemley and Lessig 2001; Crandall et al. 2002; Robinson 2002). The problem is that the deployment of DSL does require investment in the loop infrastructure. For example, lines must be conditioned to remove loading coils, bridge taps, and other attachments originally designed to optimize the circuit for voice, but which interfere with DSL service. Even more problematic is the fact that the natural resistance inherent in copper wire means that DSL service degrades in quality as the distance from the central office increases and becomes completely unusable once the distance exceeds roughly 12,000 feet (although technologies deployed later have extended this distance). As a result, Rogerson (2000b) acknowledges that DSL providers will have to use a DLC architecture for at least 56% of all their loops, with the number increasing if end users demand better performance. The net result is to make the investments needed to deploy DSL comparable to those for deploying cable modem service. The shift toward higher-bandwidth technologies like VDSL is likely to further increase the investments required to deploy DSL.

Not only does this raise the capital investments needed to provide service. It also greatly complicates the regulatory problem by forcing the FCC to allocate the limited space in remote terminals and by creating incentives for incumbent local telephone companies to design their networks for strategic reasons rather than to promote economic efficiency. The alternative would be to require the incumbent to provide access to a "virtual loop." The problem is that compelling access to a virtual loop would mandate access to facilities that are not yet built and may require significant investment and innovation, in which case the deterrent impact on investment and innovation might justify relying on competition between DSL and cable modems instead of regulation. With respect to DLC loops, Rogerson thus concedes that he is simply raising important issues without drawing any firm conclusions.

Implementing access regimes on even a portion of the industry would run afoul of the problems that have long confronted direct regulation of rates. Even worse, asymmetric regulation threatens to put the government in the position of favoring one transmission technology over the other. Lauding the benefits of one portion of the industry but not the other raises the question of which portion of the industry will be subject to regulation. As discussed above, the fact that cable modem service established the early lead and the significant capital investments needed to deploy last-mile broadband service through telephone lines renders the usual solution of burdening the legacy portion of the industry untenable. It is for these and other reasons that similar proposals for asymmetric regulation of other communications media have not been well received.[34]

Such asymmetric regulation would also be inconsistent with regulatory precedent. The FCC has repeated emphasized the importance of maintaining technological neutrality and of regulating in a consistent manner across platforms (see, e.g., FCC 2002b, 2002c, 2005d). The FCC noted that it developed its previous asymmetric regulatory efforts, which distinguished between dominant and nondominant carriers, at a time when the telecommunications industry was just beginning to evolve from one dominated by a monopoly provider into one in which a degree of competition was possible for some communications services. The FCC further noted that "this market environment differs markedly from the dynamic and evolving broadband Internet access marketplace before us today where the current market leaders, cable operators and wireline carriers, face competition not only from each other but also from other emerging broadband Internet access service providers. This rapidly changing market does not lend itself to conclusions about market dominance the commission typically makes to determine the degree of regulation to be applied to well-established, relatively stable telecommunications service markets. On the contrary, any finding about dominance or non-dominance in this emerging broadband Internet access service market would be premature." Indeed, the FCC noted that even if it were to apply its traditional dominance/nondominance analysis to broadband, the fact that cable modem systems had established the early lead dictated that it would conclude that DSL was nondominant. Thus, if anything, the asymmetric regulation would apply to the newly emerging technology and would exempt the more established technology, in direct opposition to the way that asymmetric regulation is usually applied (FCC 2005d, p. 14898 and n. 253, quoting FCC 1979, p. 309).

## C. The Different Types of Access to Broadband Networks

The debate over the regulation of last-mile broadband networks has also largely failed to take into account the differences between the different types of access sought. A close analysis reveals that each type of access has a different effect on network demand, optimal network configuration, transaction costs, the practical realities of implementation, and dynamic efficiency.

---

34 Lee Bollinger (1991) argued in favor of asymmetric regulation of print and broadcasting to allow experimentation with different policy approaches. Even commentators sympathetic to Bollinger's proposal criticized it as "too abstract, too speculative, insufficiently empirical" and concluded that it fell short of "fully grappling with some hard factual, predictive, and theoretical issues" (Sunstein 1993, pp. 111–12).

## 1. Retail Access

Retail access represents perhaps the most common form of access imposed on telecommunications providers. It provides every end user the right to benefit from the network's services on the same terms and conditions as other end users. To the extent that the carrier is a natural monopoly, retail access is usually accompanied by direct regulation of retail rates.

As we discussed at greater length in Chapter 5, one of retail access's principal effects would be to limit last-mile broadband providers' ability to manage their networks. A network owner will create sufficient capacity to satisfy projected demand and the level of reliability that customers demand. Because no forecast is ever perfect, at times network demand will exceed projected levels. The best long-run solution would be to expand capacity to meet the increased demand. The reality is that broadband capacity cannot be expanded instantaneously. Thus, the best long-run solution may be unavailable in the short run.

When expanding capacity is impossible, network owners face three options: they can preserve network performance by refusing to serve additional customers, they can allow prices to rise to ration existing network capacity, or they can allow service to degrade (by allowing the increased congestion to slow down network performance or by reducing network service in other ways) until demand shifts back into line with the available capacity. Retail access renders the first two of these options impossible, leaving the network with no option but to reduce the quality of network services even when doing so will harm consumers and lead to inefficiencies.

Direct regulation of rates can also be the source of large-scale inefficiencies. As noted in Chapter 8, regulatory authorities have long struggled with the proper manner of calculating the rate base. Approaches based on historical cost have the advantage of being more tractable, but run the risk of overcompensating capital assets that have become obsolete. Approaches based on replacement cost are more responsive to economic changes, but require undertaking the inherently speculative endeavor of updating costs to market levels. This task becomes all the more complicated if regulators base the replacement cost calculation not the structure of the actual network, but rather on the structure of a hypothetical network configured according to the best available technology. Cost-plus rate-setting regimes also fail to provide incentives for network owners to economize and, to the extent that they only allow rates of return to be earned on the rate base, can introduce a bias toward capital-intensive solutions (Averch and Johnson 1962). Experience with cable television has revealed the difficulties of regulating retail rates when the quality of the product being regulated varies, as will be the case with respect to broadband (Hazlett and Spitzer 1997; Crawford 2000).

The implementation of rate regulation also harms the competitive process in other ways. The process of developing and filing tariffs and shepherding them through any challenges that arise during the regulatory approval process imposes a degree of transaction costs and delay. Furthermore, by forcing advance disclosure of rates, the tariffing process forces all firms to give their competitors advance notice of any changes in business strategies. In addition, rate regulation facilitates collusion by making information about price more transparent, making products more homogeneous, and providing a mechanism for enforcing any deviations from the established price. The enforced uniformity inherent in tariffs reduces network owners' ability to tailor product offerings to individual customers' particular needs. In addition, it has long been understood that deadweight loss can be minimized in high-fixed-cost industries by allocating greater proportions of those fixed costs to those customers that are least price-sensitive (and thus will reduce their consumption the least in response to pricing above marginal cost) (Ramsey 1927). The nondiscrimination aspects of retail access foreclose such welfare-enhancing possibilities.

Perhaps most importantly, retail access can dampen incentives to invest in last-mile broadband technologies. Retail access will have no effect if regulators set retail access prices too high. On the other hand, setting retail access prices too low will reduce incentives for incumbents and competitors alike to invest in upgrading existing networks and in last-mile technologies. Regulators must thus thread a very narrow needle if retail access is to have any beneficial effect. Such a process would be difficult under the best of circumstances. It borders on the impossible with respect to technologies that are undergoing rapid innovation and differentiation and that are growing ever more complex.

Most importantly, the presence of intermodal competition largely obviates the need for regulatory authorities to assume the burdens of implementing retail access. It is for this reason that commentators have generally criticized the possibility of imposing retail access on last-mile broadband services (Crandall et al. 2002). Indeed, it does not appear that the FCC has ever attempted to mandate retail access to last-mile broadband services. Nor does it appear that state or local authorities have attempted to do so. Indeed, even when attempting to impose other types of access mandates, state authorities affirmatively disclaimed any attempt to regulate the reasonableness of retail rates (California Public Utilities Commission 2003).

## 2. Wholesale Access

Wholesale access is a right given to a network owner's competitors to purchase services normally sold at retail by the network and resell them to end users. The FCC initially imposed wholesale access on DSL. For example, the *Computer Inquiries* required incumbent local telephone companies offering enhanced services to make the same transmission component available to unaffiliated enhanced service providers on a tariffed basis (FCC 1998e). Furthermore, the *Advanced Services Second Report and Order* ruled that the resale requirements of the 1996 Act applied to DSL services offered to end users regardless of whether DSL was classified as telephone exchange service or exchange access. This in essence authorized competitors to lease DSL service from the incumbent local telephone company at their retail rate less the costs of marketing, provisioning, billing, and customer service usually incurred by the incumbent, but avoided when service is provided through a reseller.[35] Wholesale access was also available through special access tariffs of the type approved by the FCC with respect to GTE (FCC 1998e).

The FCC's *Wireline Broadband Internet Access Services Order* abolished both sets of wholesale access requirements. As an initial matter, the conclusion that DSL and other forms of wireline broadband represented information services and not telecommunications services rendered the 1996 Act wholly inapplicable. At the same time, the FCC also exempted DSL and other wireline broadband technologies used for Internet access from the access requirements imposed by the *Computer Inquiries* (FCC 2005d).

The situation is quite different with respect to cable. As the FCC has noted, "cable operators... have never been required to make Internet access transmission available to third parties on a wholesale basis" (FCC 2005d, p. 14887). As noted earlier, the FCC took somewhat inconsistent positions when facing calls for giving unaffiliated ISPs wholesale access to cable modem systems when approving the AT&T–TCI, AT&T–MediaOne, America Online–Time Warner, and Comcast–AT&T mergers. The agency addressed the issue more definitively in its *Cable Modem Declaratory Ruling*, when it refused to mandate wholesale access to cable modem systems (FCC 2002c).

The FCC's reluctance to mandate wholesale access to last-mile broadband systems is understandable. As discussed in Chapter 5, because total demand under wholesale access depends on two prices, its net impact on network demand is ambiguous and the accompanying increase or decrease in traffic can adversely affect network cost, capacity, and reliability. Forcing networks to externalize marketing, provisioning, and billing functions also forces networks to deviate from the transaction cost–minimizing institutional structure that represents the natural boundaries of the firm.

Indeed, last-mile broadband providers already have strong incentives to provide wholesale access. As the FCC noted, the benefits of spreading fixed costs over a larger customer base already give network owners powerful incentives to maximize traffic on their networks and the competition to capture the available network demand represents a powerful inducement to offer wholesale access voluntarily. Indeed, all of the major wireline broadband providers negotiate private wholesale access contracts

---

35  FCC (1999d), *pet. for review denied sub nom. Ass'n of Commc'ns Enters. v. FCC*, 253 F.3d 29 (D.C. Cir. 2001). DSL services offered at retail stand in stark contrast to DSL services offered to ISPs, which the FCC ruled were not subject to the 1996 Act's wholesale access mandate. Indeed, it is hard to understand how wholesale access prices to such services would be calculated. The statute provides that resale prices equal retail prices less "any marketing, billing, collection, and other costs that will be avoided." 47 U.S.C. § 252(d)(3). DSL services are offered to ISPs without marketing, billing, collection, ordering, repair, and other similar costs, because those services are expected to be provided by the ISP. There would thus be no avoided costs to deduct from the full price, in which case the resale price would be the same as the retail price.

on a regular basis at reasonable prices and have indicated their intention to continue doing so in the future. The development of VoIP and other new broadband service offerings will only cause the incentives to provide wholesale access voluntarily to become stronger. This current status of the broadband market thus alleviated any need for the FCC to compel wholesale access or to oversee the terms under which wholesale access occurs (FCC 2005d).

In addition, wholesale access hurts dynamic efficiency by eliminating demand from complementary service providers who represent the natural strategic partners for those seeking to construct alternative network capacity. The FCC noted in its *Wireline Broadband Internet Access Services Order*, "Because our rules require a particular type of generalized wholesale offering, they may reduce incentives for ISPs to seek alternative arrangements from other broadband Internet access platform providers and for those other providers to offer such arrangements." The greater flexibility and reduction in risk stemming from eliminating wholesale access also increases incentives for existing players to invest in upgrading their networks (FCC 2005d, pp. 14886, 14891, 14905).

Perhaps most problematic is the fact that the type of competition induced by wholesale access provides few consumer benefits. Under wholesale access, all of the competing ISPs employ the same equipment and thus provide the same speed, services, and access to content. Resellers thus cannot compete in terms of cost, network features, or quality of service impossible. Instead, the only way in which they can compete is through their willingness to accept thinner margins (Columbia Telecommunications Corporation 2001).

The paucity of consumer benefits underscores the extent to which wholesale access represents something of a competition policy anomaly. When confronted with an excessively concentrated market, competition policy's traditional response is to deconcentrate the problematic market, either by breaking up the existing monopoly or by facilitating entry by a competitor. Wholesale access, in contrast, leaves the concentrated market intact and instead simply requires that the bottleneck resource be shared. Such an approach may be justified if competition is infeasible, as was the case when wholesale access to last-mile broadband networks was first mandated. As the FCC noted, the emergence of competition from alternative broadband technologies essentially renders wholesale access untenable (FCC 2005d). The limited benefits can no longer offset the significant costs and the adverse impact on the incentives to invest in new network capacity.

### 3. Interconnection Access

Interconnection access is provided to horizontal providers competing to serve the same customers, giving them the right to terminate traffic originating on the other network or to have the other network terminate traffic originating on their networks. Interconnection access is considerably more disruptive to network management than retail or wholesale access. Impact on demand is ambiguous. Increasing the number of subscribers increases the value of the network, which in turn can cause network demand to increase. At the same time, interconnection access necessarily presumes that some network traffic will originate or terminate on other networks. The resulting diversion of network traffic places downward pressure on network demand. The overall impact of interconnection on network demand is thus ambiguous and depends on which of these two effects dominates.

The resulting change in network demand in turn affects the optimal network configuration. Network owners use forecasts of the magnitude, distribution, and variability of demand to design their networks to minimize cost, maximize capacity, and optimize reliability. In the process, the network owner must decide precisely where to place its links and nodes and whether it can aggregate sufficient volume to justify making capital expenditures in cost-reducing transmission technologies. Regardless of whether interconnection access increases or decreases demand, any unanticipated deviations in the level of network traffic can increase costs and affect network performance. Interconnection access prevents network owners from obtaining the information needed to make these decisions through direct observation. Instead, it must obtain that information from its competitors, which may be under no legal obligation or economic incentive to provide it.

Interconnection access also affects network design in other ways. Unlike retail and wholesale access, which only introduce traffic at locations where the network already serves customers, interconnection access requires networks to provide service at new locations within the network where the network was not previously offering service, although those interfaces are likely to be at major nodes. Interconnection access thus requires network owners to develop new systems to provision and meter usage at new points within their networks. It also introduces new flows in the middle of the network, which can be more difficult to manage than flows introduced at traditional customer locations.

The architecture of the Internet is such that last-mile providers generally do not interconnect with one another directly. Instead, DSL and cable modem providers serving the same area typically interconnect indirectly through the Internet backbone. This greatly minimizes many of the problems traditionally associated with interconnection access. Scholars concerned about promoting interconnection access have nonetheless raised the concern that backbone providers might strategically engage in discriminatory interconnection or refuse to interconnect altogether in ways that are privately beneficial, but economically harmful (Varian 1998; Speta 2002; Economides 2005; Werbach 2007).

As a recent working paper issued by the FCC Office of Plans and Policy notes, a wide variety of legitimate reasons exist for refusing to interconnect with all other backbones in a nondiscriminatory manner. For example, if a backbone with a national presence on both coasts were to peer with regional backbones only on one coast, it would allow the regional backbone to free ride on the national backbone's infrastructure investments. Asymmetries in the size of the traffic being conveyed can lead to similar problems (Kende 2000).

As we discuss in Chapter 4, network economic effects subject network providers to powerful incentives to interconnect with one another.[36] In addition, market structure plays a critical role in determining the competitive impact of a refusal to interconnect. Specifically, the models in which the refusal to interconnect to harms competition assume the existence of a dominant player. The backbone market has historically been composed of five players of roughly equal size (Kende 2000). When the market is structured in this manner, refusals to interconnect cannot plausibly lead to anticompetitive harms, since the demand-side economies of scale created by network economic effects would place any network that refused to interconnect at a decisive competitive disadvantage.[37]

It is for this reason that the FCC has traditionally declined to mandate interconnection access among backbone providers. As the agency noted in its 2001 *Intercarrier Compensation NPRM*, "The backbones appear to be successfully negotiating interconnection agreements among themselves without any regulatory intervention, and we see no reason to intervene in this efficiently functioning market" (FCC 2001c, p. 9656). The FCC followed similar reasoning in its orders clearing the Verizon–MCI, SBC–AT&T, and AT&T–BellSouth mergers, ruling that competition among five backbone providers of roughly equal size was sufficient to obviate the need to mandate interconnection access (FCC 2005g, 2005h, 2007a). Conversely, in approving the WorldCom–MCI merger, the FCC raised the concern that the merger would give one company a sufficiently dominant market share to allow it to harm competition. Consequently, the FCC conditioned its approval of the merger on the divestiture of MCI's backbone assets. Once those assets had been spun off, the agency saw no reason to mandate interconnection access. The spinoff of MCI's backbone business ensured that the backbone market would remain sufficiently competitive to obviate the need for any direct regulation of interconnection (FCC 1998c).

Competition among backbone providers has thus been sufficient to obviate any need to mandate interconnection access among last-mile broadband providers. Any move toward concentration in the backbone market is better solved by taking steps to ensure that the market remains unconcentrated than by imposing an interconnection access mandate.

## 4. Platform Access

As noted in Chapter 5, platform access occurs when the government creates a standard and requires networks to provide nondiscriminatory service to anyone

---

36  Katz and Shapiro (1994, p. 105) note that "[i]n markets with network effects, there is natural tendency toward de facto standardization."

37  Faulhaber (2005) observes that in markets with five roughly equal-sized players such as the backbone market, the large players are likely to interconnect with one another. Economides (2005) recognizes that network economic effects give firms strong incentives to interconnect. Katz and Shapiro (1985, p. 429) note that "[a]s the number of firms becomes increasingly large," equilibrium in which all firms interconnect converges to perfectly competitive equilibrium.

presenting their data configured in accordance with that standard. The FCC mandated platform access to last-mile broadband networks as part of its *Computer Inquiries*, in which it required the leading local telephone companies to "make available standardized hardware and software interfaces that are able to support transmission, switching, and signaling functions identical to those utilized in the enhanced service provided by the carrier." The *Computer Inquiries* also required the major local telephone companies to offer tariffs providing nondiscriminatory access to the network to any firm presenting its data configured in accordance with that standardized interface (FCC 1986a, p. 1039). As we discuss in greater detail in Chapters 11 and 12, many industry players and public interest groups are advocating imposing platform access to broadband networks through the cluster of policy proposals that fall under the banner of "network neutrality."

By increasing the availability of complementary goods, platform access typically causes network demand to increase, which in turn affects the network's optimal configuration, capacity, and reliability. As we discuss in Chapter 5, the normal way for network owners to protect network performance should network demand exceed expectations is to deny service to new customers. As is the case with respect to other forms of access, mandating platform access forecloses this option and forces the network either to permit network performance to degrade or to maintain excess capacity as insurance against this possibility. Both solutions necessarily either raise costs or reduce consumer benefits.

The inability to deny service to any complementary service provider becomes particularly troublesome once one acknowledges how sensitive network performance is to the magnitude and variability of demand. The introduction of particular traffic affects the network in nonuniform ways. Not only can it cause local congestion in the areas near where the traffic enters the network; as our discussion of the max-flow/min-cut theorem in Chapter 2 demonstrates, networks' ability to route traffic along other paths can also cause the introduction of traffic in one location to impair performance in portions of the network that are located far from where the additional traffic is introduced. The impact on network performance thus depends not only on the magnitude and variability of the flows being introduced into the network through platform access, but also on the configuration of the entire network, including the arrangement of elements in areas of the network quite distant from the access point, as well as the magnitude and the variability of the flows being introduced into the network by other parties. The greater the variability of the flows, the bigger the adverse impact on network performance.

These qualities make platform access to last-mile broadband networks particularly problematic. Internet traffic is notoriously "bursty," in that it often involves the brief introduction of a high volume of traffic followed by an extended period of little or no traffic. This is particularly true for certain types of applications and contrasts sharply with the flows in other types of networks, in which flows tend to be steadier and to change more gradually. The classic response to these problems is for the network owner to exercise discretion in the types of application and content providers it allows to access the network, as well as the precise locations at which it permits such access to occur. Platform access prevents network owners from exercising such discretion.

The implementation of platform access necessarily gives rise to other economic harms. For example, platform access presumes that network owners must provide access to any content or application provider that presents data in a standard format. In the extreme case, the government requires all networks to conform to that standard and prohibits networks from deviating from it. Although the standardization of Internet architecture is often praised as an unmitigated good, conventional economic theory underscores the existence of an optimal level of standardization, determined by the tradeoff between the value of the larger network size created by network economic effects and the value that end users place on the different types of services. If consumer preferences are relatively homogeneous, one would expect the entire network to coalesce around a single standard. As consumer preferences become increasingly heterogeneous, one would expect the optimal number of networks to begin to exceed one. By artificially limiting nonstandardization, platform access can prevent the network from reaching the optimal level of standardization.

Platform access is also subject to a number of practical problems. Once the government designates a standard, network owners cannot implement any changes to that standard until the government has approved those changes. Imposing platform access thus inevitably causes a degree of delay in the speed with which the network can adapt to changes in technology. In addition, platform access requires the government to designate particular locations within the network where platform access can occur. The logical course of action is for the government to choose locations at natural interfaces between different segments of the industry. The problem is that technological change can cause natural interfaces to shift or to collapse altogether. Such problems are likely to loom particularly large in industries such as broadband that are undergoing rapid technological change.

Consider the transformation that occurs when end users shift from narrowband, in which end users are reached through dial-up services, to broadband connections such as DSL or cable modem service. Long-haul transmission is provided by backbones, which provide high-speed connections among a dozen or so network access points located at key locations throughout the country. Under a narrowband architecture, end users connected to the Internet through their local telephone system, which routed Internet-bound calls to locations in individual cities spread throughout the country in the same manner that it routed conventional telephone calls. The local telephone company did not need to maintain any packet-switching capability of its own. The only difference between Internet-bound calls and conventional calls was that the former consisted of data packets encoded in an analog format by the dial-up modem and the latter consisted of voice traffic. With respect to either, the local telephone company simply served as a passthrough. The key function served by ISPs was to convert the analog signal into a digital signal and to provide the connection between the modem banks dispersed in communities throughout the country and the limited number of network access points served by the backbones. ISPs perform a number of other functions, including supplying e-mail servers, hosting end users' Web pages, offering proprietary content, and caching the popular content locally so that customers can access it more easily.

The arrival of broadband technologies has effected some fundamental changes in the Internet's architecture. Because both DSL and cable modem providers use the same infrastructure to provide two different types of service (either cable television combined with cable modem service or local telephone service combined with DSL), both types of providers must maintain equipment to segregate the two different communication streams. As discussed earlier, DSL systems route traffic through devices known as a digital subscriber line access multiplexers (DSLAMs), which separate the voice communications from the data-based communications. Cable operators employ devices known as frequency up-converters and cable modem termination systems (CMTSs) to divide the video and data streams.

Unlike what was the case in the narrowband world, last-mile broadband providers must maintain packet-switched networks in their main facilities to hold and route the streams of data packets after they have been separated from other types of communications. Once broadband networks were required to maintain their own data networks, it was a relatively simple matter for them to cut out the ISP and simply to negotiate their own interconnection agreement with a backbone provider. Indeed, given that last-mile providers already had to perform most of the functions previously provided by ISPs, in many cases it would likely be more efficient to have the last-mile provider carry out the functions previously performed by the unaffiliated ISP.

The efficiency of having last-mile providers perform the functions previously performed by ISPs is demonstrated dramatically by the manner in which the multiple ISP access mandated during the AOL–Time Warner merger has been implemented. Contrary to the original expectations of the FTC, the unaffiliated ISPs that have obtained access to AOL–Time Warner's cable modem systems under the FTC's merger clearance order have not placed their own packet networks and backbone access facilities within AOL–Time Warner's headends. Instead, traffic bound for these unaffiliated ISPs exits the headend via AOL–Time Warner's backbone and is handed off to the unaffiliated ISP at some external location. It is hard to see how consumers benefit from such arrangements, given that they necessarily use the same equipment and thus provide the same speed, services, and access to content regardless of the identity of the nominal ISP. The fact that these unaffiliated ISPs have found it more economical to share AOL – Time Warner's existing ISP facilities rather than build their own strongly suggests that integrating ISP and last-mile operations is more efficient.

In other words, the technological structure of the narrowband made the interface between local telephone systems and ISPs a natural boundary between two different providers. The architectural changes wrought by the digitization of last-mile broadband technologies caused what was once a natural interface between market players to collapse. By requiring network owners to maintain standardized interfaces, platform access runs the risk of locking existing interfaces into place long after technological changes have rendered such an interface obsolete.

Platform access can also increase transaction costs. Government establishment of a standardized interface requires considerable time and effort both by regulatory authorities and by interested parties participating in the process. To the extent that the standard developed by the government differs from the current network architecture, last-mile broadband providers will also have to incur the costs needed to reconfigure their equipment to make it compatible with the standard. In addition, because a network owner can render a platform access mandate a nullity simply by charging excessive prices to providers of complementary services with which it does not wish to do business, platform access necessarily envisions some oversight and enforcement of the nondiscrimination. The complexity of the interface means that the means of potential discrimination are likely to be myriad, which in turn means that regulatory authorities are likely to have to oversee an extremely large proportion of the dimensions of the business relationship.

Imposing platform access can also adversely affect dynamic efficiency. By guaranteeing content and applications providers access to the existing network, platform access deprives new entrants seeking to construct alternative last-mile platforms of their natural strategic partners.

Despite the seriousness of the costs of mandating platform access, it is still conceivable that such regulation might create sufficient benefits to justify its imposition. As we noted in Chapter 5, the problem with this argument is that last-mile broadband providers already possess powerful incentives to open their networks to a wide range of content and applications providers. The likelihood that the goals of platform access will be accomplished even in the absence of government intervention undercuts the case for imposing it as a regulatory mandate.

The FCC embraced much of this reasoning in its *Wireline Broadband Internet Access Services Order*. The FCC noted how platform access can adversely affect network architecture. The imposition of a standardized interface can create equipment configuration costs. Forcing network owners to reengineer general use equipment to conform with the standard requires the network owner to confront the unattractive choice between either foregoing the benefits of the equipment's full functionality or deferring deployment until the equipment is reengineered to be compatible with the standard. In addition, consumer demand and technological improvements were pushing the industry "toward equipment that integrates information service and transmission capabilities in a manner that allows functions to be performed at multiple points within a broadband network and closer to the end user than ever before." The FCC warned that its "rules should not force technological development in another, less efficient direction" by insisting on the separation of functionality and transmission that platform access presumes (FCC 2005d, p. 14889).

Platform access also impedes the network's ability to evolve to meet the needs of the increasingly heterogeneous demands of end users. As the FCC noted, standardization hinders network owners' ability to respond to individual requests for new or modified features. Refusing to impose platform access would allow more technological innovation than the "'cookie-cutter' common carrier offerings" implicit in any nondiscriminatory access mandate. Indeed, the FCC noted that the *Computer Inquiries* reflected "a fairly static picture of network development" in which innovation occurred at the network's edge or outside the network altogether and in which "a line could be drawn between the network functions and computer processing without impeding technological innovation." Policy should adapt to reflect the insight that "innovation can occur at all network points and at all network layers as well as in non-network applications and equipment" (FCC 2005d, pp. 14890, 14892, 14900).

The FCC also expressed concern about how platform access increases transaction costs. As an initial matter, the agency took seriously concerns expressed about "the inherent regulatory delay that occurs through the network change disclosure process, the web positing requirements, and tariffing requirements" as well as the costs of determining the proper regulatory classification under the *Computer Inquiry* regimes as well as the steps needed to comply with those restrictions (FCC 2005d, pp. 14890–91).

In addition, the FCC noted how platform access "deter[s] broadband infrastructure investment by creating disincentives to the deployment of facilities capable of providing invocative broadband Internet access services." The FCC found "this negative impact on deployment and innovation particularly troubling in view of Congress' clear and express policy goal of ensuing broadband deployment, and its directive that we remove barriers to that deployment." Giving network owners greater flexibility in their dealings with providers of complementary services will allow them to "take more risks in investing in and deploying new technologies." In addition, the fact that network owners are already confronted with powerful incentives to make transmission capacity available to providers of complementary services absent regulation cut against the need for imposing platform access. Indeed, such incentives are likely to become even stronger as content and applications providers develop and deploy VoIP and other innovative broadband service offerings (FCC 2005d, pp. 14865, 14877–78, 14891).

## 5. Unbundled Access

Unbundled access is a right to parts of the incumbent's network given to competitors. Cable modem systems have never been subject to unbundling. As we describe above, the FCC initially subjected DSL systems to limited unbundling requirements, but has repealed most of those requirements over time.

As we discuss at some length in Chapter 5, unbundled access disrupts network management to a greater degree than any other form of access. Unbundled access simultaneously supports complementary services, which tend to increase network demand, while diverting some traffic outside of the network, which tends to decrease network demand. As a result, its net impact on the demand for network resources is ambiguous. Network owners depend on forecasts of demand when deciding on the configuration that provides the greatest capacity and the optimal level of reliability at the lowest cost. The ambiguous impact of unbundled access on network demand makes such forecasts considerably more uncertain. The mandatory carriage aspect of unbundled access also prevents the network owner from protecting network performance by responding to any unexpected increases in demand by refusing to carry additional traffic.

Unlike other forms of access, unbundled access has the potential to introduce flows deep in the heart of a network at points that may not represent natural points of interface with other providers. As a result, the pattern of flows associated with unbundled access often bears little resemblance to the pattern of flows for which a network was designed. In addition, as we noted in Chapter 2, tying up isolated elements of a network can cause network performance to degrade in ways that are often quite unexpected. Not only can it increase congestion in the portion of the network adjacent to the elements to which network access is sought; as our discussion of the max-flow/min-cut theorem illustrates, the fact that networks attempt to minimize such distortions by rerouting traffic through other portions of the network means that unbundled access can create new bottlenecks in areas of the network that are located far from the elements to which competitors obtain unbundled access. Thus unbundled access can adversely affect network performance in ways that are sharply discontinuous and unpredictable.

Unbundled access can also greatly increase the transaction costs of network management. At a minimum, placing some of the traffic outside the network prevents the network owner from observing information regarding the magnitude and variability of network traffic directly. Instead, such information is only available from the network's competitors, who are likely to be under no regulatory obligation to share that information and may have strategic incentives to withhold it. In addition, unbundled access forces network owners to develop new processes and equipment for provisioning and metering access at just about any points within the network, even if they have never provided service at those points in the past and have no plans to do so in the future.

Unbundled access can also have a devastating impact on incentives to invest in alternative network capacity. Giving competitors the right to access elements of the existing network at cost effectively destroys their incentive to invest in third-generation wireless networks and other broadband technologies, particularly if the network owner is not allowed to charge its actual cost and is instead required to charge the cost of a hypothetical network providing the same service using the most efficient technology currently available. Requiring that any successful improvements to the existing networks be shared also substantially dampens incumbents' incentives to invest in upgrading their own networks.

This is particularly true when the success of various improvements is highly variable and hard to anticipate. Consider, for example, an incumbent that is considering whether to upgrade its network in a way that is likely to be successful in some geographic areas, but not in others, in ways that are unpredictable. Absent unbundled access, the network owner could forego determining in which geographies the innovation was likely to prove successful and instead focus on the average success rate across all geographies and undertake the investment as long as that average success rate exceeded its investment hurdle. The situation changes dramatically once unbundled access is imposed. Unbundled access gives competitors the opportunity to obtain access to only those geographies that prove economically successful and to ignore those that do not. This leaves the network owner with two relatively unattractive possibilities. First, it can spend additional resources to determine in advance which geographies are likely to prove more successful. Even if it is successful in making this determination, unbundled access guarantees that any economic benefits it obtains from these investments will be quickly dissipated. Second, it can forego the investment altogether. Either decision will have an adverse impact on network investment.

As we have discussed in Chapters 8 and 9, Justice Breyer invoked these considerations with respect to narrowband technologies in *Iowa Utilities Board* and *Verizon Communications Inc. v. FCC* and eventually saw them endorsed by a majority of the Supreme Court in *Trinko*. The D.C. Circuit extended Justice Breyer's reasoning to last-mile broadband networks when striking down the FCC's *Line Sharing Order*. The court noted that "mandatory unbundling comes at a cost, including disincentives to research and development by both ILECs and CLECs and the tangled management inherent in shared use of a common resource." In addition, the existence of intermodal competition from cable modem providers eliminated the need to impose unbundled access (*U.S. Telecom Ass'n*, 290 F.3d at 428–29, citing *Iowa Utils. Bd.*, 525 U.S. at 416–17, 427–31).

The FCC relied on many of these same insights in its *Triennial Review Order*, which eliminated UNE access to the high-frequency portion of the loop, fiber loops, and packet switching equipment. Extending unbundled access to last-mile broadband networks "would blunt the deployment of advanced telecommunications infrastructure by incumbent LECs and the incentive for competitive LECs to invest in their own facilities." The FCC repeatedly acknowledged that the market for last-mile broadband services had grown increasingly competitive. Competition is better than unbundling because of the difficulties in allocating shared costs and resources (FCC 2003d).

### D. Arguments in Favor of Market-Based Pricing

If access to broadband inputs is to be mandated, economic analysis indicates that access rates should be based on market prices. Doing so would promote allocative efficiency by giving purchasers and providers alike the appropriate signals for calibrating consumption and production levels. In addition, basing access rates on market prices would enhance dynamic efficiency by providing the incentives need to attract the investments needed to finance the deployment of the various broadband technologies. As the FCC has repeatedly recognized, issues surrounding investment and innovation are of the utmost importance when the market involved is a nascent one (see, e.g., FCC 1999c, 2002c).

Although market prices might previously have been difficult to determine, the emergence of new technologies capable of providing high-speed broadband services is making this task increasingly easy. As noted earlier, DSL and cable modem systems are currently competing vigorously for early dominance of the broadband industry. In addition, communications companies are preparing to provide broadband services through a wide variety of wireless technologies, including PCS, WiFi, WiMax, ancillary and supplemental service provided via digital television, and 3G mobile wireless devices. Although these services are still in their nascent stages, when fully operational they have the potential to provide a ready basis for determining the value of the transmission of services.

Should these alternative technologies be insufficiently developed to allow direct determination of market prices, economic theory indicates that regulatory authorities should base rates on ECPR, which sets rates as the sum of the forward-looking incremental cost and the opportunity cost associated with providing access. The opportunity cost of providing network access is determined by subtracting direct incremental costs from the retail price in the final goods market. The primary reason that the FCC has been reluctant to allow this issue in the context of DSL has been that the retail prices supposedly reflected monopoly returns. Although this position is at least arguable in the case of local telephony, it is unsupportable in the case of broadband. The FCC and the courts have recognized that vibrant competition exists, and the impending arrival of additional competitors should only cause it to intensify.

Indeed, the presence of this competition raises serious questions whether compelling access to high-speed broadband facilities represents sensible economic policy. Access requirements only make sense if there is a true bottleneck facility that in effect gives a company a natural monopoly. As noted above, when competition exists, compelling access at best accomplishes nothing, because parties who negotiate agreements on other terms will simply negotiate around access rates that are set too high. Access rates that are set too low, however, can harm allocative efficiency by creating the shortages and distortions inevitably associated with prices that are not calibrated to balance supply and demand.

Even worse, compelling access can harm dynamic efficiency by eliminating the need for firms to invest in substitute facilities. By rescuing those who need alternative means of transmission from having to invest in alternative capacity, access requirements can forestall the emergence of competition by depriving other facilities-based competitors of their natural strategic partners. Access requirements can thus have the perverse effect of cementing the existing technologies into place. Indeed, that is the clear import of the FCC's notice of proposed rulemaking underscoring the importance of taking a more functional approach from the consumers' perspective and recognizing the emergence of multiple options in providing broadband service, including cable, telephony, wireless, and satellite. Indeed, it was the emergence of this competition that led the FCC to seek comment on whether access requirements should be foregone (FCC 2002b).

If such access requirements are to be imposed, however, economic analysis indicates that rates for access should be based on market prices. Any attempt to base access prices solely on direct cost, as is currently done under TELRIC, fails to acknowledge that the market value of network access is determined by the value of the services sold through the network, not the cost of the network itself. Not only is this appropriate in light of the fact that networks are capital assets that are not consumables; it also reflects the demand-side considerations that underlie economic analysis. The presence of substitute facilities should permit market value to be determined through a comparison to actual market transactions or through the opportunity cost component mandated by ECPR. The presence of direct competition makes it unlikely that prices set in this manner will allow network owners to recover supracompetitive returns.

The Supreme Court's takings jurisprudence provides another reason for requiring that any access requirement imposed by the FCC be priced at market value. The issues are clearest with respect to DSL. Although the D.C. Circuit vacated the regulations providing that the high-frequency portion of the loop constituted a network element that was subject to unbundled access under the 1996 Act, it left intact the regulations giving requesting telecommunications carriers the right to physically collocate routing equipment on the incumbent LEC's property. As we discuss in Chapter 7, such a requirement constitutes the type of permanent physical occupation held to constitute a per se taking in *Loretto*.

Lower court precedent supports this conclusion as well. A similar issue arose in *GTE Northwest, Inc. v. Public Utility Commission*. At issue in that case was the regulatory provision enacted by the Oregon Public Utility Commission (PUC) similar to the ONA regime created by the FCC in *Computer III*. The key difference was that Oregon's regime required local telephone companies to permit enhanced service providers to physically collocate on their property. After reviewing the relevant takings analysis contained in *Loretto*, *Florida Power*, and *Yee v. City of Escondido*, the court concluded that the physical collocation requirement was properly characterized as the type of permanent physical invasion held to be a *per se* taking in *Loretto*. In so holding, the court rejected the argument that the fact that the PUC had already placed restrictions on the telephone company's ability to use its property deprived it of any historically rooted expectation of compensation. As the court reasoned, "the facts that an industry is heavily regulated, and that a property owner acquired the property knowing that it is heavily regulated, do not diminish a physical invasion to something less than a taking." The court also rejected the argument that physical collocation represented nothing more than a restriction on the use of the telephone company's property that was more properly analyzed as a regulatory taking. According to the court, the PUC lacked the statutory authority to exercise the power of eminent domain. As a result, the Oregon Supreme Court invalidated the PUC's collocation regulations as beyond the PUC's statutory authority.[38]

The analysis with respect to cable modem systems is slightly more ambiguous. Unless it mandates multiple ISP access as a general matter, the FCC need not address precisely how and where the interconnection needed for multiple ISP access should occur or how such access should be priced. None of the municipal ordinances requiring multiple ISP access set forth the parameters for interconnection or pricing guidelines; no consensus has emerged among industry participants as to where the interconnection needed for multiple ISP access should occur (Lathen 1999). If access is to provide anything more than the thin type of competition that results from resale of the same network capacity (such as occurred under the multiple ISP access mandate imposed during the AOL–Time Warner merger), access to cable modem systems will necessarily require the type of permanent physical invasion held to constitute a per se taking. Consequently, cable modem system operators who are made subject to multiple ISP access requirements will be entitled to fair market value as compensation. As noted in the discussion regarding access to DSL networks, the proliferation of technological alternatives is in the process of greatly simplifying such a determination.

---

38   900 P.2d 495, 499–501, 504, 505–06 (Or. 1995). The litigants in *GTE Northwest* framed their challenge in terms of the Takings Clauses embodied in both the federal and the Oregon constitutions. The court assumed without deciding that the analysis would be the same under either provision. Id. at 501 n. 6. Note that Sections 251 and 252 enacted by the Telecommunications Act of 1996 explicitly give state public utility commissions the right to enforce physical collocation provisions. 47 U.S.C. §§ 251(c)(6), 252. Although this in effect overturned the Oregon Supreme Court's holding with respect to the PUC's authority to enforce physical collocation, it did not in any way undercut the court's conclusion that the physical collocation provisions of the Oregon regulatory scheme constituted a per se taking under *Loretto*.

# 11

# The Regulation of Broadband Networks and the Internet: Network Neutrality versus Network Diversity

Most Internet users communicate through a suite of nonproprietary protocols known as the transmission control protocol/Internet protocol ("TCP/IP"). Widespread adoption of TCP/IP has given the Internet a nearly universal interoperability that allows all end users to access Internet applications and content on a nondiscriminatory basis. Commentators, led by Lawrence Lessig (2002), have long been concerned that cable modem and DSL systems will use their control of the "last mile" of the network to block or slow access to content and applications that threaten their proprietary operations. The concern is that the resulting reduction in interoperability will produce a less favorable environment for competition and innovation in the market for Internet content and applications.

Some regulatory proposals attempt to preserve the transparency of the Internet by regulating last-mile providers' relationships with *end users*. Other proposals seek to regulate last-mile providers' relationships with *network and content providers*. Some call for mandating interconnection of broadband networks along standardized interfaces such as TCP/IP.[1] Others argue in favor of a presumption that any discriminatory access agreements are anticompetitive, leaving the precise regulatory requirements to be developed over time through case-by-case adjudication.[2] Although these proposals vary considerably in both their terminology and details, they can comfortably be aggregated within the broad rubric of "network neutrality."

The term "network neutrality" is something of a misnomer. Adoption of any standardized interface has the inevitable effect of favoring certain applications and disfavoring others. For example, TCP/IP routes packets anonymously on a "first come, first served" and "best efforts" basis. Thus, it is poorly suited to applications that are less tolerant of variations in throughput rates, such as streaming media and

---

1 See, e.g., Lemley (1996); Lessig (2002); Werbach (2002); Cooper (2003); Solum and Chung (2004); Wu (2004); cf. Speta (2002), proposing mandatory interconnection among backbone carriers.
2 See, e.g., Weiser (2003b); Lessig (2005).

VoIP, and is biased against network-based security features that protect e-commerce and ward off viruses and spam. Contrary to what the nomenclature might suggest, network neutrality is anything but neutral. Indeed, using regulation to standardize interfaces would have the unfortunate effect of forcing the government to act as the central planner of the technological evolution of the network.

There can be no question that interoperability provides substantial economic benefits. Making Internet applications and content universally accessible increases the value of the network to both end users and providers of applications and content. Indeed, as the FCC has recognized, the benefits from network neutrality are often so compelling that the vast majority of network owners can be expected to adhere to it voluntarily (FCC 2005d[3]). Furthermore, network neutrality hearkens back to the regime of mandatory interconnection and interface standardization used so successfully by the courts and the FCC to foster competition in customer premises equipment ("CPE"), long distance, and information services, as discussed in Chapter 8. Concepts such as openness and neutrality also seem to promote such widely held values as equality of treatment and freedom of choice. The recent surge of merger activity in the cable and telecommunications industries appears to make concerns about gatekeeper control by network owners all the more plausible.

That said, in deciding whether to impose network neutrality as a regulatory mandate, the key question is not whether network neutrality provides substantial benefits. Instead, the key inquiry is whether circumstances exist in which deviations from network neutrality are so likely to be harmful that firms should be foreclosed from experimenting with them even in the absence of any demonstration of consumer harm. As the Supreme Court recognized in *Northern Pacific Railway Co. v. United States*, which represents the Court's seminal statement on when to treat business practices as categorically prohibited, a business practice should not be declared illegal per se unless the challenged practice evinces such a "pernicious effect on competition" and such a "lack of any redeeming virtue" that nothing would be lost if it were "presumed to be . . . illegal without elaborate inquiry as to the precise harm [it] ha[s] caused or the business excuse for [its] use" (356 U.S. 1, 5 (1957)).

The Court reiterated these principles in 2007 in its decision in *Leegin Creative Leather Products, Inc. v. PSKS, Inc.*, in which the Court once again concluded that "[r]esort to *per se* rules is confined to restraints . . . that would always or almost always tend to restrict competition and decrease output." Thus, "[a]s a consequence, the *per se* rule is appropriate only after courts have had considerable experience with the type of restraint at issue, and only if courts can predict with confidence that it would be invalidated in all or almost all instances under the rule of reason" (127 S. Ct. 2705, 2713 (2007) (internal quotation marks omitted)). Conversely, the Court has been reluctant to apply a per se rule "where the economic impact of

---

3   The Court of Appeals sustained the FCC's order in *Time Warner Telecom, Inc. v. FCC*, 507 F.3d 205 (3d Cir. 2007).

certain practices is not immediately obvious,"[4] when the courts lack experience with certain business relationships,[5] or when the effect of certain practices is not "so plainly anticompetitive that no elaborate study of the industry is needed to establish their illegality."[6] In the absence of clear competitive harm, the standard response under competition policy is to forbear from categorically prohibiting the challenged practice and instead to evaluate its effect on a case-by-case basis.[7]

This approach allows policymakers to steer a middle course when facing uncertainty about the competitive impact of conflicting business models. Rather than presumptively favoring one particular architecture and placing the burden of proof on parties wishing to deviate from it, adopting a more restrained regulatory posture permits policymakers to avoid committing to either side of the debate and instead let both approaches go forward until the economic implications become clearer. It would have its biggest impact with respect to practices that could possibly promote or harm competition and in which it is difficult to anticipate which will be the case. Presumptions in favor of a particular architecture effectively foreclose the potential benefits of alternative approaches even when there is no clear indication that permitting such a deviation would cause any demonstrable harm. A more restrained approach would give the benefit of the doubt to ambiguous cases and permit them to go forward unless and until there was a concrete showing of anticompetitive harm. Any other rule would short-circuit the process of experimentation with new products and alternate organizational forms that is essential to a properly functioning market. Such tolerance is particularly appropriate in light of network neutrality proponents' acknowledgement that standardization can lead to market failure, that deviating from universal interoperability and interconnectivity can yield substantial benefits, and that determining whether a particular practice will help or harm competition is often difficult, if not impossible.[8] In addition, a less categorical and more restrained approach is particularly appropriate when technological change is transforming the economic impact of various practices. A better understanding of the potential benefits of deviating from network neutrality is thus essential for any proper assessment of the relevant tradeoffs.[9] Indeed, the FCC's 2008 *Comcast* order rejected broad, categorical, ex ante rules in favor of precisely the type of case-by-case, ex post analysis that we propose (FCC 2008c).

---

4  *FTC v. Ind. Fed'n of Dentists*, 476 U.S. 447, 458–59 (1986).

5  *United States v. Topco Assocs., Inc.*, 405 U.S. 596, 607–08 (1972); *Broad. Music, Inc. v. Columbia Broad. Sys., Inc.*, 441 U.S. 1, 9 (1979); *Arizona v. Maricopa County*, 457 U.S. 332, 350 n. 19 (1982); *State Oil Co. v. Khan*, 522 U.S. 3, 10 (1997).

6  *Nat'l Soc'y of Prof'l Eng'rs v. United States*, 43 U.S. 679, 692 (1978).

7  *White Motor Co. v. United States*, 372 U.S. 253, 262–63 (1963); *Bus. Elecs.*, 485 U.S. at 724, 726; *Leegin*, 127 S. Ct. at 2713.

8  Cooper (2000); Lemley and Lessig (2001); Lessig (2002); Wu (2003).

9  The existing critiques of network neutrality are important but do not attempt to offer any extended evaluation of the underlying economics (Lopatka and Page 2001; Thierer 2005; Owen and Rosston 2006).

## A. The Economic Case for Network Diversity

The existing debate has largely overlooked how product differentiation can ameliorate both the supply-side scale economies associated with high sunk costs and the demand-side scale economies associated with network economic effects. In other words, increasing the number of dimensions along which networks compete can allow smaller producers to survive despite having lower sales volumes and higher per-unit costs. Allowing network owners to differentiate their networks can also better satisfy the increasing heterogeneity of end-user demand. Restated in terms of the Internet, network diversity might make it possible for three different last-mile networks to coexist: one optimized for traditional Internet applications such as e-mail and Web site access; another incorporating security features to facilitate e-commerce and to guard against viruses, spam, and other undesirable aspects of life on the Internet; and a third that prioritizes packets in the manner needed to facilitate bandwidth-intensive, time-sensitive applications such as streaming media and virtual worlds. Each would survive by catering to the market segment that places the highest value on a particular type of service.

Extended to its logical conclusion, this analysis suggests that public policy would be better served if Congress and the FCC were to embrace a "network diversity" principle that permitted network owners to deploy proprietary protocols and to enter into exclusivity agreements with content providers. Preventing network owners from differentiating their offerings would forestall this process. In other words, standardization on TCP/IP would have the effect of narrowing the dimensions of competition, forcing networks to compete solely on the basis of price and network size. The commodification of bandwidth would foreclose one avenue for mitigating the advantages enjoyed by the largest players.

At the same time, network neutrality threatens to reduce incentives for increased competition through the construction of new networks. Eliminating the potential for short-run supracompetitive returns would also thwart one of the primary mechanisms upon which markets rely to stimulate entry. Furthermore, by providing all applications and content providers with access to the existing network, network neutrality deprives would-be builders of alternative network capacity of their natural strategic partners. Concerns about reducing investment incentives carry little weight when last-mile competition is infeasible, as was arguably the case when interconnection and standardization were mandated with respect to CPE, long distance, and enhanced services. They are paramount when entry by new last-mile providers is ongoing and other last-mile technologies are waiting in the wings. Under these circumstances, regulation imposed to curb market concentration can turn into the cause, rather than the consequence, of market failure.

What emerges is a vision of competition that is quite different from that envisioned by the current debate. This is not to say that network diversity would be a panacea. The underlying welfare calculus is quite complex. Just to highlight a couple of considerations, the aggregate demand and the cost structure may cause the level of competition to be insufficiently robust to yield significant welfare benefits. Furthermore, the viability of network diversity depends in no small part on the relative heterogeneity of consumer preferences. If there is no variance in what end users want from networks, there will be no subsegments for smaller network owners to target. In addition, some degree of deadweight loss and redundant entry may be endemic under network diversity, and it is possible that the welfare increases associated with greater product diversity will not completely offset these losses. Furthermore, given that entry is never instantaneous, welfare analysis of network diversity requires balancing the short-run static efficiency losses from allowing network owners to earn short-run supracompetitive profits against the long-run dynamic efficiency gains resulting from stimulating the entry of competing networks. In short, whether network neutrality or network diversity would lead to a more socially beneficial outcome is a context-specific question that cannot be answered *a priori.* The absence of simple policy inferences renders the regulatory decision whether to impose network neutrality quite complex. Indeed, network neutrality proponents have suggested that many of the problems associated with network neutrality can be addressed through other means (Lessig 2002; Wu 2004).

There are, however, a number of institutional considerations that suggest that network diversity might well be the better approach. To the extent that regulatory solutions take the form of *ex ante* rules, they are poorly suited to the context-specific determinations suggested by network diversity theory. A presumption that discriminatory access arrangements are anticompetitive would contradict the growing empirical literature indicating that vertical integration and vertical contractual restraints tend to promote consumer welfare. Such a presumption would also prevent network owners from experimenting with network diversity, because they would presumably be foreclosed from adopting any practice that deviated from interoperability and interconnectivity unless they could demonstrate clear benefits. Network neutrality proponents concede the difficulties in distinguishing practices that are economically justified from those that will harm competition. Because of the inherent ambiguity of many business practices, competition policy's usual response is not to put the burden of demonstrating economic benefits on parties who wish to adopt a practice, but rather to place the burden on the opponents of the practice and to permit the practice to occur until opponents can demonstrate anticompetitive harm.

In addition, the regulatory tools needed to implement the regime of interconnection, standardization, rate regulation, and nondiscrimination implicit in network neutrality have long been criticized as difficult to implement and unlikely to be effective in industries such as broadband, where the services provided vary in quality and where technology is changing rapidly. Regulatory lag creates the danger that restrictions will persist long after the conditions that justified their imposition have dissipated. Even worse, by reducing investment incentives, network neutrality can itself become the means through which market concentration is cemented into place. Indeed, one of the principal drawbacks of regimes of mandatory interconnection and interface standardization is that they implicitly presuppose that regulation will continue indefinitely. Network diversity, in contrast, is better at facilitating competitive entry. As such, it has the advantage of having embedded within it a built-in exit strategy.

Even these arguments, although carrying considerable persuasive force, fall short of providing a definitive resolution of these issues, and the debate all too often risks collapsing into battles over ideology. Competition policy offers a potential solution by implicitly recognizing that the best response in the face of uncertainty is forbearance. Until it is clear whether adhering to or deviating from complete interoperability would be the better course of action, competition policy would counsel in favor of permitting both architectures to go forward. Intervening by mandating network neutrality would have the inevitable effect of locking the existing interfaces into place and of foreclosing experimentation with new products and alternative organizational forms that transcend traditional firm boundaries.

The decision to permit network diversity to emerge, then, does not necessarily depend on a conviction that it would yield a substantively better outcome, but rather from a "technological humility" that permits exploration to proceed until policymakers can make a clearer assessment of the cost–benefit tradeoff. Although preserving the status quo might be preferable if allowing such experimentation would inflict irreversible and catastrophic harm, neither would seem to be the case with respect to network neutrality. In this sense, network diversity is not the mirror image of network neutrality, in that it does not call for the imposition of any mandatory obligations. Rather, network diversity adopts the more modest position that regards regulatory forbearance as the appropriate course of action when confronted with ambiguity.

## 1. Vertical Exclusion and Network Neutrality

Regulations that compel access to bottleneck facilities are inherently about vertical exclusion.[10] That this is the case can easily be seen if the broadband industry is mapped onto the vertical chain of production that characterizes most industries (Yoo 2002). The initial stage is known as manufacturing and consists of the companies that create the products and services that end users actually consume. The final stage is known as retailing and is composed of the companies responsible for delivering those products and services to end users. Although it is theoretically possible for retailers to purchase products directly from manufacturers, in some cases logistical complications create the need for an intermediate stage between manufacturers and retailers. Firms operating in this intermediate stage, known as wholesalers, assemble goods purchased directly from manufacturers into complete product lines and distribute them to retailers. Formal vertical integration through

10   Werden (1987); Areeda and Hovenkamp (2008c); Lessig (2002); Wu (2004).

mergers and de facto vertical integration through exclusivity arrangements between manufacturers and retailers or between manufacturers and wholesalers are common economic features, appearing in industries varying from shoes to cars.[11]

The broadband industry fits easily into this vertical structure. The manufacturing stage is composed of the companies that produce Web page content and Internet-based services, such as e-commerce and VoIP. The retail stage includes DSL providers, cable modem systems, and other last-mile technologies. Conceptualizing the chain of distribution in this manner makes clear that the practices toward which network neutrality directs its attention, which are uniformly about last-mile providers favoring proprietary applications and content, are essentially forms of vertical exclusion.

The emphasis on vertical exclusion remains clear even if network neutrality is viewed through the "layered model" that has become an increasingly popular way to conceive of the structure of the Internet. The leading approach disaggregates networks into four horizontal layers that cut across different network providers.[12] The bottommost layer is the *physical layer*, which consists of the hardware infrastructure used to route and transmit the data packets that make up a particular form of communications. The second layer is the *logical layer*, which is composed of the protocols used to route packets to their proper destinations and to ensure that they arrive intact. The third layer is the *applications layer*, which is composed of the particular programs and functions used by consumers. The fourth layer is the *content layer*, which consists of the particular data being conveyed.

The differences between the layers can be illustrated in terms of the most common Internet application: e-mail. The physical layer consists of the telephone or cable lines, e-mail servers, routers, and backbone facilities needed to convey the e-mail from one location to another. The logical layer consists of the SMTP protocol employed by the network to route the e-mail to its destination. The application layer consists of the e-mail program used, such as Microsoft Outlook. The content layer consists of the particular e-mail message sent.

The layered model underscores the extent to which network neutrality is focused on vertical exclusion. The concern is that owners of the physical layer will use their control over the logical layer to give preferential treatment to proprietary applications and content. Network neutrality thus proposes regulating the logical layer to preserve competition in the applications and content layers.

---

11  See, e.g., *Brown Shoe Co. v. United States*, 370 U.S. 294 (1962); *White Motor Co. v. United States*, 372 U.S. 253 (1963).

12  The layered model is related to the open systems interconnection (OSI) model developed by the International Standards Organization (ISO) in the 1980s, which divides into seven different layers. Because some of these distinctions have greater relevance for technologists than for policy analysts, the four-layer model combines some of these layers (Werbach 2002; Whitt 2004). Note that other versions of the layered approach use different numbers of layers. Benkler (2000) and Lessig (2002) employ a three-layer model of physical, code, and content layers. Solum and Chung (2004) propose a six-layer model. Werbach (2005) has revised his initial four-layer model into a three-layer model. Wu (1999) proposes a different four-layer model.

One of the key insights of vertical integration and vertical restraint theory is that any vertical chain of production will only be efficient if every link is competitive (Yoo 2004b). The intuitions underlying that literature can be easily illustrated through a hypothetical example based on the Supreme Court's landmark *Terminal Railroad* decision, the seminal case for mandating interconnection to a bottleneck facility. Suppose that a railway company controlled the only bridge across the Mississippi River at St. Louis and that it was using its control of the bridge either to give preferential treatment to its proprietary rolling stock or to forbid competing carriers to use the bridge at all. One might be tempted to require the bridge owner to allow other railway networks to interconnect to its bridge and to require it to provide access to the bridge to all comers on reasonable and nondiscriminatory terms. Indeed, that is precisely the type of solution sanctioned by the Supreme Court (224 U.S. 383, 411–12 (1912)).

Competition policy theorists have pointed out that this type of compulsory sharing of a monopoly facility represents something of a competition policy anomaly. When confronted with a concentrated market, the conventional response is to deconcentrate the problematic market, either by breaking up the existing monopoly or by facilitating entry by a competitor. The elimination of horizontal concentration allows private ordering to dissipate the supracompetitive prices and reductions in output associated with monopoly (see, e.g., Areeda and Hovenkamp 2008c).

Compelling interconnection to the bottleneck resource deviates from the conventional approach by leaving the monopoly in place and simply requiring that it be shared. If shared at the monopoly price, it fails to reduce prices below or increase output above monopoly levels. If that is the case, forcing a bridge monopolist to provide nondiscriminatory access to its bridge provides no consumer benefits, because vertical disintegration does nothing to displace the bridge monopoly that is the real source of market failure.[13] In essence, the Supreme Court focused on the wrong policy problem. It makes little sense to protect the market for rolling stock. That market was already quite competitive, and the barriers to entering that portion of the industry were quite low. Rather than attempting to foster competition among railways, it should have focused its efforts on increasing the competitiveness of the market for bridges. In other words, competition policy would be better promoted if attention were focused on the level of production that is the most concentrated and the most protected by entry barriers.

The same economic reasoning holds true for broadband. Suppose that vertical integration in broadband were banned altogether and that every last-mile provider were forced to divest its ownership interests in any content or applications provider. Would doing so reduce the market power of the last-mile providers? The answer is clearly "no." The market power exercised by DSL and cable modem providers exists

---

13  Indeed, if the market for rolling stock were also uncompetitive, double marginalization theory indicates that vertical integration could actually enhance welfare (Yoo 2002).

because of the limited number of options that end users have for obtaining last-mile services. The number of options will remain the same regardless of whether last-mile providers hold ownership stakes in content and application providers and of whether unaffiliated content and application providers are granted nondiscriminatory access. Vertical disintegration thus has no effect on last-mile providers' ability to extract supracompetitive returns. Consumers will receive benefits only if entry by alternative network capacity is promoted.

This analysis emphasizes the extent to which network neutrality proponents are focusing on the wrong policy problem. By directing their efforts toward encouraging and preserving competition in the market for applications and content, they are concentrating on the segments of the industry that are already the most competitive and the most likely to remain that way. This is not to say that the previous regulations designed to foster competition in CPE, long distance, and enhanced services were misguided. Focusing on promoting competition in complementary services may make sense when entry by alternative network capacity is impossible, as was arguably the case when the FCC mandated access to network transmission in order to promote competition in CPE, long distance, and enhanced services.

The FCC has recognized, however, that the increasing availability of last-mile alternatives has undercut the continued appropriateness of this approach. For example, the FCC has ruled that the local telephone companies created by the breakup of AT&T now face sufficient competition to justify permitting them to offer in-region long-distance service in every state except Alaska and Hawaii (FCC 2008d). In addition, in eliminating the regulatory requirements imposed by the *Computer Inquiries*, the FCC recognized that those rules "were developed before separate and different broadband technologies began to emerge and compete for customers" and could no longer be justified under contemporary circumstances (FCC 2005d). Last, the FCC has acknowledged that the increase in competition has weakened the ability of last-mile providers to discriminate in favor of proprietary CPE. The FCC has concluded that the growth in competition among local exchange carriers justified abolishing its prohibition of bundling CPE with telecommunications services. Even though local exchange markets were not yet perfectly competitive, the FCC concluded that the level of competition and the consumer benefits of bundling sufficiently mitigated the risk of anticompetitive harm (FCC 2001b). The FCC has also abandoned its previous role in establishing the technical criteria for interconnecting CPE, although the FCC stopped short of repealing the interconnection requirements altogether (FCC 2000f).

The rationale underlying previous examples of mandated interconnection and standardization, as well as the evolution of regulatory policy since those restrictions were initially adopted, indicates that broadband policy would be better served if such efforts were directed toward identifying and increasing the competitiveness of the last mile, which remains the industry segment that is the most concentrated and protected by entry barriers. Restated in terms of the layered model, decisions about whether to regulate the logical layer should not be driven by a desire to preserve and promote competition in the application and content layers. Such decisions should instead be guided by their impact on competition in the physical layer.

## 2. Network Diversity and Static Efficiency

The appropriate central goal of broadband policy having been determined to be fostering greater competition in the last mile, the next logical step is to assess whether network neutrality would further or hinder that goal. The analysis will examine two different dimensions of economic performance: "static efficiency" and "dynamic efficiency." Static efficiency holds the quantity of inputs and the available technology constant and asks whether goods and services are being produced using the fewest resources and are being allocated to those consumers who place the highest value on them. Static efficiency is traditionally measured according to the most familiar metrics of economic welfare, such as the maximization of consumer and total surplus and the minimization of average cost and deadweight loss.

This analysis reveals that network neutrality may impair static efficiency in two ways. First, standardization necessarily reduces economic welfare by limiting product variety. Second, and more importantly for the purposes of this book, network neutrality can impede the emergence of competition in the last mile by reinforcing the economic characteristics that drive markets for telecommunications networks toward natural monopoly (i.e., high up-front costs and network economic effects). To the extent that network neutrality is imposed to limit monopoly or oligopoly power, it can have the perverse effect of entrenching industry concentration by short-circuiting one of the most natural ways to mitigate market failure. Network neutrality is also hamstrung by the practical consideration that the regulatory tools traditionally used to promote static efficiency are unlikely to work well in industries undergoing rapid technological change. Those tools are also unlikely to be effective when the demands that end users are placing on the network are becoming increasingly heterogeneous in terms of quality of service and content.

Although static efficiency represents the most widely accepted measure of economic performance, it begs an important question by failing to take into account the fact that the distribution of inputs and technology is itself subject to change and optimization. Such considerations fall within the realm of dynamic efficiency, which treats input availability and technology as endogenous. Put another way, whereas static efficiency optimizes placement along a production possibility frontier, dynamic efficiency also addresses the prospect that the production possibility frontier could shift outward. Indeed, the growing importance of technology and infrastructure and the accelerating pace of technological change have made dynamic efficiency an increasingly important consideration in the modern economy.

In terms of dynamic efficiency, network diversity draws on the literature exploring the impact of compulsory access on investment incentives in order to examine how mandating interconnection can discourage the build-out of new last-mile technologies. Mounting empirical evidence confirms that the imposition of interconnection and standardization regimes of the type envisaged by network neutrality proponents to redress concentration in the last mile may in fact have the opposite effect. Network diversity, in contrast, would avoid these problems and could facilitate entry by new last-mile providers.

Adoption of any set of protocols has the inevitable effect of favoring certain types of applications and disfavoring others. Standardization also has the inevitable effect of putting the government in the position of picking technological winners and losers. In addition, to be effective, such intervention would likely be required at an early stage when the underlying technology was still in a state of flux (Bresnahan 1999).

Consider TCP/IP, which remains the de facto standard set of protocols on the Internet.[14] Given the Internet's meteoric success, it is tempting to treat the status quo as the relevant baseline and to place the burden on those who would deviate from it,[15] although, as discussed later, there are significant conceptual problems associated with taking such an approach. As noted earlier, one of the distinguishing features of TCP/IP is that it routes packets anonymously on a "first come, first served" basis without regard to the application with which they are associated. It also transmits packets on a "best efforts" basis without any guarantee of success.

This approach to routing packets was uncontroversial when usage restrictions prohibited commercial use of the Internet and the network was used primarily by technology-oriented academics to share text-based communications that were not particularly sensitive to delays of up to a second. In recent years, however, the environment in which the Internet operates has changed radically (Blumenthal and Clark 2001). The transformation of the Internet from a medium for academic communication into a mass market phenomenon has greatly complicated the decisions faced by network owners. Indeed, as noted in Chapter 1, the number of possible connections increases quadratically with network size. The commercialization made possible by the privatization of the Internet has greatly increased the heterogeneity and variability of Internet usage. The shift from text-based applications, such as e-mail, to more bandwidth-intensive applications, such as Web page downloading and file transfers, has dramatically increased the volume of end-user demand. The emergence of applications that are increasingly sensitive to delay, even at the cost of lower accuracy and increased distortion (MacKie-Mason and Varian 1994), such as streaming video and virtual worlds, has created demand for even greater reliability in throughput rates and quality of service and is creating pressure for the deployment of "policy-based routers," which break from TCP/IP by assigning higher priority to packets associated with time-sensitive applications (Clark 1996; Yoo 2004b). Furthermore, as noted in Chapter 2, the unexpected interactions among network components that are the hallmark of complex systems can be quite sensitive to variability of demand. Increases in the variability

14   For a preliminary version of this argument, see Yoo (2004b).
15   Lemley and Lessig (2001); Wu (2004).

of network traffic can thus greatly impede network performance even if, on average, utilization of network capacity remains quite low (Mackie-Mason and Varian 1995b).

Furthermore, the packet anonymity inherent in TCP/IP may be interfering with network owners' attempts to add security features designed to foster e-commerce or to protect against viruses and other hostile elements that are proliferating on the Internet. In addition, the Internet's shift away from academically oriented users who enjoyed a similar degree of institutional support and shared certain common institutional norms has increased the justification for moving responsibility for system maintenance and management away from end users and toward the network's core (Yoo 2004b).

These considerations make network management quite challenging. Although it is theoretically possible for network owners to respond to some of these demands by expanding bandwidth (Lessig 2002), the fact that application designers are waiting in the wings with ever more bandwidth-intensive applications dictates that there is no compelling reason to believe that bandwidth will necessarily increase faster than demand, especially in light of the fact that the number of potential connections goes up exponentially with the number of computers added to the system. In addition, decisions about capacity expansion can be difficult when facing uncertainty about the magnitude, heterogeneity, and variability of the demand that will be placed on the network. Decision making is complicated still further by the "lumpiness" of network capacity created by the indivisibility of fixed costs and the fact that increasing network capacity typically takes a considerable amount of time.

In such an environment, it seems unrealistic to tie network owners' hands by limiting the number of ways in which they can manage network demand. An example from the early days of the Internet illustrates the point nicely. In 1987, end users began to rely increasingly on personal computers instead of dumb terminals to connect to what was then the NSFNET. The increased functionality provided by the shift to personal computers increased the intensity of the demands that end users were placing on the network. The resulting congestion caused terminal sessions to run unacceptably slowly, and the fact that fixed cost investments cannot be made instantaneously created an inevitable delay in adding network capacity. This is precisely the type of technology- and demand-driven exogenous shock that makes network management so difficult. NSFNET's interim solution was to reprogram its routers to give terminal sessions higher priority than file transfer sessions until additional bandwidth could be added (Mackie-Mason and Varian 1995b). Indeed, such solutions need not be temporary: in a technologically dynamic world, one would expect the relative costs of different types of solutions to change over time. Sometimes increases in bandwidth would be cheaper than reliance on network management techniques, and vice versa. It would thus be short-sighted to tie network managers' hands by limiting their flexibility in their choice of network management solutions.

Network neutrality can also restrict the network's functionality.[16] A close analysis of the "end-to-end argument" (Saltzer et al. 1984) – generally regarded as one of the foundations of network neutrality[17] – demonstrates this point. The end-to-end argument asserts that application-specific functionality should be confined to the hosts operating at the edge of the network and that the core of the network should be as simple and general as possible. The rationale underlying this argument is based on cost–benefit analysis. Increasing the functions performed in the core of the network can improve the functionality of the network, but only at the cost of reduced network performance. The problem is that all applications would have to bear the costs associated with the reduction in performance even if they gained no compensating benefits. This tradeoff can be avoided if the core of the network performs only those functions that benefit almost all applications and if higher-level, application-specific functions are confined to the servers operating at the network's edge.

Although the end-to-end argument is frequently invoked in support of network neutrality, such claims are misplaced. The architects of the end-to-end argument candidly reject calls to elevate end-to-end into a regulatory mandate as "too simplistic." Correct application of the cost–benefit tradeoff lying at the heart of the end-to-end argument requires "subtlety of analysis" and can be "quite complex." Indeed, the architects of end-to-end acknowledge that circumstances exist under which application of end-to-end would do more harm than good.[18] Properly construed, end-to-end calls for implementation on a case-by-case basis rather as a blanket regulatory prohibition (Bhattacharjee et al. 1997; Hatfield 2000).

There is no reason to believe *a priori* that giving preference to innovations operating at the network's edge over innovations in the network's core will prove to be beneficial in all cases. Two examples from the early days of the Internet introduced in Chapter 8 illustrate the problem. The introduction of digital transmission technologies required the deployment of protocols that were not interoperable with the existing analog network. This necessitated the introduction of computer processing into the core of the network to engage in "protocol conversion." The emergence of "voice messaging services," such as voice mail and advance calling, posed similar problems. Voice messaging services appeared to function best when their capabilities were designed directly into the telephone switch. Both developments were inconsistent with the regime of transparency and interoperability envisioned by the

---

16  The discussion that follows draws on the more extended analysis in Yoo (2004b).

17  See, e.g., Lemley and Lessig (2001); Lessig (2002); Cooper (2003); Solum and Chung (2004); Wu (2004).

18  Saltzer et al. (1984); Clark (1996); Reed et al. (1998); Blumenthal and Clark (2001). To take but one example, the desirability of end-to-end depends in part on the length of the file. If a system drops one message per one hundred messages sent, the probability that all packets will arrive correctly decreases exponentially as the length of the file (and thus the number of packets composing the file) increases (Saltzer et al. 1984, pp. 280–81).

second *Computer Inquiry* as well as the simplistic reading of the end-to-end argument. Both required specific waivers from the FCC's rules in order to be deployed. Had the FCC adhered to its policy of preserving the ability of unaffiliated providers to obtain transparent access to the network, these innovations would not have been allowed to emerge.

Simply put, any choice of standardized protocol has the inevitable effect of favoring certain applications and disfavoring others, just as TCP/IP discriminates against applications that are time-sensitive and end-to-end favors innovation at the edge over innovation in the core. As discussed in some detail below, whether mandating network neutrality would be socially beneficial is a complicated question that depends on a myriad of considerations, including the level of aggregate demand, heterogeneity of network uses, the variability in network traffic flows, end users' need for network reliability, and the extent to which technological change is reorganizing the natural boundaries between levels that were previously separated by a natural interface, notwithstanding the many claims to the contrary. In short, the desirability of complete standardization and interoperability is an empirical question that cannot be answered *a priori*.

Indeed, the nonneutrality inherent in the choice of baseline principles becomes even clearer when the debates about network neutrality are viewed through the lens of the broader debates about jurisprudence. In essence, it is the same insight driving the critique of Herbert Wechsler's espousal of so-called "neutral principles" (Wechsler 1959) as well as the failure of attempts to advance a value-neutral conception of equality (Westen 1982). The choice of the appropriate underlying baseline is an inherently normative judgment. In other words, although there is hope that principles can be neutrally applied once they have been established, the choice of foundation principles is inevitably nonneutral.

It would thus be a mistake to regard network neutrality as inherently neutral, as the engineering embodiment of a competitive market, or as the best way to reflect technological humility, as some network neutrality proponents have suggested (Lessig 2002; Wu 2004).[19] At best, it represents a casual empirical conjecture about how competition and innovation can best be promoted under current circumstances. At worst, it represents an attempt to use engineering principles to impart legitimacy to a naked normative commitment (Blumenthal 2002). Like any baseline principle, it must be supported by substantial normative and empirical justification before being imposed as an absolute mandate. Until that occurs, the more technologically humble position would appear to be permitting network diversity through nonregulation, rather than mandating the use of any particular set of protocols.

---

19  Lessig's later work concedes that no network design is neutral and instead describes network neutrality as an attempt to eliminate certain kinds of discrimination (Lessig 2005). For the reasons stated above, reconstructing network neutrality in terms of discrimination and equality simply restates the underlying normative issues in different terms without resolving them.

Mandating interconnection, nondiscrimination, rate regulation, and standard-ization could reinforce the very sources of market failure that network neutrality is supposed to redress. The central concern of network neutrality is that DSL and cable modem providers are using their control over the last mile to restrict the ability of applications and content providers to reach end users. In this respect, it is motivated by the same policy concerns animating regulatory intervention into markets for CPE, long distance, and enhanced services. Two factors are typically cited as the reasons for the high degree of concentration in markets for last-mile services. The classic source of market concentration is the supply-side economies of scale that arise when entry requires significant up-front investments. More recently, attention has also focused on the demand-side economies of scale created by "net-work economic effects," which arise when the value of the network is largely determined by the number of people connected to it. Both forces tend to give the large players a decisive advantage. In the most extreme case, they create natural monopolies.

Interestingly, mandating network neutrality can have the perverse effect of rein-forcing both of these sources of market failure.[20] In other words, network neutrality can actually make matters worse by short-circuiting one of the most promising ways that smaller players use to survive when confronted with unexhausted returns to scale. If true, this raises the specter that network neutrality could be the source of, rather than the solution to, market failure.

Allowing networks to differentiate themselves can also alleviate the economies of scale associated with declining average costs (Yoo 2003b, 2004a). It is the fact that price is the only dimension along which firms can compete that gives the largest players their decisive advantage. A different equilibrium can obtain if competitors are allowed to compete along dimensions other than price. If so, a smaller player may be able to survive notwithstanding lower sales volumes and higher unit costs (and thus higher prices) by tailoring its network toward services that a subsegment of the market values particularly highly. The greater value provided by the differentiation of the network allows a specialized provider to generate sufficient revenue to cover its up-front costs even though its volume is significantly smaller than that of the leading players.

How could such differentiation occur in the context of broadband? One way is through protocol nonstandardization, such as through the adoption of a different routing protocol. As discussed above, all protocols necessarily favor certain appli-cations over others. If discrete subgroups of end users place sufficiently different valuations on different types of applications, multiple networks will be able to coex-ist simply by targeting their networks toward the needs of different subgroups (Yoo 2004b). If demand is sufficiently heterogeneous, the greater utility derived from allowing consumers to access consumer services that they value more highly can more than compensate for any cost disadvantages resulting from the reduction in

---

20   For a preliminary sketch of this argument, see Yoo (2004b).

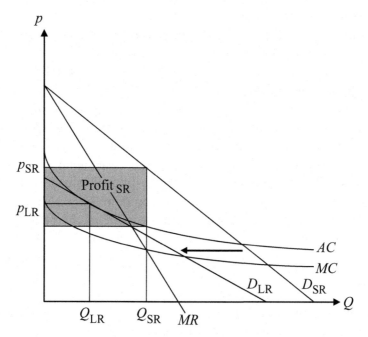

**Figure 11.1.** Short-run and long-run equilibrium under monopolistic competition.

volume. Indeed, it is conceivable that network diversity might make it possible for three different last-mile networks to coexist: one optimized for traditional Internet applications such as e-mail and Web site access, another incorporating security features to facilitate e-commerce and to guard against viruses and other hostile aspects of Internet life, and a third that prioritizes packets in the manner needed to facilitate time-sensitive applications such as streaming media and VoIP.

Network diversity allows greater experimentation with different ways to take advantage of technological differences. Consider, for example, the fact that wireless telephone networks in the U.S. have employed incompatible standards. The initial standard, known as time division multiple access ("TDMA"), is being replaced by global system for mobile communications ("GSM") and code division multiple access ("CDMA") without inconveniencing consumers to a significant degree. In some cases wireless carriers are using different transmission protocols for voice and data communication in order to utilize the characteristics of the transmission medium to meet the different technical demands of each application (Yoo 2007b). The experience with wireless telephony highlights the economic benefits that can flow from competition among standards. Had the United States followed Europe's example and adopted a uniform standard for second-generation wireless telephony, it would have precluded the realization of the benefits associated with CDMA, which supports a broader range of data services, makes more efficient use of spectrum, and provides the most straightforward migration path to the next generation of wireless technologies (Gandal et al. 2003; Weiser 2003a).

Entering into exclusivity arrangements with respect to content represents another possible means for differentiating one's network.[21] One of the best current examples is the manner in which DBS provider DirecTV is using an exclusive programming package known as "NFL Sunday Ticket" to enhance its ability to compete with cable television. Indeed, it appears that exclusive access to NFL Sunday Ticket constitutes one of the major factors helping DBS emerge as a viable competitor to cable. If regulators were to view this exclusivity arrangement solely in static terms, they might be tempted to appease cable customers who have expressed frustration at their inability to purchase NFL Sunday Ticket by requiring that the package be made available on both platforms. Doing so would reduce DBS's ability to compete by eliminating one of the primary inducements to shift from cable to DBS.[22] In other words, banning exclusivity would only serve to entrench the dominant position that local cable operators have historically enjoyed over multichannel video distribution, which has long represented one of the central policy problems confronting the television industry.

Another example that should be familiar to practicing lawyers is Lexis's efforts to differentiate itself from Westlaw. In past years, Lexis attempted to distinguish its services by obtaining exclusive access to the full-text version of the *New York Times* (Ojala 1997). More recent efforts include Lexis's acquisition of the exclusive rights to the Shepard's citator system (Liebert 1999). This exclusivity arrangement is doubtless a source of frustration to those who previously accessed Shepard's through Westlaw. That said, these exclusivity rights have helped Lexis to survive despite the significant advantages West enjoys by virtue of its role in publishing case reporters. It also has forced Westlaw to develop a new product called Key Cite to compete with Shepard's.

These examples illustrate how using nonstandardized protocols and exclusive access to content – the precise practices that network neutrality would condemn – can in fact facilitate competition in the last mile. The implication is that public policy may be better served if Congress and the FCC were to reject network neutrality in favor of a network diversity principle that would allow networks to differentiate their services in precisely this manner. It is possible that such network diversity may take some time to emerge. Indeed, the seminal analyses of production differentiation recognize that the initial industry entrants may well prefer to offer products that are quite similar (Hotelling 1929). As entry increases, providers should begin to find it profitable to pursue more targeted strategies (Steiner 1952). Thus, policymakers should avoid imposing regulations that would foreclose the emergence of network diversity even in the absence of the imminent arrival of a new entrant offering differentiated services. Humility about policymakers' ability to

21  Shapiro (1999, p. 678) notes how exclusivity "can serve to differentiate products and networks."

22  Interestingly, the NFL's decision to start its own cable network may alter the current situation.

predict which business models will prove successful further underscores the importance of leaving this possibility open.

In summary, the complexity of the interface, the increasing heterogeneity of end users' demands, and the pace of technological change are reducing the utility of the regulatory tools upon which policymakers have traditionally relied to manage interconnection, nondiscrimination, rate regulation, and standardization. It is particularly telling that two noted scholars of network industries not noted for deregulatory views have suggested that access regimes have proven so unworkable that they should be abandoned (Joskow and Noll 1999).

### 3. Network Diversity and Dynamic Efficiency

Not only would network neutrality threaten to reduce static efficiency; it also poses a serious risk to dynamic efficiency. The literature exploring the impact of mandating interconnection on dynamic efficiency in the context of antitrust,[23] UNE access,[24] and multiple ISP access to cable modem systems[25] has long emphasized how regimes mandating interconnection and standardization can discourage entry into the last mile. As a result, network neutrality would appear to conflict directly with the goal of dynamic efficiency and would instead be the source of, rather than the solution to, market failure. Conversely, embracing a network diversity principle promises to promote competition in the last mile and thereby alleviate the central issue confronting broadband policy.

The reasons that mandating interconnection is potentially problematic from the standpoint of dynamic efficiency can best be explained in terms of the hypothetical example based on *Terminal Railroad* discussed above. Suppose that access to the bridge was not compelled and that rates were not regulated. Any supracompetitive returns earned by the owner of the existing bridge would signal that the market was in disequilibrium and would provide the incentive for anyone interested in building another bridge to do so. In addition, the railroads that were unable to obtain access to the existing bridge would be clamoring for an alternative. They would thus represent the natural strategic partners for any would-be builder of another bridge.

The situation changes dramatically if access to the bridge is compelled. Granting access lets the customers who would otherwise stand ready to invest in a new bridge off the hook, rescuing them from having to undertake the risks associated with investing in alternative capacity. At the same time, the would-be bridge entrant would also find entry less attractive. Knowing that it would be forced to share the new bridge with all comers at regulated prices weakens the incentives for it to construct another bridge. Indeed, rate regulation can deprive the new entrant of the returns

---

23  Areeda and Hovenkamp (2008c); Robinson (2002).
24  Hausman and Sidak (1999); Crandall and Hausman (2000); Jorde et al. (2000).
25  Yoo (2004a); Lopatka and Page (2001).

it needs to survive.[26] Granting access thus threatens to frustrate the appearance of alternative bridge capacity that remains the central goal of competition policy in this situation. In so doing, it threatens to entrench the existing bridge monopolist in place. As the Supreme Court recently noted in *Trinko*:

> Firms may acquire monopoly power by establishing an infrastructure that renders them uniquely suited to serve their customers. Compelling such firms to share the source of their advantage is in some tension with the underlying purpose of antitrust law, since it may lessen the incentive for the monopolist, the rival, or both to invest in those economically beneficial facilities.
>
> (540 U.S. 398, 407–08 (2004)

At the same time, the obligation to share the benefits of any improvements also reduces the incumbents' incentives to undertake the investments needed to upgrade existing network technologies.[27] This dynamic is why courts and leading commentators have consistently condemned compelling access to communications networks whenever competition from alternative network platforms is feasible.[28] The need to stimulate reinvestment also undercuts asymmetric regulatory proposals that would impose interconnection mandates only on incumbents with market power.[29] Focusing on current market shares can be misleading in industries that are undergoing rapid growth, because it is future rather than current shares that are important. Even more importantly, imposing more stringent regulation on incumbents is also problematic in a world in which encouraging reinvestment in existing networks is as important as encouraging investment in new network technologies.

The same dynamics can be illustrated by considering a hypothetical town in which there is a single department store. Much like a broadband network, a department store is simply a conduit for goods and services produced by others. Upon reflection, it becomes clear that imposing a rule requiring all department stores to make space available to all manufacturers on a reasonable and nondiscriminatory basis would discourage entry by a second department store. Although entrants often

---

26  The FCC's experience with a broadcast regulation known as the financial interest and syndication rules ("finsyn") illustrates how imposing rate regulation discourages investment in alternative networks. Finsyn attempted to curb the dominant positions held by ABC, CBS, and NBC by limiting the extent to which networks could take ownership stakes in the programming that they televised. Reducing the profitability of networking had the inevitable consequence of deterring entry by new networks. This is confirmed by the fact that the Fox network was unable to enter successfully until it obtained a waiver from finsyn (FCC 1990; Chen 1996). The courts eventually struck down finsyn as arbitrary and capricious (*Schurz Commc'ns, Inc. v. FCC*, 982 F.2d 1043 (7th Cir. 1992); *Capital Cities/ABC v. FCC*, 29 F.3d 309 (7th Cir. 1994)). The rules were eliminated shortly thereafter (FCC 1995d).

27  *AT&T v. Iowa Utils. Bd.*, 525 U.S. 366, 428–29 (1999) (Breyer, J., concurring in part and dissenting in part).

28  *Brand X*, 545 U.S. at 1002; *AT&T v. Iowa Utils. Bd.*, 525 U.S. at 388–89; *U.S. Telecom Ass'n v. FCC*, 290 F.3d 415, 428–29 (D.C. Cir. 2002); Areeda and Hovenkamp (2008c, pp. 242–46).

29  Rogerson (2000a); Speta (2004).

find it profitable to enter into competition with a monopolist earning monopoly rents, this incentive is reduced if rate regulation precludes any such rents from being earned. In addition, the frustrated manufacturers who would otherwise be eager to support construction of a second department store would also lose their enthusiasm for the project. Furthermore, compelling access to the department store shelves would also limit the ability of stores to control whether an appropriate mix of goods was represented or to ensure that the goods satisfied certain quality standards. Preventing consolidation with manufacturers can preclude the achievement of real efficiencies by using tighter integration through inventory management and electronic data interchange to reduce costs. Department stores often try to promote their popularity by entering into exclusivity arrangements with key manufacturers, sometimes even establishing boutiques in portions of their stores. Requiring department stores to provide nondiscriminatory access to all manufacturers would thus prevent them from pursuing one of the best entry strategies available to new entrants. Indeed, this type of strategic partnership between manufacturers and retailers appears to have played a critical role in promoting the growth of the cable industry (Owen and Rosston 2006). This mechanism for promoting entry would be frustrated by regulations mandating open access to the retail platform.

This underscores the extent to which mandating access to a bottleneck facility represents surrender to the monopoly. The normal response of competition policy when it encounters monopolies is to break them up or at least to prevent them from getting any worse. Mandating interconnection deviates from this tradition by addressing the symptoms of monopoly power without treating its causes. Instead of breaking up the monopoly, access leaves it in place and only requires that it be shared. Furthermore, approaches that break up monopolies necessarily have built-in exit strategies embedded within them. Mandated sharing of a bottleneck facility, in contrast, implicitly envisions that the monopoly, and thus the regime of regulatory oversight, will persist indefinitely.

Such an approach might be appropriate if entry by a competitor to the bottleneck were impossible, as was arguably the case when the FCC and the courts relied on interconnection and standardization to promote competition in CPE, long distance, and enhanced services. In that event, any reduction of incentives to invest in alternative network capacity would be beside the point, because such entry would be impossible. The situation is quite different when entry by alternative network capacity is feasible. In that case, the reduction in investment incentives may short-circuit the natural process by which markets diffuse bottlenecks. In the worst case scenario, mandating interconnection can itself have the perverse effect of entrenching the existing monopolies in place. Indeed, as discussed in Chapter 8, the absence of an interconnection requirement helped drive the rapid geographical buildout of the telephone network during the early years of the telephone industry, as the Bells and the independent telephone companies competed to satisfy customers. Empirical studies have failed to provide any support for claims that mandating access helps facilitate the emergence of facilities-based competition. Empirical studies of unbundling of broadband facilities have drawn similar conclusions (Howell 2002; Kim et al. 2003; Aron and Burnstein 2003; Garcia-Murillo 2005).

It is also possible that entry by the new bridge would be wasteful if the welfare benefits did not exceed the fixed costs of creating the second bridge. The optimality of entry depends on how much of the volume captured by the new entrant consists of new surplus created either by better pricing caused by enhanced competition or by the provision of differentiated services that represent a better fit with particular consumers' preferences – called "demand creation" – or simply surplus cannibalized from the existing bridge – called "demand diversion" (Yoo 2004a).

By now, the implications for broadband policy should be manifest. The central focus in deciding whether to mandate network neutrality should be on its effect on stimulating competition in the last mile. If it were subject to mandatory interconnection, standardization, nondiscrimination, and rate regulation, any would-be last-mile entrant would realize that even if it were successful, it would be forced to make its platform available to all content and application providers under rates that would limit it to ordinary returns. In addition, the would-be builder would not find a group of content and applications providers clamoring for additional access, because mandating interconnection to the existing platform would rescue them from having to invest in alternative distribution arrangements. In the process, network neutrality risks reducing incentives to invest in new last-mile technologies to the extent that it cements the existing last-mile oligopoly in place. Although such a policy might be justifiable if entry by alternative network capacity were impossible, it is indefensible when 3G, WiFi, powerline, and other technologies are actively searching for capital to support their deployment and when the state of the art in transmission is undergoing rapid technological change. At best, the inevitable lag in enacting new regulations will cause economic losses. At worst, by destroying incentives to build new technologies and to reinvest in existing technologies, regulation might itself be the cause, rather than the consequence, of market failure. Under these circumstances, mandating network neutrality would appear to pose a serious threat to dynamic efficiency.

It is for this reason that the FCC has repeatedly stated that its decisions with respect to broadband will be guided by the principle that "broadband services should exist in a minimal regulatory environment that promotes investment and innovation in a competitive market" (FCC 2002b, p. 3022; accord FCC 2002c). The manner in which lack of interconnection can stimulate investment in new networks is eloquently demonstrated by the fact that major complementary services and equipment providers, such as Google, EarthLink, IBM, Intel, and Disney, have each undertaken major investment in alternative broadband technologies in the wake of the Supreme Court's *Brand X* decision.[30] Embracing network diversity as a policy, in contrast, would thus appear to provide substantial incentives to support the build-out of new last-mile facilities.

---

30   *Atlanta Journal-Constitution* (2005); *Broadcasting & Cable* (2005); *San Jose Mercury News* (2005); *Telephony* (2005); *Wall Street Journal* (2005a).

## B. Noneconomic Justifications for Network Diversity

In addition to the economic rationales discussed above, some commentators have invoked noneconomic rationales to justify network neutrality.[31] Drawing inspiration from the Supreme Court's admonition that "it has long been a basic tenet of national communications policy that the widest possible dissemination of information from diverse and antagonistic sources is essential to the welfare of the public,"[32] some of these scholars argue that the central rationale is to promote political discourse, even if it might be more economical to limit access.[33] Indeed, there is a long legacy of regulating network industries in order to protect access by small producers that dates back to the initial regulation of the railroads in the late nineteenth century.[34] Following the landmark Supreme Court decision in *Munn v. Illinois* (94 U.S. 113, 126 (1876)), other scholars justify the imposition of interconnection, standardization, nondiscrimination, and rate regulation requirements because telecommunications networks are "affected with a public interest" (Speta 2002, pp. 261 n. 185, 270–71; Nachbar 2008).

There is nothing incoherent about imposing regulation to promote values other than economic welfare. The problems with this approach are more practical than conceptual.[35] Unless protecting the widest possible diversity of sources is a virtue in and of itself that trumps all other values, such a theory must provide a basis for quantifying the noneconomic benefits and for determining when those benefits justify the economic costs. Our nation's experience with antitrust law has revealed that telecommunications networks are often subject to economies of scale, which in turn implies that forcing communications enterprises to remain small can exact a price. At some point, the marginal benefit associated with protecting another small voice will fall short of the marginal cost of preventing network firms from realizing the available economies of scale.

The problem is that arguments in favor of protecting small customers and speakers have historically failed to reflect any sense of optimality and have instead regarded additional diversity as an absolute good.[36] But the presence of scale economies underscores the basic fact that promoting diversity exacts a cost that must be traded off against the benefits of additional producers. As the D.C. Circuit has noted in a related context, "Everything else being equal, each additional 'voice' may be said to enhance diversity. . . . But at some point, surely, the marginal value of

---

31  See, e.g., Liebman (1997, p. 833): "Should the populist ancestry of the Sherman Act be revisited to contend with telecommunications giants?"

32  *Turner Broad. Sys., Inc. v. FCC* (*Turner I*), 512 U.S. 622, 663–64 (1994) (internal quotation marks omitted); accord *Turner Broad. Sys., Inc. v. FCC* (*Turner II*), 520 U.S. 180, 192 (1997).

33  Benkler (2000); Cooper (2003); *Turner II*, 520 U.S. at 227 (Breyer, J., concurring).

34  Rabin (1986); Hovenkamp (1988).

35  For a more general critique of attempts to build theories of media regulation on democratic principles, see Yoo (2003c).

36  FCC (1970a); Cooper (2003).

such an increment in 'diversity' would not qualify as an 'important' governmental interest. Is moving from 100 possible combinations to 101 'important'?" (*Time Warner Entm't Co. v. FCC*, 240 F.3d 1126, 1135 (D.C. Cir. 2001)). More recent pronouncements have begun to acknowledge that not "each and every incremental increase in the number of outlet owners can be justified as necessary in the public interest" and that "there certainly are points of diminishing returns in incremental increases in diversity" (FCC 2003c, p. 13631). That said, the approach has remained decidedly ad hoc. As a result, those who take seriously the admonition that it takes a model to beat a model will be decidedly reluctant to embrace such an indeterminate approach. The open-endedness of the approach and the lack of a clear notion of optimality leave it vulnerable to being redirected towards political purposes.

In this regard, the fate of the "populist" school of antitrust provides a useful object lesson.[37] This school embraced a noneconomic vision of competition policy that protected small players in order to promote democratic values associated with Brandeisian pluralism even when doing so was economically costly.[38] Over time, courts and commentators began to recognize that because many industries are subject to economies of scale, preserving small producers has a price. The problem was that populism failed to provide a basis for determining when the costs outweighed the benefits. By the end of the 1980s, even those sympathetic to the populist school were forced to concede that the economic approach to antitrust had prevailed.[39] In the process, antitrust shifted from hostility toward vertical integration in order to protect small players for largely noneconomic reasons to a more nuanced, explicitly economic approach that recognized that vertical integration can yield substantial economic benefits (Yoo 2002). Broadband policy could be well served to follow the same path and recognize the dangers of an excessive focus on preserving the freedom of consumers and content/applications providers and that permitting a degree of vertical integration can represent a better way to promote economic welfare.

Arguments justifying the regulation of telecommunications networks because they are "affected with the public interest" are similarly unlikely to prove a satisfactory basis for regulation. As noted in Chapter 9, modern courts now regard this category as analytically empty. In addition, the category was notoriously slippery.

---

37  For overviews of the conflict between the Chicago and the Populist Schools that manifest distinctly different sympathies, see Jacobs (1995); Meese (2000); Areeda and Hovenkamp (2006a).

38  For a classic statement of this position, see *United States v. Brown Shoe Co.*, 370 U.S. 294, 344 (1962) (Congress intended to "promote competition through the protection of viable, small, locally owned business" even when "occasional higher costs and prices might result from the maintenance of fragmented industries and markets"). For other similar statements, see, e.g., *Klor's, Inc. v. Broadway–Hale Stores, Inc.*, 359 U.S. 207, 212–13 (1959); *Albrecht v. Herald Co.*, 390 U.S. 145, 152–4 (1968), *overruled by State Oil Co. v. Khan*, 522 U.S. 3 (1997); *Topco*, 405 U.S. at 610–11; see also *Fashion Originators' Guild of Am., Inc. v. FTC*, 312 U.S. 457, 467 (1941) (holding group boycotts illegal and evidence of procompetitive benefits inadmissible).

39  Fox (1981); Gerla (1988); Lande (1990); Jacobs (1995).

Specifically, courts rejected the notion that exercise of the power of eminent domain or operation under a state franchise was by itself sufficient to render an industry "affected with the public interest." Instead, the inquiry was governed by a multifactor balancing test, with no one factor being dispositive.[40] Eventually, the Supreme Court rejected the entire framework as unworkable in its landmark decision in *Nebbia v. New York* (291 U.S. at 536), and the concept was thereafter regarded as "discarded."[41]

This is not to say that Brandeisian principles could not support a coherent theory of regulation. It is only to say that no one has yet articulated such a theory with sufficient clarity to be coherent. That said, the populist vision rests in uneasy tension with the modern economy. Brandeisian populism aspires to the type of small-scale economic activity typically associated with Jeffersonian democracy (Rabin 1986).[42] It also tends to value economic stability for its own sake, because instability tends to

---

40 Hall (1940). In addition, courts have repeatedly rejected the notion that private property that was initially obtained via eminent domain and is currently used to serve the public is somehow entitled to less dignity under the law. *W. Union Tel. Co. v. Pa. R.R.*, 195 U.S. 540, 569–70, 573 (1904) (noting that a right of way obtained through condemnation remains private property even when devoted to a public use); *United Rys. & Elec. Co. v. West*, 280 U.S. 234, 249 (1930) (holding that "the property of a public utility, although devoted to the public service and impressed with a public interest, is still private property"), *overruled in part on other grounds by Fed. Power Comm'n v. Hope Natural Gas Co.*, 320 U.S. 591 (1944); *Gulf Power Co. v. United States*, 187 F.3d 1324, 1329–30 (11th Cir. 1999) ("A property owner is entitled to expect that the property it acquired via eminent domain . . . came with the right all property has").

41 *Olsen v. Nebraska ex rel. W. Reference & Bond Ass'n*, 313 U.S. 236, 245 (1941).

42 In the words of Brandeis himself:

[S]ize alone gives to giant corporations a social significance not attached ordinarily to smaller units of private enterprise. Through size, corporations, once merely an efficient tool employed by individuals in the conduct of private business, have become an institution – an institution which has brought such concentration of economic power that so-called private corporations are sometimes able to dominate the state. The typical business corporation of the last century, owned by a small group of individuals, managed by their owners, and limited in size by their personal wealth, is being supplanted by huge concerns in which the lives of tens or hundreds of thousands of employees and the property of tens or hundreds of thousands of investors are subjected, through the corporate mechanism, to the control of a few men. . . . The changes thereby wrought in the lives of the workers, of the owners and of the general public, are so fundamental and far-reaching as to lead these scholars to compare the evolving "corporate system" with the feudal system; and to lead other men of insight and experience to assert that this "master institution of civilised life is committing it to the rule of a plutocracy."

(*Louis K. Liggett Co. v. Lee*, 288 U.S. 517, 565 (1933))

(Brandeis, J., dissenting))

See also *United States v. Falstaff Brewing Corp.*, 410 U.S. 526, 543 (1973) (Douglas, J., concurring) (stating that "the concentration of power leads predictably to socialism that is antagonistic to our system").

break down the citizenry. As such, it does not seem well suited to industries such as broadband, in which large-scale, rapid, and often disruptive change is a prominent feature. Although some scholars have posited that network neutrality would yield important democratic benefits, they are usually articulated too generally and too incompletely to provide a basis for regulation (Yoo 2003c).

## C. Institutional Considerations

Adoption of network diversity necessarily requires the incurrence of some degree of transaction costs. Some would be temporary, such as the costs incurred when network owners voluntarily retool their networks to accommodate different standards. Other transaction costs would be more enduring. For example, if multiple standards were to exist, end users and providers of applications and content would have to expend significant resources to verify compatibility with respect to different networks. It is theoretically possible that the resulting friction might be so severe that it more than offsets the benefits of shifting to another standard. When that is the case, society would be better off if network diversity were not permitted.

At the same time, mandating network neutrality would involve transaction costs as well. As first discussed in Chapter 5 and developed further in Chapters 8 and 10, the costs of adopting, disseminating, maintaining, and updating a standardized interface are considerable. Furthermore, imposing and updating any such interface gives rise to an inevitable regulatory delay that can be debilitating when the underlying technology is changing rapidly. Indeed, the FCC has recognized that network neutrality can actually harm consumers by forcing network owners either to delay deployment of new technologies while reengineering their networks to comply with interconnection and interoperability requirements or, in the event that they are able to do so economically, by forcing them to forego deploying the full increase in capability made possible by a particular innovation (FCC 2005d). Resolution of the network neutrality debate thus depends on a complete analysis of the transaction costs on both sides of the equation.

Entry by providers of differentiated networks will not be instantaneous. Thus, even if monopolistic competition is likely to yield dynamic efficiency benefits over the long run, the inevitable delays in entry may force the market to incur short-run static efficiency losses. As noted in Chapter 4, whether the dynamic efficiency gains will dominate the static efficiency losses depends on a myriad of factors, including the magnitude of the gains and losses, the speed of entry, and the appropriate discount rate. Determining the welfare implications of network diversity requires a multifaceted inquiry that is not susceptible to a simple policy inference.

Regulation tends to take the form of *ex ante* rules, and such rules tend to be ill suited to factually nuanced determinations. Regulation is an inherently blunt instrument that acts in a categorical, non-fact-specific manner. It is less well suited to resolving issues that demand detailed inquiry into the circumstances of individual cases. Some commentators attempt to avoid the clumsiness of *ex ante* regulation by urging the adoption of a general regulatory standard of nondiscriminatory access that leaves the details of the regulatory regime to be developed after the fact through case-by-case adjudication on an *ex post* basis. Although better able than *ex ante* regulation to take into account the context-specific considerations described above, such an approach threatens to stifle network diversity nonetheless. Even proponents of network diversity concede that deviations from interconnectivity and standardization are sometimes justified and that it can be difficult, if not impossible, to determine whether a particular deviation is justified. When that is the case, the usual policy response is to allow experimentation with different business practices and to place on those who would oppose such practices the burden to demonstrate some adverse effect on competition.

Erecting a presumption against discriminatory access and forcing owners to justify any deviations would have the effect of foreclosing practices that are ambiguous or for which evidence of actual market performance is lacking. This would have the unfortunate effect of preventing the development of network diversity even if entry by diversified network providers would be welfare-enhancing. Given the difficulties in forecasting the impact of technological change and in predicting which business models will ultimately prove successful, the humility inherent in a more restrained approach provides critical breathing room for the experimentation upon which the innovative process depends. Although the difference between the network diversity approach and the more modest, *ex post* versions of network neutrality at first glance may appear to be nothing more than a difference in emphasis or a shift in the burden of proof, allowing practices to go forward until they are proven harmful has the important consequence of permitting experimentation with ambiguous practices that would be foreclosed under a presumption of nondiscrimination.

Even if competition were not sufficiently robust to prevent network owners from undertaking anticompetitive conduct, it is extremely unlikely that the type of blanket approach to nondiscrimination favored by network neutrality proponents would represent the proper policy response. Should a local telephone company attempt to protect its core business by blocking its DSL customers from using VoIP or a cable modem provider attempt to protect its core cable television business by prohibiting its cable modem customers from accessing streaming video, such problems would justify a targeted response limited to a particular application, as the FCC mandated in *Madison River* (FCC 2005b) and endorsed in *Comcast* (FCC 2008c). Under no circumstances would such concerns support the kind of blanket restrictions envisioned under the strongest versions of network neutrality.

Regulation poses particularly grave risks in industries that are undergoing rapid technological change. When that is the case, even the most conscientious regulator will find it hard to keep up with the pace of change. Worse yet, whether imposed as an *ex ante* rule or as a presumption against discriminatory access with the specific contours of the regulatory requirement developed *ex post*, network neutrality would have the effect of foreclosing practices that are ambiguous or about which there is too little information. This is why scholars from across the political spectrum have warned of the dangers of regulatory lag in industries that are technologically dynamic (see, e.g., Posner 1969; Kahn 1971; Panzar and Willig 1977; Breyer 1982). The task confronting policy makers is especially difficult because they would have to intervene at a fairly early stage in the technology's development to make any difference, because governmental intervention after the market has settled on the optimal technology would serve little purpose.

Given the institutional considerations, how should the debate between network diversity and network neutrality be resolved? Lessig (2002, p. 47) suggests that although network management is a real problem, congestion problems can be solved by increasing bandwidth rather than by giving network owners more control over network flows. Although Lessig recognizes that this vision of a world with "infinite" bandwidth contradicts the basic economic notion that all commodities are inherently scarce, he nonetheless states, "I'm willing to believe in the potential of essentially infinite bandwidth. And I am happy to imagine the scarcity-centric economist proven wrong."

There is no compelling reason to believe that bandwidth will necessarily increase faster than demand, especially in light of the number of bandwidth-intensive applications waiting in the wings and the fact that the number of potential connections goes up exponentially with the number of computers added to the system. Relying on capacity expansion to solve the problems related to congestion is made all the more problematic by the fact that forecasting demand is inherently uncertain and capacity cannot be expanded instantaneously. Even when capacity expansion is feasible in the long run, any underestimation of projected demand will necessarily create short-run scarcity that cannot be addressed through increased bandwidth. The inherent uncertainty about future changes in demand renders it essentially impossible for network owners to rely on the expansion of capacity as the sole solution to the problems of network management. In addition, adding bandwidth and using network management techniques that reduce the transparency of the network represent alternative ways to solve the problems of congestion. Unless one assumes that the cost of capacity will necessarily decline faster than the growth in the demand for capacity, the relative attractiveness of each alternative cannot be determined *a priori*. Last, the nonstandardization and exclusivity inherent in network diversity are often designed to improve security or increase functionality, wholly apart from the desire to reduce congestion. When that is the case, the possibility of adding bandwidth is not responsive to the problem. It would thus seem to be a mistake to precommit to one approach over the other.

Second, Lessig also suggests that network neutrality might be justified by the growing level of concentration in network ownership. Indeed, Lessig is quite skeptical about the prospects that intermodal competition from alternative platforms such as DSL can provide sufficient discipline on cable modem providers.[43] This conclusion rests in uneasy tension with Lessig's faith in unlimited bandwidth as a solution to the problems of network management. Even more importantly, it is far from clear that concentration represents the threat that Lessig suggests once the precise markets that network neutrality is designed to protect have been identified.[44] The concentration is most acute in the market in which last-mile broadband providers bargain with end users. As noted earlier, preventing owners of last-mile technologies from entering into exclusivity arrangements and forcing them to employ nonproprietary protocols that permit complete interoperability would not affect this market one iota. The economic relationship between last-mile providers and end users is largely determined by the fact that most end users currently only have two options in terms of last-mile providers: the cable company and the telephone company. Mandated network neutrality would not change the makeup of this market.

Imposing network neutrality would have a significant impact on the upstream market in which last-mile providers bargain with providers of applications and content. Major Web-based providers, such as Amazon.com or eBay, are focused more on the total number of customers they are able to reach nationwide than they are on their ability to reach customers located in any specific metropolitan area. The fact that they may be unable to reach certain customers is of no greater concern, however, than the fact that manufacturers of particular brands of cars, shoes, or other conventional goods are not always able to gain distribution in all parts of the country. Manufacturers who are cut off from consumers served by a particular cable or telephone company should not face significant problems so long as they are able to obtain access to a sufficient number of customers located elsewhere (*Time Warner*, 240 F.3d at 1131–32). The FCC has similarly rejected the notion that the local market power enjoyed by early cellular telephone providers posed any threat to the cellular telephone equipment market, because any one cellular provider represented a tiny fraction of the national equipment market (FCC 1992a). The proper question is thus not whether the broadband transport provider wields market power vis-à-vis broadband users in any particular city, but rather whether that provider has market power in the national market for obtaining broadband content. In short, it is national reach, not local reach, that matters.

---

43   Lessig is candid about his bias against incumbent network owners:

Dinosaurs should die.... And innovators should resist efforts by dinosaurs to keep control. Not because dinosaurs are evil; not because they can't change; but because the greatest innovation will come from those outside these old institutions. Whatever the scientists at Bell Labs understood, AT&T didn't get it. Some may offer a theory to explain why AT&T wouldn't get it. But this is a point most understand without needing to invoke a fancy theory.

(Lessig 2002, p 176)

44   The following discussion is based on Yoo (2004a, 2004b).

When the relevant market is properly defined, it becomes clear that this market is too unconcentrated for vertical exclusion to pose a threat to competition. In the context of broadband, it amounts to the claim that a decision by the largest broadband provider to limit access to its network poses a real threat to competition in applications and content. Although such dangers might have been credible in the days in which AT&T dominated the last mile, they are considerably less compelling during an era in which the largest player controls only twenty-one percent of the national market (Yoo 2004b). Absent collusion with other providers, the interconnection decisions of even the largest player are not in a position to stifle the competitiveness of the applications and content layers.

Indeed, the ambiguity inherent in the issues surrounding concentration is underscored by comparing Lessig's concern, which is that portions of the network will be too eager to deviate from the established standard, with the concern associated more frequently with network economic effects, which is that users will be too reluctant to deviate from the established standard, thereby allowing an obsolete technology to become locked in (Farrell and Saloner 1986; Katz and Shapiro 1994). When the latter is the primary concern, the presence of large players is a potential boon, rather than a bane. Because larger players are able to internalize a greater share of the benefits created by their own technology choices, they are logical candidates to mitigate the lock-in effects caused by network externalities by becoming the sponsors of new technologies (Yoo 2002). In other words, to the extent that network economic effects create excess inertia rather than excess momentum, attempts to deviate from the existing standard should be embraced, rather than rebuffed.

In the end, Lessig's primary concern is that network diversity would hurt the environment for innovation, which he believes stems from the existence of an "innovation commons" in which applications and content providers can have access to the entire universe of potential customers without having to obtain permission from any gatekeeper. Network owners, Lessig argues, are too eager to fracture the interoperability of the Internet because they fail to internalize the benefits from innovation associated with network neutrality (Lessig 2005).[45] As noted earlier, a close reading of the economic literature reveals that the impact of network economic effects on innovation is ambiguous and that such concerns appear to be misplaced in the context of a physical network that can be owned and in an industry undergoing exponential growth. Indeed, the use of the term "commons" creates some degree of irony, because the accepted solution to the tragedy of the commons is the creation of well-defined property rights (Hardin 1968), which would be more consistent with network diversity than network neutrality. More recent scholarship on the anticommons has underscored the fact that property rights can be too small as well as too large (see, e.g., Heller 1998). The presence of innovation externalities more

---

45 This is a point that is more important to him than even the end-to-end argument. Indeed, Lessig acknowledges that even if discrimination were imposed by end users in a manner consistent with end-to-end, he would still be concerned (Lessig 2005).

properly suggests the existence of an optimal size of a property right rather than a blanket presumption in favor of an innovation commons.

As such, little insight is gained by trying to elevate the preservation of the innovation commons into a rhetorical trump. The most plausible justification resembles a version of the "precautionary principle," which argues that certain harms are so potentially catastrophic that regulators should guard against them even when it is uncertain whether they will ever come to fruition. Such an argument would claim that the potential harm to innovation associated with deviating from the transparency that now characterizes the Internet is so great as to justify imposing network neutrality prophylactically. The problem with this argument is that the precautionary principle is incoherent as an *a priori* commitment. Because there are risks in adhering to as well as deviating from the status quo, taken to its logical conclusion, it forbids all courses of action, because regulation can impose costs and foreclose beneficial outcomes just as surely as nonregulation. As a result, theorists have attempted to render the precautionary principle coherent by limiting application to circumstances in which the adverse consequences are truly *catastrophic* and in which deviations from the status quo are *irreversible* (Sunstein 2005). Neither precondition would appear to be satisfied in the case of network neutrality. As the experience in reconfiguring local telephone switches for independent long distance providers demonstrates, allowing networks to become noninteroperable is unlikely to prove irreversible. Furthermore, as important as innovation on the Internet is, reduced innovation does not constitute the type of catastrophic harm that would justify regulatory intervention in the absence of a concrete showing of competitive harm.

Ultimately, Lessig fails to provide a determinative resolution to the question. Likewise, in the absence of a clearer picture of the contextual details, the resolution proposed here is necessarily no more definitive. Short of swapping *ipse dixit* claims about better policy, how should decision makers resolve disputes in the face of uncertainty? Fortunately, competition policy offers a potential way out of this analytical limbo. It suggests that when policy makers cannot determine whether a new institutional form would help or hinder competition, the proper response is nonregulation until a practice is shown to effect a concrete harm to competition. Forbearance from either forbidding or mandating any particular solution leaves room for the experimentation upon which markets depend. Nonintervention is particularly appropriate where, as here, regulators will struggle to distinguish anticompetitive from procompetitive behavior. As noted earlier, network neutrality advocates candidly acknowledge that deviations from network neutrality are often the result of benign attempts to meet the increasingly varied demands that end users are placing on the network.

Permitting deviations from network neutrality in the absence of concrete demonstrations of competitive harm draws further support from the growing empirical literature on vertical integration and vertical contractual restraints, as demonstrated by the recent surveys described in Chapter 9. Placing the burden of proof on those who would regulate represents the proper way for regulators to show technological humility and accords with our notions of liberty and the classic vision of the proper relationship between the individual and the state (Yoo 2003c). It also allows decision making about technology adoption to be decentralized. Finally, it avoids the risks of locking the existing technological boundaries between firms into place in industries undergoing dynamic technological change. In the most extreme case, regulation can itself become the source of natural monopoly, in which case intervention would have the perverse effect of reinforcing the market failure that regulation was designed to redress.

These intuitions are also informed by the practical problems associated with mandating interconnection, nondiscrimination, rate regulation, and standardization. Experience with cable leased access and UNE access has shown how difficult such regimes are to administer when interfaces are complex and the underlying technology is changing rapidly. Viewing the history of FCC regulation through the cautionary lens of public choice theory provides an additional reason to disfavor regulatory intervention. As noted earlier, it is quite possible that regulators will give preference to the concerns of static efficiency, which have a concrete impact in the here and now, over the concerns of dynamic efficiency, which involve contingent benefits to parties who often have yet to be identified. The FCC's history in this regard is not promising. Even James Landis, the leading proponent of expertise-driven public interest regulation and one of the key architects of the New Deal, acknowledged that the FCC has been a disaster (Landis 1960).

This bias has unfortunate implications for the permanence of regulatory intervention. Compelling sharing of the existing network by mandating interconnection, nondiscrimination, rate regulation, and standardization implicitly presumes that regulatory supervision will continue indefinitely. In short, it represents a surrender to monopoly that is only justifiable if entry by alternative network capacity is impossible. In contrast, solutions that focus on dynamic efficiency have built-in exit strategies embedded within them. Once a sufficient number of broadband network platforms exist, regulatory intervention will no longer be necessary. Fostering entry and then deregulating once it has occurred seems to be a better ambition for regulatory policy than committing to the ongoing supervision of both the price and nonprice terms of business relationships that network neutrality implies.

Ultimately, network diversity does not depend upon a definitive resolution of the best substantive outcome. It adopts a humbler stance toward policymakers' ability to determine the competitive impact of particular practices and to anticipate technological change. Network diversity is not simply the mirror image of network neutrality, in that it does not call for the imposition of proprietary protocols. Instead, it adopts a more modest position that permits the experimentation upon which economic progress depends to proceed until a practice's actual impact can be determined.

*    *    *

There can be no question that network neutrality holds considerable allure. The vision of a world in which every end user can obtain access to every available application and piece of information is quite compelling. It is thus quite understandable that so many commentators have endorsed network neutrality as a concept. The economic advantages of interoperability are considerable, and interoperability would likely play a central role in the business plans of the vast majority of Internet-based businesses.

The question that must be asked is not whether network neutrality yields benefits, but rather whether the threat posed by a single network owner deviating from network neutrality is so great that regulators should prohibit it from exploring whether network diversity might make more sense. The foregoing exploration of the arguments underlying network neutrality provides substantial reason for caution. Standardization can reduce welfare both by reducing diversity and by biasing the market against certain types of applications. It can have the perverse effect of reinforcing the sources of market failure used to justify regulatory intervention in the first place. It can further entrench monopoly power by dampening incentives to invest in alternative network neutrality.

Instead, public policy might be better served if policymakers were to embrace network diversity. Doing so would permit end users to enjoy the benefits of product variety. Network diversity also has the potential to mitigate the supply-side and demand-side scale economies that concentrate telecommunications markets and to make it easier for multiple networks to coexist. The more restrained approach inherent in network diversity is also more consistent with the current understanding of the institutional capabilities of courts and agencies. It also accommodates technological dynamism and humility by providing maximum room for experimentation and development. This is not to say that policy makers should reject network neutrality once and for all. What is called for is a sense of balance and optimality that can adjust with the circumstances. But in the face of technological uncertainty, the more appropriate and humble approach would appear to favor forbearance from mandating any particular architecture.

# 12

## The Regulation of Broadband Networks and the Internet: Network Neutrality versus Network Capacity

During the Internet's initial, narrowband phase of development, Internet service providers (ISPs) pursued a variety of architectural approaches. Some ISPs, such as CompuServe, Prodigy, and America Online, initially adopted relatively restrictive policies, which only provided end users with access to proprietary applications and content and charged them for network usage on a per-minute basis. Others followed a more permissive approach, opening up their networks to all content and applications providers on a nondiscriminatory basis and allowing end users to download any content, run any application, and attach any device for a flat monthly fee. The latter approach ultimately proved more attractive to consumers, and end users became accustomed to a world in which they faced few restrictions either on the ways they could use their network connections or on the amount of bandwidth they consumed.

This same debate has resurfaced as the Internet has begun to migrate from a narrowband to a broadband architecture. Once again, network owners have begun to experiment with more restrictive approaches. With respect to end users, some network owners have begun to offer bandwidth tiers to end users, in which the amount that customers pay varies with the amount of bandwidth with which they are provided. Others have placed restrictions on end users' latitude to run certain applications or attach certain devices. Still others have considered alternative pricing relationships with respect to content and applications providers, under which transmission speed would depend on the tier of service purchased. To date, the policy decision has been framed as a choice between universal interoperability, in which end users remain free to access content, run applications, and attach devices as they see fit, and a world of "walled gardens," in which the subscribers to any particular network will only be able to enjoy the benefits of a limited number of Internet-based services.

Unfortunately, the current debate has framed the issues in too narrow a manner. The problem is that – as even network neutrality proponents concede – deviations from network neutrality may well be motivated by legitimate concerns about network management and that it can be difficult, if not impossible, to predict which architectural approach will eventually prevail. For example, as Lessig himself notes, the vast potential of the Internet was lost not only on incumbent network owners such as AT&T, but also on almost every computer science expert presented with the concept of the World Wide Web (Lessig 2002). The difficulty of predicting the future is demonstrated even more eloquently by the furor surrounding America Online's acquisition of Time Warner. Many experts warned that the merger would create an Internet juggernaut, in which the combination of America Online's Internet content with the transmission capabilities of Warner Cable would chill innovation and with which other providers would struggle to compete. Needless to say, these dire predictions failed to materialize, as the vertically integrated business model that America Online pursued with such confidence ultimately proved to be a colossal failure. In the absence of some reason to believe that policy makers will be able to anticipate which architecture will ultimately emerge as optimal, mandating one architecture over another has the unfortunate effect of foreclosing exploration of the potential benefits of alternative approaches.

Fortunately, competition policy offers a middle ground that obviates the need for policy makers to make such judgments. If the choice between two architectural approaches is ambiguous, policy makers have the option of permitting both alternatives to go forward until concrete harm to competition can be demonstrated. In other words, rather than mandating any particular architecture, policy makers can instead embrace a regime of *network diversity* that allows network owners to pursue different strategies. Unless such experimentation poses potential harms that are catastrophic or irreversible, the emerging consensus argues against imposing proactive regulation on the basis of speculation about the likely impact on competition (Sunstein 2005).

This approach places regulators in a more restrained and humble position that is better suited to their institutional capabilities. Rather than asking them to determine which architectural design is likely to prove more socially beneficial, it asks them only to determine whether a plausible case can be made to justify each possible approach and whether allowing experimentation with each approach would pose potentially catastrophic or irreversible harms. This approach is more than just a question of which side bears the burden of proof (cf. Wu 2004). Instead, it represents a true middle course that allows policy makers to avoid having to foreclose any particular alternative when confronted with a policy choice that is ambiguous.

Recast in this manner, the key regulatory question is whether the restrictions criticized by network neutrality proponents are so pernicious and unjustifiable that experimentation should not be permitted. An analysis of the economics of the Internet reveals the existence of a number of plausible arguments demonstrating that deviations from network neutrality might well enhance economic welfare.

The key to understanding why this might be the case is recognizing the fact that the Internet is subject to congestion. When networks are subject to congestion, one customer's usage of the network can degrade the quality of service that other customers receive. The primary finding of the literature on the economics of congestion is that competitive markets will reach an efficient equilibrium if each user is charged a usage-sensitive price set equal to his or her marginal contribution to congestion (see, e.g., Berglas 1976). As a result, some commentators have argued in favor of shifting all Internet services to usage-sensitive pricing (MacKie-Mason and Varian 1995a; Sidak and Spulber 1998; Wu 2003). At the same time, flat-fee pricing has persisted for a wide range of other congestible resources, such as ski lifts and local telephone service. The persistence of these practices has led to the creation of a literature exploring the circumstances under which usage-sensitive pricing might prove uneconomic. The general thrust of this literature is that transaction costs associated with a usage-sensitive pricing system can consume all of the economic benefits associated with a shift to usage-based pricing. When that is the case, economic welfare would be better served if end users were charged flat rates instead of usage-sensitive prices (Barro and Romer 1987; Helsley and Strange 1991; Lee 1991; MacKie-Mason and Varian 1995a).[1]

While the debate between flat-rate and usage-sensitive pricing is an important one, it is incomplete in that it frames the range of available pricing options too narrowly. Specifically, it overlooks the insight, derived from Ronald Coase's classic critique of the economic parable of the lighthouse (1974), that the high transaction costs associated with metered pricing can also be avoided by finding an alternative activity that can serve as a proxy for usage. If that alternative activity is easier to meter, it can provide a useful approximation of actual usage of the primary services.

Consideration of a broader range of institutional solutions to the pricing problem expands the policy space in important ways. It suggests that allowing broadband providers to impose restrictions on bandwidth-intensive end user activities could well represent a more cost-effective way to address the problems of congestion. In fact, the types of restrictions that cause network neutrality proponents the greatest concern are precisely the type of activities that tend to impose congestion costs on other users. Viewed from this perspective, bandwidth management and end user restrictions are just two points in a spectrum of alternative institutional approaches to solving the problems of network management. It is unnecessary to determine which of the many possible ways to manage congestion on the Internet will ultimately prove most economical. For our purposes, it suffices to acknowledge that the optimal solution might take on one of a range of institutional forms. The indeterminacy of the problem justifies adopting policies that do not foreclose network owners from experimenting with any particular institutional solution absent the demonstration of concrete competitive harm. Indeed, there is no reason to presume that the eventual solution will be uniform, and it is quite conceivable that different portions of the network might pursue different institutional solutions.

---

1　Barro and Romer did not initially frame their analysis in terms of congestion economics but later acknowledged the connection (Barro and Romer 1991).

This analysis also suggests that prohibiting last-mile providers from deviating from network neutrality may actually harm consumers. Simply put, the current regime of flat-rate pricing and unrestricted access discourages innovation in network management. In the process, it allows high-volume users to impose costs on low-volume users, in effect requiring the latter to subsidize the former. Taking a broader vision of consumer welfare reveals that allowing network owners to place restrictions on high-bandwidth uses can benefit consumers by making possible new ways to manage network traffic and to force those who create the most congestion on the Internet to bear the costs they impose on others. Conversely, low-volume users may well benefit from such restrictions through increases in the quality of the service they receive and decreases in the prices they pay (MacKie-Mason and Varian 1995b). Indeed, the emergence of potentially beneficial practices, such as backbone peering, content delivery networks such as Akamai, network-based spam filtering, and blocking Web sites known to be the source of viruses, attests to the extent to which the Internet is already far from "neutral."

On a more fundamental level, adoption of a more permissive approach to end user restrictions would parallel the shift in the vision of the ideal form of competition that has taken place under the antitrust laws. Prior to the mid-1970s, the Supreme Court took an extremely hostile view toward vertical integration that combined manufacturing and retail delivery under the same corporate umbrella, as well as vertical contractual arrangements (such as exclusive dealing contracts, long-term contracts, territorial exclusivity, and requirements contracts) that were tantamount to the same thing. Over time, the Court has become considerably more hospitable toward vertical integration, recognizing that vertical integration can represent an important means through which firms can minimize transaction costs. In the process, the Court rejected categorical prohibitions in favor of a more nuanced approach that evaluates the competitive impact of vertical integration and vertical contractual restraints on a case-by-case basis (*Continental T.V., Inc. v. GTE Sylvania, Inc.*, 433 U.S. 36, 52–59 & n. 21 (1977)).

The case for permitting last-mile networks to experiment with end user restrictions also draws on economic considerations separate from congestion. For example, by allowing network owners to differentiate the services they offer, exclusivity can play a key role in mitigating the sources of market failure that require regulatory intervention in the first place. Indeed, some degree of discrimination and differentiation is inevitable in any industry characterized by large fixed costs. Furthermore, close analysis reveals that access requirements such as network neutrality are less justifiable and less likely to succeed in a world in which competition among last-mile providers is growing ever more robust, natural interfaces between companies are complex and constantly changing, and the avalanche of content available on the Internet has heightened end users' reliance on media filters exercising editorial discretion.

Every deviation from network neutrality need not necessarily enhance economic welfare. It is sufficient if some deviations from network neutrality may plausibly be motivated by legitimate concerns and it is hard to distinguish procompetitive and anticompetitive uses of such restrictions, as network neutrality proponents have conceded is often the case. When it is possible that intervention may do more harm than good, and particularly when consumers do not face any immediate harm, the more prudent course would be to forego locking the network into any particular architecture. Because the threatened harms are neither catastrophic nor irreversible, competition policy supports forbearing from forbidding particular practices until specific harm to competition can be demonstrated. Any competitive problems that do emerge can be addressed through the type of targeted intervention imposed by the FCC in *Madison River*, limited to prohibiting the broadband provider from blocking access to those applications that compete directly with the broadband provider's core business (FCC 2005b). They would not justify the broad prohibition of end user restrictions envisioned under network neutrality.

Indeed, if one adopts a broader notion of consumer welfare, such restrictions may well be a benefit to consumers by forcing heavy bandwidth users to bear the congestion costs they impose on other users and by effectively lowering the prices paid by light bandwidth users who previously were forced to cross-subsidize heavier users. It also engages the broader arguments about the economics of innovation and the dangers of imposing regulation in the face of prospective harms.

## A. Sources of Congestion on the Internet

As is commonly known, the Internet is not a single network but rather a network of interconnected networks. The FCC has found it useful to divide the networks that compose the Internet into three types. *Backbone providers* provide high-speed, long distance connections between a small number of interconnection points.[2] *Middle-mile providers* provide regional distribution functions, carrying the traffic from the limited number of interconnection points served by backbone providers to the local distribution facilities maintained by last-mile providers in individual cities (which in the case of DSL are usually called "central offices" and in the case of cable modem systems are usually called "headends").[3] *Last-mile providers* convey the traffic from these local distribution facilities to the premises of end

---

2  Originally, backbones only interconnected at the four public network access points (NAPs) created by the National Science Foundation (located in San Francisco, Chicago, New York, and Washington, DC) and the Commercial Internet Exchange maintained in Santa Clara, California (Kende 2000). The NAPs have since been privatized, and backbone providers have also created a number of other public interconnection points, where any carrier can exchange traffic. In addition, backbone providers have begun to exchange traffic directly through private interconnection points (Yoo 2004b). Depending on the context, the FCC sometimes replaces the term "backbone providers" with the term "long haul communications transport facilities" to make clear that it is referring to high-speed fiber transport used for voice as well as data communications (FCC 2002a).

3  Under broadband, middle-mile and last-mile provision are often vertically integrated. This is because real efficiencies often result from such integration (Yoo 2004b).

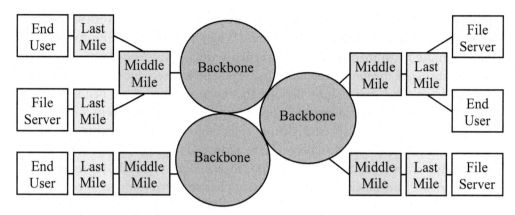

**Figure 12.1.** The basic architecture of the Internet.

users. The FCC has analogized this to a road system. Backbones represent inter-state highways, which convey traffic at high speeds and allow entry and exit only through limited access points. Middle-mile networks are the divided highways that connect interstate exits to local roads. Last-mile networks are the local roads responsible for delivering traffic to the driveways leading into individual residences (FCC 2000e).

Until recently, the protocols that govern the Internet have required that all of these providers be organized into a series of parallel hierarchies, in which each last-mile provider exchanged traffic with a dedicated middle-mile provider, which in turn exchanged traffic with a dedicated backbone (Besen et al. 2001). Each type of Internet provider in this chain must maintain some infrastructure for conveying the stream of data packets, consisting of wires, fiber optic cable, or some other medium of transmission. Each network must also have a number of computers called *routers*, which operate in the core of the network to direct packets to their destinations. Computers that store files at the edge of the network and fulfill requests for those files from other users are called *servers*.

The process can be illustrated by tracing the path of a typical Internet trans-action, such as downloading a Web page over a cable modem system. The process begins when an end user employs its computer to submit a request for a Web page. The end user's computer divides the address of the requested Web page into packets and forwards the packets to the cable modem provider serving that end user. The packets travel through the coaxial cables connecting the end user's premises to a fiber node located in its neighborhood, which aggregates those packets with other traffic and transmits them to the headend. A cable modem termination system separates the data packets from the video stream and directs them onto the data network maintained at the headend. The router on the data network located at the headend transmits the packets to a middle-mile provider, which in turn transmits the packets to one of the interconnection points served by backbone providers. The backbone directs the packets to other backbone providers until they reach the backbone connected to the middle-mile provider that serves the destination.[4] The middle-mile provider then directs the packets to the terminating last-mile provider, which passes them on to the server hosting the Web page content. The Web server fulfills the request, and the packets composing the Web page return through a similar set of steps.

Congestion results from the fact that the capacity of almost every step in this process is constrained. For example, the bandwidth of each component of the physical transmission media (e.g., the wires and fiber nodes composing the network) is limited.[5] The number of packets and requests that routers and content servers can fulfill at any time is similarly constrained. When data packets arrive at a rate that exceeds the capacity of any particular element, they form a queue. The resulting delay in the speed with which the requests are fulfilled causes degradation in the quality of service provided by the network.

Changes in the ways people are using the Internet are making these problems all the more acute. The Internet was once dominated by e-mail and other applications that placed fairly modest demands on the network, and the restrictions imposed by the National Science Foundation on backbone services limited the Internet to noncommercial uses. The subsequent privatization of the Internet has greatly increased the number of network users as well as the heterogeneity of network usage (Yoo 2004b). These changes have increased the variability of demand in ways that have made problems of network management considerably more complex. For example, the emergence of Web page downloading, which requires the transfer of images and multimedia features, has increased the intensity of bandwidth usage, as has the emergence of music filesharing and other applications involving the transfer of increasingly large files. In addition, end users are more frequently using applications that are increasingly bandwidth-intensive and sensitive to delay, such

---

4   The number of backbones involved depends on whether service is being provided under a *peering* or a *transit* arrangement. Under peering arrangements, backbones only exchange traffic that originates from the customer of one backbone and terminates with the customers of the other peered backbone. In that case, the maximum number of backbones involved is two. Under transit arrangements, backbones serve as intermediaries for traffic that neither originates from nor terminates with their customers or the customers of their peering partners. In this case, the number of backbones involved may exceed two (Kende 2000).

5   In addition to congestion in backbone and middle-mile services, cable modem customers share bandwidth both between the end users' premises and the fiber node and between the fiber node and the cable headend. As a result, both segments are subject to congestion. DSL systems have historically used dedicated circuits that were less subject to congestion. Telephone companies are increasingly deploying remote terminals that aggregate traffic and convey it via fiber to their central office facilities in a manner quite similar to the hybrid fiber–coaxial architecture of most cable modem systems. To the extent that they employ remote terminals, telephone networks may be subject to congestion effects between the remote terminal and the central office that are similar to those suffered by cable modem systems between the fiber node and the headend. The connection between the end users' premises and the remote terminal continues to be through dedicated wires that are not subject to congestion.

as streaming media and virtual worlds. Thus, guaranteed throughput rates have become increasingly important at the precise time that increases in the volume of traffic are making quality of service harder to maintain. Indeed, some technologists have come to regard the thirty-year-old suite of protocols around which the Internet is currently designed (known as TCP/IP), which routes packets on a first-come, first-served basis in precisely the manner favored by network neutrality proponents, as an increasingly obsolete technology that is ill-suited to the increasingly varied and intense demands that end users are placing on the network (*Telephony* 2006, quoting David Farber).

## B. The Economics of Congestion

The fact that the Internet is subject to congestion gives rise to a number of important policy implications. Perhaps the most sophisticated insights into congestion are provided by the branch of economics known as *club goods*, which was largely inspired by the pioneering work of Nobel laureate James Buchanan (1965).[6]

Club goods are goods that can be shared by more than one person. At the same time, they differ from infinitely shareable goods (known in the literature as *pure public goods*) in that consumption by an additional person creates congestion costs that cause the quality of the services provided to others to deteriorate. Buchanan's paradigmatic example of a club good is a swimming pool. Others have suggested that the theory also applies to a wide range of other facilities, including golf courses, theaters, laundromats, restaurants, and roads.

### 1. Congestion and the Choice between Flat-Rate and Usage-Sensitive Pricing

One of the primary issues that has emerged in the literature is whether a club should charge a single flat-rate price for membership or whether it should charge a price that varies with the intensity of each member's usage of the club facilities. The

---

6  See generally Cornes and Sandler (1996), reviewing the origins of the study of club goods. Buchanan's work is related to Charles Tiebout's earlier work on local public goods, which analyzed shared resources provided by local governments. Tiebout's model assumed that cities attempt to achieve an optimal community size, which is achieved when a city produces the bundle of services desired by residents at the lowest average cost. The posited "U" shape of the cost curve in turn presupposed the existence of some local resource that was in fixed supply, such as a beach or the total amount of land available; otherwise, there would be no logical reason to limit community size (Tiebout 1956). Although Tiebout does not specify what causes marginal cost to increase, it is analogous to the congestion costs assumed by the club goods literature. The primary difference between club goods and local public goods is the feasibility of entry. The former assumes that entry by new clubs is possible. The latter assumes that the total number of municipalities is fixed (Scotchmer 1994).

standard result is that reliance solely on flat-rate pricing will result in inefficiently high levels of congestion and in overconsumption of the club facilities (see, e.g., Berglas 1976, 1981; Scotchmer 1985).

The intuitions underlying this result are quite straightforward. Economic welfare is maximized if the market reaches equilibrium at the point where the social benefits equal the social costs. In the case of club goods, this would occur where the benefits each club member derived from the last unit consumed equalled the costs of congestion created by the last unit consumed. The problem is that if club members are charged rates that are not sensitive to usage, the private cost of consuming an additional unit is zero. That means that utility-maximizing club members will increase their consumption of club resources until the marginal utility from any further increases in usage is zero, at which point the social costs associated with the last unit consumed will exceed the benefits, and welfare is reduced.

In short, flat-rate pricing results in excessive consumption of club resources, which arises because the congestion costs represent a negative externality that individual club members responsible for causing the congestion are not forced to bear. The classic solution is to impose a usage-sensitive price that is equal to the congestion costs imposed by the last unit consumed. In this way, usage-sensitive pricing aligns incentives by bringing private costs into line with the true social costs of consuming an additional unit.[7] As a theoretical matter, usage-sensitive pricing has thus been regarded as a critical mechanism for promoting the efficient allocation of resources.

## 2. The Impact of Transaction Costs on the Choice between Flat-Rate and Usage-Sensitive Pricing

The preference for usage-sensitive pricing suggested by the theoretical literature on club goods is subject to a number of limiting assumptions and conditions. Many

---

7   Within each club, each member will calibrate his or her consumption until the utility they derive is equal. There may initially be some variation in per capita utility across clubs, with some clubs being more crowded than others. Assuming that mobility across clubs is possible, people in high-congestion clubs will seek to shift to low-congestion clubs until utility is equalized across all clubs. Furthermore, club goods theory posits the existence of an optimal club size. On one hand, increasing club size benefits members by allowing them to amortize the overhead costs needed to establish the club and to enforce exclusion over a larger membership base. On the other hand, any increase in membership causes congestion costs to rise. Clubs thus add members until the benefits of spreading costs over an additional member no longer exceed the marginal increase in congestion costs, at which point they will stop adding new members. Assuming free entry, any remaining individuals refused membership in existing clubs remain free to form new clubs. The result is an equilibrium in which the optimal number of clubs exist and in which each club member consumes the optimal amount of club services (Buchanan 1965). Subsequent work has confirmed this result regardless of whether the market structure is monopolistic, oligopolistic, or competitive (Calem and Spulber 1984; MacKie-Mason and Varian 1995a).

of these caveats are not relevant to the network neutrality debate.[8] One caveat that is applicable, however, is that the standard result depends on the assumption that exclusion and metering are costless. A literature has emerged relaxing this assumption and exploring the results that obtain when metering and exclusion require the incurrence of transaction costs. It draws on the insight that someone buying ten units of a good is indifferent between a price of $1 per unit and a $10 entry fee with a ten-unit limit per customer. In other words, the equilibrium under usage-sensitive pricing can be replicated by charging a flat-rate price set equal to the unit price under usage-sensitive pricing times the optimal number of units consumed. Given the identity of these two pricing mechanisms, providers are free to choose the pricing regime that imposes the fewer transaction costs. Thus, if the transaction costs of metering and exclusion are sufficiently high, charging a flat-rate price based on the contribution to congestion by the average club member may well prove economically superior to usage-sensitive pricing (Barro and Romer 1987; Helsley and Strange 1991).[9]

8    For example, as a purely formal matter, a club good equilibrium is only stable if dividing the overall population by the optimal club size results in an integer. When that occurs, the solution is said to be in the *core*, which in turn implies that the equilibrium is Pareto optimal, in that no individual or set of individuals can improve their situation by forming a different club. A noninteger result destabilizes the equilibrium, however, because anyone excluded from club membership will have the incentive to attempt to bid his or her way into a club by offering to accept a lower payoff than a current club member. The result is a constant shuffling of club composition. See, e.g., Pauly (1967). Fortunately, the introduction of a concept known as the *approximate core* renders the nonexistence of an equilibrium less problematic than initially appears. If the number of club members is large relative to the number of nonmembers, club members can make side payments to nonmembers to induce them not to destabilize the existing coalitions. The resulting utilities lie fairly close to core utilities. See, e.g., Wooders (1980).
     Another limiting factor is that the classic analysis of club goods assumes that consumer preferences are homogeneous. See, e.g., Buchanan (1965). If preferences are heterogeneous, each homogeneous subset of the population should partition itself into homogeneous clubs (Pauly 1970; McGuire 1974; Berglas and Pines 1981). If integer problems prevent the total population from segregating itself into homogeneous clubs, individuals with different preferences may have to form a *mixed club*. The resulting intraclub heterogeneity can lead to suboptimal provision (Berglas and Pines 1981). Later work has shown that mixed clubs may be optimal so long as crowding is anonymous and members' demands for facility size and congestion coincide at a feasible division of total economy-wide endowments (Scotchmer and Wooders 1987).
9    It is worth noting that the analyses that found flat-rate pricing preferable to usage-sensitive pricing assumed perfect information (Helsley and Strange 1991). When information is imperfect, the presence of transaction costs can lead to an adverse selection problem in which high demanders patronize facilities designed for low demanders. In such cases, no equilibrium may exist, and any equilibrium that does exist is inefficient (Lee 1991).
     In addition, existing analyses take capacity as given. Although per capita usage will be higher under flat-rate pricing, models that take capacity as endogenous also point out that capacity will be higher as well. As a result, the net impact on congestion is ultimately ambiguous and depends on which of these effects dominates. The problem becomes even more complex if one acknowledges that flat-rate pricing can cause the number of users to change as well. If

As discussed in Chapters 8 and 10, transaction costs can justify replacing a metered regime of interconnection access with a "bill and keep" or "peering" regime in which networks interconnect on a settlement-free basis. Indeed, transaction costs can help explain another of the persistent puzzles of telecommunications pricing, which is the persistence of flat-rate pricing for local telephone service. Local telephone service in the U.S. has not historically been priced on a usage-sensitive basis. Instead, subscribers can place unlimited local calls for a flat monthly fee (FCC 1996b).[10] Economists have long theorized that the fact that local calling was unmetered at the margin was inducing customers to make excessive calls and that usage-sensitive pricing would lead to welfare gains (Mitchell 1978). It is for this reason that some local telephone companies began experimenting with usage-sensitive pricing regimes generally known as "local measured service" (LMS).

The economics of congestion arguably suggest that LMS would eventually emerge as the dominant pricing regime, and yet network providers, regulators, and consumers all failed to embrace LMS. Acceptance of LMS was deterred in part because of the magnitude of the transaction costs of metering local telephone service.[11] The available data suggest that the transaction costs associated with metering and billing for local telephone service may well be substantial. Studies conducted several years ago indicate that the costs of metering and billing represent more than 50% of the costs associated with an incremental call and roughly 100% of the incremental cost of a nonpeak call, with the total cost to the industry exceeding $10 billion.[12]

The problem is further complicated by the nature of congestion on communications networks. When total network usage is relatively low and network resources are slack, the costs associated with incremental usage approach zero. It is only when demand peaks that congestion costs become significant. As a result, a first-best solution would require imposing a form of peak-load pricing in which the usage charge at any particular moment varied with the network elements being used and the level of demand being placed on those elements (Boiteux 1949; Steiner 1957; Williamson 1966). Thus, as a theoretical matter, economic efficiency would require that prices vary with each local exchange, from one moment to the next, and in different portions of the network, depending on the particular level of network demand (Kahn and Shew 1987). As a practical matter, however, the inability to make such minute adjustments prevents networks from charging prices that are

---

users can shift to alternative providers of network services, adopting a flat-rate price will cause the customer base to consist solely of a small group of intensive users with a high tolerance for congestion (MacKie-Mason and Varian 1995a).

10  This situation contrasts with the rate practice of much of the rest of the world, which generally employs usage-based pricing for local telephone service.

11  Mathewson and Quirin (1972); Mitchell (1978); Selwyn (1981); Crew and Dansby (1982); Griffin and Mayor (1987); Kahn and Shew (1987).

12  MacKie-Mason and Varian (1995b); *Telepath* (1998).

precisely calibrated toward actual usage. Instead, network owners typically divide the day into peak and off-peak periods and charge uniform prices during those periods that exceed the true congestion costs of the lower-volume segments of the period and that fall short of the true congestion costs of the higher-volume segments of the period. Variations in demand within those periods inevitably lead to some degree of economic inefficiency, because the uniformity of prices during the period will deter efficient calls during the low-volume segments of the period and will not deter inefficient calls during the high-volume segments of the period. The welfare losses created by these imperfections in the pricing regime become another source of inefficiency that offsets the welfare benefits of usage-sensitive pricing (Kahn and Shew 1987; Park and Mitchell 1987). The combination of transaction costs and the inefficiency caused by the inability to precisely tailor prices to current demand may be sufficient to render usage-based pricing uneconomical.

In addition, networks are complex systems that can adapt in ways that are hard to predict. For example, increasing a particular flow through a saturated network element by ten percent will not necessarily reduce the carrying capacity of the network by ten percent, because the network may be able to compensate by rerouting traffic through other paths. Networks' ability to compensate for changes in network flows can cause the elements that are saturated to shift in discontinuous ways that greatly complicate determining the precise impact of increasing a network flow at any particular time. Customers' aversion to complex pricing regimes further limits networks' ability to implement usage-sensitive prices (*Telephony* 1975). Furthermore, the fact that capacity expansion typically takes time and is subject to indivisibilities dictates that capacity will generally be added before it is needed. In addition, networks always maintain a certain level of excess capacity to insure against unexpected surges in demand. As a result, the network will always appear slack even when the excess capacity is simply a reflection of proper network management.

The impracticality of designing a pricing regime that was precisely calibrated to the actual congestion costs associated with an incremental call led carriers implementing LMS to adopt pricing regimes that broke the day into three discrete periods: peak, near peak (called "shoulder rates"), and off peak. Empirical studies of these experiments have split on the economic impact of LMS.[13] Some have concluded that the combination of metering costs and the misincentives created by the inability to set prices precisely equal to congestion costs were sufficient to render LMS uneconomical (Park and Mitchell 1987). Others have concluded that adoption of LMS would enhance economic welfare (Griffin and Mayor 1987), although even those favoring LMS concede that any such gains were modest (Kahn and Shew 1987). The failure of LMS to yield clear welfare benefits demonstrates how transaction costs can render usage-based pricing uneconomical.

---

13   See sources collected in Kahn and Shew (1987); and Parsons (1996).

Interestingly, wireless telephone pricing has moved in the opposite direction. When cellular telephones first appeared, carriers tended to charge subscribers on a strict per-minute basis. Thus, as a theoretical matter, the wireless industry began with a pricing regime that was a model of usage sensitivity. Over time, wireless carriers began to relax their initial approach to pricing in two ways. First, they tended to sell peak minutes in bundles, so that incremental usage was not fully metered. Second, carriers began to allow subscribers to use off-peak minutes for free. The wireless industry's abandonment of an established usage-based pricing regime in favor of one with flat-rate characteristics again attests to the complexity created by the presence of significant transaction costs.

These conclusions are not unassailable by any means. For example, it is quite possible that the replacement of mechanical switches with first electrical and later digital switches has dramatically lowered the transaction costs of metering usage (Kahn and Shew 1987; Kaserman and Mayo 1994). In addition, the persistence of usage-based pricing of local telephone service in other countries raises questions of the universality of the benefits of flat-rate pricing. The argument advanced here does not, however, depend on any definitive resolution of these debates. The sheer variety of approaches to pricing local telephone service underscores the difficulty in determining whether the transaction costs are of sufficient magnitude to render usage-sensitive pricing uneconomical and demonstrates the potential benefits from allowing network owners to experiment with different institutional arrangements.

Nor is local telephone service the only prominent instance in which communications networks have relied on flat-rate pricing. Consider the terms under which the Internet backbones exchange traffic. Backbones that are able to meet minimum traffic volumes exchange traffic through a system known as *peering*, under which the backbones do not charge each other for terminating traffic. In other words, top-tier backbones employ a pricing system that is equivalent to bill-and-keep systems for reciprocal compensation for terminating local telephone calls. Backbones unable to meet these minimum volume requirements enter into *transit arrangements*, under which they pay other backbones to terminate their traffic (Kende 2000). Backbones too small to peer with top-tier backbones have begun to avoid paying transit costs by entering into *secondary peering arrangements* with one another, which has helped to create a richer, less hierarchical set of interconnection arrangements that has weakened the dominant position of the top-tier backbones. In addition, the development of a practice known as *multihoming*, in which middle-mile providers interconnect with more than one backbone, has reduced the market power of core backbone providers still further (Besen et al. 2001).

This brief analysis reveals how transaction cost considerations have caused backbone providers to enter into a wide diversity of pricing arrangements, including many that do not depend on usage. The FCC has taken the existence of peering as an indication that flat-rate pricing regimes may at times prove economical (FCC

2001c). At the same time, the fact that backbones limit peering to other backbones of similar size does suggest the existence of circumstances under which the preferred pricing regime will be more usage-sensitive.[14]

These examples have prompted the FCC to soften its traditional hostility toward flat-rate pricing and to initiate a number of proceedings exploring broader use of pricing regimes that are not usage-sensitive. For example, the FCC had tentatively concluded in 1996 that wireless providers should interconnect with wireline providers on a bill-and-keep basis. In drawing this conclusion, it noted studies indicating that the transaction costs of metering the termination of traffic were sufficiently high to make bill-and-keep the more economically efficient pricing regime (FCC 1996c). This effort ended when the FCC opted to fold wireless-to-wireline interconnection into the proceeding to implement the interconnection provisions of the Telecommunications Act of 1996 (FCC 1996c).

The FCC's interest in non-usage-sensitive pricing has continued to grow. Prompted by a pair of in-house studies supporting broader use of bill-and-keep regimes (Atkinson and Barkenov 2000; DeGraba 2000) and by the prevalence of peering regimes for backbone interconnection and flat-rate pricing for residential local telephone service, the FCC has begun exploring whether bill-and-keep can serve as the basis for reforming the entire regime of intercarrier compensation. In the process, the FCC specifically sought and received comments on whether transaction costs might justify flat-rate pricing (FCC 2001c, 2005c).

---

14  Symmetry in traffic exchanged costs may not provide the only explanation for backbone peering. The Internet depends on some ISPs generating complete routing tables for the Internet, in order to avoid circularity problems in which links simply direct traffic along paths that feed back into themselves. The transaction costs of coordinating routing tables go up as the number of core backbones increases. This suggests the existence of an optimal number of core backbones exchanging traffic on a settlement-free basis. This also suggests that other networks must be charged for terminating traffic in order to prevent them from free riding on the core backbones' efforts to maintain complete routing tables (Milgrom et al. 2000).

Limiting peering to large backbones may also be designed to minimize another type of free riding. For example, backbones that interconnect on a settlement-free basis would prefer coast-to-coast traffic to travel on their peering partners' network to the greatest extent possible. This would mean that they would hand off traffic that they originate at the earliest possible interconnection point and would accept traffic that they terminate at the latest possible interconnection point. In other words, a backbone carrying traffic from New York to Silicon Valley would like to hand it off as early as possible and have the traffic travel across the country on its partner's backbone. Conversely, the same backbone handling traffic heading in the other direction would like the traffic to be handed off as late as possible so that again the burden of carrying the traffic falls upon its peering partner. In order to avoid this type of free riding, backbones have adopted a practice known as "hot potato routing," in which each backbone delivers packets bound for another backbone at the nearest possible interconnection point. A backbone could defeat the benefits of hot potato routing simply by maintaining a relatively small number of interconnection points located close to its customers. This possibility makes it logical for backbones to limit peering arrangements to those backbones large enough to maintain a presence at each of the major backbone interconnection points (Kende 2000; Milgrom et al. 2000).

### 3. Coasian Proxies as an Alternative Solution to Congestion

Although incorporating transaction cost considerations has yielded important insights into the choice between flat-rate and usage-sensitive pricing, the analysis remains incomplete. The problem is that framing the issue as a choice between flat-rate and usage-sensitive pricing fails to take into account the full range of possible institutional forms. In particular, it overlooks the possibility that transaction costs can also be avoided by identifying and charging for another good that can be metered more cheaply and that can serve as a reasonable proxy for usage of the good that needs to be metered.

This solution is suggested by Ronald Coase's classic critique of lighthouses as pure public goods (1974). Lighthouses have long been regarded as posing a paradigmatic example of a market failure in need of governmental redress. The standard account posits that the fact that the difficulties that lighthouse owners face in securing payment from ships that benefit from the services they provide prevents lighthouse owners from generating sufficient revenue to cover their costs. Restated in terms relevant for our purposes, the difficulties in metering the usage of lighthouse services introduce an externality that creates a wedge between private and social net product. The resulting distortion in the market for lighthouse services caused by the presence of metering costs is generally regarded as providing a classic case for governmental intervention.

Coase rebutted this account by pointing out that throughout most of the 17th and 18th centuries British lighthouses were operated by private, profit-making enterprises. Lighthouse owners were able to finance their lighthouses through tolls collected at nearby ports, because presumably only those ships that were preparing to enter port would come close enough to shore to have need of the lighthouse's services. Port usage thus represented an easily metered proxy for determining which ships had benefited from the services of nearby lighthouse. The historical record suggests that this system was quite successful. As of 1820, thirty-four of the forty-six lighthouses in existence had been built by private individuals. Over time, these private lighthouses began to be taken over by a quasi-governmental organization known as Trinity House. Even after being acquired by Trinity House, they continued to be privately financed through user fees rather than through tax revenues.

Coase's analysis of lighthouse financing suggests that framing the debate over congestion pricing as a choice between flat-rate and usage-sensitive pricing overlooks the full range of possible pricing arrangements. Although later scholars have disputed the specifics of his analysis,[15] it still serves as a useful illustration of the benefits of thinking more broadly about alternative institutional solutions to the problems of exclusion. In the process, it demonstrates how public policy might be better served if providers of club goods were given the latitude to explore the use of proxies

---

15   Van Zandt (1993); Epstein (1999); Odlyzko (2004).

that minimize transaction costs while incorporating some of the positive features benefits associated with usage-sensitive pricing.

## C. Implications of Congestion Economics for Network Neutrality

The economics of congestion offers potential justifications for many of the practices criticized by network neutrality proponents. Although these restrictions would place some limits on end users' ability to run applications, access content, and attach devices as they see fit, they could also provide a new way to internalize the congestion costs that high-volume users impose on others. They could also create consumer benefits by reducing the congestion costs and by lowering the access prices that low-volume end users must pay. Although network neutrality proponents have suggested that mandating network neutrality is essential to preserve the environment for innovation on the Internet, a close examination of the economic literature reveals that such arguments are misplaced in the context of physical networks such as the Internet, because the network owner has both the ability and the incentive to internalize any spillover benefits associated with innovative activity.

The economic attractiveness of employing usage-sensitive pricing on the Internet turns on the nature of congestion and the magnitude of the transaction costs needed to implement such a scheme. The standard result is that in the absence of transaction costs, economic welfare would be maximized if the price of incremental usage of network services were set equal to the contribution of that incremental usage to network congestion. If transaction costs are sufficiently high, it may well prove more economical to allow network providers to pursue alternative pricing regimes.

Because Internet-based communications operate on fundamentally different principles, the transaction costs associated with metering Internet traffic are likely to be even more significant than those associated with local telephone service. The protocol that composes the Internet breaks every piece of communication into smaller packets that are transmitted individually and reassembled at their destination. In addition, the Internet is connectionless, in that it does not establish a closed, dedicated circuit between the originating and terminating computers. Instead, each packet is allowed to move independently. Because routing tables are updated dynamically, it is possible for different packets from the same communications to pass through different routes on the way to their destination. As a result, multiple records are required to account for every Internet-based communication. Indeed, the number of records needed to account for the packets associated with a ten-minute telephone call over the Internet could number in the tens of thousands (MacKie-Mason and Varian 1995b). Consequently, the industry has struggled to develop workable methods for metering Internet usage (*Telephony* 2006).

At the same time, the increasingly varied and intense demands that end users are placing on the network and the rise of applications that are more sensitive to variations in throughput rates have made the need to manage congestion all the more acute. Furthermore, because any impact of the congestion costs imposed by a particular user depends upon the volume and pattern of other traffic being carried by the network, congestion only begins to degrade service when the aggregate traffic levels cause individual network elements to approach saturation. A properly calibrated usage-based pricing regime might therefore need to employ a complex version of peak-load pricing. In addition, usage-based pricing is further complicated by the fact that modern applications often access network resources autonomously, which limits end users' ability to exercise control over their total bandwidth usage.

It is thus quite plausible that the transaction costs needed to establish and run a properly calibrated usage-based pricing regime would be sufficiently large to make alternative pricing arrangements economically desirable. Furthermore, even if metering is economical in the long run, the inevitable lag in creating such a metering system may lead Internet providers to rely on alternative institutional arrangements on a transitional basis.

The significance of these transaction costs reveals why Internet providers might be interested in experimenting with alternative ways to manage the costs of congestion by forcing those who consume large amounts of bandwidth to bear the costs created by their actions.[16] From this perspective, it would be quite sensible for providers to charge higher prices to those who engage in bandwidth-intensive activities. If enforcement of these bandwidth limits proves too costly, it may prove more efficient to prohibit certain bandwidth-intensive applications altogether. Indeed, a close analysis of the specific provisions criticized by network neutrality proponents suggest that last-mile providers have experimented with tiered pricing and use restrictions in precisely the way that theory would suggest.

In advancing this argument, we do not purport to draw any firm conclusions about the optimality of any particular form of tiered access or use restrictions. A determination of the most efficient institutional form would require detailed analysis of the relevant cost data and network flows and would likely vary from network to network. Indeed, one might well expect different networks to pursue different pricing strategies. In addition, the data would need to be updated constantly in response to technological changes. The difficulties in determining the relative merits of various forms of access tiering and end user restrictions provide one of the most powerful arguments against mandating or foreclosing any particular institutional arrangement. The plausibility of economic benefits provides sufficient justification for permitting network owners to experiment

16  The most systematic review of these types of restrictions is Wu (2003). For less comprehensive surveys, see Saltzer (1999); Bar et al. (2000); Lessig (2002).

with different pricing arrangements until actual harm to competition can be demonstrated.

## 1. Prohibitions on Reselling Bandwidth or Acting as an Internet Service Provider

Consider first restrictions on reselling bandwidth, acting as an ISP, or attaching equipment that makes network service available to users residing outside the subscriber's premises. When analyzed under the framework laid out above, such restrictions make perfect sense. A last-mile provider who finds that transaction costs render deploying usage-based pricing uneconomical may find it beneficial to turn to a flat-rate price set equal to average congestion costs imposed by an average user. Even though such usage would be unmetered at the margin, the flat-rate price could be calibrated to lead to an equilibrium that approached efficient pricing. Reselling bandwidth or acting as an ISP would upset this balance by having a single connection serve multiple end users, despite the fact that the cost of service was calibrated to reflect the network demands imposed by a single user. This would in turn create economic inefficiency by allowing those end users to impose congestion costs that far exceed the amount that they pay for the service. Prohibiting end users reselling bandwidth or acting as ISPs would thus appear necessary to facilitate flat-rate pricing.

## 2. Restrictions on Home Networking

Another practice that has drawn the ire of network neutrality proponents is restrictions on home networking, either prohibiting home networking or charging those who connect more than one computer to the network more for their service. Restrictions on home networking may make sense for reasons similar to those justifying restrictions on the resale of bandwidth. Home networking technologies permit multiple computers to access the Internet through a single connection. This would be unproblematic under usage-sensitive pricing, because each subscriber would be forced to compensate the network owner and other users for the additional contribution to network congestion.

The situation is quite different if transaction costs make it more economical for network owners to rely on flat-rate pricing. In that case, the network owner sets the flat-rate price so that it equals the congestion costs imposed by the average subscriber. Calibrating this price becomes significantly more difficult if the number of computers attached to any link varies, because bandwidth usage will vary from customer to customer depending on the number of computers attached. Furthermore, the absence of any restrictions on the number of computers attached to a single connection can give rise to an adverse selection problem, as high-volume end users take advantage of information asymmetries to consume greater network resources without paying any additional compensation (Lee 1991).

The result will be to increase the flat rate charged, which simultaneously excludes some users from access and forces low-volume users to cross-subsidize those who place more intensive demands on the Internet. It should thus come as no surprise that network owners have experimented with prohibiting home networking or charging those attaching multiple computers more for their service. Such an approach is perfectly sensible when viewed through the lens of congestion economics.

### 3. Restrictions on Attaching Devices

Another area of controversy centers on restrictions on end users' right to attach devices, such as consoles for graphics-intensive computer games, Internet phones, and WiFi routers. On some occasions, network providers have prohibited the attachment of certain equipment altogether. On other occasions, providers have required customers wishing to attach such equipment to pay additional charges. The economics of congestion reveals why such measures may be quite sensible when transaction costs render usage-sensitive pricing infeasible. To the extent that online gaming consoles, Internet telephones, and home networking equipment are associated with bandwidth-intensive applications, prohibiting them or requiring end users employing them to pay more for their use may represent a sensible use of proxies for high-volume uses. The absence of such limits will increase the cost of access, thereby reducing the number of people able to connect to the Internet. It will also effectively allow high-volume users to free ride on the contributions made by low-volume users.

The restrictions on attaching devices to the Internet are in some tension with the FCC's historical approach to the attachment of handsets and other customer premises equipment (CPE) to the public telephone network. With respect to telephony, both the D.C. Circuit's *Hush-a-Phone* and the FCC's *Carterfone* decisions recognized the customer's right to interconnect any device that would improve the utility of the telephone system "so long as the interconnection does not adversely affect the telephone company's operations or the telephone system's utility for others" (FCC 1968; *Hush-a-Phone Corp. v. United States*, 238 F.2d 266, 269 (D.C. Cir. 1956)). The FCC later promulgated rules (commonly known as the "Part 68" rules after their location in the Code of Federal Regulations) that allow the interconnection of any device that complies with certain designated standards (47 C.F.R. §§ 68.1–.614 (2004)). As part of the second *Computer Inquiry*, the FCC also prohibited common carriers from bundling CPE with telecommunications services (FCC 1980a).[17]

The context surrounding these decisions was quite different from that surrounding the Internet. For example, telephone service in the 1950s and 1960s was

---

17   This order was affirmed on judicial review (*Computer & Commc'ns Indus. Ass'n v. FCC*, 693 F.2d 198 (D.C. Cir. 1982)).

provided over lines dedicated to individual residences and businesses. Placing a local telephone call thus did not place much pressure on transmission facilities shared with other users, and thus the impact that one person's usage had on the quality of service provided to other users was minimal.[18] Long-distance calling did place additional pressure on shared transmission facilities, but those effects were internalized through usage-sensitive prices.

In addition, at the time these rules were promulgated, there were no viable alternatives to the local telephone network. Because there was little point in promoting innovation and competition in transmission technologies, promoting innovation and competition in complementary services represented a sensible policy goal at that time.

The FCC and the Supreme Court have both acknowledged that the underlying technological environment has changed in ways that have undercut the basis for previous policies.[19] As an initial matter, the Internet is subject to congestion in a way that was not true with respect to conventional telephone service. The impact of congestion on other users is further exacerbated by the fact that the devices end users attach to the network have an increasingly heterogeneous impact on demand. As a result, the attachment of devices used to run bandwidth-intensive applications to the network can adversely affect the quality of service enjoyed by other end users, and these devices arguably represent situations in which restrictions on attaching devices would be permissible under both *Carterfone* and *Hush-a-Phone*. Last, the emergence of alternative transmission technologies is in the process of eliminating network owners' ability to use end user restrictions in an anticompetitive manner.

### 4. Restrictions on Operating File Servers

Similar reasoning justifies restrictions on end users' ability to operate servers holding files for retrieval by other users. Prominent examples include Web page hosting, game servers, and file sharing. These practices represent quintessential bandwidth-intensive uses of network services and are particularly problematic once one acknowledges that network owners will inevitably take the usual network usage patterns of typical users into account when designing their networks. Because most end users download a larger volume of traffic than they upload, network owners typically allocate bandwidth asymmetrically by devoting more bandwidth to downloading. As a result, allowing end users to operate servers places particular pressure on a system designed for different usage patterns, which will degrade the quality of service for other users.

---

18  Local telephone calls do require the use of a local switch, which is a shared resource. The scalability of switching capacity makes the collective impact of call usage easier to manage than transmission capacity.

19  *Nat'l Cable & Telecomm. Ass'n v. Brand X Internet Servs.*, 545 U.S. 967, 1001–02 (2005); FCC (2002b, 2002c).

## 5. Discrimination against Particular Applications

Another type of restriction that has drawn criticism from network neutrality proponents is restrictions on particular applications. Some of these restrictions are imposed against end users. For example, some acceptable use policies prohibit commercial uses outright. Others simply require end users who wish to use their connections for commercial purposes to subscribe to a higher-priced service. Still others have responded to reports that file-sharing programs are consuming an overwhelming share of the Internet's capacity by requiring those who wish to file-share to pay a higher charge or by barring the use of file-sharing programs altogether. On other occasions, network owners discriminate against particular applications on the server side, rather than the end user side, of the network. Specifically, some networks are considering deploying devices known as "policy-based routers" that will give a higher priority to traffic based on the application with which they are associated.

The defensibility of end user restrictions on certain applications again turns on whether the applications being restricted are correlated with more intensive consumption of network resources. If so, it is reasonable to ask those who make greater use of network resources and who impose greater congestion costs on other users either to forego such behavior or to internalize the costs they impose on others.

The problems of network management can also justify the use of policy-based routers on the server side as well. As discussed in Chapter 11, one natural response to capacity constraints is to give traffic associated with bandwidth-intensive, time-sensitive applications, such as streaming media or virtual worlds, a higher priority than traffic associated with less time-sensitive applications, such as e-mail and Web browsing, in which delays of a third of a second are essentially unnoticeable. Discriminating among applications may thus represent nothing more than the natural response of network owners attempting to manage congestion and latency in a world in which capacity is constrained and in which end user demands are increasingly heterogeneous and intense.

## 6. Discrimination against Particular Content

The development that concerns network neutrality proponents the most is the possibility that network owners will discriminate against particular content. The original concern was that network owners would completely block access to dis-preferred Web sites, although FCC Commissioners have repeatedly noted the lack of evidence that network owners have widely adopted such practices, and even network neutrality proponents acknowledge that port blocking does not represent a serious problem.[20] More recently, the focus has shifted away from the outright

---

20  In U.S. Senate (2006a, p. 5), Lessig calls port blocking problems "isolated." CNET News.com (2005) notes that network neutrality proponent Amazon.com acknowledged that outright blocking of sites was not a current problem and was unlikely to become one in the future.

blocking of access and toward the danger that network owners will give traffic bound for or received from preferred content and applications providers a higher priority or will inject latency into traffic associated with dispreferred content and applications providers. Although the FCC has yet to uncover any allegations that any network provider has pursued such practices, network neutrality proponents remain concerned that such discrimination might harm the competitiveness and innovativeness of markets for content and applications (Lessig 2002). Similarly, network neutrality proponents have expressed misgivings about what Professor Lessig has called "access tiering," in which content and applications pay different access charges depending on the levels of service they would like to receive. The concern is that allowing large content and applications to obtain guaranteed levels of bandwidth will restrict the opportunities of other innovators who wish to offer Internet-based services (U.S. Senate 2006a).

These arguments overlook the fact that the type of discrimination they decry represents one of the most innovative ways found to date to mitigate the problems of congestion and latency on the Internet. The following example provides an apt illustration of this point: Suppose that an end user located in Los Angeles attempts to download a Web page from a leading content provider, such as CNN.com. If CNN hosted the content itself, all such queries would be transmitted to CNN's server (presumably located in CNN's headquarters in Atlanta). The distance that the packets composing both the query and the response would have to travel guarantees that this transaction will suffer from at least some degree of latency. In addition, the network access points where backbones exchange traffic might well be congested, as might CNN's file server (Kende 2000).

A new technological solution known as "content delivery networks" has emerged that has the potential to mitigate these problems.[21] Content delivery networks dynamically store content and applications at multiple locations throughout the Internet. When a last-mile network receives a query for content stored on a content delivery network, instead of blindly directing that request to the designated URL, the content delivery network may redirect the request to a particular cache that is closer or less congested. In the process, it can minimize delay and congestion costs by taking into account the topological proximity of each server, the load on each server, and the relative congestion of different portions of the network. In this manner, content delivery networks can dynamically manage network traffic in a way that can minimize transmission costs, congestion costs, and latency. Distributing multiple copies of the content throughout the Internet also enhances network performance in other ways, by allowing content and applications providers to aggregate server capacity and by giving them added protection against denial of service attacks. Using distributed caching to bypass the backbones also weakens whatever market power is enjoyed by backbones and regional ISPs (Besen et al. 2001). Content delivery networks have proven tremendously successful. The leading content delivery network, known as Akamai, reportedly maintains more

---

21  For an excellent overview of content delivery networks, see Clark et al. (2006).

than 14,000 servers and handles more than fifteen percent of the world's Web content (*Washington Technology* 2005). Indeed, it is conceivable that content delivery networks might displace the current architecture and become *the* network, in much the same way that the Internet began as an overlay on top of a voice network and is now in the process of displacing the voice network.

Content delivery networks thus appear to be an important alternative solution to reducing network costs, managing congestion, and minimizing latency. The problem is that content delivery networks violate network neutrality. Not only does URL redirection violate the end-to-end argument by introducing intelligence into the core of the network (Clark et al. 2006; for a critique of the way the end-to-end argument has been applied to the network neutrality debate, see Yoo 2004b); the fact that content delivery networks are commercial entities means that their benefits are available only to those entities willing to pay for their services. In other words, MSNBC.com would suffer greater latency and congestion than CNN.com unless it was also willing to pay a content delivery network to assist in delivering its content.[22]

To the extent that it would prohibit networks from charging content and applications providers for higher levels of service, network neutrality would thus threaten to foreclose one of the most innovative solutions to the problems of congestion and delay. Indeed, preventing network owners from pricing bandwidth would foreclose them from employing the most widely used mechanism for allocating scarce resources in our society. In the process, prohibiting access tiering would have the unintended effect of favoring current industry players whose offerings are not particularly bandwidth-intensive or time-sensitive, while impeding the development of new applications who would gladly pay for higher guaranteed throughput rates if given the chance.[23]

## 7. The Potential Insufficiency of Capacity Expansion and Metered Pricing as Alternatives

Despite acknowledging that deviations from network neutrality may be justified by the needs of network management, network neutrality proponents still argue against such restrictions. These arguments bear close scrutiny, since it is the persuasiveness

22  Network neutrality proponents also oppose access tiering because end users will not be able to determine whether problems with latency are the responsibility of the network owner or of the content and applications provider (Lessig 2002). Interestingly, the Supreme Court has upheld a district court decision condoning the bundling of complementary services (in this case installation and service of a cable television system) with a monopoly product (in this case cable television equipment) in part on the grounds that, should problems with the system develop, consumers would be unable to determine whether the problems resulted from the equipment or the manner in which the equipment had been installed and maintained. Under those circumstances, it was reasonable to allow the provider to bundle them together during the initial growth phase of its business. *United States v. Jerrold Elecs. Corp.*, 187 F. Supp. 545, 557–58, 560 (E.D. Pa. 1960), *aff'd mem.*, 365 U.S. 567 (1961).

23  In the words of one industry consultant, "'If I have an expanding business or I create a [high-bandwidth] application, I'd gladly pay for better service'" (*CIO Magazine* 2006).

of these justifications for overriding the needs of network management that will determine the overall convincingness of network neutrality proposals.

As first discussed in Chapter 11, relying on capacity expansion to solve the problems related to congestion implicitly presumes that capacity will grow faster than network demand. Over the longer term, there is no compelling reason to believe *a priori* that that will be the case, especially given the number of would-be providers of bandwidth-intensive applications that are waiting in the wings and in light of the fact that the number of potential connections increases quadratically as the number of end users connected to the system increases. Indeed, many observers take for granted the existence of a cadre of would-be providers of bandwidth-intensive applications waiting in the wings to soak up any increases in capacity.

Relying on capacity expansion to solve problems related to congestion also ignores the problems associated with the inherent impossibility of perfect forecasting of demand and the inability to expand capacity instantaneously. Unless network owners are able to anticipate changes in demographic patterns, improvements in networking technology, and the development of complementary products that drive demand for network services, situations will exist in which network owners underestimate the growth in network demand. When that occurs, some form of network management may prove to be the only viable short-run solution. Stated more generally, capacity expansion and network management represent alternative approaches to dealing with the problems of congestion. Because the relative costs of each solution are likely to be different and likely to vary over time, there appears to be no reason to erect what would amount to a systematic preference for one solution over the other.

These problems are well illustrated by the impact of the emergence of personal computers on the NSFNET during the mid-1980s, introduced in Chapter 11. The increased functionality provided by the PC enabled users to run increasingly bandwidth-intensive applications on the network, most notably file transfer programs. As a result, terminal-based NSFNET sessions began to run unacceptably slowly. Because capacity cannot be added instantaneously, NSFNET adopted the interim solution of reprogramming its routers to give terminal sessions priority over file transfer sessions. This emergence of the PC represents an exogenous shock caused by a technological development in a related technology that is inevitable in the broadband industry and that makes anticipating the future demand for capacity difficult. This example also shows how discrimination on the basis of the application can be the preferred (and perhaps the only feasible) solution to problems of managing a network in an environment characterized by rapid changes in technology and consumer demand. Given that the costs of discrimination and capacity expansion are likely to vary from case to case, and amidst the uncertainty that the cost of adding capacity will decline faster than demand for network capacity will grow, it would seem imprudent to precommit to one solution over the other.

Other commentators urge network owners to solve congestion problems through metered pricing.[24] Although metered pricing would solve some of the problems associated with congestion costs, it would also require the establishment of mechanisms for monitoring bandwidth usage and for bringing enforcement actions against those who exceed the bandwidth limits. As a result, it would require the incurring of transaction costs quite similar to those required to implement a regime of usage-sensitive pricing. To the extent that the transactions costs are likely to render usage-sensitive pricing uneconomical, they will probably also preclude the use of tiered pricing as a solution.

## D. A Broader Perspective on Consumer Welfare

The foregoing analysis demonstrates that, contrary to the suggestions of network neutrality proponents, allowing some end user restrictions may in fact be welfare-enhancing. In so doing, it underscores the often-overlooked downside to the image of competition advanced by network neutrality proponents, in which end users and providers of content and applications are able to contract with each other freely in a constantly shifting spot market. Use of the alternative institutional forms can in fact benefit consumers by effectively lowering the prices paid by low-volume end users. In addition, increasing the economic efficiency of the overall pricing system should lower the price of basic access, which in turn should increase the number of people able to benefit from the network's services.

In this sense, the debate over network neutrality bears a number of striking parallels to the debate over vertical integration under the antitrust laws described in Chapter 4. Until the mid-1970s, the Supreme Court clearly embraced a vision of competition quite similar to that espoused by network neutrality proponents. Fueled by a scholarly literature that was largely distrustful of vertically integrated enterprises, the Supreme Court invalidated a wide range of exclusivity arrangements on the grounds that they infringed on consumers' freedom of choice.[25] The Court invalidated other exclusivity arrangements as impermissible restrictions on manufacturers' ability to access all channels of distribution.[26]

Over time, however, the Court began to realize that this atomistic vision of competition often exacted a steep price. Economic theorists began to identify circumstances under which vertical integration and vertical contractual restraints could promote efficiency, either by eliminating downstream monopoly pricing or by rationalizing the proportions of variable inputs. Even more important was the

---

24  Wu (2003); Frischmann and van Schewick (2007).

25  *Times-Picayune Publ'g Co. v. United States*, 345 U.S. 594, 605 (1953); *FTC v. Brown Shoe Co.*, 384 U.S. 316, 321 (1966).

26  *Klor's, Inc. v. Broadway–Hale Stores, Inc.*, 359 U.S. 207, 212–13 (1959); *Albrecht v. Herald Co.*, 390 U.S. 145, 152–53 (1968), *overruled by State Oil Co. v. Khan*, 522 U.S. 3 (1997); *United States v. Topco Assocs., Inc.*, 405 U.S. 596, 610–11 (1972).

realization that vertical integration and vertical restraints could also yield trans-action cost efficiencies that could not be realized in the world of unfettered buyer and trader freedom. In particular, economists began to recognize how vertical inte-gration and vertical contractual restraints that simulate vertical integration (such as exclusive dealing contracts, tying, and territorial exclusivity) can reduce the transaction costs needed to protect against opportunism.

The Supreme Court eventually embraced this emerging vision in its landmark decision in *Continental T.V., Inc. v. GTE Sylvania*, in which it accepted the reduction of the transaction costs needed to guard against opportunism as a pro-competitive business justification sufficient to support holding exclusivity agreements. In the process, the Court rejected buyer and trader freedom as independent values that justify regulatory intervention even in the absence of any showing of harm to competition (433 U.S. at 53 n. 21, 54–55) and implicitly reaffirmed the principle that the antitrust laws were enacted for "the protection of *competition*, not *competitors*."[27] If competition is sufficiently robust, the reduction in freedom of some consumers or manufacturers does not rise to the level of antitrust concern, as any consumers who wish to avoid the strictures of the exclusivity arrangement can do so simply by shifting their purchases to other providers.[28]

*Sylvania* marked a sea change in competition policy with respect to vertical integration. Following *Sylvania*, the debate shifted away from the impact on indi-vidual buyers and traders and focused on increasingly sophisticated analyses of whether or not particular exclusivity arrangements promote economic welfare.[29] Thereafter, antitrust law has become increasingly hospitable to vertical integration and vertical contractual restraints.[30]

The image of end user and application/content provider freedom that lies at the center of network neutrality is quite reminiscent of the vision of an atomized market composed of small manufacturers that dominated pre-*Sylvania* antitrust law. Indeed, network neutrality proponents often wax rhapsodic about the early days of the Internet when small innovators were important sources of new Internet content and applications (see, e.g., U.S. Senate 2006a, p. 4).

---

27 *Brown Shoe Co. v. United States*, 370 U.S. 294, 320 (1962) (offering the classic statement of this proposition). For more recent statements, see *Brunswick Corp. v. Pueblo Bowl-O-Mat, Inc.*, 429 U.S. 477, 488 (1977); *Cargill, Inc v. Monfort of Colo., Inc.*, 479 U.S. 104, 110 (1986); *Atlantic Richfield Co. v. USA Petroleum Co.*, 495 U.S. 328, 338 (1990); *Brooke Group Ltd. v. Brown & Williamson Tobacco Corp.*, 509 U.S. 209, 224 (1993); *NYNEX Corp. v. Discon, Inc.*, 525 U.S. 128, 135 (1998).

28 *N. Pac. Ry. Co. v. United States*, 356 U.S. 1, 6–7 (1958); *Jefferson Parish Hosp. Dist. No. 2 v. Hyde*, 466 U.S. 2, 11–12 (1984).

29 See, e.g., Hovenkamp (1985); Baker (1989); Jacobs (1995).

30 See, e.g., *Bus. Elecs. Corp. v Sharp Elecs. Corp.*, 485 U.S. 717 (1988); *Spectrum Sports, Inc. v. McQuillan*, 506 U.S. 447, 459 (1993); *State Oil Co. v. Khan*, 522 U.S. 3 (1997); *Leegin Creative Leather Prods., Inc. v. PSKS, Inc.*, 127 S. Ct. 2705 (2007); *Barry Wright Corp. v. ITT Grinnell Corp.*, 724 F.2d 227, 236–37 (1st Cir. 1983) (Breyer, J.). See generally Yoo (2002) tracing this shift in the vertical integration doctrine.

Shifting to the view that end user restrictions can actually promote consumer welfare would parallel the historical development of antitrust doctrine with respect to vertical integration, which transformed antitrust doctrine from a vision of competition that favored the independence of purchasers and traders to buy and sell in an open market into one considerably more hospitable toward vertical integration. That the Court has since rejected this vision and has acknowledged that vertical integration and exclusivity arrangements can often promote competition is quite striking and suggests a dramatically different model of industrial organization. This history of vertical integration thus cautions against taking too narrow a vision of competition and taking too skeptical a position with respect to exclusivity.

*   *   *

Network neutrality proponents do not simply justify their arguments by the need to preserve the autonomy of end users and providers of applications, content, and devices for its own sake. They also argue that network neutrality is essential to promoting and preserving innovation on the Internet. The concern is that without guaranteed access to markets, content and applications providers will be deterred from innovating and that network owners will make decisions that hurt the interests of the public as a whole.[31]

Both the FCC and network neutrality proponents recognize that it is typically in the best interests of network owners to maximize the value that end users derive from their network connections.[32] Indeed, competition policy has long rejected the notion that the owners of bottleneck facilities have systematic incentives to expand into vertically related markets for the simple reason that there is only one monopoly rent generated by any vertical chain of production and a monopolist can extract the entirety of that rent without vertically integrating simply by charging the monopoly price for the bottleneck facility. Although later theorists identified limited circumstances under which the one-monopoly-rent theorem does not hold, those models explicitly or implicitly assume that the relevant markets are both concentrated and protected by barriers to entry. For reasons described in Chapter 10, those structural preconditions are not satisfied in the context of broadband, which makes it far more likely that vertical integration is motivated by a desire to achieve efficiencies than it is by a desire to harm competition in the adjacent market.

One would thus expect a network owner's natural instinct would be to open up its network to all content and applications providers, because doing so would maximize the value of its network and thus maximize the amount that it could charge for network access. Because innovation in applications and content only serves to increase a network's value, network owners should have every incentive to encourage such innovation. To the extent that innovation is best promoted by an open architecture, network owners can generally be expected to embrace it

---

31   Lemley and Lessig (2001); Lessig (2002); Wu (2003).
32   FCC (2005a); Lessig (2002); Wu (2003); Wu and Lessig (2003).

in the absence of some element that leads to market failure.[33] The failure of early proprietary services provided by America Online, CompuServe, and Prodigy attests to the market's ability to discipline network owners who attempt to impose closed architectures on consumers who prefer open ones.

This underscores the extent to which the interests of network owners on the one hand and the interests of content and application providers on the other hand are aligned. Indeed, this is the same conclusion that the FCC's Network Inquiry Special Staff drew more than twenty years ago with respect to the relationship between the broadcast television networks (the analog to modern applications and content providers) and their local affiliates (the analog modern last-mile providers). Simply put, both players have a strong interest in maximizing joint profits. They will inevitably vie with one another over how those profits should be divided. Although the division of profits will be of intense interest to the parties, it raises few, if any, policy implications. From this perspective, mandating network neutrality is unnecessary at best and counterproductive at worst. If innovation is better promoted by open architectures, network owners can be expected to embrace network neutrality voluntarily, in which case regulatory intervention will be unnecessary. If innovation is better promoted by closed architectures, mandating network neutrality will only serve to frustrate the very goals that network neutrality would purport to promote.

33   Speta (2000); Yoo (2002); Benjamin (2003); Farrell and Weiser (2003).

# Conclusion

From the very beginnings of the telephone and telegraph industries, the evolution of the communications sector has fundamentally transformed social and economic relations. Virtually all collaborative work within and between organizations depends on electronic interaction. Personal communications have moved beyond simple voice communications to encompass e-mail, instant messaging, text messaging, and online virtual communities. Electronic commerce is no longer a separate category, because practically all business transactions use electronic communications, including retail, wholesale, inventories, procurement, and manufacturing. Mobile communications using computers, phones, planners, and other devices have made every individual a node in the network. The communications system is now central to every form of economic activity, including purchases, payments, music, images, video, music, entertainment, marketing, and search.

Although much public policy continues to reflect the traditional approach to telecommunications, the evolution of communications has caused some changes in the regulatory framework. The primary focus of regulatory policy in telecommunications has shifted from traditional rate regulation, which regulates the terms under which final goods are provided to end customers, to mandated access, which regulates the terms under which network services are provided to competitors. This regulatory change, as exemplified by the Telecommunications Act of 1996 and the actions of the Federal Communications Commission, has affected the entire communications sector, including local telephone networks, long-distance telecommunications, broadband networks, and the Internet. The shift has major implications for economic usage of the communications sector, including information technology generally and electronic commerce.

Understanding the continuing evolution of the telecommunications industry and public policy requires an integrated framework that combines economic and legal analysis. Network economics should be studied in the context of regulatory and legal constraints on market transactions. In turn, the legal aspects of networks should be examined in the context of economic incentives for the establishment and design of networks. Our discussion offers an integrated framework for analyzing networks in communications.

But what is access? We define access as market transactions for the services of networks. In this context, we propose a Coasian theory of networks. Network connections take the form of access when the costs of monitoring and overseeing a particular function within the boundaries of a firm exceed the transaction costs of obtaining those same services from an outside party. The boundaries of a firm's network expand to the point where the incremental costs of internal governance surpass the incremental costs of negotiating and enforcing an external market transaction. In a competitive market, networks have the incentive to establish network boundaries and interconnection arrangements in a way that maximizes economic welfare.

Because networks are complex systems, network theory sheds light on the effects of access mandates. The interaction between different network elements can yield sharply discontinuous and unexpected changes in network performance. Accordingly, we apply and extend the graph-theoretic analysis of networks to open the black box of network structure that dominates both current policymaking and legal and economic scholarship on telecommunications. Our approach offers a general framework for examining internal and external network connections that models the impact of access regulation.

The graph theory approach shows that mandatory access can significantly change a network's costs, traffic patterns, reliability, and quality of service. Regulated access necessarily affects market behavior, which in turn gives firms the incentive to change the configuration of their networks to compensate for the effects of mandatory access on how the networks function. The result is to force firms to deviate from the most efficient network configuration.

We also introduce a classification system that distinguishes among different types of access that all too often are simply treated as if they were the same. Retail access refers to transactions between network firms and retail customers. Wholesale access refers to transactions between network firms and resellers. Interconnection access refers to transactions between network firms for the origination, termination, and transit of traffic. Platform access refers to the set of transactions between network firms and suppliers of complementary services, such as programming on cable networks or Internet content provision. Finally, unbundled access refers to transactions between network firms for leasing network elements such as lines and switches.

We show how each of these types of access has a different impact on the network's optimal configuration, capacity, and transaction costs. For example, retail access alters the network owner's design decisions by preventing him or her from responding to unexpected increases in demand either by refusing to add additional customers or by allowing higher prices to allocate bandwidth when expanding capacity is impossible in the short run. The only way to restore equilibrium is to allow congestion to degrade the quality of service provided until the demand curve shifts backward so that demand once again equals the existing capacity. Network owners may have to maintain excess capacity to guard against this degradation in service, which in turn causes an inefficient increase in network cost.

The impact of wholesale access is rendered ambiguous by the fact that the impact on demand depends on two prices (i.e., wholesale and retail prices). If demand increases, wholesale access creates problems that are quite similar to retail access. A demand decrease would leave the network owner with an inefficiently high level of excess capacity and can affect the decision whether to reduce costs by deploying traffic-aggregating technologies. The Coasian theory we introduce reveals that wholesale access also has the inevitable effect of externalizing retail merchant activities that would be more efficiently performed within the boundary of the firm.

Interconnection access also has an ambiguous impact on demand. Although the diversion of some traffic off network lowers demand, the ability to access more customers can give rise to network economic effects that increase demand. This gives rise to the problems of network configuration discussed above, with some added twists. Unlike retail and wholesale access, interconnection access introduces new traffic flows into the core of the network, although such traffic is likely to be introduced at a major node. In addition, interconnection access creates transaction costs by requiring network owners to create new interfaces, as well as systems to monitor and bill traffic at those interfaces. It also has the effect of placing some of the information needed for network planning outside the network owner's control. Most interestingly, the problems addressed by interconnection access are, as a general matter, typically solved by competition, because the literature recognizes that the equilibrium in a market with five equal-sized players is one in which all of those players interconnect voluntarily.

Platform access also has an ambiguous impact on demand, albeit for somewhat different reasons. On one hand, the increase in the number of complementary services caused by guaranteeing all providers of complementary services access to the network should cause demand to increase. On the other hand, the standardization implicit in platform access can cause demand to decrease by foreclosing the emergence of new, beneficial applications that depend on a different network architecture. For the reasons stated above, regardless of its direction, the change in network demand will affect network cost, capacity, reliability, and quality of service. In addition, the standardization not only reduces product variety; it also creates transaction costs by requiring the creation of standardized interfaces and by requiring the establishment of mechanisms for changes in the interface and for setting access prices. Furthermore, it can retard technological change by effectively locking interfaces into place long after technological change has rendered those interfaces obsolete. The literature recognizes that network owners also already possess powerful incentives to provide platform access even in the absence of regulation, even when network services are provided on a noncompetitive basis.

Unbundled access also has an ambiguous impact on demand. On one hand, unbundled access is likely to increase demand by introducing flows from other providers. On the other hand, unbundled access is the form of access most likely to cause costs to increase. Introducing additional traffic at locations other than major nodes can have a dramatic impact on a network's cost, capacity, reliability, and optimal configuration and can lead to significant congestion costs. It also affects the network owner's ability to avail itself of cost-reducing, traffic-aggregating technologies. Whether demand increases depends on whether the upward pressure on demand caused by the outward shift in the demand curve is offset by the downward pressure on demand caused by the increase in marginal cost. In addition, unbundled access creates significant transaction costs by requiring the creation of interfaces and metering systems at locations other than major nodes and by taking information about projected traffic flows outside the network. It also violates the Coasian theory of networks by externalizing functions that would more efficiently be provided by the network owner.

By their very nature, market transactions for access are voluntary. They are motivated by gains from trade. Market transactions for access reflect the relative effects of market transaction costs and internal governance costs. Making access mandatory changes the terms of the transactions, including prices and product features. As a result, access-based public policy affects both the boundaries of individual networks and interactions among networks.

Mandatory access is likely to change the costs of network governance. In addition, mandatory access changes the transaction costs of market transactions. The resulting changes in the relative costs of network governance and market transactions will change the market equilibrium. Changes in costs and opportunities for arbitrage may be expected to impact all forms of access transactions: retail, wholesale, interconnection, platform, and unbundled. Such effects arise even if the regulations are confined to one type of access, such as unbundled access. The effects are extensive because they tend to alter the boundaries of networks and the pattern of interconnections between networks.

For example, changing platform access under the banner of promoting network neutrality can be expected to alter the technology and configuration of networks and the pattern of interconnections. Public policy discussions have been framed in terms of "access to information," although what is meant is access to the networks that transmit the information. Limiting a network firm's ability to control network utilization and to specify network protocols will have far-reaching effects on economic efficiency. Users of network services benefit when prices, products, and quality of service are tailored to their needs.

We also show how access regulation can reduce economic welfare by narrowing the number of dimensions along which networks can compete. Access regulation necessarily requires network providers to interconnect with any other firm that that presents its data at a designated location in a designated format. This has the effect of freezing both the location and the format of the interface into place, a consequence that is quite problematic in industries such as communications that are undergoing rapid technological change. Access regulation also commoditizes bandwidth in ways that narrow the number of dimensions along which firms can compete, which has the effect of preventing firms from pursuing niche or differentiation strategies that can allow them to survive notwithstanding the presence of unexhausted returns to scale. In so doing, it forces networks to compete on price and network size, which in turn reinforces the advantages enjoyed by the largest players.

Our analysis has implications for access policy generally. Granting access has become a public policy code word for mandatory access in a variety of areas that extend beyond communications. Access is an extension of the antitrust doctrine of essential facilities. Under the essential facilities doctrine, promotion of competition or remedies for anticompetitive behavior have led to mandatory access to manufacturing and transportation facilities. Policymakers have been tempted to mandate access to assets that are less tangible, such as intellectual property and innovations.

Mandatory access raises substantial legal questions. It must be emphasized that networks are privately owned facilities. The boundaries of the network are also the boundaries of ownership. Mandated access affects returns and control of the network owner. Without adequate compensation, access becomes a form of governmental taking. Equally important are concerns about investment incentives and dynamic efficiency. As the *Trinko* Court found, compelling telecommunications "firms to share the source of their advantage is in some tension with the underlying purpose of antitrust law, since it may lessen the incentive for the monopolist, the rival, or both to invest in those economically beneficial facilities" (540 U.S. 398, 407–08 (2004)). Policymakers were able to ignore the impact on investment in new networks when entry by new networks was infeasible. That is no longer the case today, now that digitization has broken down the barriers between communications technologies, new media (such as wireless) have emerged as important modes of transmission, and upgrading network technology has become an important way in which firms compete.

Indeed, industry analysis must take into account the increasing complexity of communications technology. Our analysis has largely been in the context of what are frequently called "managed networks," in which a handful of large actors make decisions about network boundaries and interconnections. The Internet operates on distinctly different principles. Because it is composed of a large number of autonomous systems, decisions about network configuration will be made in a more decentralized and uncoordinated manner. The shift to this more diffuse mode of governance will bring communications networks within the domain of what are often called "spontaneous networks," in which each node has the potential to act independently. Understanding market outcomes when there are spontaneous networks requires an analysis of the incentives confronting each individual node. This transformation will make analytical frameworks that capture the interaction among different network elements all the more essential to understanding network behavior and the impact of mandating access in the years to come.

Recognizing the complexity of networks strongly suggests the need for regulatory forbearance. The complexity of networks implies that policymakers cannot be expected to design ideal network configurations. The effects of public policy interventions can be more difficult to predict in network industries. Seemingly limited access mandates can impact the performance of individual networks in significant ways, changing the investment and management decisions of the network provider. As a consequence, even limited access mandates can change customer and competitor decisions and alter the pattern of network interconnections in unexpected ways. Our analysis suggests that the impact of access mandates is greatest when regulators impose requirements on platform access and unbundled access. Despite the rhetorical appeal of network neutrality, the far-reaching effects of platform access on economic efficiency make regulatory forbearance critical.

Public policy goals in communications should focus on the benefits to end users rather than on access mandates. The benefits received by end users require efficient network boundaries and interconnections and market incentives for investment and innovation. End users benefit from network diversity as well as economies of scale. Firms that offer network services and providers of content and applications have incentives to choose efficient access transactions.

Economic and legal studies benefit by opening the black box of networks. Advances in network theory offer a rich set of tools for examining the determinants of network boundaries and interconnections. Our analysis highlights how market transactions for access influence network architecture and performance. We emphasize that market transactions for network services reflect the tradeoffs between governance of networks and interconnection between networks. Our discussion demonstrates the critical role played by networks in communications.

# Bibliography

Abel, Jaison 2002. "Entry into regulated monopoly markets: The development of a competitive fringe in the local telephone industry," *Journal of Law and Economics* 45: 289–316.

Abiru, Masahiro 1988. "Vertical integration, variable proportions and successive oligopolies," *Journal of Industrial Economics* 36: 315–25.

Albon, Robert, Alexis Hardin, and Philippa Dee, with the assistance of Paulene McCalman 1997. *Telecommunications economics and policy issues: Industry Commission staff information paper.* Canberra: Australian Government Publishing Service, http://www.pc.gov.au/ic/research/information/teleeco.

Anderson, Sabra S. 1970. *Graph theory and finite combinatorics.* Chicago: Markham Publishing Co.

Areeda, Phillip E. 1990. "Essential facilities: An epithet in need of limiting principles," *Antitrust Law Journal* 58: 841–54.

Areeda, Phillip E. and Herbert Hovenkamp 2006a. *Antitrust law: An analysis of antitrust principles and their application,* 3d ed. Vol. 1. New York: Aspen Law & Business.

———— 2006b. *Antitrust law: An analysis of antitrust principles and their application,* 3d ed. Vol. 2A. New York: Aspen Law & Business.

———— 2008a. *Antitrust law: An analysis of antitrust principles and their application,* 3d. ed. Vol. 3. New York: Aspen Law & Business.

———— 2008b. *Antitrust law: An analysis of antitrust principles and their application,* 3d. ed. Vol. 3A. New York: Aspen Law & Business.

———— 2008c. *Antitrust law: An analysis of antitrust principles and their application,* 3d ed. Vol. 3B. NY: Aspen.

Areeda, Phillip E. and Donald F. Turner 1978. *Antitrust law: An analysis of antitrust principles and their application.* Vol. 3. Boston: Little, Brown.

Aron, Debra J. and David E. Burnstein 2003. "Broadband adoption in the United States: An empirical analysis," in *Down to the wire: Studies in the diffusion and regulation of telecommunications technologies,* Allan L. Shampine (ed.). Hauppauge, NY: Nova Science Publishers, pp. 119–38.

Association of American Railroads – Policy and Economics Department 2008. "Class I railroad statistics," http://www.aar.org/PubCommon/Documents/AboutTheIndustry/statistics.pdf.

AT&T 1901. *1900 annual report.*

———— 1905. *1904 annual report.*

———— 1907. *1906 annual report.*

———— 1908. *1907 annual report.*

———— 1911. *1910 annual report.*

———— 1914. *1913 annual report.*

Atkinson, Jay M. and Christopher C. Barkenov 2000. A competitively neutral approach to network interconnection. Office of Plans and Policy Working Paper No. 34, Federal Communications Commission, http://www.fcc.gov/Bureaus/OPP/working_papers/oppwp34.pdf.

*Atlanta Journal Constitution* 2005. "Battered EarthLink shifts gears: Phone services play role in makeover," 24 July.

Averch, Harvey and Leland L. Johnson 1962. "Behavior of the firm under regulatory constraint," *American Economic Review* 52: 1052–69.

Ayres, Ian 1988. Vertical integration and overbuying: An analysis of foreclosure via raised rivals' costs. Working Paper No. 8803, American Bar Foundation.

*B2Day* 2006. "Powell warns net neutrologists not to be naive," 3 April, http:business2.blogs.com/business2blog/2006/04/powell_warn_ne.html.

Bain, Joe S. 1956. *Barriers to new competition, their character and consequences in manufacturing industries.* Cambridge, MA: Harvard University Press.

Baker, Jonathan B. 1989. "Recent developments in economics that challenge Chicago school views," *Antitrust Law Journal* 58: 645–56.

Bar, François, Stephen S. Cohen, Peter Cowhey, Bradford J. DeLong, Michael Kleeman, and John Zysman 2000. "Access and innovation policy for the third-generation Internet," *Telecommunications Policy* 24: 489–518.

Barabási, Alberto-Laszlo 2002. *Linked: The new science of networks.* Cambridge, MA: Perseus Books Group.

Barnett, Stephen R. 1972. "State, federal, and local regulation of cable television," *Notre Dame Law Review* 47: 685–814.

Barro, Robert J. and Paul M. Romer 1987. "Ski-lift pricing, with applications to labor and other markets," *American Economic Review* 77: 875–90.

———— 1991. "Ski-lift pricing, with applications to labor and other markets: Reply," *American Economic Review* 81: 378–80.

Bator, Paul M., Daniel J. Meltzer, Paul J. Mishkin, and David L. Shapiro (eds.) 1988. *Hart and Wechsler's The federal courts and the federal system,* 3d ed. Westbury, NY: Foundation Press.

Bauer, Joseph P. 2006. "Refusals to deal with competitors by owners of patents and copyrights: Reflections on the *Image Technical* and *Xerox* decisions," *DePaul Law Review* 55: 1211–46.

Baumol, William J. 1983. "Some subtle pricing issues in railroad regulation," *International Journal of Transport Economics* 10: 341–55.

Baumol, William J. and Janusz A. Ordover 1985. "Use of antitrust to subvert competition," *Journal of Law and Economics* 28: 247–65.

Baumol, William J., John C. Panzar, and Robert D. Willig 1982. *Contestable markets and the theory of industry structure.* New York: Harcourt Brace Jovanovich.

Baumol, William J. and J. Gregory Sidak 1994. *Toward competition in local telephony.* Cambridge, MA: MIT Press.

———— 2002. "The pig in the python: Is lumpy capacity investment used and useful?" *Energy Law Journal* 23: 383–99.

Baumol, William J. and Robert D. Willig 1981. "Fixed costs, sunk costs, entry barriers, and sustainability of monopoly," *Quarterly Journal of Economics* 96: 405–31.

Baxter, William F. 1983. "Conditions creating antitrust concern with vertical integration by regulated industries: 'For whom the Bell doctrine tolls,'" *Antitrust Law Journal* 52: 243–8.

Baynes, Leonard M. 1995. "Swerving to avoid the 'takings' and 'ultra vires' potholes on the information superhighway: Is the New York collocations and telecommunications policy a taking under the New York public service law?" *Hastings Communications and Entertainment Law Journal* 18: 51–84.

Beard, J. Randolph, David L. Kaserman, and John W. Mayo. 1998. "The role of resale entry in promoting local exchange competition," *Telecommunications Policy* 22: 315–26.

Becker, Robert A. and Daniel F. Spulber 1984. "The cost function given imperfectly flexible capital," *Economics Letters* 16: 197–204.

Beineke, Lowell W. and Robin J. Wilson (eds.) 1978. *Selected topics in graph theory.* New York: Academic Press.

Benjamin, Stuart M. 2003. "Spectrum abundance and the choice between private and public control," *New York University Law Review* 78: 2007–2102.

Benkler, Yochai 2000. "From consumers to users: Shifting the deeper structures of regulation toward sustainable commons and user access," *Federal Communications Law Journal* 52: 561–80.

Berg, Sanford V. and John Tschirhart 1995. "A market test for natural monopoly in local exchange," *Journal of Regulatory Economics* 8: 103–24.

Berge, Claude 1976. *Graphs and hypergraphs.* New York: American Elsevier Publishing Co.

Berglas, Eitan 1976. "On the theory of clubs," *American Economic Review* 66: 116–21.

—————— 1981. "The market provision of club goods once again," *Journal of Public Economics* 15: 389–93.

Berglas, Eitan and David Pines 1981. "Clubs, local public goods, and transportation models: A synthesis," *Journal of Public Economics* 15: 141–62.

Bernstein, Jeffrey I. and David E. Sappington 1999. "Setting the X factor in price-cap regulation plans," *Journal of Regulatory Economics* 16: 5–25.

Besen, Stanley M. and Joseph Farrell 1994. "Choosing how to compete: Strategies and tactics in standardization," *Journal of Economic Perspectives* 8: 117–31.

Besen, Stanley M., Paul Milgrom, Bridger Mitchell, and Padmanabhan Srinagesh 2001. "Advances in routing technologies and Internet peering arrangements," *American Economic Review* 91: 292–6.

Bhattacharjee, Samrat, Kenneth L. Clavert, and Ellen W. Zegura, 1997. "Active networking and the end-to-end argument," *Proceedings of the International Conference on Network Protocols*, 1997, pp. 220–28.

Biggs, Norman L., E. Keith Lloyd, and Robin J. Wilson 1976. *Graph theory: 1736–1936.* Oxford: Clarendon Press.

Bird, C. G. 1976. "Cost allocation for a spanning tree: A game theoretic approach," *Networks* 6: 335–50.

Blair, Roger D. and David L. Kaserman 1985. *Antitrust economics.* New York: McGraw-Hill.

Blaug, Mark 1968. *Economic theory in retrospect.* London: Heinemann Educational.

Blumenthal, Marjory S. 2002. "End-to-end and subsequent paradigms," *Law Review of Michigan State University Detroit College of Law* 2002: 709–18.

Blumenthal, Marjory S. and David D. Clark 2001. "Rethinking the design of the Internet: The end-to-end arguments vs. the brave new world," *ACM Transactions on Internet Technology* 1: 70–109.

Bohn, Roger E., Michael C. Caramanis, and Fred C. Schweppe, 1984, "Optimal pricing in electrical networks over space and time," *RAND Journal of Economics* 15: 360–76.

Boiteux, Marcel 1949. "La tarification des demande en pointe: Application de la théorie de la vente au coût marginal," *Revue Générale de l'Electricité* 58: 321–40. Translated by H. W. Izzard 1960 as "Peak-load pricing," *Journal of Business* 33: 157–79.

Bollinger, Lee C. 1991. *Images of a free press.* Chicago: University of Chicago Press.

Bolter, Walter G., Jerry B. Duvall, Fred J. Kelsey, James W. McConnaughey 1984. *The transition to competition: Telecommunications policy for the 1980s.* Englewood Cliffs, NJ: Prentice Hall.

Bonbright, James C. 1961. *Principles of public utility rates.* New York: Columbia University Press.

Bork, Robert H. 1978. *The antitrust paradox: A policy at war with itself.* New York: Basic Books, Inc.

Bornholz, Robert and David S. Evans 1983. "The early history of competition in the telephone industry," in *Breaking up Bell: Essays on industrial organization and regulation,* David Evans (ed.). New York: Elsevier Science, pp. 8–40.

*Boston Globe* 2003. "News from the Chicago cable and telecom show," 16 June.

Bowman, Ward S. 1957. "Tying arrangements and the leverage problem," *Yale Law Journal* 67: 19–37.

Brennan, Timothy J. 1987. "Why regulated firms should be kept out of unregulated markets: Understanding the divestiture in *U. S. v. AT&T,*" *Antitrust Bulletin* 32: 741–93.

Brenner, Daniel L. 1990. "Was cable television a monopoly?" *Federal Communications Law Journal* 42: 365–412.

———— 1996. *Law and regulation of common carriers in communications.* Boulder, CO: Westview Press.

Breslaw, Jon A. 1985. Network externalities and the demand for residential long distance telephone service. Working paper, Concordia University.

Bresnahan, Timothy F. 1999. "New modes of competition: Implications for the future structure of the computer industry," in Eisenach and Lenard (eds.), pp. 155–208.

Bresnahan, Timothy F. and Shane Greenstein 1996. "Technical progress and co-invention in computing and in the uses of computers," *Brookings Papers in Economic Activity: Microeconomics* 1996: 1–83.

———— 1999. "Technological competition and the structure of the computer industry," *Journal of Industrial Economics* 47: 1–40.

Brewer, D. J. 1891. "Protection to private property from public attack," *New Englander and Yale Review* 5: 97–110.

Breyer, Stephen G. 1982. *Regulation and its reform.* Cambridge, MA: Harvard University Press.

*Broadcasting & Cable* 2005. "Plug-and-play Internet: Wall-outlet broadband attracts heavy hitters," 18 July.

Brock, Gerald W. 1981. *The telecommunications industry.* Cambridge, MA: Harvard University Press.

———— 2002. "Historical overview," in Cave et al. (eds.), pp. 3–75.

Brooks, John 1975. *Telephone: The first hundred years.* New York: Harper and Row.

Buchanan, James 1965. "An economic theory of clubs," *Economica* 32: 1–14.

Buchanan, Mark 2003. *Nexus: Small worlds and the groundbreaking science of networks.* New York: W. W. Norton and Co.

Burstein, Meyer L. 1960. "A theory of full-line forcing," *Northwestern University Law Review* 55: 62–95.

*Business Week* 2005. "At stake: The net as we know it," 26 December: 38.

Cabinet Committee on Cable Communications 1974. *Cable: Report to the President.* Washington, DC: Government Printing Office.

Caillaud, Bernard and Bruno Jullien 2003. "Chicken and egg: Competition among intermediation service providers," *RAND Journal of Economics* 34: 309–28.

Calem, Paul S. and Daniel F. Spulber 1984. "Multiproduct two part tariffs," *International Journal of Industrial Organization* 2: 105–15.

California Public Utilities Commission 2003. "California ISP Association v. Pacific Bell Telephone Co.," Decision 03-07-032, 2003 WL 21704389.

Campbell, Thomas J. 1985. "The antitrust record of the first Reagan administration," *Texas Law Review* 64: 353–70.

Campbell, Tom and Nirit Sandman 2004. "A new test for predation: Targeting," *UCLA Law Review* 52: 365–412.

Carlton, Dennis W. and Michael Waldman 2002. "The strategic use of tying to preserve and create market power in evolving industries," *RAND Journal of Economics* 33: 194–220.

Carré, Bernard 1979. *Graphs and networks.* New York: Clarendon Press.

Casadesus-Masanell, Ramon and Daniel F. Spulber 2000. "The fable of Fisher Body," *Journal of Law and Economics* 43: 67–104.

Cave, Martin E., Sumit Majumdar, and Ingo Vogelsang (eds.) 2002. *Handbook of telecommunications economics.* Vol. 1. New York: New York: Elsevier Science Publishing Co.

Cayley, Arthur 1889. "A theorem on trees," *Quarterly Journal of Applied Mathematics* 23: 376–8.

*CED Magazine* 2006. "Network neutrality: Battle royale," April.

Chamberlin, Edward H. 1962. *The theory of monopolistic competition: A reorientation of the theory of value.* Cambridge, MA: Harvard University Press.

Charnes, Abraham, William Cooper, and Glenn Sueyoshi 1988. "A goal programming constrained regression review of the Bell system breakup," *Management Science* 34: 1–26.

Chen, Jim 1996. "The last picture show (on the twilight of federal mass communications regulation)," *Minnesota Law Review* 80: 1415–1510.

———— 1999. "The magnificent seven: American telephony's deregulatory shootout," *Hastings Law Journal* 50: 1503–84.

Chenery, Hollis B. 1949. "Engineering production functions," *Quarterly Journal of Economics* 63: 507–31.

*Christian Science Monitor* 2006. Editorial, "Whose Internet is it anyway?" 24 March.

*CIO Magazine* 2006. "The net neutrality debate: You pay, you play?" 15 April.

Cirace, John 1982. "An economic analysis of the state–municipal action antitrust cases," *Texas Law Review* 61: 481–515.

Clark, David D. 1996. "Adding service discrimination to the Internet," *Telecommunications Policy* 20: 169–81.

Clark, David, Bill Lehr, Steve Bauer, Peyman Faratin, Rahul Sami, and John Wroclawski 2006. "Overlay networks and the future of the Internet," *Communications & Strategies* 63: 109–29.

Clark, John M. 1914. "A contribution to the theory of competitive price," *Quarterly Journal of Economics* 28: 747–71.

———— 1923. *Studies in the economics of overhead costs.* Chicago: University of Chicago Press.

*CNET News.com* 2003. "FCC chief dubious about new cable rules," 18 August, http://news.com.com/FCC+chief+dubious+about+new+cable+rules/2100-1025_3-5065325.html?tag=nl.

———— 2005. "Playing favorites on the net?" 21 December, http://news.com.com/
Playing+favorites+on+the+Net/2100-1028_3-6003281.html.

Coalition of Broadband Users and Innovators 2003. Ex parte communication submitted in FCC (2002e), http://gullfoss2.fcc.gov/prod/ecfs/retrieve.cgi?native_or_pdf=pdf&
id_document=6513401671.

Coase, Ronald H. 1937. "The nature of the firm," *Economica* 4: 386–405.

———— 1960. "The problem of social cost," *Journal of Law and Economics* 3: 1–44.

———— 1974. "The lighthouse in economics," *Journal of Law and Economics* 17: 357–76.

———— 1988. "The nature of the firm: Origin, meaning, influence," *Journal of Law, Economics & Organization* 4, reprinted in Oliver E. Williamson and Sidney G. Winter (eds.)
1991, pp. 34–74.

———— 1994, "The institutional structure of production," The 1991 Alfred Nobel Memorial
Prize Lecture in Economic Sciences, in *Essays on Economics and Economists*. Chicago:
University of Chicago Press, pp. 3–14.

———— 2000. "The acquisition of Fisher Body by General Motors," *Journal of Law and
Economics* 43: 15–31.

Columbia Telecommunications Corp. 2001. "Technological analysis of open access and
cable television systems," http://www.aclu.org/issues/cyber/broadband_report.pdf.

*Communications Daily* 1997. "AT&T targets local service, administrative costs and perks in
cost-cutting," 22 December.

*Communications Today* 1998. "MCI says it will scrap resale plans in favor of facilities-based
competition," 23 January.

*Congress Daily PM* 2006. "Stevens 'very close' to votes needed for telecom cloture," 27 July.

Cooper, James C., Luke M. Froeb, Dan O'Brien, and Michael G. Vita 2005. "Vertical antitrust
policy as a problem of inference," *International Journal of Industrial Organization* 23: 639–
64.

Cooper, Mark 2000. "Open access to the broadband Internet: Technical and economic
discrimination in closed, proprietary networks," *University of Colorado Law Review* 71:
1011–71.

———— 2003. "Open communications platforms: The physical infrastructure as the bedrock
of innovation and democratic discourse in the Internet age," *Journal on Telecommunications and High Technology Law* 2: 177–244.

Cornes, Richard and Todd Sandler 1996. *The theory of externalities, public goods and club
goods*. New York: Cambridge University Press.

Crandall, Robert W. 2001. "The failure of structural remedies in Sherman Act monopolization cases," *Oregon Law Review* 80: 109–98.

Crandall, Robert W. and Jerry A. Hausman 2000. "Competition in U. S. telecommunications
service: Effects of the 1996 legislation," in Peltzman and Winston (eds.), pp. 73–112.

Crandall, Robert W., Allan T. Ingraham, and Hal J. Singer 2004. "Do unbundling policies
discourage CLEC facilities-based investment?" *Topics in Economic Analysis and Policy* 4:
1136, http://www.bepress.com/cgi/viewcontent.cgi? article=1136& content=bejeap.

Crandall, Robert W. and J. Gregory Sidak 2002. "Is structural separation of incumbent local
exchange carriers necessary for competition?" *Yale Journal on Regulation* 19: 335–411.

Crandall, Robert W., Hal J. Singer, and J. Gregory Sidak 2002. "The empirical case against
asymmetrical regulation of broadband Internet access," *Berkeley Technology Law Journal*
17: 953–88.

Crandall, Robert W. and Leonard Waverman 1995. *Talk is cheap: The promise of regulatory
reform in North American telecommunications*. Washington, DC: Brookings Institution.

Crawford, Gregory S. 2000. "The impact of the 1992 Cable Act on household demand and welfare," *RAND Journal of Economics* 31: 422–50.

Crémer, Jacques, Patrick Rey, and Jean Tirole 2000. "Connectivity in the commercial Internet," *Journal of Industrial Economics* 48: 433–72.

Crew, Michael A. and Robert D. Dansby 1982. "Cost–benefit analysis of local measured service," in *Regulatory reform and public utilities*, Michael A. Crew (ed.). Lexington, MA: D. C. Heath and Co., pp. 35–50.

De Fontenay, Alain and J. T. Marshall Lee 1983. "BC/Alberta long distance calling," in *Economic analysis of telecommunications: Theory and applications*, Leon Courville, Alain de Fontenay, and Rodney Dobell (eds.). Amsterdam: North-Holland Publishing Co., pp. 199–230.

DeBow, Michael 1995. "Unjust compensation: The continuing need for reform," *South Carolina Law Review* 46: 579–94.

DeGraba, Patrick 2000. Bill and keep at the central office as an efficient interconnection regime. Office of Plans and Policy Working Paper No. 33, Federal Communications Commission, http://www.fcc.gov/Bureaus/OPP/working_papers/oppwp33.pdf.

Demsetz, Harold 1968. "Why regulate utilities?" *Journal of Law and Economics* 11(Apr): 55–65.

Director, Aaron and Edward H. Levi 1956. "Law and the future: Trade regulation," *Northwestern University Law Review* 51: 258–72.

Dixit, Avinash K. and Joseph E. Stiglitz 1977. "Monopolistic competition and optimum product diversity," *American Economic Review* 67: 297–308.

Drobak, John N. 1985. "From turnpike to nuclear-power: The constitutional limits on utility rate regulation," *Boston University Law Review* 65: 65–125.

Dutta, Bhaskar and Matthew O. Jackson 2003. *Networks and groups*. New York: Springer.

Easterbrook, Frank H. 1986. "On identifying exclusionary conduct," *Notre Dame Law Review* 61: 972–80.

Economides, Nicholas 1996. "The economics of networks," *International Journal of Industrial Organization* 14: 673–99.

———— 2005. "The economics of the Internet backbone," in Majumdar et al. (eds.), pp. 375–413.

Economides, Nicholas, Giuseppe Lopomo, and Glenn A. Woroch 1996. "Regulatory pricing rules to neutralize network dominance," *Industrial and Corporate Change* 5: 1013–28.

Eisenach, Jeffrey A. and Thomas M. Lenard (eds.) 1999. *Competition, innovation and the Microsoft monopoly: Antitrust in the digital marketplace*. Norwell, MA: Kluwer Academic Publishers.

Eisner, James and Dale E. Lehman 2001. Regulatory behavior and competitive entry. Paper presented at the 14th Annual Western Conference, Center for Research in Regulated Industries, http://www.aestudies.com/library/elpaper.pdf.

Elhauge, Einer R. 1991. "The scope of antitrust process," *Harvard Law Review* 104: 667–747.

Ely, James W., Jr. 1995. *The chief justiceship of Melville W. Fuller, 1888–1910*. Columbia, SC: University of South Carolina Press.

EP.net, "Exchange point information," http://www.ep.net/ep-main.html.

Epstein, Richard A. 1985. *Takings: Private property and the power of eminent domain*. Cambridge, MA: Harvard University Press.

———— 1997. "Takings, exclusivity and speech: The legacy of *PruneYard v. Robins*," *University of Chicago Law Review* 64: 21–56.

———— 1999. "The libertarian quartet," *Reason*, January.

Ericsson Telecom AB and Telia AB 1997. *Understanding telecommunications*. Vol. 1. Lund, Sweden: Chartwell-Bratt.

Evans, David S. and James J. Heckman 1983. "Multiproduct cost function estimates and natural monopoly tests for the Bell system," in *Breaking up Bell: Essays on industrial organization and regulation*, David S. Evans (ed.). New York: Elsevier Science, pp. 253–82.

———— 1984. "A test for subadditivity of the cost function with an application to the Bell system," *American Economic Review* 74: 615–23.

Farrell, Joseph 1996. "Creating local competition," *Federal Communications Law Journal* 49: 201–15.

———— 2006. "Open access arguments: Why confidence is misplaced," in Lenard and May (eds.), pp. 195–214.

Farrell, Joseph and Garth Saloner 1985. "Standardization, compatibility, and innovation," *RAND Journal of Economics* 16: 70–83.

———— 1986. "Installed base and compatibility: Innovation, product preannouncements, and predation," *American Economic Review* 76: 940–55.

Farrell, Joseph and Phillip J. Weiser 2003. "Modularity, vertical integration, and open access policies: Towards a convergence of antitrust and regulation in the Internet age," *Harvard Journal of Law and Technology* 17: 85–134.

Faulhaber, Gerald R. 1987. *Telecommunications in turmoil*. Cambridge, MA: Ballinger Publishing Co.

———— 2003. "Policy-induced competition: The telecommunications experiments," *Information Economics and Policy* 15: 73–97.

———— 2005. "Bottlenecks and bandwagons: Access policy in the new telecommunications," in Majumdar et al. (eds.), pp. 488–517.

Faulhaber, Gerald R. and Christiaan Hogendorn 2000. "The market structure of broadband telecommunications," *Journal of Industrial Economics* 48: 305–29.

Federal Communications Commission [FCC] 1958. "Frontier Broadcasting Co.," Memorandum opinion and order, *Federal Communications Commission Reports* 24: 251–6.

———— 1959. "Impact of community antenna systems, TV translators, TV 'satellite' stations and TV 'repeaters' on the orderly development of television broadcasting," Report and order, *Federal Communications Commission Reports* 26: 403–59.

———— 1962. "Carter Mountain Transmission Corp.," Decision, *Federal Communications Commission Reports* 32: 459–86.

———— 1965a. "Amendment of subpart L, part 11, to adopt rules and regulations to govern the grant of authorizations in the business radio service for microwave stations to relay television signals to community antenna systems," First report and order, *Federal Communications Commission Reports* 38: 683–760.

———— 1965b. "Amendment of parts 21, 74 (proposed subpart J), and 91 to adopt rules and regulations relating to the distribution of television broadcast signals by community antenna television systems," Notice of inquiry and notice of proposed rulemaking, *Federal Communications Commission Reports*, 2d Series 1: 453–95.

———— 1965c. "AT&T Co., charges for interstate and foreign communications," Memorandum opinion and order, *Federal Communications Commission Reports*, 2d Series 2: 871–5.

———— 1966. "Amendment of subpart L, part 91, to adopt rules and regulations to govern the grant of authorizations in the business radio service for microwave stations to relay television signals to community antenna systems," Second report and order, *Federal Communications Commission Reports*, 2d Series 2: 725–820.

_____ 1968. "Use of the Carterfone device in message toll telephone services," Decision, *Federal Communications Commission Reports*, 2d Series 13: 420–41.

_____ 1970a. "Multiple ownership of standard, FM and TV broadcast stations," First report and order, *Federal Communications Commission Reports*, 2d Series 22: 306–51.

_____ 1970b. "Amendment of part 74, subpart K of the Commission's rules and regulations relative to the federal-state or local relationships in the community antenna television systems fields," Notice of proposed rulemaking, *Federal Communications Commission Reports*, 2d Series 25: 50–55.

_____ 1971. "Regulatory and policy problems presented by the interdependence of computer and communications services and facilities," Final decision, *Federal Communications Commission Reports*, 2d Series 28: 267–308.

_____ 1972. "Amendment of part 74, subpart K, of the Commission's rules and regulations relative to community antenna television systems," Cable television report and order, *Federal Communications Commission Reports*, 2d Series 36: 143–325.

_____ 1975. "Proposals for new or revised classes of interstate and foreign message toll telephone service (MTS) and wide area telephone service (WATS)," First report and order, *Federal Communications Commission Reports*, 2d Series 56: 593–625.

_____ 1976a. "Amendment of part 76 of the Commission's rules and regulations concerning the cable television channel capacity and access channel requirements of Section 76.251," Report and order, *Federal Communications Commission Reports*, 2d Series 59: 294–331.

_____ 1976b. "Amendment of subpart C of part 76 of the Commission's rules and regulations regarding the regulation of cable television system regular subscriber rates," Report and order, *Federal Communications Commission Reports*, 2d Series 60: 672–86.

_____ 1977. "Amendment of Subparts B and C of Part 76 of the Commission's rules pertaining to applications for certificates of compliance and federal–state/local regulatory relationships," Report and order, *Federal Communications Commission Reports*, 2d Series 66: 380–416.

_____ 1979. "Policies and rules concerning rates for competitive common carrier services and facilities authorizations therefor," Notice of inquiry and proposed rulemaking, *Federal Communications Commission Reports*, 2d Series 77: 308–80.

_____ 1980a. "Amendment of Section 64.702 of the Commission's rules and regulations (second computer inquiry)," Order, *Federal Communications Commission Reports*, 2d Series 77: 384–522.

_____ 1980b. "MTS and WATS market structure," Report and third supplemental notice of inquiry and proposed rulemaking, *Federal Communications Commission Reports*, 2d Series 81: 177–218.

_____ 1980c. "Regulatory policies concerning resale and shared use of common carrier domestic public switched network services," Report and order, *Federal Communications Commission Reports*, 2d Series 83: 167–98.

_____ 1980d. "Policy and rules concerning rates for competitive common carrier services and facilities authorizations therefor," First report and order, *Federal Communications Commission Reports*, 2d Series 85: 1–56.

_____ 1981. "Inquiry into the use of the bands 825–845 MHz & 870–890 MHz for cellular communications systems," Report and order, *Federal Communications Commission Reports*, 2d Series 86: 469–644.

———— 1982. "Policy and rules concerning rates for competitive common carrier services and facilities authorizations therefor," Second report and order, *Federal Communications Commission Reports*, 2d Series 91: 59–75.

———— 1983a. "Policy and rules concerning rates for competitive common carrier services and facilities authorizations therefor," Fourth report and order, *Federal Communications Commission Reports*, 2d Series 95: 554–83.

———— 1983b. "Communications protocols under Section 64.702 of the Commission's rules and regulations," Memorandum opinion, order and statement of principles, *Federal Communications Commission Reports*, 2d Series 95: 584–604.

———— 1983c. "MTS and WATS market structure," Memorandum opinion and order, *Federal Communications Commission Reports*, 2d Series 97: 682–899.

———— 1984. "Petitions for waiver of Section 64.702 of the Commission's rules and regulations to provide certain types of protocol conversion with their basic network," Memorandum opinion and order, *FCC* 84–561.

———— 1985a. "Policy and rules concerning rates for competitive common carrier services and facilities authorizations therefor," Sixth report and order, *Federal Communications Commission Reports*, 2d Series 99: 1020–39.

———— 1985b. "Petitions for waiver of Section 64.702 of the Commission's rules (*Computer II*)," Memorandum opinion and order, *Federal Communications Commission Reports*, 2d Series 100: 1057–1117.

———— 1985c. "Petition of AT&T Co. for limited and temporary waiver of 47 CFR §64.702 regarding its provision of unregulated services externally to the AT&T-C network," Memorandum opinion and order, *Radio Regulation*, 2d Series 59: 505–17.

———— 1986a. "Amendment of Sections 64.702 of Commission's rules and regulations (third computer inquiry)," Report and order, *Federal Communications Commission Reports*, 2d Series 104: 958–1131.

———— 1986b. "Amendment of Part 76 of the Commission's rules concerning carriage of television broadcast signals by cable television systems," Report and order, *FCC Record* 1: 864–917.

———— 1988. "Filing and review of open network architecture plans," Memorandum opinion and order, *FCC Record* 4: 1–302.

———— 1990. "Fox Broadcasting Co. request for temporary waiver of certain provisions of 47 C. F. R. § 73.658," Memorandum opinion and order, *FCC Record* 5: 3211–17.

———— 1991a. "Reexamination of the effective competition standard for the regulation of cable television service rates," Report and order and second further notice of proposed rulemaking, *FCC Record* 6: 4545–76.

———— 1991b. "*Computer III* remand proceedings: Bell Operating Co. safeguards & tier 1 local exchange co. safeguards," Report and order, *FCC Record* 6: 7571–701.

———— 1992a. "Bundling of cellular customer premises equipment and cellular service," Report and order, *FCC Record* 7: 4028–36.

———— 1992b. "Expanded interconnection with local telephone company facilities," Report and order and notice of proposed rulemaking, *FCC Record* 7: 7369–517.

———— 1993a. "Expanded interconnection with local telephone company facilities," Second report and order and third notice of proposed rulemaking, *FCC Record* 8: 7374–473.

———— 1993b. "Amendment of the Commission's rules to establish new personal communications services," Second report and order, *FCC Record* 8: 7700–875.

———— 1994. "Expanded interconnection with local telephone company facilities," Memorandum opinion and order, *FCC Record* 9: 5154–221.

_____ 1995a. "Bell Operating Cos.' joint petition for waiver of *Computer II* rules," Memorandum opinion and order, *FCC Record* 10: 1724–31.

_____ 1995b. "Rochester Telephone Corp.," Order, *FCC Record* 10: 6776–87.

_____ 1995c. "*Computer III* further remand proceedings: Bell Operating Co. provision of enhanced services," Notice of proposed rulemaking, *FCC Record* 10: 8360–89.

_____ 1995d. "Review of the syndication and financial interest rules, Sections 73.659–73.663 of the Commission's rules," Report and order, *FCC Record* 10: 12165–73.

_____ 1995e. "Motion of AT&T Corp. to be reclassified as a non-dominant carrier," Report and order, *FCC Record* 11: 3271–376.

_____ 1996a. "Interconnection between local exchange carriers and commercial mobile radio service providers," Notice of proposed rulemaking, *FCC Record* 11: 5020–90.

_____ 1996b. "Implementation of the local competition provisions in the Telecommunications Act of 1996," Notice of proposed rulemaking, *FCC Record* 11: 14171–269.

_____ 1996c. "Implementation of local competition provisions in the Telecommunications Act of 1996," First report and order, *FCC Record* 11: 15499–16253.

_____ 1996d. "Policy and rules concerning the interstate, interexchange marketplace," Second report and order, *FCC Record* 11: 20730–822.

_____ 1996e. "Implementation of the non-accounting safeguards of Sections 271 and 272 of the Communications Act of 1934, as amended," First report and order and further notice of proposed rulemaking, *FCC Record* 11: 21905–22097.

_____ 1997. "Access charge reform," First report and order, *FCC Record* 12: 15982–16329.

_____ 1998a. "*Computer III* further remand proceedings: Bell Operating Co. provision of enhanced services," Report and order, *FCC Record* 13: 6040–121.

_____ 1998b. "Deployment of wireline services offering advanced telecommunications capability," Memorandum opinion and order and notice of proposed rulemaking, *FCC Record* 13: 15280–319.

_____ 1998c. "Application of WorldCom, Inc. and MCI Communications Corp. for transfer of control of MCI Communications Corp. to WorldCom, Inc.," Memorandum opinion and order, *FCC Record* 13: 18025–173.

_____ 1998d. "Application of BellSouth Corp., BellSouth Telecommunications, Inc., and BellSouth Long Distance, Inc., for provision of in-region, interLATA services in Louisiana," Memorandum opinion and order, *FCC Record* 13: 20599–830.

_____ 1998e. "GTE Telephone Operating Cos.," Memorandum opinion and order, *FCC Record* 13: 22466–488.

_____ 1998f. "Deployment of wireline services offering advanced telecommunications capability," Memorandum opinion and order, and notice of proposed rulemaking, *FCC Record* 13: 24012–124.

_____ 1999a. "Inquiry concerning deployment of advanced telecommunications capability to all Americans in reasonable and timely fashion, and possible steps to accelerate such deployment pursuant to Section 706 of the Telecommunications Act of 1996," Report, *FCC Record* 14: 2398–2649.

_____ 1999b. "Applications for consent to transfer of control of licenses and Section 214 authorizations from Tele-Communications, Inc., transferor, to AT&T Corp., transferee," Memorandum opinion and order, *FCC Record* 14: 3160–3243.

_____ 1999c. "Deployment of wireline services offering advanced telecommunications capability," First report and order and notice of proposed rulemaking, *FCC Record* 14: 4761–4842.

———— 1999d. "Access charge reform," Fifth report and order and further notice of proposed rulemaking, *FCC Record* 14: 14221–307.

———— 1999e. "Deployment of wireline services offering advanced telecommunications capability," Third report and order in CC Docket No. 98–147 and fourth report and order in CC Docket No. 96–98, *FCC Record* 14: 20912–1039.

———— 1999f. "Deployment of wireline services offering advanced telecommunications capability," Order on remand, *FCC Record* 15: 385–413.

———— 1999g. "Implementation of the local competition provisions of the Telecommunications Act of 1996," Third report and order and fourth further notice of proposed rulemaking, *FCC Record* 15: 3696–952.

———— 1999h. "Communications Assistance for Law Enforcement Act," Second report and order, *FCC Record* 15: 7105–50.

———— 2000a. "Applications for consent to transfer of control of licenses and Section 214 authorizations from MediaOne Group, Inc., transferor, to AT&T Corp., transferee," Memorandum opinion and order, *FCC Record* 15: 9816–915.

———— 2000b. "Interconnection and resale obligations pertaining to commercial mobile radio services," Fourth report and order, *FCC Record* 15: 13523–38.

———— 2000c. "Deployment of wireline services offering advanced telecommunications capability," Order on reconsideration and second further notice of proposed rulemaking in CC Docket No. 98–147 and fifth further notice of proposed rulemaking in CC Docket No. 96–98, FCC Record 15: 17806–91.

———— 2000d. "Inquiry concerning high-speed access to Internet over cable and other facilities," Notice of inquiry, *FCC Record* 15: 19287–310.

———— 2000e. "Inquiry considering the deployment of advanced telecommunications capability to all Americans in a reasonable and timely fashion, and possible steps to accelerate such deployment pursuant to Section 706 of the Telecommunications Act of 1996," Second report, *FCC Record* 15: 20913–1065.

———— 2000f. "2000 biennial regulatory review of Part 68 of the Commission's rules and regulations," Report and order, *FCC Record* 15: 24944–5019.

———— 2001a. "Applications for consent to transfer of control of licenses and Section 214 authorizations by Time Warner, Inc. and America Online, Inc., transferors, to AOL Time Warner Inc., transferee," Memorandum opinion and order, *FCC Record* 16: 6547–726.

———— 2001b. "Policy and rules concerning the interstate, interexchange marketplace," Report and order, *FCC Record* 16: 7418–56.

———— 2001c. "Developing a unified intercarrier compensation regime," Notice of proposed rulemaking, *FCC Record* 16: 9610–79.

———— 2001d. "Access charge reform," Seventh report and order and further notice of proposed rulemaking, *FCC Record* 16: 9923–89.

———— 2001e. "Deployment of wireline services offering advanced telecommunications capability," Fourth report and order, *FCC Record* 16: 15435–508.

———— 2002a. "Inquiry considering the deployment of advanced telecommunications capability to all Americans in a reasonable and timely fashion, and possible steps to accelerate such deployment pursuant to Section 706 of the Telecommunications Act of 1996," Third report, *FCC Record* 17: 2844–930.

———— 2002b. "Appropriate framework for broadband access to the Internet over wireline facilities," Notice of proposed rulemaking, *FCC Record* 17: 3019–76.

———— 2002c. "Inquiry concerning high-speed access to Internet over cable and other facilities," Declaratory ruling and notice of proposed rulemaking, *FCC Record* 17: 4798–872.

———— 2002d. "Applications for consent to transfer of control of licenses from Comcast Corp. and AT&T Corp., transferors, to AT&T Comcast Corp.," Memorandum opinion and order, *FCC Record* 17: 23246–353.

———— 2002e. "Review of regulatory requirements for incumbent LEC broadband services," Memorandum opinion and order, *FCC Record* 17: 27000–27.

———— 2003a. "Application by SBC Communications, Inc., Nevada Bell Telephone Co., and Southwestern Bell Communications Services, Inc., for authorization to provide in-region, interLATA services in Nevada," Memorandum opinion and order, *FCC Record* 18: 7196–324.

———— 2003b. "Application by Qwest Communications International, Inc., for authorization to provide in-region, interLATA services in New Mexico, Oregon and South Dakota," Memorandum opinion and order, *FCC Record* 18: 7325–564.

———— 2003c. "2002 biennial regulatory review – Review of the Commission's broadcast ownership rules and other rules adopted pursuant to section 202 of the Telecommunications Act of 1996," Report, order and notice of proposed rulemaking, *FCC Record* 18: 13620–4013.

———— 2003d. "Review of the Section 251 unbundled obligations of incumbent local exchange carriers," Report and order and order on remand and further notice of proposed rulemaking, *FCC Record* 18: 16978–7552.

———— 2003e. "Review of the Section 251 unbundling obligations of incumbent local exchange carriers," Report and order and order on remand and further notice of proposed rulemaking, *FCC Record* 18: 19020–23.

———— 2005a. "Unbundled access to network elements," Order on remand, *FCC Record* 20: 2533–717.

———— 2005b. "Madison River Communications, LLC," Order, *FCC Record* 20: 4295–300.

———— 2005c. "Developing a unified intercarrier compensation regime," Further notice of proposed rulemaking, *FCC Record* 20: 4685–799.

———— 2005d. "Appropriate framework for broadband access to the Internet over wireline facilities," Report and order and notice of proposed rulemaking, *FCC Record* 20: 14853–985.

———— 2005e. "Appropriate framework for broadband access to the Internet over wireline facilities," Policy statement, *FCC Record* 20: 14986–88.

———— 2005f. "Petition for waiver of pricing flexibility rules for fast pack services," Memorandum opinion and order, *FCC Record* 20: 16840–53.

———— 2005g. "SBC Communications, Inc. and AT&T Corp. applications for approval of transfer of control," Memorandum opinion and order, *FCC Record* 20: 18290–432.

———— 2005h. "Verizon Communications, Inc. and MCI, Inc. applications for approval of transfer of control," Memorandum opinion and order, *FCC Record* 20: 18433–580.

———— 2005i. "Local telephone competition: Status as of December 31, 2004," http://www.fcc.gov/Bureaus/Common_Carrier/Reports/FCC-State_Link/IAD/lcom0705.pdf.

———— 2006a. "Applications for consent to the assignment and/or transfer of control of licenses: Adelphia Communications Corporation (and subsidiaries, debtors-in-possession), assignors, to Time Warner Cable Inc. (subsidiaries), assignees, et al.," Memorandum opinion and order, *FCC Record* 21: 8203–378.

———— 2006b. "Implementation of Section 6002(b) of Omnibus Budget Reconciliation Act of 1993: Annual report and analysis of competitive market conditions with respect to commercial mobile services," Eleventh report, *FCC Record* 21: 10947–1064.

———— 2006c. "Implementation of Section 3 of the Cable Television Consumer Protection and Competition Act of 1992: Statistical report on average rates for basic service, cable programming service, and equipment," Report on cable industry prices, *FCC Record* 21: 15087–131.

———— 2006d. "Verizon Telephone Companies' petition for forbearance from Title II and *Computer Inquiry* rules with respect to their broadband services is granted by operation of law," News release, March 20. http://hraunfoss.fcc.gov/edocs_public/attachmatch/ DOC-264436A1.pdf.

———— 2007a. "AT&T Inc. and BellSouth Corp. application for transfer of control," Memorandum opinion and order, *FCC Record* 22: 5662–841.

———— 2007b. "SBC Communications Inc. petition for wavier of Section 61.42 of the Commission's rules," Order, *FCC Record* 22: 7224–32.

———— 2007c. "Qwest petition for waiver of pricing flexibility rules for advanced communications networks services," Order, *FCC Record* 22: 7482–88.

———— 2007d. "Broadband industry practices," Notice of inquiry, *FCC Record* 22: 7894–909.

———— 2007e. "Petition of AT&T Inc. for forbearance under 47 U. S. C. § 160(c) from Title II and *Computer Inquiry* rules with respect to its broadband services," Memorandum opinion and order, *FCC Record* 22: 18705–50.

———— 2008a. "Development of nationwide broadband data to evaluate reasonable and timely deployment of advanced services to all Americans, improvement of wireless broadband subscribership data, and development of data on interconnected voice over internet protocol (VoIP) subscribership," Report and order and further notice of proposed rulemaking, *FCC Record* 23: 9691–771.

———— 2008b. "High-speed services for Internet access: Status as of June 30, 2007," http://hraunfoss.fcc.gov/edocs_public/attachmatch/DOC-287962A1.pdf.

———— 2008c. "Formal complaint of Free Press and Public Knowledge against Comcast Corp. for secretly degrading peer-to-peer applications," Memorandum opinion and order, *FCC Record* 23: 13028–61.

———— 2008d. "BOC authorization to provide in-region, interLATA services under Sections 271 and 272," http://www.fcc.gov/Bureaus/Common_Carrier/in-region_applications/.

Federal Trade Commission [FTC] 2000. "America Online, Inc.," No. C-3989, Decision and order, http://www.ftc.gov/os/2000/12/aoldando.pdf.

———— 2007. Internet Access Task Force, *Broadband connectivity competition policy: A Federal Trade Commission staff report.* Washington: Government Printing Office.

Fleischer, Lisa 2004. "Minimum cost flows," in Gross and Yellen (eds.), pp. 1087–102.

Fox, Eleanor M. 1981. "The modernization of antitrust: A new equilibrium," *Cornell Law Review* 66: 1140–92.

———— 2005. "Is there life in *Aspen* after *Trinko*: The silent revolution of Section 2 of the Sherman Act," *Antitrust Law Journal* 73: 153–70.

Freeland, Robert F. 2000. "Creating holdup through vertical integration: Fisher Body revisited," *Journal of Law and Economics* 43: 33–66.

Frischmann, Brett M. and Barbara van Schewick 2007. "Network neutrality and the economics of an information superhighway: A reply to Professor Yoo," *Jurimetrics* 47: 383–428.

Gabel, David and D. Mark Kennet 1994. "Economies of scope in the local telephone exchange market," *Journal of Regulatory Economics* 6: 381–98.

Gabel, Richard 1969. "The early competitive era in telephone communication, 1893–1920," *Law and Contemporary Problems* 34: 340–59.

Gallick, Edward C. 1993. *Competition in the natural gas pipeline industry: An economic policy analysis.* Westport, CT: Praeger.

Gandal, Neil, David Salant, and Leonard Waverman 2003. "Standards in wireless telephone networks," *Telecommunications Policy* 27: 325–32.

Garcia-Murillo, Martha 2005. "International broadband deployment: The impact of unbundling," *Communications and Strategies* 57: 83–105.

Gasmi, Farid, D. Mark Kennet, Jean-Jacques Laffont, and William W. Sharkey 2002. *Cost proxy models and telecommunications policy: A new empirical approach to regulation.* Cambridge, MA: MIT Press.

Gasmi, Farid, Jean-Jacques Laffont, and William W. Sharkey 2002. "The natural monopoly test reconsidered: An engineering process-based approach to empirical analysis in telecommunications," *International Journal of Industrial Organization* 20: 435–59.

Geradin, Damien and Robert O'Donoghue 2005. "The concurrent application of competition law and regulation: The case of margin squeeze abuses in the telecommunications sector," *Journal of Competition Law and Economics* 1: 355–425.

Gerber, David J. 1988. "Rethinking the monopolist's duty to deal: A legal and economic critique of the doctrine of 'essential facilities,'" *Virginia Law Review* 74: 1069–1114.

Gergen, Ann E. 1993. "Why fair market value fails as just compensation," *Hamline Journal of Public Law and Policy* 14: 181–202.

Gerla, Henry S. 1988. "A micro-microeconomic approach to antitrust-law: Games managers play," *Michigan Law Review* 86: 892–929.

Gilder, George 1993. "Metcalfe's law and legacy," *Forbes ASAP*, September 13.

Goldberg, Victor P. 1976. "Regulation and administered contracts," *Bell Journal of Economics* 7: 426–48.

Goldsmith, Richard 1989. "Utility rates and 'takings,'" *Energy Law Journal* 10: 241–77.

Granovetter, Mark 1973. "Strength of weak ties," *American Journal of Sociology* 78: 1360–80.

———— 1985. "Economic-action and social-structure: The problem of embeddedness," *American Journal of Sociology* 91: 481–510.

Greenstein, Shane 1998. "Industrial economics and strategy: Computing platforms," *IEEE Micro* 18: 43–53.

Griffin, James M. and Thomas H. Mayor 1987. "The welfare gain from efficient pricing of local telephone services," *Journal of Law and Economics* 30: 465–87.

Gross, Jonathan L. and Jay Yellen (eds.) 2004. *Handbook of graph theory.* Boca Raton, FL: CRC Press.

Gupta, Alok, Dale O. Stahl, and Andrew B. Whinston 1997. "A stochastic equilibrium model of Internet pricing," *Journal of Economic Dynamics and Control* 21: 697–722.

Hall, Ford P. 1940. *The concept of a business affected with a public interest.* Bloomington, IN: Principia Press.

Hall, Robert E. 1973. "Specification of technology with several kinds of output," *Journal of Political Economy* 81: 878–92.

Hardin, Garrett 1968. "The tragedy of commons," *Science* 162: 1243–8.

Harris, Milton and Artur Raviv 1981. "A theory of monopoly pricing schemes with demand uncertainty," *American Economic Review* 71: 347–65.

Hart, Oliver and Jean Tirole 1990. "Vertical integration and market foreclosure," *Brookings Papers on Economic Activity: Microeconomics* 1990: 205–86.

Hatfield, Dale N. 2000. "Preface," *CommLaw Conspectus* 8: 1–4.

Hausman, Jerry A. 1995. "Competition in long-distance and telecommunications equipment markets: Effects of the MFJ," *Managerial and Decision Economics* 16: 365–83.

―――― 1997. "Valuing the effect of regulation on new services in telecommunications," *Brookings Papers on Economic Activity: Microeconomics* 28: 1–54.

Hausman, Jerry A. and J. Gregory Sidak 1999. "A consumer-welfare approach to the mandatory unbundling of telecommunications networks," *Yale Law Journal* 109: 417–505.

―――― 2005. "Did mandatory unbundling achieve its purpose? Empirical evidence from five countries," *Journal of Competition Law and Economics* 1: 173–245.

Hausman, Jerry A., J. Gregory Sidak, and Hal J. Singer 2001. "Residential demand for broadband telecommunications and consumer access to unaffiliated Internet content providers," *Yale Journal on Regulation* 18: 129–73.

Hay, George A. 1973. "An economic analysis of vertical integration," *Industrial Organization Review* 1: 188–98.

―――― 2005. "*Trinko*: Going all the way," *Antitrust Bulletin* 50: 527–48.

Hayek, Freidrich A. 1989. *The fatal conceit: The errors of socialism*, William W. Bartley (ed.). Chicago: University of Chicago Press.

Hazlett, Thomas W. 1986. "Private monopoly and the public interest: An economic analysis of the cable television franchise," *University of Pennsylvania Law Review* 134: 1335–410.

―――― 1990. "Duopolistic competition in cable television: Implications for public policy," *Yale Journal on Regulation* 7: 65–120.

―――― 2006. "Rivalrous telecommunications networks with and without mandatory sharing," *Federal Communications Law Journal* 58: 477–510.

Hazlett, Thomas W. and Matthew L. Spitzer 1997. *Public policy towards cable television: The economics of rate controls*. Washington, DC: AEI Press.

Heller, Michael A. 1998. "The tragedy of the anticommons: Property in the transition from Marx to markets," *Harvard Law Review* 111: 621–88.

Helsley, Robert W. and William C. Strange 1991. "Exclusion and the theory of clubs," *Canadian Journal of Economics–Revue Canadienne d'Économique* 24: 888–99.

Henriet, Dominique and Hervé Moulin 1996. "Traffic-based cost allocation in a network," *RAND Journal of Economics* 27: 332–45.

High Tech Broadband Coalition 2002. Comments submitted in FCC (2002e), http://gullfoss2.fcc.gov/prod/ecfs/retrieve.cgi?native_or_pdf=pdf&id_document=6513198026.

Hogan, William W. 1992, "Contract networks for electric power transmission," *Journal of Regulatory Economics* 4: 211–42.

Hotelling, Harold 1929. "Stability in competition," *Economic Journal* 39: 41–57.

Hovenkamp, Herbert 1985. "Antitrust policy after Chicago," *Michigan Law Review* 84: 213–84.

―――― 1988. "Regulatory conflict in the gilded age: Federalism and the railroad problem," *Yale Law Journal* 97: 1017–72.

―――― 1989. "The antitrust movement and the rise of industrial organization," *Texas Law Review* 68: 105–68.

―――― 1991. *Enterprise and American law, 1836–1937*. Cambridge, MA: Harvard University Press.

―――― 1993. "The marginalist revolution in legal thought," *Vanderbilt Law Review* 46: 305–59.

_____ 2004. "Antitrust and the regulatory enterprise," *Columbia Business Law Review* 2004: 335–78.

_____ 2005. *Federal antitrust policy.* St. Paul, MN: Thomson/West.

Howell, Bronwyn 2002. "Infrastructure regulation and the demand for broadband services: Evidence from the OECD countries," *Communications and Strategies* 47: 33–62.

Huber, Peter W. 1987. *The geodesic network: 1987 report on competition in the telephone industry.* Washington, DC: Government Printing Office.

_____ 1993. "Telephone competition, and the Candice-coated monopoly," *Regulation* 2: 34–43.

_____ 2002. "Washington created WorldCom," *Wall Street Journal,* 1 July.

Huber, Peter W., Michael K. Kellogg, and John Thorne 1999. *Federal telecommunications law,* 2d ed. New York: Aspen Publishers.

Hundt, Reed E. 1997. "Thinking about why some communications mergers are unthinkable," Address before the Brookings Institution, http://www.fcc.gov/Speeches/Hundt/spreh735.html.

Hylton, Keith N. 1991. "Economic rents and essential facilities," *Brigham Young University Law Review* 1991: 1243–84.

Idaho Public Utilities Commission 2003. "Qwest Corp.," Order No. 29360, 2003 WL 22417269.

*InformationWeek* 2006. "Former FCC Chairman Powell: Net neutrality 'doing great,'" 20 February, http://www.informationweek.com/news/internet/ebusiness/showArticle.jhtml?articleID=180205365.

Inman, Robert P. and Daniel L. Rubinfeld 1997. "Making sense of the antitrust state-action doctrine: Balancing political participation and economic efficiency in regulatory federalism," *Texas Law Review* 75: 1203–1300.

Interstate Commerce Commission, Bureau of Statistics 1937. *Interstate Commerce Commission Activities 1887–1937.* Washington, DC: Government Printing Office.

International Engineering Consortium. "WebPro Forums: Operations Support Systems (OSSs)," http://www.iec.org/online/tutorials/oss/topic01.html and http://www.iec.org/online/tutorials/oss/topic02.html.

Interstate Natural Gas Association of America 2007. *Interstate Pipeline Deskbook,* Washington, D.C.: INGAA, www.ingaa.org/cms/28/5928.aspx, accessed January 22, 2009.

Jacobs, Michael 1995. "An essay on the normative foundations of antitrust economics," *North Carolina Law Review* 74: 219–66.

_____ 2006. "Introduction," *DePaul Law Review* 55: 1177–90.

Jeong, Hawoong, Balint Tomber, Reka Albert, Zoltan N. Oltvai, and Albert-Laszlo Barabàsi 2000. "The large-scale organization of metabolic networks," *Nature* 407: 651–4.

Jevons, W. Stanley 1879. *The theory of political economy.* New York: Macmillan.

Johnson, Rolland C. and Robert T. Blau 1974. "Single versus multiple-system cable television," *Journal of Broadcasting* 18: 323–46.

Jorde, Thomas M., J. Gregory Sidak, and David Teece 2000. "Innovation, investment, and unbundling," *Yale Journal on Regulation* 17: 1–38.

Joskow, Paul L. and Roger G. Noll 1999. "The Bell doctrine: Applications in telecommunications, electricity, and other network industries," *Stanford Law Review* 51: 1249–315.

Jungnickel, Dieter 1999. *Graphs, networks and algorithms.* New York: Springer.

Kaestner, Robert and Brenda Kahn 1990. "The effects of regulation and competition on the price of AT&T intrastate telephone service," *Journal of Regulatory Economics* 2: 363–77.

Kahn, Alfred E. 1971. *The economics of regulation: Principles and institutions*, 2 vols. Chichester, UK: John Wiley and Sons, Ltd.

Kahn, Alfred E. and William B. Shew 1987. "Current issues in telecommunications regulation: Pricing," *Yale Journal on Regulation* 4: 191–256.

Kaserman, David L. and John W. Mayo 1994. "Cross-subsidies in telecommunications: Roadblocks on the road to more intelligent telephone pricing," *Yale Journal on Regulation* 11: 119–48.

———— 2002. "Competition in the long-distance market," in Cave et al. (eds.), pp. 510–63.

Katz, Michael L. and Carl Shapiro 1985. "Network externalities, competition, and compatibility," *American Economic Review* 75: 424–40.

———— 1986. "Technology adoption in the presence of network externalities," *Journal of Political Economy* 94: 822–41.

———— 1992. "Product introduction with network externalities," *Journal of Industrial Economics* 40: 55–83.

———— 1994. "Systems competition and network effects," *Journal of Economic Perspectives* 8: 93–115.

Kauper, Thomas E. 2005. "Section Two of the Sherman Act: The search for standards," *Georgetown Law Journal* 93: 1623–44.

Kaysen, Carl and Donald F. Turner 1959. *Antitrust policy: An economic and legal analysis*. Cambridge, MA: Harvard University Press.

Kearney, Joseph D. and Thomas W. Merrill 1998. "The great transformation of regulated industries law," *Columbia Law Review* 98: 1323–409.

Kellogg, Michael K., John Thorne, and Peter W. Huber 1992. *Federal telecommunications law*, 1st ed. Boston: Little, Brown and Co.

———— 1995. *Supplement to Federal Telecommunications Law*. Boston: Little, Brown and Co.

Kende, Michael 2000. The digital handshake: Connecting Internet backbones. Office of Plans and Policy Working Paper No. 32, Federal Communications Commission, http://www.fcc.gov/Bureaus/OPP/working_papers/oppwp32.pdf.

Keon, Neil J. and G. Anandalingam 2003. "Optimal pricing for multiple services in telecommunications networks offering quality-of-service guarantees," *IEEE/ACM Transactions on Networking* 11: 66–80.

Keyte, James A. 2005. "The ripple effects of *Trinko*: How it is affecting Section 2 analysis," *Antitrust* 20 (Fall): 44–50.

Kim, Jung H., Johannes M. Bauer, and Steven S. Wildman 2003. Broadband uptake in OECD countries: Policy lessons from comparative statistical analysis. Paper presented at the 31st Research Conference on Communication, Information and Internet Policy, Arlington, VA, http://web.si.umich.edu/tprc/papers/2003/203/Kim-Bauer-Wildman.pdf.

Kiser, Chérie R. and Angela F. Collins 2003. "Regulation on the horizon: Are regulators poised to address the status of IP telephony?" *CommLaw Conspectus* 11: 19–44.

Klass, Michael W. and Michael A. Salinger 1995. "Do new theories of vertical foreclosure provide sound guidance for consent agreements in vertical merger cases?" *Antitrust Bulletin* 40: 667–98.

Klein, Benjamin 1988. "Vertical integration as organizational ownership: The Fisher Body–General Motors relationship revisited," *Journal of Law, Economics, and Organization* 4: 199–213.

———— 2000. "Fisher–General Motors and the nature of the firm," *Journal of Law and Economics* 43: 105–41.

Klein, Benjamin, Robert G. Crawford, and Armen A. Alchian 1978. "Vertical integration, appropriable rents, and the competitive contracting process," *Journal of Law and Economics* 21: 297–326.

Kleinfeld, Judith S. 2002a. "Six degrees of separation: An urban myth," *Psychology Today* March/April.

———— 2002b. "The small world problem," *Society* 39: 61–6.

Knight, Frank H. 1921a. "Cost of production and price over long and short periods," *Journal of Political Economy* 29: 304–35.

———— 1921b. *Risk, uncertainty and profit.* New York: Houghton Mifflin Co.

Knittel, Christopher R. 2004. "Regulatory restructuring and incumbent price dynamics: The case of U.S. local telephone markets," *Review of Economics and Statistics* 86: 614–25.

Koenker, Roger W. and Martin K. Perry 1981. "Product differentiation, monopolistic competition, and public-policy," *Bell Journal of Economics* 12: 217–31.

Krattenmaker, Thomas G. and Steven C. Salop 1986. "Anticompetitive exclusion: Raising rivals' costs to achieve power over price," *Yale Law Journal* 96: 209–94.

Laffont, Jean-Jacques, Patrick Rey and Jean Tirole 1997. "Competition between telecommunications operators," *European Economic Review* 41: 701–11.

———— 1998. "Network competition. I. Overview and nondiscriminatory pricing," *RAND Journal of Economics* 29: 1–37.

Laffont, Jean-Jacques and Jean Tirole 2000. *Competition in telecommunications.* Cambridge, MA: MIT Press.

LaFontaine, Francine and Margaret Slade 2008. "Exclusive contracts and vertical restraints: Empirical evidence and public policy," in *Handbook in antitrust economics*, Paolo Buccirossi (ed.). Cambridge, MA: MIT Press, pp. 391–414.

Lancaster, Kelvin 1975. "Socially optimal product differentiation," *American Economic Review* 65: 567–85.

Lande, Robert H. 1990. "Implications of Professor Scherer's research for the future of antitrust," *Washburn Law Journal* 29: 256–63.

Landis, James M. 1960. *Report on regulatory agencies to the President-Elect.* Washington, D. C.: U.S. Government Printing Office.

Langdale, John V. 1978. "The growth of long-distance telephony in the Bell system: 1875–1907," *Journal of Historical Geography* 4: 145–59.

Larson, Alexander C. 1997. "Wholesale pricing and the Telecommunications Act of 1996: Guidelines for compliance with the avoided cost rule," *University of Florida Journal of Law and Public Policy* 8: 243–60.

Larson, Alexander C. and Douglas R. Mudd 1999. "The Telecommunications Act of 1996 and competition policy: An economic view in hindsight," *Virginia Journal of Law and Technology* 4: article 1, http://www.vjolt.net/vol4/issue/home_artl.html.

Lathen, Deborah A. 1999. "Broadband today: A staff report to William E. Kennard, Chairman, Federal Communications Commission," http://ftp.fcc.gov/Bureaus/Cable/Reports/broadbandtoday.pdf.

Le Chatelier, Henri L. 1888. "Recherches expérimentales et théoriques sur les équilibres chimiques," *Annales des Mines* 13: 157–82.

Lee, Kangoh 1991. "Transaction costs and equilibrium pricing of congested public goods with imperfect information," *Journal of Public Economics* 45: 337–62.

Lee, William E. 1983. "Cable franchising and the First Amendment," *Vanderbilt Law Review* 36: 867–928.

Leibenstein, Harvey 1950. "Bandwagon, snob, and Veblen effects in the theory of consumer's demand," *Quarterly Journal of Economics* 64: 183–207.

Lemley, Mark A. 1996. "Antitrust and the Internet standardization problem," *Connecticut Law Review* 28: 1041–94.

Lemley, Mark A. and Lawrence Lessig 2001. "The end of end-to-end: Preserving the architecture of the Internet in the broadband era," *UCLA Law Review* 48: 925–72.

Lemley, Mark A. and David McGowan 1998. "Legal implications of network economic effects," *California Law Review* 86: 479–612.

Lenard, Thomas M. and Randolph J. May (eds.) 2006. *Net neutrality or net neutering: Should broadband Internet services be regulated?* New York: Springer.

Lessig, Lawrence 2002. *The future of ideas.* New York: Random House.

———— 2005. "Reply: Re-marking the progress in Frischmann," *Minnesota Law Review* 89: 1031–43.

Levin, Stanford L. and John B. Meisel 1991. "Cable television and competition: Theory, evidence and policy," *Telecommunications Policy* 15: 519–28.

Liebert, Tobe 1999. "The new generation of citators," *Experience*, Fall.

Liebman, Lance 1997. "Foreword: The new estates," *Columbia Law Review* 97: 819–34.

Liebowitz, Stan J. and Stephen E. Margolis 1994. "Network externality: An uncommon tragedy," *Journal of Economic Perspectives* 8: 133–50.

———— 1995. "Are network externalities a new source of market failure?" *Research in Law and Economics* 17: 1–22.

———— 1996. "Should technology choice be a concern of antitrust policy?" *Harvard Journal of Law and Technology* 9: 283–318.

———— 2001. *Winners, losers and Microsoft*, revised ed. Oakland, CA: Independent Institute.

Lipartito, Kenneth 1989. *The Bell system and regional business: The telephone in the South, 1877–1920.* Baltimore: Johns Hopkins University Press.

Lipsky, Abbott B., Jr., and J. Gregory Sidak 1999. "Essential facilities," *Stanford Law Review* 51: 1187–249.

Lopatka, John E. and William H. Page 2001. "Devising a Microsoft remedy that serves consumers," *George Mason Law Review* 9: 691–726.

———— 2001. "Internet regulation and consumer welfare: Innovation, speculation, and cable bundling," *Hastings Law Journal* 52: 891–928.

———— 2005. "Bargaining and monopolization: In search of the 'boundary of Section 2 liability' between *Aspen* and *Trinko*," *Antitrust Law Journal* 73: 115–52.

Lucking-Reilly, David and Daniel F. Spulber 2001. "Business-to-business electronic commerce," *Journal of Economic Perspectives* 15: 55–68.

Lunney, Glynn S. 1993. "Compensation for takings: How much is just?" *Catholic University Law Review* 42: 721–70.

MacAvoy, Paul W. 1996. *The failure of antitrust and regulation to establish competition in long-distance telephone service.* Cambridge, MA: MIT Press.

MacAvoy, Paul W. and Kenneth Robinson 1983. "Winning by losing: The AT&T settlement and its impact on telecommunication," *Yale Journal on Regulation* 1: 1–42.

Machlup, Fritz and Martha Taber 1960. "Bilateral monopoly, successive monopoly, and vertical integration," *Economica* 27: 101–19.

Mackie-Mason, Jeffrey K. and Hal R. Varian 1994. "Economic FAQs about the Internet," *Journal of Economic Perspectives* 8: 75–96.

———— 1995a. "Pricing congestible network resources," *IEEE Journal on Selected Areas in Communications* 13: 1141–49.

―――― 1995b. "Some FAQs about usage-based pricing," *Computer Networks and ISDN Systems* 28: 257–65.

Majoras, Deborah P. 2006. Federal Trade Commission in the online world – Promoting competition and protecting consumers. Luncheon Address at the Progress & Freedom Foundation's Aspen Summit, Aspen, CO.

Majumdar, Samit K., Ingo Vogelsang, and Martin E. Cave (eds.) 2005. *Handbook of telecommunications economics*. Vol. 2. New York: Elsevier Science Publishing Co.

Mallela, Parthasaradhi and Babu Nahata 1980. "Theory of vertical control with variable proportions," *Journal of Political Economy* 88: 1009–25.

Manishin, Glenn B. 1987. "Antitrust and regulation in cable television: Federal policy at war with itself," *Cardozo Arts and Entertainment Law Journal* 6: 75–100.

Markovits, Richard S. 1970. "Tie-ins, leverage, and American antitrust laws," *Yale Law Journal* 80: 195–315.

Marshall, Alfred 1898. *Principles of economics*, 4th ed. Vol. 1. New York: Macmillan and Co.

Martin, Kevin J. 2005. "Comments on commission policy statement," news release, http://hraunfoss.fcc.gov/edocs_public/attachmatch/DOC-260435A2.pdf.

Mathewson, G. Franklin and G. David Quirin 1972. "Metering costs and marginal cost pricing in public utilities," *Bell Journal of Economics and Management Science* 3: 335–9.

Mathewson, G. Franklin and Ralph A. Winter 1984. "An economic theory of vertical restraints," *RAND Journal of Economics* 15: 27–38.

―――― 1997. "Buyer groups," *International Journal of Industrial Organization* 15: 137–64.

Mathios, Alan D. and Robert P. Rogers 1989. "The impact of alternative forms of state regulation of AT&T on direct-dial, long-distance telephone rates," *RAND Journal of Economics* 20: 437–53.

McChesney, Fred S. 1995. "Be true to your school: Chicago's contradictory views of antitrust and regulation," in *The causes and consequences of antitrust*, Fred S. McChesney and William F. Shughart II (eds.). Chicago: University of Chicago Press, pp. 323–40.

McDermott, Tom 2002. "The marriage of optical switching and electronic routing," *Lightwave*, May, http://lw.pennnet.com/display_article/143017/13/ARTCL/none/none/1/The-marriage-of-optical-switching-and-electronic-routing/.

McGowan, David 1996. "Regulating competition in the information age: Computer software as an essential facility under the Sherman Act," *Hastings Communications and Entertainment Law Journal* 18: 771–852.

McGuire, Martin 1974. "Group segregation and optimal jurisdictions," *Journal of Political Economy* 82: 112–32.

McKenzie, Lionel W. 1951. "Ideal output and the interdependence of firms," *Economic Journal* 61: 785–803.

Meese, Alan J. 2000. "Farewell to the quick look: Redefining the scope and content of the rule of reason," *Antitrust Law Journal* 68: 461–98.

Melody, William H. 2002. "Building the regulatory foundations for growth in network economies," WDR Discussion Paper No. 0201, http://www.regulateonline.org/content/view/217/64/.

Menger, Carl 1950. *Principles of economics*. Trans. and ed. by James Dingwall and Bert F. Hoselitz. Glencoe, IL: Free Press.

Milgram, Stanley 1967. "Small-world problem," *Psychology Today* 1: 61–7.

Milgrom, Paul, Bridger Mitchell, and Padmanabhan Srinagesh 2000. "Competitive effects of Internet peering policies," in *The Internet Upheaval*, Ingo Vogelsang and Benjamin M. Compaine (eds.). Cambridge, MA: MIT Press, pp. 175–95.

Milgrom, Paul and John Roberts 1992. *Economics, organization and management.* Englewood Cliffs, NJ: Prentice Hall.

Mill, John S. 1961. *Principles of political economy.* Ed. by William J. Ashley. New York: Augustus M. Kelley. [Originally published 1848.]

Mitchell, Bridger M. 1978. "Optimal pricing of local telephone service," *American Economic Review* 68: 517–37.

Mitchell, Bridger M. and Ingo Vogelsang 1991. *Telecommunications pricing: Theory and practice.* New York: Cambridge University Press.

Monge, Peter R. and Noshir S. Contractor 2003. *Theories of communication networks.* New York: Oxford University Press.

Mueller, Milton L. 1989. "The switchboard problem: Scale, signaling, and organization in manual telephone switching, 1877–1897," *Technology and Culture* 30: 534–60.

———— 1997. *Universal service.* Cambridge, MA: MIT Press.

Muris, Timothy J. 2001. "*GTE Sylvania* and the empirical foundations of antitrust," *Antitrust Law Journal* 68: 899–912.

Myerson, Roger B. 1977. "Graphs and cooperation in games," *Mathematics of Operations Research* 2: 225–9.

Nachbar, Thomas 2008. "The public network," *CommLaw Conspectus* 16: 67–139.

Nakahata, John T. 2002. "Regulating information platforms: The challenge of rewriting communications regulation from the bottom up," *Journal on Telecommunications and High Technology Law* 1: 95–142.

National Commission for the Review of Antitrust Laws and Procedures 1979. *Report to the President and the Attorney General.*

*National Journal's Insider Update* 2006. "FCC chief opens door to tiered, high-speed Internet," 6 January.

Neale, Alan D. 1960. *The antitrust laws of the United States of America,* 1st ed. New York: Cambridge University Press.

———— 1970. *The antitrust laws of the United States,* 2d ed. New York: Cambridge University Press.

New York Public Service Commission [NYPSC] 1994. "Petition of Rochester Tel. Corp. for approval of proposed restructuring plan," Opinion and order. *Public Utilities Reports,* 4th series 160: 554–617.

———— 1998. "Joint complaint of AT&T Communications of New York, Inc., MCI Telecommunications Corporation, WorldCom, Inc. d/b/a LDDS WorldCom and the Empire Association of Long Distance Telephone Companies, Inc. against New York Telephone Company concerning wholesale provisioning of local exchange service by New York Telephone Company and sections of New York Telephone Company's Tariff No. 900," Notice inviting comments on staff report, Case 95-C-0657, 1998 WL 744059.

*New York Times* 2006. Editorial, "Tollbooths on the Internet highway," 20 February.

———— 2007. "Cellphone-only homes hit a milestone," 27 August.

*Newsweek* 2006. "When the net goes from free to fee," 27 February.

Noam, Eli M. 1983. "Local distribution monopolies in cable television and telephone service: The scope for competition," in *Telecommunications regulation today and tomorrow,* Eli M. Noam (ed.). New York: Harcourt Brace Jovanovich, pp. 351–416.

———— 1985. "Economies of scale in cable television: A multiproduct analysis," in *Video media competition: Regulation, economics, and technology,* Eli M. Noam (ed.). New York: Columbia University Press, pp. 93–120.

———— 1997. "Will universal service and common carriage survive the Telecommunications Act of 1996?" *Columbia Law Review* 97: 955–75.

Noll, Roger G. 1989. "Economic perspectives on the politics of regulation," in Schmalensee and Willig (eds.), Vol. 2, pp. 1253–87.

———— 2005. "'Buyer power' and economic policy," *Antitrust Law Journal* 72: 589–624.

Noll, Roger G. and Bruce M. Owen 1989. "The anticompetitive uses of regulation: United States v. AT&T," in *The Antitrust Revolution*, John E. Kwoka and Lawrence J. White (eds.). Glenview, IL: Scott, Foresman, pp. 291–4.

North American Electric Reliability Corp. 2007. "High-voltage transmission circuit miles (230kV and above) – 2005," http://www.nerc.com/files/High-Voltage_Transmission_Circuit_Miles_2005.doc.

O'Connor, Kevin J. 1976. "The divestiture remedy in Sherman Act § 2," *Harvard Journal on Legislation* 13: 687–775.

Odlyzko, Andrew 2004. "The evolution of price discrimination in transportation and its implications for the Internet," *Review of Network Economics* 3: 323–46.

Ojala, Marydee 1997. "Online, past, present and future: Repetition, reinvention, or reincarnation?" *Online* 21: 63–6.

*Omaha World-Herald* 2007. "Big phone carriers say small firms bleed them," 16 May.

Ordover, Janusz, and William Baumol 1988. "Antitrust policy and high-technology industries," *Oxford Review of Economic Policy* 4(4): 13–34.

Ordover, Janusz A., Garth Saloner, and Steven C. Salop 1990. "Equilibrium vertical foreclosure," *American Economic Review* 80: 127–42.

Owen, Bruce M. and Peter R. Greenhalgh 1986. "Competitive considerations in cable television franchising," *Contemporary Economic Policy* 4: 69–79.

Owen, Bruce M. and Gregory L. Rosston 2006. "Local broadband access: *Primum non nocere* or *primum processi?* A property rights approach," in Lenard and May (eds.), pp. 163–94.

Page, William H. 1989. "The Chicago school and the evolution of antitrust: Characterization, antitrust injury, and evidentiary sufficiency," *Virginia Law Review* 75: 1221–308.

Panzar, John C. 1976. "A neoclassical approach to peak load pricing," *Bell Journal of Economics* 7: 521–30.

Panzar, John C. and Robert D. Willig 1977. "Free entry and sustainability of natural monopoly," *Bell Journal of Economics* 8: 1–22.

Park, Rolla E. and Bridger M. Mitchell 1987. "Optimal peak-load pricing for local telephone calls," Rand Paper No. R-3404-1-RC.

Parsons, Steven G. 1996. "The economic necessity of an increased subscriber line charge (SLC) in telecommunications," *Administrative Law Review* 48: 227–50.

Pauly, Mark V. 1967. "Clubs, commonality and the core: An integration of game theory and the theory of public goods," *Economica* 34: 314–24.

———— 1970. "Cores and clubs," *Public Choice* 9: 53–65.

Peltzman, Sam 1969. "Issues in vertical integration policy," in *Public policy towards mergers*, J. Fred Weston and Sam Peltzman (eds.). Pacific Palisades, CA: Goodyear Publishing Co., pp. 167–176.

———— 1976. "Toward a more general theory of regulation," *Journal of Law and Economics* 19: 211–40.

Peltzman, Sam and Clifford Winston (eds.) 2000. *Deregulation of network industries: What's next?* Washington, DC: AEI–Brookings Joint Center for Regulatory Studies.

Pennsylvania Public Utility Commission 2001. "Verizon, Pennsylvania, Inc.," Order, *Pennsylvania Public Utility Commission Reports* 95: 301–30.

Perry, Martin K. 1989. "Vertical integration: Determinants and effects," in Schmalensee and Willig (eds.), vol. 1, pp. 183–255.

Pindyck, Robert S. 2004. "Mandatory unbundling and irreversible investment in tele-com networks," Working Paper No. 10287, National Bureau of Economic Research, http://www.nber.org/papers/w10287.pdf.

Piraino, Thomas A. 2000. "Identifying monopolists' illegal conduct under the Sherman Act," *New York University Law Review* 75: 809–92.

Pitofsky, Robert, Donna Patterson, and Jonathan Hooks 2002. "The essential facilities doctrine under U.S. antitrust law," *Antitrust Law Journal* 70: 443–62.

Polanyi, Karl 1944. *The great transformation: The political and economic origins of our time.* New York: Farrar and Rinehart.

Posner, Richard A. 1969. "Natural monopoly and its regulation," *Stanford Law Review* 21(Feb): 548–643.

———— 1970. "Statistical study of antitrust enforcement," *Journal of Law and Economics* 13: 365–420.

———— 1972. "The appropriate scope of regulation in the cable television industry," *Bell Journal of Economics* 3: 98–129.

———— 1976. *Antitrust law: An economic perspective.* Chicago: University of Chicago Press.

Posner, Richard A. and Frank H. Easterbrook 1981. *Antitrust cases, economic notes, and other materials*, 2d ed. St. Paul, MN: West Publishing Co.

Powell, Michael K. 2004. "Preserving Internet freedom: Guiding principles for the industry," *Journal on Telecommunications and High Technology Law* 3: 5–22.

Prim, Robert C. 1957. "Shortest connection networks and some generalizations," *Bell System Technical Journal* 36: 1389–1401.

Quast, Troy 2008. "Did federal regulation discourage facilities-based entry into US local telecommunications markets?" *Telecommunications Policy* 32: 572–81.

Rabin, Robert L. 1986. "Federal regulation in historical perspective," *Stanford Law Review* 38: 1189–1326.

Ramsey, Frank P. 1927. "A contribution to the theory of taxation," *Economic Journal* 37: 47–61.

Ratner, James R. 1988. "Should there be an essential facility doctrine?" *U.C. Davis Law Review* 21: 327–82.

Rauch, James E. 1999. "Networks versus markets in international trade," *Journal of International Economics* 48: 7–35.

———— 2001. "Business and social networks in international trade," *Journal of Economic Literature* 39: 1177–1203.

*Reason Online* 2006. "A neutral panic: Why there's no need for new laws to keep the Internet open," 10 April.

Reed, David P., Jerome H. Saltzer, and David D. Clark 1998. "Commentaries on 'Active networking and end-to-end arguments,'" *IEEE Network* 12: 69–71.

Reed, Graham T. 2004. "The optical age of silicon," *Nature* 427: 595–6.

Reiffen, David and Andrew N. Kleit 1990. "*Terminal Railroad* revisited: Foreclosure of an essential facility or simple horizontal monopoly?" *Journal of Law and Economics* 33: 419–38.

Reiffen, David and Michael Vita 1995. "Is there new thinking on vertical mergers?" *Antitrust Law Journal* 63: 917–42.

Rifkin, Jeremy 2000. *The age of access.* New York: Putnam.

Riordan, Michael H. 1998. "Anticompetitive vertical integration by a dominant firm," *American Economic Review* 88: 1232–48.

Riordan, Michael H. and Steven C. Salop 1995. "Evaluating vertical mergers: A post-Chicago approach," *Antitrust Law Journal* 63: 513–68.

Risinger, D. Michael 1985. "Direct damages: The lost key to constitutional just compensation when business premises are condemned," *Seton Hall Law Review* 15: 483–540.

Robertazzi, Thomas G. 1999. *Planning telecommunication networks.* New York: Wiley–IEEE Press.

Robinson, Glen O. 1988. "The Titanic remembered: AT&T and the changing world of telecommunications," *Yale Journal on Regulation* 5: 517–45.

_____ 1989. "The Federal Communications Act: An essay on origins and regulatory purpose," in *A Legislative History of the Communications Act of 1934*, Max D. Paglin (ed.). New York: Oxford University Press, pp. 3–24.

_____ 2002. "On refusing to deal with rivals," *Cornell Law Review* 87: 1177–1232.

Rochet, Jean-Charles and Jean Tirole 2003. "Platform competition in two-sided markets," *Journal of European Economic Association* 1: 990–1029.

Rogerson, William P. 2000a. "New economic perspectives on telecommunication regulations," *University of Chicago Law Review* 67: 1489–1505.

_____ 2000b. "The regulation of broadband telecommunications, the principle of regulating narrowly defined input bottlenecks, and incentives for investment and innovation," *University of Chicago Legal Forum* 2000: 119–48.

Rohlfs, Jeffrey 1974. "A theory of interdependent demand for a communications service," *Bell Journal of Economics and Management Science* 5: 16–37.

Röller, Lars-Hendrick 1990a. "Modeling cost structure: The Bell system revisited," *Applied Economics* 22: 1661–74.

_____ 1990b. "Proper quadratic cost functions with an application to the Bell system," *Review of Economics and Statistics* 72: 202–10.

Ros, Augustin J. and Karl McDermott 2000. "Are residential local exchange prices too low?" in *Expanding Competition in Regulated Industries*, Michael A. Crew (ed.). Norwell, MA: Kluwer Academic Publishers, pp. 149–68.

Rose-Ackerman, Susan and Jim Rossi 2000. "Disentangling deregulatory takings," *Virginia Law Review* 86: 1435–95.

Rosston, Gregory L. and Roger G. Noll 2002. "The economics of the Supreme Court's decision on forward looking costs," *Review of Network Economics* 1: 81–9.

Rubin, Paul H. and Hashem Dezhbakhsh 1995. "Costs of delay and rent-seeking under the modification of final judgment," *Managerial and Decision Economics* 16: 385–99.

Saadawi, Tarek N. and Mostafa H. Ammar with Ahmed El Hakeem 1994. *Fundamentals of telecommunication networks.* New York: Wiley–Interscience.

Sackman, Julius L. 1995. *Nichols' The law of eminent domain*, 3d ed. Vol. 4. New York: Matthew Bender.

Salinger, Michael A. 1988. "Vertical mergers and market foreclosure," *Quarterly Journal of Economics* 103: 345–56.

_____ 1991. "Vertical mergers in multi-product industries and Edgeworth's paradox of taxation," *Journal of Industrial Economics* 39: 545–56.

Salop, Steven C. 1979. "Monopolistic competition with outside goods," *Bell Journal of Economics* 10: 141–56.

_____ 2006. "Exclusionary conduct: Effect on consumers, and the flawed profit-sacrifice standard," *Antitrust Law Journal* 73: 311–74.

Salop, Steven C. and David T. Scheffman 1983. "Raising rivals' costs," *American Economic Review* 73: 267–71.

Saltzer, Jerome H. 1999. "'Open access' is just the tip of the iceberg," http://web.mit .edu/Saltzer/www/publications/openaccess.html.

Saltzer, Jerome H., David P. Reed, and David D. Clark 1984. "End-to-end arguments in system-design," *ACM Transactions on Computer Systems* 2: 277–88.

Samuelson, Paul A. 1947. *Foundations of economic analysis.* Cambridge, MA: Harvard University Press.

———— 1948. "Consumption theory in terms of revealed preference," *Economica* 15: 243–53.

*San Francisco Chronicle* 2006. Editorial, "Don't undercut Internet access," 17 April.

*San Jose Mercury News* 2005. "Google offers free WiFi net for S. F.," 1 October.

———— 2006. Editorial, "Congress turns a deaf ear to need for Internet neutrality," 7 April.

Schelling, Thomas C. 1978. *Micromotives and macrobehavior.* New York: Norton.

Scherer, Frederic M. and David Ross 1990. *Industrial market structure and economic performance.* Boston: Houghton Mifflin.

Schmalensee, Richard 1973. "A note on the theory of vertical integration," *Journal of Political Economy* 81: 442–9.

Schmalensee, Richard and Robert D. Willig (eds.) 1989. *The handbook of industrial organization*, 2 vols. New York: North-Holland Publishing Co.

Schoenwald, Scott M. 1997. "Regulating competition in the interexchange telecommunications market: The dominant/nondominant carrier approach and the evolution of forbearance," *Federal Communications Law Journal* 49: 369–456.

Schumpeter, Joseph A. 1942. *Capitalism, socialism, and democracy.* New York: Harper and Row.

Scotchmer, Suzanne 1985. "Two-tier pricing of shared facilities in a free-entry equilibrium," *RAND Journal of Economics* 16: 453–72.

———— 1994. "Public goods and the invisible hand," in *Modern public finance*, John M. Quigley and Eugene Smolensky (eds.). Cambridge, MA: Harvard University Press, pp. 93–125.

Scotchmer, Suzanne and Myrna Holtz Wooders 1987. "Competitive-equilibrium and the core in club economies with anonymous crowding," *Journal of Public Economics* 34: 159–73.

*Seattle Times* (2007). "Comcast blocks some file sharing," Oct. 20.

Selwyn, Lee W. 1981. "Perspectives on usage-sensitive pricing," *Public Utilities Fortnightly*, May 7.

Shale, Roger (ed.) 1918. *Decrees and judgments in federal anti-trust cases, July 2, 1890–January 1, 1918.* Washington, DC: Government Printing Office.

Shapiro, Carl 1995. "Aftermarkets and consumer welfare: Making sense of *Kodak*," *Antitrust Law Journal* 63: 483–512.

———— 1999. "Exclusivity in network industries," *George Mason Law Review* 7: 673–84.

Shapiro, George H., Philip B. Kurland, and James P. Mercurio 1983. *Cablespeech: The case for First Amendment protection.* New York: Law and Business, Inc.

Sharfman, Isaiah L. 1931. *The Interstate Commerce Commission.* Vol. 2. New York: Commonwealth Fund.

Sharkey, William W. 1995. "Network models in economics," in *Network routing.* Vol. 8 of *The handbook of operations research and management science*, M. O. Ball, T. L. Magnanti, C. L. Momma, and G. L. Nemhauser (eds.). New York: North-Holland Publishing Co., pp. 713–65.

Shelanski, Howard A. 2007. "Adjusting regulation to competition: Toward a new model for U. S. telecommunications policy," *Yale Journal on Regulation* 24: 55–106.

Shelanski, Howard A. and J. Gregory Sidak 2001. "Antitrust divestiture in network industries," *University of Chicago Law Review* 68: 1–100.

Shin, Richard T. and John S. Ying 1992. "Unnatural monopolies in local telephone," *RAND Journal of Economics* 23: 171–83.

Shore, Stephen N. 2002. *The tapestry of modern astrophysics.* New York: Wiley–Interscience.

Sidak, J. Gregory and Daniel F. Spulber 1996. *Protecting competition from the postal monopoly.* Washington, DC: AEI Press.

_____ 1997a. *Deregulatory takings and the regulatory contract.* New York: Cambridge University Press.

_____ 1997b. "Givings, takings, and the fallacy of forward-looking costs," *New York University Law Review* 72: 1068–1164.

_____ 1998. "Cyberjam: The law and economics of Internet congestion of the telephone network," *Harvard Journal of Law and Public Policy* 21: 327–94.

Siegel, Stephen A. 1984. "Understanding the *Lochner* era: Lessons from the controversy over railroad and utility rate regulation," *Virginia Law Review* 70: 187–263.

Smiley, Albert K. 1989. Direct competition among cable television systems. Economic Analysis Group Paper No. 86-9, U.S. Department of Justice.

Sloan Commission on Cable Communications 1971. *On the cable: The television of abundance.* New York: McGraw-Hill.

Smith, Adam 1776. *An inquiry into the nature and causes of wealth of nations.* Reprinted 1998, Washington, D.C.: Regnery Publishing.

Solum, Lawrence B. and Minn Chung 2004. "The layers principle: Internet architecture and the law," *Notre Dame Law Review* 79: 815–948.

Soma, John T., David A. Forkner, and Brian P. Jumps 1998. "The essential facilities doctrine in the deregulated telecommunications industry," *Berkeley Technology Law Journal* 13: 565–614.

Spence, A. Michael 1976. "Product selection, fixed costs, and monopolistic competition," *Review of Economic Studies* 43: 217–35.

Spengler, Joseph J. 1950. "Vertical integration and antitrust policy," *Journal of Political Economy* 58: 347–52.

Speta, James B. 2000. "Handicapping the race for the last mile: A critique of open access rules for broadband platforms," *Yale Journal on Regulation* 17: 39–92.

_____ 2002. "A common carrier approach to Internet interconnection," *Federal Communications Law Journal* 54: 225–80.

_____ 2004. "Deregulating telecommunications in Internet time," *Washington and Lee Law Review* 61: 1063–1158.

_____ 2006. "Resale requirements and the intersection of antitrust and regulated industries," *Journal of Corporation Law* 31: 307–22.

Spitzer, Matthew L. 1988. "Antitrust federalism and rational choice political economy: A critique of capture theory," *Southern California Law Review* 61: 1293–1326.

Spulber, Daniel F. 1989. *Regulation and markets.* Cambridge, MA: MIT Press.

_____ 1992. "Capacity-contingent nonlinear pricing by regulated firms," *Journal of Regulatory Economics* 4: 299–319.

_____ 1993a. "Monopoly pricing," *Journal of Economic Theory* 59: 222–34.

_____ 1993b. "Monopoly pricing of capacity usage under asymmetric information," *Journal of Industrial Economics* 41: 1–17.

_____ 1995. "Deregulating telecommunications," *Yale Journal on Regulation* 12: 25–68.

———— 1996. "Market microstructure and intermediation," *Journal of Economic Perspectives* 10: 135–52.

———— 1998. *The market makers: How leading companies create and win markets.* New York: McGraw-Hill.

———— 1999. *Market microstructure: Intermediaries and the theory of the firm.* New York: Cambridge University Press.

———— 2002a. "Competition policy in telecommunications," in Martin E. Cave et al. (eds.), pp. 478–509.

———— 2002b. "Market microstructure and incentives to invest," *Journal of Political Economy* 110: 352–81.

———— 2006. "Firms and networks in two-sided markets," in *The handbook of economics and information systems*, Terry Hendershott (ed.). Amsterdam: Elsevier, pp. 137–200.

———— 2008a. "Consumer coordination in the small and in the large: Implications for antitrust in markets with network effects," *Journal of Competition Law and Economics* 4: 207–62.

———— 2008b. "Unlocking technology: Innovation and antitrust," *Journal of Competition Law and Economics* 4: 915–66.

Squire, Richard 2006. "Antitrust and the supremacy clause," *Stanford Law Review* 59: 77–130.

*Statutes at Large* 1910. Vol. 36, pp. 539–57. *Mann–Elkins Act.*

———— 1921. Vol. 42, pp. 27–28. *Willis–Graham Act.*

———— 1934. Vol. 48, pp. 1064–105. *Communications Act of 1934.*

———— 1978. Vol. 92, pp. 33–36. *Communications Act Amendments of 1978.*

———— 1984. Vol. 98, pp. 2779–806. *Communications Policy Act of 1984.*

———— 1992. Vol. 106, pp. 1460–504. *Cable Television Consumer Protection and Competition Act of 1992.*

———— 1993. Vol. 107, pp. 312–685. *Omnibus Budget Reconciliation Act of 1993.*

———— 1996. Vol. 110, pp. 56–161. *Telecommunications Act of 1996.*

Stehman, J. Warren 1925. *The financial history of the American Telephone and Telegraph Company.* Boston, Houghton Mifflin.

Stein, Clifford 2004. "Maximum flows," in Gross and Yellen (eds.), pp. 1075–86.

Steiner, Peter O. 1952. "Program patterns and preferences, and the workability of competition in radio broadcasting," *Quarterly Journal of Economics* 66: 194–223.

———— 1957. "Peak loads and efficient pricing," *Quarterly Journal of Economics* 71: 585–610.

Stigler, George J. 1968. *The organization of industry.* Homewood, IL: R. D. Irwin.

———— 1971. "Theory of economic regulation," *Bell Journal of Economics and Management Science* 2: 3–21.

Sullivan, Lawrence A. 1977. *Handbook on the law of antitrust.* St. Paul, MN: West Publishing Co.

———— 1996. "Elusive goals under the Telecommunications Act: Preserving long distance competition upon baby Bell entry and attaining local exchange competition: We'll not preserve the one unless we attain the other," *Southwestern University Law Review* 25: 487–534.

Sullivan, Lawrence A. and Warren S. Grimes 2006. *The law of antitrust: An integrated handbook*, 2d ed. St. Paul, MN: Thomson/West.

Sunstein, Cass R. 1993. *The partial Constitution.* Cambridge, MA: Harvard University Press.

———— 2005. *Laws of fear: Beyond the precautionary principle.* New York: Cambridge University Press.

Tardiff, Timothy J. 2007. "Changes in industry structure and technological convergence: Implications for competition policy and regulation in telecommunications," *International Economics and Economic Policy* 4: 109–33.

Taussig, Frank W. 1922. *Principles of economics*, 3d ed., vol. 2. New York: Macmillan Co.

techFAQ 2009. "What is SCADA?" http://www.tech-faq.com/scada.shtml. (accessed January 22, 2009).

*Telecommunications Reports* 1998a. "MCI abandons reselling residential local service to focus on facilities-based business offerings," 26 January.

———— 1998b. "AT&T's Armstrong says Bells' discounts delay competition," 16 February.

*Telepath* 1998. "Billing systems market reaps huge growth: How telecom carriers handle phone bills can make or break their customer base," 5 January.

*Telephony* 1975. "Usage sensitive pricing: Studies of a new trend," 10 February.

———— 2005. "Intel gets behind BPL," 5 September.

———— 2006. "Point of no return," 3 April.

Telser, Lester G. 1990. "Why should manufacturers want fair trade?" *Journal of Law and Economics* 33: 409–17.

Temin, Peter 1987. *The fall of the Bell system.* New York: Cambridge University Press.

Temkin, Oleg N., Andrew V. Zeigarnik, and Danail Bonchev 1996. *Chemical reaction networks: A graph-theoretical approach.* Boca Raton, FL: CRC Press.

Thierer, Adam 2005. "Are dumb pipe mandates smart public policy: Vertical integration, net neutrality, and the network layers model," *Journal on Telecommunications and High Technology Law* 3: 275–308.

Thompson, George V. 1954. "Intercompany technical standardization in the early American automobile industry," *Journal of Economic History* 14: 1–20.

Tiebout, Charles M. 1956. "A pure theory of local expenditures," *Journal of Political Economy* 64: 416–24.

Tribe, Laurence H. 1988. *American constitutional law*, 2d ed. Mineola, NY: Foundation Press.

U. S. Canada Power System Outage Task Force 2004. *Final report on the August 14th blackout in the United States and Canada: Causes and recommendations*, https://reports.energy.gov/BlackoutFinal-Web.pdf.

U. S. Department of Commerce, Economics and Statistics Administration 2003. *Digital economy 2003*, https://www.esa.doc.gov/2003.cfm.

U. S. Department of Commerce, Bureau of Economic Analysis 2008. "Annual industry accounts: Advance estimates for 2007," *Survey of Current Business*, May 2007, http://www.bea.gov/scb/pdf/2008/05%20May/0508_indy_acct.pdf.

U. S. Department of Justice 1968. "Merger guidelines," 4 Trade Reg. Rep. [CCH] ¶13,101.

———— 1984. "Merger guidelines," *Federal Register* 49: 26823–37.

———— 1992. "Merger guidelines," *Federal Register* 57: 41552–63.

———— 2007. "Ex parte filing," filed in FCC (2007d), http://www.usdoj.gov/atr/public/comments/225767.pdf.

U. S. Department of Transportation, Bureau of Transportation Statistics 2008. *National transportation statistics 2008*, http://www.bts.gov/publications/national_transportation_statistics/pdf/entire.pdf.

U. S. House 1921. *Consolidation of telephone systems.* 67th Congress, 1st sess. H. R. Rep. No. 109.

———— 1934. *Federal Communications Commission: Hearings on H. R. 8301 before the House Committee on Interstate and Foreign Commerce*, 73d Congress, 2d sess.

———— 1939. *Investigation of the telephone industry in the United States*, 76th Congress, 1st sess. H. R. Doc. No. 76–340.

———— 1984. *Congressional Record* 130, no. 20 (1 October): p. 27975.

———— 1995. *Communications Act of 1995.* 104th Congress, 1st sess. H. R. Rep. No. 204.

———— 1996. *Telecommunications Act of 1995.* 104th Congress, 2d sess. H. R. Conf. Rep. No. 458.

U. S. President's Task Force on Antitrust Policy 1968. *Report of the White House Task Force on Antitrust Policy.* Washington, DC: Bureau of National Affairs.

U. S. Senate 1934a. *Study of communications by an interdepartmental committee.* 73d Congress, 2d sess. Committee print.

———— 1934b. *Federal Communications Commission: Hearings on S. 2910 before the Senate Committee on Interstate Commerce*, 73d Congress, 2d sess.

———— 1983. *Congressional Record* 129, no. 12 (13 June): p. 15459.

———— 2006a. *Net neutrality: Hearing before the Senate Committee on Commerce, Science & Transportation*, 109th Congress, 2d sess.

———— 2006b. *Reconsidering our communications laws: Ensuring competition and innovation: Hearing before the Senate Committee on the Judiciary*, 109th Congress, 2d sess.

———— 2007. *Internet Freedom Preservation Act.* 110th Congress, 1st sess. S. 215.

Uri, Noel D. 2001. "Monopoly power and the problem of CLEC access charges," *Telecommunications Policy* 25: 611–23.

Vail, Theodore 1913. "Public utilities and public policy," *Atlantic*, March.

Van den Heuvel, Paul 1986. "Nonjoint production and the cost function: Some refinements," *Journal of Economics* 46: 283–97.

Van Zandt, David E. 1993. "The lessons of the lighthouse: 'Government' or 'private' provision of goods," *Journal of Legal Studies* 22: 47–72.

Varian, Hal R. 1989. "Price discrimination," in Schmalensee and Willig (eds.), pp. 597–654.

———— 1998. "How to strengthen the Internet's backbone," *Wall Street Journal*, June 8.

Verizon Communications Inc. 2007. "All about Verizon FiOS–Fact sheet," http://newscenter .verizon.com/kit/fios-symmetrical-internet-service/all-about-fios.html.

Vernon, John M. and Daniel A. Graham 1971. "Profitability of monopolization by vertical integration," *Journal of Political Economy* 79: 924–5.

Vickrey, William 1961. "Counterspeculation, auctions, and competitive sealed tenders," *Journal of Finance* 16: 8–37.

Vogt, Gregory J. 1999. "Cap-sized: How the promise of the price cap voyage to competition was lost in a sea of good intentions," *Federal Communications Law Journal* 51: 351–401.

*Wall Street Journal* 2002. "Washington created WorldCom," 1 July.

———— 2004. "Rules change could alter the fate of long-distance giants," 11 June.

———— 2005a. "Disney to enter cellphone market, with kids in mind," 6 July.

———— 2005b. "Neutral ground: As Web providers' clout grows, fears over access take focus," 8 August.

———— 2006. Editorial, "Stuck in neutral," 8 March.

Wallis, W. D. 2000. *A beginner's guide to graph theory.* New York: Springer.

Walrand, Jean and Prayin Varaiya 2000. *High-performance communication networks.* San Francisco: Morgan Kaufmann.

Walras, Leon 1936. *Études d'économie sociale: Théorie de la repartition de la richesse sociale.* Lausanne: F. Rouge et cie.

———— 1954. *Elements of pure economics.* Trans. by William Jaffé. Homewood, IL: George Allen and Unwin Ltd.

Warren-Boulton, Frederick R. 1974. "Vertical control with variable proportions," *Journal of Political Economy* 82: 783–802.

*Washington Post* 2006. Editorial, "The Eden illusion," 13 March.

*Washington Technology* 2005. "Slimming from 170 to one: DHS wants to consolidate portals and Web sites, now it's looking for the right tools," June 6.

Wasserman, Stanley and Katherine Faust 1994. *Social network analysis: Methods and applications.* New York: Cambridge University Press.

Waterson, Michael 1982. "Vertical integration, variable proportions and oligopoly," *Economic Journal* 92: 129–44.

Watts, Duncan J. 1999. *Small worlds: The dynamics of networks between order and randomness.* Princeton, NJ: Princeton University Press.

_____ 2003. *Six degrees: The science of a connected age.* New York: W. W. Norton and Co.

Webb, G. Kent 1983. *The economics of cable television.* Lanham, MD: Rowman and Littlefield Publishers.

Wechsler, Herbert 1959. "Toward neutral principles of constitutional law," *Harvard Law Review* 73: 1–35.

Weiman, David F. and Richard C. Levin 1994. "Preying for monopoly? The case of Southern Bell Telephone Company, 1894–1912," *Journal of Political Economy* 102: 103–26.

Weiser, Philip J. 2003a. "The Internet, innovation, and intellectual property policy," *Columbia Law Review* 103: 534–613.

_____ 2003b. "Toward a next generation regulatory strategy," *Loyola University Chicago Law Review* 35: 41–86.

_____ 2005. "The relationship of antitrust and regulation in a deregulatory era," *Antitrust Bulletin* 50: 549–88.

Werbach, Kevin D. 2002. "A layered model for Internet policy," *Journal on Telecommunications and High Technology Law* 1: 42–67.

_____ 2005. "Breaking the ice: Rethinking telecommunications law for the digital age," *Journal on Telecommunications and High Technology Law* 4: 59–96.

_____ 2007. "Only connect," *Berkeley Technology Law Journal* 22: 1233–301.

Werden, Gregory J. 1987. "The law and economics of the essential facility doctrine," *Saint Louis University Law Journal* 32: 433–80.

Westen, Peter 1982. "The empty idea of equality," *Harvard Law Review* 95: 537–96.

Westfield, Fred M. 1981. "Vertical integration: Does product price rise or fall?" *American Economic Review* 71: 334–46.

Whinston, Michael D. 1990. "Tying, foreclosure, and exclusion," *American Economic Review* 80: 837–59.

Whitt, Richard S. 2004. "A horizontal leap forward: Formulating a new communications public policy framework based on the network layers model," *Federal Communications Law Journal* 56: 587–672.

Wibe, Soren 1984. "Engineering production functions: A survey," *Economica* 51: 401–11.

Wiley, John S. 1986a. "A capture theory of antitrust federalism," *Harvard Law Review* 99: 713–89.

_____ 1986b. "After Chicago: An exaggerated demise?" *Duke Law Journal* 1986: 1003–13.

Wilkie, Simon 2004. Open networks: The roles of regulation and competition. Paper presented at the Silicon Flatirons Conference on the Digital Broadband Migration: Towards a Regulatory Regime.

Williamson, Oliver E. 1966. "Peak-load pricing and optimal capacity under indivisibility constraints," *American Economic Review* 56: 810–27.

——— 1972. "Dominant firms and the monopoly problem: Market failure considerations," *Harvard Law Review* 85: 1512–31.

——— 1976. "Franchise building for natural monopolies: In general and with respect to CATV," *Bell Journal of Economics* 7: 73–104.

——— 1987. "Delimiting antitrust," *Georgetown Law Journal* 76: 271–304.

Williamson, Oliver E., and Sidney G. Winter (eds.) 1991. *The Nature of the Firm: Origin, Meaning, Influence*. Oxford: Oxford University Press.

Willig, Robert D. 1979. "The theory of network access pricing," in *Issues in public utility regulation*, Harry M. Trebing (ed.). East Lansing, MI: Michigan State University Press, pp. 109–52.

Wilson, Robin J. and Lowell W. Beineke (eds.) 1979. *Applications of graph theory*. New York: Academic Press.

Wilson, Wesley W. and Yimin Zhou 2001. "Telecommunications deregulation and subadditive costs: Are local telephone monopolies unnatural?" *International Journal of Industrial Organization* 19: 909–30.

Wooders, Myrna 1980. "The Tiebout hypothesis: Near optimality in local public goods economies," *Econometrica* 48: 1467–85.

Woroch, Glenn A. 2002a. "Local network competition," in Cave et al. (eds.), pp. 642–719.

——— 2002b. "Open access rules and the broadband race," *Law Review of Michigan State University Detroit College of Law* 2002: 719–42.

Wu, Tim 1999. "Application-centered Internet analysis," *Virginia Law Review* 85: 1163–204.

——— 2003. "Network neutrality, broadband discrimination," *Journal on Telecommunications and High Technology Law* 2: 141–76.

——— 2004. "The broadband debate, a user's guide," *Journal on Telecommunications and High Technology Law* 3: 69–96.

Wu, Timothy and Lawrence Lessig 2003. "Ex parte letter," submitted in FCC (2002e), http://gullfoss2.fcc.gov/prod/ecfs/retrieve.cgi?native_or_pdf=pdf&id_document= 6514683884.

Yaged, Bernard 1972. "Minimum cost routing for static network models," *Networks* 1: 139–72.

Yarrow, George K. 1996. "Dealing with social obligations in telecoms," in *Regulating utilities: A time for change?* M. E. Beesley, Stephen Sayer, and Bryan Carsberg (eds.). London: Institute of Economic Affairs, pp. 60–68.

Yoo, Christopher S. 2002. "Vertical integration and media regulation in the new economy," *Yale Journal on Regulation* 19: 171–300.

——— 2003a. "New models of regulation and interagency governance," *Law Review of Michigan State University Detroit College of Law* 2003: 701–16.

——— 2003b. "Rethinking the commitment to free, local television," *Emory Law Journal* 52: 1579–1718.

——— 2003c. "The rise and demise of the technology-specific approach to the First Amendment," *Georgetown Law Journal* 91: 245–356.

——— 2004a. "Copyright and product differentiation," *New York University Law Review* 79: 212–80.

——— 2004b. "Would mandating broadband network neutrality help or hurt competition? A comment on the end-to-end debate," *Journal on Telecommunications and High Technology Law* 3: 23–68.

——— 2005. "Beyond network neutrality," *Harvard Journal of Law and Technology* 19: 1–78.

_____ 2006. "Network neutrality and the economics of congestion," *Georgetown Law Journal* 94: 1847–1908.

_____ 2007a. "What can antitrust contribute to the network neutrality debate?" *International Journal of Communication* 1: 493–530.

_____ 2007b. Innovation in wireless telephony: A case study in network diversity. Paper presented at the Free State Foundation Conference on the "Federal Unbundling Commission," Washington, D.C.

_____ 2008. "Network neutrality, consumers, and innovation," *University of Chicago Legal Forum* 2008: 179–262.

Zacharias, Lawrence S. 1988. "Repaving the Brandeis way: The decline of developmental property," *Northwestern University Law Review* 82: 596–645.

Zolnierek, James, James Eisner, and Ellen Burton 2001. "An empirical examination of entry patterns in local telephone markets," *Journal of Regulatory Economics* 19: 143–59.

Zupan, Mark A. 1989. "The efficacy of franchise bidding schemes in the case of cable television: Some systemic evidence," *Journal of Law and Economics* 32: 401–56.

# Index

Note to index: An *f* following a page number denotes a figure on that page; an *n* following a page number denotes a note on that page; a *t* following a page number denotes a table on that page.

# Table of Cases

Printed in the United States
by Baker & Taylor Publisher Services